SUNDERLAND COLLEGE

S104186

Shiney Row Learn.

.book is due for return on or before
be aware that fines a
online: http
R

Theatre Management

D1407078

Theatre Management

Producing and Managing the Performing Arts

David M. Conte

Stephen Langley

ENTERTAINMENTPRO

an imprint of Quite Specific Media Group, Ltd.
Hollywood, California

To artists and dreamers and thinkers

CITY OF SUNDERLAND, COLLEGE
LEARNING CENTRE

ORDER NUMBER	LS/30906
DATE OF ACCESSION	2/2009
ACCESSION NUMBER	5104186.
RECOMMENDED BY	Carol Mead

First published 2007
© 2007 by David M. Conte

All rights reserved. No part
of this publication may be
reproduced, stored in a
retrieval system, or transmitted,
in any form or any means,
mechanical, recording or
otherwise, without the prior
permission of the publisher.

ENTERTAINMENTPRO
an imprint of
Quite Specific Media Group, Ltd.
7373 Pyramid Place
Hollywood, CA 90046
(323) 851-5797 v. (323) 851-5798 f.
Email: info@quitespecificmedia.com

ISBN 0-89676-256-4

Quite Specific Media Group, Ltd. Imprints:
Costume & Fashion Press
Drama Publishers
Jade Rabbit
By Design Press
EntertainmentPro

www.quitespecificmedia.com

Brief Table of Contents

Detailed Table of Contents

Chapter 2: Place of Performance   19

Chapter 3: Personnel for the Theatre   49

Chapter 4: Commercial Theatre

75

Chapter 5: Not-For-Profit Professional Theatre

Chapter 6: Community Theatre   141

Chapter 7: College Theatre   153

Chapter 8: Stock and Dinner Theatre   173

Chapter 9: Presenters and Presenting Organizations   181

Chapter 10: Budget Planning 211

Chapter 11: Cost Control Strategies 249

Chapter 12: Box Office, Ticketing Systems, and Other Earned Income

Chapter 13: Fundraising and Contributed Income

Chapter 14: Marketing

Chapter 15: Publicity and Media Relations

Chapter 16: Advertising and the Sales Campaign 387

Chapter 17: Facility and Audience Management 415

Appendix   437

Bibliography 549

Index 567

Preface

THIS BOOK DELIVERS A BROAD, comprehensive, wide-angle view of theatre and performing arts management. The material is written for people who are starting or are already running small- to medium-size performing arts operations. These could include dance, theatre, or opera companies; a performing arts festival; a single production; or a venue. The basics laid out here apply to all. This book is a text for theatre management or arts management classes, and any given chapter might be the basis for a full course.

The first chapter addresses the basic idea of a company or production and the duties and training of its managers. Subsequent chapters address place of performance, personnel, not-for-profit organizations, mission statements, legal organization and structure, personnel, budgeting, box office/ticketing, fundraising, marketing, public relations, advertising, and performance management. The chapters that deal with commercial, not-for-profit, community, college, and stock theatre remain exclusive to legitimate theatre, but the lion's share of the content here is applicable to all the performing arts. Those theatre-specific chapters begin with brief histories in order to familiarize the reader with how those producing methods began and how they have developed.

This book is closely based on the 1990 edition of Stephen Langley's *Theatre Management and Production in America*. Revising and updating it was necessary because of, among other things, the emergence and influence of technology and the Internet. References to websites and software needed to be added.

In 1990 "going on line" to purchase tickets to a hot attraction meant standing in a line—*on line* in New York—for what might be an hour or more because the box office was then the main ticket-selling and distribution hub for theatre. Yes, telephone purchase was available. But now it is expected that tickets can be bought *on line*, via the Internet, for just about any performance, anywhere in the world. And that is just one example of the technological changes that have emerged in the intervening fifteen years. Simply put, we do things differently now. This book reflects those changes. Also, while some organizations have disappeared during the past sixteen years, new organizations have emerged.

Obsolete organizations were replaced. Ticket scales and budgets have also been adjusted to reflect current prices and costs.

A change that has evolved over the years, less operational and more organic, is the blurring of the lines between the for-profit and not-for-profit theatre in America. Once seen as two distinct forms, one high-art, the other crass commercial entertainment, these two have developed a symbiotic relationship that benefits each.

The chapter on Place of Performance has been expanded to include information about constructing new theatre spaces and adapting spaces for theatrical use. The explanation of the language and the process that architects and theatre consultants use should prove particularly valuable. It won't make the reader an expert in the design, construction, and renovation of theatre spaces, but it will at least prepare her or him for the long, complex process.

Presenters and Presenting Organizations, Chapter 9, now includes material on standard deal types and the booking process from the booking agent's perspective. Also new in the Appendices to that chapter are a list of items to be considered when hosting a production in one's own theatre and a checklist for presenting and international touring companies.

As comprehensive as this book is, it is not the last word on any given topic. This is not a "how-to" book although specific examples and illustrations are included both within the text and in the expanded Appendices. Anyone involved in a specific performing art should know the details and minutiae of it. For example, there is no information about music stands for recital halls or specs on how to build a sprung floor for dance. Broad topics that apply to all the performing arts are the stuff of this book. The bibliography can point readers to other texts and the Internet is a wonderful resource. More importantly, creative managers and producers continue to find new and better ways of doing just about everything. And they are thanked for that.

It is hoped that producers and managers and trustees will refer to this book in order to avoid the shoals while heading for deeper, safe water and that it will provide clear sailing for them and their organizations.

The author gratefully acknowledges permission to reprint granted from the following:

The logo for The Muny is used with permission of The Municipal Theatre Association of St. Louis (The Muny)

The logo for the New Jersey Performing Arts Center is reprinted by permission; design credit: Sussman/Prejza & Company

The artwork for Big Deals is reprinted by permission of the New York City Opera; photo credit: George Owen

The logo for Lincoln Center Theater (design by Jim Miller) is reprinted by permission of Serino Coyne Inc.

30-second radio commercial script printed with permission from the producers of the Broadway production of *Steel Magnolias*. (Writer: Ruth Rosenberg, Serino Coyne Inc.)

The logo for *Twelve Angry Men* and Roundabout Theatre is reprinted by permission of Roundabout Theatre

The ticket samples are reproduced by permission of Barbara Caporaso of TicketCraft, Merrick, NY

The *Love Hurts* newspaper advertisement is reprinted by permission of the New York City Opera: Wallace Whitworth, Director of Marketing; Peggy Pettus, Art Director, McCaffrey & McCall, Inc.; Jeanie Stein, Copywriter, McCaffrey & McCall, Inc.

The sample press releases are reprinted by separate permission of Nicholas Gordon, Joan Walden, Kevin McAnarney

The *Bonne Chance!* newspaper advertisement is reprinted by permission of the Les Miserables Company (Copyright © 1988 CMOL)

The *Tonight* newspaper advertisement is reprinted by permission of The Phantom of the Opera Company (Copyright © 1989 R.U.G. plc)

The logo for The Kennedy Center is used by permission of The John F. Kennedy Center for the Performing Arts

The *Rent* and *Avenue Q* logos, used by permission

The Sample License Agreement for Renting a Facility to an Outside Group and the Sample Technical Information Sheet in the Appendices are reprinted by permission of the Brooklyn Center for the Performing Arts at Brooklyn College (BCBC)

Making it Real, Standard Marketing Timetables, reprinted by permission of National Arts Marketing Project, Arts & Business Council of Americans for the Arts

Suzanne Gooch, Director of Presentations at The Metropolitan Opera, for her Checklist for Presenting and Touring International Companies

The Clark Transfer logo used by permission

The *Shock Headed Peter* logo used by permission of Gavin Evans

Photo credit, back cover: Anita and Steve Shevett

The Joyce Theater Foundation mission statement used by permission of The Joyce Theater

The Oregon Shakespeare Festival mission statement used by permission of the Oregon Shakespeare Festival

The Living Theatre mission statement used by permission of the Living Theatre

Houston Ballet Foundation mission statement used by permission of the Houston Ballet Foundation

The illustrations of types of stage configurations are used by permission of Trizart Alliance

Introduction
and Acknowledgments

THIS BOOK AND ITS PRIOR THREE EDITIONS are part of the legacy left by Stephen Langley who died in June of 1997. He was a professor of theatre at Brooklyn College and worked with and nurtured many students who came through the program in theatre management, which he started there. The books that he wrote grew out of his class lectures and the student internships that he had arranged and supervised. He was successful in placing his students in the top performing arts operations in the City of New York and was understandably proud of them and his role in helping them. In addition to teaching at Brooklyn College, Stephen was also the general manager of the campus performing arts center for ten years. And in the 1960s and 1970s he was the managing director of the Falmouth Playhouse on Cape Cod, which was a leading summer stock theatre in its day. That's where we met, and we remained friends until his death.

In the summer of 1966, between my first and second years at the University of Rhode Island, I was on the Cape looking for a summer job when Stephen bravely opted to hire me as a box office treasurer—ticket seller is more accurate. I had no experience of any practical value, but I dove into the job and liked it, but more importantly, I was intrigued by the new world that I had entered. I remember reading a copy of *Variety* and being dazzled by the lingo and recognizing a name or two and being pleased because I was a part—albeit a tiny one—of that world, too. I returned to Falmouth for three more summers and I added to my box office responsibilities those of business manager, a rather lofty title because all I really did was pay bills and prepare a small payroll.

At some point in the autumn of my senior year of college it became a relatively safe bet that I would graduate in June 1969 with a degree in business administration. Not surprisingly the question came up as to what I was going to do after graduating. I was open to suggestions. Undaunted by my unimpressive academic record, Stephen suggested that I investigate various graduate programs in theatre management. In those days there weren't many, but the leading program was—and still is—at the Yale School of Drama. I took his advice, applied, and to my surprise and good fortune was accepted into the

Theatre Administration program. I had a wonderful time there and graduated with a Master of Fine Arts degree in 1972.

In the thirty-plus years from 1972 to the present, I've worked as a production manager at the American Conservatory Theatre in San Francisco, as the company manager for musicals on the road, and as the general manager for the Bolshoi Ballet and Opera touring in America. I've opened and managed plays on Broadway and Off-Broadway and managed the Joffrey Ballet during its last season in New York.

I currently work on Broadway as the manager of the Gerald Schoenfeld Theatre— formerly known as the Plymouth Theatre, and I am also the vice-president for special projects for Clark Transfer, Inc., America's leading theatrical hauling and logistics company whose motto is appropriately, "Let's get the show on the road."

My point of view comes from my work experience and differs substantially from Stephen's: I have no students and I'm not a professor of theatre. As Stephen did, I, too, have reached out to knowledgeable professionals and colleagues for advice and information as I was putting this volume together. I'm delighted and grateful that everyone I contacted was exceedingly gracious. Because I asked a lot of questions of so many people, I have a long list of people to thank.

Thanks go to my wife, Suzanne Ouellette, for listening and for her help and patience during this process of writing and rewriting. Next, thanks go to Ralph Pine of EntertainmentPro for having faith in me and for agreeing to publish an updated version of what we will forever call "Stephen's Book." Thanks go to Ellen Lampert for helping Ralph and me get together.

I'd like to thank theatre consultant John Tissot for his significant help in Chapter 2, Place of Performance, and Steven Schnepp, president of AWA Touring Services, for his writing and editorial contributions to Chapter 9, Presenters and Presenting Organizations. Roger Tomlinson was kind enough to review my work on box office and ticketing, Chapter 12, and I thank Herman E. Krawitz for the time he spent helping me with the section on organized labor in Chapter 3. Bill Wright, now retired from Michigan State University's Wharton Center, was very generous in sharing his knowledge on a range of topics. My friend, the designer Ralph Funicello, kindly provided valuable information about college theatre, as did Julie Angelo of the American Association of Community Theatre on community theatre. Robert A. Boyar and Margery Boyar were very patient as they guided me through the section on insurance. Glenna Gordon was my right hand throughout.

Numerous people lent me materials that I've included, either in the text or in the appendices, and I'd like to acknowledge them also:

For art work: Frank "Fraver" Verlizzo, Susan Lee, Stephanie Santoso, Jane M. Goolong, Laura DiLorenzo, Catrina Boisson, David Steffen, David Kitto, Alan J. Benson, Tim Grassel, Jeffrey Seller, and Francois Morrison.

I hope that I'm not forgetting anyone, but in no particular order I'd like to thank Marion Mooney, Len Alexander, Stacey McMath, Timothy O'Leary, Maria D. Watson, Louis P. Filippelli (CPA), Paul Eacuello, John Copeland, Lex Poppens, Mary Johnson, Steven E. Chaikelson, Douglas McLennan (ArtsJournal.com), Paul Morer, William Baker,

Norma Deull, Jonathan Deull, Ed Denning, Paul Schierhorn, Robert V. Kenyon, CC Conner, Mitch Weiss, Ralph Boeckemeyer, Carol Wasser, Seth Marquette, Christopher Wilson, Christopher C. Smith, Seymour "Red" Press, Linda Shelton, Bernard Carragher, Joel Ruark, Lonnie Carter, Elaine Ng, Joe Traina, Ken Bloom, David Frost, Joanna Kyd, Maria Somma, Barbara Hauptman, G. Wayne Hoffman, Paul Blake, and Leonard Stein. For the photo of me on the back cover, I'd like to thank Anita and Steve Shevett. During the time I've been working on this book my classmate from Yale, Ellis M. Pryce-Jones, died, so I must thank him, unfortunately, posthumously. Finally, the biggest thanks, again sadly and posthumously, go to my friend and mentor Stephen Langley for entrusting his book to me. It is a great honor.

Despite all the correct information I've received from myriad sources, if there are any errors, mistakes, or pieces of misinformation in this book, they are mine alone, and I take complete responsibility for them.

David M. Conte

CHAPTER I

Theatre Management and the Performing Arts

F OR READERS OF THIS BOOK, the word *theatre* includes all the performing arts because, from a practical point of view, all of the performing arts have the same core issues: producing or presenting artistically satisfying works in accord with their missions, finding and keeping an audience, providing for the financial and creative well-being of an organization or production, and maintaining good personnel and public relations.

Indeed, all of the performing arts are more alike than different. An artistic director functions in virtually the same capacity across the arts. If live music is necessary and musicians are engaged, be it in a pit or symphony orchestra, similar rehearsal, personnel, and labor issues emerge. Although scenery and costume elements are almost always missing from most classical and chamber music performances, they can be major budget items in opera and ballet. Virtually all have boards of trustees and all operate under the same set of accounting and budgeting principles. Performance licensing issues are similar even if particular costs vary from one performing art to another. And audiences everywhere require the same kind of attention and management.

The title *manager* appears in many guises in this book, or more accurately, many kinds of managers appear: general, business, marketing, programming, house, company, and more. These jobs, with slightly different titles, are central to all the performing arts.

The steps involved in founding and managing a theatre/performing arts entity is the stuff of this book. But before going into the specifics of *how* to manage a theatre or a company, an initial *why* needs to be asked. Any performing arts project requires a great deal of time and effort and love and, frequently, a small army of people, so it's very important to be clear *why* it's being undertaken.

Some people believe that theatre is where art can happen, where knowledge can be attained at least as well through the medium of ballet or plays as it can through a mathematical equation. An artist seeking to provoke awareness in others is a person as passionately committed to the discovery of truth as is the scientist. And while not everyone who works in the theatre needs to strive to be an artist, everyone should possess a notion of the nature of art and its aims.

The pursuit of art and truth is the first requisite for serious theatre and it allows little room for self-serving social, financial, or political motivation. Nevertheless, people are motivated by different *whys*, and it is a combination of *whys* that people bring to theatre projects. Let's look at some of these.

The *Why* of the Theatre

Money

It is obvious that Broadway shows aim to earn profits for their investors, but it is not so obvious but equally true that most community and amateur productions also aim to make a "profit"—even when the show or project is organized under the aegis of not-for-profit status. Their goal can be to raise money for a local cause, such as new uniforms for the football team.

Fame

Some people involve themselves in the performing arts in order to gain recognition and prestige. Being a producer, for example, or being cast in a community theatre production may admit the participant into a certain social circle or bring attention to the person. Performing arts facilities have been financed by generous gifts from wealthy benefactors who wish to increase their social prominence, and the community is the better for it.

Service

Service-oriented, or purpose-oriented, theatre takes such diverse forms as:

> The industrial show/corporate theatre, which is used to demonstrate or promote products such as cars or laptops.

> Drama therapy, which is used as a psychologist's device by which patients may express and/or recognize their problems by funneling their emotions through ostensibly fictional characters.

> The agit-prop production, which is created to disseminate propaganda by theatrically agitating an audience and thereby moving it to take future action, and guerrilla theatre, which is also political in content and propagandistic in purpose. Both, virtually the same, are alive and well and can be seen on the television news when, for example, groups protest at international conferences on monetary policy or global warming. Both can be very effective tools for getting attention for a cause.

Fun

For some people, making theatre—be it hanging lights, soliciting program ads, sewing costumes, or building scenery—is just plain fun. They enjoy the idea, the process, and the people involved. Some develop the fun element into making a living, others keep busy in their community theatres, others just buy tickets—lord love them—but they all do it simply for the fun of it. Related to the fun motive, is "connectedness": people involved feel connected to fellow playmakers, people they like and with whom they share like interests. Another connection is to the art form itself—dance, or opera, or theatre. Yet another connection might be to the space. Some people like being in theatres, large or small, well equipped or bare bones. Whatever the connection, being part of the art makes them feel good. Period.

The *What* of the Theatre

Getting from the *why* to the *what* of the theatre is the next step.

The *what* could be the residents of a community deciding to make a form of live music available and ultimately putting up a tent on the town square or in a field as a venue for the music. The *what* could also be actors from a drama department producing a season of one-acts in a church basement. The possibilities are endless. But at some point what the project will be needs to be decided.

What it is should be defined in the *mission statement*. The idea that is expressed in the mission statement serves as the standard by which a venture is ultimately judged to be a success or failure. It can be thought of as the constitution or conscience of the operation. A mission statement is in fact a legal requirement when a group incorporates and applies to the Internal Revenue Service for tax-exempt status, which virtually all performing arts entities have. It is what it is all about.

An Example of a Mission Statement

The mission of The Joyce Theater Foundation, Inc. is to serve and support the art of dance and choreography, to promote the richness and variety of the art form in its fullest expression, and to advance the public interest in, and appreciation of, dance and the allied arts of music, design, and theater. The Foundation's programs embrace the entire spectrum of movement styles and traditions, from the time-honored to the untried, and are designed to encourage, sustain, and educate a diverse audience.

At this point in the process, perhaps more than at any other time in the life of an organization or project, unity of purpose is paramount. Unless everyone involved is in agreement with the purpose or mission, problems lie ahead. Particularly important is the need for a unified vision between management and artistic leadership. Without it, half of the organization will labor under false or wrongly interpreted assumptions, or worse, none at all and people will be working at cross-purposes. This is not to say that a clear statement guarantees harmony and bliss, but it is a vital early step toward harmony.

The Essentials

The four basic elements for theatre and the performing arts are quite simple:

At the very least, (1.) a *performer* to present or interpret (2.) some *material* in (3.) a *place* before (4.) an *audience* is necessary.

The *performer* could be a dancer, musician, actor, or singer. The *material* could be old—a script by Euripides or a motet by Hildegarde of Bingen—or new—an improvisation. The *place* could be the back of a truck or Carnegie Hall. The *audience* is made up of witnesses to the event.

The Manager

To whatever extent responsibilities are shared with others, a theatre or arts manager is any person who plays a part in bringing together or facilitating two or more of the above four elements, thereby contributing to the realization of a theatrical performance. From an economist's point of view, a manager is any person who helps bring labor and capital together in order to produce an end product. To a sociologist, a theatre manager may be anyone who has influence over the organizational behavior of a given internal and/or external theatre environment. Thus a manager may be an agent who finds performers to interpret a particular script, a publicity director who finds an audience for the performers, a theatre operator who provides the place where the performance is held. A general manager is one who supervises the entire process from beginning to end. This person typically supervises a number of departments and functions.

A manager, then, is a matchmaker who helps bring together the idea, the artist, the place, and the audience. More specifically, a manager is anyone involved in the following functions:

1.) Planning
2.) Organizing
3.) Staffing and casting
4.) Supervising
5.) Controlling

1.) *Planning*

The commercial producer decides on a property to produce—a play, a musical, a one-person show—and a venue in which to produce it. The board of a not-for-profit company determines the mission or overall artistic goals, policies, and objectives for the company. Supporting managers must then attempt to devise the best strategies to insure the greatest and most appropriate kind of success. This requires setting priorities, establishing major deadlines, and creating a budget. These actions mark the real beginning of how an idea is turned into a reality via a plan.

2.) *Organizing*

Once a plan has been drawn up, available resources must be organized to maximize their value. How, for instance, should authority and responsibility be delegated? This would be a good point at which to design a line chart or table of organization that indicates all job titles and the chain of command. This, too, would be subject to change. During the hiring and job orientation process, it may be found that one person can do what had been planned as two jobs, that two valued employees work best when they work apart; or that a particular position is unnecessary. Many of these decisions are best made as a situation evolves.

Organizing includes a legal structure for the operation. The question will be to form a not-for-profit organization, eligible for tax-deductible contributions from *donors*, or a for-profit entity, designed to pay dividends to *investors*. The former is the heart of not-for-profit organizations; the latter is the heart of commercial theatre.

3.) *Staffing and Casting*

It is the prerogative of the commercial producer not only to hire a general manager and all the leading artists, but also to have veto power over all hiring and firing in connection with the project at hand. In reality, some producers play a very active role while others leave everything except play selection and financing to a general manager. In nonprofit operations, the board hires one or two people to take artistic and managerial leadership and, except for giving advice, should then allow that leadership to select the repertoire and do the hiring.

4.) *Supervising*

The aim of effective personnel management is to orient everyone in the same direction, to encourage everyone to embrace the main goals of the project, to understand the product, and, in short, to be sure that everyone is on the same page. Everybody needs a boss. People, no matter how dedicated, need to be supervised, with their time and work needs measured and evaluated. Are the scenery and costume people on schedule? Are the bills being paid? Are all the roles cast? Contracts signed? Brochures designed? Is everyone pulling together, working toward the same goal?

After the major goals have been set, the play or season selected, the financing secured, and the staff and cast employed, all subsequent decisions are secondary. At this point the major decisions have been made and, short of starting all over, they are largely irrevocable. Projects have met failure simply because their *raison d'etre* was forgotten or fatally compromised. A good supervisor is able to keep an eye on the final goal and to encourage the team-work and productivity necessary for achieving it.

While individual department heads in both the artistic and administrative areas must supervise their specialized support staff, top management must be concerned with coordinating these departmentalized efforts so that they will all fit into a single completed puzzle.

5.) *Controlling*

The business of controlling a project is a matter of identifying, analyzing, and correcting the weaknesses and of finding and bolstering the strengths. It is a matter of checking and balancing, of shifting and adapting, of inspecting and evaluating as the project moves toward a single goal.

Making changes or corrections in how an organization is run, usually results in making someone unhappy. Forcing an employee to retrain for a job, demoting an old-time staffer, or firing people is not enjoyed by any manager— but that is the job.

Because the human condition is central to all artistic work, it is perhaps easier to hurt someone's feelings in the arts than in other fields. However, it is sometimes necessary to fire the director or the leading lady or the marketing director or designer. The real trick is to perceive *when* a project is in trouble, *why* it is in trouble, and *what* precisely needs to be done to correct the situation.

The ideal method for managing any project is to organize the fundamental elements so thoroughly and well that, once it is underway, its directors and managers can devote their full attention to coping with minor or unexpected developments.

Becoming a Manager

According to Len Alexander, Partner, Management Consultants for the Arts, Inc., the following advertisement for an executive director position is typical of the higher end of arts administration jobs. It would likely be for a performing arts operation with a budget in the ten to twenty million-dollar range, supervising a staff of fifty to seventy-five. And the candidate would have to bring ten to fifteen years of experience in increasingly complex organizations. Given the level of experience sought here, it can be assumed that the candidate would have earned a degree in arts administration, the likely entree to one's first position, or bring the equivalent in experience and expertise. Mr. Alexander also notes that the title of executive director in large organizations is losing favor to president and CEO.

The executive director will be the CEO of the company, reporting to the board of trustees through its executive committee, and will be responsible for the development and implementation of operational strategies and tactics that enhance and advance the company's mission. The executive director will oversee policy planning, day-to-day operations, program development, and fundraising activities and will be expected to:

Inspire confidence through the exercise of executive leadership for all aspects of the company's endeavors;

Create a vision for approval by the board of trustees of the type and direction of the company's programs and activities;

Provide a management structure and managerial style with which to support and encourage fulfillment of the company's goals. Attract, cultivate, develop, and hire key staff as necessary;

Establish and maintain a regular, open, and supportive system of communication throughout the organization;

Ensure that successful annual fundraising strategies are employed to achieve support of current and future operations;

Represent the company in its relationships with all major constituencies.

George Bernard Shaw said that every artistic director in the theatre should be followed around by a hard-minded businessman whose main job would be to cut all production budgets by half. That was essentially what managers did, thereby creating a villainous, penny-squeezing, Scrooge-like image of theatre managers and producers that is happily on the wane, if not entirely gone. While economics remain important to managers, they must assume other responsibilities if the arts are to survive.

Today's arts manager is ideally:

. . . a person who is knowledgeable in the art with which he is concerned, an impresario, labor negotiator, diplomat, educator, publicity and public relations expert, politician, skilled businessman, a social sophisticate, a servant of the community, a tireless leader—becoming humble before authority—a teacher, a tyrant and a continuing student of the arts.

(The Performing Arts: Problems and Prospects)

Education and Training for the Arts Manager

What type of background, education, and training is apt to produce a person with the qualities and abilities to guide the performing arts successfully?

It is necessary to have an undergraduate diploma. And while an undergraduate concentration in theatre management is not necessary, a single course in this subject might be advisable to make students aware of arts management as a viable career and to make them aware of graduate programs to train professional arts managers. The syllabus in Appendix A suggests appropriate units of study in a department of theatre. This syllabus could easily be adapted to fit the needs of music or dance majors or anyone in a performing arts field.

After college, the options are to:

1.) Enroll in a graduate program
2.) Serve an internship
3.) Attend specialized workshops, seminars, and conferences
4.) Travel and pursue self-instruction
5.) Seek on-the-job training
6.) Aim to combine some or all of the above

Not everyone is able to proceed immediately from undergraduate to graduate school; some will never find graduate school necessary. But if graduate school is chosen, the student must decide what type of program to enter and where. MBA programs in graduate schools of business or management and MFA programs that specialize in arts administration are both viable alternatives. It is now common to read as part of a job description in this field: "graduate degree in arts administration preferred."

A master's program in arts management typically requires two to three years of study and includes fieldwork and supervised internships at arts companies and organizations. The program may include long-established courses in economics, law, business, fine arts, with a few specialized seminars peculiar to arts organizations taught by adjunct faculty who are practicing professionals. Classroom work should emphasize analytical and original thinking; current practices should be challenged by new and different theories. The list of course titles in Appendix B suggests a credible graduate program in performing arts management.

This announcement recently appeared in *Jobs in the Arts* (www.nyfa.org):

Internships

Excellent opportunity for an organized, highly motivated college or post-collegiate intern looking to build a career in arts administration. Assists Artistic Director, Managing Director, Production Manager, and Marketing Director in all areas of opera administration at a critically acclaimed and quickly growing company. Assists with artists' contracts, grant writing, fundraising, marketing, ticketing, press, and board relations. Must have strong writing and computer skills. Flexible schedule with minimum commitment of 32 hours per week. Travel & meal stipend provided. Send resume, cover letter, and one writing sample to Elaine Ng, Managing Director, by email at intern@gotham-chamberopera.org, or by mail to Gotham Chamber Opera, 410 West 42nd Street, New York, New York 10036.

Internships in the performing arts, as in virtually all companies and organizations, commercial or nonprofit, have interns working in almost every management area. Larger organizations have intern departments. An internship is a good place to observe an operation (and field) first hand; it is not unusual for internships to grow into permanent positions. For the sponsoring organization using an intern is an opportunity to engage an eager and interested person at relatively low cost. Paid interns typically earn less than full-time employees. But an internship can be worthwhile for the intern to get that all-important first job.

Workshops, seminars, and conferences that deal with specific facets of arts management—finance, marketing, fundraising—or with specific skills—internet marketing or corporate grant research—are frequently offered by arts service organizations, membership associations, arts councils, and colleges. They provide ways for the neophyte to test the waters, for the arts management student to get additional instruction, for the practitioner to brush up, and for those in leadership positions to acquaint themselves with the skills needed by their staff members. More importantly, they present nationwide if not worldwide networking opportunities.

Foreign travel that includes instruction is likely to be memorable for most young adults. Many colleges have arrangements with foreign institutions to study abroad. Familiarity with other cultures and languages is an asset to any manager because the performing arts have increasingly become internationalized with touring activities, festivals, cultural exchange programs, and media exploitation.

Management Positions in the Performing Arts

All the following management positions are held by people who make decisions, supervise at least one other person, and fulfill other management functions. In most cases assistant and support staff positions have not been listed although some are also managerial positions, often filled with volunteers.

Board of Trustees Officer and/or Member

The trustees are responsible for the legal, fiscal, and overall conduct of not-for-profit corporations. They serve without salary, appoint the head artistic/managerial employees, determine long-range policy, and provide advice and assistance to key staff members. They may also directly or indirectly contribute money or in-kind services to the organization.

Government Arts Council Chairperson and/or Member

There are over fifteen hundred city, local, and community arts councils that receive ever-diminishing funding from state councils, as well as from local government and private and corporate sources. All government-appointed council members serve without salary and have no legal authority. Their primary responsibilities are to provide subsidies in the form of grants or "contracts" to individual artists, projects, and organizations, provide technical assistance, present arts programs, and disseminate information about the arts.

United Arts Fund Volunteer Executive

United arts funds are service organizations that raise money through federated or joint appeals to individuals, corporations, foundations, and government sources. Volunteer executives often supervise a salaried staff, which solicits funds on behalf of its constituents. How funds are distributed and to whom can have considerable impact on arts policy in the given community.

Private Foundation Board Officer and/or Member

Organized as nonprofit corporations and governed by a board of trustees, most private foundations are small and administered by a lawyer or other individual on a part-time basis. Larger foundations have a president or chairperson of the board as well as a professional support staff. Some, such as the Rockefeller Foundation, are endowed with funds from the private sector, while others, the Ford Foundation for example, are funded by commercial corporations. Board members in the Rockefeller model tend to be family members or close associates, while those in the Ford model are generally recruited from the corporate world.

Benefit or Special Events Chairperson

Most boards for nonprofit arts organizations have auxiliary committees of volunteers who raise money by sponsoring special events, which may include dinners, receptions, golf tournaments, tours, benefits, raffles, and auctions. Although headed by a volunteer chairperson or director, they may have some salaried support staff. The funds they raise are usually vitally important to the project or company they are intended to support.

Union, Guild, or Professional Association Officer and/or Board Member

A board drawn from the organization's membership almost always heads these nonprofit corporations. The work of these volunteers includes setting goals for labor-management contract negotiations, overseeing pension and benefit funds, monitoring compliance with existing contracts that apply to members, and representing the organization to the industry and the media.

Freelance Producing Managers

Impresario

Impresario is an outdated term for producers who rarely own their own theatres, who usually concentrate on the fields of opera, dance, and music, and who organize world-class tours of performing artists and ensembles.

Producer

In the British theatre a producer is the person who stages and directs the play; on the continent this position would be that of a *regisseur* or *metteur en scene*. In the American theatre a producer is the person who initiates a theatrical project by finding a property and securing the performance rights to produce it in a desired venue and raises the capital necessary to get the project to opening night. In not-for-profit organizations, the institution itself is the producer; it has the ultimate fiscal responsibility.

Theatre Operator

Distinct from a landlord who owns, maintains, and rents out a theatre facility without necessarily participating in its use, a theatre operator owns or rents a theatre and may also produce or book in the entertainment presented in it. This does not always entail initiating the productions, but it does involve taking the lion's share of legal and financial risk, promoting the entertainment locally, hiring and supervising a resident staff, and assuming many other responsibilities that qualify the theatre operator as a producing manager or presenter.

Presenter/Promoter

There are thousands of theatres, civic centers, and college and community performing arts facilities that book and present entertainment. The vast majority of these operate under the umbrella of a nonprofit organization and thereby qualify for tax-deductible contributed income. Taken as a whole, these venues probably do more to support serious music and dance, and the artists involved, than any other branch of the industry—live or electronic.

Freelance General Manager

Freelance general managers are peculiar to the commercial theatre. They are independent professionals who often maintain a permanent office and core staff and are hired by producers to take general management responsibility for specific shows or projects. Typically, the general manager negotiates the theatre license, hires the necessary staff, formulates a budget, oversees all financial transactions, negotiates all contracts, and serves as the producer's representative and troubleshooter.

Artistic Director

The artistic director is the person who has full artistic and in some cases managerial authority over a not-for-profit organization. The responsibilities of the artistic director are numerous, but the most important are the setting and maintaining of artistic policy and the selecting of repertoire.

Executive Director or President/CEO

The chief executive of large not-for-profit organizations reports to the board of trustees. All non-artistic departments report to the executive director.

General Manager (on a staff)

A general manager has full management responsibility for all nonartistic aspects of a production or an organization.

General Director

A general director is a person, most often employed in opera, with both artistic and managerial authority.

Managing Director

It is most common for a managing director to work in a not-for-profit organization. Because the managing director has overall nonartistic authority, the position can be equated with that of executive director.

Actor-Manager

The title actor-manager is anachronistic, and the title is seldom used today. Few people fit the definition of actor-manager as did nineteenth-century Henry Irving or David Belasco, or even twentieth-century Eva Le Gallienne or Laurence Olivier. The rarity of actor-managers today may be explained by the fact that artistic leadership in the theatre has shifted from actor to director, and more theatre companies are now formed by directors than by actors. The single exception these days may be that of actor Kevin Spacey as artistic director of the Old Vic in London.

Director of Theatre/Performing Arts

Academic departments or arts centers that embrace several art forms may appoint someone with the title director of theatre/performing arts.

Chairperson of Theatre/Music/Dance

This person is the head in a relevant academic department in a school, college, or university.

Financial Managers

Director of Finance

The director of finance is the chief financial officer in any large operation.

Controller/Comptroller

The controller is someone with all accounting responsibility for a company.

Accountant

The accountant has business/accounting responsibilities.

Business Manager

Often found in smaller companies, this manager may serve as a one-person department, which is responsible for paying bills, executing payrolls, etc. The business manager may also double as personnel manager.

Fundraising Managers

Development Director

The development director is responsible for all fundraising activities and is employed exclusively in the nonprofits.

Associate Director of Fundraising

A large organization might employ a number of associates, each with his or her own support staff, to take charge of such specific tasks as proposal writing, grants research, membership, government grants, corporate grants, individual donor campaigns, and planned giving.

Special Events Director

This manager coordinates the various efforts to raise contributed income by a friends' group, a guild, or a benefit chairperson.

Director of Volunteer Services

The director of volunteer services manages and coordinates all volunteer activities.

Marketing and Income-Related Managers

Director of Marketing

The director of marketing conducts research, develops a marketing plan, and supervises a staff to accomplish the marketing goals.

Director of Membership

The director of membership supervises the special services and benefits offered to members and donors in not-for-profit organizations.

Director of Audience Development

The director of audience development works to increase attendance and ticket sales in every possible way, executing both long- and short-term strategies.

Director of Public Relations

The title director of public relations can be ambiguous as it might mean director of press relations or director of public information. Regardless of the specific title, this person has the responsibility to place information before the public in a manner that upholds the goals and image of the company.

Press Representative

This person is responsible for distributing information to all media.

Director of Community Relations

The director of community relations maintains and strengthens the relationship between the institution and the community, which could include running artists-in-the-schools programs, touring programs, etc.

Director of Advertising Sales

This person is responsible for generating revenue through the sale of advertising space in playbills and souvenir programs.

Director of Publications

It is this person's job to supervise and direct all publication activity, including playbills and souvenir books.

Ticketing Services Manager

This person might also have the title of customer relations manager and supervises the processing of tickets and subscriptions and deals with customer/member complaints, special requests, and all things related to customer relations and tickets.

Box Office/Ticketing Manager

This person has overall supervision and responsibility for the operations of a box office.

Head Treasurer

A box office treasurer, who is also a ticket seller, supervises other treasurers in day-to-day procedures.

Group Sales Manager

This person directs and supervises group-sales activities.

Subscription Sales Manager

This person supervises the development, assignment, distribution, and follow-up services related to the sale of series or subscription tickets.

Merchandise-Marketing Manager

The merchandise-marketing manager supervises the creation and sale of merchandise such as T-shirts, tote bags, and umbrellas, etc.

Concessions Manager

The sale of concessions are supervised and directed by the concessions manager.

Production and Operations Managers

Director/Manager of Information Systems (MIS)

An expert in computer technology, this manager runs and maintains all aspects of computer software and hardware.

Literary Manager/Dramaturg(e)

The literary manager advises the artistic director in play selection and new script development. The manager's other activities might include doing research for directors and writing program notes and educational materials, such as study guides.

Production Manager

This person supervises the construction, load-in and load-out, and operation of the physical production on stage. The responsibilities include controlling production costs, coordinating schedules, managing crews, and possibly supervising touring productions.

Facilities Manager

This title may also be operations manager or building manager because this person oversees maintenance, security, house management, space allocation, rentals, concessions, and all purchases related to these areas.

Human Relations/Personnel Manager

In large organizations, this person supervises employee relations, including benefits, compensation and salary reviews, grievances and labor law compliance.

Stage Systems Manager

This specialist, who is usually found in very large, complex stage operations, is expert in theatre stage systems such as rigging and automation.

Company Manager

The company manager is responsible for dealing with company members and is responsible for travel and housing on tour. When not touring, this manager is responsible for payroll, company ticket requests, payment of bills and royalties, and sundry management issues for a production or company.

House Manager/Theatre Manager

The house manager or theatre manager is responsible for all front-of-house operations, which include supervising the staff, dealing with customer problems, and preparing a house payroll. On Broadway the house manager also completes a weekly company settlement.

Production Stage Manager/Stage Manager

The stage manager supervises rehearsals, assists the director, and takes charge of the stage, performers, and crew during performances. The stage manager serves as liaison between the performers and management and interfaces with house management when necessary. The person must be a member of Actors' Equity Association when union actors are employed in the legitimate theatre; it is the same position in opera and ballet.

Technical Director/Technical Supervisor

The technical director is the person who supervises all the technicians and craftspeople involved in creating a theatrical production and who attempts to carry out the design of the production designers.

Tour Manager or Tour Director

When not filled by a company manager, the person occupying this position deals with schedules and arranges transportation and housing and other details for a company while on tour.

Advance Stage Manager

This person precedes a touring production as it moves from theatre to theatre and makes the subsequent load-in, company arrival, and opening performance as smooth as possible. Now rare, this position was once common during the heyday of touring summer stock productions.

Internship Director

This person interviews, selects, orients, and generally supervises interns in large organizations.

School Director or Administrator

A school director is the person who coordinates student recruitment and enrollment, faculty appointments and supervision, and scheduling of classes and facility usage.

Director of Security

The director of security implements and supervises on-site security personnel and systems.

Maintenance Supervisor

The maintenance supervisor supervises the physical plant maintenance personnel, supplies, and services.

These titles are the ones most commonly used in the theatre and performing arts organizations and suggest the wide range of managerial positions. There are likely other titles and jobs that could be added as could the large corps of available consultants who are expert in virtually every area of the performing arts from board of trustees relationships to marketing to audience surveys. They can present valuable information and insight: from time to time it can be worthwhile to get input from outside sources.

Summary

Theatre and all the performing arts share the same core values, particularly those arts in the not-for-profit world. And although titles may vary from art form to art form the responsibilities and duties are essentially the same: planning, organizing, staffing, supervising, and controlling. The training and development of managers is similar as well, be it formal training, internships, or on-the-job training. It is a rich world, full of fascinating people and problems.

CHAPTER 2

Place of Performance

I DEALLY, PRODUCERS AND ARTISTIC DIRECTORS should be free to select the community and the building in which they believe their productions have the best chance to thrive artistically and economically. Probably the best documented attempt to suit artistic goals to a community was undertaken by Tyrone Guthrie, Peter Zeisler, and Oliver Rea and culminated in the opening of the Tyrone Guthrie Theatre in 1963 and the establishment of the Minnesota Theatre Company at Minneapolis-St. Paul. This success, even after the departure of its founders, should encourage producers and artistic directors not satisfied with utilizing performance spaces merely because they are available. Of course, not every producer or artistic director has the time and money to invest in a lengthy nationwide search for the ideal community. When assessing a potential theatre site the advice of professional consultants is often helpful in gathering information. However, like the business of selecting plays and casting actors, the final decision about the place of performance may also, without apology, be based upon a degree of intuition about a particular building or community. Consultants, feasibility reports, and architects are helpful and necessary adjuncts to the process of creating new theatres, but they should never be allowed to dominate the process.

Whether the plan is to buy, build, lease, or share a theatre, what factors regarding the site and community in which it is located should be taken into consideration?

Audience Potential

Statistical surveys have shown that somewhere between one and three percent of our population attends live theatre performances and that the ratio of theatregoers to non-theatregoers is higher in metropolitan areas. Take the population of a given city and the area immediately around it, then calculate one to three percent of that total figure to see whether or not that number of people would be sufficient to fill all the seats of all the performances of each anticipated production.

But audience potential is more than a numbers game. Factors other than numbers will impact the percentage of the local population that attends a particular theatre or production. The typical American performing arts attendee is white, college educated, middle-aged or older, a current or retired white-collar worker in a middle- or upper-income category. This is, indeed, the profile of a typical Broadway audience. However, it does not necessarily describe those attending experimental, campus, multicultural, or special-interest productions or international festivals

If a company wishes to attract a particular audience, it makes sense to be located as close to that audience as possible. On the other hand, if a particular attraction offers a potent enough lure, people will travel hundreds of miles to it. Nonetheless, the theatre building and its locale will always be a powerful influence on who and how many people attend performances there. There is always the issue of the right or wrong side of the tracks: will people go into a particular neighborhood? Is it okay to be a pioneer in a locale?

Proximity to Transportation

If a theatre site is located in a large metropolitan area, accessibility to public transportation —subways, buses, trains—must take precedence. Can a majority of the potential audience members reach the theatre easily, quickly, and safely? If not, will authorities cooperate to improve the transportation systems? Are parking facilities available or will costly provisions be required to handle a maximum number of automobiles? Can cars be accommodated for both evening and matinee performances? Is the theatre located on a major thoroughfare or is it difficult to find?

Theatregoers in the eastern states are not willing to drive as far to theatres as those in the rest of the nation, but in either case the process of finding one's way to a theatre should not take on the challenge of a treasure hunt. What are the federal and local regulations about placing directional signs on nearby roads and highways? Special permits are always required, unless a sign is located on the business site itself and meets local specifications. When a theatre is located in a remote area, even road signs may not always be sufficient. Local and state police should be informed about the location of the theatre, and every attempt should be made to have the name of the theatre appear on as many road maps as possible as well as on small, local maps such as those printed on restaurant placemats, in tourist guides, and in chamber of commerce literature. These should include those distributed through a public service, and in order to facilitate a safe flow of traffic, many cities and townships are willing to cooperate with theatre managers by allowing a few regulation-size road signs. However, signs for commercial operations are outlawed on federal highways, and state and local governments continue to tighten regulations that deal with outdoor advertising.

Transportation will also affect the operating cost of a theatre. Theatres located in remote locations will inevitably incur more transportation expenses than those in metropolitan areas. Large professional operations find it necessary to transport everything from scenery to actors.

The Competition

In general, competition in the performing arts is healthy if it does not involve frequent duplication of similar entertainment or programming. Theatregoing is a habit. It can be cultivated by patrons attending school and community theatres and then be applied to professional theatregoing. But theatregoing is not a habit that is quickly acquired. A history of theatregoing in a given area is desirable and so, without question, a new theatre should consider locating itself in a play-going community; it is easier to share an established audience than to create one. But there is an obvious, and real, difference between sharing and dividing.

How large is the potential audience for a particular kind of entertainment? Can metropolitan areas that possess similar performing groups work to coordinate their programming? What should be said about having three or four summer performing arts festivals all trying to attract the same type of ticket buyer? Can there be too much of a good thing?

When possible, it is best to coordinate programming with the competition to avoid conflicts. It is not necessary for two theatres to revive the same musical in the same season. Perhaps one theatre might present the original drama upon which the musical was based and the other the musical itself. Whatever the outcome, certainly communication and cooperation are preferable.

The Local Media

Finding a community with a good potential audience is one thing; reaching that audience is something else. If audience potential is extremely high and people are in the habit of going to the theatre, the job of selling tickets may be as simple as disseminating information about the play, the admission prices, and the curtain times. More often, people have to be enticed to attend, but the most efficient way of reaching an audience will differ with each community. Direct mail, email, telemarketing, the distribution of posters and handbills, newspaper advertising, television, or some other channel of communication may prove successful at one theatre, but unimportant at another.

Theatres located outside large metropolitan areas may be in communities with no local radio or television station, and a newspaper that does not reach a majority of the potential audience. This situation requires a wider and more expensive advertising campaign and creates greater difficulty in determining the audience profile and then communicating with that audience. And, of course, the farther away a newspaper or radio station is from a theatre, the less likely it is to provide free publicity space or time because your audience isn't *its* audience. Communicating with potential theatregoers in resort areas also presents special problems: the year-round residents follow the local newspapers while the tourists ignore them. Fortunate indeed is the operation that can reach most of its audience through one or two media outlets.

Local Organizations

It would be good to ask what groups exist within a given community that might offer assistance to your theatre. Helpful in the area of publicity and promotion are chambers of commerce, tourist bureaus, information centers, and travel agencies. Senior citizen and service clubs and civic and charitable organizations can be good sources of volunteer personnel for nonprofit theatres. What sort of philanthropic record is maintained by local individuals, businesses, and corporations? Is there a community arts council, and what is the record of the state arts council? Do nearby schools and colleges represent potential sources for group sales?

The Local Economy

Another yardstick for predicting the success of a theatre or performing arts venture is to determine whether or not potential attendees can afford the price of admission. What is the average income in the area? How much are people currently spending for live entertainment? How much can they afford to spend? Can group sales be anticipated from large businesses, schools, and religious organizations? Has there been growth or decline in the general economy of the area over the past decade or so?

The records in the local tax assessor's office will provide answers to some of these questions, as will interviews with chamber of commerce officials, managers of local movie theatres, and other businesspeople. Long before a theatre opens its doors, the producers should take a hard look at the local economy and ask whether or not its planned ticket prices are within a range that the market can bear. Even though the answer may be positive, it does not mean that a community will buy tickets. If the answer seems doubtful, can high-priced performances be alternated with low-priced or free-admission performances? How much income is it reasonable to expect from nonticket sources?

If the local economy will affect theatre business, then theatre business will also affect the local economy. This fact may provide a selling point and help to rally local support, including concessions and subsidies from local government and business. It is, nevertheless, unfortunate that the arts need to justify themselves in economic terms.

Weather

Weather conditions can seriously affect the business of theatre. What will general weather conditions mean in terms of heating and cooling an auditorium? What will this cost in terms of energy? Many a summer theatre has been bought during the winter when it is easy to forget or underestimate cooling the theatre. No theatre can be easily tested for comfort until it is in use.

Weather conditions are, of course, most germane to tent and outdoor theatres. Not a few open-air amphitheatres are standing idle because it was discovered, too late, that the local climate was either too unpredictable or too uncomfortable for regular use. Theatres-under-the-stars need careful scrutiny: downpours mean canceled performances and lost income.

Local Attitudes

Even when all conditions appear favorable for a theatre, local attitudes may ultimately determine its success or failure. What, it must be asked, is the local community's reaction to the idea for a theatre? Is it hot, lukewarm, or cool? What is the history of previous theatre projects in the community, and have these projects encouraged or discouraged local attitudes?

Communities comprised largely of well-educated and cosmopolitan people may appear ready to support a performing arts venture, but it should be remembered that such communities may have deeply entrenched concepts of what the arts should be and how a theatre should be operated. This would be a decided liability for experimental groups. Taking the performing arts to the hinterlands is noble but fraught with difficulties. Local attitudes have to be studied carefully, but a newly found and formed audience may prove to be extremely loyal and exciting.

Finally, it is important for those associated with the theatre to ask whether or not they will be comfortable and happy working in a particular community. If it is fair to ask that a community accept the theatre and its workers, it is equally fair to expect the theatre workers to accept the community.

Existing Spaces: Buying, Renting, Sharing

Buying a Theatre

Any piece of real estate should first be considered in terms of size, structure, location, age, history, and fair market price. What is the building's potential resale value? Is it structurally sound, or will major renovations and repairs to its heating, cooling, plumbing, electrical, and other physical support systems be necessary? Few buyers are sufficiently expert to judge these matters for themselves, so it is wise to secure a detailed inspection report from a professional building engineer.

It is generally believed that it is less expensive to renovate than to build from scratch, but this is not necessarily true. Every attempt should be made to discover the reasons why a building is for sale. The building records of the previous owners should be studied; past owners, managers, and employees should be quizzed about the building, as should neighboring and other business people in the community. Does the building have a reputation or image that will affect future business adversely?

Renting (or Leasing) a Theatre

Before signing a lease, the lessee needs to consider the building as if planning to purchase it. Indeed, if the plan is to operate the theatre for a long period of time, an option to buy the property at a stipulated maximum price would be desirable. Negotiating a lease is complicated and usually requires legal counsel, but everything in a lease will be related to one of two questions: what does the landlord provide and what must the tenant provide? Also, as a practical matter, nothing should be assumed—everything should be in writing. The agreement between producers and landlords of Broadway theatres is not called a lease but, rather, a license agreement. Instead of rent, it calls for a house share, which is a negotiated guarantee of an agreed weekly sum, usually with an additional percentage of the gross box office receipts to be paid to the landlord, or more accurately, deducted from the box office revenues. In addition, the production pays all expenses.

For practical purposes, the producers and the landlord are partners *of sorts*, because both benefit directly from the grosses. Of course, the laws of supply and demand determine the terms of a Broadway theatre license. When there are more theatres available than productions to fill them, more favorable terms for the production may result. Or when a successful transplanted production is to be booked, the landlord may offer more generous terms, anticipating a long occupancy. On the other hand, when most houses are booked, the price goes up.

The Off-Broadway theatre lease, also written on a per-production basis, is also unusual in that it typically requires about four weeks guaranteed payment, even if the tenant production is a flop and vacates after one week. It is usually a simple "four-wall lease," meaning the tenant is provided with the space inside the four walls, and nothing else, in exchange for a flat, weekly rent. This is in sharp contrast to an agreement made between outside producers or performance groups and colleges or civic groups to rent their theatres. Here, almost everything and everyone necessary to the operation of the facility may be provided for a price, except for the artists and the physical production.

When negotiating to occupy a nontheatre space, such as a loft or warehouse, the theatre has the option of signing a short-term lease—a one-year rental after which it could be evicted or face a sharp rent increase—or a longer term lease—three-to-five-year, which would offer more property control, tax benefits, and a fixed cost with minor built-in increases. Or the theatre might be able to negotiate a lease-option in which payments go toward a stipulated purchase price for the building at some future date. Another favorable arrangement for a tenant would be to establish occupancy payments as a percentage of the box office gross without a minimum guarantee, though this would require a very sympathetic or very desperate landlord. Whatever the terms, it is critical that the agreement clearly states what both parties must provide. The advice of a real estate attorney should be sought.

Sharing a Theatre

Companies just starting out rarely have the resources to buy, build, or even rent the theatre of their dreams. This leads them to examine less obvious alternatives and, invariably, it leads them to compromise. But creative solutions to their space needs may be found without altering the primary mission and artistic objectives of the project. Sharing a space is one such solution. It is not unusual today to find a theatre group offering performances in a church, a public or private school, or in commercial establishments such as hotels, restaurants, and cafes. The landlord-host may charge very low fees, believing that the theatre will bring in new people to his or her establishment and that the cultural or entertainment activity will enhance the image of that establishment. But, as with any liaison, there are risks and problems. How will the image of the host establishment reflect upon the theatre's image? Will the host place restrictions on the type of productions the theatre will present? What restrictions will be placed on the scheduling of rehearsals and performances?

A troupe should search out theatres, auditoriums, and other potential performance places that are not being fully utilized. Museums, for example, with available space might be happy to include theatre performances among their public activities. Many office buildings have ground-level atriums open to the public, and the corporate landlord might welcome and subsidize noontime theatre.

The Architectural Design Team

As one of the four fundamental requirements for the performing arts, the place of performance is an element that will deeply and unequivocally influence every other aspect of the operation. The best possible venue and design should be sought. While producers and artistic directors know the general architectural and physical requirements for their project, they need to seek specific advice from professionals on such topics as the nature of the building, real estate, and funding.

Theatre construction and renovation projects require an architectural design team, comprised of an architect and a variety of engineers and other professional consultants. Each member of this building team should contribute specific expertise to complement the skills of the other collaborators. The importance of selecting and assembling the appropriate architectural team applies both to new-building construction as well as to renovation projects. The number of experts will, of course, vary by project and will be dictated by the details such as the project's size, purpose, and building site.

New construction and/or renovation designs cannot proceed very far without the involvement of professional designers. Any attempt to save on design fees by excluding necessary consultants can result in costly mistakes. If a building permit is necessary, participation by licensed design professionals is almost always a legal requirement.

A theatre consultant and an architect must first be found to translate artistic and economic goals into the reality of a building or performance space. Unfortunately, many architects are unfamiliar with the details of theatrical needs and structures and although they are artists in their own right, they should not be allowed to design building elements that impose unnecessary limitations on the artistic work or function of a theatre. Theatre consultants can usually assist prospective owners and their architect in avoiding these design problems. A theatre is an integrated collection of literally hundreds of details that affect performance functions, and there are just a few ways to execute these details properly. In all likelihood, other design professionals will also be required for the execution of the design, as discussed later in this chapter. By working in close collaboration with one another, artistic directors, architects, and consultants can create performance spaces to facilitate a company's theatrical goals and advance its artistic mission.

Theatre Consultants

The services, project experience, and expertise offered can vary greatly from one theatre consultant to another in this unlicensed business. Some may specialize in programming studies, while others may work only in the field of performance equipment design. And yet, professionals working in these different disciplines may all appropriately call themselves theatre consultants.

Full-service theatre consultants typically participate in a wide range of tasks that include programming and space allocation, site planning, auditorium design, seating and sightlines, backstage, which is also called back of house or BOH, and front-of-house or FOH, functionality, performance equipment design, coordination of building systems, identification of theatre-specific code issues, and inspections of performance equipment installations. Some consultants also provide services after the theatre is open to ensure continuity in the execution of the ideas that had evolved. The client—owner, user, group, or company—should expect a theatre consultant to:

1.) Represent and protect the interests of the theatre owner and users during the design and construction processes. This requires that the consultant understand the artistic and commercial missions of the producing entity to ensure that the execution of the building's details supports the company's goals. First-hand experience of theatre practice and an appreciation of the company's artistic policy are necessary.

2.) Serve as a bridge between the theatre world and the architectural/engineering worlds. Unfortunately, many architects and engineers have never been in a live-performance theatre and, although there are notable exceptions, most do not understand a theatre's unique needs. Some architects or engineers may have experience in a few theatre projects, but do not necessarily appreciate that each performing arts project is unique. Hence, the consultant should act as a translator or facilitator, explaining theatre terminology and interpreting theatre artists' needs and expectations.

For best results, the company or owner rather than the architect should hire the theatre consultant because a consultant's candor could be compromised when contracted by anyone other than the owner.

Finding a Theatre Consultant

There are at least two approaches to finding a theatre consultant. One is word-of-mouth recommendations. Speaking with colleagues who have completed major renovations or new construction can be valuable. It is better to speak with them after the theatre has been running for a while and after they have had time to address any emerging problems.

Another approach is to contact the American Society of Theatre Consultants (ASTC) (www.theatreconsultants.org), a professional organization of theatre consultants. Note that the ASTC is an organization of individuals, not consulting firms, and membership is not an endorsement of qualifications or experience. It should also be noted that there are many qualified consultants who are not members. Finding the right consultant may require work, but the right consultant can make a considerable difference to the outcome of the building or renovation project.

As part of the screening process, it is standard to request a consultant's qualifications in writing. Assuming the material submitted is satisfactory, an interview should be arranged, references requested and checked, and proposed services and fees spelled out in writing. Consultants may charge by the hour, the day, or the project.

Architects

The role of the architect is indispensable in practically all processes involved with assessing, acquiring, renovating, or designing a building. Besides leading the design team and executing the appearance of the building, the architect is responsible for a wide variety of functions including the incorporation of all building features, coordinating the diverse building infrastructure and systems, and ensuring compliance with relevant building codes.

Peer arts groups with recent experience in architectural ventures or theatre and acoustic consultants can act as references for architects. Alternatively, the local chapter of the American Institute of Architects (AIA)(www.aia.org) can supply a list of theatre architects or a number of architects can be invited to submit proposals for the project. One form of invitation is a Request for Qualifications (RFQ) and the other is a Request for Proposal (RFP).

The RFQ is an owner's statement of intent for an upcoming project, which invites architects/design teams to participate in a selection process. The statement asks professionals to identify their interest in the project and to submit their qualifications for consideration. The RFQ typically casts a wide net and ultimately the number of respondents has to be whittled down to a manageable number, the aptly named "short-list" of candidates. It is appropriate that the owner reply to all RFQ respondents even though most will be politely refused. The short-listed respondents should be told that they will be contacted for an upcoming RFP.

The RFP is a more focused invitation than an RFQ. The goal is to invite relatively few architects and/or design teams to propose services and fees related to a well-defined project scope. Proper crafting of a good RFP is probably worthy of a book in itself. Suffice it to say that the RFP should identify details of the intended building project or study including: the purpose of the project; the history of the arts group; the nature of professional services requested; the time frame for completion of work; the phases and/ or goals of the project; and a number of other items to gain as much comparative information from respondents as possible.

Engineers and Other Design Consultants

Assessing existing spaces or designs for new construction inevitably requires a number of engineering consultants. Both scenarios require separate engineers specializing in, at least, structural, mechanical, electrical, plumbing, and fire protection. In some cases, other consultants may be required to complete the design team. They might include: civil engineers (for site conditions), landscape architects/consultants, building code and ADA consultants, cost estimators, architectural lighting consultants, audio-visual/projection consultants, communications/data consultants, and others depending on the scope of the intended project. For better or worse, this is an age of specialization and technology.

Structural Engineer

All new construction projects require the services of a licensed structural engineer. As the job title suggests, these professionals are responsible for designing building structures, foundations, rigging beams, technical catwalks, and all of the other—seen and unseen—structural elements of a building. Structural engineers are essentially responsible for the "bones" of the building. They can also assess existing buildings for structural integrity. Anyone contemplating the purchase or renovation of an existing building should take advantage of their expertise.

For existing structures, there are two areas where structural engineers are necessary:

First, a structural engineer can uncover any hidden issues that might compromise a building's intended use—is it safe to be an occupied structure? When there is a change in use and/or owners, building authorities may require a professional's review of the structural integrity before granting a legal Certificate of Occupancy (C of O). Structural defects, can be among the most costly and disruptive to correct, so it's best to know what, if any, there are before committing to the project. One of Murphy's Laws is "Anything is easier to get into than get out of."

Second, a structural engineer can determine the feasibility of any modifications proposed for a newfound space or renovation changes imagined for an existing theatre building. With an understanding of the scope of a renovation, a structural engineer can identify the feasibility of dreams and offer cost-effective solutions and alternatives. It is wise to consult a structural engineer early and often while the plans are being developed.

Mechanical/Electrical/Plumbing Engineers

Mechanical, electrical, and plumbing engineers (M-E-P for short) provide indispensable professional design and oversight services for the building systems and infrastructure, which include many items that are out of sight and taken for granted until they don't work properly.

Mechanical engineers work at HVAC—heating, ventilating, and air conditioning. Their expertise is essential for new-construction design, investigations into the "health" of existing building systems, and for proposed renovation work.

Electrical engineers design and assess conditions for virtually everything using electricity. Their scope starts at the building's service entrance—the power entry point from the utility company—and includes participation in all electrical systems within the building such as lighting, power receptacles, fire and security alarm systems, building management systems, machine, and motor, and elevator power. Many electrical engineering firms also provide architectural lighting design services.

Plumbing engineers assess existing water systems and design new building systems involving water, which includes toilets, sinks, showers, water fountains, floor drains, and roof drain piping. Their scope may also include fire protection sprinkler systems, which can address life-safety codes, insurance issues, and proper integration of sprinklers within the building fabric.

Any construction or renovation project, and/or any serious investigation into a building acquisition must involve MEP engineers. The temptation to use contractors instead of independent licensed engineers for construction/renovation in public assembly venues should be resisted as it is asking for trouble. Bypassing engineers is almost always a false economy. First-rate contractors certainly contribute to the details of construction projects, but in most cases engineers will be required to protect the interests of the owners long before the contractors enter the picture. Engineers will provide unbiased professional assistance with legal requirements, planning construction budgets, identifying project scope for bidding, review of bids to contractors, and oversight services for the actual construction work. Like the structural engineer discussed above, it is best to involve MEP engineers as early as possible in building ventures of any description.

Acoustical Consultants

Acoustical consultants typically work in three main disciplines of performance venue design: room acoustics, sound isolation, and noise control. Many acoustical firms are also involved with sound system designs. It is important to select an acoustical consultant experienced in theatre work since the general scientific field of acoustics also embraces industrial design and other esoteric applications. A theatre company should be concerned with:

1.) Room acoustics, which involves determining the design criteria for spatial volumes, auditorium geometry, architectural finishes, audience-seating relationships, and other variables of a stage and auditorium design that affect how sound energy will be transmitted to the audience. This is an important issue to get right for both speech intelligibility and the use of amplified sound for public events.

2.) Sound isolation, which consists of preventing outside noise from penetrating the stage or auditorium where it can create background noise levels that interfere with performances.

3.) Noise control addresses and prevents background sounds generated within the building from interfering with performances. Heating/cooling systems, elevators, plumbing, roof drains, performance equipment, adjacent building activities, and a variety of other building-related functions can create intrusive noise that requires isolation from the performance space.

Architectural Lighting Consultants

Working in concert with the electrical engineer and architect, lighting consultants work on the selection, distribution, and control of architectural lighting fixtures. Like theatrical lighting designers, they reveal what is seen and conceal what is not during public events. Although lighting consultants are often involved with auditorium or house lighting, most do not have the expertise to provide designs for performance lighting systems. Performance lighting and its control are usually the domain of theatre consultants.

ADA Consultants

The Americans with Disabilities Act of 1990—known as ADA—introduced new federal requirements enabling individuals with disabilities to participate fully in all aspects of society. For theatre design this essentially means the building design must provide equal access to people with impairments of all kinds. The law made significant and sweeping changes that will forever affect all publicly accessible buildings in the U.S.

Since the enactment of ADA, the details of access requirements are gradually being better defined through court decisions in response to lawsuits brought by the disabled and their advocates. ADA compliance for theatres is now a large part of theatre design. All public areas are affected: theatre entrances and exits, audience seating, restrooms, box office, hall and door details, theatre dressing rooms, and staff and technical areas.

Certainly all new buildings must address this special code, but it is also an issue to consider when investigating theatre acquisitions, renovations, and/or found spaces. Modifications required to comply with ADA regulations can be costly, and in the case of some existing structures may prove either unfeasible or impossible. The ADA issue is further complicated by the proliferation of more stringent requirements and initiatives developed by individual states and municipalities, where the local ADA code may supersede the national requirements.

In most cases an architect and/or theatre consultant will be very familiar with the requirements of the ADA and can help in anticipating and solving problems. However, some projects may require the assistance of an ADA consultant who specializes in this new field.

In addition to the building design professionals, the building-acquisition process should involve other professionals, institutions, and agencies to achieve the goals in opening a new theatre. A sample of those that might be required follows.

Management Consultants

Assistance may be needed from management consultants for board development, long-range business planning, and/or marketing of a company or arts group. Theatre consultants typically address the physical planning for phased construction and company growth, but most do not offer the business management advice that is necessary to position a company in a particular community. Nor do many theatre consultants offer services to advise on phased business growth. There are arts consulting groups that specialize only in the organizational, business, and marketing concerns of performing arts companies.

Although there may be benefits in seeking arts management services from one of the few theatre-consulting firms that offers both business planning and building design services, the arguments for separating the consulting discipline of arts management from building-design services is equally persuasive. Diversifying these services allows a group to sample different perspectives.

Fundraising Consultants

When considering a new building or expensive renovations, assistance is frequently required in raising capital to pay for the anticipated work. Capital funding for construction usually needs consultants specializing in the development and execution of fundraising strategies for nonprofit groups and the performing arts.

Fundraising of the magnitude required for major construction work typically proceeds slowly, so one needs to be realistic and patient. There is so much more to know about fundraising than targeting a few significant donors. The relatively small fees involved with hiring a specialist can be paid back many fold with a successful campaign, which will be discussed in more detail in Chapter 13: Fundraising. It is generally regarded as unprofessional to structure fees for fundraising as a percentage of monies pledged. Don't plan to pay for fundraising services on a pay-as-you-go basis from the proceeds of the fundraising effort.

Facility Management Services

In a new, or newly renovated, building it may be wise for a theatre company to divest itself of the daily responsibilities of maintaining the building and grounds. In particular, it might be most effective to hire a property management company to handle the daily cleaning and upkeep of a building in addition to the maintenance of building systems, such as the heating and cooling plant. An operating budget should take into consideration how both the mundane and technical tasks of operating the new premises will be managed.

Theatre Construction and Renovation

Building design or the adaptation of existing structures requires knowledge and experi-ence that most performing arts professionals do not have. The expertise required for building planning is as unique to the architectural world as theatre management and production skills are to the theatre world. Building design disciplines have their own vocabularies, processes, and division of labor. Groups contemplating a building acquisi-tion should proceed slowly and educate themselves about this new world. The terminol-ogy used will seem foreign at first, and small details often matter significantly to the future theatre operation. As the rest of this chapter shows, a theatre building is a unique type of real estate, which, like any performance or production, must bring together a complex and diverse number of elements to work as a unified whole.

The Architectural Design and Construction Process

Architectural practice in North America is a largely standardized process by which these design professionals take a building from initial concept through the various stages of design, including bidding and construction, to completion. The process involves specific phases of development and completion in which levels of detail are layered on top of previous decisions and conclusions. This process produces increasingly detailed drawings and specifications and increasingly refined construction-cost estimates.

The names and duration of each of a project's phases may vary depending on the scope of the project, and they may differ for renovations as compared with new con-struction. However, all building design involves the sequential, orderly development of ideas, which increasingly narrows the focus from "big picture" issues down to tiny de-tails. All projects have established schedules to control and monitor the project.

Although the design and construction phases vary in duration according to the project, generally speaking, theatre buildings require longer to complete than other building types. It is not at all unusual to spend eighteen months in the design phase. Unusually short design or construction periods should be viewed as suspect as they may indicate that the complexity of the project has been underestimated. Delays and inter-ruptions in the project's schedule can occur at any point in the process, but most of them result from a conflict between what is desired for the building and the ability to pay for those desires.

The design and construction processes seem slow, particularly compared with show production schedules. Companies entering into building projects must anticipate protracted design and construction delays and setbacks. Theatre managers must be espe-cially aware of these frustrations because renovation may prove disruptive to an upcoming season. Producing companies involved in a building project would be well advised to plan a conservative timeline for their design/construction periods. In general, troupes should have contingency plans for unforeseen, and largely inevitable, circumstances delaying their productions and/or disrupting ticket sales.

New building construction is usually divided into the following sequential steps, commonly called *phases*:

Programming Phase (also called Preschematic Phase)
Schematic Design (SD) Phase
Design Development (DD) Phase
Contract Documents (CD) Phase
Bidding/Bid Negotiations Phase
Construction Administration Phase
Commissioning/Owner Occupancy and Fit-Out Phase

Programming Phase

Program is the architectural term to describe a building's use. Depending on context, program can mean: the various purposes and functions of a building; the specific activities or tasks expected to serve the functions; and/or the physical spaces allocated within the building to house both functions and activities.

The programming phase is typically the earliest phase of a theatre building design that defines the fundamentals and will guide all future decisions for the next months or even years of work. When, for instance, challenges of insufficient space or budget emerge, the early program decisions are used to guide later solutions.

The end-product of the programming phase should include a clear understanding and documentation of the size of the building; the performance conditions; the quantity, size, and purposes of the building's rooms; an identification of surrounding site conditions; and the definition of other variables that will help to determine the probable cost of the building.

Schematic Design Phase

Once the owner accepts the recommendations and design parameters, the project moves into the schematic design (SD) phase. During SD, architectural drawings using single lines to express interior layouts of rooms, corridors, stairways, and other features appear. The building's exterior design and relationship to its surroundings also begin in this phase. Early ideas for architectural finishes and the building infrastructure are also typically identified in narrative or schedule form.

As these drawings and concepts are developed between the design team consultants and the owner or client, the drawings become increasingly detailed. Although the process can be time consuming and frustrating, fine results can be achieved if the design team and client communicate and work well together. The people who will eventually work in the building should study the design plans repeatedly, and those people should attempt to visualize just how well the place will function. One should "walk through" the design plans—as an audience member, a performer, a manager, a technician, and so forth. When problems are encountered, they should be discussed and resolved as early in the process as possible.

At the end of schematic design phase, the work is usually submitted to an experienced cost estimator. Although the drawings and narratives developed by the design team will understandably be lacking in detail, a good estimator should be able to develop reasonably accurate construction-cost projections based on knowledge of the building trades, local conditions, trends in the construction market, and experience. One should be prepared for "sticker shock." The SD process may have resulted in expanded program concepts, which are translated into expanded costs. It may be time to rethink the program or budget and to compromise in order to keep the project moving.

Design Development Phase

As soon as budget hurdles are cleared, the project design moves into design development—the DD phase. Architectural drawings now become much more detailed. At this point reversing prior decisions becomes disruptive and/or impractical for the design schedule. Building code issues are addressed in detail. Building systems are reflected in detailed drawings based on the early narratives and evolving architectural details. Engineering drawings completed during this phase show the placement of the heating and cooling physical plant, related duct routing, electrical equipment, plumbing fixtures, building structural steel, and details for all the other infrastructure.

The drawings for the performance space(s) will also show more details of audience seating and sightlines, auditorium and stage features, rigging systems, performance lighting systems, sound and production intercom systems, and others.

In short, the details developed during the design development phase are reflections of the comprehensive planning and design of all the building features. The end of the DD phase usually results in yet another cost-estimation based on the larger volume of drawings, schedules, and draft specifications.

Contract Documents Phase

The purpose of the contract documents (CD) phase is to prepare the final drawings and specifications to be used by the building trades for bidding and construction of the project. Although there may be some small details to address, the building design is largely locked in and no major redesigns are expected by the time the CD phase begins.

The majority of effort expended in this phase involves the time-consuming process of developing a detailed bid package, which assures that the bid process will be clear and efficient. The goal is to provide sufficiently detailed documents so no ambiguity will cause confusion or, worse, loopholes that can be exploited by unscrupulous contractors.

The contract drawings and written specifications developed in this phase are legally binding documents. Combined drawings and specifications complement one another in explaining the project, and are legally inseparable as the record guidelines for the bid process, construction procedures, and expected outcome of the final project.

All of the various design consultants typically contribute drawing sheets, as well as written chapters or sections to the specification. For medium- to large-scale theatre construction projects, the compiled drawing sheets can easily number in the hundreds—more even than the drawings required for the most elaborate Broadway musical. The specification volumes identifying contractual relationships, construction administrative procedures, building trade details, acceptable products, construction sequences, or theatre performance equipment/systems, for example, can be six or more inches thick.

Upon completion of the contract documents phase, the final drawings and specifications are bundled together and released as a single package for bidding by construction trades. The formal design phases of the project are now completed, barring any redesign work that might result from major cost surprises in the bids. The project now enters a phase that involves the construction trades.

Bidding/Bid Negotiations Phase

The bid phase is an interim period when neither design nor construction work occurs. Construction work begins only after a contract is signed between the project's funding-entity, or the owner, and a construction company, either a general contractor or a construction management firm. The construction contract primarily expresses what is being built, the cost of construction, and the schedule for building. The contract is usually signed by the owner and architect and builder. Obviously, the owner should seek legal counsel during all steps in this process.

Although the building contract is typically between only two parties, owner and contractor, the contractor's obligation includes the work of many subcontracting companies that together form the construction team for this one project only. Each of the subcontractors provides specialty building-trade work under separate agreements with the builder/contractor, who coordinates the subtrades' work. During construction, the *owner's* only contractual relationship is with the single construction company that heads the construction team, not with each of the subcontractors.

The organizational structure of the construction team and the process leading to the negotiations of construction costs can vary greatly depending upon the details of the particular project. For example, contract details for privately funded projects are often very different from those for public projects or those projects funded by government bodies using taxpayers' money. Public projects, for instance, often require legal acceptance of the lowest bid after a competitive, sealed-bid submittal process.

Other types of projects may use a negotiated arrangement with a single construction management company that is either assigned to the theatre work as part of a developer's larger project, or is hand-picked by the theatre owner after an interview process. Whatever the case, many theatre projects now engage a construction management company during the early design phases, thereby avoiding the builders' competitive bid process. The construction manager in this instance works with the design team for many months before any construction work is let to the trades. This approach benefits the owner and design team by providing construction solutions and periodic cost estimations, while acquainting the builder with the owner's goals.

Suffice it to say that after some process of gathering all of the trades' bids, a single price proposal is offered and then negotiated. The purpose of the contract negotiations is to identify less expensive solutions to the CD details, to more clearly define the work of individual trades, and to make a legal agreement regarding the scope, schedule, and details of what is to be built.

Construction Administration Phase
The period required for the physical construction work of theatre buildings is typically longer than that for other building types of comparable square footage. This is because of the nature of the detail-laden building and the proper sequence required to build/install those details. In turn, this is the reason that the square-foot construction costs of theatre buildings far exceed those of most other structures.

During the construction period the design team plays an active role in monitoring the construction work, which is why in architectural parlance this phase is called construction administration. Typically the design team is retained by the owner during construction to answer the contractors' questions and to review shop submittals and the work as it progresses on site. Shop submittals are the trades' final drawings, product sheets, and other paperwork, which reflect the trades' interpretations of the contract documents. It is important that the design team makes sure the trades have interpreted the drawings correctly. When a submittal strays from the original intent, the designer suggests appropriate action by the individual trades. Although seemingly a burdensome process, shop submittals protect owner, contractors, and the design team against the liabilities arising from misinterpreted contract documents.

Commissioning/Owner Occupancy and Fit-Out Phase
As the construction process nears completion, the designers and owner enter a busy period. The design team inspects all completed work, which results in compiling lists of defects room by room and trade by trade. These are called punch lists, and are submitted to the contractors with instructions for remedial work. Punch lists are inevitable with even the best of contractors.

As punch lists are cleared through contractor repairs, the major building systems are commissioned—tested—and final adjustments are made. Local authorities responsible for enforcing building codes inspect the building in anticipation of occupancy. Following the necessary legal inspections, a Certificate of Occupancy (C of O) is issued, or as often happens a temporary, or conditional, C of O is issued until the inspectors' list of issues has been addressed by the design and construction teams.

During these final months, the owner is busily preparing for the move into the new building. There are many weeks of work in arranging the details of equipment, fixtures, and furnishings that are not purchased under the construction contract. The process of getting these items into the building and installing them is often referred to as "the owner fit-out;" theatre companies should plan on several months for this effort.

There is no such thing as a "turnkey" theatre building. Part of taking occupancy involves learning about the building, debugging systems, and resolving new operational details before a production can be mounted. Theatre owners and managers must not assume that a show can smoothly move into rehearsal or production in a newly occupied building. Productions have enough challenges to overcome without simultaneously attempting to resolve the many building issues that will inevitably appear. Owners would be well advised to schedule ample time for shakedown work before starting their inaugural performance season.

Fast-Track Building Projects

Fast tracking is a process of *shortening* the time from the start of design to project completion. This is accomplished, in part, by starting on the construction phase before the design has been completed. Implausible as it sounds, this concept is often used because it allows a new building to open sooner.

Fast-track construction became popular in the 1980s and 1990s when real estate developers found that they could make profits on commercial ventures sooner by overlapping the design and construction phases. For buildings in which the floor plans are repeated on successive floors, fast tracking makes sense. In office and condominium towers the vast majority of the upper floors are identical.

Theatre buildings do not have repeat floor plans and each space within a theatre is specific and different from those on adjacent floors, so by definition, fast tracking is a poor fit. Further, because with fast tracking the structural systems are immediately underway, architectural features are locked in by the structure. The process is akin to making decisions on the run; therefore, some fast-track theatres may never reach optimum solutions because the iterative process of good theatre design has been cut short.

Also, more money may be needed sooner than a proper capital campaign can deliver, as there wouldn't be time for lengthy periods of nurturing and developing donor-relationships. More than one performing arts project has been scuttled or stalled because of capital drives that could not keep pace with fast-track design and construction schedules.

Given that fast tracking is so far from ideal, why would any company choose to deal with it? There are several possible reasons. If a theatre project is part of a mixed-use development—office, retail, and residential spaces in one structure—a schedule may well be fast tracked and the theatre would have to stay on the developer's schedule or be left behind. Another reason might be the time limits imposed on a project by municipalities or funding agencies. Although good theatres can be fast tracked, most organizations that have gone through this process feel that it was an obstacle to overcome.

Construction Costs

There are at least four budgets that need to be anticipated in a construction or renovation project. They are typically referred to as 1.) hard costs, 2.) soft costs, 3.) performance equipment, and 4.) owner fit-out.

1.) Hard costs represent the "bricks-and-mortar" costs paid to contractors to construct the physical building or to renovate an existing building.

2.) Soft costs include land acquisition, consulting fees, legal costs, project expenses, permit fees, testing costs, and a range of other procedural costs borne by the owner.

3.) Performance equipment includes all of the specialty equipment required to support the performance program for the theatre. This includes rigging systems, performance (show) lighting, sound systems, production communication systems, and other areas including audience seating. Performance equipment budgets may or may not be included in the overall construction budget.

4.) Owner fit-out costs are more accurately referred to as Furniture, Fixtures, and Equipment (or FF&E), which cover a variety of items that are best purchased directly by the owner. Although comprised of some obvious and mundane items, such as office furniture, trash cans, and wall clocks, the budgeting category may also strategically reduce construction hard costs. FF&E may be used to account for installed items that are required for theatre operations but where contractor coordination is not required. For example, cabinetwork or counters may be more efficiently purchased from a local cabinetmaker after the general contractor has left the site. Owner fit-out budgets can be quite substantial and they should not be overlooked when projecting total costs.

Renovation Costs

New construction is easier to price than renovation work because there are fewer unknowns. Even in the earliest phases of designing and budgeting a new construction project, one can reliably base costs on locale, market conditions, project precedents, and some educated guesses by a good architect and theatre consultant.

Renovation projects, on the other hand, may require more investigation into the details in order to understand likely costs. For example, more professional consultants are needed at the outset to poke into an existing building to determine the conditions of its infrastructure, maintenance, and building code status to name a few.

In renovating an existing structure it may be necessary to anticipate such expenditures as long-term replacement costs of aging systems and possible asbestos removal. Either item, alone, can break a budget if not anticipated.

The Budget in Crisis

Value Engineering

The antidote to budget overruns is a euphemistic expression called *value engineering*. In its original and pure form, value engineering was intended as a way of examining a building design to find less costly solutions to achieve desired results—a way of getting more bang for the buck.

Value engineering now involves revising building details and/or program functions to square the cost projections with the construction budget. Virtually all performing arts buildings go through this painful process one or more times during the design process.

In order to accommodate the budget, a value engineer might suggest that portions of the building be "shelled." A shelled space is one that is left as raw, unfinished space to be completed at a later time when more funding is available. The concept is used to maintain a building's original program and its architectural integrity while awaiting sufficient funding. For instance, it is common to shell rehearsal halls so that the main theatre area may be completed.

Shelling spaces is but one of many strategies that a value engineer may suggest. Other solutions might range from downgrading finishes to cutting whole areas such as trap rooms, offices, or storage. As a prospective owner, the decisions involved with value engineering can be tough, but they are often the only way to move a project into its next phase. For better or worse, value engineering has become a part of the design process and prospective owners need to work with it. Significant compromises may be necessary, and delays in the design schedule must be anticipated.

Programming and Feasibility Studies

There are ways to start the process of new construction or renovation slowly with relatively few risks in terms of time, commitment, and money. Projects can begin with a programming study to explore the first pre-schematic phase of the work that determines or tests the fundamentals or basics of the building. The work is intentionally limited by the time and funds dedicated to it in order to keep its scope manageable. Although the findings will also be limited, a properly structured programming study can provide insight for future thinking and help to align a prospective owner's expectations with likely funding.

However, for a study to be useful as the first step in a process, and not just an end in itself, it is important to involve the correct composition of professionals to identify issues that a company might not have considered. Because theatres are very expensive to build, two assessments that have to be made are the minimum space required for a company's program or needs and an estimate of likely costs to consider for future capital campaigns. Armed with that information a group can then decide if it wishes to proceed to the next step.

A feasibility study is similar in that it is an exploratory probe to find out if a given building can be renovated to be compatible with the owner's use, budget, and artistic goals. Like programming studies, feasibility studies offer low-risk methods of investigating the possibilities of a specific building and solidifying a prospective owner's thinking about operating conditions, future growth, costs, capital campaign, and artistic mission.

For instance, a structure being considered for renovation may have building code violations that are "grandfathered in" under the building's current use. It is not uncommon for buildings to have violations that predate revisions to building codes. However, the start of a renovation may trigger the need to bring the building up to current codes. Although some discoveries may require relatively minor fixes, others may include such costly repairs as fire protection, egress, handicapped access for ADA, and asbestos abatement. Bringing the building up to code may significantly deplete a budget intended for addressing program issues, which are the real focus of the renovation. Without input from building professionals experienced in the scope of a study, these discoveries could sink a renovation project.

Theatre Design Options and Requirements

Of all of the many decisions faced by boards of trustees, artistic directors, and executive directors, the choices leading to a new theatre space probably have the most enduring consequences because these decisions are likely to outlast the careers of the decision-makers. Building professionals typically view the life expectancy of a new theatre building to be at least fifty years, so it's important to get it right.

The rest of this chapter identifies some of the all-important early decisions affecting the physical attributes of a new theatre. There are no formulas or answers to offer because each company's needs will be unique. However the following topics are essential for all companies to discuss in deciding what should be built or found. The company's mission and its ability to raise funds have to guide these discussions. To help inform these discussions, Appendices C and D, Space List and Checklist for Theatre Design Criteria, can be used.

The Architectural and Performance Program

As discussed earlier in this chapter, the word *program* embraces a spectrum of guiding principles that include the building's purpose, expected activities and functions, and spaces to be built. Once completed, the program is the first record of the conceptual building, and it is both the launching pad and the touchstone for all building design and construction decisions.

Long before there are discussions about likely sites, funding-sources, and defining spaces within the future building there are more fundamental decisions to be made. What are the producing company's goals and what is the new building's purpose? These early decisions to determine the program are the most important.

By the time an organization is contemplating a new home it should have a mission statement and ties to a greater community. However, nothing can be taken for granted. The mission statement should be reviewed and then revised as necessary. Are the activities and productions still in line with the mission statement? Determine the nature and proportions of production types that have already been produced and the demographics of the audience.

Next, realistically project the company's goals five, ten, or more years into the future. An artistic mission statement is not an academic exercise. It focuses decision-makers, informs others, and is the first step in establishing a program document that will guide future building decisions.

Operating Pro Forma / Program Portfolio

If a mission statement is the key to a company's artistic identity then the company's operating *pro forma* is the key to its ideal building. Dictionaries define *pro forma* as describing something provided in advance to prescribe form. In architectural terms it suggests planning documents that call upon the company's history to identify the means and methods of how the group will work in its future building.

The objective of these early discussions should be to develop a written *program portfolio* that can be used with the executive board and advisors and move the project into the programming phase of the project with the design professionals. The portfolio should identify things such as the mission statement; performance types, both past and future; plus pertinent records regarding the productions, cast sizes, venue details, length of runs, audience sizes, and other similar production information. Equally important are financial records and projections for income and operating expenses in the proposed building.

Organize the portfolio information so it can also address administrative staff; technical staff, both salaried and freelance; likely hours of operation/activities; rehearsal and load-in periods; sources of scenery, costumes, and props; and other details of technical

support. The program portfolio cannot be too detailed in terms of either historical prece-
dent or future expectations. The information will be instrumental in helping the company
to recommit to its mission statement as well as leading it to the next level of decisions
regarding the new building. The conclusions reached in the program portfolio will ultimately define the goals for building size, the spaces to be included, and details of the
performance and support spaces. While the immutable realities of building budgets, site
conditions, and other constraints are not yet factored into the building's design, the job
of defining the physical goals has to start somewhere and it's best to start with the company's mission and operating needs.

Seating Capacity

The seating capacity of an auditorium will greatly influence both the business and artistic
potential of a theatre. Audience capacity will determine the potential box office income,
and therefore the total theatre budget. It may also help to dictate appropriate types of
productions and artistic goals. Organizations are often tempted to make drastic compromises in suiting a particular production to a particular theatre, such as a tiny show in a
huge house or a very large production on too small a stage. It is not always understood
that the theatre itself is an integral element of the art. Change the place of performance and
the performance also changes—a principle not far removed from Marshall McLuhan's
theory that the medium, not its message, determines what is communicated.

Note that audience size also affects many other factors of the company's business
from the length of production runs, to the marketing efforts needed to fill seats, to
staffing requirements for ushers, box office, and housekeeping. As audience capacity
increases more square feet are required to accommodate that audience, with higher
attendant construction costs. The relationship of audience size to theatre volume may be
obvious, but also consider how audience size has an impact on other parts of the building design. Audience size determines lobby size, number of restrooms, number of parking places, and other similar demands on public amenities including infrastructure support. As building volume increases, so do the requirements for HVAC capacity, lighting,
and other infrastructure, which are reflected in both higher capital costs and associated
operating costs.

Theatre Configuration/Types of Stages

Some theatre practitioners would argue that any play or presentation could be adapted
to any type of stage. However, many plays lend themselves better to certain stage configurations. For instance, fully staged musicals, such as *Oklahoma!*, need a quantity of
scenery that can be quickly and seamlessly changed to support the flow of the performance and the multilocation story line. It's hard to imagine that such a musical would be
as easy to mount in a theatre-in-the-round as it would be on a proscenium stage, where
traditional scenic technologies more easily conjure theatrical illusions.

In fact many theatrical pieces are created with a particular staging format in mind. Again in the case of traditional American musicals, the structure of the book and score often favor proscenium formats. The order of scenes is chosen partly to accommodate scene changes. For example, a full-stage scene is often followed by an intimate scene downstage—an in-one scene—to cover scene changes occurring upstage. This is then followed by another full-stage scene with all new scenery. This technique is common in ballet and opera as well.

Each type of stage, therefore, will suggest a certain repertoire and style of production, just as it will suggest what scenic and technical support will be necessary, and what staff will be required to create, manage, and operate it. In turn, the details of necessary production staff may lead to conclusions regarding building needs for offices and workshops, and also for budget lines to pay for related production, operating, and construction costs.

As the result of much trial and error and long tradition, most theatre practitioners concede that each style of production dictates some workable range for audience size. Although there are no hard and fast rules, the convention of matching a performance with house size is partly a function of economics and partly a result of appropriate scale for the performance piece.

The economics of house size are fairly straightforward: a fully produced traditional musical is clearly more costly to mount and run than an intimate drawing room drama with a cast of four. A musical typically requires far more actors, scenery, stagehands, and musicians. Quite obviously larger productions require a higher seat count—at the same ticket price—than smaller productions because of the greater costs.

The issues of appropriate theatre *scale* for a production are a bit more subjective, but successful live performances require a certain level of intimacy between audience and performers. It's one reason that audiences prefer sitting in the orchestra rather than in the balcony. Intimacy relates, in part, to objective ergonomic functions, such as viewing distance, field of vision to the stage, acoustic presence, and other innate perceptions that people use for judging comfort in their environment. One's sense of intimacy is also somewhat elastic and perceptions can be manipulated by the energy level of a performance. A musical, for instance, may have a very large dynamic range because of the numbers of performers onstage, their movement, decibel and illumination levels, and the overall modulation of performance energy broadcast to the audience. Therefore, many musicals can easily fill very large theatres with enough energy to sustain a connection with the audience. This phenomenon is perceived as, or confused with, intimacy, even though the auditorium is not physically intimate. In contrast, a realistic interior drama performed in an overly large house may risk having its stage energy diffused. Naturally, there are elements other than size that contribute to a sense of intimacy and these can be skillfully used to mitigate large volumes. These other elements include acoustics, sight lines, décor, seating arrangements, and general comfort—all of which contribute substantially to the appropriateness and desirability of any performance space.

Concepts of performer-audience relationships have varied over the centuries, but many theatres today favor a more intimate relationship than the one offered by a traditional proscenium theatre. Partly because the cinema can accomplish lifelike illusions so much better than live theatre, fewer productions are encased within a proscenium arch. It is not uncommon for the scenery to cross through the proscenium arch—in effect bringing the audience and stage closer together. In more recent theatre history there are other factors that have affected trends in staging and theatre construction.

In the three decades following World War II designers of theatres seemingly lost sight of some of the critical elements of intimacy that contribute to good performer-audience relationships. Why this happened must include changes to modern building codes. When one compares the physical intimacy of a nineteenth-century British play-house with a modern American playhouse, the differences are enormous. For a theatre with the same seating capacity, the modern theatre auditorium has grown physically larger. As a reaction to tragic theatre fires, building codes now dictate significantly larger seat, aisle, and egress dimensions—all of which have contributed to greatly enlarged auditoriums.

Partly in response to these large post-war auditoriums, theatre practitioners of the 1960s and 1970s began to move away from proscenium presentations. A generation of theatre directors and designers revived some of the forgotten historical forms of theatre staging, as well as inventing entirely new formats. Since then, thrust and arena staging have become fairly common. The more common forms of the many staging formats, or types of stages, are pictured in Appendix E.

Ultimately, the choice of staging format and theatre configuration comes down to a company's repertoire and the preferences of the artistic staff. There are also business issues to be considered before making this key decision.

The Dark Theatre

Most companies have an annual performance season that lasts for a predictable number of months, after which public activities end and the theatre space goes "dark." Dark the-atres are anathema as they continue to rack up expenses: utilities, mortgages, upkeep, etc.

To solve this dilemma some theatres are rented out in their dark periods to main-tain a revenue stream. An example might be a symphony concert hall that runs an an-nual summer film festival. Another example might be a theatre company that rents its space to a local business college to produce corporate seminars. To pursue such opportunities successfully requires a certain degree of forethought when selecting a theatre configura-tion and before such income appears in a business plan.

For instance, say that a theatre company has determined that its seven-month sea-son is best presented in a proscenium stage format. It has also determined that there is an off-season rental market for modern dance companies to occupy the building. The rental income would help the company and fill a local performing arts need for suitable dance space. Sounds like a win-win situation. After committing to building a theatre with a thirty-foot wide proscenium opening, the owners might discover that no dance com-pany could use their space because the dancers require a minimum forty-foot wide prosce-nium. Another example: a drama group builds a theatre with a thrust stage and plans to run a film festival during the off-season. It later discovers that two-thirds of the seats are outside the acceptable viewing angles because there is only one possible screen position. Knowing these issues in advance may not have kept these companies from their theatre configuration choices, but it would be better to know about the limitations in advance.

Black Box/Multiform Theatres

One concept developed during the experimental 1960s and 1970s was the "black box" theatre, created to allow audience-performer configurations to be changed to suit each production. Black box is not the most apt description and to counter this some advocates now call them, more appropriately, *multiform theatres*. The most common configurations used in multiform theatres are end stage, arena, and thrust, but other arrangements are also possible.

The ability of multiform theatres to change the audience-performer relationship is very attractive to many groups. Relatively low construction costs and renovation-friendly found spaces also add to their attraction and proliferation. At least on paper, multiform spaces appear to offer maximum flexibility and for some companies they are ideal. However, multiform theatres do have limitations and these restrictions should be discussed and understood before a company chooses it as a theatre design.

One limitation, or issue, of the multiform theatre is the time and labor-intensive changeover that is required to rearrange a configuration. Because of the extensive amount of time and manpower required to rearrange spaces, most black boxes are unchanged for years at a time. Although the inherent and underlying flexibility of a multiform theatre remains, production schedules and budgets often do not allow full use of that flexibility.

Another limitation is the seat count. By definition, these spaces typically have relatively low seat counts, with 200–300 seats being the high range. There are examples with fewer seats—100 or fewer—and a few examples with more seats. These usually have expensive automated changeover systems to reconfigure the space.

All except the most expensive, technology-driven multiform theatres have a somewhat casual or temporary appearance because of the very nature of movable platforms, steps, and railings. As efforts are made to make the components look more like architecture, there is usually some loss in the flexibility of the components and/or configuration schemes. Although an informal, workmanlike appearance may be appropriate for some programs, many require a more formal or finished appearance.

One last item to be considered is ticketing. It is virtually impossible to give a subscriber the same seat for each production because any given seat location (J 101, for example) can be in a different part of the room with each new configuration.

Backstage Areas

The amount and type of backstage area required are determined by the type of presentations a particular theatre is designed to accommodate. Will the stage be too large and costly to operate in relation to potential box office income? Are rehearsal rooms necessary? Does the same rehearsal and dressing room space have to service more than one performance or production at a time? Can rehearsal areas be utilized during performance hours?

Technical Support Areas

Space and facilities for the construction of scenery, costumes, and props are assets in any theatre building that supports resident productions. When the landlord is also the producer, facilities for both construction and rehearsal will be necessary either in the building or elsewhere. An operation that is centralized under one roof is always more desirable. If located away from the theatre, scenic construction may be more costly because of the necessity to transport it and more difficult to control from the administrative point of view because out of sight/out of mind. Similarly, having offsite costume construction would involve transporting performers to costume-fittings.

Scenic production facilities, which require an enormous amount of space and a large capital investment, are impractical for organizations that do not create new shows on a regular basis. If the theatre building does not contain shop facilities, it is possible to rent lofts, bowling alleys, warehouses or other low-cost spaces. The place for and cost of scenic construction should be studied carefully when theatre plans are being formulated.

If it's determined that scenery and costume fabrication work should be offsite, the theatre building will still require some dedicated backstage areas for technical support. Costumes will always require maintenance, laundering, and last minute modifications. Scenery and props will also require adjustments during load-ins and technical rehearsals, as well as maintenance over a run. Each of the several production support disciplines should at least have some dedicated maintenance space within the building.

Costume maintenance may need a laundry room—wet area—and another "dry" space for fittings, repairs, and ironing. Scenery and prop maintenance may need a small workshop, with a few basic floor tools, a workbench, and storage cabinets for supplies and portable tools. An area should be provided near the stage, with slop sinks, to accommodate the scenic-painting work that is invariably required for touch-up painting after load-in.

Backstage storage space is another issue to be studied carefully. Requirements vary widely with each company's needs and wherewithal. Most production staffs would agree that they have never seen a theatre with enough storage space. The issues of how much storage space and where to put it run largely parallel with those for the technical workshops—onsite space versus offsite space. The production staff should be consulted and involved in these decisions. And certainly, storage space should be allocated in the primary venue. Storage space is relatively inexpensive because it needs minimal finish treatments and because of its lack of building services (e.g., HVAC).

Administration Areas

The members of a management staff in an active theatre are usually required to work long hours. With a little planning, simple and inexpensive solutions can enhance administrative environments, which will greatly improve working conditions and staff productivity.

The single most important issue in designing administrative offices is their location within the theatre. When considering a building layout, the owners should see that the management areas are positioned out of the main traffic flow of performers, technicians, and deliveries in order to avoid distractions. Similarly, offices should be isolated from the many noisy activities involved with rehearsals and production work. Natural light, normally to be avoided in the theatre itself, should be encouraged in the office areas to promote healthy working attitudes and to mitigate fatigue. Therefore, an ideal location for management areas is on the building's exterior walls. Wrapping the relatively quiet offices around the theatre space may act as an acoustic buffer preventing street noise from penetrating the performance areas.

A separate entrance to the administration offices is highly desirable, both to segregate the production/performer environments and to create a calm first-impression for visitors.

Space allocation within theatres always involves difficult choices. Nothing in a theatre can replace adequate space, so in planning a new home the owner should be sure to allocate sufficient space, which should include space for growth, for the administrative staff and management team, including new staff, interns, and volunteers. Consider areas to accommodate guest artists, board meetings, and private, sensitive conversations—even if these are not prominent in your current operational needs. (Additional considerations for the administrative areas of the theatre are included in checklist form in Appendix C.)

The administrative areas should receive as much attention to detail as do the performance or audience areas. After all, without a management staff working efficiently the theatre would not be in business. Should anyone suggest moving the management offices off-site, view this as a solution of last resort. Consolidating all of the diverse company activities under one roof cannot be underestimated.

Summary

For place of performance the most important issue is the selection and composition of the design team and consultants who can guide a group and its board, through the mazelike process of renovating or constructing new theatre space. Important, too, is the realistic match of what an organization wants and needs versus its ability to pay. Because of the complexity and expense involved in the process, a programming or feasibility study can be a very enlightening first step.

CHAPTER 3

Personnel for the Theatre

T HIS CHAPTER DEALS WITH THE GENERAL PRINCIPLES of personnel management, unpaid and paid, including union members. If a member of actors' equity
association were asked to define a professional actor, the response would likely
be "a professional actor is a member of Equity." And most union members would agree.

However, there are many skilled and talented theatre people—directors, designers,
managers, and actors—who earn a living from their specialization and do not belong to
unions. For this reason, a "professional" may better be defined as someone who earns
money—a living—from his or her work. A nonprofessional, then, is someone who works
without financial compensation, although there may well be other types of reward.
Professional also implies that the work produced is of a high quality.

Humphrey Bogart is credited with saying: "A professional is a guy who does his job
well—even when he doesn't feel like it!" And that's not a bad definition.

Divisions of Theatrical Labor

The upcoming chapters discuss different types of theatre in America and how each is
usually organized and staffed. But no matter how a theatre is organized, the work that
needs to be done falls into three distinct categories: artistic, production, and administration.

Each category requires workers who possess definably different sets of skills, attitudes, and interests. It may even be said that each requires a certain temperament. Some
people are happiest on stage and others are nervous just meeting someone new. So an
important objective of personnel management is placing workers into the jobs they will
do best.

Theatre productions and companies are comprised of three levels of personnel and
three divisions of labor:

1.) LEADERSHIP LEVEL
   Producer/Board/Theatre Owner

2.) MANAGEMENT LEVEL
   Artistic/Managing Directors

3.) STAFF LEVEL
   Artistic, Production, Administration

In nearly all cases, the chain of command in the theatre—progressing from top leadership down—is as vertical as it appears in the chart opposite. But there have been alternatives. Historically, many eighteenth-century European and American theatres were operated as share-holding companies in which the actors were the main shareholders, and decisions were made by vote. Today, few companies are organized as collectives in which all matters—artistic and managerial—are discussed and agreed to by most or all members: this is a very cumbersome style of management.

Defining Staff Requirements

Organizational Structure

Each basic theatre organization type—commercial, nonprofit, educational, and community—dictates its own personnel requirements. Unlike the commercial theatre, for example, a nonprofit theatre must have a board of trustees, usually has an artistic director as well as a managing director, and employs fundraising personnel. If the theatre hires union workers, certain jobs will be *covered employment* but union employees will be limited—or more accurately, specified—in regard to the hours and types of tasks they are permitted to perform. *Covered employment*, usually—but not always—refers to fringe benefits *coverage*: health insurance, pension and annuity contributions that union workers receive through their negotiated contracts. Enlightened managements will provide *covered employment* for all its employees, regardless of union membership. *Covered employment* may also refer to positions protected by union agreements.

If the theatre is a constituent of a larger institution, personnel requirements may vary greatly from those in an independently operated theatre. This is especially true in college theatre: all salaried positions may be paid by the college budget and filled by people such as instructors, technicians and custodians whose main jobs are other than working in a theatre.

To begin defining what jobs must be created and how the operation will function in terms of a chain of command, a table of organization must be drawn up. This is also called a line chart because it clearly delineates the lines of authority.

After the line chart is developed, each job title is shown, often in a little box; with a line connecting that position to that of a supervisor above and, perhaps, to that of staff

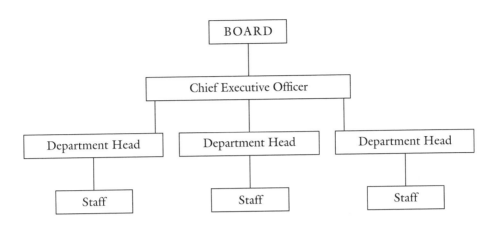

people below. To inform personnel how the organization is structured, a line chart can be distributed with job orientation materials or displayed in the reception area. The danger is that such charts can encourage an overly rigid style of personnel management. They do not take the human element into account and may tempt management to avoid creative solutions such as combining jobs or redefining job titles and responsibilities or changing the chain of command. And from the employee's point of view, no one wants to be put into a box. So, organizational charts may be a useful planning tool but should probably be kept in the manager's desk drawer.

Minimum Staffing Requirements

The following chart demonstrates that as professionalism in the theatre increases so do the number of jobs required to produce the final product.

The *type* of production being produced also has a major impact upon staff requirements. Musical theatre, including opera, almost always requires more artistic and production personnel than nonmusical theatre. Productions of Shakespeare or classical theatre usually require more actors and staff than contemporary theatre productions. And, of course, the larger the performance facility, the more people needed to run it.

Job Combining

Combining several jobs into one position may be frowned upon by large institutions or may violate union agreements, but it is a practice common to many theatre and performing arts organizations because of their limited finances or because it encourages greater efficiency. For example, it is reasonable to assume that an employee should be able to take on more work and responsibility as time goes on. Most people respond well when given new challenges in addition to familiar work. Big industries have recognized this and many have reassigned the one-task assembly line worker to multitask, beginning-to-end production work.

AN 800-SEAT, NON-MUSICAL THEATRE: TYPICAL STAFF REQUIREMENTS IN DIFFERENT THEATRICAL ORGANIZATIONS (Excluding Performers)

Non-professional community theatre (multi-production season)		Stock theatre using AEA company (multi-production season)		Broadway theatre (one production)	
Full-time operating staff (non-salaried)	Part-time or on fee, royalty or optional	Full-time operating staff (non-union)	Part-time or on fee, royalty or optional	Full-time operating staff (union)	Part-time or on fee, royalty or optional
Artistic Director	Board of Directors	Producer or Artistic Director	Board of Directors (if nonprofit)	(Producer's Staff)	Director*
House Manager	Committees	General Manager	Attorney	General Manager	Author*
Box Office Treasurer	Executive Secretary	Business Manager	Accountant*	Company Manager*	Scenic Designer*
Stage Manager	Business Secretary	House Manager	Director*	Stage Manager*	Costume Designer*
Master Electrician	Publicity Chairman			Assistant Stage Manager*	
		Secretary	Author*	Stagehands*	Lighting Designer*
Properties Master	Ticket Sales committees	Box Office Treasurer	Group Sales Manager	Fly crew*	Scene builders*
Stage crew	Legal Counsel	Assistant Treasurer	Ushers	Light crew*	Scene painters*
Makeup crew	Director*	Publicity Director	Ticket takers	Makeup artist*	Costume builders*
	Author*	Janitor(s)	Doorman	Hairdresser*	Wig makers*
	Scenic, Lighting and Costume Designer	Production	Poster crew, etc.	Wardrobe Supervisor*	Prop builders*
	Scene and costume construction crews	Stage Manager*	Security Guard	Press Agent*	Scene transporters*
	Ushers	Scenic Designer	Hairdresser and wig specialist	Dressers*	Attorney
	Ticket takers	Lighting Designer	House Physician	(Landlord's Staff)	Accountant(s)
	Prompters	Costume Designer	Matrons	House Manager*	House Physician
	Maintenance crew	Properties Master.		Treasurers*	Ad Agency
		Technical Director		Ushers*	Group Sales
		Carpenter		Doormen*	
		Stitcher and Wardrobe Supervisor		Carpenter*	
		Master Electrician		Electrician*	
		5-15 technicians or apprentices		Property Master*	
				Cleaners*	
				Matrons*	
				Heat, air-conditioning and other maintenance	
				Fireman*	
				Watchman*	
				Porter	

*Working under union or other collective bargaining association contract.

It would not be wise, however, to combine a backstage position with a front-of-house position, a leading performance job with any other, any two jobs that have similar hours or require the person's being in two different places at the same time, or any two full-time jobs. Some of the most frequent and successful job combinations are:

Producer and Director
Producer and General Manager
Producer and Business Manager
Producer and Publicity Director
Director and Designer (common in opera)
Stage Manager and Lighting Designer
Assistant Stage Manager and Properties Master
Scenic Designer and Costume and Properties Designer
Scenic Designer and Lighting, Costume and Props Designer
Lighting Designer and Electrician
Scenic Designer and Technical Director
Publicity Director and House Manager
Publicity Director and Assistant Box Office Treasurer
Publicity Director and Assistant to the General Manager
Publicity Director and Assistant to the Producer
Business Manager and House Manager
Business Manager and Associate Producer
Business Manager and Assistant Manager

Job combining is frequently a way to offer a person the highest possible salary, the fanciest job title, and the greatest set of challenges. Successful job combinations, however, always depend upon the interests, qualifications, and abilities of the individuals for whom they are designed. Because one person may perform several jobs simultaneously in a superb manner, it does not mean that a replacement can ever be found or, necessarily, should even be sought. Jobs must be suited to people, not people to jobs.

Who Will Hire Whom?

Employees inevitably reflect the people who have hired them. And hiring and casting decisions will go a long way in determining the success or failure of an organization or a production. In the commercial theatre, the producer contracts all the leading artists and may veto casting decisions made by the director. The general manager hired by the producer usually hires the administrative personnel, except those hired by a Broadway theatre owner. In professional nonprofit theatre, hiring power is usually split between the managing director and the artistic director. And in campus and community theatre, outside of the casting process, a committee usually does the hiring. However, in large nonprofit theatres, presenting organizations, and performing arts centers, hiring power may be given to department heads. The marketing director, for instance, may hold both hiring and firing authority for the entire marketing staff. This will probably mean that the staff will feel more loyalty and perhaps respect for the marketing director than for the general manager. Giving power to department heads creates a potential danger for divisiveness and for the creation of little fiefdoms, but the advantages of delegating authority in large organizations outweigh the disadvantages. In small organizations all staff members are best hired by the top manager in order to create unity and the single-ness of purpose, style, and character that will help determine the public profile of the organization.

Attracting Applicants

Writing the Job Description

The first step in finding the right employee is to create the right job description. No matter how familiar the hiring agent is with the organization and the job in question, it is always best to put the job description in writing, even if it's not going to be published or distributed. This forces the employer to review what the job has entailed in the past, what different tasks and responsibilities it might now entail, and what qualifications are necessary. Salary range, title, and benefits should be listed. Once written, the job description should be discussed with appropriate employees in the organization and, per-haps, with the person who is leaving the position. Does it reflect the true nature of the job? Has anything been left out? Vague or misleading job descriptions, if published, will waste the time of many applicants as well as that of the hiring agent. While a salary range is commonly omitted because the employer hopes to hire someone for less than the organization can afford, this tactic should be avoided. Many overqualified or underqualified applicants may apply, and it can be tempting for an employer to make a salary offer higher than originally intended. If the salary range is stated up front, mistakes and confusion can be avoided. The following is a sample of a job description that is sufficiently detailed and worded in an honest style:

ARTS ADMINISTRATION POSITION
Assistant to General Manager/Company Manager

Responsibilities include assisting General Manager in all areas of operation for a LORT B regional theatre in Houston, Texas; supervise building mainte-nance, coordinate special events, handle purchasing of equipment and supplies and other inglorious duties. Position also entails making travel and housing arrangements for visiting artists and others. Salary low 30s plus benefits. Must have own car, be proficient in Excel, Word; theatre experience is a plus. Email resume to jjones@texrep.org. Visit our website: www.texasrepertorytheater.org

When a theatre is preparing a general or seasonal announcement of job openings, the descriptions should be complete and honest. For example:

STAR PLAYHOUSE: Located near Aspen, CO, Star Playhouse is a nonprofit summer theatre producing an annual season of six plays performed by non-Equity actors and offering college credit through the University of Colorado summer school. Auditions held in April in Denver, Chicago & LA for 6 resident actors ($400 per week) and 10 apprentice actors (nonsalaried). Other openings for technical and administrative positions (salary range: $200 to $600 per week). Send pictures and/or resumes to: Michael Boulder, 1000 Vale Ave., Denver, CO 00000 or email: Personnel@starplayhouse.org. Visit our website: www.starplayhouse.org

If the above listing were published in the appropriate theatrical websites and periodicals, Mr. Boulder could expect to receive hundreds of responses from many parts of the country, if not the world. While resumes and photographs are helpful, it is even better in such cases to have all applicants complete a standard application form. Perhaps this could be put on the theatre's website. This insures that the exact information of greatest interest to the employer will be put in writing, and it provides a means to compare applications quickly and intelligently. The following standard items should be included on most application forms for administrative positions:

Applicant's name
Present address and zip code—if temporary, until what date
Permanent address and zip code—if different from above
Present home and work telephone numbers
Education:

> High school and year completed
> College: degrees and when completed
> Major subjects
> Professional training
> Workshops attended, etc.

Driver's license?
Owner of automobile?
Computer skills?
Date available for employment?
Date when applicant must terminate employment (if seasonal)
Statement of career goals
Listing of theatre experience and positions—or attach resume

Names, addresses, and phone numbers of three people who may be asked
   to provide statements about the applicant
List of hometown and college newspapers (for publicity department)

It should be noted that questions regarding race, age, sex, and marital status are illegal. The application form should be accompanied by information that describes the goals
of the organization, its artistic accomplishments, the type of employees it is seeking,
the nature of the working and living conditions and other details that may generate
the applicant's interest. But, again, the information should be honest. If, for example,
"apprentice actors" are really used only on production crews and never—or very rarely—
permitted to act in the main productions, this should be clearly stated, as should salary
range, special housing problems or costs, and other such matters.

Broadcasting the Job Opening

Most job openings are first announced by the employer who may contact known and
trusted colleagues to refer qualified applicants to him or her. This explains why the job
may already have been filled by the time a job announcement is published. All government and tax-supported employers, however, must advertise openings and process applications according to equal opportunity employment guidelines. And all employers are bound
by federal antidiscrimination laws pertaining to hiring, work conditions, promotion,
and firing. Additional laws of this type vary according to city and state.

The classified sections of local newspapers and the state employment agency are
rarely good sources for finding theatrical workers. But trade publications such as *Backstage* or *Variety* and related websites can be very effective. And a number of arts service
organizations provide job listings and referral services, including Theatre Communications Group's Artsearch, at www.tcg.org and www.artjob.org, a service of Western
States Arts Foundation (www.westaf.org).

Other sites that might be helpful are:

www.playbillarts.com
www.playbillonline.com
www.backstagejobs.com
www.backstage.com

Many of these sites have useful links to other sites, so there are many places to post positions. And while on the web, it's often worthwhile to check what other organizations are
posting and paying.

Search Firms and Employment Agencies

Search firms, or "headhunters," as they are also called, may be engaged to conduct a search that will end by filling a particular job. These companies work for and are paid by the employer, usually to find top-level executives as opposed to junior staff. The most established search firms that specialize in finding management personnel for arts organizations are Management Consultants for the Arts, www.mcaonline.com, and Arts Consulting Group, www.artsconsulting.com. But more generalized companies may also be used. While the employer hires search firms, employment agencies work for the job-seeker and are utilized by the hopeful employee, who pays the agency a percentage of the first year's salary if a job is secured.

Talent and Casting Agents and Contractors

Talent agencies are specialized private employment agencies that represent artists such as performers, writers, directors, designers, and musicians.

They must be licensed by the state in which they do business, and some must also be franchised by the labor union to which their clients belong, such as Actors' Equity Association. There are many talent agencies throughout the country that have long been recognized by producers and directors as a primary source of artist employees. Agents receive their compensation as a percentage of the salaries received for jobs that they arranged. Large agencies that represent a diversity of talent may offer a producing organization a "package" in which they represent the playwright as well as the director and perhaps even the leading performer. Although tempting and convenient, beware. A problem with one individual can easily become a problem with all the personnel represented by a single agency.

Casting agents, like search firms, work for the producer/employer to identify and secure all the performers required for a particular script. They are a common and influential presence in film and television production today and are common both on Broadway and Off-Broadway.

Contractors are private business people who supply union performers—mostly musicians—to Broadway shows, road shows, cabarets, nightclubs, orchestral groups, and others. They are located in every major city and can be the best source of local musical or specialty performer talent.

The Hiring Process

When an organization invites resumes and applications from potential employees—whether the job is administrative, production, or artistic—it should be prepared to answer every response it receives. It is inconsiderate and unprofessional to ask for applications and then to ignore them. Of course, not every applicant need be interviewed or auditioned, but all should at least be acknowledged.

Interviewing the Applicant

An interviewee's first visit and personal contact with an organization and its directors creates an impression that will last throughout the person's employment and serve as a foundation for it. Few theatres are so large that every candidate cannot be given a personal tour of the building and an introduction to the appropriate department heads. If the job opening is for a leading position, the interview should be spread over several days to allow the applicant time to meet as many people as possible. Before such an applicant is hired, the hiring agent and employees who met the applicant should confer. The candidate's qualifications and personality should be discussed, especially in regard to how he or she might get along with others in the operation.

Auditioning the Performer

Seasoned producers and directors can easily become jaded about auditions, but courtesy and politeness should always be extended to the performers. Even the most seasoned actor may find that auditioning causes acute anxiety. Auditioning is a very personal, uncertain, and risky exposure of ego and ability. People who conduct auditions should always keep this in mind. This means a polite greeting, a few words of encouragement to help the performer relax, and a pleasant thank-you at the end. More time may be required to audition nonprofessionals because they are unaccustomed to the audition prcess. But courtesy and sensitivity should always be shown to nonprofessional and professional auditioners alike.

For the majority of theatrical productions, auditions are held locally and for that single production. But some professional resident theatres hire a company of actors to perform in a series of productions throughout a season of many weeks. If that theatre is in Minneapolis, for example, it may hold auditions in New York or Los Angeles or both, and these auditions may be lengthy and complex since the artistic director is seeking actors who can play a number of roles and work well in an ensemble. Other large theatres hold regional auditions each year in four or five cities throughout the country. This enables them to see a large number of people in a short time. Also, several professional associations, such as the University/Resident Theatre Association (U/RTA), may arrange regional auditions together with interviews for administrative and production jobs for their member theatre groups. Two- or three-dozen artistic directors and managers may attend the audition held in their region to watch auditions by hundreds of hopeful participants. It is a very efficient hiring technique.

Checking References

Before an applicant is hired the hiring agent must check his or her references and qualifications. A colleague who knows the applicant well will provide the most dependable reference. Someone the agent knows by reputation will supply the next best reference. But even checking with people unknown to the agent can provide information that will be helpful. Rarely should any staff position be filled based solely on the hiring agent's intuition. Casting decisions, however, are often based largely on a director's intuition about a performer. The ability to perceive talent is a gift in itself, so casting decisions tend to be more private than most others in a hiring process.

Letters of Agreement, Contracts

Countless employees have worked years without written agreements with their employers, but such arrangements are invitations for the distress of one party or both. It is far better to define, even loosely in a letter of agreement, such basic terms of employment as salary, scheduled increments, promotion, hours, duties and responsibilities, title, benefits, severance notice and pay, and the like. In the case of high-salaried positions with performing arts companies, or institutions, a formal agreement should be drawn up and checked by lawyers for both parties.

Union members work under a collective bargaining agreement of some kind. It provides the most detailed terms of employment and the strongest guarantee that such terms will be upheld.

Job Title, Salary, and Perks

Employees who work under collective bargaining agreements are guaranteed a minimum rate of pay, various minimum benefits, and fair working conditions. These minimum terms, then, mark the starting point for negotiations between the hiring agent and the candidate. The employer, whether in a commercial or nonprofit operation, generally hopes to give *no concessions* above the union minimums, and the candidate hopes to get as *many concessions* as possible. Academic and civil service positions provide the most rigid job protection, which often includes tenure, while nonprofessional and largely nonunion professional companies offer the least. In the latter case, management has the greatest latitude in its hiring and employment practices.

Often, a candidate's salary demand may be negotiated down in exchange for benefits and opportunities. Or the candidate may accept a lower salary in exchange for a particular job title, job location, working hours, travel benefits, or entertainment allowance, for example. In short, money is not the only type of payment for labor.

Some theatre personnel, including directors and designers, have traditionally been paid on a fee basis. Minimum per-production or per-design fees have been established by the Society of Stage Directors and Choreographers (SSDC) and United Scenic Artists (USA) respectively. When such artists work on Broadway, they receive a fee plus a weekly royalty. When they are hired to be in residence and work on a series of productions, however, they are usually paid a weekly salary. A few staff members might also be offered a percentage above their salaries. For example, telemarketing people, those who sell tickets by phone, or group sales people might be given a percentage of their sales.

Just as the job applicant must remember that the salary offered will not be the amount he or she takes home after taxes and other deductions, so the employer must remember that the salary offered is less than the amount an employee will actually cost the operation. Over the base salary, the employer must pay matching social security taxes that are based on the gross salary. Further payroll costs may include payments for medical insurance, unemployment insurance, disability insurance, worker's compensation, and pension and welfare contributions. Generally, payroll taxes and benefits will add at least eighteen percent to the base salary; it can be more depending on the benefits package. Royalties will add even more, as can housing allowances, per diems, and travel reimbursement. But there is a hidden cost involved with hiring certain people that must also be considered.

A company may be able to pay a designer's or director's fee, yet be unable to support the style or manner in which that person works. Just as it would be foolish to buy a car without having enough money for gas, so it would be foolish to hire a top-flight costume designer, without having the facilities, staff, and budget to buy fabrics and build the costumes he or she has designed. This type of management mistake can be avoided by doing a bit of research. The first question that should be asked regarding any new hire is why do we want to hire this person? The next question should address his or her reputation, questions such as "Is the person thrifty or a spendthrift?" Is he or she a pain in the neck to deal with, but brilliant, nevertheless? What kind of experiences have other organizations had with this person? Depending on the answers one might wish to proceed with the hiring process or move on to another talent.

It's best to know the playing field well before an offer is made and discussions begin. Based on knowledge that the organization has obtained, if it feels that it can provide the size of budget and meet the other requirements that a designer or director is likely to present, then there should be no—or few—surprises. Some designers and directors require assistants. Some require more work space than others, some more equipment and materials, more sophisticated technology, more phone calls, more travel or whatever. Experience, professionalism, and high standards usually mean high quality results and high costs. The point is not to be blindsided by someone's style and/or method of working.

Job Training and Orientation

Staff Orientation

Some managers expect new employees to plunge headlong into the work; others prefer to put them through a period of special training, but usually, all training is done on the job. If the position is new, the employee may have to learn by trial and error. Otherwise, the departing staff person may help train the incoming employee, providing that the departure is amiable and that the employer wants the job done as it has been in the past.

Most nonartistic jobs in a theatre—from general manager to building custodian—should be clearly and specifically outlined in a work manual that describes all the responsibilities and peculiarities of a particular job or department. The Sample Manual for Box Office Treasurers and Ticket Sellers in Appendix F provides an example. Every ongoing theatre operation should maintain periodically updated manuals that cover general management, business management, marketing and promotion, fundraising, box office operations, house management, company management, production supervision—costumes, scenery, lighting, props, sound, makeup, technical supervision—tools, supplies, stage equipment, and facility maintenance and operation. In outline form, each manual should deal with work hours, supervisory responsibilities, procedures to follow under both normal and emergency conditions, and lists of relevant vendors and service companies with their phone numbers. Each department head should update the appropriate manual at least annually and submit it to the general manager, perhaps with recommendations for improvements and purchases. Manuals make the orientation of a new employee easier and more efficient. Supervisors should remember, however, that no two people work in the same manner. A given system may suit one person but not another, and it must be remembered that there is always a better way of doing anything. Procedural flexibility is desirable, and a work manual should be used as a guide and history of operations, not as a bible.

When an entire staff has to be hired to begin work for the first time—as would be the case with a new theatre or at the beginning of a new season—a general orientation meeting involving all personnel is essential to clarify and state goals and objectives, to set the right tone, to establish a sense of unity, to introduce people to one another, and to establish the chain of authority. This should be followed by breakout meetings for each department or area in the operation and finally by one-on-one discussions and instruction among supervisors and staff members. When a new employee comes into a functioning operation, the same process should be followed, though less formally. It always pays management to spend a little extra time and effort with new employees so they will become an integral part of the team as soon as possible.

The Rehearsal Process

Rehearsing is a unique form of job orientation invented to avoid the embarrassment of on-the-job training in front of an audience. While the director of the production is the overall rehearsal supervisor, the production stage manager attends to the details, the union rulebooks, and assists the director. Because the stage manager on a Broadway show puts together the prompt book that contains the stage directions, he or she may later work with a publisher in creating the acting edition of the script that will be used in future nonprofessional productions. Also, the stage manager often rehearses replacement cast members once the show is in production and may typically direct road versions of the show; and so it is that many stage managers become directors themselves.

When a theatre or production has a company manager, this person serves as management's representative in dealing with cast and rehearsal needs and problems. When there is no company manager, the theatre's general manager, the producer, or the college theatre department's chairperson must fill this function. Most directors prefer that rehearsals be kept closed to everyone not directly related to the production. However, the producer or management should make its presence known by being supportive of the artistic process. Performers work harder during the rehearsal period than at any other time and they feel most vulnerable at this time—management and staff need to keep this in mind.

Personnel Supervision

Three of the leading goals in personnel supervision are the economical organization of the workers' time, control over the quality of their work, and the achievement of optimum output. How each employee is judged differs according to the person's job. For example, a time-quality-output-efficient box office treasurer would be one who can process fifty to sixty telephone and window ticket sales per hour without making a mistake. A time-quality-output-efficient Equity actor is one who performs a given role with equal brilliance eight times a week. The manager's efficiency is judged by the people whom he or she has hired and supervised. The success of the theatre organization as a whole, however, will be measured either in economic terms—how many tickets are sold and how much profit is made—or in terms of its stated goals—to produce outstanding new American plays—or a combination of both. The more efficiently each employee performs, the more likely the whole organization will succeed.

Leadership

Leadership goes beyond management, beyond figuring out how to accomplish something. Effective leadership understands why the something is being done and inspires those under him or her with the value of what they are doing. Good leadership qualities are desirable in anyone who holds a supervisory position, from the office manager to the board president. Employees appreciate a supervisor who displays common sense, fairness, humor, and who also keeps them mindful of the why and the value of their labor. Poor leadership or the lack of leadership at the head of an organization or production almost always leads to malaise, if not malfunction. The effective leader is able to inspire and enthuse, to teach and explain, and to share both power and responsibility. This last quality is perhaps the most difficult to learn and so is rare in ambitious, young supervisors. Sharing requires great self-confidence, but when done in good faith, generates respect and indebtedness from others.

Delegating Authority and Responsibility

All employees should understand from day one the limits of their authority and responsibilities and should also feel secure that no one is going to usurp them. There is no quicker way to convert a productive worker into a careless drone than by subverting that person's authority. Supervisors may do this by making decisions or taking actions that fall within the worker's purview, by dealing directly with that worker's support staff or crew or by being critical of that worker to others. Any decision, problem, or policy should be forced up or down a ladder of responsibility, one step at a time. This procedure not only respects the authority of each staff member, it also insures the most thorough examination and treatment of the matter at hand.

As workers grow in experience and ability, they should be given additional authority and responsibility or be promoted. An important part of a supervisor's job is to assess continually when and how rewards of this type should be made and, of course, to whom. When a job offers no possibility of growth, which it inevitably will, that person should probably be placed in another job or encouraged to leave the organization. Job mobility within the organization helps maintain the nucleus of a permanent staff and avoid excessive turnover. Nonunion and low-salaried workers are particularly apt to be tempted away, as are volunteers. The first step in retaining such people is to treat them well and reward them with such things as tickets to a dress rehearsal or social events.

Communication

Communication is a two-way process. It involves receiving signals as well as sending them. Indeed, the successful manager probably spends more time listening than talking. Sound decisions are informed decisions. It may also be said that information is a form of power, so the ability to gather it well and share it wisely is important.

Lines of communication within an organization should follow lines of authority, with systems put into practice that insure that information will be sent up the ladder as well as down. No worker or department in the organization should feel isolated, as can happen in a theatre operation. Do the box office treasurers have a chance to see the productions? Do they see the press releases that describe the upcoming productions for which they are selling tickets? Does the stage carpenter know the show he is building? Have the actors been greeted by the producer or general manager?

While meetings sometimes can be a waste of time, they can also be informative, productive, and even stimulating if they are well organized and run. The key to running a successful business meeting—whether the group is large or small—is advanced planning. An agenda should be drawn up, perhaps discussed with an assistant, revised and then followed closely with as few digressions during the meeting as possible. A little humor should be encouraged and those present should feel they have made a contribution. At the end, the organizer should instill the group with a sense of accomplishment by summarizing what progress or decisions have been made—even agreeing to disagree is a decision.

Position papers, announcements, and memos, written in a succinct but friendly style, should be distributed on a regular basis. Mail and information received in the front office should be shared with or referred to appropriate staff members.

And, of course, social events are a proven way to encourage and improve communications within an organization. Parties and receptions are a good way to bring together artists and staff members, who would otherwise never meet, to relax tensions, and to reward hard, usually underpaid labor. However, there can be too many parties, and non-professionals in particular can begin to believe that the theatre is all play and no work. Also, care must always be taken to insure that no one is overlooked when the invitations are made. An everyone-or-no-one party-policy is the best.

A staff retreat is a popular management tool. The object of a retreat is to have a group meet away from its usual environment, often for several days, in order to brain-storm in a think-tank atmosphere that will produce more clear-headed results than might otherwise emerge. Sometimes an outside consultant or discussion facilitator is hired to lend objectivity and serve as a neutral moderator. Retreats are especially helpful for a board of trustees or a group of executives when long-range planning is on the agenda.

The most skillful supervisor is the one who can prevent trouble before it begins. Early and minor corrections of problems are always easier than dealing with an issue that has grown into crisis proportions. To recognize problems early on, supervisors must be sensitive to what is going on among the staff: what is the power structure among the employees; who are the instigators; how and along what lines are the employees being divided? The more dominant, aggressive employees should be guided so their energies will be channeled in a positive way and so that the less aggressive employees will be able to more fully express their opinions and abilities. A negative attitude is always dangerous to the health of a group and is best squelched, as early as possible, even if it means firing someone. Factions or cliques within the staff should be similarly discouraged. Such situations can quickly erode the morale and productivity of a group.

Employees will always respect steadiness and a good degree of predictability from their superiors, factors that contribute greatly to a sense of job security. Conversely, the surest way to abdicate authority is to practice backstabbing, hypocrisy, or favoritism. And supervisors should remember, too, that criticism is constructive only when it helps the person at whom it is directed to work more happily and efficiently. People should not be expected to accomplish things that are beyond their training or capabilities—they should not be given such assignments in the first place.

Job Reviews

In the corporate world and academia, job reviews are common practice. The CEO, area head, or department chairperson looks through the employee's personnel records and then arranges a private meeting with the employee, which may result in an evaluation report written by the supervisor and placed on file. The meeting allows the employee to express grievances, discuss problems, and make observations about the work and the organization. This may provide the basis for a promotion, a raise, or, of course, termination. It also offers the employee a sense of being valued and it invariably provides the supervisor with useful feedback. All managers of ongoing companies should consider adopting some form of the job review process. It assures that the door between staff and management will remain open and that at least some time will be set aside to recognize, analyze, and evaluate the people who are making the company work.

Job Termination

Union employees work under contracts that provide a considerable amount of job security, including protection against being fired unjustly. Managers who hire nonunion personnel should provide them with some kind of written agreement that states the start and end dates, the terms for compensation, resignation, layoff, retirement, and involuntary termination. What are the grounds for termination? How much notice must be given, if any? What is the severance pay, if any? There may also be special stipulations. For example, department heads at stock and resident theatres who are hired on a seasonal basis may be asked to maintain a written inventory of equipment, tools, and supplies and then be held accountable for those goods before being given their final paychecks.

In a perfect world, all jobs should happily come to an end, and both the manager and employee should work toward that outcome. The performing arts world is small and most of its workers hold many different jobs in the course of their careers. Taking care to leave each job with good feelings can greatly help to extend those careers.

Fundamentals of U.S. Labor Law

A majority of professional theatre productions in America employ the members of at least one labor union—namely Actors' Equity Association (AEA). Broadway theatres, large operas, dance and symphony orchestras, as well as large presenting organizations, may have agreements with a dozen or more unions. It is prudent, then, for all managers in the performing arts to understand the basis for labor law in this country, as well as the collective bargaining agreements of specific theatrical labor unions, which will be discussed later.

Labor legislation enacted by the United States Congress is essentially aimed at ensuring fair labor standards for employees and employers. These standards include freedom of speech and assembly, equal rights, and the right to sue, among others. While the Norris-LaGuardia Act (1932) outlawed the use of injunctions in labor disputes for a time, and the Wages and Hours Act (1938) established minimum work hours and pay in basic industries, the three congressional acts most germane to organized labor practices are the National Labor Relations Act, also called the Wagner Act (1935), the Taft-Hartley Act (1947), and the Landrum-Griffin Act (1959).

Although greatly modified by the two subsequent acts, the Wagner Act established the National Labor Relations Board (NLRB), which continues to serve an important function today. The NLRB resembles a court that hears complaints that cannot be settled by other means and that are brought to it by a union, an employer, or an employee. It does not deal with matters pertaining to supervisors or managers, although it now handles complaints filed *by employers* against unions and their members. With nearly fifty offices around the country, its main function is to investigate charges of unfair labor practices by employers and unions and to render decisions. If the parties concerned disagree with NLRB rulings, they may take their complaints to the U.S. Court of Appeals. The NLRB is authorized to issue cease and desist orders against unfair practices affecting interstate commerce (not until 1961 did a federal ruling establish that the theatre industry *is interstate commerce*) insure the right of workers to bargain collectively, and settle union-organizing issues. Although the NLRB has been a frequent target of criticism, its success in settling countless labor problems over the years has been remarkable.

The Taft-Hartley Act introduced an eighty-day injunction procedure in labor disputes that affect national welfare. It also prohibits the closed shop, permits employers to sue unions for breaking contracts, forbids union contributions to political campaigns, and requires unions to provide sixty days' notice before going on strike. The closed-shop provision means that a person does not need to belong to a union to be offered a job in a union shop. But once the job is offered and accepted, that person must join the appropriate union within thirty days, provided that the union invites the person to join. If asked to join and the employee refuses, then the individual's employment will be terminated. If, on the other hand, the employee is not invited to join the union, the employee may continue to work.

The Landrum-Griffin Act weakens the central power of unions as a byproduct of its attempt to remove corruption and marginalize autocratic union leaders. It also attempts to assure that unions will be run democratically, by stipulating that the union membership has the right to vote on all key decisions made by its officers. That right, however, has unfortunately reduced the authority and effectiveness of union officers, in some cases. There are also a variety of labor laws on the state level that may affect labor practices, but federal law always supersedes these.

Broad efforts to organize workers in the United States and Canada began in 1881 with the formation of the American Federation of Labor (AFL), a fairly loose coalition of craft unions that initially opposed being organized by industry. As a result, a splinter group formed the Congress of Industrial Organizations (CIO) in 1935 to unionize mass-production workers by industry rather than by craft. The CIO often criticized the NLRB for favoring its AFL rival. However, these two organizations were united in 1955 to form a single, national labor union organization: the AFL-CIO. This body grants charters for different categories of craft and industrial workers to form national labor unions. Actors' Equity Association is a national labor union. The national office, in turn, can establish branch offices wherever there may be sufficient membership.

If an actor joins AEA through a branch office, or local, he or she is usually granted automatic national membership. So if an actor joins Equity in Chicago, that actor can also work as a union member in New York or anywhere and can enjoy the hard-won benefits for which that union has bargained. No branch or local is permitted to strike without permission from national headquarters, however, but the local may negotiate its own agreement.

As unions grew in strength, people who represented the ownership of the service and manufacturing industries—collectively known as "management"—had to devise strategies for dealing with them. Huge companies with huge profits, such as General Motors or General Electric, could hire expensive lawyers to negotiate with the unions and could even sustain strikes and lockouts periodically. In the theatre industry, only the

Shubert producing organization was in this league during the early years of union growth. But as workers learned that there is strength in numbers, so did employers. Hence, numerous employer/management associations were formed to negotiate collectively with labor unions on behalf of a segment of an industry in which no single employer had any clout.

Common Labor Relations Terminology

Most of the following terms are in common usage, but some have specific meanings in labor-management parlance.

Arbitration: Both parties in a dispute agree in advance to abide by the decision of a single arbitrator or board of arbitrators. A board is often comprised of three people—one chosen by the union, one by the employer or management association, and a third by the other two.

Boycott: When people refuse to work or patronize a place of business, picket that place, and encourage others to act as if there were a strike in progress.

Closed shop: A place or type of employment in which only members of a particular union are eligible to work. The Taft-Hartley Act outlawed this.

Fact-finding: An investigation that ends with a recommendation. Although the recommendation lacks the legal clout of a decision by an arbitration panel, the opinion contains strong moral suasion for public relations purposes.

Fire for cause: Terminating employment on grounds specified in the union contract, such as failure to appear for work, failure to perform work, gross abuse of discipline, cheating, or dishonesty. Firing for artistic reasons is rare and difficult to justify. When proof of misconduct can be produced, the employee need not be given notice or severance pay.

In good faith: A genuine attempt to resolve differences.

Injunction: A court order to stop doing something.

Local: The branch of a national union.

Lockout: When the employer refuses to permit its employees to work.

Mediation: An attempt to make peace between two opposing factions, with strong moral suasion.

To serve: To start legal proceedings by giving someone a subpoena.

Settlement: When an agreement is reached or work resumes.

Sidebar: When both parties in a dispute or negotiation authorize representatives to go off alone, to explore what each really wants and what each will settle for.

Strike: A concerted refusal to work by employees—approved or not approved by the union, if there is one—until certain labor demands are met by the employer.

Strikebreaker: A person who attempts to break up a workers' strike by supplying scabs—replacement workers, or those who cross a picket line to work—or intimidating the strikers. It is illegal for an employer to participate in such activity or otherwise impede workers' attempts to organize and to bargain collectively.

Unfair labor practice: Any attempt to interfere with the rights of employees to organize, select representatives, and bargain collectively. Any form of discrimination in hiring, employment, or firing policies.

Union busting: An attempt to subvert the jurisdiction of a union.

Union shop: A place of employment where all workers of a given type must belong to the appropriate union.

Wildcat: A worker who is on strike without permission from the union.

Collective Bargaining

Labor/Capital/Management

Labor, capital, and management are the three necessary elements in any economy, be it that of a nation, an industry, or an individual company. Without the direction supplied by management, labor and capital, or workers and money, are merely untapped resources. But when creative management attempts to bring them together for the purpose of producing some service or commodity, a dynamic peculiar to the human species comes into play. This dynamic evolves around, on the one hand, a system of give and take, of bartering time, skill, and talent for personal income, and, on the other, of investing time, thought, and capital for private or public profit. It is easy to believe that money alone will determine the strength of an economy, yet economies are also fueled by such intangible resources as inspired leadership, human energy, and strongly shared goals. Trade unions attempt to equalize the balance of power between employee and employer. In recent years, however, union strength has declined.

The Negotiation

All labor-management contracts have a limited life span once they are ratified—in harmonious times, four to five years is the norm, though shorter periods may be negotiated under especially difficult circumstances or in periods of high inflation or economic instability. It is customary, of course, to begin negotiating a new contract before the old one has expired. How soon before that expiration date may itself be negotiated because the less time allowed, the more pressure may be felt by both sides to reach a new agreement and thereby avoid a job action. Depending on the circumstances and the timing and the economy, a job action—be it a lockout on the part of management, or a strike, on the part of labor—can be an effective tactic. For example, in 2003, a musicians' strike on Broadway was very successful in bringing about a quick settlement because the stagehands and actors walked out in sympathy and refused to cross the musicians' picket lines.

Generally speaking both parties at a contract negotiation are usually represented by a delegation of people headed by a chief negotiator, who may be an attorney, a union officer, a corporate officer, someone appointed by a trade association, or the head manager of a particular company. Several other officers, association members, or managers are selected to complete the negotiating team. There may also be present silent witnesses from the union's rank and file or from the trade group's membership. The press and the public are usually excluded and those present may be admonished not to discuss the proceedings with anyone outside. When the media is involved, negotiators try to mislead or intimidate their adversaries by what they say to the public and how they say it, using rhetoric instead of meaningful information. Both sides usually look and act tough and although armchair negotiators with little patience or understanding of the process hold that the posturing and ritual is a waste of time, the reality is that it allows for the venting of problems and issues of genuine interest to each side and therefore it allows the air to be cleared so that genuine negotiations can proceed. The process, after all, is important.

Contract negotiations traditionally begin with each side presenting a list of demands to the other. These demands will have been discussed and developed by a union council or management leaders prior to the commencing of negotiations. Each side's demands typically exceed their true expectations and usually include at least a few that are, for practical purposes, "throw-a-ways." But throw-a-ways can be useful when something needs to be conceded: better to concede a demand of minor importance.

With spiraling medical expenses, health care coverage has taken on greater importance in negotiations, regardless of the industry. Demands for pay increases are also omnipresent; so these two issues are usually the most difficult to settle. Additionally, unions are always interested in increasing employers' pension and annuity contributions. In hard times, job security and work-rules changes can also be major topics for negotiation.

Both sides come to a negotiation aware of the recent history of other union settlements. If a dominant group won a four percent wage increase, it is unlikely that their peers will settle for less. Similarly, if one union made a concession, it's likely that management will demand a like concession from another union. Although there may not exactly be a domino effect, negotiations are not conducted in vacuums, and so what happens in one part of an industry is likely to have an impact on another part of that industry.

The entire negotiation process is one of give and take and is ultimately a matter of how much management is willing to give and how little the union is willing to accept in an attempt to adjust for cost of living increases and prior inequities.

Ratification and Implementation

Once a new contract—the terms of which always build upon previous contracts—has been approved by the negotiating teams, the union's council or its full membership must vote in order to ratify it. Membership or council approval is not automatic. Similarly, there may be objections from the management side. An owner, the board of governors for a nonprofit organization or trade association, or an executive director must ultimately sign off if the agreement is to be binding. If the agreement fails, it's back to the negotiating table.

Once the union membership ratifies a contract and top management approves it, management must implement it as of the expiration of the old contract. If it has already expired, the terms of the new contract are retroactive to that date, so that pay increases, for instance, would have to be made retroactively. The implementation of a new contract should also involve informing both workers and supervisors about changes that have been made.

Maintaining Union-Management Relations

When employees are unionized, it is tempting, albeit unwise, to condone an adversarial atmosphere of Them against Us,—Union versus Management. Successful, creative managements understand the necessity of cooperation and collaboration based on mutual need and based on what is good of the industry. This may merely involve bringing employees into the managerial decision-making process, or it may go all the way to employee ownership of a company. According to Herman E. Krawitz, former assistant general manager of The Metropolitan Opera and head of labor management affairs, some form of cooperation is essential as it serves both sides' mutual self-interest.

General principles of personnel supervision discussed earlier in this chapter should not be forgotten when dealing with union members. Every group of union workers— the actors in a particular production, the carpenters in a particular scene shop—typically elect a deputy or steward to represent any grievances they may have either toward management or toward the union. It is very important, then, that management establish the best possible working relationship with these people and cultivate good feelings to withstand the thorny problems that are certain to arise. Having said that, it is important to keep in mind that stewards are merely elected *representatives: they are not officers of the union and they have no real authority.* They are messengers: not more, not less.

Managing Unsalaried Personnel

Volunteers

Volunteers range from the board chairperson of a high-profile nonprofit institution to young people helping to drum up support for their favorite cause. They are people who provide labor without receiving financial compensation, but who expect to receive other rewards for their efforts. When those rewards are not forthcoming, neither is the labor. This is the main point that supervisors of all unsalaried personnel must remember: labor must be rewarded if it is to be productive. Money is the easiest resource with which to reward labor. Gratitude, appreciation, and psychic and emotional rewards are among the most difficult. In other words, managers and supervisors usually have to work harder to extract labor from volunteers than from salaried employees.

The paradox involved with volunteer leadership positions, such as the trustees or board members of all nonprofit organizations and, especially, the officers within such boards, is that they must manage themselves. They alone are ultimately responsible for the fiscal and legal conduct of the organization they serve. They may hire professional managers to carry out their objectives, but such *managers do not manage the board*, try as they may. They are hired to implement the board's policies and organization. So board members of nonprofit corporations, as discussed in Chapter 5, are a special breed of volunteer.

The majority of volunteers, however, work at the low end of the totem pole, in the nonprofit sector. Unlike students, they are not primarily involved in order to learn about something nor to advance their careers. They are involved because they believe in the cause or the institution. Their greatest reward is to see the goals of that cause or institution advanced. But their next greatest reward is to feel that they are a meaningful part of that advancement process, so they must be supervised with the kind of parental devotion that elicits loyalty as well as obedience. No easy job, ask any parent.

There are myriad websites available to help with the management of volunteers. A useful place to begin is www.mapnp.org/library/staffing/outsrcng/volnteer/volnteer.htm. Also helpful, if not dizzying, is searching the web for "volunteerism."

Interns and Apprentices

Apprentices have been a fixture in the theatre, especially in summer stock theatres, for many years. While some may receive free room and board, most apprentices work for no salary; sometimes they even pay tuition or housing fees. Many successful careers began on the apprentice level and, indeed, being an apprentice can offer an opportunity to learn a lot in a short time. Most theatre apprenticeships center around the scene shop and on crews—all the work involves long hours. But distributing posters, ushering, and serving as a "go-fer" may also be part of the work. The danger is that supervisors may treat apprentices as little better than slaves. Yet, they can be of great value to an organization when treated with respect, given the necessary training, and rewarded with appreciation.

Interns are apprentices, though the term internship has come to imply a somewhat more responsible position, usually in one area or department and usually in administration or management; frequently it includes some pay. Virtually all nonprofit arts organizations and, many commercial offices have eagerly incorporated interns into their salaried staffs. Some are paid small stipends; most are given specific responsibilities at least of entry-level weight and receive professional supervision. Interns may be undergraduate or graduate students in arts management programs or others, or they may have sought out this type of learning experience independently. Because most are fairly mature and hope that their internships may lead both to jobs and careers—perhaps even in the company where they are interning—some on the staff may feel threatened by them. The primary compensation they seek, of course, is training and a high-quality learning experience. When supervisors provide this for them, interns tend to return these opportunities with loyalty and meaningful job performance.

Students

Students at all levels are also trainees in a sense. Certainly, their participation in campus theatre productions provides hands-on, practical experience. This is often designed to enhance classroom instruction and study, thereby adding another dimension to the learning process. Since students either pay tuition or attend tax-supported institutions, they have a right to expect more expert and valuable instruction than they would receive in the workplace. The ramifications of supervising students in campus theatre departments are discussed in Chapter 7.

Managing the Artistic Temperament

Although often protected by unions and collective bargaining agreements, artists in the performing arts are perhaps the most uncharacteristic of all unionized workers. Despite all the rules and regulations, artistic creativity and output itself cannot be regulated. The performer, for instance, does not turn off his or her creative energy when the rehearsal is over; the scenic designer who met great success with designs for *Othello* cannot be ordered to design an equally brilliant *Saint Joan*. The stage director cannot be expected to inspire a good production of a script that is anathema to him or her. Rules must sometimes be bent or broken to accommodate the artistic process.

The biggest problems encountered by performing arts management and production people will not have to do with money or unions: they will have to do with people

—very special people known as artists. All the money, rules, and good press in the world cannot guarantee artistic achievement. They can, however, help to form a support system for the artist, a system constructed and maintained by good management. This excludes attitudes and behavior that is patronizing, indiscriminate, or condescending.

Such attitudes tend to isolate artists, positioning them against management, if not against society at large. These attitudes are never productive. Management has an obligation to nurture and protect talent, as it is one of humanity's great resources. Too often, however, the artist has been treated as the servant rather than the master in his own house. Managing artistic talent well means respecting it, if not loving it, for the insight and the joy it provides for others. It means understanding the artists' fears of taking risks. It means, even when such understanding and respect are not present, management must put the artists' concerns above those of all others. If this perspective is lost, everything else can be lost along with it.

Summary

In Chapter 1 we discussed the *why* and the *what* of theatre. Personnel is the *who* of theatre: those who do the jobs, either for love or money, either as a member of organized labor or as an individual. In either case, workers should be treated fairly and equitably and given proper supervision, guidance, and feedback.

Writing job descriptions, getting the word out, collecting applications, conducting interviews, checking references, and writing letters of agreement are all part of the process of finding employees. The next, and perhaps harder, part is keeping good employees interested and engaged in their work. Turnover is costly and disruptive. No one wants to run or be part of an operation where there is a so-called revolving-door policy. Employees, be they artists or technicians, may be an operation's greatest assets. Every manager should protect these assets.

CHAPTER 4

Commercial Theatre

T HE COMMERCIAL THEATRE OPERATES without subsidy and is centered in New York City—on Broadway and Off-Broadway and its behavior in terms of product, talent, and box office influences all other theatre activity in America; it even has an impact on film and television. Before discussing how the commercial theatre functions today, it might be helpful to review how it functioned in the past and to remember some of its leading figures.

Background

The Beginnings: 1752 to 1792

One of the earliest known professional theatre companies in the Western Hemisphere was headed by Francisco Perez de Robles, who brought a company from Spain to Peru in 1599. But the first professional company of any consequence to reach North America was headed by Lewis Hallam and arrived in Williamsburg, Virginia, in 1752; the twenty-one-year-old George Washington may have seen the troupe during his visits there. Both theatre companies were organized as profit-sharing or shareholding ventures. A common means of financing theatre companies, this system provided that each actor own a percentage of the company, thus entitling that actor to a proportional share of any profits. The organizer of the venture, usually its leading actor who was general manager as well, held the greatest number of shares by virtue of having made the largest initial investment or because of his extra managerial duties. The number of shares allotted to actors might be determined by issues such as the number of costumes they could provide, whether they could play leading as opposed to supporting roles, whether they owned and played musical instruments, whether any children who might be traveling with them could also be pressed into serving the muse, and whether or not there were family or romantic ties with the head of the company. Occasionally, playwrights and musicians were also shareholders.

Although many European companies were organized on a shareholding basis, the system presented several disadvantages and was not long favored by either American actors or actor-managers. Actors disliked the arrangement because it meant their incomes were uncertain—providing there was any income at all; and actor-managers disliked the system because it deprived them of absolute authority and control. Virtually all theatre managers at that time were also actors. The roles of actor, manager, director, and producer did not emerge as clearly separate positions until the twentieth century. Until then, both managerial and artistic control usually rested with the leading actor in the company, the so-called actor-manager.

Despite Calvinist and Quaker resistance to stage plays, and despite the fact that public theatres were officially closed by Congress from 1774 until 1783, professional theatre managed to establish a foothold in America by the end of the eighteenth century. Generals on both sides of the Revolutionary War produced theatrical performances to keep their troops entertained; David Douglass,who married Hallam's widow during the war, built the nation's first permanent brick theatre in Philadelphia in 1776; and George Washington, when President, attended the theatre two or three times a week, sometimes accompanied by John Adams, who had picked up the theatre-going habit in Paris.

A 300-to-400-seat playhouse at that time, admittedly a rather flimsy structure, could be built for a cost of less than $2,000, an investment that could be recovered from the box office receipts of four performances. Would that you could build a theatre today and pay it off in four performances! Nor did other expenses begin to approach what they are today: actors were required to provide their own costumes, the scenery and props were meager, and there were no royalties, fees, lawyers, or accountants to pay! And during the first forty years of professional theatre in America, theatrical real estate was regarded as no more important than scenery. So actors shared both the profits and the losses of their company, and very few attempts were made to conduct the business of theatre in a businesslike manner.

The Era of the Independent Stock Companies: 1792 to 1860

By 1792 the shareholding system appears to have died a natural death. Until the end of the Civil War, actor-managers and their investors took full financial and managerial responsibility for the theatre company, while the other actors received set wages—ranging from ten to fifty dollars per week—together with the proceeds from occasional benefit performances.

The heyday of the independent stock company—with its relatively permanent resident acting company, stock supply of scenery, and repertoire of classical plays and then-current melodramas—occurred during the first half of the nineteenth century. Edwin Forrest, the nation's first great, native-born actor, made his debut in 1820. Some companies wandered from town to town playing short engagements; others remained in one city and operated from their own theatres. The companies that stayed home were often met with lethargic audiences overly familiar with their bag of theatrical tricks; those who traveled encountered other problems. When Joseph Jefferson and his company tried to play Springfield, Illinois, in the late 1820s, for instance, a local ordinance prevented them because there was a religious "camp meeting" in progress. But a young lawyer pleaded before the city council on their behalf and got the law repealed. His name was Abraham Lincoln.

Character portrayals were drawn from stock, as was the scenery. Most actors specialized in character types, or "lines," which varied only slightly during their entire careers. Nonetheless, stock companies often provided the only organized entertainment in a town, and most actors developed a cadre of fans who returned week after week to cheer them on-much as TV viewers today follow their favorites in soap operas or weekly sitcoms, or theatre groupies see the same Broadway show countless times.

To breathe more life into the local stock companies and to increase business, managers hired touring stars from abroad. From roughly 1820 to 1860, American stock companies were visited by a parade of highly touted English actors: Edmund and Charles Kean, Charles Mathews, Charles and Fanny Kemble, Junius Brutus Booth, and William Charles Macready for example. Nor did the language barrier dampen the touring success of such stars as Sarah Bernhardt, Adelaide Ristori, and Ernesto Rossi. They came across the Atlantic in the wake of their managers and advance men, whose main task was to whip the American press and the public into a fury of anticipation that would translate into ticket sales at the box office. Many made considerable profits, primarily because they had so little competition from the natives. But if the stock system was less than ideal for both actor and audience, the advent of visiting stars made matters worse. To draw an audience it became almost essential for a star to appear with a company. The public was encouraged to ask, "Who's in it?" rather than, simply, "Shall we go to the theatre?" This was ostensibly the beginning of the star system.

Because the salaries and percentages demanded by stars were so high, the salaries granted to resident actors had to be lowered. In short, the appearance of stars, however more skillful they may have been, did not do much to improve the overall integrity of theatrical production.

The Era of the Combination Companies: 1860 to 1896

The sudden growth of the American railway system changed the single traveling star system and virtually killed resident stock companies. In the decades immediately following the 1848 Gold Rush, thousands of miles of rail track were laid that connected the major cities of the nation and presaged an era of previously undreamed of mobility. During the first half of the century, it would have been impractical for a star to travel with a complete supporting company plus all the necessary costumes and scenery, but by the 1880s, the "combination company" dominated the industry. The "combination company" travelled with scenery, props, and costumes. Some historians credit actor-manager-playwright Dion Boucicault with having organized the first combination company sometime around 1860. In any case, the idea caught on quickly and soon undermined the century-old stock system. For the first time, actors were not tied to a particular resident company, had no control or interest in the theatres in which they played, and performed in a single play for long periods.

As more and more towns and cities sprang up on the American frontiers, the demand for entertainment became larger. It has been estimated that there were only about forty permanent theatres at the time of the Gold Rush, but by the end of the nineteenth century there were over five thousand theatres. About one-fourth of these were vaudeville houses, while the others played host to resident companies, touring combination troupes, and touring stars playing with resident companies. Theatres along the frontier sometimes doubled as saloons or brothels — talk about mixed-use facilities — while the larger western cities anxiously sought to establish their respectability by constructing elaborate opera houses to engage some of the world's most celebrated performing artists. It was a period of phenomenal expansion and wild and woolly extremes in the American theatre.

Aside from the broad appeal of such uniquely American family entertainments as minstrel shows and vaudeville, live theatre experienced an unprecedented increase in attendance during this period thanks to two vastly different attractions: *Uncle Tom's Cabin*; and the operettas of W. S. Gilbert and Arthur Sullivan. George Aiken first dramatized Harriet Beecher Stowe's novel in 1852; he didn't need her permission, nor did he have it. Suddenly God-fearing Christians, who had been brought up to believe that the theatre was "the devil's own drawing room," were being encouraged by their own preachers to see this production. There were literally hundreds of companies performing *Uncle Tom's Cabin* across the country, and thousands of people were converted to become regular theatregoers. In 1866, the manager of New York's fashionable Niblo's Garden adopted an entire French ballet troupe that had been booked into the Academy of Music, which suddenly burned down, and inserted it into his new melodrama, *The Black Crook*. This is regarded as the first American musical. Of course, Stephen Foster was already writing for the minstrel stage but, beginning with the 1878 Boston premier of *H.M.S. Pinafore*, Gilbert and Sullivan took the country by storm. Soon there were three hundred companies performing the piece. Then came *The Mikado*, which inspired both the Britons and Americans to buy everything Japanese. And, incredibly, there was no British-United States copyright agreement until 1905, so that no royalties were paid for producing these extremely popular works.

The Centralization of Power: 1896 to 1914

In both England and America, the nineteenth century actor-managers who were also stars were mostly impractical businessmen and women; their inflated egos fostered such traditions as the long-running engagement, an emphasis on contemporary comedies and melodrama, productions that were often tasteless, and a financial structure that usually teetered on the threshold of bankruptcy. To avoid debtors' prison they revived a particular tour de force that audiences always turned out to see.

If famous stars were ill equipped to cope with the new demands of the modern age, so were the smalltown actor-managers. The growth of touring combination companies, the continuation of the star system, the advent of vaudeville and the striking proliferation of playhouses during the closing decades of the nineteenth century necessitated more than the then-current haphazard planning and management. With the disbanding of local resident companies, theatre buildings fell under the ownership of local bankers and investors whose primary concern was to make a profit from the property. This situation placed a local manager, usually a nonactor, in charge of selecting and booking touring performers and productions. It also made play producing separate from theatre managing.

Because of the complexities in routing companies from city to city, local managers welcomed the appearance of centralized booking offices, which sprang up in New York City around 1880. Before long the booking agents were also selecting and producing the plays, which had long been the prerogative of the actor, as well as serving as the actors' agents and establishing themselves as distinct functionaries in the emerging entertainment industry. Because they often took fees and commissions for services not rendered, and because employment was nearly impossible without their assistance, actors disliked them. And, initially, these agents maintained a three-sided advantage, since they could extract a booking fee from the local manager, a casting fee from the producer, and a job-finding fee from the actor. Despite having signed contracts and agreements, booking agents were notoriously unscrupulous. Companies were rerouted at the last minute, leaving local theatre managers without an engagement; tours were canceled midway, leaving actors stranded without return fare to New York. (See also Chapter 9, Background.) The famous story about the lost company of *Blossom Time* is no myth—the Shubert brothers canceled the show when it was playing in the Northwest, and it took most of the actors years to work their way back home. Actors never received a salary for rehearsal time and were required to furnish their own wigs and costumes, which sometimes cost more than they could expect to earn during their engagement. In this lamentable fashion, New York City became the nation's theatre capital; theatrical booking, producing, and casting became highly centralized, and profits were taken by middlemen rather than by the actors and playwrights. The era of the business tycoon in the theatre had begun.

In 1896, three of New York's booking offices merged into one and thereby created the infamous Theatrical Syndicate—also called the Theatrical Trust—a partnership comprised of Sam Nixon, Fred Zimmerman, Al Hayman, Charles Frohman, Marc Klaw, and Abraham Erlanger. Less interested in standards of production than in making large profits, these gentlemen set out to gain absolute booking control over the nation's theatres, and within a few years succeeded. Such extreme centralization naturally fostered numerous evils, and the monopoly was bound to meet opposition. In 1902, the well-known actress Minnie Maddern Fiske and her husband, Harrison Grey Fiske, established the Independent Booking Agency, which attempted to break Syndicate control. Comparatively few actors of note were willing to join the Fiskes, who were often forced to perform in barns and skating rinks because the Syndicate controlled most of the theatres.

David Belasco also waged a valorous campaign against the monopoly, but the people who finally did manage to topple the Syndicate were the Shubert brothers.

Beginning modestly in upstate New York and following the untimely death of brother Sam in 1905, Lee and J. J. Shubert proclaimed themselves the liberators of the American theatre, demanding "open door" booking and casting policies. Enough people in the industry swallowed this bait to make the Shuberts successful. But everyone soon woke up to the fact that they had simply replaced the Syndicate as ruling tyrants of the American theatre. There was, however, one difference—the Shuberts amassed an empire in theatrical real estate, thus making their power more complete.

Today the founding brothers are dead; many Shubert-owned theatres across the nation have been sold or demolished, and others were sold when the Shuberts lost a federal antitrust suit in the mid-1950s. Despite this, the Shubert Organization is the largest theatre operator on Broadway, fully owning sixteen Broadway theatres—plus a fifty-percent interest in a seventeenth—two additional theatres in Boston and Philadelphia, and the Tele-Charge ticketing system. In addition, it manages the National Theatre in Washington, D.C. It should be mentioned that while the Syndicate and the Shuberts certainly took advantage of a business opportunity and milked it for all it was worth, they did not create that opportunity. They did not engineer the westward movement of America's population or encourage the demand for entertainment and the initial growth in theatre construction. Nor did they invent the star system or combination companies. They did not destroy the independence of resident stock companies and they did not build the railway system. They simply grasped an opportunity that few actor-managers understood.

Rather than fighting for artistic and economic control over their profession, actors embroiled themselves in a more fatalistic battle for workers' rights. It is interesting to wonder what the industry might be like had George M. Cohan and others succeeded in their efforts to prevent theatrical unionism. But attempts to organize a collective bargaining association for actors persisted. The first was the Actors' Society of America, formed the same year as the Syndicate, in 1896. Then the American Federation of Labor chartered the Actors' International Union, which fell under the control of the White Rats, a union of vaudeville performers. Vaudevillians had formed the White Rats to fight a five-percent kickback of their salaries to managers that had been imposed through the Vaudeville Managers Protective Association, an organization formed by Keith and Albee, who came to monopolize vaudeville at the same time the Shuberts monopolized legitimate theatre. Since the AFL can only grant one charter for any given trade or craft, a conflict arose when legitimate stage actors organized under the banner of Actors' Equity Association in 1913. But, after a three-month strike in 1919, when the union won its first meaningful contract with producers, it eventually won a charter.

Playwrights and composers were also busy securing protection for their creative output. Victor Herbert, at the turn of the twentieth century, was dining in a fashionable restaurant when he heard the orchestra play his music, for which he was not entitled to a cent in royalty payments. Not wishing to die penniless in the Bowery, which had been Stephen Foster's fate, he began a four-year court battle to receive royalty payments that ended when the Supreme Court ruled in his favor. In 1914 Herbert helped to organize the American Society of Composers and Publishers (ASCAP), which is today the world's largest music licensing organization having agreements with millions of music users in the U.S. and with music societies in forty countries. Its primary function is to monitor music use on behalf of some 240,000 members and to collect and distribute royalty payments. Of course, this would not be possible without the copyright protection guaranteed by the congressional legislation that began in 1909 and covers all types of creative work. Playwrights began to organize in 1878, when Steele MacKaye helped establish the American Dramatic Authors' Society; this was followed in 1891 by the American Dramatists Club, although neither made much progress. In 1911 the Authors League of America was established, and playwrights were included in its membership. Finally, following the Equity strike, a playwrights' committee at the League grew into the Dramatists Guild, which signed its first contract with producers in 1921. Ironically, as theatre artists began to gain better compensation and working conditions, their prospects for employment were rapidly diminishing.

The Decline of Commercial Theatre: 1914 to 1960

The phenomenal growth of electronic entertainment got under way in 1915 with D.W. Griffith's film, *Birth of a Nation*. By that time there were approximately ten thousand movie theatres scattered across the country, a figure that doubled by 1920; the average price of admission was fifty cents while the cost of the average theatre ticket was two dollars. The advent of network radio shows around 1925, and of talking pictures in 1927, greatly increased the competition that threatened live theatre. During World War I, America mobilized its railroads for the war effort and, while shipping a can of film was easy, rail travel for theatrical companies was often impossible.

Statistics vary greatly, but it seems feasible to claim that between 1900 and 1932 the number of theatres presenting live entertainment decreased from about five thousand to as few as one hundred—thirty-two of which were located in New York City. And only six of those were operating at one point in 1932. The stock market crash in 1929, and the subsequent depression, also contributed to the near demise of commercial theatre in America. Because of increasing union costs and royalty payments—not to mention the insidious growth of income taxes—few producers were rich enough to finance a commercial production out of their own pockets, which had been the rule before the Great Crash. Afterward, most producers had to seek outside investors or "angels" or, as we'll soon discuss, invent other financing schemes. The days of the truly independent producer, as typified by Florenz Ziegfeld, Arthur Hopkins, and Jed Harris, had come to an end.

Fortunately for the future of American theatre, several developments outside the commercial arena—the growth of the "little theatre movement," the first federal assistance to theatre, the growth of college theatre, and factors that will be considered in later chapters—did much to kindle both our theatre and our written drama. Beginning as noncommercial and largely experimental ventures, such groups as the Provincetown Playhouse, the Theatre Guild, and the Group Theatre uncovered an impressive amount of talent as well as a new audience to support it, much of which was quickly fed into the commercial Broadway theatre.

While Greenwich Village had long provided the space for experimental theatre, the history of the Off-Broadway movement begins with Jose Quintero's 1952 production of Tennessee Williams's *Summer and Smoke*, which starred Geraldine Page at the Circle in the Square on its original site in the Village. This was the first downtown production to receive a major review in the *New York Times*. The Off-Broadway movement subsequently received increasingly greater publicity, which didn't escape the attention of Actors' Equity, and soon the union won its first contract with the League of Off-Broadway Theatres and Producers, an event doubtless hastened by the 1960 opening of the first big moneymaking Off-Broadway hit, *The Fantasticks*. Originally offering a showcase where producers could operate without union employees and at low cost, in less than two decades many Off-Broadway productions, both in content and economic structure, belonged to the commercial genre. Nonetheless, the comparative economy and freedom offered by Off-Broadway brought new blood to commercial theatre and encouraged a new generation of producers and playwrights. But with the actors' unionization of Off-Broadway came the inevitable: increased production costs and increased commercialization. Just as inevitable, perhaps, was the subsequent birth and development of Off-Off-Broadway—small, nonprofit, nonunion theatres, which began in the early 1960s with groups such as Ellen Stewart's Cafe La Mama in lower Manhattan, and proliferated rapidly in New York and other cities. Once again, actors, directors, playwrights, and producers—many with professional credentials—had showcase opportunities for their talents. And, once again, beginning in the mid-1970s, Equity began to push for jurisdiction over these theatres—first by the introduction of the Showcase Code, which gained only carfare for its members, then minimum weekly salaries were established. In recent years, many small nonprofits that worked under the Showcase Code when they were first producing have grown as organizations and are able to produce on LOA and LORT contracts that are similar in salary scale to Off-Broadway scale, or at times have used the actual Off-Broadway contract. The Showcase Code is used by both commercial and nonprofit producers to develop productions.

Retrenchment: 1960 to 1990

Ironically, the most productive and important period of American drama occurred during the 1930s when the American theatre was at its lowest economically, yet it brought forth the works of Eugene O'Neill, Maxwell Anderson, Lillian Hellman, S. N. Behrman, Robert Sherwood, Elmer Rice, and Kaufman and Hart. The leading playwrights of the 1940s and 1950s—Arthur Miller, Tennessee Williams, and William Inge—kept alive the promise of serious American drama, but the next generation could only boast the works of Edward Albee, who may be considered the last major American playwright to write serious pieces expressly for the commercial theatre—unless one counts Neil Simon. Commercially successful authors such as Tony Kushner and Richard Greenberg now have relationships with nonprofit companies so that their work can be developed and not close in one night. As the Broadway theatre became more tourist-oriented, commercial audiences were turning to comedies and musicals, with an emphasis on the latter. At least this was the case on Broadway and the road. In part because this commercial situation frustrated so many theatre artists—especially directors—the 1960s and 1970s saw nonprofit resident theatre companies not only grow in numbers but actually surpass the commercial theatre in terms of jobs and professional theatre production.

The remarkable thing about this, historically, is that for the first time two distinctly different methods of producing professional theatre in America were being practiced concurrently: the commercial method and the nonprofit method. Until the 1970s the nonprofit sector often borrowed plays, stars, directors, and designers from Broadway. Perhaps significantly, it rarely borrowed Broadway producers or managers. But by the mid-1970s, the balance of payments, as it were, had shifted so that Broadway was relying on the nonprofits for both product and talent, in addition to managerial innovations. Virtually all serious dramatists today are nurtured and sustained by the nonprofit theatre: David Mamet, Christopher Durang, Sam Shepard, John Guare, Marsha Norman, Terrence McNally, Landford Wilson, and the late August Wilson among others. And when their plays are produced on Broadway, a nonprofit theatre company is often the producer or co-producer. This allows the plays to receive the developmental attention that they deserve, and the profits in turn help to sustain the producing organizations from which the plays originated.

The commercial theatre has always had a high failure rate. However, the industry is making an attempt to revitalize Broadway attendance and there have been some actual accomplishments in recent years. For example, The Theatre Development Fund (TDF) operates two discounted ticket booths in New York City, where producers can sell remaining tickets, day-of, at a twenty-five- to fifty-percent discount. There are similar programs in San Francisco, Boston, Washington, D.C., and Atlanta. This has been incredibly successful in boosting capacity, but some producers and theatre owners argue that the presence of so many discounted tickets in the market is training audience members not to buy full-price tickets in advance. TDF has also introduced a program through which they sell discounted tickets to their members before a show's opening, which helps to boost advance sales. It also has a subsidy program for commercial producers that provides funding for commercial productions in exchange for discounted tickets for its members. New York State legislation was introduced to permit investors to put money into blind pools, which producers may invest in many productions. Commercial productions have begun to work with audience-development specialists to target certain audiences, such as youth or audiences of color, in the way that nonprofits have for years.

In fairness, it must also be said that Broadway executives are hampered in ways in their efforts to sustain and improve the commercial theatre. Most would argue that the industry is overregulated in terms of investing, financing, insurance, the selling and distributing of tickets, ticket pricng, and union jurisdiction and regulations that escalate costs. Most commercial theatre executives argue that the nonprofit theatres benefit from an unfair tax advantage. And Broadway landlords resent the fact that over two-thirds of the existing thirty or so Broadway theatres have been given landmark designations, thereby preventing their demolition, and in some cases even their interior renovation to accommodate specific production requirements. The development potential of the Broadway theatre district was further limited in 1988, when the city reduced allowable building density because of the Times Square development project. In fact, the Shubert, Nederlander, and Jujamcyn concerns joined forces that year and filed suit against the city to revoke the landmark status. A landmark theatre housing an empty stage, they claim, serves nobody. Many would disagree with that characteristically commercial attitude, because for every landmarked theatre in America there have been a hundred demolished, and the craftspeople necessary to rebuild them are as rare as the giant Wurlitzer organs in bygone movie palaces.

1990s to the Present

Probably the most significant theatrical event of the 1990s was the opening of the stage version of Disney Theatrical's successful animated film *Beauty and the Beast* on April 18, 1994 at the Palace Theatre. Not only did it introduce a new major corporation to the New York theatre scene, but the show's huge success immediately established Disney as a major player on Broadway and later on the road. Disney's desire for a permanent home on Broadway led to its taking over the refurbishment of the New Amsterdam Theatre on 42nd Street. This single action catapulted the formerly seedy 42nd Street into a very desirable theatrical and business thoroughfare. Soon other theatres, such as the Ford Center—now the Hilton Theatre—which opened with the musical *Ragtime*, were renovated; later, Roundabout Theatre Company relocated to the American Airlines Theatre, and corporations such as Clear Channel Communications, Inc. started taking an active role on Broadway.

The late 1990s also saw the closing of a number of long-run "British invasion" musicals such as *Cats* (7,485 performances), *Les Misérables* (6,680 performances), and *Miss Saigon* (4,097 performances), freeing up prize musical houses for new productions. There was another British invasion when British directors took a revisionist look at classic American musicals, *Cabaret, Carousel, Oklahoma!*, and more recently, *Fiddler on the Roof*, each with varying degrees of success.

Drama on Broadway came mostly in the form of imports or revivals, with American playwrights finding comfort in nonprofit theatres such as the New York Shakespeare Festival, Playwrights Horizons, the Manhattan Theater Club, Lincoln Center Theatre Company, or regional theatres across the country.

The highest-profile dramatist of the period was the playwright August Wilson, who wrote a ten-play cycle dealing with African-Americans in his native Pittsburgh, with each play set in a different decade of the last century. With the staging of the tenth and final play in the spring of 2005 at the Yale Repertory Theatre, Mr. Wilson completed his cycle.

In every area of creative talent—directors, choreographers, librettists, composers, and lyricists—the attrition rate of Broadway musical theatre talent has been significant. Arguably, the last musical theatre genius left is Stephen Sondheim, who turned seventy-five in March 2005. His work is mostly viewed in revival these days; his last Broadway musical endeavor was *Passion* in 1994, and his latest, the 2003 *Bounce*, played Chicago and Washington, D.C. but never reached New York.

Singular exceptions notwithstanding, there is so little fresh material to present, producers have turned to the *jukebox musical* or *catalog musical* which takes the catalog of a popular composer, such as ABBA, Burt Bacharach, or the Beach Boys, and fashions a story around the songs. Choreographer Twyla Tharp made a variation on this idea with *Movin' Out*, employing Billy Joel music and telling a Tharp-inspired story all in dance to the delight of both Tharp and Joel fans.

The formerly common practice of adapting stage plays and musicals into film has been reversed and so in addition to the Disney examples (*Beauty and the Beast*, *The Lion King*), Broadway theatregoers have been treated to *The Producers*, *Hairspray*, *The Full Monty*, and *Thoroughly Modern Millie*, Tony Award winners, all.

As it enters the twenty-first century, Broadway is, as it has always been, that strange mixture of commerce and art with its one overarching constant, *unpredictability*. There really is no knowing or predicting who the next Rodgers and Hammerstein will be, or where the next hit will come from. Broadway randomly reinvents itself, and with every new hit a new generation of audience members is born, and the fabulous invalid—defying her Cassandras—rises again.

Finding a Property to Produce

Anyone, given the somewhat crazy urge, can produce for the commercial theatre. One needn't have a lot of money, free time, connections in high places, experience, taste, or even knowledge of how the commercial theatre works. Other people can be and usually are hired to provide those elements. All that a person must have to be a producer is something to produce and, of course, the legal right to produce it. This may begin merely as an idea in for translating some nondramatic work into a piece for the theatre. It may begin with a performer, such as John Leguizamo, Whoopi Goldberg, or Lily Tomlin, whom the producer wants to present in a one-person show. It may begin as an idea for presenting an individual in monologue form—Harry Truman, Mark Twain, Gertrude Stein, and Golda Meir are some examples. Or the producer may be lucky enough to obtain the right to produce a finished, original play. From the performer's point of view, a script is a "vehicle," a medium that allows his or her ability to be displayed before an audience. From the producer's point of view, a script is a "property," or a piece of theatrical-literary real estate that has the potential for making money. Perhaps it is indicative of how deeply commercialism has pervaded the theatre that in no other branch of the performing arts is the artist's creative work referred to as a "property." The term is a striking reminder to playwrights and producers that a script has financial as well as artistic potential.

The business of finding a property to produce, then, is the producer's first and most important responsibility. Rarely does a promising script appear unsolicited on a producer's desk. The producer must usually do a lot of reading, traveling, theatre-going, movie-going, and searching before a viable idea or property shows up. Or some commercial producers have even nurtured a working relationship with a writer, such as Emanuel Azenberg has enjoyed with Neil Simon, or Cameron Mackintosh with Andrew Lloyd Webber. In any case, from the time a producer decides upon a property until the first day of rehearsal, many months, and sometimes many years, can pass.

Federal Copyright Law

When searching for material to present on the stage, the producer should be mindful of laws that pertain to literary ownership. However, copyright laws and their application are among the most complex in the entire legal field, and an attorney should always be consulted when one is attempting to purchase or protect literary rights of any kind.

Copyright law in the United States is now based on the Copyright Act of 1976, which stipulates that any creative work or expression of an idea is the property of its author or creator for the duration of that person's life plus fifty years. The 1909 copyright law that had previously been in effect stipulated that a work would enjoy copyright protection for only twenty-eight years. But, if the copyright was renewed during the twenty-seventh year, protection could be extended for an additional twenty-eight years and, at a later point, this extension was increased to forty-seven years for a maximum of seventy-five years. As a result of that bothersome condition, many works fell into the public domain —they could be used freely by anyone—at the end of the first twenty-eight years.

In 1988, federal legislation approved American participation in and conformity with the Berne copyright treaty. This extended protection to American copyright holders in nations with no direct treaties with the United States so that pirated American works could no longer be reproduced in these nations with impunity. The treaty also eliminated previous requirements for obtaining a copyright. Because a copyright now occurs at the moment of creation, the work no longer needs to be registered with the Library of Congress, nor must copies of the work be deposited there. However, in order to invoke protections of certain copyright laws in court—copyright infringement litigation, for example—the work must be registered. Also, copyrighted works no longer need to display the copyright symbol, ©. Other points that may be helpful to bear in mind include:

1.) All literary rights are extinguishable and cannot be owned by anyone in perpetuity.

2.) Ownership of a basic property is not divisible; one may own, sell, or give away all of it or none of it.

3.) The copyright holder, however, may grant or sell licenses giving others the right to use the copyrighted material in a particular way, as in the case of granting the dramatization and attendant performance rights for a novel, and to share income generated from those particular uses with the holder.

4.) Copyrights cannot usually protect the title of a work nor may one copy-right an idea.

Broadway, for example, has seen three or four productions titled *South Pacific*, two titled *Speed-the-Plow*, and two musical productions entitled *The Wild Party*, both based on a poem by the same name and both produced in the same season. However, titles may be protected under tort law and under the Lanham Act if they have acquired secondary meaning.

5.) Only the expression of an idea may be copyrighted, not the idea alone.

6.) The Library of Congress merely files copies of work when these are sub-mitted to it, unlike the U.S. Office of Patents, which verifies that an invention is original and unique before it issues a patent. Any copyright dispute, therefore, must be settled in a court of law.

7.) When obtaining any license, agreement, or permit, it should always be remembered that anything not specifically withheld is given away. For example, if the license does not state that the producer controls the televi-sion rights to his or her property, then these rights have probably been forfeited by default, and the producer has no control over the property as far as television production of it is concerned.

Theatre-related works that enjoy copyright protection include plays; lyrics; musical scores; directors' notes; choreography and choreographic notations; scenic, costume, and lighting designs and/or plots; sound designs; advertisements; and photographs.

Types of Theatrical Property

Most common theatrical properties in both the commercial and nonprofit sectors include, for example:

An original copyrighted work—*Our Town* and *The Odd Couple* when they were first produced

An adaptation of a copyrighted work—*Cats* from a poem by T. S. Eliot and *La Cage Aux Folles* from a French film

An original copyrighted work that was commissioned—*A Chorus Line* was developed, in effect, commissioned, by the New York Shakespeare Festival, and *Nixon in China* commissioned by the Brooklyn Academy of Music and its underwriters

A revival of a work in the public domain—*Hamlet* or *The Pirates of Penzance*
A revival of a copyrighted work—*42nd Street* or *Gypsy* in their subsequent Broadway productions

An adaptation of a work in the public domain—*Dracula*, adapted from the 1897 romance novel by Bram Stoker, and *West Side Story*, adapted from Shakespeare's *Romeo and Juliet*

A translation of a foreign language work in the public domain—*The Cherry Orchard* from the Russian or *Cyrano de Bergerac* from the French

A translation of a copyrighted work—*Six Characters in Search of an Author* from the Italian or *Irma La Douce* from the French

But the work of discovering a property, or rediscovering it—a revival, if you will, or commissioning it to be written, and then putting the property together with the right interpretive artists at the right time in the right theatre is very, very difficult to accomplish—hence, the very high failure rate.

Securing Production and Subsidiary Rights

Once a producer has decided to present a particular script or commission a script to be written based on an existing work, legal action must be taken to secure the necessary production and subsidiary rights. It is advisable to hire an attorney to conduct a title search in order to determine who, if anyone, owns the copyright of a basic property that is to be adapted. Since 1921, playwrights, book writers, lyricists, and composers working on Broadway have usually been members of the Dramatists Guild and have usually negotiated with producers through the Dramatists Guild Minimum Basic Production Contract (MBPC). Because of rising production costs, however, it became increasingly difficult to attract investors, especially since the terms of the MBPC meant that investors could not earn back their investments for months or years. Hoping to find a way to recoup their expenses more rapidly, producers came up with the idea of creating a royalty "pool."

Why should playwrights, the reasoning went, be earning full royalties if the production was only breaking even and investors had yet to see a dime returned? During the early 1980s legal action between the Dramatists Guild and the League of American Theatres and Producers was threatened on the basis that the other group violated the Sherman Antitrust Act. The matter was dropped when both parties agreed upon the Approved Production Contract (APC) in 1985.

This agreement is now the basis of most contracts between producers and writers for all live, first-class productions on the speaking stage in the United States, its territories, possessions, and in Canada. Essentially, this boils down to Broadway and first-class productions in major cities and on tour. It is important to note, however, that the APC has not been renegotiated in twenty years, which means that it is horribly out of date. While the components of the agreement are still referred to, the contract itself is not used to the letter in the way that contracts with unions such as Actors' Equity or the Stagehands Union are. The agreement itself is acknowledged, and an additional rider is written and agreed to by the lawyers or general managers representing the author and the producer.

The Dramatists Guild Approved Production Contract (APC)

The Approved Production Contract, as originally published by the Guild, is a fifty-page document that ostensibly has a provision for every aspect of the relationship beween a producer and the writer(s) of a production. In fact, there are really two APCs—one for plays and one for musicals. Just as salaries are at the heart of all employee contracts, so option and royalty payments are at the heart of contracts with creative, nonemployee artists.

From the artistic standpoint, the Dramatists Guild and the APC exist in order to insure the writer's integrity and intent. They serve to prevent unapproved changes being made in the script or performance, unapproved additional authors being brought in, and other unapproved decisions being made that might alter the creative intent. These are mighty hard matters to regulate. It is very likely that both the Guild and the League are in violation of antitrust laws. Yet, until somebody comes up with a better solution, they are the best service organizations for their constituents.

Subsidiary Rights

The APC stipulates that the producer has until midnight on the first day of rehearsals to select one of four alternatives for sharing the income from certain subsidiary uses that the property may eventually enjoy. If the producer fails to notify the Guild of this choice, then the author may make the selection or, if both ignore the decision, then one of the alternatives automatically goes into effect. However, all such income will belong to the author unless the production runs for a determined number of performances and thereby permits the production company to share in any subsequent profits. The APC covers the following subsidiary rights:

1.) Media Productions: Audio-only recordings and radio use, plus those uses covered below;

2.) Audio-Visual Productions: Motion pictures, television, videocassette, video disc, and all other types of audiovisual production excluding foreign local television production outside the U.S. and Canada;

3.) Commercial Use Products: Wearing apparel, toys, games, doll figures, novelties, books, souvenir programs, and any other physical property in any way associated with the play, its title, or characters;

4.) Stock Performances: All performances of the work in English presented under an AEA agreement for stock, resident theatre, university resident theatre, dinner theatre, or guest artist agreement and the equivalent of such performances outside the U.S.;

5.) Amateur Performances: All performances in English performed only by nonprofessional actors who are not members of a performers' union or guild either in or outside of the U.S.;

6.) Ancillary Performances: Any performances in English presented in a condensed or abbreviated version, so-called concert tours, plus any musical version based on the work, plus foreign language performances of all kinds both here and abroad, plus performances presented under AEA agreements for theatre for young audiences, small professional theatre, nonprofit theatre codes and their equivalents outside the United States;

7.) Revival Performances: All performances of the play in New York City after the producer's rights to present that work have expired, plus all performances outside the city after the producer's rights have expired, providing there are revivals in at least three different cities.

Section 22

The standard procedure when negotiating a Broadway author's agreement is to write a rider to the APC, which allows the producer and author, under Section 22 of the contract, to make changes to the contract for their mutually agreed upon purposes. These riders can be quite extensive, and at present, modify the terms of almost all of the clauses of import in the APC. The rider can—and does—modify the following elements of the agreement:

Option and Advance Payments
Royalties
Payment for Developmental Productions and Tryouts and Future Companies
Additional Representations and Warranties
Billing
All Subsidiary Rights

Many riders to the APC also contain, as an insurance policy, a clause that states that if the League and the Guild renegotiate the APC before the first public performance of the play, the producer has the right either to adopt the changes—if they are more beneficial to the producer than what was negotiated—or to keep the contract as it is. The likelihood of the League and the Guild renegotiating a contract anytime soon, however, is unlikely.

If the APC is not used, as when the writer is foreign, deceased, or not a Guild member, or when the play is not being produced on Broadway, the producer or producing organization will want to make certain that its attorney draws up an agreement with the authors that covers the above subsidiary rights. But if that production subsequently moves to Broadway, it can convert to an APC at that time. Subsidiary rights are of vital concern to both producers and their backers as well as to playwrights because they may eventually bring in a tremendous amount of money. In fact, a number of shows have failed to break even on Broadway and yet have earned high profits for their participants because of subsidiary earnings.

While the original producer usually produces the first-class national touring companies of the show—as well as the initial first-class productions in foreign capitals—other producers may buy the rights to present subsequent productions of the show. The rights to publish an "acting edition" of even remotely successful plays that have received first-class productions are bought by a play publishing company, such as Samuel French or Dramatists Play Service, Inc., which in turn administers the stock and amateur rights, collects royalties, and then turns over the appropriate portion of these to the Dramatists Guild, which extracts its fee and the remainder to the author or author's agent, who would extract yet another fee. The rights to the majority of Broadway musicals are administered by such publishers as Tams Witmark, Inc., Music Theatre International, and the Rodgers and Hammerstein Music Library. These companies also rent or sell scripts and musical scores and musical accompaniment for the properties they control.

To make a recording of a Broadway show, the cast and musicians must each be paid one week's salary.

Forming a Production Company

Let's quickly review the options currently open to a commercial producer who is about to set up a production company.

Sole Proprietorship

Prior to the stock market crash of 1929, the sole proprietorship of a production company was a common method of producing. It provided the greatest independence for a producer, who put up all the capital and took all the risks along with full, personal liability. This method has virtually disappeared from commercial producing.

Private Corporation

Offering the advantages of limited personal liability and perpetual existence, a private corporation is theoretically controlled by a board of directors, who may be family members or friends and, in reality, exercise no say whatever. Private corporations are commonly used as the legal structure for commercial stock and dinner theatres, companies that package road shows and tours of all kinds, and by theatrical service and production companies. Individual artists and managers sometimes incorporate in order to gain certain tax advantages.

Sub-Chapter S Corporation

Commonly called an "S Corporation," this small business corporation is taxed as if it were an individual proprietorship, in effect allowing the corporation to avoid the corporate tax, but instead allowing the corporation's losses to be claimed by the shareholders on their individual tax returns.

Public Corporation

The possibility of financing a Broadway show through the device of a public stock offering has intrigued producers for years. It was finally put to the test during the 1970s by Joseph Tandet to produce a musical adaptation of *The Little Prince*. Unfortunately, the show was not a hit, so it doesn't provide much of a case study. Advantages with this approach include the ability of the company to enter easily into other ventures, to raise money in one fell swoop through block stock sales to an underwriter, and to tap a vast number of small investors whose risk is minimal and who wouldn't ordinarily invest in theatre. The company can also take advantage of retained earnings, since profits need not be distributed as they come in. The disadvantages include locking the production into a set budget because there is no "overcall" provision—meaning that the investors must put up additional monies, if asked to do so; having high start-up costs for attorneys, accountants, and underwriters, having the Securities and Exchange Commission act as a watchdog; and making stockholders subject to double—corporate and personal—taxation, which is not the case in a partnership.

However, recently a company producing on Broadway and in Canada called LiveEnt —Live Entertainment—took advantage of a public corporation's ability to retain earnings—not only did it retain them, its officers embezzled the earnings, and the corporation purposefully misrepresented its earnings, inflating the numbers so that the company should seem more profitable, making its shares more valuable. When LiveEnt filed for bankruptcy, its vendors and shareholders were horrified to learn of the company's practices. Most Broadway productions are watched carefully by their investors, and a quarterly statement of operations and regular distribution of capital and profit are expected by and rightly provided to its investors.

General Partnership or Joint Venture

The joint venture arrangement typically involves two, three, or four entities—corporations and/or individuals—that provide the full capitalization, somewhat like that of a sole proprietorship with several owners. The diffusion of control, however, can present a danger as it is always more complicated when decisions are shared by a group than when made by an individual. To determine how decisions will be made and by whom, the amount of capital needed, how much each party will contribute, how profits will be distributed, and the conditions under which a party may withdraw, a joint Venture Agreement must be drawn up by an attorney. It is not necessary to become involved with the Securities and Exchange Commission (SEC). Each of the three major Broadway theatre landlords has often entered into a joint venture with an independent producer or corporation because it is the most expedient way to keep their theatres occupied. In a general partnership, the parties are personally liable for the losses of the venture—as in a sole proprietorship—but in a joint venture, the liability is limited to the corporations that are members.

Investment Pooling

In 1988 a bill was introduced in the New York State Legislature that provided an alternative to the way in which Broadway and Off-Broadway productions could be financed. Previously, producers were only permitted to raise money for a specified production and had to repeat the process for each new production they hoped to stage. The law permits producers to set up a "blind pool"—somewhat like a mutual fund—into which investors put money that can then be used for a number of unspecified productions. Unfotunately, the original law required that all investments in a pool be spent within two years, making the scheme highly impractical without a lot of money in a pool and, even more unlikely, a lot of potential hits to produce. While new legislation may eventually correct this problem, only those few producers with solid track records are likely to attract such investors. Producers often offer investment opportunities to particular individuals because they think that the investor will be attracted to the product, and attracting investors to a pool has proven difficult for even the most high-profile producers. Additionally, profits from a hit show can easily be lost on a succession of flops. Nonetheless, investment pooling is a creative attempt to revitalize commercial production. This is a topic of much discussion, but unfortunately, neither the success rate nor profit margin in commercial theatre is high enough to attract investors who don't want to put their money in a particular property.

Limited Partnership

Some commercial New York theatre productions are organized around a Limited Partnership Agreement, the terms of which differ from agreement to agreement but have basic similarities that appear to offer the best legal and tax advantages for both producers and investors when shares are offered publicly through the SEC. For example, investors in a partnership can deduct the full amount of any loss in the year it occurs, whereas corporate shareholders can deduct only a part of the loss in each of several years and may never be able to deduct the full amount lost. Similarly, profits from a partnership are taxed only to the individual partners, while corporations pay taxes on their profits, and then shareholders are taxed when the same profits are distributed as dividends.

A Limited Partnership Agreement provides for two types of partners: limited partners and general partners. The former, who are the investors, provide the funds to cap-
italize the production, but don't have control over the affairs of the partnership. Their
liability is limited to their investment plus an additional "overcall" amount—usually ten
to twenty percent of their investment—in the event that it is needed. The general partners, who are the producers, assume all control over the affairs of the partnership and all
the legal risks and financial liabilities, including personal responsibility for the losses of the
company. For this reason, the Limited Partnership has been replaced relatively recently
by the Limited Liability Company.

The Limited Liability Company

The Limited Liability Company is similar to a Limited Partnership, except that none of
the members, general or limited, is personally liable for the losses of the company.
Commonly referred to as the LLC, it is easier to form than a corporation and can be dissolved more easily. The members are designated as limited—those who contribute capital
but are not responsible for the management of the company—or general—those who manage the day-to-day affairs of the company. Members can be individuals, corporations, or
other LLCs. It is possible for someone to be both a general partner and also a limited
partner.

In New York State, some productions have gone back to the LP model because of
the large annual tax payment that is required by each member of the company of an LLC
model. While a show is running on Broadway, investors may not mind paying such a
tax, but when the income becomes minimal yet is still enough to keep the company from
dissolving, the tax makes a Limited Partnership—where the general partners are represented by sole-member Limited Liability Companies and therefore are not personally
liable for losses—a more reasonable and cheaper alternative.

As in a Limited Partnership, the LLC members are liable only for the dollar-
amount of their investment plus, in most cases, overcall. Ordinarily, the limited partners
collectively provide the total capital required to finance the production but share only
fifty percent of the profits, with the other fifty percent going to the general partners.
This means that if a limited partner has paid, or invested, ten percent of the total cost,
or capitalization, that person will share in only five percent of the profits.

The producers—general partners or members—of the company begin with fifty
percent ownership interest but seldom retain it because they usually deem it advisable or
necessary to sell or otherwise forfeit a portion of it for several reasons. At times, a general member will transfer a portion of his or her share to a limited partner in exchange
for a larger investment, or for "front money," the only funds which can be spent before the
company is completely capitalized. Front money is the riskiest investment because those
monies may be spent, whether or not the project materializes. (See Appendix G.)

If a capitalization higher than originally stated in the Limited Liability Agreement
is required, the general partners may have to sell part of their fifty percent share in the

company, because they are prohibited by law from issuing additional limited shares that would decrease the value of the original limited partners' shares.

The limited partners' chief obligations and benefits are:

1.) To contribute a specified amount of money to the company;

2.) To contribute a further specified amount if requested to do so, provided this is stated in the investment agreement;

3.) To have no other financial or legal obligation or liability in connection with the company;

4.) To share fifty percent of any profits with the other limited partners according to the amount of their investments—profits usually include money earned from the sale of subsidiary rights though, again, such matters must be spelled out in the agreement.

The general partners' chief obligations to the limited partners and to the company are:

1.) To guarantee that they have the legal right to produce the property in question;

2.) To guarantee that they actually intend to produce the property, provided the necessary capital is raised;

3.) To guarantee the safekeeping and legitimate expenditure of all invested capital;

4.) To return all invested capital in full if the amount specified in the agreement is not raised within a stated length of time;

5.) To desist from spending any invested capital until the full amount required has been raised, unless otherwise stated and specifically agreed to by the investor, as in the case of front money;

6.) To guarantee that the total capitalization stated in the agreement is sufficient to finance the production and that, for the purpose of determining the value of each share, it shall not be changed;

7.) To repay the limited partners' investments before the general partners begin to share in any profits.

Because they possess full control over the company, the general partners may dissolve it at any time provided they can show reasonable cause for so doing.

Now let's make up some simple figures to illustrate how a Limited Liability company works:

An Off-Broadway show organized as a Limited Liability Company is capitalized at $500,000:

There are 100 units offered, each valued at: $5,000

The total potential weekly gross of the theatre is: $125,000

The total weekly operating cost of the show is: $50,000

How many weeks of full-capacity business will it take to break even, or pay back its capitalization?

From each week's gross, in this case $125,000, the weekly operating expenses must first be taken, leaving a balance of $75,000—$125,000 less $50,000— available to be applied toward repaying the capitalization.

Assuming that each week's gross is the same $125,000 and the operating expenses hold at $50,000, it will take 6.67 weeks to pay back ($500,000 ÷ $75,000).

Once the show has paid back the capitalization, how much could an investor with a ten-percent interest in the show expect in weekly profits? Royalty recipients would now be eligible for their royalty share of the gross. Let's say that the show carries a twenty-percent royalty burden, spread out among authors, director, designers, underlying-rightsholders, and producers. So to the operating expenses of $50,000, the royalty package of $25,000—twenty percent of $125,000—must be added. Now the total weekly operating expenses are $75,000.

After deducting $75,000 from a full-capacity gross of $125,000, a weekly profit of $50,000 is left. Because of the 50/50 split the general partners' weekly share of the profits is $25,000.

The investors—all one hundred percent of them—are entitled to the other fifty percent, or in this case $25,000. A ten-percent interest then is ten percent of $25,000, or $2,500.

NOTE: This example assumes that the royalty recipients have *waived*, not deferred, their royalties until the show has paid back its capitalization. If they had *deferred*, instead of waiving, the total amount of money deferred would have to be repaid, sooner or later, depending on the original royalty terms. The greater the weekly expenses, the longer it will take to pay back the capitalization. In some cases, shows may run for years and never fully pay back their capitalizations.

It may appear at first glance that a fifty percent share in a company is excessive for a person who doesn't invest a cent in it. While the producer is entitled to be reimbursed by the company for option money advanced to the playwrights, for office expenses, and other such costs, there are no provisions for reimbursing that producer for all the time, travel, and entertaining that were necessary to obtain the property in the first place. Nor may producers, general partners, be reimbursed for expenses incurred to attract investors. Several years often elapse from the time a play is optioned until it opens in New York, and it may take another year or more of capacity business before it begins to realize a profit. Whatever money a producer may finally earn is, indeed, well earned.

Raising the Capital

How a production company is organized, as suggested in the preceding section, also determines how it will be financed. When just a few individuals and/or corporations are supplying all the needed capital, the process is simple. But, as in the case of most Limited Partnership Agreements, it is often necessary to attract dozens of investors. After obtaining a property, the producer must finance the venture, which is the producer's second most important function.

Offering papers, which provide a synopsis of the play and short biographies of the producer, author, and any leading artists committed to the project, are distributed to potential investors. The papers must also describe in detail the financial and legal organization of the company and contain a statement about the risks of theatrical investing, even giving the percentage of Broadway (or Off-Broadway) shows that failed during the previous New York season. Legal requirements such as these are designed to protect investors from unknowingly investing in highly speculative ventures, and nobody can deny that producing for the commercial theatre is highly speculative.

Offering papers are often accompanied by a promissory letter that the producer hopes the potential investor will sign and return. The sample that follows shows its typical content. However, it should be emphasized that this form letter merely precedes or accompanies a Limited Partnership Agreement and is not a substitute for it; nor should it be used until the agreement has been filed with the attorney general. The care that a producer must take when attempting to comply with the numerous laws and regulations related to producing for the commercial theatre cannot be overstated. A few reference works, such as the four volumes edited by Donald Farber, *Entertainment Industry Con-*

tracts (Albany, New York: Mathew Bender and Company, 1987), describe these regulations in greater detail than is appropriate here; but the producer is best advised to retain a reputable attorney with experience in the field of theatrical law.

To sell shares in commercial theatre productions the producing team invites potential investors to a rented theatre, hall, or private home to witness an informal presentation of scenes read from a script or songs sung from a score by professional performers (not necessarily the ones who will appear in the actual production). This is called a backers' audition. The producer, author, and others are present to answer questions and help promote the venture. Scenic design models or sketches may be displayed, and generous amounts of food and drink may be served. Few investors are capable of judging the commercial value and theatrical effectiveness of a play merely by reading a script, so a backers' audition can help them to visualize better and, of course, when well stage-managed, can also help them part with their money. However, few producers wish to take investments from people who cannot afford to lose that investment in full.

Negotiating for a Theatre

The success or failure of a production is partially determined by the theatre in which it is performed. Is the city, the neighborhood, and the address of the theatre "right" for the production at hand? The annals of theatre are filled with examples of intimate plays that got lost in huge theatres and of grandiose plays and musicals that were stifled in small houses. When considering a theatre space, whether on Broadway or in Toronto, the selection should be based first on artistic considerations and second on economic reasons. Most Broadway theatres have a similar aesthetic, though, so it may be difficult to find a venue with a nontraditional feel.

New York commercial theatre is basically divided into two categories: Broadway and Off-Broadway. Each designation is determined by the seating capacity of the theatre and by its location. Most theatres located in the general area of Times Square that have more than 500 seats operate as Broadway theatres under the Actors' Equity Production Contract or on a LORT A+ contract (see Chapter 5), and also have contracts with the other theatrical unions discussed later in this chapter. The AEA Off-Broadway contract roughly applies to theatres below 34th Street in Manhattan that seat fewer than 499 people and have been designated union houses. In theatres that have not been so designated, a producer can choose how to produce the show, either on an Off-Broadway contract, using members of Equity and other unions, or as a Showcase or with a Mini-contract with either union or nonunion members. The Showcase or Mini-contract were devised by AEA to cover runs limited to four weeks—Showcase—or commercial productions—Mini—in theatres with fewer than one hundred seats.

Before proceeding too far with contractual commitments to actors and others, the producer or general manager must begin the negotiations to rent a theatre. The rental agreement is not a lease but a license. The Off-Broadway producer can choose from a variety of theatres and often has considerable bargaining flexibility in the type of license that is concluded with the landlord. Many Off-Broadway theatres are rented according to the "four-wall" agreement. Here the producer is provided only with the building, with no personnel, no special equipment, and no operating costs paid by the landlord; but the producer pays only a fixed rental fee. The producer may also be required to pay rent for a certain number of weeks, even if the production closes during the first week. The League of Off-Broadway Theatres and Producers negotiates the minimum Off-Broadway contract terms with AEA.

In other Off-Broadway houses and most Broadway theatres, the relationship between the landlord and the tenant-producer is more like a partnership, in which both may share in the box office income and both gain from a successful, long-running production. All terms in a theatre license are negotiable and depend on what the landlord sees as the potential for success in a certain show and on how many shows are seeking to use that theatre. When a new show proves to be a great hit in London, for example, New York landlords may bid against one another to offer the producer the best terms, which may even include extensive interior renovation of the theatre as demanded for the musical *Cats*, for example. While various union employees are contracted to the landlord, the producer must pay for their salaries plus the other operating costs for the theatre. These costs may be included in a flat rental fee negotiated between the producer and the landlord, or the parties may negotiate a minimum guaranteed rent plus a percentage of the gross over a stipulated break-even figure. Another unique characteristic of the Broadway theatre license is the *stop clause*, a weekly box office gross amount that is agreed to in the license. If the show fails to realize this amount—usually for a period of two consecutive weeks—the landlord has the right to evict the production and/or the tenant may vacate without cost or penalty. The agreement may exempt the show from the stop clause stipulation for certain periods, such as the two weeks before Christmas or the first three weeks of January. The producer cannot logically arrive at a figure for the stop clause, however, until the total capitalization and the weekly operating cost for the production have been determined. (See Chapter 10: Setting the Stop Clause in a Commercial Theatre License.)

However, the situation is usually dire for a landlord to evict because the production has hit the amount in the stop clause—often the decision to close is made by the producer after the landlord has allowed the show to run for weeks or months below the negotiated amount.

Producers with an established record of success or who own a "hot" property are in the strongest bargaining positions. The star, or lack of one, is a primary factor in negotiating with Broadway landlords, and a license frequently requires the producer to use a certain star as promised. The landlord may have the right to terminate the license if a particular star fails to appear or leaves the production for any reason; or the landlord may have the right to veto the hiring or replacement of the star and certain featured players. For reasons such as these, the producer cannot effectively begin negotiating for a theatre until the production plans are well under way and leading artists' contracts have been signed. But the producer also does not wish to sign too many contracts until the license for a New York theatre is assured In other words, a commercial producer must often play both ends against the middle; time, luck, and shrewd judgment are critical, to say the least.

Employees in the Commercial Theatre

In order to bring a commercial production to opening night, a producer must hire an array of employees. In general, the LLC will contract a commercial general manager, who will handle contract administration, negotiations, ticket sales, and the coordination of press, marketing, advertising, and production. A general manager may have several productions that he or she is responsible for managing at one time and will generally hire a company manager to oversee payroll, the payment of invoices, nightly box office statements, and other day-to-day details. In addition, there may be an assistant general manager or assistant company manager to help in the administration of the production. The general manager will work with the producer to hire an advertising agency, a marketing firm, and a press agent. In addition, an audience development specialist or group sales agency may be brought on board to focus on ticket sales. The general manager will also hire a production manager, technical supervisor, stage managers, and production assistants. Generally the producer will hire the casting director, director, and designers and work with them to round out the creative team, which includes performers and may include a dramaturg, a composer, an arranger, an orchestrator, a music copyist, and design assistants. Some employees will be hired either by the theatre or the producer, depending on union jurisdictions; these include a box office staff, a house manager and house staff, musicians, technicians, and others. Some of these employees will be on the payroll just until opening night, while others will continue on with the production for the duration of the run.

As discussed earlier, not all commercial productions employ solely union employees. A producer must engage union employees if the union in question has negotiated a contract with the theatre owner in which the performance is to take place, or if there are creative and technical individuals who belong to the union that the producer specifically wishes to employ. In certain Off-Broadway theatres, for example, the actors are Equity actors because an agreement exists between the theatre owner and the union, but there may be no agreement with the musicians' union or the stagehands' union. The union status of employees is important to know from the earliest stages, as pension and welfare payments, as well as union bonds, significantly impact payroll costs.

Contracting Union Employees

The only person allowed to sign contracts with union employees is the one who has posted a bond with the union or that union's authorized representative. Questions regarding union jurisdiction, contracts, and regulations should be addressed directly to the appropriate union office, since many contractual terms involving salaries, benefits, and working conditions change each year and special concessions must be negotiated directly with a union. In any case, producers and managers are well advised to establish cordial relationships with union representatives. The following organizations maintain their headquarters in New York City, though some also have offices in other major cities.

Contracts Made by the Producer

1.) Dramatists Guild, Inc. This is not a union but a professional association to protect the rights of authors, including playwrights, bookwriters, lyricists, and composers, of dramatic and dramatico-musical works. Most works by living American playwrights presented on the New York stage, except those in public domain, are performed under a Dramatists Guild Approved Production Contract, as negotiated by the producer and author(s) with Guild guidance and certification.

2.) Actors' Equity Association (AEA). Equity derives its charter from the Associated Actors and Artists of America—known as the 4 A's—which in turn is chartered by the AFL-CIO. Its jurisdiction covers all professional actors—principals, chorus members, and extras—as well as stage managers and assistant stage managers.

3.) Society of Stage Directors and Choreographers (SSDC). This is a union to which virtually all directors and choreographers active in New York legitimate theatre belong. It sets minimum fees, royalty percentages, and employment conditions for its members; each conract is negotiated individually by the producer and the artist before seeking SSDC approval.

4.) United Scenic Artists of America (USA), Local 829. Most scenic, costume, and lighting designers working in New York legitimate theatre belong to this union. It requires all members to pass a lengthy and difficult examination before gaining membership, although producers may hire nonmembers who are then required to join the union but are exempted from the exam.

5.) Wardrobe Supervisors and Dressers, Local 764. Although producers or stars may hire whomever they wish in these two job categories, the new hires must join the union within thirty days if they are not already members.

Contracts Made by the Theatre Landlord

It is important to note that while some contracts are held by the theatre landlord, and therefore often negotiated by him or her—with assistance from the producers—this does not mean that the landlord bears the cost of the union employees. The theatre owner pays the union employees and bills all of the costs back to the producer as part of the weekly settlement.

1.) International Alliance of Theatrical Stage Employees (IATSE), Local 1. This union, representing all carpenters, stagehands, electricians, sound technicians, and property crewpeople, is contracted to the theatre. The number of employees required is determined by the theatre's agreement with the union and the type of production in residence.

2.) Treasurers and Ticket Sellers, Local 751. This union is also contracted by the theatre, and the number of employees required depends upon the theatre's seating capacity.

3.) Porters and Cleaners—Service Employees in Amusement and Cultural Buildings, Local 32-BJ. This union includes all cleaners, matrons, elevator operators, and porters.

4.) International Union of Operating Engineers, Local 30. This union includes all heavy equipment maintenance personnel, heating, and air-conditioning engineers.

5.) Ushers, Ticket-Takers and Doormen—Legitimate Theatre Employees Union, Local 306. This union has jurisdiction over all ushers, directors of ushers, ticket-takers, and front and back doorkeepers.

Contracts Made with Both the Producer and Theatre Landlord

1.) Association of Theatrical Press Agents and Managers (ATPAM), Union No. 18032. The producer contracts with the company manager and press agent, both of whom must be employed in conjunction with every Broadway and first-class touring production for the full length of its engagement. The landlord contracts with the house managers.

2.) American Federation of Musicians, Local 802. Some theatres have agreed to employ a minimum number of musicians whenever there is a musical production in residence or when more than four minutes of taped music is used. Additional musicians required, if any, are determined by the demands of the score and are contracted by the producer.

All collective bargaining agreements with the above organizations are negotiated between them and the League of American Theatres and Producers every two or three years on average. Even so, producers and landlords can and often do negotiate independently for special concessions or modifications in regard to a particular employee or production. Rarely, however, do such concessions reduce the minimum terms as spelled out in the standing collective bargaining agreement. Each of the unions now have their collective bargaining agreements available online. (See Appendix H for their web addresses.)

Authors and composers receive royalties from the income generated by their work on Broadway, as well as all subsequent uses of that work, such as on road tours or television adaptations. Other leading artists—directors, choreographers, designers, and star performers—may also negotiate a contract in which they earn a percentage of a show's Broadway box office income in addition to their fee or salary. While actors must negotiate any such percentage from scratch, SSDC and designers' contracts stipulate minimum royalty payments for its members. Some leading artists also negotiate terms whereby they share in subsidiary income that the show may generate beyond its Broadway run.

Royalty Pools

For many years the creative artists connected with a Broadway production negotiated contracts with the producer that stipulated they would receive a percentage of gross box office income from the very first performance week, or at least from the first week after opening night. This meant that these people earned royalties before the show reached its break-even point and, therefore, before the investors earned back any of their investments. As the cost of Broadway production skyrocketed, it became increasingly important to devise ways for shows to break even faster so that investors would not desert the industry. This was when the royalty pool was introduced into the commercial theatre.

To expedite the return of capitalizations to investors, royalty pools typically replace all negotiated percentage royalties. A royalty pool is a negotiated agreement between the producer and each and every person entitled to a percentage of net box office receipts. For example a director entitled to two percent of the gross might also negotiate two-and-a-half points in the royalty pool. If each point is valued at a minimun weekly guarantee of $500, the director will earn at least $1,250 per week until the show pays back its capitalization.

It is common that once 110 percent of the production's capitalization is reached, the pool might either dissolve with the pool-participants receiving the percentages of net box office income originally agreed—two percent, in the case of the director, above—or the pool might continue to operate, but with an increased amount of allocated profit, which would depend on how the production is organized. In the latter scenario, because the amount of money going into the pool has increased, each pool-participant will receive more money each week. If business later declines it is possible that the royalty pool might be reactivated.

Understanding the Actors' Union

Actors' Equity Association Jurisdiction and Membership

Equity is an open union in the sense that no one can be denied membership if offered a job under a standard Equity contract. Nonetheless, it is difficult for nonmember actors to

TABLE OF ORGANIZATION
FOR A TYPICAL BROADWAY MUSICAL

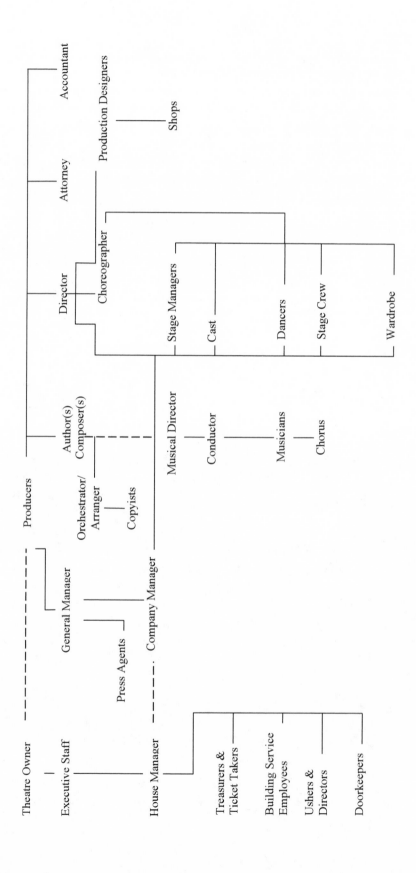

gain access to directors, agents, and casting directors even though Equity auditions are now more open to nonmembers. In 1988, the union was called before the National Labor Relations Board and told that its audition system discriminated against nonunion members and was therefore illegal. An agreement was finally reached that admits non-Equity members to Equity auditions, providing they can prove minimum professional employment as actors during any one year. This minimum is defined as two weeks of salary and benefits at the Theatre for Young Audiences contract minimum—the lowest among standard AEA contracts—as a performer in theatre, radio, television, or film. Aside from gaining employment through the audition process, one may join Equity by being hired as a stage manager or assistant stage manager for an AEA production, or through the Equity membership candidate program in which one becomes a full member after fifty weeks of work. Finally, there is a "side-door" membership by which members of other performers' unions—AGVA, SAG, etc.—who have belonged to that union for at least one year and can document at least three days work under contract, may then gain Equity membership. Once a member, a person may work either as an actor or stage manager regardless of how membership was gained.

From its beginning in 1919 until 1956, the Chorus Equity Association—generally independent from AEA—represented chorus performers. The two organizations merged in 1956 under the single banner of Equity, which now represents both principal and chorus performers. Both enjoy the same basic employment protection and benefits, although there remain a few minor differences between a "white contract"—used for principals—and a "pink contract"—used for chorus. One area of jurisdiction that is sometimes challenged concerns vaudeville-like performers in burlesque shows or revues where both Equity and the American Guild of Variety Artists (AGVA) might claim authority. Equity is only vested with jurisdiction over live and so-called legitimate stage productions, even though it shares the 1919 AFL charter—granted to the Associated Actors and Artists of America, or the 4 A's—with the following unions:

1.) AGVA, the American Guild of Variety Artists, covers performers in nightclubs, vaudeville, special acts, burlesque, etc.;

2.) SAG, the Screen Actors' Guild, covers cinema and certain television productions;

3.) SEG, the Screen Extras' Guild, covers cinema performers who do not have speaking roles—jurisdiction is only on the West Coast;

4.) AFTRA, the American Federation of Television and Radio Artists, covers most performers, newscasters, and participants on the television screen or in front of a television or radio microphone;

5.) AGMA, the American Guild of Musical Artists, covers performers in dance, opera, concert, and the serious music field;

6.)   IAU, the Italian Actors' Union, is for actors who perform in Italian;

7.)   HAU, the Hebrew Actors' Union, is for actors who perform in Yiddish;

Geographically, Equity's jurisdiction extends throughout the United States. Until 1976 it also extended throughout Canada, but as of that date an independent Canadian Actors' Equity Association was created to represent English-speaking actors and the Union des Artistes was formed in Montreal to represent French-speaking actors, although special reciprocal membership privileges continue between these unions. However, there is no reciprocal agreement with British Equity or actors' associations in other foreign countries, so American Equity cannot guarantee or assist its members in gaining employment abroad. Indeed, labor unions both here and abroad always favor contracts for their own citizens. If a Broadway producer wishes to employ a performer who is not a U.S. citizen, Equity usually requires proof that the role in question cannot be played by an American. The same would be true, in reverse, in England. When certain star performers bring unique talents and personalities to a role, then the union is likely to permit their employment despite their alien status, but usually with the stipulation that they must be replaced by a native performer within a few months' time. Nonresident aliens are never permitted to replace American actors. In other cases, when a British actor is allowed to work in the United States, for example, either the producer or British Equity is made to promise equal employment of an American actor in England. In the best of all possible worlds, artists should be able to work wherever they wish, and international cross-fertilization in the arts should be common, but that won't happen soon. Meanwhile, unions do at least permit whole ensembles, or "unit companies" from foreign lands to perform wherever they earn bookings, as artistic ensembles that cannot be separated without destroying their character. So the union does not attempt to force American performers into a visiting Kabuki, Teatro Picolo, or Royal Shakespeare production.

Types of AEA Contracts and Agreements for Commercial Theatre

A visit to the Equity website, www.actorsequity.org, provides a complete overview of and access to all of its thirty-plus contracts. All Equity contracts are subject to the constitution and by-laws of the union. Most of the rules and regulations are essentially the same for all segments of the industry; the items that vary most, not surprisingly, are those related to salaries, benefits, and the use of nonprofessionals. Each collective bargaining agreement clearly spells out the definitions, jurisdiction, and length of that particular contract, and, as these can vary widely, it is important to read the entire agreement carefully if one plans to produce or manage an Equity production.

The Production Contract

The AEA Production Contract is normally negotiated every three years by the League of American Theatres and Producers. It reflects the terms of the Standard Production

Contract and the Run of the Play Contract to which all principal and chorus actors and all stage managers are signed on Broadway. It also governs AEA employment for first class and bus and truck tours and sit-down—open-ended—runs in any of the Equity-office cities. The Production Contract is the basic agreement from which all other Equity contracts and agreements are derived. Familiarity with the Production Contract, its terminology, and types of regulation, greatly assists in understanding any type of Equity contract. The producer members of the league, incidentally, negotiate the Equity contracts, while the landlord members negotiate with those unions that represent treasurers, building service employees, and others.

The Off-Broadway Contract

The contract between Equity and the League of Off-Broadway Theatres and Producers provides minimum salaries based on five different sets of potential box office grosses as well as five different seating capacities. The Off-Broadway contract applies to theatres in Manhattan with fewer than 500 seats. For categories A and B, 100–199 seats and 200–250 seats respectively, the more money a production earns at the box office, the more the actors must be paid until a certain maximum gross is reached. For capacity categories C (215–299 seats), D (300–350 seats), and E (351–499 seats) the salary is the same regardless of the box office gross. Minimum salaries for Equity members are, of course, lower Off-Broadway than on Broadway. Nonprofessionals may not be used under either contract.

The Theatre for Young Audiences Contract

During the 1975 negotiations for the AEA contract governing children's theatre, the official name of the agreement was changed to the Theatre for Young Audiences, and the name of the management association representing producers in this field became the Producers' League of Theatre for Young Audiences (PLOTYA). Equity defines young audience productions as those presenting material expressly prepared or adapted for children up to and including the twelfth grade with performance time not exceeding an hour and a half, including intermissions. Actors may work by the week or by the performance, but in both cases minimum salaries are comparatively low, although additional compensation is required when the actor:

1.) Performs in a theatre seating more than 300;

2.) Is required to travel beyond points that can be reached by one fare via local public transportation;

3.) Is required to travel to more than one theatre during the same day;

4.) Is required to sleep away from home;

5.) Is required to work overtime;

6.) Is required to perform more than nine performances a week on the weekly contract.

Except when agreed to in writing with AEA, nonprofessionals are no longer permitted in Theatre for Young Audiences productions. Because of the special nature of children's theatre, this is one of the most flexible AEA contracts, and modifications are often granted to producers by the union.

Before the first agreement was negotiated in 1953, Equity had more or less stayed out of children's theatre because so few were profitable. But when permanent children's theatre companies comprised of adult actors were formed and their organizers began to realize sizable profits, Equity began making an effort to guarantee basic rights and wages that most actors in this branch of the business were denied. Of course, there remain a great number of nonprofessional children's theatre companies and productions that continue to work outside union jurisdiction.

The Showcase Code

In order to deal with Equity members who choose to work without salary in Off-Off-Broadway theatres in New York or similar theatres in other cities, the union developed the Showcase Code. This permits producers to collect contributions from the audience or charge a limited ticket price, but restricts the budget, the number of performances to sixteen, and the size of the theatre to fewer than one hundred seats. Even though they are unsalaried, Equity members must be reimbursed for basic expenses during the rehearsal and performance periods. There are no restrictions on the number of nonprofessionals who may be used in a Showcase production.

While there is no Off-Off-Broadway producers' association as such, there is a service organization called the Alliance of Resident Theatres/New York (ART/NY), which was formerly the Off-Off-Broadway Alliance or OOBA, in which many such producers are members. The vast majority of Off-Off-Broadway companies are nonprofit, yet works that are showcased may end up in the commercial sector. For this reason, Equity stipulates that if a Showcase—or other Equity Code or other-than-standard contract—production is produced under a standard contract within a certain period of time, which depends on the contract to which the production is converting, all Equity actors in that showcase must be offered the same roles or paid a number of weeks salary at the minimum rate of the contract under which the new production is playing.

Workshop Productions

Usually organized as a method of trying out and developing a property for eventual commercial production, the AEA-approved workshops stipulate that only union actors may be used, that they may receive a smaller than standard production salary, that the workshop consist of six to twelve weeks of rehearsal, during which twelve rehearsals may be played before an invited audience, and that rehearsals may be interrupted for as much as two weeks to permit rewriting time. Then there may be three weeks of limited performances, again without admission charge. The hitch is that actors will receive a percentage of any income the property may generate for the next eighteen years.

Needless to say, both the Showcase Code and the Workshop provisions have stirred up a terrific amount of controversy. A number of prominent playwrights refuse to allow their work to be produced under either arrangement because the cost, which is paid from their royalties, could become too great. And factions of Equity's own membership have loudly protested the union's growing jurisdiction over developmental production projects: actors want opportunities to perform and be seen; playwrights want opportunities to get produced and develop their work based on actors' input and audience reaction. The union, on the other hand, is trying to protect its members from being exploited. The controversy is not likely to go away soon.

Special Situations

There is most likely an agreement for practically any and every theatrical situation. In the event that there is not, the leadership at Equity will happily sit down to arrange such an agreement.

General Aspects of Employment Regulated by AEA

Auditioning and casting for a production are the director's responsibilities. Although producers and playwrights often have veto power over casting decisions, and professional casting directors have recently diminished directors' involvement in this process, it is still the director's most important responsibility. The union mandates that interviews/auditions be held for all Equity productions and that these be open to all AEA members as well as nonmembers who can prove professional credentials. However, as with the other labor organizations in theatre, Equity is opposed to its members doing any extensive work until a contract is signed. There are separate interviews/auditions for principals and chorus; no stars or other actors may be summoned or sent by agents until the open auditions have been completed. Auditioning cannot be delegated to a stage manager or minor functionary; at least one person with casting authority—producer, director, choreographer, casting director, etc.—must be present as well as an AEA representative. Auditions for AEA productions are held in the Equity office city that the producer indicates as the "point of origin"—New York, Los Angeles, San Francisco, or Chicago.

Equity maintains a list of actor agents and personal representatives in good standing that it has franchised to seek and oversee employment for its members. Actors are not required to pay an agency commission if they settle their terms of employment directly with the producer; and agents traditionally don't accept commissions from performers holding chorus contracts.

If signed to a Standard Minimum Contract, performers may find that the rehearsal period serves as a probationary trial period during which they may be replaced, if they receive the proper notice and severance pay. Or actors may receive a Run of the Play Contract, which carries a higher minimum salary but perhaps one not so high as actors can demand if the play proves to be a big hit after it has opened. Stars are usually signed to long-term contracts from the outset, making it more expensive to replace them before the termination date.

Provisions in AEA contracts stipulate that actors and stage managers must receive extra compensation or insurance coverage for the performance of special tasks or feats, such as being responsible for the transportation of costumes, performing a risky feat on stage, or playing a second role.

Supervising the Production

Tryouts and Previews

During the nineteenth century nearly all shows opened first in New York, if only for one or two performances, and were then sent on the road so they could use the magical phrase "direct from New York!" in their advertisements. Later the situation was reversed and nearly every commercial show began outside New York. It now seems safe to say that neither "prior to Broadway" nor "direct from New York" attracts many ticket buyers. For this reason, and even more because of the high cost of touring, a less frenzied method of trying out a show became popular during the 1960s: the New York "preview." Of course, eliminating the pre-Broadway, out-of-town engagement meant that many shows would never be seen outside New York. But lower operating costs and the belief that preview audiences in New York are more representative of Broadway audiences made the preview system the choice of many producers. Of course, this method tends to exclude theatrical properties developed over a fairly long period of time, usually by a nonprofit theatre company. Out-of-town tryouts seldom earn enough revenue at the box office to pay the expenses of the tour. Nonetheless, they do permit the production company to work away from the glare of Broadway publicity and potentially damaging word of mouth. The most recent practice to develop a new property is the "enhancement deal," in which a commercial producer licenses the rights to a property to a nonprofit company, where it is developed and presented, in exchange for a donation that subsidizes the production. (See Chapter 5.) This allows for a more intense period of development without the exorbitant cost of an out-of-town tryout.

The purpose of tryout or preview performances is to examine a production as it plays to an audience and to make whatever adjustments are deemed necessary and possible. Like casting, this kind of artistic analysis and decision-making is difficult—producers and directors who have mastered it are at the top of their professions. When a show is "in trouble," it is rarely a simple matter to figure out exactly what the problem is—the writing, directing, designing, performing, or perhaps even the marketing. In some cases a "play doctor" or consultant will be brought in to make changes. In other cases, the producer may have to "buy out" the contract of one or more of the leading artists. This may be very costly since the producer might have to pay both a weekly salary and a percentage of the gross throughout the New York run, as in the case of dismissing a star who signed a Run of the Play Contract. A dismissed director would be entitled to the full contractual fee plus a percentage of the show and subsidiary rights, as specified. Or it may be deemed necessary to scrap the scenery or costumes and build anew.

The Opening Night

On Broadway, as in any community theatre in any American city, opening night of a production is likely to be the least typical night of the show. The house is usually packed with well-wishers, relatives, critics, and, perhaps, backers and celebrity hounds. Little wonder that opening-night jitters have become part of the tradition. Performances can easily suffer and the perception of audience members may be equally off balance. From the first preview performance to opening night and beyond, it is the role of management to do whatever is reasonable to create a stable and secure workplace for the company, while also helping the audience and the press to feel that they're having the time of their lives. But there are no union rules that stipulate how this can be accomplished.

Maintaining a Production

Because so much energy and anxiety go into opening night, the second night's performance may well be the most difficult. Seasoned professionals understand that they must go on night after night and maintain a uniformly high level of performance. Nonprofessionals tend to relax their efforts and lose their concentration as time goes on—this is true on both sides of the footlights. Keeping a production alive and fresh for an extended number of performances is an obligation shared by both the artists and the management. If the price of admission remains the same, so should the quality of the production.

On Broadway, SSDC requires that directors and choreographers attend performances of their productions approximately every eight weeks and redirect or re-rehearse them without additional compensation if necessary. They may even forfeit half of their royalties if they fail in this responsibility. It is difficult to win judgments against performers on artistic grounds, but not impossible. Most serious complaints leveled against actors by producers are likely to be leveled against stars, whom the union is not so disposed to protect as vigorously as supporting players. Stars, after all, earn a great deal of money and don't require minimum levels of salary, housing, transport, and other compensations. More likely, they require protection against exploitation, harassment, anxiety, self-aggrandizement, boredom, alcohol, hangers-on, or drugs, and that is a management function.

Fortunately, most professional actors work hard at keeping their performances fresh. Many continue taking lessons, develop daily memory or sensory exercises, and spend considerable time "getting into character" before each performance. Others just seem blessed and, as was once said about pianist Artur Rubinstein, never need to practice. Whatever the case may be, the integrity of the theatre profession hangs on the profession's being able to engage the full attention and admiration of an audience. So everyone seriously involved in theatre has to be committed to maintaining this integrity.

Dissolving a Production Company

Once the media critics' views are known, the New York commercial producer must almost immediately decide whether or not to continue the production. If the reaction is unfavorable, a closing notice might be posted after opening night—or even before—in order to terminate all contracts and other financial obligations as quickly and inexpensively as possible. But when the critical reaction is mixed, when there is a large advance sale or when audience reaction appears to indicate the possibility of extending the run, then the producer may decide to absorb a degree of loss in order to "turn business around." In the event of rave reviews, of course, the producer's decision is both obvious and easy.

When closing a commercial production in New York and dissolving a joint venture or Limited Partnership Agreement, the producer must dispatch all obligations as quickly as possible and render a final accounting of the enterprise to all partners.

Putting the Show on the Road

(See also Chapter 9: Presenting Organizations.)

National touring companies, also called first-class touring companies, are generally organized and controlled by the original producer. This may be a commercial Broadway producer, such as Cameron Mackintosh, or a nonprofit institution, such as the New York Shakespeare Festival or Lincoln Center Theater. When ticket demand is high, two or three national companies of the same show may be sent on the road simultaneously while the original production is still playing in New York. In such cases, each company will perform in a major city—Boston, Los Angeles, or Chicago—for many months. National companies are signed to the AEA Production Contract, which spells out all the rules and regulations regarding actors away from home.

Unlike national companies, bus and truck companies may give only a few performances at each theatre they visit. National companies are usually under the supervision of the original producer, director, and creative team whose aim is to stage carbon copies of the New York hit, but bus and truck tours tend to be more modest, though not necessarily less effective.

Summary

The commercial theatre in America has always been a speculative business. During some periods it has just managed to provide livings for the people who work in it. During other times it has made large profits and provided more than subsistance livings. Ostensibly, commercial theatre has continued to exist without the benefit of subsidies, but a closer look reveals that it is ever dependent upon the noncompensatory time and energy invested by nearly everyone who has worked to be a part of it, and by many fortunes in private capital that have been invested and lost. Nevertheless, the commercial theatre continues to maintain its position of influence because of its product and talent and its importance to theatres outside of New York City.

CHAPTER 5

Not-For-Profit
Professional Threatre

T HE GROWTH OF THE NOT-FOR-PROFIT, nonprofit, professional theatre
sector over the past few decades has been astounding, not only in its number but
also in its impact on where and how theatre is produced. The Theatre Communications Group, an arts service organization serving American not-for-profit theatres,
estimates that there are between 1,300 and 1,500 nonprofit theatres in the United States.
While many of these theatres may resemble the resident stock companies of the 1800s,
they grew out of a completely different tradition; indeed, they have created their own
tradition in American theatre. The not-for-profit theatres are governed by boards of
trustees and artistic directors who, unlike the actor-managers of yesteryear, have their
sights fixed on artistic and organizational rather than commercial goals, although the lure
of a commercial transfer often looms large.

This chapter will consider governmental structures and special concerns of not-for-
profit theatres, and then will look at the different types of union contracts under which
they may operate.

Background

The Seeds are Planted: "47" to '47

The foundation upon which today's nonprofit professional theatre rests was laid between
1912, when George Pierce Baker first offered an influential playwriting course numbered
"47" in the Harvard catalog, and 1947, when Margo Jones's Theatre '47 in Dallas and
Nina Vance's Alley Theatre in Houston provided models for many of the artistically motivated theatre companies that were to follow.

The early drama courses and theatre programs that appeared on college campuses
grew simultaneously with what is called the Little Theatre Movement. Both were stim-
ulated by an interest in the drama of such playwrights as Ibsen, Strindberg, Chekhov, and
Shaw, and by the innovative productions their works were receiving in Europe under

the direction of such men as Antoine, Stanislavsky, and Meyerhold. The first important, nonprofessional theatre companies in America were the Washington Square Players (1914) and the Provincetown Players, which produced O'Neill's *Bound East for Cardiff* on Cape Cod in 1916, during the group's first season; subsequently they set up permanent headquarters in New York's Greenwich Village. On a professional level, the Theatre Guild (1919) was founded to produce serious plays for subscription audiences in a number of major cities. Americans such as Kenneth Macgowan, Robert Edmund Jones, Joshua Logan, and Elia Kazan traveled abroad to observe the work of Stanislavsky and others, while Europeans such as Lee Strasberg and Herbert Berghof, who had been exposed to the Free Theatre Movement abroad, immigrated to America and became its proponents here. In both playwriting and staging, two essentially new styles were developed—realism and expressionism—which by the 1940s gave the theatre an altogether new look, even transforming operetta into the distinctly American, musical theatre.

Eva Le Gallienne attempted to revive the repertory system* with her Civic Repertory Theatre, which she founded in 1926; and the Group Theatre was established in 1929 by several defectors from the Theatre Guild. Outside New York, the most ambitious, pioneering groups included the Cleveland PlayHouse (1917), Jasper Deeter's Hedgerow Theatre (1923), the Pittsburgh Playhouse (1933), and Robert Porterfield's Barter Theatre (1933).

Between 1935 and 1939 the administration of Franklin D. Roosevelt provided indirect subsidy for the arts through the Works Progress Administration (WPA), the main purpose of which was to create jobs for a nation in the throes of the Great Depression. Several million dollars were earmarked for four programs to benefit painters, writers, musicians, and theatre writers respectively. Theatre artists were organized under the Federal Theatre Project, headed by Hallie Flanagan. Aside from the well-documented productions and talents that the Federal Theatre project introduced, it also inspired the creation of the National Theatre Conference, a collection of theatre people—many inspired by George Pierce Baker—who sought to reduce the dominance of commercial Broadway theatre and encourage artistically challenging work, not tied to the profit motive. The conference also sought to create a network of community theatre centers across the country and lay the groundwork for a national federation of theatres. But the Federal Theatre Project became entangled in a web of political controversy, and federal support was abruptly withdrawn. While most of its ambitious plans were never realized, the project helped plant the seeds for the growth of serious professional theatre in America, as well as for more meaningful and direct government subsidy of the arts that would last for a number of decades.

Much of the hope and passion engendered by Federal Theatre Project activities seem to have taken root in the work of Margo Jones and her Theatre '47 in Texas, helping to inspire the subsequent proliferation of professional theatres outside of New York

---

* A repertory theatre produces a series of productions that are performed in "rep," or, utilizing the same space to house multiple productions performing at alternate times, and often employs a company of actors who perform in all of the productions. Some companies had either a repertory system or a repertory company; some had both.

City. Having worked for the Federal Theatre Project in Houston, taught at the university level, and directed on Broadway, Jones combined the attributes of intelligence, professionalism, and dedication to artistic integrity that remain the cornerstones of the majority of nonprofit theatres today. Aside from presenting the first productions of plays by such writers as William Inge and Tennessee Williams, her theatre was also a model for arena-style staging, which was adopted or adapted by many of the nonprofit theatres that followed.

The Birth of the Nonprofit Theatre Movement: 1950 to 1965

Arena Stage in Washington, D.C. was founded in 1950 by Zelda Fichandler, who was a disciple of Margo Jones, by Fichandler's husband Thomas, and by Edward Mangum. From its humble beginnings in a converted movie house, Arena Stage eventually moved into its own, multimillion-dollar facility, to become one of the most venerated of the nonprofit companies. Ms. Fichandler resigned from her position at Arena Stage in 1991 to assume the role of dean of the theatre school at NYU. Under the leadership of Molly Smith, Arena Stage has continued to be one of America's bellwether nonprofit theatres. Circle in the Square (1951) was the nonprofit model upon which many of the Off-Broadway companies was based; it eventually moved from Greenwich Village to Broadway and became one of the first nonprofit companies to invade the citadel of commercialism.

Rising production costs also prompted the growth of another alternative to the commercial theatre, Off-Off-Broadway, which was fueled by the experimental energies of such innovators as Judith Malina and Julian Beck and their Living Theatre, Ellen Stewart, Maria Irene Fornes, Al Carmines, and Joseph Chaikin, among others. But the catalyst that turned all this considerable activity into what soon became identified as a nonprofit theatre movement was the commitment of the Ford Foundation in 1957 to give almost sixty million dollars to the arts over a short period of years—the first such philanthropic undertaking in American history. As director and later vice-president of this program, W. McNeil Lowry can be said to have influenced twentieth century theatre in this country more than any other individual. Money was also given to opera and dance companies, symphony orchestras, and schools, but these had already been established both as "serious" endeavors and as nonprofit institutions. The theatre, however, was still regarded, for the most part, as a frivolous form of entertainment that could and should pay its own way—not an uncommon attitude even today. Nonetheless, the Ford Foundation arts program made one thing clear for the first time: if a theatre wished to receive a philanthropic gift, it had to operate as an ongoing, nonprofit organization. In other words, it had to be an institution, such as the Cleveland Symphony Orchestra, the Lyric Theatre of Chicago, or the Boston Museum of Fine Arts. Furthermore, it had to be professional, both in terms of its objectives and its employees. To this end, Ford also funded an arts management internship program, probably the first to provide professional training in this field.

As a result, theatre groups that had been loosely structured began incorporating and applying for nonprofit status, and newly formed groups used the nonprofit model from the outset. Then, in 1961, again at the instigation of Lowry, and with additional money from the Ford Foundation, Theatre Communications Group (TCG) was established in New York to provide networking and support for the increasing number of diverse nonprofits, which soon included the Guthrie Theatre in Minneapolis (1963), Trinity Square Repertory Company in Providence (1964) founded by another Margo Jones disciple, Adrian Hall, the Actors Theatre of Louisville (1964), The Eugene O'Neill Theatre Center in Connecticut (1964), and the American Conservatory Theatre (ACT) in San Francisco (1965). Individual donors and subscribers in addition to the grants supported these theatres; the Guthrie allied itself with a group of society women who sold hundreds of subscriptions on its behalf before the theatre had even opened.

Needless to say, all this new activity did not escape the attention of Actors' Equity, which felt that a new contract should be drawn up to accommodate this new category of theatre, not because these theatres were nonprofit, but because they made demands upon actors that were different from the demands made by Off-Broadway or stock theatres. To negotiate with the union, a group of managers from the larger and more established nonprofits formed the League of Resident Theatres (LORT), which is responsible for negotiating contracts with unions on behalf of its member theatres.

The year 1965 is a landmark for the arts in America because that was the year President Lyndon B. Johnson signed the legislation that created the National Endowment for the Arts (NEA). The establishment of the NEA had followed the publication of the Rockefeller Panel Report, *The Performing Arts: Problems and Prospects*, which had made a compelling case in favor of federal subsidy for the arts. Now subsidy had become a reality, with state and local arts support just around the corner. But, as with private and corporate contributions, only nonprofit organizations were eligible to receive government funding. This was how the nonprofit professional theatre movement in America was first nurtured, then formalized.

The Dominance of Nonprofit Theatre: 1966 to the Present

Beginning in 1966 with a meager congressional allocation of $2.5 million, the NEA began its grant-giving process. The first AEA/LORT contract went into effect. William J. Baumol and William G. Bowen published "Performing Arts: The Economic Dilemma," which documented the inherent inability of the arts to become cost efficient, and in that way reinforced the argument in favor of subsidy. From 1966 to 2004 the number of significant nonprofit, professional theatres in America increased from a handful to over 400.

Throughout the 1970s the movement continued to grow, and very soon the nonprofit professional theatre was the largest branch of the American theatre industry, offering more productions and providing more weeks of employment each year than any other. As time went on and government subsidy waned, nonprofit theatres began extensive fundraising campaigns to cultivate corporate and individual donors, as well as to work with foundations that, following the example of Ford and Rockefeller, were willing to give to the nonprofit theatres. Theatres gained status in their communities as respectable arts organizations, and across the country, boards of directors oversaw the construction of new venues, the implementation of new programs, and the support of innumerable artists and projects in their initial stages.

While it is outside the purview of this volume to document all the activities and accomplishments of the nonprofit theatre during recent years, they have been impressive. It has even been said that nonprofit professional theatres, collectively, form a national American theatre since they represent all the cultural, social, ethnic, political, aesthetic, and philosophical diversity that constitutes America in a way that no single national theatre company could. Each theatre has created a relationship with its community and is responsible for maintaining that relationship and the essential support of local subscribers, vendors, and donors. Theatres have also created relationships with playwrights and directors, offering them the opportunity to develop their work in an environment less volatile than that of the commercial theatre.

Most ongoing nonprofit companies have had the opportunity to synthesize their fundamental artistic goals and build local support systems before establishing themselves as fully professional, high-budget entities. A singular, dynamic artist who possessed both a vision and the ability to lead founded each of these theatres. However, as groups evolved into institutions, and as founding artists departed, the company's survival was often threatened when the leadership role was not properly filled.

The nonprofit theatre and the commercial theatre have become dependent on each other for growth. Nonprofit theatres depend on the revenues from transferring their productions to commercial venues, and Broadway producers depend on new and fully developed products to produce. Despite criticism from both industries suggesting that commercial and nonprofit theatre should function independently, the combination of business models is more economically realistic and viable for both parties.

Organizing a Not-For-Profit Company

There is no formula for producing successful theatre in the nonprofit sector any more than there is within the commercial sector. It would be lovely if the motivating idea for a theatre always led to a clearly articulated mission statement, which would then stimulate a terrific volunteer board of trustees working to attract top artists and managers to sign on to and produce brilliant works, which would then attract sell-out business and unlimited eternal contributions. But, not so; there is no foolproof way to organize a nonprofit theatre, but there are guidelines that can be followed and common mistakes that can be avoided.

Leadership

As discussed in Chapter 1, most theatre companies begin from the ideas of a single person, who is usually an actor or director motivated by a need to create theatre with a specific vision. A theatre company may also be formed to fill a vacant or planned facility, which is rather like the cart drawing the horse, but this can and does work. Additionally, some companies have been formed to celebrate a particular playwright, such as Shakespeare, Shaw, or O'Neill. Even more difficult than forming a new company may be the task of reorganizing and revitalizing a failed company or one that is in serious trouble. Each of these different scenarios requires a different type of leadership, of which there are four prototypes:

1.) An artist-driven company
2.) A board-driven company
3.) A management-driven company
4.) Shared leadership

When a company, or any organization for that matter, is firmly controlled by one dynamic and capable person—whether artist, board chairperson, or manager—the chain of authority is clear. Everyone knows who's in charge. But when authority is shared, lines of authority can become blurred, and the community, workers, or public may be unsure as to who's in charge. Uncertainty in management is dangerous. Nevertheless, there are three essential components in the structure of a nonprofit theatre company, and it is difficult not to think of them in a triangular relationship:

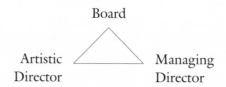

In some cases, the artistic director might also be the board president or chairperson, or the artistic and managerial leadership might be combined in one person, but usually a different person fills each of the three leadership roles. The managing director may report to the artistic director who, alone, reports to the board. In many cases, both report to the board and have equal status; this situation mandates a true partnership based on a mutual respect, easily said, but less easily achieved. Extreme examples of shared leadership are found in companies such as Mabou Mines, which is comprised of five individuals who not only share the roles of artistic and producing director, but also make up the majority of the board of directors, and Theatre de la Jeune Lune, which is also organized as a collective.

No matter how authority is assigned in a nonprofit theatre company, none of the three leadership components can be neglected. Law requires a board of trustees; theatre production requires artistic direction; and the process requires management. It may seem awkward to ask trustees to accept fiscal and legal responsibility for a company while requiring them to keep quiet about any artistic decisions; or to ask a managing director with twenty years' experience to report to a young, unproven genius who was just appointed artistic director; or to ask the proven genius to play second fiddle to a business manager. Yet, people in nonprofit theatre are frequently asked to accept such relationships. When that is the case, it would be wise for the board to monitor relationships closely and permit them to evolve in terms of position, salary, title, and authority based on what works best for the company and the people in it.

The Mission Statement

In Chapter 1 the importance and use of a mission statement, or statement of purpose, is discussed. But what characterizes a good mission statement? Ideally, it should:

1.) State the company's central philosophy, thrust, or goal in one concise sentence or brief paragraph;

2.) Be unique and recognizable, unsuitable for any other company;

3.) Be exciting and inspiring, especially to company participants and to the targeted audience;

4.) State the company's primary objectives so that they may be measured according to the company's terms.

Yet, one must bear in mind that the mission statement, or something closely resembling it, will appear in the company's papers of incorporation and its IRS tax determination, both of which are bothersome and expensive to change after they have been filed and accepted. If anything a company does is carved in stone, this is it. So particular care should be taken writing it. Based on this statement, the IRS will decide whether or not to grant nonprofit status and may also decide, at a later date, to remove that status if the company is not living up to the statement. For example, if the statement declares that the company is organized on a membership basis—as with a collective or a community theatre—and then company policy changes, there is a possibility that the 501(c)(3) status will be forfeited. An organization must be very certain of its basic goals before beginning the process of incorporation.

Here is a sample mission statement for a dance theatre company.

The Spanish Dance Theatre is committed to reviving Spanish dance as a theatre art and to bringing this art to all sectors of the American public. The goal is to create ballets, that is, theatre works with a story line, using the Spanish dance idiom. The Spanish Dance Theatre also seeks to establish itself as the "premiere" Spanish dance company of the City of Miami.

This sample would seem to meet the four characteristics of a good mission statement, but the company may decide to delete the last sentence because it might eventually decide to make its home in another city.

The next sample shows a rather general statement for use in corporate papers, followed by a few specific objectives to be promulgated in-house, on grant applications, and at fundraising events:

> The Black Caravan Theatre is dedicated to the support of a professional theatre company, the presentation of works that dramatize and enrich the Black experience, and the development of a broad-based audience. Objectives of the Black Caravan Theatre include:
>
> 1.) To establish and maintain at least ten artists/technicians/administrators on a full-time basis each season;
>
> 2.) To present at least four full-length productions each season;
>
> 3.) To perform for audiences in the City of Detroit at a permanent theatre space as well as through a touring program in parks, schools, churches, and social centers.

Notice that this statement does not restrict participation to Blacks or Black audiences or to a narrow repertoire of plays. And, of course, the specific objectives can be changed or adapted to suit the purposes at hand.

It is also common for nonprofit theatre companies—especially the larger ones—to operate under a very broad mission statement:

> To present classical and modern drama in a way that is relevant to contemporary audiences.

And, in fact, this is just what many of the best nonprofit companies do. So, general statements are appropriate for some institutions, but a highly defined statement can also serve a company well. For example, the Second Stage Company in New York City is dedicated to giving American plays that were not originally successful a second, professional production in addition to developing new work and expanding theatre audiences. Other companies are dedicated to developing playwrights, actors, or directors; and still others are dedicated to presenting only the plays of Shakespeare or some other dramatist.

The mission of a theatre company is important as it tells participants, audiences, grant-givers, and critics what to look for and how to judge the company's performance. (See examples of Mission Statements in Appendix I.)

Forming a Corporation and Gaining Nonprofit Status

To gain permission to operate under the 501(c)(3) provision of the Internal Revenue Code and qualify as a nonprofit organization, the group in question must state that its primary purpose is not pecuniary, although it may make money in order to further its non-pecuniary goals. Excluding salaries and other normal operating costs, no assets or income belonging to the organization may be used to benefit its participants.

To gain nonprofit corporate status, an attorney should be engaged to:

1.) Choose, clear, and reserve a corporate name;

2.) Prepare a Certificate of Incorporation, which must state the organization's goals, among other items;

3.) Secure approvals from the appropriate administrative and judicial state officials;

4.) File the completed Certificate of Incorporation and the necessary supporting documents with the Secretary of State.

Because law firms accept a limited number or *pro bono* clients, fledgling nonprofit theatre companies should always seek out such an arrangement with a law firm. Many non-profits that are just starting out find a lawyer to sit on their board of directors because corporate laws vary from state to state. But once corporate status for a group has been legally recognized in a particular state and the group's goals can be established as non-pecuniary, it should immediately proceed to apply for tax-exempt 501(c)(3) status. This process will again require an attorney to file applications with the appropriate finance and tax departments of the city and state in which the organization plans to make its head-quarters. Legal counsel should also be sought to assist with the preparation of an organization's constitution and by-laws and to provide advice regarding a variety of other legal obligations to which an organization must conform.

Volunteer Lawyers for the Arts (VLA), an organization in New York City, helps connect individual artists and small arts organizations with lawyers seeking *pro bono* arts work. Through several funded programs, they offer a walk-in clinic, where lawyers can consult on contracts; a law telephone hotline; a not-for-profit incorporation program; and case placement within large firms. The organization depends completely on volunteer attorneys and is a great resource for companies just starting out. Many cities in America have local versions of VLA.

Fiscal Sponsors

If a new company is uncertain about its future and does not wish to incorporate formally, a *fiscal sponsor* (or *fiscal agent*) can serve as the recipient of contributions on behalf of the group. The sponsor, a not-for-profit organization, will receive and administer funds on behalf of the group, usually for a small percentage charge to cover administrative expenses. Fiscal sponsorship also allows artists to apply for government and corporate grants limited to 501(c)(3) organizations. There is a good deal of information about fiscal sponsors available on the Internet.

Developing a Board of Trustees

The terms *board of trustees, board of directors*, and *board of managers* are frequently used interchangeably. Many feel that the title of *trustee* is the most appropriate because of the trust role that those individuals have.

The first question to be asked in forming a new board is how large should it be? Although the law may only require three or four members to fill the roles of president, vice-president, secretary, and treasurer, there are no limits on how large the board may be beyond those imposed by its own by-laws. For most organizations with an annual budget under $5 million, a board of fifteen to twenty-five members is common as well as sensible. However, many artist-led companies begin with a small board comprised of the artist's friends and relatives who are merely asked to lend their names to the papers of incorporation. These could be called "paper boards" or "dummy boards." If the company grows and requires more sophisticated leadership, especially in regard to fundraising, then such boards are usually replaced or increased in size.

A board member should offer one or more of the three "W's" to an organization: Work—*pro bono* legal counsel, accounting services, or press representation are some examples; Wisdom—experience above and beyond that of the staff of the organization and the sound advice that comes with it; and Wealth. Traditional wisdom dictates that board membership should reflect the organization's main areas of concern: artistic development, finance, marketing, fundraising, operations, planning, education, and so forth. At least one person who is an expert in each of these areas should be invited to join the board and head a committee that advises and supports the equivalent staff director. When the marketing director needs contacts in the media world, for example, the board's marketing committee should be able to provide them. While this method of board development provides a very clear structure, it may also encourage board interference in the day-to-day management of the company. Small companies with fairly small boards may dispense with the formality of the committee structure and allow its board to function as a committee of the whole.

While it is necessary to include successful and influential members of the community, a board should also reflect the character of the theatre company and the fact that it is an artistic endeavor. A few board members should either be artists or understand the arts well enough to interpret the special needs of arts organizations to other board members. Even the board presence of an unusual local personality is sometimes useful for representing viewpoints not ordinarily expressed at board meetings. Companies are regularly approached by enthusiastic supporters who want to do something to help, and candidates for the board may be found among these people. Frequently, professionals who have worked in theatre make great board members because they are thrilled to be back in the world of the arts and they bring with them contacts from their particular professional communities.

Another key question in board development is how long board members should serve. Most experts agree that membership should be limited to three to five years, even though many nonprofit organizations impose no time limitation. But having an open-ended length of term risks stagnation. Also, once trustees have tapped their best contacts, especially potential contributors, they are less likely to repeat their effort. Boards should have rotating terms so that no two members leave the board at the same time. A board's by-laws can also incorporate a board review policy whereby at a specified interval, normally one or two years, each board member is reviewed to determine if he or she is meeting the obligations of a board member.

The biggest fiscal responsibility of board members is the amount of money they are expected to raise or contribute each year; this is often called the minimum "give or get." Most small or developing arts organizations fail to clarify or even mention raising or contributing money when recruiting new board members; the organization fears that potential members will be turned off and decline. Yet, insuring the fiscal health of the organization is a primary responsibility of trusteeship, and a trustee who does not contribute to this health is usually dead weight. Trustees should be required to bring in a certain dollar amount each year, and this should be made a clear condition of their service.

In addition to this, typical board responsibilities include:

1.) Making and/or approving policy (executive committee and full board);

2.) Approving large capital expenditures and leases (executive committee and full board);

3.) Developing long-range plans (planning committee);

4.) Hiring artistic and managerial staff heads (executive committee and search committee);

5.) Approving and monitoring the budget (finance committee);

6.) Seeking and nominating new board members (nominating committee);

7.) Raising the needed unearned income (fundraising committee);

8.) Assisting with special events and benefit functions (special programs committee);

9.) Promoting ticket sales and other sources of earned income (marketing committee);

10.) Helping to keep the organization solvent and within the law according to prudent management strategies while helping to support the artistic goals of the company.

A trusteeship, then, is not an honor to be accepted lightly. It carries with it real obligations, including personal liability under certain circumstances. In fact, some board members take out insurance to protect themselves against possible damages. The law requires that trustees act with diligence, care, and prudence. If they are negligent and cause loss or damage to the institution, they may be held personally liable and may even be prosecuted if their dissent does not appear in the board minutes, or if the suspected illegality was reported to the state's attorney general.

While the first board of trustees for a new nonprofit corporation is handpicked by the organizers of the enterprise, future members are generally nominated and elected by the sitting board. Of course the artistic director, manager, or other company member may also suggest nominees. The original organizers also have the luxury of writing the by-laws—usually with an attorney's guidance—that will determine the structure and governance of the board and the organization. Future boards, of course, may amend these, but the basic character of an organization is very difficult to alter once its profile has been shown in public.

Artistic Boards

Many companies, especially experimental companies, have an "artistic board" as well. These boards are often comprised of established artists who wish to support a company but are unable to do so financially. Artistic boards, however, can provide introductions to other artists, connections in the theatre world, and advice about the planning of a season or the construction of an artistic team. This is an excellent way to utilize individuals who support a company's work but may not be able to work with the company directly or contribute financially.

Junior Boards and Advisory Groups

Considering the obligations and liabilities that most trustees must assume, it is hardly surprising that many are socially and/or professionally well established. Rather than weaken a board by excluding these established members of society for younger more hip members, it may be more effective to create a junior board or advisory group of some kind. Although such an advisory board has no legal decision-making power, the members will be committed to and involved with the company and will therefore attend performances on a regular basis and also involve their friends. Their involvement might take the form or post-performance social gatherings. Junior boards hold regular business meetings to plan such events and may also plan and help run telethons, benefit parties, and other special events and fund-raisers.

While the organization and supervision of junior boards is labor-intensive, the investment is worth the effort. As government and corporate support for the arts dwindles, along with that engendered by young and new audiences, any strategy that engages fresh converts is good. Professional opera companies and symphony orchestras have a long-established record with junior boards, and theatre companies are beginning to follow suit. Aside from providing a way to bring in new audiences, these groups are perhaps the best way to train and identify future leadership for the regular boards of trustees.

Organizational Structures

Large Theatre Company Organization

Large nonprofits with annual operating expenses of more than $10 million usually have a board comprised of several dozen people, who are divided into committees in order to capitalize on their expertise for the benefit of the institution. Likely committees are Executive, Development (sometimes includes Benefit Committee), Nominating or Board Governance (recruits new members), Audit, Finance, Education, Planning, Marketing, and Artistic. Here, as in smaller organizations, success depends upon the caliber of the people on the board and its committees and their working relationship with the artistic director and the general manager.

Medium-Size Theatre Company

Nonprofit theatre companies with annual operating budgets of more than $3 million but less than $10 million lack the resources for the large number of specialized personnel found in companies with higher budgets. There may also be a less formal board structure.

Small Theatre Company

The majority of nonprofit professional theatre companies have annual budgets under $3 million. As they grow from having no budget to $100,000 and more, such companies must frequently agonize over how to divide up their limited payroll resources. For instance, they have to decide whether to hire a technical director or a development director; whether to increase seating capacity and/or ticket prices and possibly graduate into the next higher category of Equity salaries (if applicable); whether to continue business as usual; whether the time has come for the artistic director to share, actually share, the power and the glory with a managing director.

Artistic Policy Choices for Nonprofit Theatres

The following policies are especially important to nonprofit professional theatres in terms of setting artistic character and direction. While policies should only be put in place after careful study and deliberation, policies should also be given sufficient time and support

SAMPLE TABLE OF ORGANIZATION
Large Nonprofit Theatre Company Budgeted Over $10 Million Annually

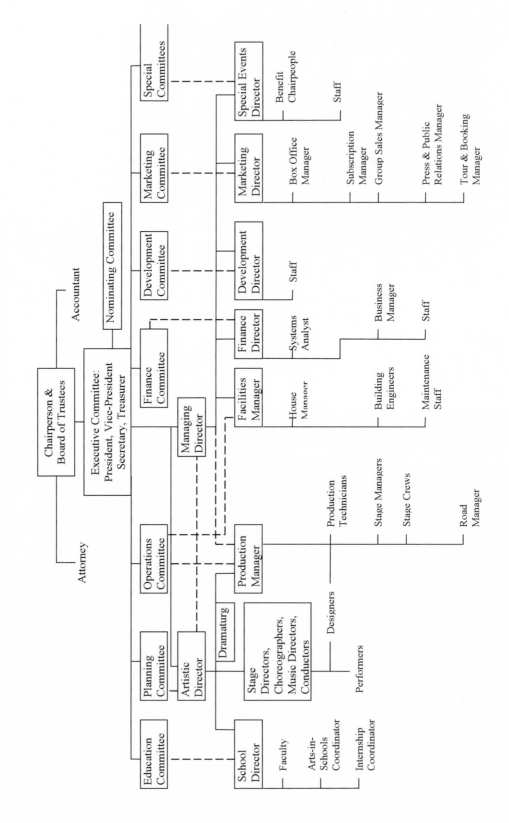

NONPROFIT PROFESSIONAL THEATRE
SAMPLE TABLE OF ORGANIZATION
Medium-Size Theatre Company Budgeted Between $3 Million and $10 Million

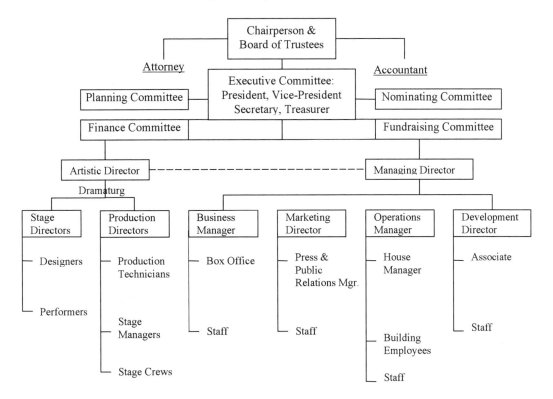

SAMPLE TABLE OF ORGANIZATION
Small Theatre Company Budgeted Under $3 Million Annually

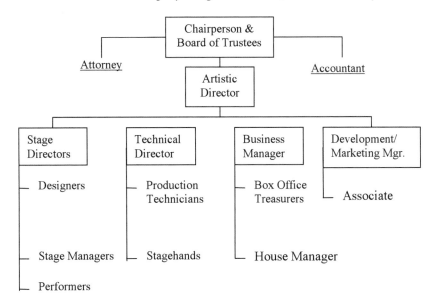

to prove themselves. If they do not prove successful, then they should be dropped or altered. And, of course, policies must be flexible enough to accommodate the abilities and desires of their leading exponents. For example, when a new artistic director is brought in, it is reasonable to assume that he or she will bring along a few policy changes, which should be made clear to the board in advance.

Production Policy

In the early years of the nonprofit professional theatre movement, many artistic directors believed that serious theatre should follow the model of ballet and opera companies and adopt the repertory rotation method of production. This means that after a production is mounted, all the costumes and other physical elements are kept in the theatre or in a convenient storage location, and the cast is kept under contract, at least for a season, so that the piece can be performed alternately with others. A resident company of actors performs in all productions, although guest performers may be jobbed in for some roles. Many American companies still contain the word repertory in their names, even though they no longer practice rotating repertory as few companies can afford to hire a company for an entire season, and the continuous changeover of productions in a theatre is very costly.

The opposite of repertory rotation, of course, is the single, open-ended run as practiced in the commercial theatre. Most medium- to large-size nonprofit companies produce a three- to eight-month season of five to twelve productions that are performed in sequence, a system aimed at attracting a large, permanent audience of subscribers. On rare occasions, if there is sufficient demand, an extra performance or two may be added each week—at extra cost. In some cases, it may be possible to revive the most successful production of the season for a nonsubscription audience and perform it at the end of the regular season. A season comprised of a set number of limited runs, as discussed here, may also allow for the creation of a resident company and provide the opportunity for ensemble development.

Some companies have two production facilities, usually a 500- to 1000-seat theatre and a smaller studio, or black box space. This permits productions to be tested in the smaller space and then, if successful, transferred to the larger space and given a full production. The largest nonprofit theatre companies in New York City, like The New York Shakespeare Festival, The Manhattan Theatre Club, and Lincoln Center Theatre have a number of performance spaces at different locations that operate under different ticket policies for different types of audiences: subscripion, membership, free theatre in the park, subsidized performances for public school students, and so forth.

Whatever the production policy, its goal should be to present the highest quality performances possible.

Play Selection Policy/Dramaturge

Dramaturges, or dramaturgs, have a long history in European theatre, but they earned particular distinction and publicity during the 1960s with Kenneth Tynan's work as literary manager of England's National Theatre. Because fundraising demands more of the artistic director's time, many nonprofit companies in this country now employ a full-time dramaturg(e), or literary manager, to assist the artistic director in searching for works to produce; to research all matters that pertain to selected works for the purpose of enhancing their interpretation; to assist the marketing department in the preparation of publicity material and program notes; and to assist the touring and schools programs in the preparation of special educational materials. But while a dramaturg's contributions to the work of a company can be varied, his or her primary value often lies in selecting plays. Larger nonprofits often employ a literary manager to select the plays, and a dramaturg to do the necessary literary work to bring the projects to fruition; this may include the identification of artists who are available and interested in certain projects.

Large institutions can afford to be more universal in their appeal than smaller ones-or this may be mandated by their need to attract a wide patronage. In the public mind, the largest theatre companies may represent nothing more specific than quality and diversity, which would certainly fulfill an important mission. But the smaller theatre companies often succeed best with an audience-specific mission that evolves around a particular genre, style, culture, philosophy, or movement. The artistic director usually has the final say on which plays to select, but rarely does the same person direct all of them. Suitable guest directors must then be found. If one is not available, the play selections should be changed or postponed. The availability or unavailibility of particular actors might also cause changes to be made.

Some theatre companies follow a play-scheduling tradition that dictates other scheduling; for example, each season might begin with a comparatively light piece and end with a musical. Or, just as many ballet companies present *The Nutcracker* during the winter holiday season, so some resident theatre companies have found that *A Christmas Carol* is a reliable moneymaker each year. Other productions must of course be scheduled around these.

The artistic goal of play selection is to choose works for which the best interpretive artists can be employed; the management goal is the efficient organization of the selections both in terms of production and marketing.

Casting Policy

Nonprofit theatres that employ Equity actors must first select one of the four cities with a union office in which to hold auditions. Actors may then be hired according to the rules of the contract under which the theatre is operating. LORT contracts allow the theatre to choose between signing actors to standard contracts for the length of a production's run or to seasonal contracts, which must offer between twenty-four and fifty-two consecutive weeks of employment. The audition process is described in Chapter 4.

These and other union regulations have a direct impact on casting policy and, of course, on payroll costs. If there is a resident Equity company, then seasonal contracts may be the most economical, providing that all actors on such contracts are utilized in all productions. When the proposed list of productions for a season is studied from the casting viewpoint, changes or substitutions may again be necessary. Casting questions such as, "What roles other than Hedda Gabler can be performed by the actress we have in mind?" may be asked. "Shouldn't we schedule the three-character play at the beginning or end of the season so that contracts for the other actors can be written for a shorter season?" "Should the guest directors sit in on the seasonal auditions?"

None of the nonprofit professional theatres in New York City sign actors to seasonal contracts because there is such a large pool of available talent. However, the artistic directors of these theatres and others elsewhere who do not maintain a true resident company often hire many of the same actors over and over and thereby create a sense of company, even without seasonal contracts.

Nonprofit theatres must also consider whether or not to engage "name" or star performers. It is assumed that name actors will sell more tickets, athough this is often not the case. Also, training audiences to attend the theatre because of stars rather than the overall quality of production can be counterproductive: what does one do when a production has no star?

The artistic goal of casting is to bring together a group of performers who will illuminate the playwright's script both through their individual work and as an ensemble; the management goal is to provide the resources and environment in which this will be possible.

Outreach Policy

Most activities that fall outside the business of producing and performing one or more productions yet involve the theatre company's personnel may be classified as "outreach" programs. These activities include sending artists into schools, sending the whole company on tour, running special workshops, or running a whole conservatory. Such activities are discussed elsewhere in this volume. But as a matter of policy they must be considered in terms of the amount of personal energy and other resources they will cost the organization. How will such activities affect the quality of the company's primary mission and production schedule? Do available personnel really have the expertise to perform these activities? For example, a person who is a good technical director is not necessarily good at teaching a course in stagecraft.

The temptation to sponsor outreach activities usually arises from the need for more income. But running a school and going on tour are demanding projects and if they are not done well could seriously tarnish the company's public image. Nonetheless, nonprofit professional theatres have a greater responsibility than commercial theatres to provide services to the community because most receive grants from public tax monies. Nonprofits are also set up to function for many years. To do this, they must think about educating future audiences, future employees, future trustees, and future donors, and this is best accomplished through outreach programs.

The artistic goal of an outreach policy is to elevate standards of theatre practice and audience appreciation in ways that are impossible through stage productions alone; the management goal is to cultivate future audiences for the institution.

Types of Actors' Equity Contracts Used by Nonprofit Theatres

LORT A+, A, B+, B, C, and D

The League of Resident Theatres negotiates an agreement with AEA every three years. Six categories of theatres are covered in the agreement: A+, A, B+, B, C, and D. The A+ category was added during the most recent negotiations with Equity in order to address the fact that nonprofits producing on Broadway were unable to pay their actors Production Contract salaries. This category is determined by the weekly gross of the theatre averaged over the previous three-year period, with A+ theatres having the highest gross and D the lowest. Salary scales covering actors, stage managers, assistant stage managers, and Equity professional interns are adjusted downward from the A+ to D categories. Actors may be signed to a standard or a seasonal contract. A limited number of nonprofessional actors may be used—except in A and A+ theatres in New York and Los Angeles—according to a formula based on the LORT category and the number of full Equity members under contract for the production in question. A similar formula exists for the employment of professional theatre interns. Interns are actors who can prove professional training and/or experience, but are signed to a standard Equity contract at seventy-five percent of the minimum salary in the appropriate theatre category.

Other Equity Contracts Used by Nonprofit Theatres

A theatre company may use any Equity contract it feels appropriate, provided it meets the requirements stated in the contract, regardless of whether or not the contract is intended for nonprofits exclusively. Contracts are renegotiated by various collective bargaining units and on their own schedules; the best way to get information on the contracts is to visit www.actorsequity.org, where all of the contracts can be downloaded and answers to frequently asked questions are available.

Special arrangements are frequently negotiated with AEA by individual theatres or producing companies. This may involve adapting one of the standard agreements to suit individual production or company needs, or it may involve writing a special letter of agreement. In any case, the possibility of special concessions should always be explored and discussed with AEA and any other involved union.

Actors rarely have claims to the income from subsequent productions of plays in which they performed under Production, Off-Broadway, LORT, or Stock contracts. However, under the contracts and agreements for which actors receive what the union considers substandard compensation, the actors, under complex provisions, have the right either to re-create their roles, if the production is subsequently produced under a standard contract, or to receive four to five weeks of minimum salary under the Production Contract. Regulations covering conversion and contingent rights are found in Showcase, Workshop, 99-Seat Theatre, SPT, LOA, and Funded Nonprofit Theatre agreements as well as in special agreements. Regulations may vary somewhat and are subject to change; details should be obtained directly from AEA.

Contracts:

1.) Off-Broadway (Chapter 4): The Off-Broadway contract is most frequently used for commercial productions, although some nonprofits have used it. It serves as the model upon which special agreements are designed to accommodate other nonprofit companies.

2.) Theatre for Young Audiences (Chapter 4).

3.) Stock Contracts (Chapter 8).

4.) The Showcase Code and the Seasonal Showcase Code (Chapter 4).

5.) Workshop Productions (Chapter 4).

6.) Cabaret Theatres (Chapter 4).

7.) Small Professional Theatre Contract (SPT): This contract was designed for nonprofit theatres that have a seating capacity of 349 or fewer seats and are not located in Chicago, New York, or Los Angeles. These theatres may not have operated under a standard Equity contract during the previous year. There are ten categories of SPT theatres based on box office income. Until recently, many theatres now operating under the SPT contract merely had a letter of agreement with Equity. It was the union's hope that such theatres would graduate in terms of size and income into LORT categories, but this happened so infrequently that SPT was conceived.

8.) 99-Seat Theatre Plan: During much of the 1970s and 1980s, Equity more or less ignored the sizable number of theatres in Los Angles that had less than one hundred seats. After a great deal of controversy, the local Equity membership voted to institute a 99-Seat Theatre Plan to replace what had previously been called the Equity Waiver Theatres. The plan is modeled after the Off-Broadway contract, although, like the SPT, it features ten salary categories based on box office income and may be applied to single-unit productions or full seasons.

9.) Chicago Area Plan (CAP): This is similar to the 99-Seat Theatre Plan that is in effect for the Los Angeles area. Equity had waived jurisdiction over theatres with fewer than one hundred seats, then beginning in 1988 CAP covered these theatres.

10.) Letter of Agreement (LOA): The LOA was designed for small, developing, limited income theatres in New York City that intend to convert within the next few seasons to a LORT contract. Start-up companies just about anywhere also use it.

Second Theatre

When a company has a second theatre facility in the same city as its first, the Equity contract category will be determined by the weekly box office gross of the second theatre. When productions from the second theatre go on tour, they are governed by the rules that apply to the main theatre. Actors on a seasonal contract are permitted to perform in both theatres, but the salary of an actor moving from a larger to a smaller theatre may not be reduced. The salary of an actor moving from a small theatre to a larger one must be increased to the minimum for the larger facility. Similar provisions apply when there are more than two performance spaces operated by the same theatre company.

Local Tours

Many companies sponsor outreach programs that send actors to schools or community centers. When on these tours actors are not required to spend the night away from home and are within a specified amount of travel time from their home theatre, they are said to be on local tours. In such cases actors are permitted to give ten performances per week, providing each performance does not exceed one-and-one-half hours in length. Local tour rules are similar to those found in the Theatre for Young Audiences Contract.

Other Unions

Nonprofit theatres may also have to negotiate with other unions, such as Local 802, the musician's union, The Association of Theatrical Press Agents and Managers (ATPAM), or any of the IATSE, stagehands, locals. If a nonprofit is producing on an A+ or A scale, it is likely that it will be negotiating with most if not all of the Broadway unions, especially if it is presenting in a Broadway theatre. When opening a new theatre, a nonprofit must consider whether the unions have jurisdiction and whether it wants to hire union employees; if a nonprofit is presenting in a theatre that is not its own, it will need to ask the theatre owner about any union obligations. Outside of New York City, this is not an issue.

Transferring a Production

One of the first productions transferred from a LORT theatre to Broadway was Howard Sackler's *The Great White Hope*, which opened in 1968 after a successful premiere at the Arena Stage in Washington, D.C. Unfortunately, there were no provisions made for the Arena Stage to share in the play's subsequent earnings—an oversight to be avoided by any nonprofit company. In recent years, the transfer of productions from nonprofit theatres to Broadway, Off-Broadway, and the road have been relatively common. Yet, there are many factors to consider before a popular production is moved.

The first factor to be studied is the possibility of extending the run where the production originated. This is by far the most economical solution to extending a run, and, in fact, may require no additional costs at all, outside of increased marketing expenses. The most common problem with this is that the company is locked into a production schedule that is already sold to a subscription audience. Or certain actors who are considered indispensable to the play's success aren't available for a longer run. If it is decided to move a production intact to another theatre, the faster this can be accomplished the cheaper it will be; and, perhaps, less artistic momentum and energy will be lost. Ideally, the curtain would fall on Sunday at one theatre and rise on Tuesday at the new one. This would avoid lay-off and rehearsal costs, as well as an interruption in publicity, audience interest, and ticket sales.

There are several methods by which a nonprofit professional theatre may transfer one of its productions:

1.) The nonprofit company may license the first-class production rights to a commercial producer, who then takes on all the responsibilities in exchange for a royalty payment, a cash advance and, perhaps, payment for any physical elements that will be carried over into the new production.

2.) The nonprofit company may act as producer of the production at the new venue but hire a professional general management firm to execute the details.

3.) The nonprofit company may go into partnership with an independent producer or theatre landlord and become a co-producer in exchange for certain services, financing, or concessions in the theatre license.

4.) The nonprofit company may serve as both its own producer and general manager at the new venue.

Enhancement

The most popular collaboration between commercial producers and nonprofit theatres in recent years has been the *enhancement* deal. Commercial producers sometimes "invest" in nonprofit companies by providing what is called *enhancement* money. This is in the form of a contribution to help develop a particular property that the producer hopes will transfer to Broadway; of course, he or she also hopes to share in any future revenues as a participating producer, co-producer, or investment partner. Frequently, the commercial producer will hold the rights to a property and will provide the nonprofit with the difference between the actual cost of the production and what the nonprofit would have spent on that slot in their season. An example is the puppet musical *Avenue Q*, which was developed as a collaboration between the relatively small New Group and The Vineyard Theatre, with the financial and artistic assistance of commercial producers Robyn Goodman, Kevin McCullum, and Jeffrey Seller. The show sold out during its Off-Broadway run, thanks in no small part to the Vineyard's subscribers, and generated word of mouth that led to a successful Broadway run. After it moved to Broadway it won the Best Musical Tony Award.

The enhancement process is a good way for a commercial producer to gauge audience interest in a production without having to pay the costs of an out-of-town tryout, while allowing the nonprofit access to Broadway-bound writers, directors, and designers. The object of transferring productions from nonprofit theatres to Off-Broadway or production contracts is twofold: to share the company's artistic achievement with the widest possible audience and to gain additional revenue for the institution. So long as such revenue is invested in the furtherance of the nonprofit company's stated goal, there is nothing illegal or unethical about making money in the commercial sector. Is there a not-for-profit that wouldn't want its own *A Chorus Line*?

Co-Productions, Shared Productions, and Commissions

It has become apparent to most nonprofit professional theatres that neither earned nor contributed income can keep pace with rising costs, at least not for long or not without certain fairly drastic changes in production policy. One possible solution to the never-ending economic squeeze is to transfer their "hit" productions to other venues, where they can enjoy open-ended profitable runs. Another is to permit the nonprofit to extend the run in its home theatre. Other companies may opt to cut back on their production schedules or cut back on their more daring work and increase the production of popular works; however, such policy changes seriously compromise artistic standards and risk allowing the nonprofit theatres to backslide into stock-company tactics. Hard times require creative economic solutions.

Another solution that has become increasingly common is for two or more nonprofit theatres to share the cost of a production that is presented on both of their stages. A production could originate at one theatre and then be transferred more or less intact to the other theatre. But a true co-production is one that is a cooperative endeavor between two or among several producing companies from the beginning. These theatres would share the artistic decisions as well as costs. Also a production could be co-produced by a nonprofit company and a commercial producer in an attempt to develop the property for a Broadway run.

In recent years, collaborations between nonprofit theatres here and abroad have allowed productions to originate in other countries and travel to the United States. The Donmar Warehouse in London and the Public Theatre have collaborated on projects such as Richard Greenberg's *Take Me Out*, which opened at the Donmar in London, moved to The Public for a successful run, and then transferred to Broadway, winning the Tony Award for Best Play. The Public Theatre has also collaborated with regional theatres, such as the Berkeley Repertory Theatre, co-producing plays that appear as part of the season at both not-for-profits. Collaborations are profitable for all the participants because:

1.) Sharing costs is cheaper than picking up the full tab;

2.) Sharing a production increases the number of performances it can be guaranteed and, therefore, the size of the audience;

3.) Increased performances bring increased work for the performers and production staff;

4.) By moving a production to several theatres, rehearsal time may be increased and the dark periods between engagements may provide the creative team with valuable time to fine-tune the project;

5.) Sharing production costs may permit larger, more ambitious works than would otherwise be possible.

The disadvantages of sharing productions include loss of autonomy in decision-making, conflicts in scheduling, and the dilution of profits. The conflicts that commonly plague shared productions are usually costly, both artistically and economically. For example, the stage director may have to move on to another project after opening night and not be available for needed rehearsals; major reconstruction may be required to move the production to another venue; the company may have to be paid while waiting for the next available performance date.

But co-producing can also make the commissioning of new works much more feasible. Of course the process involves considerable risk because it involves buying something that does not yet exist. Before a commission payment of any kind is extended, therefore, the producer or institution should draw up a contract with the artist that spells out what must be delivered or shown and when, and this contract should allow for payments to be stopped or a production denied at any point in the development of the material. The contract must also stipulate any future rights that may be enjoyed by the signatories.

Co-producing among different institutions and even between the commercial and the nonprofit sectors of the industry provides a viable economic alternative to suffering penury alone.

Summary

The nonprofit professional theatre today encompasses the largest and most dynamic activity in the profession. Its growth since the early 1950s has amazed even those who helped to pioneer the movement. Its accomplishments in terms of discovering, supporting, and developing theatrical talent in all areas have been outstanding. In fact, without nonprofit companies, it is doubtful that there would be a recent body of work worthy of being called "American drama" or a record of productions worthy of being called "American professional theatre."

The not-for-profit professional theatre movement was nurtured by contributions from government, corporate, and private sources, which created fairly reliable patterns of support during the 1960s and 1970s. But now the combined reduction of government support and tax incentives for private and corporate giving has created substantial funding concerns for not-for-profits. This in part accounts for nonprofits' interest in co-productions and commercial alliances and transfers. Over time, both foundation and corporate giving has been so drastically reduced that nonprofit companies have significantly increased their development and have also turned to special events and non-box-office earned income. Some companies have taken advantage of the national trend called "branding," which allows a product or company to place its name on a venue or series. A large corporation will donate a small percentage of its advertising budget to allow a theatre to build, expand, or keep its doors open in exchange for its name appearing on the venue or series. For example, in 2000 the Roundabout Theatre opened on Broadway in a house named The American Airlines Theatre.

Nonprofit theatres continually face the challenges of shrinking audiences, increased costs, and slowing donations but they are the lifeblood of the American theatre. The commercial theatre relies more and more on mission-driven organizations for satisfying product, and nonprofits are more regularly transferring their productions in order to take advantage of a successful Broadway run.

The relationships between commercial and nonprofit theatres in this country are constantly being reinvented; they must be if the theatre as an industry is to survive, both financially and artistically. The enhancement deal, while eschewed by some nonprofit purists, allows a theatre company with limited resources to produce the kind of work that interests it, as well as opening the possibility of wide exposure and future income if the production transfers. For commercial producers, enhancement is a way to place a show in an artistic community, knowing that it will be nurtured by a mission-driven organization. Any financial contribution made as part of an enhancement deal is significantly less than the cost of a try-out. Both sides win.

The 2006 Tony Awards revealed just how beneficial a collaboration between a non-profit theatre and Broadway can be: *Jersey Boys*, Best Musical, originated at La Jolla Playhouse; *The History Boys*, Best Play, came from the National Theatre of Great Britain; *The Pajama Game*, Best Musical Revival, originated by the Roundabout Theatre Company; *Awake and Sing*, Best Play Revival, produced by Lincoln Center Theater— nonprofits, all. Although smaller nonprofits continue to struggle, creative solutions such as co-productions and enhancement deals allow nonprofits to endure, and under the right circumstances, prosper.

CHAPTER 6

Community Theatre

ALL THEATRE, FROM ANCIENT TIMES TO THE PRESENT, has been rooted in amateur activity that reflects people's urges to imitate and their delight in watching others engage in this activity.

The theatre amateur is a person who does not receive financial remuneration, although amateurs may be highly knowledgeable about their theatre work and even gifted. They have simply chosen not to earn their livings in the theatre. Community theatres, or civic theatres, are either largely or exclusively comprised of nonsalaried amateurs who usually represent a cross section of residents in a given area and perform only in that area for its other residents. It is wise to remember that the word *amateur* comes from the Latin, *amare*, to love; and so an amateur is a lover.

Background

Amateur theatricals unrelated to a distinct theatre organization have long been common in America. Judge Samuel Sewall, the Pepys of New England Puritanism, wrote in his diary in 1687 that a maypole had been set up in Charlestown, Massachusetts, that public dancing was seen, and that a stage fight occurred in the streets. During the same year, Increase Mather noted "much discourse of beginning Stage-Plays in New England." By the early 1700s amateur theatricals were being offered in the southern colonies, and one Tony Ashton, the first professional actor to perform in the colonies, was paving the way for the arrival of Lewis Hallam's company in 1752. When public theatres were inactive during the Revolution, the spirit of theatre was kept alive by amateur theatricals performed in military camps and organized by such eminent "producers" as generals Howe, Burgoyne, and Clinton. So began the nation's tradition of amateur theatre, but community theatre as considered in this chapter did not really evolve until the last century.

Both community and educational theatre sprang from the same sources of inspiration. Both began at about the same time, in the years immediately before and after

World War I, and both had considerable influence upon the development of resident and Off-Broadway theatre, which in turn influenced the commercial theatre. The little theatre movement—also referred to as the "tributary theatre" or "nationwide theatre" or, simply, "community theatre"—was a reaction against the flagging commercial theatre, a vote in favor of the European Free Theatre movement, and, not insignificantly, an indication that, as average Americans gained leisure time, they lost certain puritanical standards.

Inspired by the genius of men such as Reinhardt, Stanislavsky, and Craig and by the example of the Abbey Theatre in Dublin and American tours by the Irish Players, countless little theatres began to organize in communities throughout the nation. Initially, their resources were slight, their leadership practically nonexistent, and their activities primarily aimed at pleasing their participants rather than their audiences. By the mid-1920s, however, many community groups could boast a salaried, year-round director and, perhaps, several other salaried workers. Many had acquired or constructed permanent homes for their productions and achieved sizable membership and audience support. Unfortunately, the growth of community theatre was curtailed by the Great Depression and, later, by World War II. But with the creation of the Federal Theatre Project in 1935, there was renewed theatre activity nationwide. Many audience members in the forty states where federally sponsored theatres were located were exposed to live performances for the first time. This helped establish the idea and the feasibility of local theatre.

As community theatre found its own voice through the meetings and publications of organizations such as the Drama League and the National Theatre Conference, its standards and goals became more ambitious and well defined. The American Association of Community Theatre is a membership organization with a great deal of helpful information available at its web site (www.aact.org).

Central Elements of a Community Theatre

Leadership

A successful community theatre depends no less on strong, imaginative leadership than does a commercial theatre, a resident theatre, or a college theatre. Theatrical productions don't spring fully formed out of the ground or from good intentions. They are the result of the hard work of many people under the guidance of a clear-minded leader. Because an energetic, knowledgeable theatre director is not always available, there may be frequent gaps in local leadership. This is especially true when the organization does not employ a salaried director. To avoid the problem, every attempt should be made to groom directors before a crisis necessitates a changeover. When events conspire to leave a group without effective leadership, the organization should consider a temporary suspension of major productions. This might dampen membership enthusiasm and weaken audience loyalties, but it is a more honest and ultimately more rewarding policy than that of presenting productions that are inferior to established standards. The membership, during such times, can remain active in other areas or can present less ambitious productions. And meanwhile, of course, it should search for a new artistic director who is able and willing to assume leadership.

Membership

When there is talk about forming a new community theatre or about reactivating one that has been dormant, the leading organizers should question their motives to be certain that they wish to establish a long-term venture. Perhaps they are merely enthusiastic about producing a particular script for a particular cause, in which case they should limit their sights accordingly. Or, they might produce a play as a trial venture preceding the formation of a community theatre group in order to test local support, attract potential leaders and participants, or serve as a rallying point. A trial production uncovers problems that, subsequently, can be dealt with intelligently when writing the constitution and by-laws for the new organization.

Most community theatres provide for several types of membership. Full members usually pay annual dues, serve on committees, work on the productions, and are eligible to serve as officers and directors. Associate members may be comprised of all those who buy a season ticket or a block of tickets but are not eligible to vote. Patrons or sponsors may be comprised of people or businesses that donate money or materials to the group or purchase program advertising.

The important thing is to maintain a large nucleus of enthusiastic and active members. To do this, the organization must offer a wide-enough range of activities to satisfy the diverse abilities and desires of its membership. Not everyone will want to perform on stage, and those who do should not be regarded as so "special" that other workers and activities are made to seem unimportant or unnecessary. It must become known throughout the community that the organization serves the interests of many individuals and that it welcomes the nonactor as readily as the actor.

Capital

Before writing by-laws or planning productions, the organizers of a community theatre should estimate how much their activities will cost. Where will the money come from? Ticket sales, patron donations, membership dues, advertising revenue? How much money can be reasonably expected from each source? Does the anticipated revenue indicate that the proposed activities of the group are too costly for it to support? Should ticket prices and dues be increased? How much money will be required before any ticket income is generated? What provisions can be made for a reserve fund? Whatever the answers to these questions, they will determine the early activities and plans of the organization. To realize the best legal and financial advantages, a community theatre should be formed as a nonprofit organization. (See Chapter 1.)

Theatre Facilities

Like the availability of capital, the availability of physical plant facilities will dictate a great deal about what a community theatre can produce, how frequently, and at what cost. Often, the organization may negotiate for free or low-cost usage of a school or civic auditorium. Or it may use a professional theatre's facilities during its off-season or nonperformance periods. The owners of such theatres may welcome off-season usage for several reasons: the rental income, the fact that it may introduce new audiences to the theatre building, the fact that it may reduce the landlord's maintenance and security problems. Some community theatres are sufficiently established and resourceful to own theatres.

Constitution and By-laws

After stating the goals and objectives of the organization, the constitution and by-laws of a community theatre should set out the basic operating rules and organizational structure while allowing sufficient flexibility to accommodate change and future developments. Legal counsel should be obtained before the document is finalized. While basic operating rules and organizational structure should be defined, enough flexibility should be provided to accommodate changes and future developments. The by-laws for a typical community theatre might include details related to the following:

1.) General
Name and location
Preamble
Legal counsel
Bookkeeping and audit procedures corporate status
Amendment and repeal procedures
Rules of procedure

2.) Officers and Board of Directors
Election procedures
Terms of office
Powers
Duties
Replacement during absences and vacancies
Indemnification

3.) Members
Definitions
Types of
Dues
Obligations
Powers
Privileges

4.) Meetings
   Annual
   Special
   Purposes of
   Quorum requirements
   Advance notice for
   Order of business
   Time and place requirements, if any

5.) Committees
   Standing
   Types and purposes of
   Membership
   Chairmanship
   Membership changes
   Appointment or election
   Powers
   Duties

6.) Amendments

An operating manual, referenced in the by-laws, can then address the details of the operation, such as membership, dues, meetings, committees, etc.

The revised edition of *Roberts' Rules of Order* is generally recognized as the authoritative guide for parliamentary procedure, a democratic and efficient system of regulating discussions especially for large meetings or those that are meant to result in formal, important actions and decisions.

Although it is possible to run an organization without an official constitution or organizational documents, it isn't advisable. Particular problems may arise when the group wishes to open a checking account or establish credit. Some groups have worked around this by becoming an arm of an existing organization, such as a city recreation department, church, arts council, or arts center.

Administrative Structure

The Board, The Officers, and The Committees

When a nonprofit corporation is established as the legal base of an organization, there must be a board of directors or trustees, and a set of officers to control it. If the board is a large one, it may appoint an executive committee comprised of a few of its members, together with the president of the group and its leading managers. An executive committee can help to facilitate the rapid transaction of routine business. The fundamental responsibilities of a board of directors in a civic or community theatre might include the following:

1.) To set long-range goals and objectives;
2.) To safeguard and improve physical and financial assets, including funding;
3.) To insure the legality of the organization's activities;
4.) To engage a managing director;
5.) To receive regular, timely reports from all leading officers and standing committees;
6.) To approve annual budgets;
7.) To manage community relations.

A board of directors should not officially concern itself with any of the routine, day-to-day business of the organization. If a salaried artistic director is employed, he or she should be given power and flexibility in all areas of artistic decision-making. If the board is unhappy with the results, it can decide not to renew the artistic director's contract.

While the following tables of organization show typical structures for community theatre groups, different structures are possible. The number of standing and special committees will be determined by the number of active members and, of course, by their interests. Large groups might operate a publications program that, among other projects, should write and distribute frequent newsletters to keep the membership informed about activities and, more importantly, maintain a high level of membership support and enthusiasm.

When a production is being prepared, the artistic director must organize workers under his or her immediate supervision, as shown in the second chart. If the group is sufficiently active, some of these workers may come from standing committees. For example, there might be a standing design committee that studies problems and techniques in scenic and costume design and then applies its knowledge to the organization's productions. The same could hold true in the areas of publicity, makeup, and house management. When there are groups of people permanently working in such areas, it is easier to organize a production staff and it guarantees more knowledgeable workers. Following each production, the appropriate committees and workers should analyze their results to learn as much as possible from their experiences. Suggestions and written reports should then be submitted for the benefit of future production workers. Too many community groups virtually disband between productions. Unless there is loyalty to and participation in the organization itself, little growth and development will be possible. Each production will have to be staffed anew, each will make the same mistakes as the last, and each will face the same ponderous difficulties.

TABLE OF EXECUTIVE ORGANIZATION
COMMUNITY THEATRE

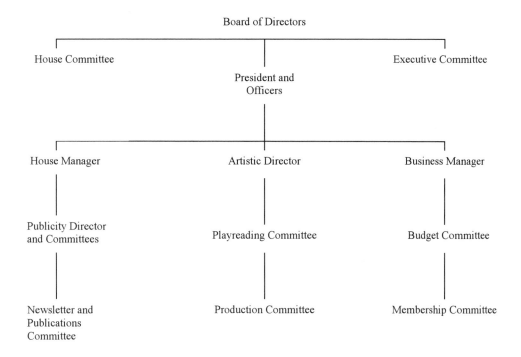

TABLE OF PRODUCTION ORGANIZATION

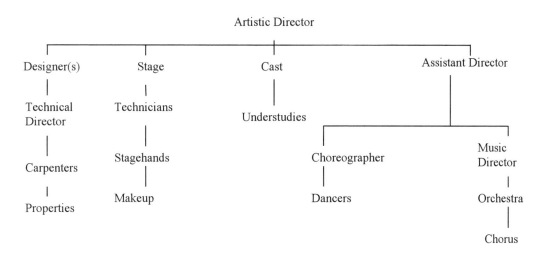

Affiliations with Other Organizations

To strengthen theatre activities and standards on the community theatre level, local organizations should devise both informal and official methods of working together. Sometimes a community arts council or some other umbrella group can serve to coordinate, sponsor, or fund broad-based community programs. However it is done, community theatre should benefit in terms of material and personnel resources when it works with local school, college, or civic groups.

Public Schools

Members of the high school theatre club and members of the community theatre probably face many of the same problems. This may be especially true in regard to such areas as scenic design and construction, makeup, and publicity. Some high schools give credit or out-of-school time to students who participate in community projects as this type of work deserves encouragement.

High school and community theatre groups may find it possible to coordinate their productions and thereby create a local "theatre season" and tickets could be sold as a series. Or the community theatre, assisted by a budget allocation or fee from the school, might present special performances for public school audiences. Whatever the affiliation, cooperative efforts between local arts organizations are important to strengthen the arts and to strengthen the community, itself.

Colleges

Formalized programs may be arranged between college and community theatres to share facilities, audiences, materials, personnel, and experiences. The community theatre may be pleased to accept student workers, who should receive credit for their fieldwork, and in some cases the theatres may be able to provide them with small fees or salaries. And, conversely, the college theatre may welcome and benefit from the involvement of community theatre members.

Civic Organizations

Many community theatres become affiliated with a civic agency or organization in order to secure theatre facilities. A town recreation center may include a theatre, auditorium, or space suitable for stage productions that the local theatre club can rent for a modest fee. By working under the umbrella of a city agency, the theatre may benefit from using the agency's personnel, fiscal resources, mailing lists, public information services, and space facilities. Conversely, such a marriage may detract from the desired independence of the theatre group, by forcing many compromises in regard to space usage and even in regard to play selection.

A community theatre may affiliate itself with a local service club, business, or charity that offers it sustaining support. Although security of this kind is tempting, it may be accompanied by compromise and outsiders' attempts to impose their vested interests upon the theatre organization.

Relationship of Community Theatre to Professional Theatre

The quality of work produced by community theatres reflects the quality of interest its members have toward professional quality theatre and, indeed, toward life itself. If the membership of a group is comprised largely of people who are merely seeking ego satisfaction, the productions are unlikely to satisfy audiences. Nor, in the long run, are they apt to provide much personal satisfaction for participants. It is not contradictory for nonprofessional groups to aim for professionalism. People who join ongoing community theatres should have an ongoing interest in the arts as well as a desire to develop as individuals. There is a big difference between the dedicated amateur and the dabbling dilettante. To keep the standards and goals of professionalism ever before it, a community theatre may establish relationships with professional artists and organizations.

A standing or special committee could be formed within the community theatre organization to assist and encourage its members to attend professional plays and events. This committee could negotiate with professional theatres for group rates, arrange for backstage tours and lectures, and invite professionals to speak at membership meetings. When the community theatre is located many miles from professional theatres, it should arrange annual trips to visit distinguished professional theatres. Most professional managements are extremely gracious about providing backstage tours, will frequently arrange for groups to be addressed by leading artists or craftspeople, and willingly make special arrangements when requested to do so. The same may be said of college theatres, which also stand ready to receive touring groups and provide special lectures.

When as a group, members of a community theatre attend outside productions and activities, they should follow up with discussions to analyze and evaluate their experiences. Also, thank-you letters should be sent to the host theatre, a courtesy that is often overlooked.

Sponsorship of Professional Events

There is no reason why a community theatre should not sponsor a professional series of public events with its productions. This may take the form of a lecture series featuring well-known speakers, a poetry- or play-reading series or a series of seminars. If there is strong membership and local support, events like these can be self-sustaining and, if they are tied in with the sale of tickets for the organization's regular productions, may increase general ticket sales. Guest speakers and individual guest performers may be engaged through direct negotiation or, more simply, through agencies such as the American Program Bureau (www.apbspeakers.com) or the Premiere Speakers Bureau (www.premierespeakers.com), which offer speakers for nationwide bookings.

An ambitious community theatre might also sponsor or co-sponsor professional touring companies. The only caveat being that a community theatre acting as a presenter must understand all the risks involved. It is quite possible to lose money presenting an attraction.

Employment of Professional Guest Artists

While a civic theatre organization may hire professional actors, stage directors, designers, conductors, choreographers, and others without negotiating an entire union contract, the professionals would be better served by some arrangement with their respective unions that would provide at least some level of health or pension benefit contribution.

A professional's association with an amateur group can afford considerable opportunity for its members to learn about professional attitudes and techniques. Not all actors, however, are anxious or suited to this type of engagement, and an effort should be made to avoid the employment of guests who are interested only in the salary they will receive. The community theatre group should know why it wants or needs the services and talents of a professional, and the professional should have good reason for working with a community organization. Perhaps it offers the artist a role that he or she might not play elsewhere, an opportunity to experiment in some way, or the gratification and satisfaction of teaching and assisting others.

Cooperation with Professional Competitors

As mentioned earlier, theatregoing is a habit and, generally speaking, the more that theatre is available the more theatregoing that will take place. A number of different theatres and performing organizations can live comfortably together in the same community and, furthermore, contribute substantially to each other's success if performance scheduling, play selection, and related matters are well thought out.

Obvious areas for cooperation between theatre groups include the sharing of mailing lists, fundraising campaigns, plant facilities, and material and personnel resources. Mutual endeavors can be organized without loss of image or independence to any of the participating groups. By keeping lines of communication open between various arts organizations in a community, opportunities for joint endeavors and benefits will be discovered. An energetic community arts council can be especially helpful in promoting such activities and increasing public support.

Summary

Community theatre is grassroots theatre that offers many of the nation's audience members and artists their first theatre experiences. The higher the quality of community theatre, the higher the demands will be on the professional theatre.

Community theatre in America has yet to reach full maturity. Because of the living and moving patterns of Americans and the resulting impermanence of American communities, civic theatre may never reach its full potential. Limited financial and personnel resources make many community theatres dependent on assistance and cooperation from educational and professional theatres and organizations. So a primary responsibility of community theatre leaders is to secure the best outside help available. There may be also local or community arts councils ready to give assistance and financial support to serious community theatre groups with good track records.

CHAPTER 7

College Theatre

POETS, PHILOSOPHERS, AND EDUCATORS since Plato and Aristotle have been concerned with the educational and moral values of theatre. Does the drama have an obligation to teach and enlighten its audiences? How deeply and in what ways can the living theatre influence its audiences? Questions such as these have pragmatic as well as academic relevance. Until the twentieth century, schools and colleges in the Western world were concerned with theatre almost exclusively as an instrument for teaching, especially in connection with classical subjects. In other words, educational theatre was for the participant and not for the audience. The first plays written and performed in English were the products of British schools such as Oxford and St. Paul's. In the eighteenth and nineteenth centuries, theatre was recognized only as an extracurricular school activity and as an appropriate addition to commencement and assembly programs. Not until the twentieth century were theatre courses included in British and American college curricula, and not until recently have American theatre programs begun to recognize an obligation to campus and community audiences as well as to student participants. The history of educational theatre, therefore, is largely modern history.

Background

Early Theatre Schools: 1871 to 1914

Nearly forty-five years elapsed between the establishment of the first schools to train professional actors in America and the introduction of the first four-year theatre program in an American college. Among those who had an early impact on the growth of professional schools was Steele MacKaye, one of the most inventive and innovative men the American theatre has ever known. Influenced by Francois Delsarte and the Paris Conservatoire, MacKaye established a school of acting at the St. James Theatre in New York in 1871. Although it failed after several months, he went on to found the School of Expression on Union Square in New York City in 1877, the declared purpose of which was "to instruct and elevate society beyond merely entertaining it." MacKaye was the school's only teacher and again the venture collapsed, but in 1884 he tried again as the major force behind the establishment of the Lyceum Theatre School, an institution that evolved into the present American Academy of Dramatic Arts. Early management of the Lyceum School was assumed by Franklin Sargent, with Charles Frohman as business manager and a faculty that included David Belasco.

During the 1870s classes in acting were offered by other schools, such as the New York Conservatory of Music and James E. Frobisher's College of Oratory and Acting. Subsequently, more acting schools opened, especially in the eastern part of the nation. Most were privately sponsored and a few, such as the Lyceum, the Empire, and the Madison Square schools, were affiliated with a producing theatre.

Early theatre schools were founded to provide students an alternative to the traditional method of learning theatre by joining a stock or repertory company. As stock companies disappeared in the early twentieth century formal school programs became increasingly accepted and influential. At first, curricula included courses such as body movement, mime, vocal expression, and, later, diction, stage effect, makeup, elementary dance, ballet, and fencing. Many schools adopted the Delsartian Life Study approach to acting, which advised the student to look to life and nature as a basis for dramatic characterization—a method well suited to the contemporaneous plays of Ibsen, Chekhov, and Shaw. Little if any attention was paid to technical aspects of the theatre, and schools of elocution that emphasized the verbal and oral elements of interpretation continued to be popular.

As the little theatre movement increased its activity, the new European drama became known to Americans and the nation's colleges slowly began to incorporate the dramatic arts. The Wisconsin Players was founded in 1911, though it was only unofficially identified with the university. George Pierce Baker began his '47 Workshop at Harvard University in 1912, and in 1914 the first four-year program in theatre leading to a baccalaureate degree was inaugurated at the Carnegie Institute of Technology in Pittsburgh.

The Growth of Theatre Programs on the Campus: 1914 to 1950

Theatre courses and performances on the campus increased tremendously after World War I and again after World War II. Part of these increases, like so many other changes in American life, can be attributed to the liberalizing effect that foreign postings had on young Americans. This is not to imply that college theatre programs in America are designed after European models. In European colleges and universities the performing arts are treated either as extracurriculars or highly academic subjects. Training performers abroad is done in a conservatory, a special school, or through apprenticeships with professional performance organizations. College degree programs in theatre are uniquely American.

At the outbreak of World War I and in the following two decades, American theatre schools could be divided into four categories: (1) professional training schools, (2) schools of expression, (3) community and art theatre-affiliated schools, and (4) college theatre programs. The first type, similar to the Lyceum School, was often affiliated with a professional theatre or designed to offer specialized training in some aspect or method of theatre. Examples include the National Dramatic Conservatory of New York, the American School of Playwriting, founded by William T. Price, and Richard Boleslavsky's Laboratory Theatre School, founded in 1924 and modeled after the Moscow Art Theatre School. Those affiliated with operating theatres included the Henry Jewett School of Acting in Boston and the Detroit Civic Theatre. Both the Washington Square Players and the Theatre Guild operated schools for a brief period of time.

Schools of expression, offering a slightly more refined and "respectable" approach to the drama, were concentrated in Boston. Inspired by Professor L. B. Monroe of the Boston University School of Oratory, Charles Wesley Emerson founded the Boston College of Oratory (later Emerson College) in 1880; Anna and Samuel Curry founded Curry College, and the Leland Powers School was founded in 1904. All were schools of expression that, nonetheless, reflected the influence of Delsarte and the Lyceum School.

Noncommercial community and art theatres that operated schools included the Pasadena Community Playhouse, founded by Gilmore Brown in 1917; the Cleveland Playhouse, organized in the late 1920s under the guidance of Frederic McConnell; the Goodman Theatre, affiliated with the Chicago Art Institute; and the Neighborhood Playhouse in New York. Following on the heels of the first college theatre department at the Carnegie Institute of Technology were those at New York University, University of Iowa, Northwestern, Cornell, and Yale. Often a department was inspired by the activities of a campus theatre club, such as the Carolina Playmakers, which had started in 1918 at the University of North Carolina.

From the beginning the trend was to offer college courses that emphasized theatre practice as well as history and theory. The study of dramatic literature and playwriting, rather illogically, generally continued to be taught in English departments. Practical training required the use of actual theatres and it took many years for plays to be presented before audiences. Brander Matthews at Columbia, Alexander Drummond at Cornell, Edward Mabie at the University of Iowa, and Frederick Koch at North Carolina were among the first notable professors to establish this practice.

The first large campus playhouse opened in 1926 at Yale, which enticed George Pierce Baker to join its faculty. Like European colleges, Harvard refused to create a separate theatre department and, after a fire destroyed Baker's laboratory theatre, it also refused to provide him with a new theatre for his '47 Workshop students. When Baker transferred his energies from Harvard to Yale, the headlines in the Harvard Crimson read "Yale 47, Harvard 0!"

During the 1930s, large and well-equipped theatres were constructed on one campus after another: Iowa, Stanford, Amherst, and Indiana. Also, during the decade, theatre began to emerge as a separate academic discipline. Organizations such as the National Theatre Conference, the American National Theatre and Academy, and the American Theatre Association (ATA) gave voice to the standards and goals of campus theatre and provided an important wedge that helped make theatre study distinct from other disciplines, such as English and speech. To this day, however, many theatre programs both in colleges and high schools remain tied to nontheatre departments, budgets, and regulations.

The Professionalization of College Theatre: 1950 to Present

Theatre came into higher education through the back door. A major justification for the study and practice of theatre was that it offered the best approach to the appreciation of drama and, under the guidance of college dons, a far more responsible approach than that of attending commercial theatre productions. Little wonder that the academic world long disassociated itself from the commercial and professional theatre. But as higher education in general came to recognize and use the knowledge of professionals, first in the sciences, then in all disciplines, its attitude toward professional theatre began to change. Practice was mixed with theory; the practitioner was heard beside the professor, and the laboratory was used as well as the library. More and more theatre programs became vocationally oriented. More and more they replaced instruction that had previously occurred in independent schools and institutes. The professional became a frequent lecturer on the campus. Visiting artists, entire theatre companies, and professionals-in-residence became almost commonplace.

In 1962 the Association of Producing Artists (APA), under the direction of Ellis Rabb, took up residence at the University of Michigan. New York University, with a large grant from the Rockefeller Foundation, established a professional theatre-training program, and Stanford University, with another Rockefeller grant, hired nine professional actors to form two resident companies to work with its students. The University of Minnesota offered credit-generating internships for its theatre students at the Tyrone Guthrie Theater; Indiana University operated a showboat on the Ohio River; the University of Kansas established an exchange program with acting students from Yugoslavia; the University of Missouri (Southwest Missouri State campus) operated an annual summer tent theatre; the University of Missouri at Kansas City inaugurated a summer repertory program, as did many other colleges.

Several campuses even established professional LORT theatres to produce plays on a regular basis and to supplement the instructional programs by providing work experiences of various kinds. As Dean of the Yale School of Drama, Robert Brustein founded Yale Repertory Theatre in 1966 but eventually left that institution and in 1979 founded the American Repertory Theatre at Harvard—providing a nice turnaround to the George Pierce Baker defection over fifty years earlier. Meanwhile, the new dean and artistic director at Yale Rep, Lloyd Richards, brought considerable distinction to the company with the transfer to New York of such productions as Athol Fugard's *The Road to Mecca* and August Wilson's *Fences*. La Jolla Playhouse, which is associated with the University of California, San Diego, has transferred *The Who's Tommy*, *How to Succeed In Business Without Really Trying*, *Dracula, the Musical*, and *Jersey Boys*.

Today's list of professionally oriented theatre programs offered by colleges is long. Most were inaugurated during the 1960s and 1970s and many were accompanied by ambitious plans for the construction of new campus theatre facilities, of which the Krannert Center for the Performing Arts at the University of Illinois is among the largest and most elaborate. Such facilities were often built as a result of the dreams and labor of senior faculty members, long frustrated by inadequate theatres and budgets, and by theatre programs still tied to other departments. Once a new campus theatre or performing arts center had become a reality, however, it often required professional management that faculty members were not prepared to provide. Not unlike the manner in which actor-managers lost control of their profession to businessmen, many academicians and theatre departments lost considerable autonomy when they moved into new facilities and found themselves "under new management," as it were.

Shortly after the American Theatre Association went bankrupt in 1986, several dozen educators founded the Association for Theatre in Higher Education, www.athe.org, which attracted a large membership and now sponsors an annual convention. The University/ Resident Theatre Association, www.urta.com, continues as an independent organization to service campuses that operate resident, often professional, acting companies.

Types of College Theatre Programs

Extracurricular Theatre Activities

Support for the arts in public education has never been great. More often than not, the arts take a backseat to athletic activities; and public schools provide little if any money, faculty expertise, or special facilities to promote the arts in education, much less arts education itself. And without strong arts programs at the secondary level, fewer promising students will appear as arts majors at the college level.

Theatre production can serve young people in a number of unique ways. Aside from demonstrating the importance of teamwork, coordination, and leadership, theatre provides insight into literature and history, as well as into the student's own personality. When properly guided, it can also teach self-confidence, self-awareness, and sensitivity.

When guided badly, it's merely another channel for extroverted students to show off or for others to develop fantasies about becoming stars. Extracurricular theatre clubs and productions are common on the college campus, where they may or may not coexist with an academic theatre program. There should always be faculty guidance to insure continuity from year to year and to provide a liaison with the faculty and administration. The success of such organizations, however, always depends on student leadership and involvement. The first test of this may well be the ability of the student officers to gain a fair budget allotment from their student government organization or whoever administers the student activities fees that are collected by most colleges precisely to support extracurricular initiatives. Again, sports activities are usually favored. When there is a theatre department or theatre program, an extracurricular club can help encourage interest in theatre courses and in becoming a theatre major. It may feed volunteers into departmental production crews and it can also serve as a helpful safety valve that permits students a place to get rid of any complaints they may have with the department. They may, for example, not like the department's choice of productions or its casting policy. The student theatre organization might also be the best venue for producing experimental, original, or unusual material. There have also been educationally creative instances when students have cast faculty members in their productions and reversed traditional relationships—usually to everyone's advantage.

Elective Theatre Course Offerings

Theatre productions are usually extracurricular on campuses where there is no theatre major and little thought that students may enter theatre as a profession or pursue graduate work in the field. Courses and productions on these campuses are designed to complement a liberal arts education or concentration in some specialized field of study. Only one or two faculty members are needed to teach these courses, but ideally, they should have a special background and experience in theatre.

Liberal Arts Theatre Programs

A liberal arts program offering a Bachelor of Arts degree with a concentration in theatre is often the best undergraduate study plan for students interested in this field. This assures a broad-based education, while introducing the student to theatre and, hopefully, the wide range of dramatic literature. Although the student unrest of the 1960s prompted academia to loosen or drop many curricular requirements and make course content more "relevant," many such changes were reversed in the 1980s with the reintroduction of a required core curriculum at many institutions. Theatre courses in this type of program are usually open to majors and nonmajors alike, as are department stage productions. Two or more full-time theatre instructors are necessary, and they should also be qualified to direct the productions.

Vocationally Oriented Undergraduate Theatre Program

A number of college theatre programs offer a Bachelor of Fine Arts degree in theatre. This allows the student more theatre courses that are usually of a vocationally oriented nature, fewer course requirements in the humanities and sciences, no foreign language requirement, and perhaps more production opportunities than in a B.A. program. Yet the student receives a broader education than at a professional theatre school and more intense exposure to theatre than in a B.A. program. B.F.A. programs, such as those used by the Juilliard School and Oberlin College, attempt a conservatory approach to professional training. The faculty for such programs should be comprised of four or more full-time instructors as well as guests and part-time adjuncts from the professional theatre. Concentrations in acting, musical theatre, design, and theatre education are appropriate for B.F.A. programs. Concentrations in directing and theatre management, however, are not ideal at the undergraduate level because students interested in these disciplines should first gain a broad knowledge of theatre and its repertory.

Vocationally Oriented Graduate Theatre Programs

Graduate schools offer theatre programs that lead to the master of arts, master of fine arts, doctor of education, doctor of fine arts, and doctor of philosophy degrees. The M.A. is usually a one- or two-year program and serves as a stepping stone toward a doctoral degree. The M.F.A., however, is considered a terminal degree, which means that it is considered the highest degree necessary for professional certification in fields such as acting, directing, design, and arts management. Most colleges, for example, accept it in lieu of a doctoral degree for purposes of hiring and promoting faculty. M.F.A. theatre programs are two to three years in length and aim for an intensive, conservatory approach to training that provides a great deal of laboratory, workshop, and production work. Students may also work as interns on campus or with professional theatre companies and organizations off-campus. In fact, the strongest graduate theatre programs are associated with one or more professional groups, include established theatre professionals on their regular faculty, and make frequent use of visiting guest artists and lecturers from the profession.

Doctoral theatre programs—the Ph.D. is the degree most commonly offered—are primarily designed for students interested in education, history, criticism, and/or dramaturgy, although graduates who hold doctoral degrees have a wide variety of other career choices as well. Doctoral programs emphasize research and scholarship as opposed to practice and application. Information about both undergraduate and graduate theatre programs is available at the website of the Association for Theatre in Higher Education, ATHE, www.athe.org, and the Association of Arts Administration Educators, www.artsadministration.org.

Management of the College Theatre Department

The Department's Position within the Institution

The manner in which an academic department is positioned within the structure of the institution will determine a great deal about its programs, its faculty, and its students. The weakest theatre programs are those housed within a department of another discipline, such as speech or English. Fortunately, this type of situation is not nearly so common as it used to be. The strongest theatre programs are those housed in their own school of theatre and headed by a dean who has direct access to the college president and the college budget. But few universities are willing or able to elevate the study of theatre to such a position in the academic hierarchy. A number, however, have established a school of the arts to embrace departments in both visual and performing arts disciplines. Others have a school of fine and applied arts or a school of communication arts and sciences that includes departments of television and journalism, as well as the visual and performing arts. Smaller institutions may make similar configurations within a department rather than a school. While such arrangements may not seem important at first glance, they, in fact, can have a very significant and far-reaching impact. Structuring an academic institution is somewhat like creating a family out of a group of strangers, or having the opportunity to pick all of one's relatives. It mandates that certain people and disciplines will have to learn to live and work together and, just as important, that others won't. Academic planning must answer questions such as, "Should theatre majors be required to take film and television courses, and vice versa?" "Should dancers study acting?" "Can actors and singers be combined in the same voice and diction classes?" Similar questions emerge in regard to interdisciplinary faculty relationships and the shared use of performance, production, studio, classroom, office, and other campus facilities.

More and more theatre programs are recognizing students' desire to train in theatre, film, and television. M.F.A. design departments are also recognizing and addressing the very large field of "themed entertainment." There is general recognition that the professional theatre cannot adequately employ the vast numbers of students graduating from the M.F.A. theatre programs nationwide. Consciously applying the talents and training found in a theatre-training program to affiliated fields is therefore a necessity.

Theatre departments within a more general structure, as in a school of humanities or an institution where there is no theatre-school structure at all, may find it more difficult to defend their interests because they must compete directly with larger and therefore more powerful departments, such as economics or education. Size and power in academia are almost always based on numbers of students and the faculty-student ratio. The economics of education is based on the price of admission and the number of admissions. Theatre departments also require much greater cubic footage per student to accommodate their theatres, rehearsal studios, graduate design studios, etc. Of course, personalities and campus politics can also contribute to how a department is treated by the administration and the college community at large. In other words, it would help if the president were a theatre or music or opera or dance buff. It must not be forgotten that six to ten musical theatre majors can be far more useful as entertainment at a college fundraising dinner than a similar number of star mathematics students.

The degree to which a theatre department controls its facilities is also of major importance. Lucky is the department that has exclusive use of a fully equipped theatre. More often, it must share performance, rehearsal, classroom, and production spaces with other departments, if not also with outside bookings and special events. This tends to be the case when there is a large auditorium or a performing arts center on campus. When facilities are controlled by the administration, faculty must often battle to see that academic priorities take precedence over others.

Finally, how a department is funded and how much control it has over the money it generates from box office receipts are major factors in determining how it controls its facilities. As a general rule, the more hands money passes through on its way to any project for which it was originally intended, the less will arrive there. So the department or school head wants to be as close as possible to the source—the state legislature, the board of trustees, the college president, the provost, or the dean. Control over box office income is critical to campus theatre production because it often represents the only "soft money," money that can be spent without having to secure it through the lengthy and uncertain requisition process. Many items and services related to theatre production require immediate or quick payment, although few college budget officers are able to grasp this.

Faculty versus Student Control

The sudden explosion during the 1960s of campus riots, ethnically oriented demonstrations, and forceful student demands had a measurable effect on higher education. Students were granted participation in such fundamental areas as curriculum planning and development, faculty hiring and promotion, budgeting, grading, and admission procedures. During this period there were huge turnovers of college presidents, a widespread change in college admission policies, and a general move toward community service and away from research and relationships with the so-called military-industrial complex. While there has been a recent trend to restore a more traditional curriculum, campus governance continues to require student representation in most areas and levels of decision-making. Many faculty members and administrators have been pleasantly surprised to find that such student involvement has actually been helpful; certainly it bespeaks a new partnership on the campus.

Because of the collaborative nature of putting together a production, student-teacher relationships in a theatre department have always tended to be less rigid and more personal than in most others. Yet lines of authority must be drawn and maintained. Faculty members must often work hard to keep the learning process to the fore, as opposed to the production, entertainment, or gratification process alone. Students may have control of an extracurricular theatre organization and participate in campus and department management, but faculty must control the teaching as well as maintain leadership in campus governance.

The Committee System

Most colleges and universities operate though a system of committees. This may hamper individual decision-making and initiative because it makes it so easy to avoid personal responsibility; one can always "defer to the decision of the committee" or hide behind the cloak of anonymity provided by group membership. But while committees may give the appearance of democratic distribution of power, very little democracy or government by consensus may actually be at work.

Department chairpersons in large institutions usually inherit an administrative structure that they are powerless to change, while at small institutions chairpersons may be able to establish their own systems. However, in both cases some type of committee system will be necessary. The advantages of management by committee are:

1.)   Decentralization of political power;

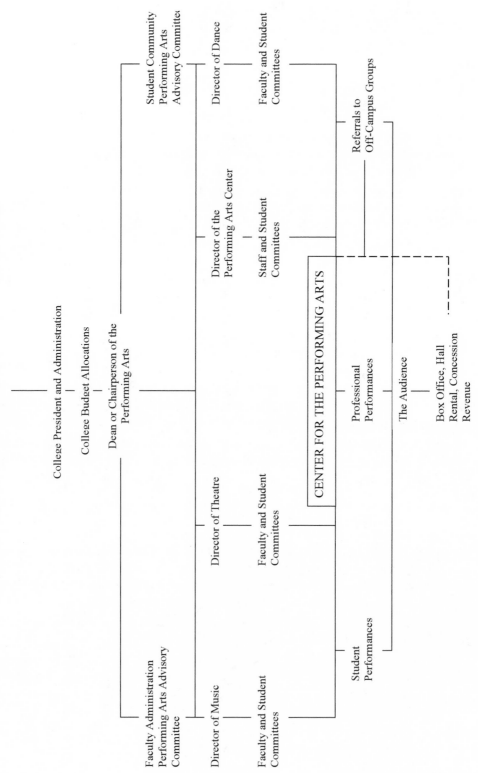

ORGANIZATIONAL CHART

A School Department of Performing Arts Within a University College

College President and Administration

College Budget Allocations

Dean or Chairperson of the Performing Arts

Faculty Administration Performing Arts Advisory Committee

Director of Music

Faculty and Student Committees

Director of Theatre

Faculty and Student Committees

Student Community Performing Arts Advisory Committee

Director of Dance

Faculty and Student Committees

Director of the Performing Arts Center

Staff and Student Committees

Referrals to Off-Campus Groups

CENTER FOR THE PERFORMING ARTS

Student Performances

Professional Performances

The Audience

Box Office, Hall Rental, Concession Revenue

2.) Majority rule;

3.) The guarantee that minority opinions will be heard.

The usual disadvantages include:

1.) Time-consuming delays;

2.) The discouraging of individual initiative and responsibility, which of course retards action, change, and development;

3.) Decisions often lack the personal commitment of the people who must carry them out.

Any system for managing an academic department should aim for clarity of purpose and reasoned leadership, with a fair distribution of faculty and students representation on all committees.

There are some aspects of a theatre department's work that obviously defy management by committee. A committee may select the plays that will be produced, for example,

ORGANIZATIONAL CHART
COLLEGE THEATRE DEPARTMENT

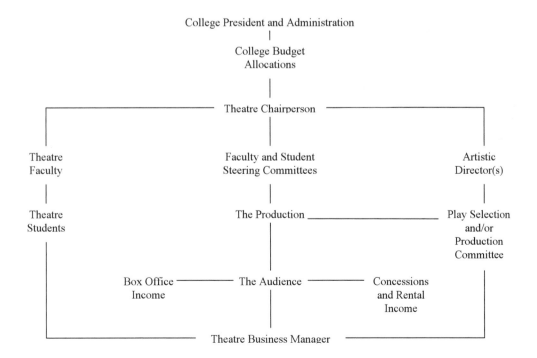

but it cannot direct those plays. The direction must be done by an individual who has autocratic authority over the production. And there are times when a chairperson must stand alone and make difficult decisions such as canceling a production before it opens, replacing the set designer, bringing in a play doctor, or canceling a performance because of some emergency.

The principles of personnel management discussed in Chapter 3 are as applicable to college theatre as to any other, although the college administrator may be burdened with more bureaucracy and institutional red tape. And on top of all the details and responsibilities that go into play producing, the managers of college theatre programs must add the challenges of teaching.

Play Production in College Theatre

Play Selection

Chapter 5 defines certain criteria that may be applied to play selection and the business of planning a season. Decision-making in this area is surprisingly casual for many theatres. It is especially unfortunate when college theatres engage in random methods of play selection, because in no other branch of theatre do the people involved enjoy such job security and leisure for planning. Most students are in residence for three or four years, and most faculty members are likely to have tenure or long-term contracts. The problems of paying the rent, breaking even, or showing a profit are seldom urgent, although they may be factors in budgeting. A college theatre faculty is in a unique position to analyze its strengths and weaknesses, formulate policy, and activate long-term projects. If a campus theatre program is primarily extracurricular, its major obligation is to the audience. If it is vocational and aimed at training students for the profession, the student participants must receive high priority in terms of play selection.

In either case, four years is a natural time cycle because of the length of time most undergraduates are in residence. What, it should be asked, will be produced over each four-year period? How well do the plays selected represent the repertory of world drama? How well do the plays selected suit the talents and abilities of the available student and faculty participants? What experiences, both as audience and participant, will the student walk away with at the end of four years? In commercial, resident, stock, and community theatre, four years usually seems like an eternity—four months is a long season, and four days can make or break the entire operation.

College theatre departments traditionally favor the classics: Sophocles, Shakespeare, Congreve, Wilde, Ibsen, Shaw, Strindberg, Brecht; and, the American dramatists O'Neill, Miller, and Williams. I am not sure if this is still true, but it is as it should be because academia has an obligation to protect the masterworks of civilization and to encourage each generation to rediscover them. But new, obscure, or controversial plays also have a place on campus. Most theatre departments of any size have access to a smaller performance space in addition to their main stage. This smaller space may simply be a large room with its walls covered with black velour—thus the term "black box" theatre —and with flexible staging and seating possibilities.

College theatre seasons can easily lend themselves to a festival format in which play selection is related to a particular dramatist or theme: Shakespeare's history plays, the American musical theatre, new voices in the theatre, whatever. A few colleges even announce their main-stage production schedules four to five years in advance. This approach has the advantage of enabling other departments and the local schools to adapt their course content to the study of plays in production. Background materials, production information, study kits, and teaching aids can be prepared well in advance and made available to teachers whose students will attend the performances. College theatre departments can do much to coordinate productions with classroom study and utilize them as teaching opportunities for theatre and nontheatre majors on campus and off.

Whatever standards for play selection are applied, students should be involved in the decision-making. Educational priorities should be honored as well as long-range goals; these should be understood by both faculty and students. Nowadays, there is an unspoken emphasis on minority plays, hiring, and casting. Also it is an accepted fact that most undergraduate theatre departments contain many more female acting majors than male, which makes casting Shakespeare, for example, difficult.

Casting

The casting process presents special problems in nonprofessional theatre, where favoritism, real or imagined, can be a factor. Yet what do faculty directors do when the number of really capable student actors is limited to just a few? Or when academic policy requires that acting majors be cast a certain number of times each year, even to the exclusion of others who give better auditions? Or when a faculty member is cast instead of a student? The solution often lies in adopting a standard departmental casting policy, of making this well known to the students, and then sticking to it. If policy requires teachers of acting to take on roles in campus productions periodically, then students will accept such casting.

Many theatre departments hold annual or semester auditions to which all its majors are required to participate and nonmajors may also be invited. From these general auditions, faculty and students who are directing upcoming productions call back certain actors to audition again for specific roles. Before casting is finalized, all directors meet to discuss their choices and resolve the inevitable conflicts. This system helps insure an even distribution of acting opportunities and, more importantly, permits the student actors to integrate their academic work and other activities accordingly.

A card or computer catalog system that indexes all the department majors and keeps their production credits up-to-date can be an indispensable casting and crewing device. It can also be consulted before play selections are made, not for precasting but as an indication of talent and crew resources. It can serve as a record of student activities and accomplishments that may be consulted when a letter of recommendation is requested, when a grievance is being voiced, or when award time rolls around. It is also a helpful resource for new faculty members and for student counseling purposes.

Double or alternate casting can substantially increase the number of acting roles available to students. Of course, directing two casts for the same production is difficult and time consuming, costuming is more expensive and time consuming, and so on. But some educators feel that the advantages of alternate casts performing on alternate nights far outweigh the disadvantages. Another valuable educational technique is to switch the roles that actors in the same cast are to perform, to give them experience in different roles on different nights. While such policies may bring about somewhat uneven or inconsistent performances, the actors' development must be considered at least as important as the audiences' reactions. Most campus audiences, even when they pay admission, understand this.

As a final note about casting, it should be said that college theatre is in the best position to avoid typecasting. Indeed, training programs for actors have an obligation to provide students with roles and experiences they might not gain elsewhere. As a rule, more is learned by casting against type than by playing it safe—provided there is a purpose to the experiment and that good coaching and some kind of safety net are available.

Managing the Campus Theatre and Production Personnel

When the theatre or performing arts department does not have exclusive use of the campus theatre, which is often the case, then that facility is usually managed and staffed by professionals who are accountable to the administration rather than to an academic department. Most such facilities also are the venues for professional performing arts companies and other performances for the general public. These facilities, together with other types of presenting organizations, are discussed in Chapter 9.

Small campus theatre facilities, however, are often staffed entirely by faculty and students, in which case management and production may be less professional, but life and learning are likely to be a whole lot easier. Even when there is a large performing arts center on campus, a sizable theatre department would benefit from another, smaller performance space that it can call its own.

Whenever possible, productions should be related to class work and student participants should largely be drawn from such classes. All theatre majors might be required to work on a certain number of productions each semester. Students in theatre management classes, for example, would serve in box office and publicity jobs. Students in stagecraft classes would be assigned to set construction jobs, and so forth. In order for this system to work well with a busy production schedule, a crew coordinator must be appointed to visit classrooms, describe personnel needs, sign up crews, monitor crew performance, keep time sheets, collect grades or other assessments of students from the crew supervisors, and hand all such information back to the classroom instructor, who may use it to help determine a final grade.

Some theatre departments also grant credit for production work. This is justifiable when such work is meaningful and accomplished under direct faculty supervision. It is similar to fieldwork that might be conducted for credit in any academic discipline. The only drawback is that the more credits a student earns this way, the fewer he or she will earn from classroom course work.

When the department operates a theatre facility, it must assign faculty members to take responsibility for the primary functions, which include:

1.) Production Coordination: The faculty supervisor will be in charge of scheduling of space, coordinating efforts of design and technical personnel, assigning student crews, supervising production purchases, supplies and inventories, serving as liaison with department chairperson and college administration in appropriate areas, assigning personnel, and supervising stage and house management.

2.) Business Coordination: The supervisor will be in charge of long- and short-term budgeting, preparation of production budgets, annual financial reports, individual production reports, box office operation, banking, production requisitions, payment orders, account ledgers, and departmental grants administration.

3.) Technical Coordination: This supervisor will be in charge of all personnel and activity in the technical production shops, will oversee requisition, purchasing, and maintenance of all production equipment and supplies, will have the ability to operate all power equipment, as well as sound and lighting equipment.

4.) Marketing Coordination: This person will be in charge of working with appropriate campus and performing arts center offices to coordinate information gathering and distribution in regard to theatre productions: playbills, posters, on- and off-campus advertising, press releases, seasonal brochure design and distribution, subscription sales, and group sales.

These responsibilities should be included in job descriptions and when a theatre department is hiring new faculty. Some institutions excuse instructors from a full teaching load in exchange for nonteaching duties. When this is not possible, faculty must volunteer to take on extra responsibilities in order to make theatre production possible. Faculty and administrators outside the department rarely understand the time, expertise, energy, talent, or money required to produce good theatre. Getting a budget line to hire a technical director, an electrician, or a guest artist can be a major battle. College administrators who understand the need to build a well-equipped chemistry lab won't see the need for a well-equipped theatre. They will understand an accounting class with seventy-five students, but refuse to permit an acting class with fewer than twenty students. And they'll view box office income with the greed of Silas Marner and wonder why the theatre department can't use the same sixteen-week requisition process that all other departments do.

The four job functions previously listed could, of course, be handled by nonfaculty personnel, but the use of faculty insures that the facility will be used more fully as a teaching laboratory and that production work will have close ties to classroom instruction.

In addition, many of these duties should be executed by students, which would then allow faculty to perform major functions such as directing, designing, choreographing, and conducting as part of their regular duties. A department chairperson usually functions in a manner similar to that of the artistic director of a nonprofit theatre company.

The Professional on Campus

The use of experts, professionals, and celebrities in the college classroom has increased so tremendously in recent years that some institutions have been accused of being short on professors of substance. There is little doubt that star performers attract attention and sell seats; and as long as their academic credentials and teaching abilities are acceptable, there is nothing wrong with including them on the faculty. However, if they are given favored treatment—especially regarding their appointment, promotion, or tenure— other faculty will have legitimate grounds for complaint.

Professionals as Full-Time Faculty

Because they are committed to providing the best professional training possible, many academic departments—especially on the graduate level—hire well-known, established professionals believing that such people will be valuable learning resources. In most cases they are, but there is a difference between hiring a professional who is still working and one who has effectively retired. The difference will be the amount of service the college receives from the professional. Because few successful people in the performing arts ever retire by choice, special problems arise when the theatre department hires an actor, director, or designer who is still in demand professionally. What happens when a major film offer comes through mid-semester? Or a directing offer comes from Europe? Or involvement with professional or government committees requires frequent trips? A department's solution may be to hire the professional on a part-time or half-time basis, or to compress that person's teaching schedule into a short period. But all of these scenarios present complications. It would be preferable to hire retired professionals on a full-time basis, even though they are not always the most glamorous choices available. Retired professionals, however, may remain on the faculty for twenty years or more, making their professional experience and contacts outdated by the end of their teaching careers. Further, many "retired" professionals are folks who fell out of favor or may never have been very successful, and might now be jaded and bitter. Although professionals on campus can have value, each situation should be judged carefully.

Adjunct Faculty

Adjunct faculty is usually hired to teach one or two courses and is brought in because the regular faculty is either insufficient or unqualified to teach courses or section being offered. Adjuncts are sometimes hired from other departments on campus, from another campus, or from the profession. They are the best solution to limited or short-term teaching needs, and the college administration regards them as a bargain because they often get paid less and receive fewer benefits than the regular faculty. And when they are respected experts, they lend a professional tone to the department and may also provide valuable job contacts for students. The disadvantage of adjuncts is that they are not so available to students as full-time faculty, and some have little interest in the ongoing work of the department or the institution.

Guest Lecturers

Campuses located more than a few hours' drive from a major city sometimes hire guest lecturers for more than a single lecture. The person might run a day-long workshop for selected students or deliver several lectures or also, in the role of a consultant, may prepare a special report for the department or the college administration.

Wherever a campus is located, the faculty and chairperson should always be open to special guest opportunities. What successful professional could they personally invite to the campus? Who is visiting the area on other business? Who are the local experts in a given field? What members of the faculty and administration might provide an interesting guest lecture? The possibilities are endless although, of course, guests should not be overused nor should they distract from good, solid instruction.

While it is always correct to pay guest speakers a fee or an honorarium, this may not always be possible or necessary. Most people feel honored to be asked to teach or lecture at a college or university. For very successful people who have already received money, awards, and acclaim, teaching may offer gratification that is its own payment.

Endowed Chairs

A few universities have established endowed chairs in directing, acting, or design. The independent funding for such positions removes them from some of the usual constraints placed on professor apppointments and may enable the university to attract top flight, active professionals to teach by offering top level salaries, full benefits, flexible schedules, and multiyear appointments.

Artists-in-Residence

Artist-in-residence programs provide that an individual artist or whole company of performing artists be contracted to spend as little as a day to several weeks on a campus conducting lectures and workshops and often also putting on a public performance. This practice is now a major source of income for most American dance companies, which generally try to arrange such residencies as a regular part of their touring schedule. This is also true for string quartets. It is less common for theatre companies, because so few are available to tour in the first place. However, it is not unusual for a theatre department to arrange for a playwright to be in residence while his or her work is being produced on the campus, and there are many instances in which a professional director has been brought in to stage a production. In fact, most leading actors and directors have plays they are itching to do but will probably never get the chance in the professional theatre. They might embrace such opportunities on campus—and for very reasonable fees.

The AEA Actor-Teacher Contract

Members of Actors' Equity who accept teaching positions of any kind can do so without AEA involvement. When an Equity member is hired by a college as a performer or as a performer/teacher, he or she usually signs one of two agreements devised primarily to insure that actors receive compensation and treatment equal to that of the institution's faculty, which also must be the minimum guaranteed by an Equity contract.

The University Actor-Teacher Agreement is a simple form that specifies the following terms of employment:

1.) Preknowledge of the productions and courses the actor will be assigned;

2.) All rights and privileges accorded to the college faculty will be accorded to the Equity member;

3.) Agreement to length of employment—no week may exceed an average of forty hours of work and must include at least one full day of rest;

4.) Agreement on salary, which must be no less than the minimum salary for faculty members of comparable status;

5.) Agreement on pension, medical, and insurance coverage—the actor will be covered by Equity provisions in these areas until such time as university coverage becomes effective.

The AEA Guest Artist Agreement

Equity members who are hired exclusively to perform on a campus are signed to an AEA Guest-Artist Agreement, which is issued on a quadruplicate contract form similar to other Equity contracts. Such actors usually perform with a student cast. The same agreement is used when an AEA member is hired to perform with a community theatre cast.

Resident Performing Companies

If a college wishes to maintain an entirely professional resident theatre company on its campus—as has been done at the University of Michigan, in Ann Arbor, at the University of Texas, in Fort Worth, at Yale, and at Harvard—it may employ the actors on a Guest-Artist Agreement or, more likely, it may operate under a League of Resident Theatres (LORT) Contract. Sometimes the professional or partially professional company operates within the university structure; at other times it is a separate corporation with greater autonomy.

Maintaining a professional theatre company is expensive and may garner some bad press for the host institution, but the educational opportunities it affords students in affiliated academic programs can be considerable. Students can observe and work with accomplished professionals who may also serve as classroom instructors. Professional theatre companies on campus also reinforce the future of resident, regional theatres that concentrate on a serious repertory.

Summary

During the years that have elapsed since the creation of the first college-theatre program in 1914, the study of theatre has become an accepted part of higher education. Vocationally oriented theatre programs have increased tremendously; colleges have allocated many millions of dollars for performing arts facilities and instruction; and many campuses have become important centers for the professional arts. There is increased dialogue and understanding between the educational and professional branches of the theatre— an encouraging trend away from the old academic attitude that theatre is an extracurricular plaything, and a move toward professional recognition of the validity of academic training. Hundreds of campus productions each year entertain college and community audiences and help maintain life in the world's drama.

Yet the arts continue to be treated inequitably when budget allocations are made, whether in the halls of government or the halls of ivy, whether in public or private education. The challenge of making politicians, bureaucrats, and administrators understand the life-sustaining value of the arts and their need for subsidy is a supreme challenge to arts educators at all levels. But this should become easier as campuses become entrenched as the cultural centers of their communities, as communication increases between the academy and the professional world, and as a new generation learns about the essential value of the arts.

CHAPTER 8

Stock and Dinner Theatre

STOCK AND DINNER THEATRES ARE BEST VIEWED in retrospect, as the heyday of each has come and gone. Most stock theatres, dinner theatres, and outdoor drama productions that still exist are nonprofessional and most, if not all, are not-for-profit operations. There are both summer and winter operations in all three categories, although we tend to use the phrase "summer theatre" or "summer stock" as a general label. Those interested in the complete history of summer stock should read the informative and engaging *Summer Stock* by Martha LoMonaco.

A Brief History

The Rebirth of Independent Stock Companies: 1914 to 1935

Chapter 4 of this book outlines the story of independent stock companies during the nineteenth century and tells how, during the years prior to World War I, they virtually disappeared. Chapter 5 outlines the growth of nonprofit professional theatres as encouraged by academics and others interested in giving high quality productions of serious drama. The stock theatre companies that came into existence after World War I were more in the tradition of nineteenth-century stock theatres, except that most were located in resort communities and only operated during an eight- to twelve-week summer or winter season.

While serious drama was sometimes included in a season of plays, the emphasis was decidedly on light entertainment and on providing young people with opportunities to learn the craft of theatre. Like the Lakewood Playhouse, which was established in 1901 in the resort town of Skowhegan, Maine, the "born again" stock theatres were independent operations that utilized a resident company of amateur actors with a resident director and staff. They operated on a seasonal basis and produced a different play every week or two; usually in a humble playhouse that resembled or actually was a converted barn. Such companies were often organized and run by enthusiastic college students. One example was the University Players Guild that operated during the summers from 1928 to 1932 in Falmouth, Massachusetts, under the leadership of several Princeton students. Other summer stock theatres employed young talents who would later become famous: Henry Fonda, Joshua Logan, Myron McCormick, Mildred Natwick, Kent Smith, James Stewart, and Margaret Sullivan.

During the 1920s, men such as Richard Aldrich, Milton Stiefel, and Guy Palmerton, who later became the scions of summer theatre establishments, were searching among the resort communities of New England for hospitable places to establish amateur resident companies. Aldrich founded the still-functioning Cape Playhouse on Cape Cod in 1926 and later operated the now-vanished Falmouth Playhouse and the Cape Cod Melody Tent, which still presents musical attractions, but no "book musicals." The Ivoryton Playhouse in Connecticut opened in 1930—Katharine Hepburn performed there. The Westport Country Playhouse was founded by Lawrence Langner as an informal laboratory for Theatre Guild activities in 1931, and the Ogunquit Playhouse was started in Maine in 1932. By the 1930s there were hundreds of stock companies that, collectively, served as the training grounds for future Broadway and Hollywood actors. And the movement spread from its New England beginnings to the South and Middle West. Some stock theatres lasted only a season, others continued for years on an amateur basis, and yet others negotiated with Equity and began hiring professional actors and stars. Winter stock, typified by the elegant Royal Poinciana Playhouse in Palm Beach and the Coconut Grove Playhouse, also in Florida, further expanded the activities.

The Heyday of Stock; History Repeats Itself

Most of the better-known summer theatres were started during the 1930s and 1940s and followed similar patterns of development. They progressed from amateur-resident companies to Equity-resident companies, to Equity-resident companies with visiting stars, to roadhouses for Equity-nonresident-touring package productions—the same pattern as that followed by the independent stock theatres of the nineteenth century.

When the Stock Managers' Association negotiated its first contract with Actors' Equity in the early 1930s, only about a dozen summer theatres were under union jurisdiction. By 1950, that number had increased to about 130 and continued to grow. As always with the unionization of a new branch of the industry, minimum salaries were low at first and Equity also permitted a rather liberal use of nonprofessionals.

It appears that the first "star" in this century hired to perform with a resident stock company was Jane Cowl, whom Richard Aldrich in 1935 paid $1,000 to appear for a week in *Romance* with his company at the Cape Playhouse. Many stock managers were horrified by such extravagance but, since the experiment paid off at the box office, the idea soon caught on; once again, audiences were asking, "Who's in it?" before buying tickets. And, once again, the shady townships of rural America were brightened by the seasonal visitation of theatrical luminaries: ZaSu Pitts, Billie Burke, Bea Lillie, Gertrude Lawrence, Cedric Hardwicke, Helen Hayes, Lillian Gish, and the perennial Tallulah Bankhead were among the atypical tourists. Star salaries climbed as high as $5,000 per week, forcing managers to pinch pennies in other areas. Providing something of a vacation for the star, if no one else, the system usually required the star to spend several weeks rehearsing with the resident company before the performance week. Soon, however, stars began traveling with several featured players, and by the 1950s they generally carried their entire company—which was cast, directed, rehearsed, and costumed in New York City—and spent only the performance week itself at each theatre. The "package system" had begun and was just like the combination companies of the previous century, except for the name and the fact that package shows seldom traveled with the necessary scenery. This was constructed at each theatre in order to accommodate greatly different stage dimensions and production capabilities. As a result of packages, the professional resident stock system once again virtually ceased to exist.

While stock theatres never fell under the control of a syndicate—although some producers operated several theatres simultaneously—the stock managers who opted for the package system lost most artistic control over their product and, in effect, became presenters rather than producers. Only a limited number of top attractions—that is to say, big-name stars or hit shows fresh from New York—became available each season. Most managers wanted the same attractions and therefore booked almost identical seasons. The Stock Managers' Association was replaced in the 1950s by a similar organization of summer and winter theatre managers, the Council of Stock Theatres (COST), which negotiated the Equity agreements and also served as a central booking exchange. Stock companies that still maintained a professional resident company formed the Council of Resident Stock Theatres (CORST) and also negotiated with Equity.

Perhaps the best known of the CORST operations is the Williamstown Theatre Festival in Massachusetts, operated for thirty years under the artistic direction of the late Nikos Psacharopoulos. Its tradition of bringing in stars to play with a resident company harkens back to the earlier days of stock but is also similar to the policies of other nonprofit professional companies. Admission into its apprentice program is seen as a jewel for would-be actors, directors, and techies.

During its heyday, stock often provided a testing ground for new plays, a function now filled by the nonprofit professional theatres. Among the many plays that traveled through stock on their way to becoming hits were *Life with Father*, *The Fourposter*, *A View from the Bridge*, and *Barefoot in the Park*.

The 25th Annual Putnam County Spelling Bee by William Finn and Rachel Sheinkin opened Off-Broadway in the spring of 2005, after it premiered at the Barrington Stage Company, in Sheffield, Massachusetts. It is mentioned here because of the rarity of a production today moving from stock to New York.

The most obvious attempt to cash in on the popularity of stock theatre took the form of large tent theatres, which began operating in the 1950s using real tents or more permanent structures. A number of so-called tent theatres seating one thousand to two thousand people were put up from Boston Harbor to San Francisco Bay, and another stock managers' organization was formed to deal with Equity—this was the Musical Theatre Association (MTA). Initially, the tents presented popular musicals and operettas, which were performed by a largely resident company, chorus, and orchestra, and

ORGANIZATIONAL CHART

Medium-size Commercial, Nonresident Stock Theatre

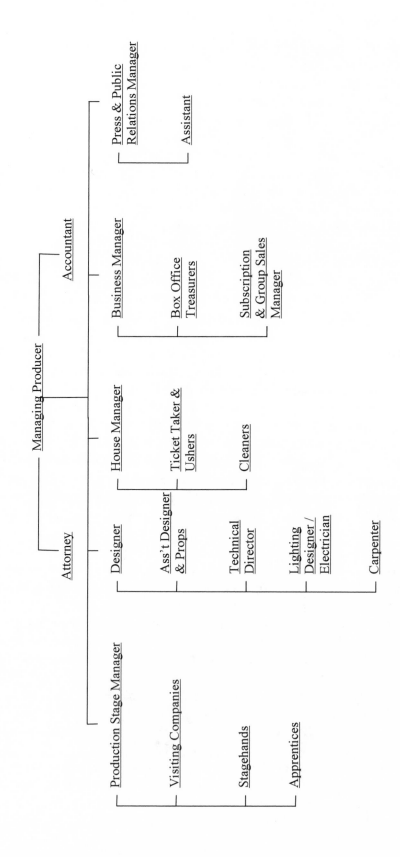

aimed to please the entire family at low prices. The prototype of all tent theatres was the Music Circus in Lambertville, New Jersey, founded by St. John Terrell; the largest and most successful operations involved the simultaneous management of several tent theatres, such as John Lemar Price, Jr.'s Musicarnival, Inc., begun in 1954, which controlled a summer theatre in Cleveland and a winter theatre in Palm Beach. Messrs. Guber, Gross, and Ford operated five tent theatres just south of New York City during this period. But the popular appeal for such attractions as *The Student Prince* began to dwindle by their third or fourth revivals, and Broadway simply wasn't keeping up with the demand for new hit musicals. Not surprisingly, tents began to engage stars in their productions and began to supplement their seasons with special performances by rock groups or nightclub and TV personalities. Ticket prices went up, and tent theatres found themselves ensnared in the star-package system and all the attendant problems. Furthermore, because of the large potential grosses at the tents, many stars adjusted their salary demands upward and became unavailable to the smaller, proscenium stock houses.

Dinner Theatre

A novel approach to commercial theatre is that of the dinner theatre format, somewhat like that of a nightclub, in which food and beverages are served in the same room where the production is performed.

In the 1960s and 1970s dinner theatres sprang up throughout the nation. Most operated like nonresident stock theatres, except for their food policy and the fact that their shows usually ran longer than one or two weeks. Like professional stock theatres, they declined in number during the 1980s and also suffered from the lack of new hit comedies and musicals. There are very few dinner theatres operating these days.

Outdoor Theatre

Completing the spectrum of largely tourist-oriented theatre operations are the outdoor drama festivals and productions. Only a handful of these operate under an Equity contract of some kind, but many pay salaries to all or some of their participants nonetheless. Of the nearly one hundred companies in this category, most are members of the Institute of Outdoor Drama, headquartered in Chapel Hill, North Carolina, even though this association does not involve itself in collective bargaining. Outdoor drama productions—which have been popular in all sections of the country for much of the twentieth century—often center around an American folk hero such as Daniel Boone, Abraham Lincoln, Mark Twain, or Stephen Foster. Many are passion plays or are based on religious themes; some are pageants, like The Mormon Miracle Pageant. These outdoor drama companies represent the closest thing this country has to grassroots theatre and many have maintained their successes while other tourist-oriented theatres have fallen by the wayside.

Despite the overall decline of summer stock operations, there are a few exceptions. The most notable is the MUNY in St. Louis. Founded as The Municipal Theatre Association of St. Louis in 1917, it is now stronger than ever with 31,000 subscribers. It performs

ORGANIZATIONAL CHART

Musical Stock or Outdoor Theatre Compnay

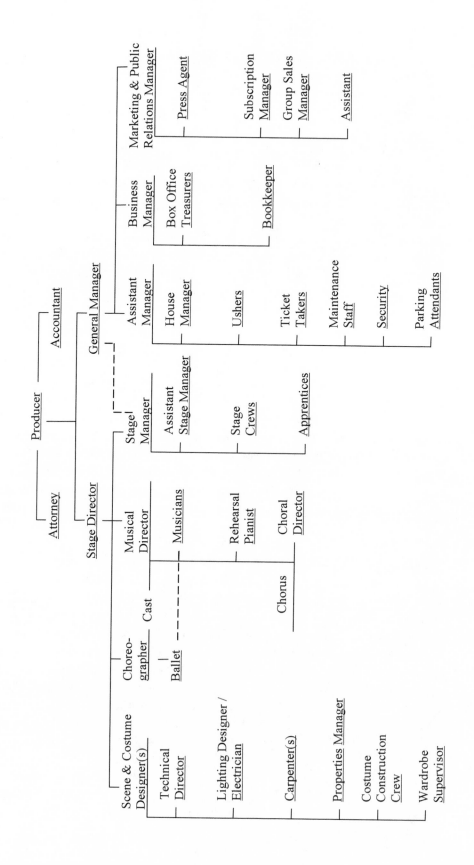

in an outdoor amphitheatre that seats in excess of 11,000 and is located in a large urban park—Forest Park. Its season of seven musicals is selected from the standard Broadway catalog. However, in the last few years, under the leadership of executive producer Paul Blake, new musicals have premiered to some acclaim. They include stage musical versions of the films *Roman Holiday*, *Breakfast at Tiffany's*, and *White Christmas*.

The other exception is the emergence and popularity of Shakespeare festivals. Usually occurring in the summer and situated outdoors in a park setting, there are Shakespeare festivals all over the country. They can be found from the Hamptons on Long Island to San Francisco, from Dallas to Vermont, and across the Midwest and into the South. Although Shakespeare is part of their name, it is common for these organizations to present works both classic and contemporary.

Apprentice or Intern Systems

Apprentices have long been a feature of American stock theatres and the demise of stock theatres translates into a reduction of learning opportunities for young people wishing to work in the theatre. It was—and to a small extent is—entry-level theatre.

Applicants for apprenticeships should closely examine programs. In some cases the program's claims are not what are actually delivered. The most common undelivered promise is that of performing opportunities.

Some theatres have experimented with apprentice programs that offer college credit, or with apprentice schools that offer formal classes. These make sense when they are well run and when they are part of the operation's mission, as opposed to being merely a device to earn extra income. An apprentice or intern policy needs to be thought out carefully in terms of the time, expense, and energy it will require as compared to the benefits that may or may not accrue.

Summary

Stock theatre in America has enjoyed two lives, both of which were largely provincial geographically and largely commercial artistically. The star system and overcentralization contributed to the demise of the nineteenth century's professional stock theatres. The star system, escalating costs, and changing tastes led to the demise of professional stock theatres in the twentieth century. Stock's greatest contribution was that it was a place to learn the realities of the profession, a place to experience the grind of working. Those able to associate themselves with the few existing operations will surely be better for the experience. The glimmer of hope is surely the growth of Shakespeare festivals where learning opportunities still can be found.

CHAPTER 9

Presenters and Presenting Organizations

ALTHOUGH THIS BOOK FOCUSES ON THE PROCESS of producing theatrical productions, there are literally thousands of theatres and administrators who concern themselves almost exclusively with presenting productions that have been produced by others. These people are called *presenters*.

Theatrical presenters come in all shapes and sizes—from nonprofit presenting organizations, such as city-supported performing arts centers, state-supported university theatres, community-supported resident theatres, civic centers, museums, student organizations, religious organizations, libraries, and community centers, to commercial-presenting organizations, such as theatre landlords, Broadway series presenters, independent promoters, casinos, and nightclubs. The administrators of such theatrical presenting organizations, whether not-for-profit or commercial, are known by a wide variety of titles including presenter, president, executive director, sponsor, vice-president of programming, or owner.

So who supplies these theatrical presenters with shows, concerts, and performances? The answer—producers. (See Chapters 4 and 5.) Producers also come in a variety of sizes from nonprofit producers, such as regional theatres, dance companies, opera companies, and ballet troupes, to Broadway entrepreneurs, limited liability corporations, and large publicly traded entertainment corporations. More often than not, producers hire representatives to manage and distribute their work to theatrical presenters. These representatives include booking agents, general managers, personal managers, company managers, and other production companies.

There are several points that should be made clear at the outset about theatrical presenting:

1.) Many theatrical presenters sponsor all types of performing arts events, including Broadway musicals and plays, dance performances, music concerts, lecture series, celebrity acts, and multicultural programs.

2.) Administrators of presenting organizations must be particularly skilled in marketing, finance, personnel supervision in addition to having a broad and current understanding of the various performing arts disciplines. Presenters at not-for-profit organizations must also have a keen understanding of fundraising and managing a board of trustees.

3.) Some of the larger and more ambitious presenting organizations may occasionally commission and produce a production that is included among their presentations. (See Chapter 5, Commissions.)

4.) Some of the producers who supply product to various presenters are themselves presenters.

To untangle this seemingly contradictory branch of show business, let's consider how it started.

Background

The First Presenters: 1830-1900

The American tradition of presenting live entertainment that has been produced by others can be traced back to the lyceum bureaus, the Chautauquas, and various theatre circuits that fostered touring stars and companies during the nineteenth century. Touring has been a fundamental part of the presenting process since the system began.

Popular for several decades prior to the Civil War, lyceum groups disseminated information for adults about history, politics, science, and the arts by offering lectures, concerts, and other presentations. The lyceum bureau in a given community would select which speakers and events to offer. Derived from a French word meaning "school" and from a Greek word meaning "gymnasium," such as the one in which Aristotle taught in ancient Athens, American-style lyceums gained respectability during the 1830s—even in such puritanical cities as Boston. In fact, in many communities a lyceum or "musee" offered the only theatre or dance presented, usually under a pious-sounding title that promised instruction rather than, heaven forbid, entertainment. Theatre performances, for example, might have been Shakespearean tragedies rearranged to illustrate a moral lesson, and "dance" recitals were often little more than a series of *tableaux vivants* in which well-draped performers stood stock-still to depict some edifying historical moment, real or imagined.

Chautauqua institutions, like the lyceums, were devoted to adult education in both religious and secular subjects. The first Chautauqua was established in upstate New York in 1874 as a summer activity, and thousands attended this eight-week event, taking courses in religion, arts, and humanities. Chautauqua publications were written to accommodate groups of people who could not attend the institute, and lecturers were sent on the road to enhance their literature. Eventually, several hundred Chautauqua institutes were formed around the country, and each engaged speakers, musicians, and various types of entertainment. In 1912, the movement was organized as a commercial enterprise: entertainers and speakers were offered on a contractual basis, touring circuits were formed, and the system enjoyed considerable popularity until the mid-1920s.

While the advent of Chautauquas encouraged the careers of local promoters and community lyceum (or booking) bureaus, they were a comparatively unsophisticated forerunner of today's professional presenting organizations. The participants of a Chautauqua program traveled together by train and the event, comprised of both lectures and entertainments, usually took place in a tent—resembling something between a revival meeting and a country fair. However, parallel with the growth of the Chautauqua movement was the growth in popularity of the touring combination companies, organized to present full-length theatrical productions with professional actors, including a number of stars from England and the continent. These troupes also traveled by rail, but they performed in permanent theatre buildings that had been vacated by resident companies forced out by the demand for visiting stars and companies. In essence, landlords of such theatres became presenters, dependent upon the offerings put together by booking agencies in New York City.

Aside from the theatre managers on the road and the booking/producing agencies in New York City, there was also a kind of hybrid promoter/presenter known as an impresario. One pioneer in the art of promoting, touring, and presenting on a grand scale was Phineas T. Barnum, who in the 1850s made a fortune managing the American tour of the Swedish singer Jenny Lind. Barnum proved there was a vast American market for foreign attractions and unusual spectacles. In the 1890s, after failing as a theatre operator, a German emigrant named William Morris opened the performers' agency that still bears his name and also served as a leading booking agency for vaudeville acts. Morris thus established a link between artist representation and booking that is still practiced. Impresarios of later times purveyed offerings that were somewhat more refined, but their taste for profit was equally keen: Florenz Ziegfeld, Billy Rose, and the quintessential impresario of the twentieth century, Sol Hurok. Yet impresarios are a breed apart; they usually combine the functions of booking and presenting and, therefore, do not share profits or losses with another party. The day of the impresario may well have passed, however, and it is now rare to find the functions of both booking and presenting in one operation, either on an individual level or at a corporate level: bookers book and presenters present.

Booking and Producing Monopolies: 1900–1955

Given the uncertainties of travel, as well as a general attitude of mistrust, the first booking offices often made simultaneous engagements; local theatre managers would then book two or three attractions for the same date to cover themselves. These practices caused a chaotic situation that was partially addressed when three New York booking offices joined forces in 1900 to form the Theatrical Syndicate; they soon controlled most of the nation's legitimate theatres and bookings. A similar situation developed in the field of vaudeville.

Starting in the 1880s vaudeville became an immensely popular form of entertainment. It consisted of unrelated songs, sketches, and acts, or what we call today a variety show. Its end, officially or not, came about when the Palace Theatre in New York became a motion picture house. A number of different vaudeville circuits, each comprised of a string of theatres, were eventually absorbed into the Keith-Albee circuit, just as legitimate theatres fell under Syndicate control. The vaudeville monopoly did business out of B. F. Keith's United Booking Office (UBO), which was managed by E. F. Albee, whose adopted grandson is the playwright Edward Albee.

By the time the Shubert Brothers began to gain prominence both as producers and theatre landlords, theatre production in America was on the decline. By the mid-1920s, the Shuberts had secretly become a majority shareholder of UBO and controlled well over half of all legitimate theatre bookings in the nation. They also produced about twenty percent of all road shows. By the early 1950s, they had gained control of virtually all theatres still operating outside of New York City, and the UBO had become their central booking office. Even when they merely booked a theatre, they took as much as fifty percent of the box office; and when box office receipts fell below a minimum, they simply booked in a new attraction and avoided any serious loss.

Organized Audience Support: 1920–1960

Methods for organizing audience support on the road—as opposed to organizing control over theatres and bookings—were pioneered during the 1920s in the theatrical field when the Theatre Guild invented a subscription plan that guaranteed support for its productions. Aside from being the dominant producing company on Broadway during the 1920s and 1930s, the Guild could boast 30,000 subscribers in cities outside New York. In the concert field, two far-sighted promoters in Chicago, Dema Harshburger and Ward French, came up with a subscription plan that was eventually adopted by thousands of local music clubs. A permanent, nonprofit concert association in each city ran an intensive, annual, one-week membership drive that was directed by a professional organizer. The money raised became the budget for that year's attractions. Single admissions were not sold, and only members could attend the concerts. The plan was first tried in Battle Creek, Michigan, in 1920; by 1930 it had been successfully introduced in numerous cities and its operation became centralized when the two leading artist management organizations of the day, Columbia Concerts Inc. and National Artists Service, gave it both financial and artistic support.

Until the early 1990s Columbia Artists Management, Inc. included the Community Concerts division that packaged artists and ensembles for most of the community concert series throughout the country, particularly in small communities that presented four to six events annually. Over the years, community concerts provided countless soloists and ensembles while serving as a highly successful inspiration for the development of subscription audiences in all branches of the performing arts. In a later decade, the Ford Foundation became so convinced that subscription audiences were the key to a stable performing arts economy, that it hired a special consultant, Danny Newman, to help a number of nonprofit companies develop a ticket sales plan. This plan is outlined in his book *Subscribe Now!* Following the demise of the community concerts division of Columbia Artists, efforts to replicate the idea were not successful and artists began to be represented by boutique agencies, many of whom specialized in a specific arts discipline such as jazz, classic solo recital, chamber music ensembles. The 1990s also saw a decrease nationally in the number of local community concert series as the population increasingly gravitated to the popular musical arts or Broadway type productions.

The history of theatrical road tours was abruptly altered in 1955 when the federal government began its antitrust action against the Shuberts. By the next year, the courts put an end to the Shuberts' monopoly by forcing them both to sell a number of their theatres and also to stop operating the United Booking Office. When that office was closed in 1956, it created a wide-open opportunity in the theatre industry. Several groups jumped into action, notably the League of New York Theatres and Producers (League); the Legitimate Independent Theatres of North America (LITNA), a group of theatre managers from outside New York City; and Columbia Artists Management, Inc. (CAMI).

The League incorporated the Independent Booking Office (IBO) in 1956 as a central booking office for touring legit shows. The hope was that all theatre owners and operators would join IBO, but instead, LITNA attempted to conduct its own booking activities. It charged five percent of the gross box office receipts as its booking fee, while IBO introduced a rather modest flat fee to be paid both by the presenter and the producer. In 1957 after inevitable conflicts, the two organizations consolidated their booking interests under the IBO banner. It served the road business by booking and contracting shows as well as collecting and sharing pertinent information with its client theatres. There were twenty board members, ten from the League and ten from LITNA. While the number of playing weeks on the road fluctuated widely in the 1960s and 1970s, IBO continued to function primarily as a booking agency until the early 1980s, when its main work evolved into serving as a computerized national clearing-house for performing arts touring information. In 1985, however, IBO was dissolved, and its assets were transferred to the League for the purpose of forming a professional resource center to assist producers and presenters both on Broadway and the road. To reflect this change in its membership and services to the industry, the League of New York Theatres and Producers became the League of American Theatres and Producers, a national membership organization, not a booking agency.

In 1955, just twenty-five years after the founding of IBO by Arthur Judson, CAMI, anticipating the demise of IBO, created the Columbia Artists Theatricals Corporation

(CATC). Modeled after Community Concerts, CATC maintained a professional central staff in New York to work with volunteers in seventy-eight cities—these volunteers were people who were members of such service organizations as the Junior League. Each volunteer group was comprised of a nucleus of members who chaired committees dealing with finance, publicity, venue rental, hospitality, and, of course, subscription sales. Each member was expected to bring ten other volunteers into the organization to assist with sales. Prior to each season of four productions that CATC sent on the road—typically, there would be two musicals, a comedy, and either a serious drama or a mystery—a representative from the New York office would visit each city. The season would be announced at an annual dinner.

CATC's primary responsibility to its local constituents was to contract the services of producers who would organize the four productions each year and provide the volunteer presenters with the necessary support material and information. In 1958 Ronald Wilford was invited into CAMI as general manager of this network or circuit of theatrical presenters, known at this time as the Broadway Theatre Alliance—later renamed the Broadway Theatre League. CATC never intended to produce its own productions, although it was eventually forced into this activity to fulfill its commitments. Perhaps because of such complications, CATC, in 1961, sold its interest in the national subscription series to an independent producer, Harlowe Dean, and became a temporarily dormant corporation. After a single season, the Broadway Theatre League was acquired by Julian Olney, who renamed it the National Performing Arts Company. By the mid-1960s, however, the circuit members no longer paid annual fees to a central booking agency and were free to develop their own series. For the first time in the history of touring in America, the road became decentralized. Individual presenters were free to pick and choose attractions from the agencies or producers they chose.

Diversity and Expansion: 1965–Present

A significant factor in the decentralization and growth of the road was the construction of thousands of new performing arts facilities in the 1960s and 1970s, most on college and university campuses. As these were often too lavish and expensive to maintain for student use alone, the universities opened their doors to professional performing arts presentations of every kind in order to generate needed revenues. As a result, the campus often became the cultural center of its community. And, predictably, many new booking agencies and producers anxious to cash in on a widening national audience sprang into operation.

In 1965 Tom Mallow founded American Theatre Productions (ATP) and quickly became preeminent in the theatrical touring market. Mallow worked closely with local promoters and presenters without attempting to centralize road management. Then ATP created a subsidiary corporation, Janco Productions, which served as the production arm of its booking operation, thus eliminating the middleman position of the booking agency and strengthening conrol over both product and contract flexibility. By 1970, ATP was virtually the sole bidder for the touring rights to Broadway shows. Shortly thereafter, however, CAMI decided to revive its theatrical touring activities, in part because it happened to own the touring rights to the Tony Award-winning musical, *1776*. Kenneth Olsen, who had worked with Tom Mallow at ATP, was recruited to head CATC and soon revitalized its reputation by importing such prestigious companies as The Young Vic, The Royal Shakespeare Company, and the Cómedie-Française, while also vying for the rights to New York hit shows.

In the mid-1980s the advent of the mega-musical had a major impact on touring productions. *Cats*, *The Phantom of the Opera*, and *Les Misérables* led the way and helped increase theatre attendance and subscription audiences all over the country. Alan Wasser Associates (AWA) was founded to manage these productions in New York and book them for the road. AWA continues to be one of the primary general management and booking agencies for road product. Shortly thereafter, Disney Theatricals was founded to produce *The Lion King*, *Beauty and the Beast*, and *Aida* for the New York stage and for national tours. These mega-musicals resulted in a change in the usual one- or two-week runs in major cities to eight- to twelve-week runs—and often longer—and required two to three weeks for load-in and restoration.

As Broadway product and the demand for that product increased throughout the 1990s, a number of booking agencies were founded to handle the demand, many of them also being involved with the original production of the shows for the Broadway stage. As the new century started, the primary booking agencies for Broadway theatricals included Big League Theatricals, The Booking Group, Columbia Artists Theatricals, Disney Theatricals, Dodger Touring Limited, On The Road, The Road Company, AWA Touring Services—the booking agency arm of Alan Wasser Associates—and William Morris Agency. Like virtually all booking agencies and producers of touring productions, these are commercial, for-profit outfits, even though they often sell their products to nonprofit presenting organizations.

Most, although not all, producers of touring productions and booking agencies are members of the League of American Theatres and Producers. As discussed in Chapter 4, this organization negotiates with Actors' Equity Association and other theatrical unions.

Non-Equity Tours

Until the mid-1990s, the only tours playing major markets were full union tours. The actors were members of Actors' Equity Association, and the balance of the company, musicians, and stage crew were members of their respective unions, AFM and IATSE, SSDC. (See Chapter 3.) The producers of these Equity tours were typically the original producers —members of the League of American Theatres and Producers—and because they had agreements with all the appropriate theatrical unions, they were accordingly bound to engage union personnel—read Equity—for their tours. The appropriate Equity contract for a tour would be the Broadway Production Contract.

Non-Equity tours played one-nighters and split weeks and were ostensibly below the radar. Producers of non-Equity tours, obviously had no Equity agreement, but did have agreements with other theatrical unions. And so, there were two separate touring worlds: Equity and non-Equity.

However, those two worlds were moving closer together. League producers needed to cut costs because presenters were reducing their guarantees. The League's response was to look to non-Equity performers as a cost-savings device. (Equity claimed that the real issue for producers was not so much a response to reduced guarantees, but simply an attempt to make more money at the expense of its members.) Whatever their reasons, League producers, unable to engage non-Equity performers themselves because of their existing agreements, *licensed* their shows to non-Equity producers or repackagers, such as NetWorks, Troika Productions, and Phoenix Productions to begin playing major markets. The repackagers could put out tours and operate them less expensively because they used modified union agreements and also because they used revised light plots, redesigned set pieces and scenery, and virtual orchestras—computers that simulated the sound of live musicians, thus reducing the number of touring players, if not eliminating them entirely. In short, they attempted to replicate a Broadway production at substantially reduced costs. Although there was a large economic advantage to using non-Equity performers, they could not use excellent Equity performers because these actors were barred from working in non-Equity productions. Therefore, production quality varied from show to show.

Equity needed to get its members back on tour, and so during the 2004 Equity-League contract negotiations, an experimental "tiered" agreement was reached that allowed Equity performers to work for wages and benefits below those normally required under the Production Contract. That agreement imposed conditions on the producers: the guarantee received by producers had to be below an agreed amount, the tour could not play in one city for more than a certain number of weeks, and there had to be a minimum of forty people in the company. Because of this agreement forged between the League and Equity, Troika and NetWorks have now signed pacts with Equity as well.

Presenters' Organizations

Formerly the Association of College, University and Community Arts Administrators (ACUCAA), the Association of Performing Arts Presenters (APAP), headquartered in Washington, D.C., has the largest national membership for managers and administrators in the presenting field. It holds an annual conference in New York City, provides workshops there and at other locations around the country, and supports research and publication.

APAP members bring performances to over two million audience-goers each week (www.artspresenters.org/about/index.cfm). No other association membership rivals the breadth of creative expression, representing disciplines ranging from all forms of dance, music, theatre, and family programming to puppetry, circus, magic attractions, and performance art.

The National Association for Campus Activities (NACA) and the International Society of Performing Arts Administrators (ISPA) also represent presenters; the latter having an international membership and holding conferences both in the U.S. and abroad.

Regional associations and consortia devoted largely to management issues and block-booking for presenting organizations include Southern Arts Federation, in Atlanta; New England Foundation for the Arts, in Boston; Arts Midwest, in Minneapolis; Mid-Atlantic Arts Foundation, in Baltimore; Western States Arts Federation, in Denver; Consortium for Pacific Arts and Cultures, in Honolulu; and CAPACOA, in Ontario. Most of these organizations hold an annual conference for members in their regions, which offer seminars on areas of interest in presenting the arts and resource/exhibit halls where the agencies display their offerings and book upcoming seasons. Many states also have consortium organizations, such as the Montana Performing Arts Consortium, Arts Northwest, and the Ohio Arts Presenters Network, which meet to discuss current issues in the presenting world and to block book attractions.

Until the 1970s few funding agencies regarded nonprofit presenting organizations as eligible for grants; most awards went directly to the artists and not-for-profit producing companies. The NEA, state arts councils, and other granting entities came to realize that without the theatres, audiences, and fees provided by presenting organizations, few ongoing performing arts companies could survive. About one-third of most presenting organizations' budgets is spent on artist fees. Commercial presenters are not eligible to receive grants or contributions.

By the 1980s, the business of presenting theatre and other types of performances had become a major part of the entertainment industry. The nation's sprawling performing arts centers, from Lincoln Center to the Kennedy Center to the Los Angeles Music Center, had become the jewels in what is a very impressive "presentation" crown sitting atop the performing arts colossus in America.

Types of Theatrical Tours

Touring was invented as a means of increasing audiences and revenues for productions beyond what they could attract by staying in one place. Let's look at the current type of tours that make up theatrical presentations.

National Tour

Also called a first national company or a first-class touring production, the national tour of a New York production that has received critical acclaim or audience interest is usually sent on the road concurrent with the New York run or immediately after its close. It is almost always organized and controlled by the original New York producers. If one of these producers is the Shubert or Nederlander organization, which owns theatres in New York and several major cities, the first national company or companies may be obliged to play these cities first. Similarly, if one of the producers is Clear Channel Entertainment (now Live Nation), the production will play these venues first because of the large number of markets it books and/or controls. The same holds true with the group of presenters known as the Independent Presenters Network (IPN).

National companies are generally booked into theatres according to one of two schemes:

1.) *Open-ended run*: The production will continue at the theatre as long as it earns a minimum weekly amount at the box office, similar to how a Broadway theatre license works, or continues to run profitably. This arrangement works only in large metropolitan areas and is increasingly uncommon. Open-ended runs are generally restricted to shows that fall into the mega-musical category, such as *The Phantom of the Opera*, *The Lion King*, or *Wicked*.

2.) *Fixed run*: The production is booked into a theatre for a specific, limited run, usually ranging from one to twenty-six weeks in length. Like the open-ended run, fixed runs are mostly in big cities, usually for very popular musicals or star-driven plays.

Bus and Truck Tour

A bus and truck tour may also be called the second or third national company. The *bus and truck tour* derived its name from the tradition of transporting the performers by chartered bus and the scenery and costumes by truck(s). Today, several buses—and occasionally commercial air carriers—are used to transport the actors, musicians, and stagehands; two to eight trucks are generally used to haul the scenery, wardrobe, lighting rig, sound package, and goods. Such companies are booked into venues for fixed runs according to one of three schemes:

1.) *One-week to two-week runs*: These might be in cities such as Seattle or St. Louis or even larger cities like Boston or Chicago.

2.) *Split-week runs*: The production plays in two to three venues during the same week, usually in such secondary markets as Kalamazoo or Scranton.

3.) *One-nighters*: One or two performances in a single day, in still-smaller, tertiary markets like Lima, Ohio, or Sioux City, Iowa.

As mentioned already, a major shift has occurred in touring shows since the early 2000s with the growth of nonunion touring companies. In addition, playing schedules in various cities have changed, and although the one-week to two-week formula still holds, it is increasingly common for the non-Equity tour to play for one, two, or more weeks in any given market. It all depends on how many weeks a market can realistically support a show, whether it be a new title fresh from Broadway or a new production of a revival.

When there is only one company on the road—either Equity or non-Equity—it will usually play four weeks in a major city, two weeks in a mid-size city such as St. Louis, and one week in a smaller city such as Louisville. Most tours start with an Equity first national company, and, after exhausting the roster of the full-week markets, will often be remounted as a smaller production to play the split weeks, and finally adjusted down to play one-nighters. By the time a show gets to the one-night circuit it is almost certainly nonunion.

International Productions

First-class productions of Broadway hits outside the United States may be organized and controlled by the original producers, or more likely be licensed to local producers in non-U.S. cities. These occur in foreign capitals and either employ U.S. performers or citizens of those nations. Sometimes, fully American productions are sent to foreign territories as part of the U.S. touring schedule. The engagements in foreign parts are always for a fixed run. Occasionally, U.S. tours are hosted in foreign territories as part of a cultural exchange program or as part of an international festival.

Company-Booked Tours/Shared Tours

LORT theatres and dance companies sometimes organize limited tours or support special small or junior troupes that perform for school and community audiences. Most companies whose mission is to perform for young audiences tour regularly; similarly there are professional repertory companies for adult audiences such as The Acting Company and The Tyrone Guthrie Theater.

American Ballet Theatre and the David Parsons Company are two of several hundred professional dance companies that operate their own in-house booking departments to sell and manage annual tours for both the U.S. and international markets. A slight variation of the company-booked tour is the shared tour. In this example, a group or consortium of producers will mount a show with the support of its members. Many of these are the CLO's (Civic Light Opera companies) such as those in Pittsburgh, Sacramento, Atlanta, and Houston. In these, the producers and presenters are the same entities. They each take on a pro-rata share of the pre-production expenses, pay the relevant weekly operating expenses, and each keeps its box office revenues. The shared tour model is often used for mounting revivals.

Types of Venues

When you first attended a theatrical production, chances are it was mounted in a community theatre, high school auditorium, or school gymnasium. Theatres exist as gathering places for people to come together and share a common experience. But that experience can happen in different types of venues.

Commercial Road Houses

Theatres in this category are the backbone of touring theatre. They are usually considered legitimate theatres in large markets outside of New York City. They include the Forrest in Philadelphia, the Colonial in Boston, the Cadillac Palace in Chicago, the Curran in San Francisco, and the Pantages in Los Angeles. These venues book shows on their way to Broadway and shows that have been Broadway hits. Engagements in these theatres range from two weeks to six months or even longer and generally represent the first national company of a tour.

Major Performing Arts Centers

Multifacility performing arts centers such as the Los Angeles Music Center, Tampa Bay Performing Arts Center, or the Orange County Performing Arts Center may be owned by a municipality and leased to a nonprofit operating corporation. They may have constituent performing arts companies—symphony orchestras or opera companies—in residence, but operate as presenters at least part of the time. They may also make their facilities available to outside groups with fixed runs of one to six weeks. These venues often host bus and truck touring companies.

College and University Performance Facilities

Campus facilities may be large performing arts complexes equipped with state-of-the-art technical systems. The Krannert Center at the University of Illinois is this type of complex. An example of a more modest, single-use theatre is the Spingold at Brandeis University. Most are used for both student productions and in-house booked professional attractions. These venues generally book one to two nights of Broadway shows, family, music, and dance attractions. The exceptions are the larger universities, such as Arizona State University and the University of Texas at Austin, that book week-long engagements of touring Broadway musicals.

Mixed-Use Commercial Facilities

Gambling casinos and hotels in Atlantic City or Las Vegas, or the Mohegan Sun or Foxwoods in Connecticut are famous for their lavish entertainment. Las Vegas has become a small center for either sit-down or open-ended Broadway musicals, albeit often in abbreviated form, called a *tab version*. *Tabs* are presented so that customers can see a show and then get back to gambling.

Although one would not consider Cirque du Soleil legitimate theatre, it certainly has made an impact on the entertainment front in Las Vegas, with five different shows currently running. Other musicals that have played or are now playing, in either full-length or tab versions are *Mamma Mia*, *Hairspray*, *Chicago*, and *The Phantom of the Opera*. They typically sit down in Las Vegas for months at a time.

Festivals

There are several hundred annual performing arts festivals in the United States and Canada, including the Spoleto Festival USA in Charleston, South Carolina, and the Chicago International Theatre Festival, and the Stratford Festival in Canada. These may operate as producers or presenters or both. Internationally, there are thousands of such festivals, and American artists and companies are becoming increasingly involved with them.

Civic Centers, Auditoriums, Halls, and Other Facilities

Built by a city or county and operated with civic funds, these facilities are usually part of a civic complex and service a variety of functions: town meetings, conventions, public performances produced by amateur groups, or professional performances booked in by local promoters or community arts bureaus. These can also include older theatres and former movie palaces that have been purchased by the city, restored, and now operate under city jurisdiction or as a not-for-profit organization.

Public School Facilities

Many auditoriums, gymnasiums, and cafeterias in public schools are used for student activities, as well as for community meetings and public performances.

Mixed-Use Noncommercial Facilities

Hospitals, clinics, libraries, community centers, senior centers, museums, war memorials, multicultural centers, religious facilities, and social-service clubs often make their buildings available for both amateur and professional performances, especially in small or developing communities.

In addition to these types of venues there are many others. Any given venue might be right for one attraction and completely wrong for another. Matching the attraction to the venue is an essential part of presenting.

The Presenter

The presenter must perform a sophisticated juggling act: selecting programs and productions that will satisfy the local audience artistically and make some sense financially. More juggling is required in regard to contracting the attraction, renting the theatre, setting up the box office and phone rooms, arranging for local publicity, placing local advertising, greeting the artists, and finally settling the finances with the producer. Plus, an opening night reception for the company is a nice extra that presenters often organize.

The Local Scene

The presenter must know that a particular performance space is available and must also know its exact seating and production specifications. In addition, the presenter must be very familiar with the audience and its financial potential. Obviously, this is easiest with experience and when there is a subscription audience, which guarantees a financial base at the outset of an engagement. Knowing what the scale of ticket prices will be — and whether or not this may be raised or lowered to suit particular attractions—means knowing the gross potentials for each performance or series of performances. Finally, the presenter must have a close approximation of all the expenses required to operate the venue and manage the season. Only when armed with this information is the presenter ready to begin negotiating.

Presenter Responsibilities

The presenter usually furnishes and pays for all the local facilities, services, and personnel required to present the production locally. Specifically this can entail the following:

1.) Enter into a theatre lease, providing use of the theatre, which will be clean, fully staffed, and supplied with appropriate heat and/or air-conditioning. The stage and orchestra pit must be cleared and ready for the production.

2.) Pay the salaries of local stagehands, wardrobe attendants, security personnel, teamsters, loaders, and forklift operators for the take-in, performances, and take-out.

3.) Pay the salaries of local musicians required for rehearsals and performances. In some cases the producer will bring a few orchestra members so the presenter will have to pay for only the local players.

4.) Pay for theatre ushers, ticket takers, house manager, security and medical staff, cleaners, and other theatre personnel.

5.) Other special arrangements specific to a given production including quick-change booths, sufficient hemp, counterweights, and pipe. Also, the production usually requires the use of washing machines and clothes dryers.

6.) The presenter must also set up the box office at least four to eight weeks in advance of the first performance. This includes scaling the house and negotiating box office commission structures. In addition, the presenter must pay for all the costs associated with the operation of the box office —telephone charge sales, website, subscription sales, and group sales.

7.) Pay for a local press agent and marketing staff.

8.) Purchase or trade advertising time on television and radio outlets and secure space in the print media. The producer often provides generic copy, layouts, and commercials, which are localized for the specific market by the presenter.

9.) Comply with all terms of the Technical Rider (see Appendix J).

10.) Provide a printed program free of charge to every member of the audience.

For each attraction, it is essential that the presenter has a good understanding of and is able to maintain a complete record of the projected costs and income. This is best accomplished by keeping a form that details all of the expected expenses and the income potential so that the two can be compared to see if the attraction is going to be viable.

The following is an example of the type of report that can be useful in contract negotiations:

Event *Pro Forma*

The *Pro Forma* puts all costs and income for a single event on one page and allows one to manipulate the various items in determining the financial feasibility of an event. All costs associated with the event are on the left side of the page and all income items are on the right side. There is a column for including the "actual cost" following the event. This is historically valuable in looking at future events of the same type. Here are some definitions of each category on the Pro Forma:

Projected Expenses

ARTIST/PRODUCER FEES
Fee, Performance
Negotiated fee amount per the contract with booking agency
Fee, Education
An amount that the artist may require to provide involvement in arts education activity
Lodging
Cost of hotel accommodations that may be required by artist
Transportation
Cost of airfare and local limo service that may be required by artist
Artist, Other
Any other costs associated directly with artist

HOUSE COSTS

Stage Rental

Cost to rent the theatre

Equipment Rental

Cost to rent special equipment needed for this show, such as house sound and lights or extra washer and dryers

Equipment Purchase

Cost of equipment purchase, such as lighting gels and dry ice, etc.

Piano Tuning

The fee paid to the piano tuner, after moving the piano into place

Space Rental

Rental fees for front-of-house spaces, such as lobbies or rehearsal rooms

Ushers/Ticket Takers/Security

Direct cost of ushers, ticket takers, and security

Hospitality

Cost of receptions, postconcert meet & greets, etc.

Flowers/Décor

Costs for stage flowers or decorations, artist finale bouquets

Special Services

Baby-sitting, chiropractor, medical services, etc.

Other

Any cost directly associated with the production, such as signed interpreters

PRODUCTION LABOR

Stagehands

Estimated cost of stagehands, wardrobe attendants, and loaders for load-in, load-out, and running show, based on the artist/production technical rider

Musicians

Local musicians needed, based on the artist/production technical rider

SERIES MARKETING

Season Promotion

Pro-rata share of season brochures, design, printing, and mailing; these costs are usually reimbursed through a box office commission

Box Office Set-up

The cost to program the ticketing system for ticket sales, plus the cost of ticket stock

Programs

The cost, if any, of producing a program for patrons; display advertising often covers these costs

ADVERTISING AND PUBLICITY

Advertising

Direct cost of all media advertising (print, radio, television) including costs to create the ads, add voice-overs to radio and television spots, plus direct mail and promos; this is often a separate budget with a detailed breakout of expenditures

Placement Commission

Agency or in-house fees or salary to develop materials, place advertising buys, and negotiate in-kind advertising

Publicity

Costs to create press kits, duplicate photos, and releases, plus car service for actor interviews

BOX OFFICE

Telephone

Fees charged by credit card companies for purchases over the telephone

Subscriptions

A percentage of the series subscription ticket that contributes to series marketing

Credit Card Charges

Fees charged by credit card companies for purchases at the box office

Group Sales

A percentage of group sales that contributes to the overhead costs of group sales personnel

TOTAL EXPENSES

The total sum of Artists Fees, House Costs, Production Labor, Series Marketing, Advertising and Publicity, and Box Office.

PRESENTER PROFIT

This is a negotiated amount that the presenter may claim as profit after all the show expenses have been paid. In reality, the presenter may have year-long overhead expenses that are not reflected in the event pro forma. This "profit" helps defer these costs.

ROYALTIES

Although this customary deal term due the artists/producer is quoted as a "royalty," in reality it is an amount due the artist and often has little to do with an actual royalty paid to the rights holder.

LEAGUE FEES

This is a fee that the League of American Theatres and Producers charges, usually on a weekly per show basis.

Projected Income

SCALE

This *Pro Forma* provides the option of four different ticket price zones that represent seating in four different areas of the theatre.

SEAT DISTRIBUTION

This is an estimate of the total number of seats sold in each category—series subscriptions, public (nonsubscription), student, and groups. The total number of seats must equal the theatre's capacity.

ESTIMATED GROSS INCOME

This chart multiplies the corresponding Scale and Seat Distribution numbers and multiplies them together to give a dollar value of anticipated sales.

WEEKLY GROSS INCOME

The figure is the total sum of zones A–D, multiplied by the number of performances given in the week.

PROJECTED PERCENTAGE OF HOUSE SOLD

This is a key number. Seldom is every seat sold. In this model we have used an eighty-five percent figure.

PROJECTED NUMBER OF SEATS SOLD PER HOUSE

This figure represents the total house capacity multiplied by the Projected Percentage of House Sold.

PROJECTED NUMBER OF SEATS SOLD PER ENGAGEMENT

This figure represents the Projected Number of Seats multiplied by the number of performances in the week.

ESTIMTED GROSS INCOME

This figure represents the Weekly Gross Potential multiplied by the Projected Percentage of House Sold.

NET INCOME AFTER EXPENSES

This figure is the Estimated Gross Income less the Grand Total of Expenses.

AFTER EXPENSES SPLIT

These percentages are part of the financial terms negotiated with the booking agent. This figure is the split of the Net Income After Expenses.

ESTIMATED TOTAL TO ARTIST/PRODUCER

This figure is the sum of the Artist/Producer Fees, Royalties, and producer's share of After Expense Split.

ESTIMATED TOTAL TO PRESENTER

This figure is the Estimated Gross Income less the Estimated Total to Artist/Producer.

VENUE: THE THEATRE

THE PROFORMA

EVENT:	Broadway Show
VENUE:	GREAT HALL
AGENCY:	The Agency
Contact:	The Agent
CONTRACT BASIS:	Negotiated

DATE:	April 12 - 17, 2005
TIME:	Broadway Schedule
	8 performance week

This proforma is an estimate only based on assumptions relative to performance costs and income.
(NAGBOR: Net Adjusted Gross Box Office Receipts)

PROJECTED EXPENSES

PROJECTED EXPENSES	Actual	Budget
ARTIST / PRODUCER FEES		
Fee: Performance		$ 250,000
Fee: Education		$ -
Lodging		$ -
Transportation		$ -
Artist Other		$ -
Subtotal		$ 250,000
HOUSE COSTS		
Stage Rental		$ 28,000
Equipment Rental		$ 4,000
Equipment Purchase		$ 1,000
Piano Tuning		$ 1,000
Space Rental		$ 400
Ushers/TT's/Security		$ 16,000
Catering/Hospitality		$ 2,500
Flowers/Decorations		$ -
Special Services		$ 500
Other Interpreters		$ 1,000
Subtotal		$ 54,400
PRODUCTION LABOR		
Stagehands/Wardrobe		$ 55,000
Musicians		$ 12,000
Subtotal		$ 67,000
SERIES MARKETING		
Season promo/Subscriptions		$ 10,000
Box Office Setup		$ 2,600
Programs		$ 2,000
Subtotal		$ 14,600
ADVERTISING & PUBLICITY		
Advertising, Promos & Prod.		$ 50,000
Placement Commissions		$ 8,500
Publicity		$ 2,000
Subtotal		$ 60,500
BOX OFFICE COMMISSIONS		
Telephone 7%		$ 10,534
Subscriptions 12%		$ 33,599
Credit Card Charges 4%		$ 2,000
Group Sales 10%		$ 5,814
Subtotal		$ 51,947
TOTAL EXPENSES:		$ 498,447
Presenters Profit		$ 15,000
Royalties (10% of NAGBOR)		$ 66,239
League Fees		$ -
GRAND TOTAL:		$ 579,686

PROJECTED INCOME

	A Series 10% discount	B Public No discount	C Student 20% discount	D Group 10% discount	Total Seats
Scale:					
Zone 1	$ 47.25	$ 52.50	$ 42.00	$ 47.25	
Zone 2	$ 42.75	$ 47.50	$ 38.00	$ 42.75	
Zone 3	$ 38.25	$ 42.50	$ 34.00	$ 38.25	
Zone 4	$ 22.50	$ 25.00	$ 20.00	$ 22.50	
Seat Distribution:					
Zone 1	700	300	0	0	1,000
Zone 2	100	300	0	200	600
Zone 3	100	450	50	0	600
Zone 4	0	100	100	0	200
Total	900	1150	150	200	2,400
Estimated Gross Income:					
Zone 1:	$ 33,075.00	$ 15,750.00	$ -	$ -	
Zone 2:	$ 4,275.00	$ 14,250.00	$ -	$ 8,550	
Zone 3:	$ 3,825.00	$ 19,125.00	$ 1,700.00	$ -	
Zone 4:	$ -	$ 2,500.00	$ 2,000.00	$ -	
TOTAL	$ 41,175.00	$ 51,625.00	$ 3,700.00	$ 8,550	

WEEKLY GROSS POTENTIAL (A+B+C+D)*8 shows	$ 840,400
Projected % of House Sold:	85%
Projected # Seats Sold Per House:	2,040
Projected # Seats Sold Per Engagement:	16,320
ESTIMATED GROSS INCOME:	$ 714,340
NET INCOME AFTER EXPENSES:	$ 134,654

AFTER EXPENSES SPLIT		
Producer	60%	$ 80,792
Presenter	40%	$ 53,862

ESTIMATED TOAL TO ARTIST/PRODUCER

Artist / Producer Fees	$ 250,000
Royalty	$ 66,239
After Expenses Split	$ 80,792
	$ 397,031.63

ESTIMATED TOAL TO PRESENTER $ 317,308.37

Types of Deal Terms

According to Steven Schnepp, president of AWA Touring Services (www.awatouring-services.com), deal terms for touring musicals and plays come in three structures:

1.) A guarantee deal, plus a "royalty" percentage of box office receipts
2.) A co-promote arrangement
3.) A four-wall arrangement

To analyze which deal is more favorable for each party, one has to look at each deal in the form of a settlement. Assume in all three models that eighty-five percent of the capacity has been sold, which is the same capacity used in the estimates of the Pro Forma.

Guarantee Deal

The deal outlined in the Pro Forma is termed a "$250,000 Guarantee to producer with a ten percent royalty percentage of NAGBOR and a backend split after local expenses of sixty percent to producer, forty percent to presenter." Net Adjusted Gross Box Office Revenue (NAGBOR) is the total gross ticket sales less local and/or state taxes, commissions paid to the presenter for subscription and group sales, and commissions collected by credit card issuers for the use of credit cards either at the box office or in telephone sales.

Here's how the Guarantee deal looks at the postperformance settlement:

In this deal, the producer takes away $414,792—fifty-eight percent of the Gross Income—while the presenter takes $299,548—forty-two percent of the Gross Income. The Guarantee deal is the most common, widely used financial deal for touring Broadway productions. The key advantage of this deal to the producer is that it provides for a secured tour. Because the cities booked on the tour will be paying a Guarantee to the producer, regardless of the number of tickets sold, the producer can count on consistent income over the life of the tour. Within each guarantee payment, there is an amount set aside to repay the capitalization or the start-up costs to mount the tour. By securing a series of Guarantee deals, the producer ensures a stable tour that will most likely repay the capitalization costs to the investors, pay the weekly operating costs of the tour, and provide some profit for the producer. Using this example, if the producer's actual weekly operating costs are $300,000, he or she would make $114,792 and apply that to capitalization costs. If those have already been repaid, then the $114,792 is profit.

In a Guarantee deal, the presenter also benefits from having a stable tour. Once the show has been booked and announced to subscribers and the local media, nothing could be worse than a cancellation. When a show is booked on a Guarantee, a stable tour route prevails, ensuring the production will arrive in each market as scheduled. It also allows the presenter to plan a budget with a fixed package of expenses—"house costs" in the Pro Forma—that usually contains some overhead expense.

GUARANTEE SETTLEMENT

Percent of Capacity	85%
GROSS INCOME	**$714,340**
LESS BOX OFFICE COMMISSION TO PRESENTER	($51,947)
NET GROSS BOX OFFICE RECEIPTS (NAGBOR)	**$662,393**
ARTIST/PRODUCER FEES	
Guarantee	$250,000
10% of NAGBOR	$66,239
TOTAL COMPANY GUARANTEE	**$316,239**
HOUSE COSTS	
Rent, Ushers, Electricity	$54,400
	$54,400
PRODUCTION LABOR	
Stagehands & Wardrobe—In / Out / Running	$55,000
Musicians—Rehearsals and Performance	$12,000
	$67,000
ADVERTISING & PUBLICITY	$60,500
	$60,500
TOTAL THEATRE OPERATING COSTS	**$181,900**
TOTAL ENGAGEMENT OPERATING COSTS	**$498,139**
BALANCE TO SPLIT	$164,254
60% Producer	$98,552
40% Presenter	$65,702
	$0
TOTAL PRODUCER SHARE	**$414,792**
% of GROSS INCOME	58%
TOTAL PRESENTER SHARE	**$299,548**
% of GROSS	42%

Co-promote Deal

A Co-promote or Co-pro is an arrangement wherein both the presenter and producer share the risk in presenting the engagement. In this arrangement, each party estimates

CO-PROMOTE SETTLEMENT

Percent of Capacity	85%
GROSS INCOME	**$714,340**
LESS BOX OFFICE COMMISSION TO PRESENTER	($51,947)
NET GROSS BOX OFFICE RECEIPTS (NAGBOR)	**$662,393**
ADVERTISING & PUBLICITY "Off The Top"	$60,500
	$60,500
BALANCE TO SPLIT	$601,893
80% Producer	$481,515
20% Presenter	$120,379
	$0
TOTAL PRODUCER SHARE	**$481,515**
% of GROSS INCOME	67%
TOTAL PRESENTER SHARE	**$232,825**
% of GROSS INCOME	33%

its actual expenses; those expenses are then expressed as a ratio that the parities use to share in the NAGBOR.

In a Co-promote, the presenter customarily pays out of its share all the presentation expenses—the ones listed on the left side of the Pro Forma including box office, house costs, stage hands, and musicians—and the producer pays all the production expenses, such as the salaries of the traveling actors, stagehands and musicians, sets, costumes, and lighting. It is common practice to remove advertising, the presenter's largest single expense, from the presenter's list of expenses. The advertising amount is then, in effect, "taken off the top," thus reducing the NAGBOR. It is from that reduced NAGBOR figure that all splits of box office revenues will be taken.

In the Co-promote deal, the producer walks away with $481,515—sixty-seven percent of the Gross Income—while the presenter takes home $232,825—thirty-three percent of the Gross Income. Notice that the producer is receiving $66,723 more than he did in the Guarantee deal, even though the producer's costs are the same. The risk to the producer is higher in the Co-promote. For the Co-pro, the agreed upon ratio split after advertising that was paid was eighty percent to the producer and twenty percent to the presenter. But what if the agreed upon split was sixty percent to the producer and forty percent to the presenter? The outcome would be $361,136 to the producer and $240,757 to the presenter. Continuing with the example that the producer's actual weekly operating costs are $300,000, in the eighty/twenty split, the producer can apply $181,515 toward the capitalization and profit, while in the sixty/forty example, only $61,136 can be applied. It's all a matter of risk verses reward.

If this is how the deals affect the producer's bottom line, how do the Guarantee and Co-promote deals impact the presenter's bottom line? In the Guarantee deal, the presenter took $299,548. Out of that sum, the presenter paid the local costs to run the attraction including box office staff costs, credit card commissions, ushers, theatre rent, electricity, local stagehands, and local musicians. Plus, the presenter paid expenses not listed on the settlement such as staff overhead and office expenses. Although the presenter collects some reimbursements from the show settlement, not all are covered. Notice, too, that the presenter's Series Marketing budget line from the Pro Forma is not directly reimbursed on the settlements. It's in the presenter's best interest to lower the actual paid-out expenses as much as possible.

In some cases, the presenter may negotiate with the artists that the house costs will be expressed as a fixed amount rather than line-by-line negotiated items; in the Pro Forma example, the house costs fixed amount would be expressed as $54,400. With the fixed house costs negotiated, it is to the presenter's advantage to lower the actual paid-out costs. Those saved monies go directly to the presenter's bottom line. For example, the presenter may take a reimbursement for credit card commissions of five percent, but the deal with the bank that issues the credit cards may only be three percent—the presenter may then apply the two percent difference to improving the bottom line. Further, if the presenter provides the services of an advertising agency in-house, a customary agency commission of fifteen percent is often charged; the commission figure helps defer the year-long presenter costs of maintaining an in-house marketing department.

Four-Wall Deal

In a Four-Wall deal, the producer rents the theatre from the presenter, thereby assuming all financial responsibility for all expenses of both the attraction and the presentation—but keeping all box office revenue.

In a Four-Wall deal the local presenter has no risk, but neither does she or he have the potential for making extra profit. The most money the local presenter can make is the rental figure, plus some minimal mark-up profit from credit card fees and advertising commissions. Under certain circumstances, if the presenter feels that it is an attraction that his audience will want to see, he might well agree to those terms. If a venue hosts a Broadway series for example, the presenter would most likely want to include the latest hot musical from Broadway in the series, and the Four-Wall arrangement might be the only way that a community could see that production. Most "mega-musicals" are presented using the Four-Wall agreement or a variation thereof. "Mega musicals" are shows that are very large and very expensive, but also very good for subscriptions and very good for single ticket sales. Four-Wall deals are typically used for multiweek engagements. However, as mentioned above, the disadvantage to the presenter is the reduced reward, meaning that even if the attraction sells every single ticket, the presenter's share is fixed at the agreed rental figure.

FOUR-WALL SETTLEMENT

Percent of Capacity	85%
GROSS INCOME	**$714,340**
LESS BOX OFFICE COMMISSION TO PRESENTER	($51,947)
NET GROSS BOX OFFICE RECEIPTS (NAGBOR)	**$662,393**
HOUSE COSTS	
Rent, Ushers, Electricity	$54,400
PRODUCTION LABOR	
Stagehands & Wardrobe—In / Out / Running	$55,000
Musicians—Rehearsals and Performance	$12,000
	$67,000
ADVERTISING & PUBLICITY	$60,500
	$60,500
TOTAL THEATRE OPERATING COSTS	**$181,900**
BALANCE TO PRODUCER	$480,493
TOTAL PRODUCER SHARE	**$480,493**
% of GROSS INCOME	58%
TOTAL PRESENTER SHARE	**$233,874**
% of GROSS	33%

It is necessary to compare all three deals by viewing them side by side. All start with the same Gross Income figure but end with different results. Note how both the Producer Share and Presenter Share vary. In the Four-Wall example, the riskiest of all deals for the producer, she or he takes away a sum of $480,493—sixty-seven percent of the Gross Income—while the presenter walks away with only $233,847—thirty-three percent of the Gross Income. The Producer's Share is greater than in the Guarantee deal, as expected.

But given its risky nature, why in our examples does the Four-Wall deal produce less money for the producer than the Co-Pro—$480,493 versus $481,515? It all comes down to the percentage (amount) of tickets sold. If in our settlement ninety-five percent of the tickets were sold, rather than eighty-five percent, the Producer's Share of Four-Wall would be *approximately* $564,000 as compared to the Co-Pro share of $548,000. This

COMPARISON OF THREE DEALS

	Guarantee	Co-promote	Four-Wall
PRODUCER	$414,792	$481,515	$480,493
PRESENTER	$299,548	$232,825	$233,847

illustrates that while risky, the Four-Wall deal is best for the producer on a hot-selling show.

On the other hand, because the Producer assumes little to no risk in the Guarantee deal, the reward is substantially less than in the other deals: $414,792 versus $480,493 and $481,515. But low risk for one side is not low risk for the other. The Presenter is the guarantor of the Guarantee to the Producer, and so the Presenter is on the hook for the guaranteed sum, in this case $250,000, regardless of what the actual sales turn out to be, plus 10% of the NAGBOR, plus all of the presentation expenses.

There are as many variations to the Guarantee, Co-promote, and Four-Wall deals as there are productions. The deal arrangements described above apply to touring musicals. In the concert world, the flat fee or Guarantee is the norm.

The Producer's Team

The Booking Agent

The booking agent is the producer's liaison between the show and the presenter. The main task for the agent is to secure and set up engagements all across a specific territory. For each tour, a geographic order known as routing is set up. The booker must pay careful attention to the travel time and distance between venues. It's much more efficient to move in a steady, direct route, than to zigzag north, south, east, and west. This is as true for small dance companies as it is for large musicals. For example, it is better to move from Boston to Philadelphia to Washington, D.C. for three consecutive playing weeks than to go from Boston to Atlanta to Chicago. Because theatrical tours pay their personnel for eight performances per week, whether they are played or not, the booker makes every attempt to secure engagements that will allow eight performances per week in each city.

Although staring at a blank booking calendar can be daunting for a beginner, an experienced booking agent sees it as an opportunity. The process begins with a "ghost route," an ideal tour that makes the most sense geographically with reasonably short jumps from venue to venue. Reality sets in as a few "anchor dates" are settled on. Anchor dates are in those key cities that consist of multiweek engagements operated by experienced presenters who know how to market and present an attraction. Next the agent has to fill in bookings from anchor to anchor. Ideally this will be done with no down time or layoff weeks; layoff weeks cost the producer money as many of the normal operating costs cannot be eliminated for a limited layoff. The key to the process is thinking of the tour as a chain, with no, or very few, weak links.

For attractions that will play split-weeks and one-nighters, bookers usually begin with one geographic area—Texas, for example—and assign a specific time period to it. Large booking agencies assign specific agents to specific territories so that the agents can be informed about the particular markets they are selling in and get to know the presenters in their market. The goal is to acquire as many dates in as small a geographic area as possible. As above, shorter travel distances are better than long.

When a number of different presenters in a geographical area share similar programming interests that are normally limited to one-night or split-week engagements, they can negotiate with booking agents as a group to strengthen their bargaining clout. By giving agents a block of time that can be booked solid with reasonable traveling distances between venues, the consortium can usually buy attractions at reduced rates and can be assured that the dates will be firm. Michigan Presenters Network, Ohio Presenters, the Pennsylvania Presenters Network, and other statewide consortia have undertaken successful block bookings.

One of the major problems that a booking agent faces is that oral commitments sometimes fail to develop into contractual commitments. Presenters may express interest in a product, and may even hold time for it, but in the end might have to release the date because of other commitments or because they've changed their minds. Sometimes presenters play the odds, which results in their failing to release dates in a timely fashion. This then leaves the booking agent with an unfilled date and no revenue for the attraction for that particular week. Conversely, the booking agent may hold more than one venue for a particular date, which can cause havoc in the presenters' world. Clearly, a direct approach to booking, holding dates, and the speedy execution of contracts is in the best interest of both the presenter and the booking agent.

Contracting the Tour

Bookers have standard form contracts that are mostly fill-in-the-blank. There is almost always some type of technical rider that becomes part of the agreement. Copies of the signed documents go to the presenter, booker, producer, company manager, and any other relevant player in the process. (See Appendix K, Sample Artists' Contracts.)

The Producer/Mounting the Production

Most tours rehearse from three to six weeks prior to their first engagement, and the tour producer must follow the same steps as other theatrical producers. But there are a few matters unique to tour management that deserve mention. Especially germane to tour producers are the duties and responsibilities of three key managers who work for him or her: the general manager, the company manager, and the production stage manager.

The General Manager

The general manager slot may be filled by an associate or employee of the producer, by an independent general manager, or even by the producer who would then serve in a double role. In any case, the general manager works with the producer on production expenses and with the booker on local theatre expenses to determine what costs and other obligations are necessary to the attraction in question. If the attraction is a current or recent theatre production, this process may have to begin with a check on the initial set of production contracts to discover which, if any, of the original creative team members have the right of first refusal to work on subsequent productions. Also the general manager may have to determine the size of the royalty package those contracts mandate in terms of road performances. Other factors that may have a major influence on the cost of a tour include:

1.) The size of the physical production. What are the costs involved in re-designing or adapting existing scenery? Will the current scenery withstand the necessary travel, load-ins, and load-outs? In recent years great strides have been made to bring the same production quality that exists on Broadway to audiences outside New York, and accordingly, expenses have risen, as well.

2.) The number of trucks necessary to move the production.

3.) The number of stagehands necessary to load, unload, assemble, and operate the show. How long will the load-in take?

4.) Costumes: Will new costumes need to be designed or redesigned and built; or, can they be rented?

5.) Orchestrations: Can the existing Broadway orchestrations be used? Or can they be adapted to fewer musicians without losing the desired effect? How many musicians will travel with the production? Will local players need to be hired for each engagement?

The general manager or a production coordinator may also work with designers and a technical supervisor or master carpenter to put together a technical rider to the booking contract rider. (See Appendix J.) This will give local presenters a complete idea of the costs and expenses related to such matters as dressing room requirements, star amenities, and the number of stagehands and musicians who must be hired locally. Stagehands may have to be members of IATSE, in which case the show is called a "yellow card" attraction. The presenter will be informed about how many IATSE workers must be hired in such areas as electrics, sound, props, wardrobe, and carpentry for the load-in, performances, and load-out. The appropriate union members are then pulled from the ranks of the local IATSE and sent to the job. Touring musicians are usually AFM members; often, additional players are needed to augment the traveling group. If so, local AFM members are hired through a local contractor who specializes in supplying talent for visiting shows.

Depending on the complexity of the attraction, it may be necessary to send an advance carpenter or crew to do a site survey. This means that a technical supervisor or his designee checks out the theatre to be sure that there is enough room onstage for the production.

Whatever happens on stage, the general manager continues as an active off-stage player throughout the tour. All of the traveling personnel—artistic, technical, and managerial—must be cared for, managed, and paid. Fees and royalties must be collected, adjustments dictated by penalties and lost performances must be made, disbursements must be handed out, and disagreements must be resolved. And all such responsibilities must observe deadlines dictated by curtain times and union rules, even though the general manager is sitting in an office hundreds of miles away.

The Company Manager

A company manager is responsible for booking the company and crew housing and travel. In recent years, several agencies have emerged that handle all housing and travel arrangements for touring companies. Because of the amount of business that they conduct with various hotels and motels across the country, they are often able to secure very good discounted rates for the show. Booking hotel rooms for any tour can be a very time-consuming task, so if there is a reasonable way to off-load that task, it's wise to do so.

Once the production is actually on the road, the company manager is the producer's top on-site representative. He or she must be very familiar with contracts in order to represent accurately the producer's interests at settlement time. There should be daily phone and email contact between the general manager and the company manager. Financial settlements, box office statements, programs, check registers, petty cash reconciliations, and media reviews must be sent to the general manager weekly.

In addition to his or her other duties, the company manager has as a top priority weekly payroll preparation, which is rarely a routine matter. Factors such as percentage royalties, overtime, additional services, and missed performances always prevent any two payrolls from being identical. There are companies—Castellana Payroll Services, for example—that are set up to prepare theatrical payrolls and using one of these services is highly recommended. They not only cut payroll checks and/or direct deposits, they also make appropriate tax deposits and some can prepare union reports if necessary.

The Production Stage Manager

The production stage manager who travels with the show also serves as a vital link with the producer and general manager, especially in regard to artistic, personnel, and technical matters. Together with the company manager, the stage manager helps to set and maintain company morale. Often the grueling and narrowly focused life on the road causes people to lose perspective, and it is very helpful if someone in the position of authority can defuse and manage any situations that might arise.

Promotional Support and Marketing

The booking contract usually states a minimum amount of money that the producer agrees to absorb for the local "media buy." The producer's office or press agent works with the local presenter or marketing director to coordinate this buy. In addition, the producer supplies fliers—also known as heralds—posters, logos, advertising copy and copy for news releases, radio and television commercials—the latter may be actual prerecorded audio or digital (video) tapes. The star may also record telephone interviews with local radio stations well before the show arrives. On tour, the press agent works closely with the company manager and stage manager to maximize the limited amount of time the star gives for interviews and promotional appearances. Reports on box office "wraps"—money taken in each day—and advances from the venues where the attraction has been booked are used to determine where additional advertising and publicity are necessary. Promotion experts either from the producer's or the booker's office may be sent to venues where single ticket sales need beefing up. The marketing process for a touring production may involve researching population demographics in order to select the prime venues for a particular attraction. (See Suzanne Gooch's Checklist for Presenting and Touring International Companies in Appendix L, and Hosting the Attraction, Appendix M.)

Summary

This chapter has dealt with presenters, those special managers who have a feel for their audiences and the work they must undertake in hosting a tour. That juggling act of finding a space, contracting for an attraction, handling the marketing, and providing all kinds of staffing requires a special kind of person because presenting is a risky business. There is no law of nature that guarantees an attraction will play to packed houses in one city because it did in another. There is no accounting for snowstorms, blackouts, and other kinds of disasters, natural or otherwise, that can mess up a really wonderful booking. Maybe there should be a warning on every show similar to that on mutual funds: Past performance is no guarantee of future results.

The history of presenting is virtually a history of the road, those theatres, opera houses, and performing arts centers all over the country where attractions take on yet another life, after or even during their initial runs in New York or elsewhere. Although this chapter uses touring musicals as the key examples, the principles apply to any type of touring production. Note that the concerns of the booker are the same as those for anyone planning a trip: getting from here to there via the most efficient/cost-effective route, although the cost of being late is substantially greater than being late for dinner. And notwithstanding the cooperation among producers and bookers and presenters, the discussion has demonstrated that a dollar won on one side of the transaction is a dollar lost on the other.

CHAPTER 10

Budget Planning

BUDGET IS A FINANCIAL ESTIMATE of future income and expenses. It is one element in the plan of operation in projecting how much will be spent and how much will be earned. Budgeting entails using the best judgment, based partly on past experience, combined with an investigation of current cost factors.

A financial statement is documentation of past expenses and revenues over a finite time period: monthly, quarterly, or annually. The financial statement is normally audited and prepared by an independent auditor and becomes a part of the filing for the IRS Form 990 that is required of all nonprofit organizations. For-profit performing arts companies use audited statements as part of their annual corporate tax preparation. Form 990 becomes a public document and can be accessed over the Internet at www.guidestar.org. Financial statements give a history and should, to the extent possible, be truthful in reporting income and expenses for the organization.

Budgets and financial statements are among the most important tools in the exercise of sound management. This chapter will discuss the opposites in the budgeting process: costs and revenues.

General Budgetary Considerations

Planning and Using a Budget

Financial planning is a process that should be approached seriously—and somewhat conservatively—before work begins on the project and certainly before commitments are made or contracts are signed. Accurate financial planning depends on the experience and expertise of those who devise it. In order to maximize accuracy and control, every department within an organization that will eventually have an impact on expenditures or earnings should be involved in the budget-planning process. While methods for doing this are discussed in the next chapter, it ought to be said here that, once adopted, no budget can be adhered to with fanatical zeal. As policies, plans, costs, and income change, the figures in the budget should be revised. A budget must be flexible enough to deal with unanticipated emergencies and unforeseen expenses. Nonetheless, when used as a well-informed and intelligent projection, a budget is a good barometer for measuring the fiscal health of a particular project or the organization.

Zero-Based Versus Incremental Budgeting

Unless an operation is absolutely static, meaning that there is no change in the operation or program from year to year, a combination of zero-based and incremental budgeting will be used in the development of a new budget. Pulling out the previous year's budget or financial statements often starts the annual budget process. Then, figures for the new budget are simply based on the past year's figures, taking into account inflationary and operational growth increases. Such incremental budgeting can work when the financial climate is steady, and when the company wishes to continue the same policies and methods of operation as in the past. But when this is not the case, zero-based budgeting probably offers a better approach. This requires that every budget item be justified from the first dollar. This encourages more sophisticated analytical thinking about finances and, hence, about policies and priorities.

Because the largest budget area for a performing arts company is that of production, and because each production tends to be unique, most of the budgeting in this area is zero-based. Therefore, operating budgets might be designed incrementally while the production elements are designed using zero-based methods. Clearly when a company operates under the umbrella of a larger parent institution or has an endowment that generates significant income, a higher level of budget security is added. However, this does not negate the need to plan diligently and monitor the overall budget. Production budgets, such as those illustrated later in this chapter, are often problematic in that a series of productions is being budgeted for the same season. This encourages comparative analysis and also permits more flexibility than if each production were planned independently. Resources can be manipulated between productions—i.e., resources from production number one might be put into production number two—or if there are residual resources from an early production, they might be used to enhance a production later in the season.

The Contingency

Budgets should contain both a "miscellaneous" and a contingency or reserve fund. The miscellaneous category can be based on experience and provides funds for minor but unanticipated costs due to inflation, staff overtime, and equipment repair. The contingency or reserve category should be no less than ten percent of the total budget. The contingency is a hedge against the unknown and is the primary budget insurance against a downturn in box office receipts, canceled productions or performances, costly equipment replacement, and temporary loss of facility usage because of natural disasters.

Unfortunately, some budget allocations, such as those from college, university, and government institutions or agencies, do not recognize or provide contingency or reserve funds. In this case, the organization or department making budget requests is virtually forced to overestimate its costs and thereby create a built-in contingency. Once such allocations are received, if the amounts were not purposely inflated, the recipient must usually readjust budget commitments to provide for miscellaneous and unexpected costs. When every dollar is closely and specifically budgeted, slavish adherence to the budget is a likely—and undesirable—result.

Deficit Spending

While it usually "takes money to make money," it is a peculiarity of fundraising that it may take a deficit to gain more revenue. Many nonprofit organizations believe that if they maintain sizable cash assets and are therefore known as "rich" organizations, they will not attract contributions. And, while it might be possible for a nonprofit company to build up its cash reserves by economizing, what would this do to the quality of its work? The money that comes in is meant to further its stated mission and goals, not to compromise them. The line between solvency and bankruptcy is often very thin; the line between quality and mediocrity is very broad. Deficits, consequently, are a fact of life for many nonprofits. Most have the ability to carry a limited deficit all of the time and a large deficit some of the time. An organization may seek to dramatize its financial need through the press or other publicity as a way to attract grants and contributions. Normally there must be a strong justification for a subsidy before one is granted. On the other hand, if the organization cannot prove its value to society as well as its financial need, and demonstrate the strength and wisdom of its management, then fundraising efforts will seldom be successful. Most donors want to be associated with success and will give to a successful organization before giving to one that is always on the brink of insolvency.

Cost Averaging

Operations that offer a season or series of different productions often plan in terms of average box office income and average costs so that popular shows can carry less popular ones, and expensive productions are balanced by inexpensive ones. This permits a greater range of production than is possible on Broadway where each show is a separate enterprise. It is also a practice that emphasizes the overall picture or season, rather than each production. And it provides an average weekly or per-production-operating figure that may serve as a break-even point for the purpose of paying royalties and percentages, or for the purpose of estimating profits, which are also called "marginal revenue." Royalties and percentages are variable costs determined by the actual box office gross. Let's say that a performer is guaranteed a weekly salary of $2,000 against a percentage of twenty-five percent over the break-even point. If the theatre determines its break-even —weekly operating cost—at an average of $18,000, the performer will earn a percentage of box office income only if the break-even exceeds $18,000, but his or her $2,000 weekly salary is assured regardless of the box office receipts. If that agreed *average* weekly operating cost for that particular week was higher than the *actual* operating cost, then management got a bargain, as no additional payments need be made.

Cost averaging helps to show a broad, general profile of projected or actual costs and revenues. figures are averaged over a series of units, which may be performances, weeks, productions, or whole seasons.

The Variable Cost

In large commercial operations and presenting organizations especially, many costs, such as rent, performer fees, booking fees, and royalties paid to the creative team, are tied to the actual box office gross and cannot be determined until that figure is known. Small professional companies and most nonprofessional groups usually pay flat royalty amounts for performance rights, which are based on the number of performances or size of the theatre; rarely are they involved in percentage deals.

Variable costs suggest or imply that there will be a difference between the fixed weekly operating cost and the actual weekly operating cost for a producion. Basically, this means that the higher the box office gross, the higher the royalties and percentage payments. So the estimated weekly operating cost is not a static figure. The fixed costs plus the variable costs, based on the actual box office gross income, comprise the total, actual costs.

The Marginal Cost

An operating budget is always based on the assumption that the producing organization will present a certain number of productions and a certain number of performances per production, per week. When the cost of doing this is averaged out among all the performances, the resulting figure represents the "per-unit cost" of producing a product. In theatre the unit is a single performance, a week, or a season of performances.

As any manufacturer knows, it is cheaper to produce one hundred units of the same product than one hundred different products. Live theatre's inability to do this is the core of its economic dilemma. Hollywood can produce one hundred prints of the same film for release in one hundred different movie houses simultaneously and all for about the same investment and the same number of employee hours required to produce a single print of the film.

The performing arts, on the other hand, cannot even contemplate such economies of scale. However, there are several ways live theatre may decrease its per-unit cost. One of these, when business warrants it, is to increase the number of performances presented in a given week or the number of productions presented in a given season at the same theatre. Capital, operating, and production expenses remain essentially the same whether a theatre presents four or eight performances per week.

If the budget is based on a schedule of eight performances per week, and the show is a hit, the producing organization might want to know how much an extra performance would cost during that same week.

The figure that answers this question is called the marginal cost and is illustrated in the budget for a twelve-week community theatre season at the end of this chapter. It shows how the per-unit cost decreases as production of the units increases.

Variables in Cost-Estimating

The most common variables to be taken into account when drafting a budget for a theatrical project are:

1.) Does the project operate under union agreements?
2.) Is it affiliated with some other group or institution?
3.) Does it plan a single production or a series of productions?
4.) Does it rent or operate its own facility?
5.) Is it commercial or nonprofit?
6.) What are the general overhead and maintenance costs?
7.) What is the seating capacity of the facility?
8.) What is the physical condition of the facility?
9.) What is the location of the facility?
10.) What is the nature of the production(s) being offered?
11.) What is the number of performances (per day, week and season)?
12.) What are the total anticipated revenues from all sources?

Theatre budgets share similarities with all budgets. For instance, all federal withholding taxes are computed in the same manner, as are union benefits. But there are variables that deserve special attention.

The Larger the Capacity, the Higher the Cost

The volume of space within the physical plant will influence the dollar amount of many budgetary items. Larger buildings require more maintenance, more heat and air-conditioning, greater repair and renovation costs, more powerful and extensive machinery and electronic systems, and, of course, a larger staff and more complicated security provisions.

The Newer the Theatre, the Higher the Cost

Old buildings invariably present operating problems that account for high costs, especially in the areas of maintenance and repair. Poor plumbing and wiring, leaking roofs, and aging equipment often inspire the tenants of an old plant to lease or build a new one believing that it will be less expensive to operate. A new building should offer greater operating efficiency than an old one, but only at a price. A new building will probably contain more electronic systems, more electrical wiring, more plumbing, and more computer technology than an older building. New surroundings and new features can be wonders, but are they assets or liabilities? A new facility, like a new employee, must be broken in—this requires both time and money. Perhaps it will be necessary to correct the acoustics in the auditorium, enlarge the box office, or hire pole climbers from the circus to change the light bulbs in the chandelier. In short, replacing the old with the new can sometimes amount to little more than swapping one set of frustrations and expenses for another.

The new or beginning organization may be more costly to operate because it must spend more on marketing to build a nucleus of loyal customers and inform the public of its location and what it is doing. A young organization will sometimes unavoidably make expensive mistakes: mistakes in staffing, in programming, in production policy, in the choice of vendors. Inexperience can be expensive.

A new building or newly established operation also invites myriad inspectors and officials who may ignore or go more gently with established operations. Labor unions may demand that more of their members be used where nonunion employees were previously hired. Building and public safety inspectors will almost certainly make thorough investigations of the building, and these investigations may result in unexpected costs. Building codes and operating regulations are often more stringent for new buildings or for extensively renovated ones than for existing structures.

However, while a new building may indeed result in higher operating costs, it may also result in increased income during the two- to three-year "honeymoon" period, when many people will attend the theatre solely because it is new. This can offset the higher operating costs during the initial occupancy and give the company an opportunity to match its operating budget to the new space.

The More Geographically Remote, the Higher the Cost

Operations located off the beaten path may spend a lot merely to call attention to their existence and to direct customers to their doors. They may also have high transportation costs for personnel and supplies and it may be difficult to find convenient housing for artists and staff. If located away from shopping centers, it can become a time-consuming safari to run a simple errand.

The More Unusual or Esoteric the Fare, the Higher the Cost

Because the general public is hesitant about what is new or unfamiliar, extra marketing is usually necessary to promote unique or esoteric types of entertainment. Generally speaking, opera is more difficult to sell than musical comedy, William Shakespeare more difficult than Neil Simon, the new play more difficult than the established hit, the unknown actor more difficult than the household name. Unusual productions often require employees who possess special skills or training and who therefore command higher salaries. Novelty, sophistication, or extravagance may also require special or additional equipment in terms of stage lighting, scenery, sound systems, costumes, and properties, and possibly insurance. The extra expenses may pay off at the box office, but rarely unless the elements that mandate them can be justified artistically. Also, if the play or musical is a new work, extra rehearsal time will be required as the writers adjust the script. In addition to this there will be increased fees or commission for the new work.

Affiliations Can Lower the Cost

Often, two or more theatres will join in the production of a play or musical—co-producing the work and moving it between theatres. Both theatres share the production costs and they can be spread over a longer run of the show. While the cost involved in moving the production must be taken into account, as well as designing the production for what might be two stages of different size and technical capabilities, the savings in rehearsal and production costs, professional technical and theatrical personnel and marketing can be substantial. Sharing a production should always be seriously considered.

Three Important "Don'ts"

Don't Spend Income before It's Earned

Most earned income in the performing arts is derived from the sale of tickets. A theatre ticket is a rental agreement—license—that entitles the buyer to a particular seat in a particular theatre, at a particular time and date, for a particular performance, at a particular price—possibly featuring particular performers. Those are a lot of particulars! If for any reason the producer cannot deliver on them as promised, the price paid for that ticket may have to be refunded.

Owing to this possibility, ticket revenue

1.) Should be held until the performance for which it was paid has concluded.
2.) Should never be regarded as money earned until the performance has occurred.

In other words, one should recognize the fundamental difference between earned revenue and deferred revenue—money that has been received but not yet earned. These deferred revenues constitute a production's "advance sale," meaning money that is taken into the box office for future performances yet to be played.

This distinction is especially clear in regard to Broadway productions, because the law requires that producers and their backers—limited partners—provide all the capital necessary to finance the production up to and including its opening night. Advance ticket revenue, which can be considerable, is held in order to pay for weekly operating costs. If the weekly ticket sales are insufficient to cover weekly operating costs, the show is usually closed—or the producers must lend money to the production in order to meet the week's expenses. If a production closes, all money being held for future performances is refunded to ticket holders for those canceled performances.

But if weekly sales do cover weekly operating costs, any excess ticket income is used to first repay the investors who put up the money for the initial production—capitalization; any excess revenue thereafter is paid out as profits to the producers and investors.

As a practical matter, it is impossible for a production to tap into its advance on Broadway because the production only receives the dollar amount earned for that week's performances as reflected by the box office statements. The theatre owner holds the advance money.

In a situation, however, where advance money can be accessed, it is always tempting to dip into it. In large operations, season tickets or subscriptions may be sold as much as a year in advance and the amounts of money can be substantial, and all the more tempting. Only the interest earned on that money could safely be spent. But the wisest policy is to regard such income as money being held in trust and to keep it in a safe and separate (insured) savings account, and to transfer it into an operating account only as the daily or weekly box office reports show that it has been earned.

Most theatres or performing arts organizations commit themselves to a minimum number of performances per production, regardless of what they may earn at the box office—a policy that presents considerable risk. Whether or not tickets are sold, the show goes on and the attendant expenses are incurred.

In the case of commercial ventures, the producer or promoter should have the personal resources to underwrite any losses or find another person or company to agree to assume this risk in exchange for a percentage of any profits.

If the operation is a nonprofit, it should arrange to cover anticipated losses with contributions of various kinds. Few corporations or foundations, however, will long support an operation that fails to earn at least fifty or sixty percent of its costs at the box office. But revenue from such sources as well as from individuals—as long as it is promised in writing—is like money in the bank and may be spent immediately, within the limits of any conditions attached to it. Although concessions and merchandise income may supplement box office receipts, caution should be used in estimating potential revenue from such sources as program advertising, parking lots, or food and beverage concessions. Profits rarely meet expectations.

When an organization or company has estimated its costs and sees that it will need its contributed income plus more than sixty-percent-of-capacity business in order to break even, it is usually a sign that its costs should be reduced, its revenue increased, or its plans revised or abandoned.

Don't Spend or Budget the Same Dollar Twice

There is always a need to stretch a dollar as far as possible, but there is a limit to how much this can be done. Optimism or inexperience sometimes leads people into the illusion that the same dollar can be spent twice. For example, many theatre companies must post bonds with unions before they can sign contracts with members of those unions. The bond may be in the form of cash, a savings account book, or some other security. Although the person or company posting the bond is entitled to receive any interest it earns, the principal, itself, will not be returned until after the production or the season has concluded. And, if there is unfinished business or a dispute between the two parties involved, the bond will be held until everything is settled. Bonds are returnable and represent a cash asset, but they do not represent readily available cash and, indeed, could eventually be lost because of arbitration or litigation.

Sales tax collected as part of ticket or merchandise sales—or payroll tax withheld from salaries—belongs to the government. If spent by the organization, it would be money spent twice. And budgeting for labor costs also holds possibilities for spending the same dollar twice. For example, it may be assumed that one employee can fulfill the functions of both receptionist and box office treasurer, but handling box office and front office traffic simultaneously may prove impossible for one person.

Don't Get Into the Boat Unless You Can Afford to Sink

If a project is initiated and financial commitments are made before there is good assurance that the necessary capital will be forthcoming, a lot of money is likely to be lost, and a lot of reputations damaged. Because theatre is so highly speculative and because so many unexpected things can happen to increase expenses or prevent productions from taking place, producing organizations must always keep the possibility of financial disaster in mind and protect themselves, their investors, and the ticket buyers accordingly. Of course, it is sometimes necessary to take calculated risks. The New York producer may never be compensated for the time and money she or he spends trying to secure an option on a certain property. The organization trying to establish an acting company or construct a new theatre building may never see its efforts pay off.

Estimating the Expenses

Most performing arts operations must absorb four basic types of expenses, and four different types of budgets traditionally reflect these:

1.) Capital Budget includes one-time business and facility expenses, such as incorporation, board development, feasibility studies, facility design construction, renovation, and new equipment.

2.) Annual Operating Budget includes ongoing business and facility expenses that continue over an entire season or year without being greatly influenced by what productions are offered—these include utilities, real estate taxes, in-house staff, insurance, and office supplies.

3.) Preproduction Budget—sometimes called a Production Budget—includes one-time expenses related to the preparation of a theatrical production, such as auditions, rehearsal salaries, director's fee, costume and scenic construction, seasonal or preopening marketing, nonartistic production personnel, and the opening night party.

4.) Production Operating Budget—sometimes called an Operating Budget—includes ongoing expenses per week or per performance that are directly related to the stage show itself—these include royalties, performers' salaries, advertising, stagehands, company transportation, per diems, and equipment rentals.

While a single production company or organization may absorb all the items covered in all four budgets, it may not have direct responsibility for estimating and controlling them. For example, the cost of operating a Broadway theatre and the corporation that owns it is paid by the tenant production company to the landlord in the form of rental fees. But the production and operating costs for a bus and truck company are paid as fees by the promoter or presenting organization to a commercial producer. The presenting organization may control its own facility and therefore control its own capital and annual operating budgets, or it may rent a facility and pay for such costs in the form of rental fees. Or a resident stock company or a LORT theatre that operates its own facility and originates its own productions would have control over all four budgets listed above. Because separating expenses greatly clarifies the planning process, such budget categories are often maintained even when the same company or organization controls all four.

Capital Budget

Virtually all producers or groups that seriously intend to organize a professional production or a company must form a legal entity of some type. This process is discussed in Chapter 1. Not surprisingly, this process requires money and the services of an attorney. Drawing up a limited partnership agreement or limited liability corporation, an offering prospectus, a set of bylaws, or other one-time obligations related to setting up a business will also require a lawyer. Generally, independent not-for-profit organizations will have a statutory board of directors or trustees, with the board having the ultimate responsibility for the financial health of the organization and the ultimate liability for any losses or law suits, as well as the having the responsibility of hiring and firing the chief executive officer. Organizations that are part of a larger entity, such as an institution of higher learning or a municipal cultural center, may be covered under the legal umbrella of the larger organization and may not be required to have a separate statutory board.

Such start-up costs are shown in the capital budget or, in the case of a commercial production, in the preproduction budget, which is the capital budget for the show as well as for its single-purpose production company. Most ongoing theatre companies must also find a more or less permanent theatre space in which to present their work. As discussed in Chapter 2, there are a variety of buying, renting, or sharing possibilities for the production space. Many a theatre company starts out in a modest, rented space and later acquires its own home. So initial start-up costs may be minimal—limited, perhaps, to the cost of incorporation, which can easily be absorbed into the first annual operating budget; or they may be very high because they might include such things as buying and renovating an old movie theatre or warehouse. Or, a theatrical entrepreneur may begin by purchasing an existing theatre and then producing or booking the productions that will perform in it.

The budget related to renovation or new construction costs should be separate from those related to production and operating expenses. The acquisition of a new facility may require a separate public relations and fundraising campaign as well as paying for consultants who are not directly related to regular production activity. The producing organization that is already presenting plays should not endanger its production activity by committing its operating capital to other uses. Eventually, construction, renovation, and other capital costs will appear in the operating budget in the form of plant amortization. If a mortgage or loan has been secured, the payments will constitute the organization's rent or "occupancy cost." Organizations that operate in campus or civic facilities may not be required to contribute directly to capital expenditures. But when financial responsibility for facility acquisition and renovation does rest with the producing organization, then a capital budget must be developed. At the beginning, the capital plan, although based on expert advice and containing detailed numbers, is only an estimate. If it is a new or remodeled facility, consultants should be engaged to give specific numbers to the special requirements that will allow the development of a detailed estimate for bidding and construction. Often, this stage is undertaken prior to a major fundraising campaign in order to provide the visual materials for the campaign and to determine, with some certainty, the capital costs of the project.

Using the hypothetical example of a professional nonprofit theatre company, let's look at sample budgets of the four basic types and then see how each contributes to the total annual cost of the operation. Later in the chapter, we'll examine how this company might also estimate its income to determine whether or not its plans are realistic. The sample budgets that follow cannot provide full details of actual circumstances, but they show the major items and should suffice to illustrate the budgetary process.

Sample Capital Budget
(Nonprofit Professional Theatre)

Capital fundraising drive	$175,000
Purchase price of building	1,230,000
Title search, legal fees, etc.	12,000
Permits, licenses, etc.	7,900
Consultant fees	30,000
Architect's fees and costs	45,000
Renovation costs (interior)	500,000
Renovation costs (exterior)	115,000
Landscaping	64,000
New, permanent stage equipment	562,100
New, permanent office equipment	109,000
Miscellaneous	50,000
Contingency	100,000
Total Estimated Capital Expenses	$3,000,000

Annual Operating Budget

Once the occupancy cost has been determined, whether in the form of a mortgage or loan payments or rent payments to a landlord, then the organization must estimate its annual operating expenses. How much will it cost to operate the facility, including an amortized portion of the capital cost? A successful fundraising campaign may provide all of the required funds, thereby letting the company occupy the building free of any payment for borrowed funds. In a very successful campaign, an allocation for one year of operating expenses will be included in the initial start-up costs. This enables the company to work without compromising its artistic vision. Personnel and staffing will account for a large portion of ongoing, annual expenses. These items in an annual operating budget have little flexibility. They will essentially be the same whether the theatre presents five or eight performances a week, or six or sixteen productions during the year. Like the rent or occupancy cost, the total of all annual operating costs may eventually be amortized or averaged over each week in the year or season, or into the cost of each production, whichever will better assist the planning and evaluation process.

Sample Annual Operating Budget (Nonprofit Professional Theatre)

Mortgage payment	$120,000
Interest	6,000
Salaries:	
Artistic (annual contracts)	500,000
Administrative (annual contracts)	165,000
Technical (annual contracts)	190,000
Security and maintenance (annual contracts)	85,000
Payroll taxes and benefits	376,000
Company vehicles expense	27,000
Utilities	68,000
Insurance	39,000
Legal and auditing	32,000
Licenses and permits	56,000
Maintenance and repair	42,400
Internet technology	85,000
Plant opening and closing	25,000
Office and building supplies	78,000
Travel and transportation	39,000
Seasonal marketing expenses	400,000
Seasonal development expenses	69,000
Equipment rentals	29,000
Board meetings and expense	3,600
Postage (general)	5,000
Miscellaneous	60,000
Total Estimated Annual Operating Expenses:	$2,500,000
AEA and ATPAM Bonds (returnable)	55,000

Production Budget

A production budget contains the one-time expenses involved in mounting a specific production, which makes it the capital budget for that production.

Thus far, the cost of acquiring a facility and operating that facility have been estimated, but the theatre is still dark. A third budget, which would estimate the cost of putting together a stage production, must be drawn up. There should be a separate production budget for each show that is being planned. Items included in such budgets will be determined in part by how goods and services are contracted. If production supplies such as lighting supplies, scene paint, and lumber are purchased annually in order to take advantage of bulk-rate discounts, they may be shown in the annual operating budget. The same might also be true for personnel—including directors and designers—hired for a whole year or season rather than for a single production. Again, the budgeting and accounting system that most helps the decision-making process is the one to use.

Productions being mounted on a one-time basis—as for Broadway and the road— are budgeted as independent, one-time ventures. It is comparatively easy to isolate the cost of each item because the full cost of virtually all items can only be charged to the one production. On the other hand, budget items for ongoing, multiproduction companies or institutions, can more easily be manipulated in order to create a particular impression. In fact, the same figures can and sometimes are organized into several different budgets for different public information purposes: the press, the state arts council, the IRS, and major donors/grantors. The same may also be done with financial reports.

The budget sample that follows reflects the costs for a professional nonprofit theatre that does not maintain a resident acting company.

Sample Production Budget
(Not-For-Profit Professional Theatre: Nonresident, Nonmusical,
Five-Character, One-Set Show)

Fees:

Director	6,000
Set designer	2,500
Costume designer	1,500
Lighting designer	1,500
Salaries (rehearsal):	
Actors (5 × 5 wks × $600)	15,000
Stage manager(5 wks × $425)	2,125
Ass't stage manager (5 wks × $380)	1,900
Ass't set designer	1,000
Ass't costume designer	800
Ass't lighting/sound	800
Ass't director	500
Payroll taxes and benefits	3,450

Rehearsal & Audition Expenses:

NYC studio	2,000
Audition stage manager	500
Stage manager's rehearsal expenses	200
Scripts, parts, and duplicating	200
Rehearsal props	225

Per Diems:

Director	1,500
Designers and assistants	3,000

Company Travel:

R/T from NYC	750
Local transportation	600

Physical Production:

Scenery	38,000
Properties	2,000
Costumes and accessories	4,100
Electrics	400
Sound	200

Marketing/Promotion:

Advertising	6,500
Brochures, flyers, mailings	2,100
Press kits	200
Graphics, design	1,500

Miscellaneous:

Box office expenses	1,000
Departmental	1,500
Opening night party	1,500
Contingency	10,000

Total Estimated Preproduction expenses:	$115,050

Operating Budget

An operating budget projects those costs directly related to the performances of a work after it has been designed, constructed, and rehearsed. Naturally, the production that requires twenty rather than two actors will be more expensive. Musicals and recent hits carry higher rights costs than other shows while works in the public domain—excluding recent translations, adaptations, or revised versions—carry no rights expenses at all. The use of accomplished and well-known actors, directors, and designers not only requires high fees or salaries but also may require other expenditures in order for them to work at their highest levels of achievement. In short, the manner—shoestring or deluxe—in which an organization chooses to produce its productions is the most flexible budget element. While most actors will work for the Equity scale appropriate to the classification of the theatre—e.g., LORT C—seasoned professionals and stars will be able to negotiate higher salaries and perhaps a percentage of the gross ticket sales.

Ongoing theatre productions from Broadway to nonprofit professional theatres are budgeted and operate on a weekly financial basis, typically Monday through Sunday. Touring productions that play split weeks or one-night engagements are sold to presenters on a per performance basis even though the company's producer thinks of the production in terms of its *weekly* expenses.

The production operating budget is designed to represent how much performances will cost, apart from capital and ongoing theatre-operating costs. By isolating this part of the operation, it is possible to compute the cost of extending the run of a certain production. As most standard Equity contracts cover eight performances per week, it seldom makes economic sense to offer fewer than that number. Capital, annual operating, and production budgets all involve fixed or inflexible estimates. The amount spent on each item can be determined in advance with reasonable accuracy. Marketing expenses, for instance, may go up or down depending on the show and the advance ticket sales, but those expenses can nonetheless be controlled and determined in advance. On the other hand, any production's operating expenses often include variable or flexible costs, such as royalties, that are directly tied to the box office gross income and can only be determined once the actual gross is known. While the following operating budget shows only fixed costs, a method for computing the break-even point that takes variable costs into account is discussed later.

No two production or operating budgets are ever exactly the same, because no two performing arts works are the same. The budget sample that follows might be for a non-musical, five-character play with one set.

Sample Weekly Operating Budget
(Nonprofit, Professional Theatre: Show #1, Five-Character, One-Set musical)

Salaries:

Actors (2 × $5,000 & 3 × $1,750)	$15,250
Stage managers	1,700
Crew	4,000
Wardrobe/makeup	800
House staff	1,500
Payroll taxes and benefits	5,813
Royalties	4,000
Local transportation (company)	500
Maintenance of physical production	500
Laundry and cleaning	250
Marketing/promotion	6,000
Printing and postage	100
Playbill printing (commission deal)	0

Box office expenses	500
Contingency	2,000
Sundry	1,087

Total Estimated Weekly Operating Expenses:	$44,000

It is likely that a typical nonprofit company would produce more than one production per season. For example, the company in this case study is planning four major productions, each with a five-week run for the upcoming twenty-week season. The first of these has just been budgeted: a five-character, one-set, nonmusical play.

Assuming that there are no variable costs and that the remaining three productions have been budgeted in detail, the budget summation for this theatre's upcoming season might look something like the following:

	Production Expenses	Weekly Operating Expenses	# of Weeks	Total Operating Expenses	Total Operating + Production Expenses
Show #1	$100,000	$44,000	5	$220,000	$320,000
Show #2	43,000	39,000	5	195,000	238,000
Show #3	83,000	41,000	5	205,000	288,000
Show #4	50,000	35,000	5	175,000	225,000
Totals	$276,000	$159,000		$795,000	$1,071,000
Average Cost	$69,000	$39,750		$198,750	$267,750

One can see at a glance that not all productions are equal in terms of their demands on the budget. The budget of show #1, a five-character play, indicates that two of the parts are being played by high-salaried performers. Perhaps show #2 is a revival of *A Christmas Carol* and will use sets and costumes from storage and have no stars; show #3 could be a contemporary comedy, and show #4 could be a five-character expressionist play with virtually no scenery. But, again, if different scripts mandate different costs, then different artistic approaches to the same play also generate different—even wildly divergent—costs; this underscores an essential principle in regard to theatrical budgeting: the budget figures must reflect the standards and goals of the leading artists involved with the production. This presents a challenge to the manager because it requires translating what a designer or artistic director wants into probable dollar amounts, or the contractual demands of a performer into expected costs. Production plans conceived in the artistic imagination must be translated into dollars in the business office, and this is the point when artistic-managerial dialogue must become one of give and take in order to meet the artistic goals of the company while retaining overall fiscal responsibility.

With all the production plans and cost estimates set, it might be tempting to hold auditions and begin rehearsals. But the projected costs represent only one side of the budgetary coin. A detailed estimation of all income it can reasonably anticipate during the same season has to be completed. It is essential that total expenses be determined prior to beginning the process of estimating income because it is on the income side that adjustments might be made to compensate for costs through ticket scaling and the development of sponsorship and gift plans.

Estimating the Income

Commercial ventures do not as a rule receive contributions; they rely exclusively on ticket sales to fuel their activities and, hopefully, to distribute as profits as well. The only exceptions might be a merchandising or promotional sponsorship, or perhaps a company might provide advertising in conjunction with its own advertising. For example, American Express sometimes provides advertising for Broadway shows, so that its Gold Card holders can purchase choice tickets.

Nonprofit companies, however, initiate appeals, which they hope will attract grants and contributions, called "unearned income." There are many types of nonmonetary contributions—in-kind services, volunteer labor, donated land, corporate tie-ins—that provide free advertising, free housing for visiting artists, and pro bono services from professional arts support groups such as lawyers and accountants. But this chapter is only concerned with monetary income. What are all the different sources of earned and unearned income that an organization can reasonably count on? In the case of a theatre production or an ongoing performing arts group, the primary source of income is the box office.

Ticket Pricing

Once the total operating costs have been determined, moving the ticket scale up or down can help meet the anticipated expenses. For instance, if a star is used in a production, then a higher ticket price may be necessary and justified. The public is usually willing to pay a higher price for a higher quality product.

If the goal of the company is to maintain standard ticket prices across all productions, then extra effort may be required to secure sponsorships and gift income in order to balance expenses with income.

Ticket prices are often based on intuition, what a producer feels a community will pay. And, in truth, it is difficult to judge whether there will be price resistance until the tickets are actually on sale. Experience has shown that there is virtually no price resistance if the public wants to see a particular production. On the other hand, a not-for-profit company will sometimes have a low-ticket-price policy in order to provide the greatest possible access for its community. Consider for example, free Shakespeare in the Park.

Decisions about ticket pricing generally boil down to an estimation of the elasticity of demand for tickets. What is the top price the consumer will pay? How many consumers will pay it? How much are comparable attractions charging? What is the pricing history in the community? Assigning ticket prices that answer those questions correctly will result in optimum ticket sales for the production being priced.

Scaling the House

The diagrams of different seating arrangements in Chapter 2 suggest that ticket prices might reflect these differences: for example, there could be one price for the orchestra, another for the mezzanine, and another for the balcony. Assigning different prices to different sections of the theatre is known as "scaling the house," and the result is the price scale chart that is usually advertised and posted next to the box office and on relevant ticket-buying websites.

Some theatres have a long stretch of uninterrupted rows of seats; therefore, it may be necessary to select an arbitrary point at which the price changes. If rows of orchestra seats proceed from A to Z, for instance, the producer may decide to cut ticket prices beginning at row N. To make such an arbitrary decision obvious to customers and ushers, different colored seat covers might be used. It is best to avoid row I when designating rows because the letter *I* is easily confused with the number one. Many theatres label the first few rows of the orchestra by using double letters—row AA, row BB—and commence anew with row A farther back in the orchestra. Some theatres and ticketing systems use a zoned numbering system to indicate various sections of the auditorium, such as Zone 1, Zone 2, etc.

If there are fewer than five hundred seats, it makes sense to have a single ticket price. Otherwise, prices should decrease for seats farther from the stage. When sightlines are poor in certain sections of the house—often the case in arena theatres that have elliptical stages—ticket prices should be adjusted accordingly. Tickets for these locations are usually stamped "obstructed view" or "partial view" and scaled downward according to the degree of obstruction. When selling a "partial view" ticket, the buyer typically asks, "How much of the show am I going to miss?" The answer should be, "It's a fine seat and there are just a few unimportant moments that you won't see."

Because auditorium and ticket terminology varies from one theatre to another, it is not surprising that many customers are confused when it comes to ordering tickets. How, then, should the various sections of a theatre be labeled? Some terms are preferred because they sound more elegant than others, i.e. "terrace" instead of "first balcony," "family circle" instead of "second balcony." While the fancy labels may be desirable, more accurate terms are probably better in most cases. Almost any box office treasurer will attest that a surprising number of ticket buyers don't even understand the term "orchestra." Suffice it to say that theatregoing should be made as easy as possible. The following are the most commonly used seating terms:

Front Auditorium	Middle Auditorium	Rear Auditorium
Orchestra	Mezzanine	Balcony
Stalls (England)	Dress Circle	Rear Orchestra
	Front Balcony	Family Circle
	First Balcony	Second Balcony
	Boxes	Rear Balcony
	Side Terrace	The Gods (England)
	Side Balcony	Second Tier
	Loge	Second Terrace
	Parterre	
	Galleries (England)	
	First Tier	

Estimating Potential Box Office Income

Once the seating arrangement has been determined and the various sections have been labeled, a price is assigned to each seat and the potential gross is determined as follows:

Section	# of Seats	Price Per Ticket	Total
Orchestra and Front Mezzanine	500	$55	$27,500
Mezzanine	200	$45	$9,000
Balcony	100	$20	$2,000
			$38,500

There may be times when the scale is reduced for early-in-the-week evening performances, matinees, or special audiences, such as young people's performances. The following shows the same house as above, but with the price scale,

Section	# of Seats	Price Per Ticket	Total
Orchestra and Front Mezzanine	500	$45	$22,500
Mezzanine	200	$40	$8,000
Balcony	100	$15	$1,500

TOTAL POTENTIAL GROSS
FOR A SINGLE MATINEE PERFORMANCE: $32,000

A common way to create a lower scale is to make the top price of the lower scale ticket equal to the second price level of the higher scale ticket: $55/45/20 would become $45/20/x. How should the balcony be priced?

In this case, instead of the mezzanine selling at the balcony price of $20, a $40 mezzanine price was created in order to keep the potential gross high, and a new price of $15 was created for the balcony: $45/40/15. The new price configuration succeeds in that all sections are priced lower than in the first format.

If the production is scheduled for a limited run of less than a week, the total potential gross for the entire run can be computed and then set aside for study once the estimated production costs have been determined. But if the same or different productions are offered as an ongoing policy, then a weekly potential gross can be determined as follows:

	Income	Number	Total
Evening Performances	$38,500	6	$231,000
Matinees	$32,000	2	$64,000
Total Weekly Potential Gross:			$295,000

TOTAL SEASON
POTENTIAL GROSS: 20 weeks: $5,900,000

As well as having different price scales for evening and matinee performances, a theatre may elect to increase its ticket prices for opening night, gala performances, weekend and holiday performances, for musical productions, or for those that feature an especially popular star.

The gross potential is almost never reached because of the following, all of which must be considered when projecting income:

1.)   Complimentary tickets
2.)   Press seats
3.)   Discounted season or subscription tickets
4.)   Discounted group sales tickets
5.)   Commissions paid to group sales agents and other salespeople
6.)   Disputed credit card charges
7.)   Difficulty in selling single, scattered seats
8.)   Service charges imposed by credit card companies
9.)   Ticket printing charges
10.) Ticket mailing costs
11.) Charge backs for bad checks

It is common practice to offset some of these losses by adding a handling charge, which in part will cover the credit card charges, mailing costs, and ticket printing expenses. In some cases, standing room or additional chairs can be sold for a sold-out performance.

In the case of not-for-profit operations, the return of unused tickets for resale can cancel out the complimentary ticket income loss.

The following can diminish ticket sales:

1.) Negative reviews in the media
2.) Poor word of mouth
3.) Adverse general publicity
4.) Illness and/or nonappearance of leading performers
5.) Interruptions in public transportation
6.) Interruptions in media coverage (local disaster)
7.) Severe weather conditions
8.) National emergency or heightened security alerts

Given all of the things that can go wrong to adversely affect box office income, it's prudent to estimate only fifty to sixty percent of the total potential box office gross. In rare instances, with a production with exceptionally wide appeal, the percentage might be raised to eighty percent. If the actual grosses exceed those estimates, pats on the back to all concerned.

In states that impose a sales tax on theatre tickets, price scales and estimates of gross must take this into account by providing "net" and "tax" categories for each price. And the taxable portion of all income should be deposited separately into a special escrow account, until paid to the appropriate tax collector. This practice helps to avoid the temptation of spending those dollars for other purposes.

Income Earned Outside the Box Office

There are countless ways a theatre organization may earn money apart from the sale of tickets. These are discussed in Chapter 12, but it is necessary to show how income that is earned outside the box office might fit into the budget process. Sometimes this income is called "subsidiary" or "concessionary" income.

While it has become increasingly important for the survival of many professional theatres, it is nonetheless unwise to count on such revenue when it is minimal.

Just as capital and operating expenses must be estimated in regard to acquiring and running both a facility and a theatrical production, so they must be estimated in regard to stocking and running a concession—although inexperienced theatre groups are often tempted to anticipate the earnings and forget that there are usually expenses involved. For example, a "simple" little soft drink concession might entail the following costs:

Sample Concession Budget: Soft Drink Bar

Capital Costs:
Electric 100-cup coffee maker $95
Double hot plate   50

Four carafes	65
Small refrigerator	215
Large cooler chest	275
Caps and aprons for employees	100

TOTAL CAPITAL COSTS $800
amortized over 20 operating weeks = $40/wk

Weekly Operating Costs:

1000 paper napkins	$10
1 gross stirrers	5
1 gross hot drink cups	20
1 gross cold drink cups	30
2 cases half-&-half cream containers	17
20 pounds of coffee	60
200 tea bags	10
25 cases of cola	250
25 cases other soda & juices	250
12 lemons	5
6 limes	3

AMORTIZED CAPITAL COSTS $40

2 workers at $125 each + 15% tax	288
Total Estimated Weekly Costs	$988

One can see at a glance that, if both hot and cold drinks are sold for one dollar each, it would take 988 sales each week just to break even—which means that if this 800-seat theatre plays to fifty percent capacity for eight performances, every 2.2 customers would have to buy a drink.

Furthermore, sales for this concession will fluctuate greatly because of such factors as:

1.) Outside weather conditions
2.) Changes in the inside temperature
3.) General age of the audience
4.) General affluence of the audience
5.) The nature of the stage production (with or without an intermission)

If the air-conditioning system breaks down, if the audience includes five hundred children or six hundred senior citizens, if the play is a high-spirited comedy in which champagne is frequently served or a serious drama about alcohol abuse, then certain concessions will suffer a sudden drop in revenues. Spoilage, theft, and embezzlement are also common problems in concession management. And don't forget that any losses may have to come out of the hard-earned box office revenue. So before going into the wet goods business, theatre managers consider the alternative of leasing concession space to private operators on a flat fee basis. And even in that situation, a percentage deal in which the theatre shares a portion of any profit with the concessionaire requires almost as much surveillance of the operation as if the theatre ran the juice bar itself.

Only when concessions have been in operation over a period of weeks or, better still, seasons, should a theatre feel reasonably confident in estimating the revenue—unless this is purely rental income. For example:

Sample Concession Expense and Income Summary

Concession	Estimated Expense	Estimated Revenue	Differential
Soft drinks	$988	$700	$(288)
Parking	200	1,600	1,400
Coat lockers	50	75	25
Souvenir programs	425	1,200	775
Estimated Totals	$1,663	$3,575	$1,912

PROJECTED SEASON TOTAL ($1,912 × 20 weeks) $38,240

Aside from concessions, there may be other important sources of earned income. Again, any operating expenses must be figured in before profits (or losses) can be projected:

Sample Income Projection Other Than Box Office & Concessions

Other Earned Revenues (Annual)	Est. Income After Expenses
Endowment Fund Interest	$6,000
Savings Account Interest	2,100
Income from Rentals	23,500
Tuition from Acting School	-4,600
Fees from Artists-in-the-Schools Program	-1,500

TOTAL ANNUAL OTHER EARNED REVENUES $25,500

If the above figures cover all sources of potential income, and if the prudent manager of our hypothetical theatre company plans on taking in 50 percent of the potential box office gross, the income summary so far would appear as follows:

Sample Income Summery (All Sources)

Est. season box office income	
($295,000 × 20 wks = $5,900,000 @ 50%)	$2,950,000
Est. concessionary income after expenses	38,240
Est. other earned income after expenses	25,500
TOTAL ANNUAL ESTIMATED INCOME	$3,013,740

Let's tally all of the expenses so far:

Annual Operating:	$2,500,000
Preproduction for four shows	276,000
Production Operating	
(four shows, five weeks each)	795,000
Bonds (Returnable)	55,000
TOTAL PROJECTED ANNUAL EXPENSES	$3,626,000

Comparing the expenses of $3,636,00 to the income of $3,013,74, there is a short-fall of $612,260.

Fortunately, this is a nonprofit company that cannot only sell things to earn money but can also appeal to a variety of sources for grants and contributions.

Estimating Potential Contributed Income

The methods for raising unearned income are covered in Chapter 13. At the moment we are only concerned with illustrating how such revenue figures into the financial planning process. Fundraising expenses have already been addressed: fundraising costs for the capital budget were included in the capital budget, and fundraising costs to offset operating and production expenses were included in the salary and development items in those budgets. It is only necessary to revisit them if costs have risen above the previous estimates.

Fundraising activities are generally conducted well in advance of opening night. In fact, when contributed income is necessary to fund a particular project, work on that project should not begin until such funds are assured. So the fundraiser is likely to begin work at least a year or more prior to the time when it is hoped that the project can be initiated. While there will be many turn-downs, it will eventually become clear whether funding sources are interested in the project and how much money they are willing to promise. The results of a fundraising campaign aimed at numerous individuals for small donations are difficult to predict, although experience with such appeals lends validity to any estimation.

Contributed income estimations—based on past success and careful projection of increases based on new initiatives—can be summarized as follows:

Sample Summary of Projected Annual Contributed Income

Government	
Municipal Agencies	$10,000
City Arts Council	5,000
State Arts Council	8,000
NEA	4,000

Foundations

    Foundation A   6,000

    Foundation B   24,000

    Foundation C   2,500

Corporations

    Corporation A   125,500

    Corporation B   30,000

    Individual Donors Subscribers   16,000

Trustee Donations   75,000

Friends Campaign   10,000

Major Benefactors   15,000

TOTAL ANNUAL PROJECTED

UNEARNED INCOME $331,000

A sizable portion of contributed income is likely to be earmarked for specific purposes, such as commissioning a new work or a particular production or a tour. Similarly, budget allocations from a parent institution, such as a civic center, a university or a municipal agency, are usually limited to specific types of expenditures, such as office supplies, full-time salaries, part-time wages, and equipment. Such encumbrances, which limit the manner in which an organization can spend its money, are discussed in the "cash flow" section of the next chapter.

Projecting Profit or (Loss)

Commercial managers talk in terms of profit and loss, while nonprofit managers use the terms surplus and deficit. From a bookkeeping standpoint, such distinctions mean little. The bottom line in a budget shows whether a given company or project is expected to come out with a profit or a loss, and the bottom line in a financial statement shows whether or not it did. The following budget summation for our hypothetical theatre company projects a troublesome, though hardly gigantic, deficit for an operation of its size.

Sample Projection of Income and Expense
(Nonprofit Professional Theatre, 20-Week Season)

Protected Expenses

Annual Operating Budget

(Including Amortized Capital Costs) $2,500,000

Preproduction Expenses (4 shows)   276,000

Production Operating Expenses

(4 shows, 5 weeks each)   795,000

Total Bonds (returnable)   55,000

Total Projected Annual Expense	$3,626,000
Projected Income	
Total Box Office Income	
(50% of $5,900,000)	$2,950,000
Total Concessionary Income After Expenses	38,240
Total Earned Income from Other Sources	25,500
Total Grants and Contributions	331,000
TOTAL PROJECTED ANNUAL INCOME	$3,344,740
Income Less Expenses	-281,260
Plus Refundable Bonds	55,000
Differential (Shortfall)	-226,260

The bottom line for this company—-$226,260—doesn't look too bad, providing that the board of trustees and the management have faith in the planning process. Still, no company should start a season with a projected deficit. The goal should always be to have a balance between income and expenses. Alternative plans should be explored, and proposed revisions should be studied in terms of their impact on production standards and goals. In other words, back to the drawing board.

Budget Balancing Alternatives

The basic alternatives to a projected deficit are very simple:

1.) Increase income—earned or contributed
2.) Decrease expenses

Balancing a budget can be tricky, largely because it is tempting to make false assumptions. For example, it is easy to assume that if ticket prices are raised, the theatre will continue to draw fifty percent of its capacity. This may not be the result. Or perhaps the decision is made to produce three rather than four productions over the twenty-week season, thereby lowering production costs. But this makes the dangerous assumption that more ticket buyers can be found to support the additional performances of the remaining three productions and thereby maintain revenue at the level estimated from four shows.

Most budgeting involves a certain amount of robbing from Peter to pay Paul. Money is borrowed from one item to pay for another. But realism must be brought to bear. For instance, if it is decided to hire only two box office treasurers rather than three, can the box office still service customers without a loss in ticket sales? If the set designer is told not to construct a revolving stage unit, will additional stagehands have to be hired to move scenery manually?

Substantial revisions of estimated expenses or income almost always translate into substantial revisions of policies and priorities. Managers and boards must be mindful of this fact when looking at the budget-balancing alternatives. How much financial compromise is possible before the artistic mission and integrity of the project are threatened?

Increasing the Earned Income

The first budget-balancing alternative to consider is increasing ticket prices. A simple raise of ticket income by only ten percent would bring in another $295,000, which would wipe out the deficit. This is a slippery slope, however, because at this point in the process these are only numbers on a page. What is the real impact of a ten percent ticket price increase? Will the ticket-buying community go along with it? Will there be a drop off in sales? Or what if the board is simply adamant about holding prices at the current level? Some alternatives would be to:

1.) Increase prices or sales in relation to other sources of earned income— i.e., charge $2.00 for a soda or add a T-shirt concession.

2.) Increase the number of performances for the planned production(s). This would also increase expenses, but the marginal revenue could be worth it. Additionally performances might be given at the home theatre, at another theatre, or on tour.

3.) Increase the number of productions and performances. This would usually entail the most extra costs, unless the productions were revivals that could use costumes and scenery from storage and, perhaps, actors already rehearsed in their roles.

Some alternatives obviously carry a higher degree of risk than others. Experimenting with alternatives can provide valuable lessons for future planning.

Increasing the Contributed Income

While the fundraising director may already feel overburdened, necessity may inspire increased productivity from this person's efforts. Present donors, from board members to subscribers, could be asked to donate more. Funding agencies could also be asked for additional money, although many of them are locked into annual budgets themselves, which they cannot exceed. New funding sources could always be approached. However, at this point, it may be too late to start looking for new sources of donated funds. While new sources are always an option, the company would have to be certain that the potential sources are real and not fantasy.

Factors such as urgency and merit are important in seeking additional or new funding. But as with the business of increasing sales, the business of increasing contributed income will also entail added expenses.

Decreasing Expenses

Nobody likes to have to economize, much less produce in impoverished circumstances. Unfortunately, most arts organizations, and the dedicated people who work for them, frequently must function under such circumstances. Many companies never rise above them. Doing more with less is a well-known exercise for theatres.

If we look at the production budgets and the programming plans for our hypothetical theatre company, it's clear that many cost-saving measures could be adopted. What remains the big point of conjecture is how such measures will affect production activities and results. Artistic considerations aside, let's make a few cuts, and see how they affect the bottom line.

Merely by not using stars in the first production and thereby reducing actors' salaries to $7,500 per playing week—saving $9,300 in weekly salaries plus payroll taxes—and by substituting two plays that don't carry royalty payments for two that do, the season's costs are reduced by $69,300. Any number of changes and combinations of cost reductions can be fed into the computer and the results seen instantly. Each new set of results will stimulate new discussions between the artistic and managerial leadership, or at least this is how it should be. Each new budget cut will threaten somebody's territory, each will affect the quality and standards of the operation in some way, each will alter the navigational direction of the operation—even if this is perceptible only to the keenest observer.

One option might be to look at the entire season and question each play or production choice. Might some be substituted with less expensive works, without compromising artistic integrity? Perhaps selecting pieces with smaller casts or less scenery might help.

Another idea might be to co-produce with another company and thereby reduce the expense of the productions.

The Free Admission Policy

Ironically enough, the policy of eliminating box office revenue is sometimes the best way to balance the budget. Of course this policy could only be adopted by a nonprofit organization because it is based on the theory that if audience size can be substantially increased by giving all tickets away, contributed income will be increased proportionately. From a per capita standpoint, free tickets may actually reduce losses—a good argument to use in grants applications. For example, if the weekly operating costs for a production are $10,000 a week, and 1,000 people per week are paying two dollars and fifty cents each to see that production, then each person is being subsidized seven dollars and fifty cents. But if no admission is charged and, as a result of this policy, the production plays to 5,000 people weekly, each person is then being subsidized by only two dollars. This is a logical rationale, providing that the goal is not to make money. Also, the larger the audience served by a theatre group—regardless of ticket policy—the more favorably that group is likely to be regarded by potential funders. If some libraries, parks, and museums are free to the public, why shouldn't free theatre also be made available? Experiments with this policy, such as The New York Shakespeare Festival's Shakespeare in the Park productions each summer in New York, show that free theatre attracts hundreds of thousands of first-time theatregoers. This is a phenomenon that makes politicians, as well as government and corporate funders, sit up and take notice.

However, this is an extreme example, requiring substantial financial commitments from funding sources. The danger in an ongoing operating policy of this nature is that when the economy takes a downturn, government grants, sponsorships, and major gifts tend to either dry up or shrink substantially, putting the company at risk.

Two Special Equations

Setting the Stop Clause in a Commercial Theatre License

Most tenants who rent spaces typically negotiate leases that allow occupancy for a specific length of time at a specific rental. A Broadway theatre license, however, frequently calls for a percentage of the box office gross against a minimum guaranteed usage—rental or license—fee. Rarely is there a specified date when the production must vacate the theatre, unless the attraction is booked for a specific limited engagement. The date when the production will actually vacate the theatre is usually determined by the so-called stop clause—or a mutually agreed closing date, typically because of poor sales.

The stop clause is a provision in the theatre license stipulating that when weekly box office revenue falls below a certain negotiated figure—usually for two consecutive weeks—either the landlord or the producer may serve notice on the other in order to terminate the lease. Termination notice must be given within a preagreed number of days after the gross has dropped below that predetermined figure.

What box office figure should be used in the stop clause? If the weekly break-even point is projected at $273,973, perhaps that figure should be used because the producer doesn't wish to lose money. On the other hand, what if bad weather or illness of the star or some other occurrence results in business that is only temporarily bad? The producer obviously doesn't wish to give the theatre owner the right to close the production. In most cases, the Broadway producer selects a figure slightly below the break-even point. The reasoning is that if business is going to be permanently bad, it will probably get worse quickly. If receipts fall to $200,000 one week, for example, they will probably fall much lower the following week. But the producer who must sustain a continuing weekly loss that is above the stop clause figure is in serious trouble. After the capitalization has been exhausted and previous profits spent, further losses probably have to come out of the producer's own pocket. Hence, it is important to set the right stop clause amount. (See Chapter 4, Commercial Theatre.)

Computing the Break-Even Point When There Are Variable Costs

When all operating costs are fixed, it is a simple matter to estimate the revenue dollar amount at which there will be neither profit nor loss, the so-called break-even point. But what if there are also variable costs in the form of percentages, the dollar costs of which can only be determined by the exact revenue earned? In this case, the point at which the fixed and variable costs equal the gross income is the break-even point. Furthermore, if revenue exceeds the break-even point, expenses will increase because of the percentage payments. If revenue is less than the break-even point, then the actual operating cost will be lower than the break-even point. How then can a break-even point be determined without first knowing the actual revenue? To illustrate the equation that provides the answer, isolate the items in a Broadway production weekly operating budget that involve both fixed and variable costs.

The formula below provides a way to compute the actual operating cost, the break-even point. It divides the fixed cost by what may be called the marginal income ratio—the margin of profit that can be gained after variable costs are paid. In this example, the producer has given away twenty-three percent of every dollar that will be taken in at the box office, leaving seventy-seven percent of marginal income.

The fixed cost—$249,500—divided by the marginal income ratio—seventy-seven percent equals the break-even point, or $249,500 divided by 77% = 324,026.

For the sake of clarity, the following figures have been lowered and rounded off:

	Fixed	Variable
Theatre Rent	$12,500	6%
Star	$25,000	5%
Authors	$6,000	6%
Director	$2,000	2%
Choreographer	$2,000	2%
Prior Production	$2,000	2%
Other Fixed Costs	$200,000	
Total Fixed Costs	$249,500 plus 23% of NAGBOR	

Fixed Cost	$249,500
Marginal Income Ratio	1−23%

$$\frac{\$249,500}{0.77} = \qquad \$\,324,026$$

This budget shows fixed weekly operating costs at $249,500. But the producing company would have to take in well over that amount in weekly revenue in order to show a profit because of the twenty-three percent variable cost.

Gross Income	$324,026	
Less:		
Variable Cost (23%)	$74,526	(23% of $324,026)
Fixed Costs	$249,500	
Total Costs	$324,026	
Profit or Loss	$0	

If the total potential weekly gross at the theatre where this show is playing is $500,000, then at capacity business it can earn a $135,500 weekly profit, as follows:

Gross Income:	$500,000	
Less:		
Variable Cost	$115,000	(23% of $500,000)
Fixed Costs	$249,500	
Total Costs	$364,500	
Profit	$135,500	($500,000 minus $364,500)

But the profit exists only after the capitalization, or preproduction expenses, have been paid off.

If this preproduction amount is $6,000,000, then the show must play at capacity for over forty-four weeks before any true profit can be realized:

$6,000,000/$135,500 = 45 weeks

Under this scheme the producer and backers must wait until the capitalization is repaid before they earn a profit even though the theatre landlord, the star, and others earn their percentages from the first ticket sold. Under the Dramatists Guild Approved Production Contract, percentage payments to the creative team are lower before the capital costs are recouped so that the investors can be paid back sooner and begin to share in profits earlier. Notice that actual operating costs of a production vary according to the actual box office income.

If the total weekly potential gross is $500,000 but the actual weekly gross is seventy-five percent of $500,000, or $375,000, then the actual cost for that week will be:

Gross Income	$375,000	
Less:		
Variable Costs	$ 86,250	(23% of $375,000)
Fixed Costs	$249,500	
Total Costs	$335,750	
Profit	$ 39,250	($375,000 less $335,750)

If the show opens at and maintains this $375,000 weekly gross, it will take over 152 weeks to pay off a $6,000,000 capitalization.

To reflect these figures in terms of profit dividends—assuming that the producer is sharing profits equally with the limited partners at a $375,000 weekly gross—the producer can earn no more than $19,625 per week after 153 weeks or just under three years of waiting, plus all the time spent before the show went into rehearsal. And the person who bought a ten percent investment in that show—$600,000 of the total $6,000,000 capitalization—will earn $1,963 per week, ten percent of $19,625. (See Chapter 4.)

Stepped Percentage Costs

The above example uses a simple twenty-three percent variable cost. However, there is a scenario in which the percentages change with the amount of money taken in.

Rent: Five percent over $12,000, ten percent over $15,000

Royalties: Seven percent plus ten percent over $24,000

In this case the rent is free until the gross hits $12,000, then five percent is charged. Once the gross reaches $15,000, the percentage charged jumps to ten percent.

Royalties begin at seven percent and then increase to ten percent at $24,000 of income.

The following example starts with the production budget and includes that of the operating budget:

Sample Production Budget

PHYSICAL PRODUCTION:

Scenery	$50,000	
Costumes	$20,000	
Props	$2,500	
Electric and sound	$15,000	
Instrument rental	$1,100	
Sub Total		$88,600

FEES:

Authors	$6,000
Director	$8,000
Scenic designer	$5,000
Costume designer	$5,000
Lighting designer	$5,000
Choreographer	$6,500
Casting	$3,500
General manager	$15,000

Orchestration	$4,000	
Sub Total		$58,000
SALARIES:		
Equity	$21,400	
Crew/wardrobe	$4,000	
Musical director	$5,000	
Musicians	$6,000	
Press agent	$4,200	
Sub Total		$40,600
REHEARSAL EXPENSES:		
Audition/rehearsal hall	$4,000	
Scripts and scores	$500	
Departmental	$500	
PREOPENING:		
Hauling	$3,000	
Take-in and out	$25,000	
Box office	$1,000	
Opening night party	$10,000	
Sub Total		$ 44,000
ADVERTISING:		
Newspaper and radio	$120,000	
Posters, printing, etc.	$12,000	
Radio spot	$10,000	
Sub Total		$142,000
ADMINISTRATION:		
Office fee	$2,400	
Legal	$15,000	
Accounting	$4,500	
Payroll/fringes	$10,700	
Insurance	$500	
Sub Total		$33,100
TOTAL PRODUCTION COSTS:		$406,300
BONDS/DEPOSITS:		$40,000
CONTINGENCY:		$48,700
CLOSING COSTS:		$5,000
TOTAL CAPITALIZATION:		$500,000

FIXED COSTS

SALARIES:

Cast	$4,400	
Stage manager and ASM	$1,480	
General manager	$1,500	
Press agent	$1,100	
Stagehands	$1,500	
Wardrobe/makeup	$700	
Musicians	$3,600	
Company manager	$1,100	
Total Salaries		$ 15,380

PHYSICAL PRODUCTION:

Light/sound rental	$2,000	
Physical production maintenance	$400	
Instrument rental	$1,100	
		$ 3,500

ADVERTISING:

Print and radio	$15,000	
		$ 15,000

ADMINISTRATION:

Office	$250	
Legal	$250	
Accounting	$250	
Insurance	$300	
Payroll taxes, etc.	$2,100	
		$3,150

THEATRE OPERATING:

Rent	$6,000	
House staff	$4,000	
		$10,000

TOTAL FIXED COSTS: $47,030

Fixed Costs: $ 47,030

VARIABLE COSTS

Rent: 5% over $12,000, 10% over $15,000
Royalties: 7% plus 10% over $24,000

Break-even point =   S = Sales at break-even

Fixed Costs + Variable Costs
$47,030 +   .05(S-12,000) + .05 (S-15,000) + .07S + .03(S-24,000)
          $47,030 -(600 + 750 + 720)/1.0-.2
          $47,030 2070/1.0-.2
$44,960/1.0-.2
$44,960/.8
          $56,200

Gross income			$56,200		

Expenses
  Fixed: $47,030

  Variable:

Rent
Gross income			$56,000		
less		×	$12,000		
	0.05		$44,200	=	$2,210

Gross income			$56,200		
less			$15,000		
	0.05	×	$41,200	=	$2,060

Royalties	0.07	×	$56,200	=	$3,934
less			$24,000		
	0.03	×	$32,200	=	$966

Total Expenses $56,200

Note: Total Expenses: $56,200 is equal to Gross Income: $56,200

Both the rent and royalties are calculated in two formula steps:

Rent: Five percent of all income (sales) over $12,000 plus an additional five percent, or ten percent, on all income above $15,000. In this case, the first $12,000 is exempt—the free rent.

Royalties: Seven percent from the first dollar of income, plus an additional three percent, or ten percent, on all income above $24,000.

After computing the break-even point, one should be certain that none of the sales levels at which a percentage begins are higher than that break-even figure. If that is the case, the break-even figure will be inaccurate. For instance, if the above example were changed to add an additional ten percent royalty for all sales over $24,000, this would invalidate the break-even figure. Many contractual percentages or increases are negotiated after the break-even point has been figured so it is important to remember this.

With a $45 average ticket price, at fifty percent capacity, the producer, unenviably, will need to dig into her or his own pocket to meet that week's expenses. All of the box office proceeds, $53,820, are not enough to meet the expenses of $56,200.

Sample Gross Potentials
(For an 8-performance week in a 299-seat house
with a $56,200 weekly break-even point)

Capacity: 299
Weekly Break-even Point: $56,200

Average Ticket Price	% Capacity	Gross Expenses	Total Weekly Expenses	Weekly Profit (Loss)	# of weeks to pay off Capitol of $500.000	Weekly Break-even as % of Gross Potential at different Capacities
$55.00	100	$131,560	$71,272	$60,288	8	43%
	65	$85,514	$62,063	$23,451	21	66%
	50	$65,780	$58,116	$7,664	65	85%
$50.00	100	$119,600	$68,880	$50,720	10	47%
	65	$77,740	$60,508	$17,232	29	72%
	50	$59,800	$56,920	$2,880	74	4%
$45.00	100	$107,640	$66,488	$41,152	12	52%
	65	$69,966	$58,953	$11,013	45	80%
	50	$53,820	$55,724	($1,904)	N/A	104%

Summary

A great deal of time and effort must be invested in financial planning if the final budget is to bear a reasonable resemblance to the final financial report. Happily, spreadsheet programs make the mechanics much easier than in the past. Financial scenarios are merely financial exercises and "what ifs," but the adopted budget will be a document with a great deal of importance.

Variances between estimated and actual figures will directly affect the tenure of employees, which productions will be produced, and ultimately whether or not the organization will succeed or fail. Hence, it is important to think long and hard when making budgets and financial plans.

When projected income doesn't meet the necessary expense threshold, a particularly seductive trap is to raise ticket prices. It's very easy to change a few numbers (ticket prices) in a spreadsheet. It's not so easy to sell a ticket, however, at any price.

Measured against realistic income and expense projections, decisions should be judged as safe, reasonable, or risky. But still there is no accounting for luck: good or bad. All one can do is make the best choices based on the best information available at the time.

CHAPTER 11

Cost Control Strategies

ONCE THE ARTISTIC MISSION OF A PRODUCTION or theatre company has been set and budget planning has projected the expenses and income that will support that mission, a system of checks and balances should be put into place to safeguard the project. While accountants and bookkeepers have devised cost control systems to suit every type of theatre and performing arts operation, such systems are only as trustworthy as the people who supervise and operate them. Most important is the comptroller, or controller, the person who actually does the accounting and is responsible for the financial operation of the company. It could be the producer, general manager, business manager, or finance director, who, acting as the chief financial officer of the company, will maintain records and follow accepted accounting procedures in monitoring all of the income and outflow of company funds.

The Business Manager

The person whose daily routine is keeping financial records, paying bills, making deposits, or supervising such activities usually has the most accurate and up-to-the-minute picture of the organization's financial health. This person's input is essential on any matter involving the financial operation of the company. A business manager should not merely be a bookkeeper, but someone regarded as one of the principal executives in the company. This person is often given the title director of finance to indicate where she or he fits in the hierarchy of the company organization.

A business manager is typically responsible for the following aspects of the operation:

Box office (if not a part of the marketing operation)
Banking
Purchasing
Insurance
Payroll
Taxes

Accounting and financial reporting
Interfacing with outside independent auditors

The business manager also assists and advises on the following:

Budgeting
Concessions (particularly outside contractors)
Fulfilling contract and license obligations
Contract and union negotiations
Endowments/Investments
Personnel policies (salary, benefits, disciplinary actions)

The business manager serves as the primary liaison with the business community in order to gain and maintain goodwill and trust.

The Business Office

The business office should provide privacy, security, and quiet. Privacy is required because of the confidential nature of discussions about personnel, finances, and policy. Security is an important factor for safeguarding equipment and records. Given the fact that business office personnel will often spend hours in front of computer monitors, dealing with complex spreadsheets, the space should be designed with these factors in mind. It must be well lighted and have furniture appropriate to the task. In no operation of the company is an "ergonomically" designed work area more important.

Internal Control

As a precaution against both errors and fraud, every business involving more than one person should establish internal control. This entails introducing a variety of devices to protect the company's assets, the most important of which is the separation of duties so that more than one person is involved in each transaction. While cash is the most vulnerable asset, methods to protect inventories of goods and supplies should also be in place. Just a few administrators run many theatre operations, so a reasonable balance must be struck between division of duties and effective internal control. The most common internal control practices include:

1.) An annual audit conducted by an outside independent CPA who reports directly to the Chief Executive Officer or the board. This should include an audit of all the accounts and financial records, including the box office, concessions, and endowments. Certified audits can be quite costly. The legal requirement for not-for-profits to conduct certified audits varies from state to state. Private corporations are not obligated to conduct such audits.

2.) Bonding employees, especially those who work in the box office and handle cash. All insurance should be reviewed annually; and, as appropriate, the company should seek bids from competing companies on a regular basis.

3.) Making sure that under no circumstances are personal and business funds ever co-mingled. The business manager should never be asked to manage the personal accounts of employees.

4.) Daily cash deposits in which cash, checks, and credit card slips are sent to the bank exactly as they were received. Cash, checks, and credit slips should be received and recorded by one person and later recounted and re-recorded for deposit by another person.

5.) Check signing should not be authorized for employees who handle cash or keep financial records, unless there is a system of countersigning all company-issued checks.

6.) Reconciling bank accounts against bank statements to maintain ongoing knowledge of cash assets and assurance that the reconciliation is being conducted properly by the chief financial officer and verified by a second senior person.

7.) Making sure that all tax money received, withheld, or owed as a liability is not counted as an asset and is not budgeted or spent. Tax money must be escrowed for later payment to the government.

8.) Disbursing payment for an original invoice to avoid duplicate payments.

9.) Using purchasing requisition and purchase order forms.

10.) Using tax exempt forms when permitted.

11.) Providing timely (monthly) budget reports to other principals in the organization, such as marketing, development, and production, who have budget responsibility.

12.) Never making invoice payments or box office refunds in cash. Use company checks or debit cards for all payments.

13.) Backing up the accounting systems information and storing it at a secure location off-site. This can normally be done electronically by sending it to another computer system or to a company that provides this service.

Comparative Budget Analysis

At the very least, a budget should be examined and analyzed (1) before it is adopted, (2) during the period when it is in effect, and (3) after all the actual costs are known. Nowadays, a program such as Quickbooks Pro, for example, makes it possible to conduct such analyses on an hourly basis, if that is desirable.

Once preliminary cost estimates are formulated, they should be checked against current retail prices and services to be sure they are accurate and on target. Next, department heads should be given an opportunity to review their estimates to be certain they can and will work within any revisions.

When the project is under way and purchasing has begun, a comparative budget should be drawn up to show *actual* costs subtracted from *budgeted* costs and the unexpended balance. Is there enough money to cover the necessary remaining costs? Do the original estimates appear too high or too low? Can the organization anticipate a budget surplus or deficit? Is it necessary to take corrective measures? The sample budget analysis sheet that follows could also provide columns to show "final costs" and the "final difference" between budgeted and actual costs. Original, interim, and final budget reports such as these are sometimes required by foundations and government agencies as a part of an initial grant application and as a final report to the granting agency.

Sample Budget Analysis Spreadsheet

As of: (date)

Items	A	B	C	D	E
	Original Estimate	Actual to Date	Balance Remaining	Estimate to Complete	Difference
1 Box Office Income					
2 Concessions Income					
3 Grants and Contributions*					
Total Revenue					
Less:					
4 Total Operating Expenses					
5 Surplus (deficit)					

* Should include interest, endowment, or investment earnings

Variance Analysis

An effective management tool for evaluating the financial performance of a business organization and its component departments is to make a comparison between actual costs and budgeted costs. Its purpose is to compare budgetary projections with actual costs and revenue, to determine the differential, and thereby make possible an analysis of the accuracy or inaccuracy of earlier estimates.

In large and complex business organizations, management often decides where to focus its investigations by locating the greatest variances from an original estimate. For instance, a general variance report—estimated versus actual costs—might show that overall costs for an operation are currently exceeding the overall estimates. (See Chart A.)

A detailed variance report for each area or department in the operation will show exactly where the greatest variance occurs. For example, the cost for scenery and lighting was estimated at $5,000, but $7,400 was actually spent. The scenery budget included amounts or allocations for lumber, muslin, paints, hardware, and lighting equipment. The $2,400 overage, almost fifty percent more than the original estimate, shows that either there was a significant problem or oversight in the original estimate, or that those who executed the scenery did not follow the original plan. In either case, this now becomes an issue that must be addressed by management. The cause of the overage and those responsible for the project will likely be required to review the process that led to the overage so that corrective action can be taken on the next project.

In any case, management should know the reasons for budget over-runs and any employees who may be responsible for them. There may have to be adjustments in the next production's budget to account for the current overage. Further, it shows that closer scrutiny must be given to each production element, from start to finish.

Chart A: Sample Variance Report (College Theatre Production)

Item	Estimated Cost	Actual Cost	Differential
Tickets	$100	$135	($35)
Publicity	$900	$1,150	($250)
Programs	$300	$275	$25
Costumes	$3,500	$5,000	($1,500)
Scenery and props	$5,000	$6,900	($1,900)
Trucking	$200	$300	($100)
Lighting	$1,000	$590	$410
Royalty	$500	$500	$0
Makeup	$200	$177	$23
Scripts	$400	$500	($100)
House manager	$200	$300	($100)
Sound	$200	$89	$111
Reserve fund	$1,000	$1,000	$0
TOTALS	$13,500	$16,916	($3,416)

Chart B: Sample Variance Report (College Theatre Production)
(College Theatre Production; as per Chart A)

Vendor	Item	Est. Cost	Actual Cost	Differential
ABC Lumber Co.	lumber	$3,220	$3,100	$120
ABC Lumber Co.	lumber	$0	$1,900	($1,900)
Acme Color Co.	scene paint	$175	$250	($75)
J & J Rental Co.	prop rentals	$100	$325	($225)
Joe's Hardware	nails, braces, etc.	$60	$78	($18)
Lighting Assoc.	gels	$1,000	$900	$100
Local Electrics Co.	projector rental	$75	$200	($125)
B & B Fabrics	muslin	$70	$145	($75)
Transfer Assoc.	prop transport	$200	$300	($100)
Miscellaneous		$100	$211	($111)
TOTAL		$5,000	$7,409	($2,409)

Cash Flow

It can safely be said that all businesses are about cash flow: money coming in, money going out. The key is *when*. When will the funds be available? When will they be needed?

If a theatre began its season or fiscal year with all the necessary income for that period, it would be an easy matter to spend that money whenever necessary. But rarely is annual income accumulated all at once, so the business office must plan ahead to insure that money will be available when it is needed. The best device for doing this is called a cash flow chart. It's basically a money calendar or money schedule. It helps avoid unpleasant cash-crunch surprises.

A cash flow chart shows *when* income from all sources will be received, and when monies for expenses incurred will need to be paid out. Companies that do not utilize this type of planning are often in crisis—always, for example, scrambling just to meet the weekly payroll. Cash flow charts can predict cash shortages and thereby provide time to secure a loan, cut expenses, change plans, speed up the subscription campaign, or take other measures that will avert a crisis.

The sample that follows in Chart C could, of course, show the expense categories in greater detail, but it serves to illustrate how a cash flow chart can be designed. It might, for instance, be helpful to show payroll, tax, and loan payment obligations for each month since these cannot usually be postponed.

Most accounting software packages, such as Quickbooks Pro, contain programs for creating a cash flow chart. Recording payables and revenues on a calendar basis will show how much money will be needed when. Most performing arts companies will incur most of their expenses at the beginning of a season or the beginning of a production period. Depending on the particular cash situation, a cash flow chart can be set up to show quarterly, monthly, weekly, or even daily periods.

Sample Cash-Flow Projection
(Professional Nonprofit Theatre Company; 4 productions, 5 weeks each, November through March)

	July	August	September	October	November	December	January	February	March	April	May	June	Projected Annual Gross
REVENUES													
Box Office Income	$ -	$ -	$800,000	$500,000	$400,000	$500,000	$350,000	$200,000	$200,000	$ -	$ -	$ -	$2,950,000
Concession Net Income	$0	$0	$0	$0	$10,000	$10,000	$2,500	$7,500	$7,500	$740	$0	$0	$38,240
Grants and Contributions	$0	$0	$25,000	$31,000	$50,000	$75,000	$100,000	$50,000	$0	$0	$0	$0	$331,000
Bond Return												$55,000	$55,000
Other Earned Income	$500	$500	$5,500	$2,000	$2,000	$2,000	$2,000	$2,500	$2,500	$1,500	$500	$4,000	$25,500
Total Income	$500	$500	$830,500	$533,000	$462,000	$587,000	$454,500	$260,000	$210,000	$2,240	$500	$59,000	$3,399,740
EXPENSES													
Capital and Annual Operating Expenses	$208,333	$208,333	$208,333	$208,333	$208,333	$208,333	$208,333	$208,333	$208,333	$208,333	$208,333	$208,333	$2,500,000
Pre-Production Expenses	$ -	$ -	$40,000	$75,000	$75,000	$16,000	$40,000	$20,000	$10,000	$ -	$ -	$ -	$276,000
Operating Expenses	$ -	$ -	$ -	$ -	$126,000	$130,000	$133,000	$164,000	$121,000	$121,000	$ -	$ -	$795,000
Bonds (Returnable)				$55,000									$55,000
Total Expenses	$208,333	$208,333	$248,333	$338,333	$409,333	$354,333	$381,333	$392,333	$339,333	$329,333	$208,333	$208,333	$3,626,000
OPERATING INCOME (Deficit)	($207,833)	($207,833)	$582,167	$194,667	$52,667	$232,667	$73,167	($132,333)	($129,333)	($327,093)	($207,833)	($149,333)	($226,260)
Add: Loan Proceeds													$0
Less: Loan Principal Repayments													$0
Beginning Working Capital	$1	($207,832)	($415,666)	$166,501	$361,168	$413,834	$646,501	$719,668	$587,334	$458,001	$130,908	($76,926)	
Ending Working Capital	($207,832)	($415,666)	$166,501	$361,168	$413,834	$646,501	$719,668	$587,334	$458,001	$130,908	($76,926)	($226,259)	($226,259)

Assumes a $30 top and a total potential annual gross of $3,360,000, shown here at 50%

SAMPLE CONCESSION INVENTORY AND SALES REPORT FORM

Concessioner

Week Ending

ITEM	Merchandise Received								Opening Inventory This Week	Less Closing Inventory	Allowable Credits	Total Units Sales	Unit Selling Price	Amount of Sales
	Mon	Tues	Wed	Thurs	Fri	Sat	Sun	Total						
TOTALS														

Inventories

Everything that belongs to an organization should be listed in an inventory, copies of which should be kept in the business office with a back-up copy stored off-site. Digital cameras come in especially handy for creating an inventory. For insurance purposes, it is helpful to send inventories of all insured items—together with the dollar value of each item—to the insurance company, which should also be notified when expensive new items are acquired. When the physical assets of an organization are extensive, or when items are stored in a variety of locations, appropriate inventories should be available to department heads who may check to see what is on hand.

The properties department, for example, should not rummage through five cluttered storage rooms to determine whether or not the theatre owns a seltzer bottle. Each department head should be responsible for keeping its inventory up to date. At the beginning and end of each season, the department head, together with a representative from the business office, should check the inventory. Then department heads should be held responsible for all items—within the boundaries of common sense. A master carpenter, for instance, will be more likely to lock up all tools at the end of each day when the cost of any missing tool may be deducted from his or her next paycheck. Even when no financial penalty is imposed for missing or broken items, it is good business practice to verify the inventory with the appropriate staff member before that person receives a final paycheck.

Expendable and salable items should also be inventoried: the cash on hand in the box office, postage stamps, theatre tickets, candy and soda in concession booths, or anything that represents a cash asset to the company. Remaindered items—unsold tickets, unsold candy bars—should be checked periodically against cash receipts. When records don't balance, an investigation should be conducted. A method of auditing the box office is provided in Appendix P. If an organization operates a concession, it should utilize a concession sales form maintained and checked not by sales personnel but by the operation's business office.

Methods of Payment

Once an item or service has been selected, the method of payment has to be chosen. There is often more than one way to pay. Delayed payments may involve interest or service charges that can amount to a considerable sum. Prompt payments may be rewarded with discounts; this is often the case with advertising bills. Other considerations, such as the interest being earned on cash assets, also may help determine when payments should be made.

A Tickler System

A good management technique for being certain that things are done in a timely fashion is to establish a tickler system. For a low-tech example, one could set up a file drawer that contains a separate folder for each workday of the year. As invoices are received, they can be filed by the date they are to be paid. Memos about loan repayments, tax and budget deadlines, and even personal reminders might be similarly filed. At the beginning of each workday, one simply takes out the folder for that date to see what must be accomplished that day. This system not only "tickles" the memory of the person who maintains it, more importantly, it enables another worker to step in and take over if necessary. Most accounting packages have a calendar program and/or an alarm to alert the user to deadlines and payment dates. For small companies, writing deadlines on a calendar is a helpful reminder.

Processing the Payment or "Is it okay to pay this bill?"

When the business office receives a bill, an original invoice, it should proceed as follows:

1.) Check the bill for mathematical accuracy.
2.) Check the bill against the purchase order. Did the vendor supply what was ordered?
3.) Check the purchase order against the requisitions. Did the order request what was requisitioned?
4.) Check to be certain the merchandise or service was received in proper condition. To accomplish this in a large operation, a "receiver of goods" form may be sent to the appropriate theatre employee who must then verify that the merchandise or service was actually received.
5.) Issue a check for payment of the invoice, or file it for future payment.

To the extent possible, get verifications and payment authorizations in writing so that there will not be a contest later for a mistake caused by a faulty memory.

Payments should only be made from original invoices or bills, never from statements sent by the vendor. Paying by check allows more time to study bills than paying with cash. It also allows time to examine merchandise and correct mistakes. While computer systems have removed much of the human error in billing, a careful check of each invoice is nevertheless prudent.

In the future, check or credit card payments may become obsolete as direct electronic transfer of funds becomes more prevalent. This will, in the end, save time in the business office, however the business manager will have to be extra vigilant in monitoring these transactions, and in making sure that there are sufficient funds available to handle automatic withdrawals.

The Petty Cash Fund

A petty cash fund is a separate cash—loan or advance—fund set up to cover small expenses. It might be, for example, a fund of one hundred dollars to pay for postage or delivery charges or to reimburse employees for mileage or food. Under no circumstance should the company pay for such items with box office money because this practice greatly increases the possibility for error in accounting for ticket income.

The better method is to keep a petty-cash box from which small amounts are paid in exchange for signed and itemized receipts. The total money plus the receipts should always equal the amount originally consigned to the box, in this case one hundred dollars. When the cash gets low, a check is made payable to the custodian of the fund to "buy back" the receipts on hand. As money is disbursed from the petty-cash fund, the receipts taken in should be marked "paid" so that it won't be reused, either fraudulently or by mistake.

There may be a need for several petty-cash funds to accommodate employees who must often put out cash for minor expenses. The publicity director, the properties director, and the production stage manager are logical candidates. Or workers may be asked to spend limited amounts from their own pockets and then be reimbursed periodically upon surrendering receipts. Whichever method is used, cash payments should only be made as a last resort and only for small amounts.

Credit Cards

Some positions require the constant expenditure of monies, and paying in cash is either awkward or impractical. Using company credit cards, with individual account numbers issued to employees, solves this problem. Credit cards provide a "cash float"—the time between when the charge is incurred and the time it must be paid—and they provide for better record keeping. Also, it's easier to return/credit goods purchased on credit cards.

Types of Checking Accounts

Money should always be kept where it will cost the least and earn the most for its owner, within the boundaries of what is legal and prudent. At the very least, most theatre organizations of any size should maintain interest-bearing checking accounts, if not savings accounts and certificates of deposit. The safety of money is paramount. Similarly, low-fee or no-fee banking is most desirable. A credit union instead of a commercial bank could provide for the operation's banking needs. The type of bank will depend largely on the size of the theatre operation. Also, the relationship between the bank and the theatre company becomes more important if the theatre carries a "line of credit" with the bank, or encourages the use of bank credit or debit cards in its box office operation.

Any operation that has income and expenses should establish two types of checking accounts, each with its own checkbook, account number, and name. These two are:

1.) Box office account
2.) General operating account

The box office account should begin each fiscal year with a zero balance and take in only the income from ticket sales. All ticket income should be deposited into this account, so that an exact record of paid ticket sales is maintained. In the case of a single production, the final balance in the account should be exactly the same as the final total gross shown on the box office statement. For theatres that operate a multiproduction season, the cleanest way to maintain records is to transfer—by check—the total weekly gross or individual performance gross from the box office account into the general account. At season's end, the box office account should be back to a zero balance, excluding service charges. One fundamental principle should always be observed: all box office income—and only box office income—must be deposited into a separate box office account before it is disbursed for any reason whatsoever.

Ticket revenue collected before the start of the season by subscription or early ticket sales, should be escrowed and not made available until the season start date. A trap that many companies fall into is spending the next season's money in its current season, which inevitably leads to a shortfall in funds the next season. This can be compounded over a number of seasons, expressed as an accumulated deficit, and become a black hole from which there is no return. (See Chapter 10.)

From the general operating account all disbursements are made. It may also be desirable to maintain other checking accounts to handle payroll, payroll taxes, and other budget categories where isolated accountability is helpful. When a theatre maintains several checking and savings accounts, it is good practice to use different banks. This practice helps establish credit ratings as well as good relations with the local business community. In any case, each checking account should use different colored checks to avoid mistakes and confusion in the business office. All checks should provide space to itemize or describe the transaction. Payroll checks should provide the employee with a detachable stub where gross wages, taxes, and other deductions may be itemized.

A separate account for the deposit of all donated income is desirable, especially income destined for endowment funds. This helps keep the lines clean between earned and unearned income, and provides a secure place for endowment gifts that will eventually be invested in long-term securities. This also precludes the possibility that these funds will become co-mingled with operating funds.

Payroll Procedures

A paycheck is based on an agreement between an employer and an employee. This agreement should never be limited to an oral agreement because oral agreements are difficult to verify and are easily misinterpreted. Further, they are problematic if an employment issue needs to be adjudicated. It is always better for both parties if the conditions and benefits of employment are spelled out in a written agreement. This employment agreement then becomes a contract with terms and conditions that the business office can use to write a paycheck.

Special Features of Theatrical Payrolls

Several features of payroll calculation are mandated by law and are standard for all salaried employees in a given state and city, but the preparation of a theatrical payroll often involves additional features that, while not all unique to this profession, do complicate the process. For example, Actors' Equity Association takes upon itself the responsibility for determining a "parts breakdown" regarding the roles and performance functions of its members during the rehearsal period of many Equity productions. If an actor performs two different parts, some special feat such as a pratfall or a slide, or some dangerous feat such as walking a tightrope, the actor may be entitled to more compensation than the base salary in that actor's contract. The same might also be true for a member of IATSE or AFM who is required to work on stage during the performance. While parts breakdowns are not necessary for all productions, they are commonplace when it comes to musicals, variety shows, and plays with numerous characters.

Royalty payments and certain other payments that may be tied to percentages of actual box office receipts are also common in the professional theatre. This almost always involves star performers—perhaps a fee against a percentage of the gross—as well as directors, composers, lyricists, book writers, designers, and producers, who usually receive only fees and/or the royalty payments. Theatres that provided initial tryout or workshop productions that contributed to the development of the work are also on the list of those who might receive royalty payments.

Daily or weekly per diem amounts are often paid to employees who are on tour with a production, sleeping "away from home." It is important to establish exactly where is "home," meaning a city, not a street address. These payments are not part of the taxable wage. Current wage scales and per diems are available on the Actors' Equity website, www.actorsequity.org.

The business office must also scrutinize each performer's contract for special riders that mandate such amenities and costs as baby-sitters, tutors, traveling companions, dressers, maids, chauffeurs, or hairdressers—all of these would also add to the payroll. Other riders may stipulate food services, dressing room décor, or anything else that the performer's agent is able to negotiate. The process of payroll preparation for a professional theatre company can, indeed, be complex.

Payroll computation, remittance, and government reporting is best done by a payroll service, for example, Paychex or QuickBooks Pro Payroll Service. Not only are these services relatively inexpensive, they also remit federal and state payroll taxes directly and they guarantee that any tax penalties and interest for late or incorrect payment of required deposits will be paid by them—provided cash was available at the time a required deposit payment was due.

Direct Deposit

Ongoing companies should consider paying their permanent employees by direct deposit, a payroll method that has become the norm in business. Typically, a computer connection is established between the employer and its bank and transfers are made directly into the bank accounts of the employees. A little bit of set-up work is required in terms of entering bank routing numbers and account numbers, but it's an especially good way to get money to people working on tour. They can immediately access their accounts via ATMs.

There is one negative aspect of direct deposit—once the Send button is hit, the payroll is done and gone. Whereas if a check is drawn incorrectly and needs to be voided and redrawn, a stop-payment order to the company's bank has to be issued. There is no voiding a direct deposit. For that reason, it's best to pay retroactively, once it's clear how much each person is to be paid and the pay week/work week has ended.

Cash Payrolls

Cash payments are rare these days, but if used, a single check should be drawn from the general account for the total amount of the cash payroll. The business office may then instruct the local bank to divide the total into appropriate cash amounts. The bank may request the organization to fill out pay envelopes, showing each employee's name and the amount of salary, but most banks are willing to insert cash into the individual envelopes. Upon receipt of the envelope, the employee should be required to count the money and then sign a payroll sheet or receipt to indicate that it is correct. In all other ways, the cash payroll process is the same as a standard payroll.

All forms regarding payroll can now be downloaded from the United States Government websites: www.fedforms.gov/ or www.irs.gov/.

The W-2 and W-4 Forms

Payroll information is provided from the w-4 form, required by the federal government and filled out by each employee and submitted to the business office. It requires the employee to state his or her name, permanent address, Social Security number, and the number of exemptions being claimed. This is a mandatory procedure and necessary in order for the employer to prepare payroll tax returns and w-2 forms, which show the gross annual amount earned by each employee, at the end of each year. Both forms are available free of charge from any IRS office, or they can be downloaded.

INS Form I-9

The Immigration Reform and Control Act of 1986 and subsequent revisions attempt to discourage illegal entry into the United States by denying employment to illegal aliens. The law requires all employers to do five things:

1.) Have employees fill out their part of Form I-9 when they start work;

2.) Check employee documents to verify identity and eligibility to work;

3.) Properly complete Form I-9;

4.) Retain the form for at least three years. If the person is employed longer than that, the form must be retained until one year after employment terminates;

5.) Present the form for inspection to the Immigration and Naturalization Service (INS) or the Department of Labor upon request.

In the post-September 11 world, I-9 forms have taken on greater importance than in the past.

The Independent Contractor

An independent contractor is a person or group paid by a fee from which no tax deductions are made. The responsibility for paying all income taxes, therefore, falls on the independent contractor and not upon the employer. The independent contractor must, nevertheless, fill out and submit a w-9 form; it is highly recommended that the contractor sign a statement certifying that he or she is working as an independent contractor. Many times insurers of the performing arts company will require that such independents provide the company with certificates of insurance as evidence for liability and/or worker's compensation coverage being in place for the independent. Should such evidence of this type of insurance coverage by the independent be lacking, the insurer may assess an additional premium to the company as a result of the independent not having proper insurance coverage, when required. The obvious advantage of classifying payments for labor as independent contractor payment is that no matching tax or Social Security contributions will be required as they are for other salaried employees. Many artists and consultants who earn large amounts of money work as independent contractors, forming their own corporations into which all their earnings are deposited. In such cases, the fee is made payable directly to the corporation and the corporation then becomes responsible for declaring its earnings and paying taxes at the end of the year. This system often provides an individual with a more advantageous tax situation than working for a regular salary, but only when very large earnings are involved. The company that pays independent contractor fees must indicate this on Form 1099 when filing tax records with the government at the end of each calendar year. Royalty recipients almost always get 1099s at the end of each year.

In many states, out-of-state persons receiving a salary or fee in return for services must pay state taxes to the state in which they were earned. The responsibility for reporting the salary or fee is usually the theatre company's. The state will then contact the recipient of the salary or fee for the required taxes.

Strictly speaking, the Internal Revenue Service does not regard any individual as an independent contractor unless that person is incorporated, such as an accounting firm or a consulting firm, and working for the corporation. This means that all people working under union contracts and all casual or part-time laborers are employees, subject to employee tax laws. If an unincorporated person who is not legally authorized to receive a fee as an independent contractor is discovered, and if that person fails to pay the appropriate taxes, the employer may be held liable both for the employee wage deductions and the employer's Social Security tax contribution. This frequently happens when a nontaxed, ex-employee applies for unemployment benefits.

Depository Receipts for Withheld Taxes

Present-day accounting packages or payroll services accomplish the following automatically, but should the company be involved in producing a payroll manually the following must transpire. A federal depository receipt, Treasury Department Form 8109, which is a record of payroll taxes withheld, must be completed and paid to the federal government by the employer. The monies are paid to the Federal Reserve Bank or to a depository bank at the end of each payroll week. The payment should be made by a check drawn on the general operating account and sent to the bank with a completed Form 8109, which will show the employer's name, address, registration number, and amount being paid. However, for payroll tax remittances over $200,000 per year, the U.S. Department of the Treasury requires that such funds be remitted electronically using the Electronic Federal Tax Payment System.

Employer Identification Number

All corporations must have an Employer Identification Number, also known as the Federal Employer Identification Number or EIN, assigned by the IRS. Even nonprofit organizations that have no employees on payroll must comply with this obligation. The number will be used on such documents as union employees' contracts, w-2 forms, and the like. Think of it as a Social Security number for a business. It is assigned by filing an Application for Employer Identification Number, Department of Treasury Form ss-4, with a local office of the IRS, from which the blank form may be obtained, or downloaded from the U. S. Government website: www.fedforms.gov.

Withholding Tax and Social Security Forms

By the end of each month after the close of each calendar quarter, Form 941 must be filed. By January 31 of the following year, the law requires that Form w-2 be filed for each employee. To facilitate this, an individual payroll record should be kept for each employee.

There are three ID numbers that must be obtained by the business office or the accountant; they are frequently used on employee forms and records:

1.) Employer's Registration Number (EIN)
2.) Federal Insurance Contribution Identification Number
3.) State Unemployment Insurance Identification Number

Failure to Submit Withheld Taxes

The following information makes clear the advantages of an up-to-date bookkeeping system. Late submission of payroll taxes to the IRS carries a significant penalty and interest. In rare instances where the corporate shield does not protect an individual that manager may be held personally liable for any decision in which he or she was involved not to remit payroll taxes. Even bankruptcy does not discharge that liability in regard to tax payments. It is worth restating that at no time should a corporation use with-held tax money for operating expenses. The wisdom of transferring such money to a Federal Reserve Bank at the end of each pay period is that the employer will not then be tempted to budget or use that money for other purposes. The Internal Revenue Service rigorously enforces tax collection and is quick to impose penal-ties on defaulting corporations.

Methods of Accounting

The Role of the Accountant

An accountant or accounting firm is necessary for permanent theatre operations of any size. As mentioned earlier, the accountant should be directly responsible to the producer or the board of trustees. Nonetheless, the accountant works closely with the business manager in organizing the financial record-keeping system and providing financial advice. The most user-friendly accounting software packages available on the market today, such as QuickBooks or Peachtree, automatically record the minutia of bookkeeping and accounting, meaning that the work of the accountant in recording and summarizing transactions can now be done in very short order.

The outside accountant will be primarily concerned with filing the neces-sary tax forms, preparing annual reports, conducting evaluation and related reporting of the books and the box office, and reconciling the checkbooks with bank statements. Where problems or discrepancies arise, the accountant reports these directly to the producer or the board, together with recommendations for corrective measures.

Balance Sheets

A balance sheet is designed to show what an organization owns—its assets—and what the organization owes—its liabilities—as of a specified date. It does this according to the following formula:

Assets = Liabilities + Capital, or Owners' Equity

Assets consist of all the cash, material, and other resources owned by the business to which a dollar value can be assigned. Liabilities consist of all outstand-ing financial obligations the business has at a given moment. Capital represents the owners' or the nonprofit corporation's equity or proprietorship. Capital equals assets less liabilities. The assets shown on a balance sheet are always equal to the total liabilities and fund balances.

Notice in the following sample balance sheet that deferred revenue, or money that has already been received for future performances, is shown as a liability. A conservative balance sheet would also show accrued expenses as a liability. These are materials and services incurred but not yet paid. On the other hand, deferred expenses, which represent prepayments for materials and services not yet received, show up as assets, as do accounts receivable, which is accrued income, or money earned but not yet received.

Sample Balance Sheet
(Nonprofit Professional Theatre Company)

As of June 30, 20xx

ASSETS:

Cash:			
	Checking Accounts	26,100	
	Savings Accounts	31,108	
		57,208	
Marketable securities		396,997	
Accounts receivable		1,054,035	
Prepaid expenses		36,627	
Deferred operating expenses		90,000	
Total current assets		1,634,867	
Equipment at cost less depreciation and amortization		308,840	
			$1,943,707

LIABILITIES & FUND BALANCES

Accounts payable	150,160	
Deferred revenue	1,428,557	
Total liabilities	1,578,717	
Current fund balances	364,990	
		$1,943,707

Depreciation and Amortization

Depreciation is the proportional part of the cost of an asset that has been allocated to a particular period, such as a year. The same is true about amortization, although the latter is generally used for intangible assets such as copyrights, patents, franchises, and good will, whereas depreciation is the allocation attributable to wear and tear on a tangible asset, such as a computer or an automobile. Some financial statements simply show amortization, although depreciation is included. In any case, it is easy to understand that amortization offers a neat way to manipulate figures up and down. For example, an item may be amortized over five years or over twenty, and such allocations can be changed from year to year or even month to month.

Chart of Accounts

Every financial asset and liability, and every type of income and expenditure for an operation should be assigned a code or line number. The numbering or coding system that is adopted should be tailored to fit the specific organization and, once adopted, should remain uniform throughout the life of that organization. The following list provides one manner in which accounts may be named and coded:

Assets: Code 100
To include cash assets, petty cash, accounts receivable from patrons, employees and others, returnable bonds and deposits, prepaid expenses, land, building supplies, and machinery

Liabilities and Capital: Code 200
To include all accrued withholding and payroll taxes payable, insurance, bonds, accounts and notes payable, mortgages, capital stock, retained earnings, etc.

Income: Code 300
To include box office gross receipts, income from interest, concessions, program advertising, income from grants and contributions

Capital Costs: Code 400
One-time expenses to include acquiring and renovating a building, the purchase of major equipment, etc.

Annual Operating Expenses: Code 500
Ongoing costs of operating a facility: paying rent, administrative salaries and costs, marketing, fundraising, legal and accounting costs, etc.

Preproduction Costs: Code 600
Costs for designing, building and rehearsing stage productions, including artist fees and salaries up to opening night

Production Operating Costs: Code 700
To include all salaries, fees, and royalties for performers, other artists, stage-hands, ongoing cost of equipment and costume rental, and, if desired, certain front-of-house costs such as ushers and box office personnel.

This system is designed to complement the budgeting system for a professional nonprofit theatre as described in the previous chapter. If this were a seasonal operation, there might be a final code category named Closing Costs: 800. Each code in the above system can have one hundred subdivisions, and even more if letters are introduced—Code 105-A, 105-B, etc. While coding should be specific, it should not be any more complicated than necessary.

The reason for establishing different accounts and budget lines is to facilitate fiscal analysis and to provide a clear picture of assets, liabilities, income, and costs in each area. Multiproduction operations should adopt a letter code, such as A, B, or C, for each production to be used next to the number in codes 600 and 700. Hence, 721-C might quickly translate into "properties, rental items for *Tartuffe*." At the end of the season, all the A expenses can be tallied, then all the B expenses, and so forth, to determine the actual cost of each production. Subdivision items can also be tallied to reveal the total costs in such areas as stage properties, royalties, travel, or whatever. Any number of reports and combinations of figures are possible in an instant with today's accounting packages.

The Strength in the Numbers

In this day of accounting scandals, there is a not-so-amusing story about an executive who is interviewing an accountant for a staff opening:

Executive: "How much is two and two?"
Accountant: "How much would you *like* it to be?"

When figures are made to lie, it is deceitful at best and criminal at worst. Sometimes, however, figures unintentionally present a wrong or misleading picture. And other times figures are manipulated to present a certain impression that supports someone's position or viewpoint but does not constitute an illegal or unethical act. In fact, *whenever* figures are organized in some visible format, they will give a particular impression that would change if they were organized differently. The ironic thing about numbers on a printed page is that we tend to think of them as objective and irrefutable, whereas they are often highly subjective and debatable.

The person who designs the chart of accounts, makes decisions that will strongly influence the organization's financial profile. For example: How will deferred income be treated? Will production costs and income be averaged out or not? Which expenses will be allocated to which departments? Will anticipated grants and contributions be shown as assets before the money is in hand? Different answers to such questions result in different presentations of the very same sets of figures. And these differences can make the same employee or department look either frugal or irresponsible, either productive or counter-productive, either an asset to the organization or a liability.

While producers and boards of trustees vary greatly, most are result-oriented and most, like the rest of us, prefer good news to bad. This suggests that sanguine financial management should be pessimistic in its projections—always underestimating income projections and always overestimating cost projections; never showing or even crowing about possible grants and contributions until the contract or the check is in hand; always, in short, putting the bad news into the budget so that the annual financial report will look like good news! In other words, costs will turn out lower than projected, and income will exceed the expectations.

Legal Precautions

All businesses are subject to examination by the Internal Revenue Service in connection with tax liabilities; and all businesses may on occasion be required to present their fiscal records—including receipts, canceled checks, and ticket stubs—to insurance companies, arbitration panels, or courts of law in order to establish a claim for theft, embezzlement, or bankruptcy, or for any number of other similarly depressing reasons. Financial records should always be kept in safe and secure places. Unsold tickets, ticket stubs, and receipts should be kept for at least three years before being destroyed, and books of accounts and canceled checks for seven years.

For-profit and not-for-profit theatres are both subject to IRS audits. For the non-profit organizations the test is relatively simple in that it must continuously demonstrate that it does not make a profit even though the success of some productions may result in substantial surpluses. For theatres that have accumulated reserves, which in some cases may look like profits, it is essential that the theatre be able to demonstrate how those reserves serve the nonprofit mission of the organization. Reserves in these cases are usually typified as insurance against deficits caused by any number of things, including a downturn in the economy, a poor season at the box office, or increases in the cost of labor and production.

Annual Financial Reports

Producing companies and performing arts organizations are required by law to prepare annual financial reports for distribution among investors, partners, directors, trustees, and officers, as well as with state and federal tax agencies. These are often in the form of a year-end balance sheet. Usually, such reports are prepared by and accompanied by the opinion of a Certified Public Accountant, although the producer or the board may only see these reports. Even modest community and amateur theatre groups should compile annual reports. The annual report will be a summary of earlier box office reports as well as a statement of current assets and liabilities. It may also include audience attendance figures, production photographs, statements from top board, artistic and management leaders. It may be reproduced on a copy machine or it may be a costly pamphlet in many colors on glossy paper. It may be designed to impress investors or contributors or to attract new ones. At the end of the day, however, it is just a useful business document.

Summary

There is nothing particularly mysterious about good financial management, but it does require a little bit of special knowledge and experience. Many techniques of business management can be acquired and handled by people with no special training, provided they have proper supervision. And the availability and ease of use of current accounting packages makes what used to be large, time-consuming tasks a piece of cake, particularly the creation of various reports, but those packages, as good as they are, are not a substitute for an accountant.

CHAPTER 12

Box Office, Ticketing Systems, and Other Earned Income

THE BOX OFFICE OF THE OLD DAYS, meaning pre-Internet, was the traditional front line of the theatre-going experience. Although the Internet has changed the process of ticket purchasing and distribution, a box office is still the physical place where tickets purchased on-line or on the telephone can be picked up, and in some theatre operations it is still the only place to purchase tickets.

Whether it serves only as a will-call window or as a place where tickets are actually sold, the box office must be secure, well organized, and managed with attention to accuracy and detail. It, along with those who staff it, should be regarded as a primary factor in creating the image of the theatre.

General Box Office Considerations

Design

The design and layout of the box office, even in many new theatre facilities, is often too small and cramped, with steel bars or heavy glass separating the treasurers from the public, making communication difficult. Such elements reinforce the suspicion and distrust with which customers often approach a box office. Box office design could benefit from the example of the banking industry. Although once built like granite fortresses and decorated with locks, keys, and steel cages for each worker, banks have developed a much friendlier and more open image.

Location

A box office should be easily accessible to the public, located so that customer lines do not obstruct the flow of people into the auditorium at performance times, and operate independently of the main lobby or other large areas of the building. This often requires that the box office be located off an intermediary lobby between the street and the main lobby. The design should also protect both customers and treasurers from drafts and outside extremes in temperature.

Ideally, the box office should adjoin the business office or connect to an inner room without windows or public access that can be used for banking and clerical work. One public window or service counter is generally sufficient to service a five-hundred-seat theatre, and more windows should be added according to the same ratio. Two windows can be useful, however, even for a small theatre, especially if there are many tickets to be picked up just prior to curtain. In that case, advance sales will stop until the performance begins. Drive-up windows could be a plus for some large theatres and performing arts centers.

In any case, the process of buying a ticket should be made as easy as possible for as many people as possible. A checklist of other considerations regarding box office design is provided in Appendix D.

Equipment and Supplies

The equipment and supplies required to operate a box office efficiently will largely be determined by the volume of potential sales, the number of people involved in box office work, and whether or not a computerized ticket system is used. The basic requirements for each station or window should include:

> Ticketing computer: if a computerized ticketing system is not being used, then ticket racks will be required to store the inventory of hard tickets. Also, without a computerized system, a calculator, price scales, and price multiplication charts will be required at each station
> Ticket printer
> Credit card imprinter or swiper
> Telephone
> Cash drawers/box
> Ticket envelopes
> Theatre map (seating chart)
> Season briefing book: Ticket sellers communicating directly with ticket buyers should have at their fingertips a briefing book to answer questions concerning the performance, principal cast, and running time of the show. They should be able to answer questions on where to park, what telephone numbers can be left with baby-sitters, and directions to the theatre. Information about local restaurants is also helpful to those not familiar with the neighborhood.

Ideally, the equipment and supplies should be arranged so that the treasurer never needs to turn away from the customer and never needs to take a step. This requires careful design but increases efficiency.

Ongoing box office operations should maintain an inventory of the following equipment and supplies:

Safe or vault
Quiet secure area for accounting functions
Stationery
Box office statement forms
Group sales forms
Bank deposit forms and deposit bags
Credit card charge slips
Credit card deposit summary slips
Lockable ticket stub boxes for ticket takers
Wastebaskets
Paper shredder
General office and clerical supplies

Security

Closing the customer windows and locking a single door can usually secure box offices designed in the traditional manner. If the box office is designed as a largely open space, sliding panels or metal security gates may be needed or ticket racks and other equipment may be designed to slide into a wall or adjoining room. Obviously, complete security is required for ticket and cash storage. Burglar alarm systems may be installed and designed to alert the local police precinct in the event of a break-in. Good protection is provided if the entire box office and the safe are visible from a busy street through a glass wall, in which case lights should remain on all night. Another inexpensive security device is the installation of a box office microphone wired to an amplifier that can be heard by a security guard or someone's nearby. When the box office is closed, the system is turned on to pick up the sound of intruders—low-tech, but effective.

When there are no security guards on staff, a police escort or private security agency should be used whenever large cash deposits or payrolls are being transported to and from the theatre. Most managers, however, stop short at keeping guns on hand. Employees should always be instructed not to resist thieves in the event of a robbery. And, of course, as little cash as possible should be kept on hand. Box office income should be deposited in a bank periodically throughout the day if business is brisk, or shortly after the curtain goes up on each performance, using night deposit bank facilities when necessary.

The Box Office Treasurer and Ticket Sellers

Qualifications

A box office treasurer is a salesperson. Because of this, treasurers and perhaps the entire box office operation can come under the supervision of the marketing director. More often, the box office is the responsibility of the business manager or finance department. On Broadway, treasurers belong to Local 751—Treasurers and Ticketsellers—and are contracted by the theatre owner. They should be honest, efficient, courteous, and well groomed. While treasurers don't require any special training in theatre, they should have an interest if not an enthusiasm for the productions they are selling, which means they should see a performance as early in the run as possible.

To encourage them to feel like valued partners in the enterprise, rather than like prisoners in a cell, treasurers should not only see performances, they should receive copies of all news releases and advertisements, be invited to appropriate staff meetings, and be included in social functions. Stars and other artists who earn a percentage of the gross should be encouraged to introduce themselves to treasurers to increase their enthusiasm for the production. Treasurers must be informed about local transportation routes to the theatre, local parking, restaurants, and even hotel accommodations.

Management can easily train box office personnel provided they possess the right qualities and potential: sales experience, ability to think and act quickly, dedication to detail and accuracy, and a friendly and helpful attitude toward others are important qualifications. Treasurers with previous experience are not always assets. They may resist unfamiliar business systems and styles and, regrettably, their experience may include box office embezzlement techniques. Good management will eliminate any temptation to pilfer cash and tickets that a subordinate may have. Also, bringing in fresh and enthusiastic workers helps keep the overall morale high.

In many not-for-profit organizations volunteers are often recruited to work in the box office; they are primarily used as window or telephone agents. The theatre volunteer will normally have a vested interest in the success of the theatre, will be familiar with the local area, and know many of the ticket buyers. They can be a large asset in a small organization and help to maintain the integrity and congeniality of the paid staff.

Duties

Treasurers' duties depend on the size of the box office staff and the type of theatre in which it functions. In all cases, one person should be appointed as box office manager, ticket manager, or head treasurer, and be directly responsible to the business manager, general manager, or marketing director. A large operation might include the following positions:

Box office manager (head treasurer)
Assistant treasurer(s) (ticket seller(s))
Subscription or season ticket manager
Mail order treasurer(s)
Group sales manager

At least two treasurers should be employed in all but the smallest operations and should share responsibilities related to Internet orders, mail orders, telephone orders and information, customer window service, ticket counting, and box office statement computation. Box office hours should fit the convenience of potential customers, and treasurers should give their full concentration to their work. No box office business should be carried out of the box office, and no other business should be carried into the box office.

Treasurers must be responsible for keeping the box office clean and well organized because maintenance personnel should never be allowed in the room. Treasurers should also keep themselves well informed about productions so they can provide accurate information to the public. It is never advisable to be vague or dishonest about answering such questions as, "Is it appropriate for children?" "Is it a comedy?" If treasurers are asked questions they cannot answer, they should seek the information requested from the appropriate source and report back to the customer. And, as mentioned, copies of all press releases, brochures, and advertisements should be given to the box office customer because comments, questions, or complaints about such material will come to the box office, not to the press office. The house manager or stage manager should provide the box office with running times and intermission times.

Selling Tickets

Selling tickets, by whatever process, is at the heart of theatrical management, producing, and arts administration. Tickets can now be sold over the Internet or over the counter in the traditional manner or with a combination of both. Which method one chooses depends upon the scale and complexity of a given performing arts operation. A one-off production or a relatively simple season in a relatively small auditorium needs not go electronic, but as the scale of activities and the organization grows, the Internet and computerized ticketing and its attendant options will likely be seen as desirable and maybe even essential. This chapter will deal with both methods.

The Theatre Ticket

London's Drury Lane Theatre reportedly issued the first theatre tickets printed in English in 1703. Since then they have served as a convenience for both theatregoers and managers; in addition, they have been the objects of fraud, theft, speculation, and profiteering.

A theatre ticket is a rental agreement, a license, that guarantees whatever is printed on it will be delivered. Should the theatre be unable to furnish what is promised on the ticket, it must offer a refund. It may suggest that the ticket be exchanged or donated, but it cannot demand this. When a series of different attractions is being offered, it is wise to omit from the printed ticket the names of productions and performers but include the disclaimer "program subject to change" both on the ticket and in the advertising. When this is done, refunds and exchanges will not be necessary for program or performer changes, as long as substitutes are offered at the same time, place, date, and price as printed on the ticket.

A ticket may be bought or sold anywhere where there is a market for it, although there are laws that regulate where tickets may be sold, by whom, and for how much. Such laws are especially stringent in New York State, although they are largely unenforceable. If a ticket is lost or stolen from a box office, it is exactly the same as if money were lost or stolen. If the treasurers cannot account for a ticket, they must pay for it. A box office may contain tickets or ticketing systems that represent thousands or even millions of dollars. Treasurers and ticket sellers must be taught to handle each ticket as if it were a hundred-dollar bill.

Traditional Ticketing

Traditional ticketing refers to the selling of "hard tickets," tickets preprinted by a ticket printing house, not ticket stock—aka "soft tickets—used in ticket printers kept in the box office for a computer-based system, known as "point of purchase" printing. Nevertheless, many of the same principles apply to computerized ticketing.

Ordering Preprinted Theatre Tickets

Tickets should be ordered from a bonded ticket printer, such as TicketCraft, www.ticketcraft.com, or Globe Ticket and Label Co., www.globeticket.com. These companies are experienced and can provide the service and expertise required.

Unreserved tickets should be printed with the relevant event information—name, address, date, time, but no seat location. These tickets are much less expensive to buy and easier to sell because customers select their seats from the unoccupied ones, as in a movie theatre: first come, first served. Unreserved tickets may be ordered in roll form, like those used by most movie theatres, or they may be ordered as separated tickets. They should be numbered from one to the capacity number of seats in the house, and ideally sold in that order, if separated. Just look at the number on the next ticket to be sold to find out how many tickets have been sold, so far. Couldn't be easier.

Reserved seating tickets—with specific section, row, and seat locations, known as "variable information"—may be ordered in a variety of formats. When a series of programs is being offered and customers buy the entire series, it simplifies ticket processing to order these tickets in booklet or sheet form. Tickets for the same location—Orchestra section, Row J, Seat 101—at different dates in the series are bound in a booklet or printed together. This saves the box office the considerable work of having to pull individual tickets for a number of performances out of ticket boxes and then arranging them in a series. Tickets not sold as a series are separated by the box office and sold for individual performances.

Most tickets come in a standard size that should fit easily into a wallet. Reserved seating tickets should include the following information:

Name and address of the theatre
Performance day and date and curtain time
   (Friday, November 1st, 2xxx, 8:00pm)
Section (orchestra, balcony, etc.)
Row (number or letter) and seat (number)
Aisle number (optional)
Title of production (optional)
"No refunds or exchanges" (optional, but good practice)
"Program subject to change" (optional, but good practice).

Orders for tickets should be made in writing. The first order for reserved tickets should include a detailed seating plan—map, chart, or diagram—of the auditorium, showing every seat in the house and indicating seat numbers, rows, sections, and aisles. It will be kept on file by the printer for future orders. Other factors to consider when ordering tickets are the following:

1.) Tickets should be notched or perforated to permit easy and uniform tearing by ticket takers.

2.) For ease of identification, each price category should be printed in a different color. When a single admission price is used for a large theatre, different colors may be used to indicate different sections of the theatre. If there are price differences between matinee and evening, or weeknight and weekend performances, completely different color sets should be ordered to indicate such differences.

3.) Ticket colors should be changed from season to season. Printing companies keep a record of past color schemes.

4.) Tickets should be ordered in pastel colors or white. Printing on dark or vibrant colors is difficult to read.

5.) All-important information should appear twice on each ticket, so that both the stub retained by the customer and that retained by the theatre are the same.

6.) Ticket takers should tear the ticket so that three-fourths of the ticket goes to the customer; the shorter portion into the box.

Audit Stubs

The ticket samples that follow show that tickets may be ordered with perforated, detachable portions (or stubs). These may be left on the ticket for customers to use for parking

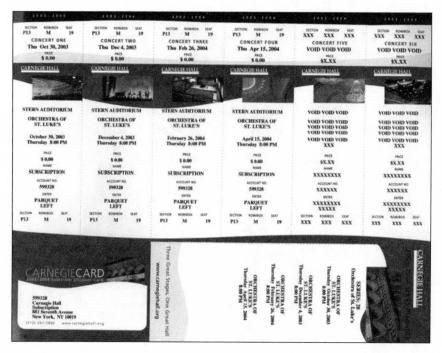

Example of series ticket with subscriber discount card and series reminder card.

PINEAPPLE HEIGHTS THEATRE 222 Pineapple Drive	PINEAPPLE HEIGHTS THEATRE 222 Pineapple Drive
Location	Location ....
Row	Row ....
Seat	Seat ....
Date	Date ....
Price	Price ....
Number 2901	Number 2901

Example of hardwood ticket.

or coatroom services, or they may be removed by the box office when the ticket is sold. In the latter instance, the audit stub serves as a record of ticket sales. When the ticket is sold, the stub is placed in a locked box and all stubs are tallied at the end of the day and checked against window income. This system, however, makes ticket refunds, exchanges, and discounts very cumbersome. Also, after repeated handling by treasurers, audit stubs tend to loosen and fall off. As a practical matter, audit stubs have become obsolete. Computerized ticket-selling systems provide all necessary ticket sales data, so there is no need to count stubs.

Left to right, examples of a softwood ticket, a single audit stub ticket, and a ticket envelope.

Hardwood

A hardwood ticket is a numbered blank form on which authorized managers or treasurers may fill in the appropriate seating information to issue to the customer in lieu of an actual ticket. Hardwood tickets may be issued for standing room or additional chairs, or when a customer claims to have lost a ticket. This should not be issued unless there is a record of the customer's name and purchase. In this latter case, it would be wise to print a disclaimer on the pass that "this is not a ticket of admission and will be revoked if the actual ticket is presented."

For control purposes, only one or two people should be authorized to issue hardwood; they must always record the names of the recipients and the performance information before actually giving out any replacement ticket.

Deadwood

Deadwood is the term used for all unsold tickets that remain after the performance for which they were valid. In the event that actual tickets are substituted by hardwood, the actual tickets then become the deadwood—representing "dead," or unsold, seats that have been assigned but not paid for—or paid for at a different price. When such transactions occur, the actual tickets must be placed in an envelope and marked "dead" so there will be no possibility of selling them.

Deadwood has been made all but obsolete, however, with computer ticketing systems, which print tickets on an as-needed basis. Unsold tickets or, more accurately, locations—J 6-14, for example—will remain as unsold in the electronic computer inventory for that performance.

Selling the Ticket

Before a box office is open to the public, it should be prepared to operate in the most efficient manner. If it has been closed for a substantial amount of time, it should be thoroughly cleaned and dusted; all tickets, correspondence, and other items not related to
current operations should be removed; price charts and multiplication charts should be
drawn up in addition to seating plans and other necessary forms.

After the tickets have been ordered and received, ticket boxes should be lined up in
chronological order and checked against the ticket confirmation order sheet for accuracy
of dates, colors, prices, and numbering. Once tickets have arrived in the box office,
nobody except the people bonded with the insurance company should be allowed to cross
the threshold, and the room must be kept either locked or staffed from then on.

Before placing tickets in the racks, the treasurers should pull all permanent locations, or all sets of tickets that are to be withheld from sale to the general public. These
may include:

1.) House seats: seats held for the use of the landlord or producer or company as authorized.

2.) Press seats: seats for opening nights and other performances as authorized
by the press agent or publicity director.

3.) Dead seats: seats that may not be used at all because they have obstructed
views or because they have been removed to make space for musicians or
some other purpose.

4.) Agency seats: seats permanently assigned to be sold by ticket agents,
which are paid for by the agency or released for general sale at a specified
time prior to each performance.

5.) Special seats: tickets held until a specified time by the star, the director, or
others and to be paid for by them or by the persons authorized to claim them.

A master seating plan should be drawn up to indicate those seats that have been
pulled, or removed from general sale, as permanent locations. Most of these should be
located in the first twelve rows and on aisles in the orchestra section; they should be
grouped in twos and fours. They should also be somewhat scattered, so if most of them
are unoccupied at a given performance, they will not leave a noticeable block of empty seats.

After pulling permanent locations, series or subscription seats may be assigned, if
tickets are sold in this manner. Series ticket buyers should be given the seats of their
choice whenever possible and, also, the same seat numbers should be recorded for easy
access, in case a customer misplaces the ticket or wishes to exchange it at some point.
This record also serves as a basis for processing renewal orders and for serving as a list of
most favored patrons.

Once season tickets, permanent locations, and advance theatre party orders have been pulled from the ticket boxes, then the tickets are "racked," and the box office is ready to open to the general public.

Helping Make Up the Customer's Mind

Few people approach a box office knowing exactly where they wish to sit. Their uncertainty is compounded when they are unfamiliar with the layout of the auditorium. For such reasons, a diagram of the auditorium should be displayed near the box office where customers can study it. Equally customer-friendly is to have a seating chart in the box office so that the ticket seller can point out to the buyer the locations available.

Small producing organizations that offer only a few performances of each production might consider adopting what the airlines used in the precomputer era in regard to seat selection and maintain one seating chart for each performance. As tickets are sold, they are crossed off on the chart and thereby permit both treasurers and customers to see the unsold seats at a glance.

Treasurers and ticket sellers should be courteous but firm when discussing seating availability. If, for example, the treasurer asks, "Where would you like to sit?" a long discussion will probably ensue. If, on the other hand, the treasurer says, "I can give you two excellent seats in the tenth row center," the transaction will proceed more quickly. While treasurers should not mislead customers about seating locations, they should attempt to sell the highest-priced tickets. Hence, when the customer asks, "Do you have three for tonight?" the answer might be, "Yes, I can give you three nice seats in the orchestra," with no mention of lower-priced balcony seats unless the customer requests such tickets. When quoting ticket prices, treasurers should always quote the highest-priced ones last, since that is the figure the customer will recall first.

Once the permanent locations and group orders have been put aside, tickets should be sold on a first-come, first-served basis. Customers should be discouraged from walking into the auditorium to study seating possibilities. The theatre may be poorly lighted, and accidents could occur, or the theatre may not have been cleaned after the previous performance, or a rehearsal may be in progress. This practice also prolongs ticket transactions. After all, the customer is going to occupy a theatre seat for only a few hours, although many behave as if they were going to build a house on the site.

Dressing the House

When it appears that a performance is not going to sell out, the treasurer should scatter the customers throughout each section rather than pack them together. Fifty people scattered throughout ten rows appear to be a much larger audience than fifty people squeezed into five rows. Also, when there are empty seats, patrons will move themselves for greater comfort. When dressing the house, however, treasurers should not scatter the audience so much that the feeling of audience is destroyed, as this will diminish a unified, group response to the performance.

Papering the House

A house that is "papered" is one in which a number of seats have been given away. Some producers and managers feel that when ticket sales are poor, it is better to fill the house with nonpaying guests than to have many empty seats. Others believe this policy will reduce the number of paying customers in the long run, because it may give the impression that business is bad because the production is bad. It's a choice; one is neither right nor wrong.

Some tickets must be given away for legitimate business purposes—to the press and important visitors, for example. If local businesses display a theatre's promotional material or provide the theatre with free or discounted services, free tickets might be a reasonable exchange. Nonetheless, comps—complimentary tickets—should be given out very sparingly and selectively, and when possible, they should be limited to performances that are unlikely to sell out. It is unadvisable to give away those tickets that you can sell.

When the decision is made to paper a house, the theatre should look for individuals and groups who can't afford to buy tickets, who are unlikely to buy tickets or who don't reside in the local community. Comps should also be given out with an eye to their publicity value and the good they might accomplish in terms of community relations. For example, inviting all the office workers from a nearby corporation or college might create favorable word or mouth that could stimulate their bosses to buy seats. City or county workers can be good targets for papering, too. Or members of the town police department might be given comps just to insure that they will know where the theatre is. Among other groups and institutions a theatre may contact when giving away blocks of seats are senior citizens, noncommissioned military personnel, hospital outpatients, schools and camps, Boy Scouts, or Girl Scouts. If papering, it is always a good idea to thank cast and crew and others who have worked on a production with comps.

Making Change and Handling Cash

Other than using major credit cards, a box office should not extend credit or allow tickets to be charged to a so-called house account. An exception to this practice includes the case of a box office that accepts ticket vouchers from authorized ticket agencies for which it is paid later. It may also extend short-term credit to an organization that has agreed to sell a large block of tickets, and it may permit actors and other salaried employees to take tickets, the price of which will later be deducted from their paychecks. Another exception is the "company charge," when the tickets will be paid by the production. This can only be done with the company manager or producer's prior approval. But, in general, the fewer credits allowed, the fewer mistakes and problems.

Personal checks from customers may be accepted with proper identification. Similarly, traveler's checks and money orders may be accepted with proper identification. Other helpful practices include:

1.)   Releasing tickets to the customer only after payment has been received;

2.) Leaving any cash payment on the counter until change has been made and checked by the customer;

3.) Posting a sign next to the box office window that reads, "Check your tickets and your change—no refunds or exchanges";

4.) Training treasurers to look at a price multiplication chart every time a total ticket price is quoted or entered into a cash register.

Sample Ticket Multiplication Chart

Number of Tickets

1	2	3	4	5	6	7	8	9
35.00	70.00	105.00	140.00	175.00	210.00	245.00	280.00	315.00
30.00	60.00	90.00	120.00	150.00	180.00	210.00	240.00	270.00
28.50	57.00	85.50	114.00	142.50	171.00	199.50	228.00	256.50
22.00	44.00	66.00	88.00	110.00	132.00	154.00	176.00	198.00

Telephone and Credit Card Sales

Most professional theatres can easily arrange to institute a credit card system of payment through their local bank, which will supply any necessary charge slips and deposit-summary forms plus, for a small deposit, the imprinting machine. The bank will credit the theatre's account with the credit card sales and will also deduct a percentage of such sales—usually four-to-six percent, depending on the credit card company. The service charge percentage decreases if sales volume reaches a specified amount. Automated credit card systems allow instant verification by simply keying in—or swiping—the card-holder's number and the transaction amount.

Accepting credit cards for telephone and fax orders gives the customer a secured reservation that does not need to be claimed until curtain time, and it gives the theatre the income even if those tickets are never claimed. Tickets ordered with credit cards over the phone are best mailed to the customer if time permits; this reduces traffic at the window at performance time.

Taking Ticket Orders

Operations should accept as few unpaid advance ticket reservations as possible, although this may be impossible without the ability to make credit card purchases over the phone. Looking at a large number of to-be-paid reservations can be very disconcerting as curtain time approaches. Will they or won't they actually be picked up?

As a general rule, at least ten percent of all unpaid reservations will never be claimed; and, when the weather suddenly turns bad, or events command public attention, that percentage can be higher. Therefore, customers should be required to pick up reservations as far in advance of the performance as possible-an hour, a day, a week, depending on when the reservations are made.

The higher the demand for tickets, the more stringent the pick-up policy should be. It is a difficult feat to sell every seat in the house and this may even require taking more reservations than there are tickets available, although this is a risky practice. To sell every ticket, or "go clean," inevitably requires some couples or parties of theatregoers to accept seats separated from each other, or it may involve selling some seats that offer a limited view. While treasurers should be honest about selling such locations, their sales abilities are of particular importance in selling those last ten or twelve tickets that make it possible to put up the SRO sign.

All ticket orders and reservation envelopes should carry the following information:

Name and address of theatre
Customer's name and initials
Performance date
Matinee or evening performance
Number of tickets being held
Price per ticket
Time when customer was told to claim tickets
Paid or due, or unpaid amount

Theatres with inexperienced treasurers and ticket sellers should order ticket envelopes with a preprinted form on the face, so that crucial information is not omitted. Ticket envelopes may be ordered from general printing companies or from ticket printing companies, which may provide them without charge if permitted to display their advertising on them. Or the theatre may sell such advertising space itself or print its own ad copy on the envelopes.

Unclaimed, paid tickets held at the box office should never be resold. They are held forever. However, as curtain time draws near, it might be wise to check unclaimed tickets—especially blocks of tickets—that remain in the box office against whatever records exist, to be certain that there was no error in pulling the tickets. It is best if a cell phone number for a group contact person is in the files and a call can be made to clear up any mystery.

Box office telephones should be answered promptly and courteously. Transactions should be brief but clear. As many telephone lines as required to handle customer calls should be installed in the box office. To avoid the risk of taking orders and then misplacing them, there should be no extensions outside the box office. An answering machine or voice mail can be used to provide ticket information when the box office is closed. When a large portion of the audience comes from outside the theatre's telephone area code, a toll-free number should be made available.

Mail Orders

Although mail orders have effectively been replaced by telephone sales and Internet sales, they do occur. As with all box office business, mail orders should be double-checked, preferably by two different people. The marketing department should always consult with the box office staff when designing mail order forms for brochures and newspaper ads, to be certain the information being requested is sufficient, correct, and efficiently presented.

Customers should be directed to include a stamped, self-addressed envelope if they wish to have their tickets mailed to them. Mail order correspondence should only be opened and processed in the box office or an adjacent workroom to avoid losing or misplacing orders. All pertinent information should be written in red ink on the order form or letter; this should include the price, number of tickets, total amount, method of payment, performance date, matinee or evening, seat locations, and whether tickets were held at the box office or mailed and on what date. This should be done even when the customer has already provided such information. All correspondence and order forms should be filed where they are readily available to the box office. Mistakes and complaints about mail orders will occur and, most likely, will occur during the busy rush just before curtain when treasurers have little time to rummage through ill-kept records and files.

Season Tickets/Series Tickets/Subscriptions

Because it is easier and less expensive to sell one hundred tickets once, than to sell one ticket one hundred times, any system that encourages multiple tickets per order is desirable. The more tickets sold in a single transaction the better. When a theatre offers a season of nonrepeating productions, each playing the same number of performances on a uniform schedule of days and times, the business of selling a series ticket is simple. The customer merely selects a day and performance time and buys a ticket for the same seat for each production in the season.

But when several different attractions are presented, as in a festival, or when performances are scattered unevenly over a long period of time, then confusion is bound to result. Should the theatre select an arbitrary number of performances to comprise a series, or should the customer be allowed the freedom to choose? When the theatre selects the dates in each series, it can boost the sales for less-popular productions by including these in a series with a blockbuster.

When a series of performances extends over a long period, it is likely for customers to experience changes in their plans. A liberal policy of ticket exchange may solve this problem to the customers' satisfaction. Or customers may be invited to give tickets they can't use back to the box office as a tax-deductible donation. Ideally, the box office then sells them again and earns a bonus, essentially selling the same set of tickets twice. Technically, the income for the money from the second sale is a contribution by the customer to the organization. There may be a problem for the donor, however, because the IRS may demand proof that the seat was actually sold—a difficulty when the house is not sold out. Some theatres sell an open series that permits customers to select specific tickets for each production up to twenty-four hours prior to the performance if tickets are still available. Although plans like this are attractive to ticket-buyers, fulfilling them can be a nightmare and the last thing the customer wants to hear is that the request cannot be satisfied. It is better to sell specific seats to specific performances.

Group Sales

Most operations of any size and permanence obtain much of their business from theatre parties or groups. These may be drawn from schools, clubs, corporations, or special interest groups. They may be organized for purely social reasons; or in order to raise money for some cause or purpose, in which case they are called "benefits," and a tax-deductible donation is added to the ticket price and eventually paid, after expenses, to the beneficiary in question. In major theatre cities, there are group sales agencies or companies that serve theatre group and party clients as brokers in arranging for blocks of tickets and, perhaps, other matters such as dinner reservations, chartered buses and lodging, or a meet-and-greet with the cast following the performance.

Theatres court agents by inviting them to performances—sometimes paying their expenses to see a performance in another city prior to its local engagement. And many tour operators involved in the tourist industry put together packaged tours. These may be bus companies, airline companies, or travel agencies, and they, too, should be contacted by alert marketing directors in order to convince them to include a theatre performance in local tours or, at least, offer it at extra cost to the tour participants.

Most multiple ticket sales, however, result from the efforts of a group sales manager who receives promotional support materials from the marketing department and ticket service from the box office. Group sales work in the theatre requires coordinated efforts as well as a coordinated policy that clarify such matters as which shows or performances, if any, can be offered at discounted ticket prices, which can be offered for groups at full price, which groups should be approached for which productions, and how the agreement between the theatre and the group should be formalized. The sample group sales contract that follows provides a typical model.

It is important to have a clear payment and change policy regarding group sales contracts. What are the payment terms—how much is due upon signing and when is the balance due? When will unpaid group contracts be cancelled? Will an agent be able to increase or decrease the number of tickets on a contract? If so, by what date? By how many?

Ticket Agencies

The theatre may operate a ticket agency, staffed by theatre employees, or independent agencies may be selected by the theatre to serve as authorized ticket outlets. Ticket agencies in many states must obtain a special license from the city or state in which they operate and must conform to a number of laws and regulations. In New York the licensed agent is permitted to charge the customer a service fee over the face value of the ticket—the same fee regardless of the ticket price.

Sample Group Sales Contract

Account #:	xxx		Performance:	*The Show*
Organization:	Multi-Cultural Development		Day/Date/Time:	Friday, November 14, 20xx, 8:00pm
Contact:			Order Id:	198975
Address:	555 Fifth Street		Space Reserved:	
City, State, Zip	Kokomo		Type of Reception:	
Day Phone:			Notes:	
Evening Phone:				
E-mail:			Billing Info:	
Fax:			Corporate Sponsors	Yes No

Reservation Requested   Full Price

Total # of Tickets	Zone	Public
20	1st	$26.00

Discount Price

Group	$23.40	
Student*	$22.10	$442.00

*Age 5–high school and full-time college students w/ID

Once all tickets have been received, all group sales are final, nonrefundable, and cannot be exchanged. There must be twenty tickets total to qualify for a group discount (when applicable) on public tickets. A nonrefundable deposit of **$0.00** is due by n/a.
Seating will be released or charged to your credit card if we do not receive payment by n/a.

Final Ticket Counts

# of Tickets	Zone	Price
Group		
Stu Group		
Public		

Settlement Total	Total $

		Received On
$5 processing fee		
Deposit		
Final Payment		

Make check payable to: State University.

Please do not send multiple checks for deposit and final payment.

Final Balance Due: Sept. 30, 20xx   JVE 21-3130
                                            912
                              Dep. P.A.F.P

Seat Locations	H 75-82	J 75-80
Box Office Use Only	K 75-80	

Order entered by GLA   9/11/200x

Accounting for the Tickets

Ticket Stubs and Deadwood

Before each performance the ticket taker should be provided with an empty, locked box into which all the stubs can be deposited. The shorter portion of the ticket should be placed in the box, the longer given back to the customer.

The deadwood—unsold tickets remaining in the box office after each curtain time—have to be used to determine actual ticket sales; they are subtracted from the capacity of seats at respective prices, and the difference is entered on the box office statement as the number sold. The ticket-stub count should correspond closely to this number, although it is common for a few ticket holders not to show up for any given performance.

Obviously, the total deadwood and stubs should never exceed the capacity. Tickets should be recounted and statements rechecked until all discrepancies have been resolved. Stubs and deadwood should be counted and banded in piles of fifty or one hundred soon after the curtain goes up. The stub count may or may not appear on the box office statement, depending on the amount of information desired. Each count and computation should be done by at least two people working independently of each other until both can agree on the results. When the statement has been finalized, the stubs and dead tickets should be placed in a box or bag, labeled, and stored in a safe place for at least two years.

Discounted and Complimentary Tickets (Comps)

The fewer discounts or "specials" that are offered, the better: less chance for mistakes at the box office. Treasurers should keep a written record of all discounts and comps that are issued. When the statement is being computed, this record is compared against all the signed house orders for complimentary and discounted tickets that were given to the box office by the producer, manager, or press agent. Box office personnel, of course, should never be authorized to issue either comps or discounted seats without a written order, which should be kept and stored with the tickets. All complimentary ticket locations, along with the name of the person ordering them and the recipients, should be written on one or more Pass Lists and signed by the various parties in position of authority: theatre manager, producer, company manager, treasurer. (See Appendix N.)

Box Office Reports

The theatre might find several types of reports necessary. These might include:

1.) Master Statement
A Master Statement shows the complete and total number of seats available for sale at each price and the total potential gross per performance.

2.) Box Office Statement
A Box Office Statement is a report that shows the final accounting of tickets sold for a particular performance. Copies of the statement are usually submitted to the producer, the business manager, and the accountant. (See Box Office Statement: Appendix O.) It also shows any adjustments to the gross income, such as credit card commissions, agency sales commissions, group sales commissions, subscription discounts, etc. After all deductions from gross sales, the resulting figure is NAGBOR: Net Adjusted Gross Box Office Receipts. That is the figure upon which all royalty payments should be made.

3.) Daily Wrap
The Daily Wrap shows how much money was taken into the box office that day. It includes all monies from all sources, including telephones, Internet, groups, mail, and window for *all performances* of *all productions* on sale. If there is more than one production on sale, without a computerized ticketing system and without audit stubs, it can be difficult to ascertain how well each individual production is selling. One method is to count all the tickets remaining at the end of each day and subtract that number from the number of tickets on hand at the start of the day. The difference between those two totals should be the number of tickets sold during the course of the day. That number multiplied times the various price categories should equal the day's sales, less any commissions. This is practical only in very small theatres.

4.) Weekly Box Office Summary
A Weekly Box Office Summary is a report reflecting one week's worth of box office statements, showing the number of tickets sold and the resulting gross sales.

5.) Seasonal Box Office Summary
A Seasonal Box Office Summary is a report that shows all box office sales figures for a given season, as they will also appear in the accountant's annual financial report.

6.) Ticket-Stub Report (also called a Box Count)
This report shows the ticket-stub count, made after each curtain has gone up, and may be the responsibility of the head usher or the house manager.

7.) Season Ticket Report
After subscription series or season ticket sales have ended, a complete record of these sales must be made for each performance in the series in order to determine how much money is to be deducted from each box

office statement, assuming there is a discount. The report is also useful as a tool to see how well each series sold in relation to the others, and which performance days/times sold better than others.

8.) Group Sales and other Discounts Report
When the sale of discounted tickets is frequent and varied, a separate report of tickets for each performance may be required. Analyzing this report can be useful in determining where the groups originated and perhaps where more group sales can be generated.

9.) Advance Sales Report
This shows ticket sales for one or more performances in the future. Such reports are easily generated by a computerized ticket system; to accomplish this manually, however, would require an audit of every ticket in the box office and is, therefore, not feasible on a regular basis. Audit stubs can be very useful here.

Box Office Auditing

An audit of the box office should be conducted at the end of each production or season and any other time a notable discrepancy appears between the number of tickets missing and the amount of income. The audit should be conducted or at least supervised by the accountant and not by the business manager or the treasurers. Essentially, an audit involves counting all the unsold tickets on hand, then making up a box office statement that shows income-to-date for all future performances. This total amount, together with income shown on statements for past performances, should be the same as the total of all deposits for ticket sales made into the box office bank account. If income cannot be closely reconciled with the figures shown on the statements, the audit should be redone. It is easy to forget details, such as discounted tickets, petty cash borrowed from the box office, and so forth. The audit will never balance exactly. Even the most honestly and efficiently managed box office may show a one to four percent discrepancy as the result of honest human error. If a treasurer makes change for thousands of dollars each day, it stands to reason that a few mistakes will be made. In fact, an audit that balances income with tickets sold to the exact penny is more suspicious than one that shows a small discrepancy. An audit system that can be adapted to suit most theatres is provided in Appendix P.

Computer Ticketing Systems, Customer Relationship Management (CRM), and Internet Ticketing

For organizations of a certain size, with certain needs, computer ticketing systems are wonderful things. No more deadwood to count, instant reports, and information about your customers, sliced and diced and packaged in ways to thrill any marketing department, plus the ability to sell tickets 24 hours a day, while your box office is closed and your staff is at home, asleep. Some systems even offer sample views of the stage from the seats that your customers are contemplating buying. Sound too good to be true? It is good and it is true. And its gets better: there are numerous systems and providers.

Research

Appropriately enough, the Internet and specifically INTIX, International Ticketing Association, is a good place to start researching systems and providers. It is an international not-for-profit trade association with over 1,400 members. The association is dedicated to the improvement, progress, and advancement of ticket management. It has an interactive web site at www.intix.org, which will enable you to go to the websites of its members: ticketing service providers. It annually conducts surveys, provides educational programs, sponsors trade shows, and produces publications on box office management. INTIX also provides professional development grants to assist organizations that do not have the budget to cover professional development costs. Another good source aimed at the not-for-profit sector is www.ticketing.org.uk. Even though this site is aimed at European users, it provides a hive of useful information and many of the suppliers and systems reviewed are in the US. It is necessary to register because the funders of this site want to know who visits it.

Be sure to visit www.ticketlife.com, the online community of box office managers and the ticketing industry. Its archive of articles on the subject is especially helpful. See also, www.connectedcourseware.com/ccweb/prodrevs.htm for informative articles by Patrick M. Finelli.

Another way to research the topic is to search "Ticketing Systems" or "Ticket Systems" or "Box Office Systems" or "Performing Arts Tickets" or any variations of these words. Each of these searches will bring up new websites and new information, and the numerous options and choices will begin to take shape. (See Appendix Q, Ticketing Software and Systems.)

And, of course, there is the old-fashioned way—visit colleagues at other venues to see what equipment they are using and what they like and dislike. It is not necessary to reinvent the wheel.

The core ticketing issue is the process of selling tickets and any system can accomplish that. It does seem to surprise people however that systems do the same task in different ways and that not all can handle subscriptions or donations and fundraising. Each has its own operating characteristics and quirks, and some are more user friendly than others, but beyond that, or more accurately *before* that, one fundamental question must be answered.

How Much Control over the Ticket-Buying Process Does the Organization Wish to Have?

Roger Tomlinson (www.ticketing.org.uk then > Systems > Choosing your solution) writes:

> You want to control how your tickets are sold; you want purchasers to deal with you, your way, to buy tickets; you only offer sales channels you control so purchasers are within your brand and values; you regard your customer care as a fundamental part of closing the sale and selling the ticket; you want to ensure customers are charged the price you set and judge your value on the price/product equation; you want to build a relationship with ticket purchasers, capturing their details, and relating to them as customers who may come back and buy again.

These are really important and basic issues. Agreeing with them basically eliminates one half of the solutions available and makes the choice for an "in-house" system. It is a system—software—that is purchased or licensed from a vendor. This powerful tool will be available for all aspects of customer relationship management that integrates marketing, subscriptions, and communications. It could also include fundraising and volunteering, as well as delivering on-line sales and e-marketing. The Rolls Royce version of this type of system is Tessitura (www.tessiturasoftware.com). A competitor is Theatre Manager by Arts Management Systems (www.artsman.com).

Alternatively, if the above issues don't resonate with the theatre's management team, they can choose a *hosted* system. The customers will have Internet access to tickets; they will, of course, have to pay a fee to a ticketing service, but there will be little or no cost whatsoever to the theatre. For some organizations the cost consideration could drive the decision to opt for a hosted system instead of an in-house system.

Internet Ticketing

What follows is a brief description of online ticket sales or Internet ticketing. As mentioned earlier, there is a truly vast amount of information available on the Internet, and it is the best place to go for up-to-the-minute information and advice.

Virtually every organization, large or small, has a website. And a growing proportion of the public has become accustomed to making online purchases. eBay and Amazon have led the way in helping Americans feel comfortable buying online. No surprise, then, that many customers expect to be able to purchase tickets online and it is notably the purchase-method of choice for a young audience. Tickets are a perfect product for selling on the Internet.

A Hosted Ticketing Service

There are two ways to sell tickets online when using a *hosted ticketing service*, invisible or visible; once that has been decided, the next question is "Will the sales be live from inventory or from an allotment?"

Using the *invisible* method, customers click on a button at the theatre's website to be taken to the ticket service's website, for example (tix.com), *but* they will continue to be looking at what they think is the theatre's website. As a practical—visual—matter, customers believe that they never leave the theatre's website and continue to see only the organization's logo and propaganda.

Using the *visible* method, customers click on the theatre's website and are instantly taken the ticketing service's website, for example (ticketcentral.com). Once there, customers will then need to find the listing and all the ticket-buying choices before them.

Whichever method management chooses, their next decision has to do with what tickets will be available for online buyers? Will customers be able to select from your "live" total inventory of available tickets just as if they were standing at the window? Or will an allotment be assigned to the ticketing service and be replenished as needed? The consideration is one of control. If the service is "selling live," the ticket inventory will constantly be changing and be outside of the box office control. A theatre may decide to hold back a few rows for a pending group order only to find that they've just been sold, so regular reporting and monitoring are essential.

All hosted ticketing services will see to it that the ticket sales revenue is credited to the proper bank account and will, if time permits, mail the tickets to the customer. If there is not enough time, the theatre box office will receive email notification of the sale and the tickets will be printed in the box office and held for pick up.

Hosting services can be of particular value to organizations selling hard tickets, with no Internet ability. Even without a website, the theatre can make an allocation to a hosted ticketing service and have tickets available for purchase all over the world. They will then be either held at the box office for pick up, or mailed out by your company, time permitting.

Fees

Although there may be no costs to the theatre for selling tickets through a hosted service, the theatre's customers will be charged service fees for the transaction and that money will go to the ticketing service. If only a relatively small number of tickets are involved, that might not be much of a consideration, but if during the course of a season, thousands of tickets are being sold online, that could amount to a good deal of money not going to the theatre.

In-House Box Office

The second way to conduct Internet ticketing is to sell tickets through an in-house system via a link on the theatre's website. This option is moot unless there is an in-house box office system, as discussed in the prior section. If the software and hardware are available to execute the selling of tickets, the fees that would be paid to the host service would be paid to the theatre. Some organizations are cool toward charging fees to its customer base; others see it as a source of additional revenue.

Hybrid

For additional market reach, some portion of the tickets might be handled by a large, nationwide hosted ticketing system (tickemaster.com). An allocation might be very appropriate, in that case.

What to Consider in Regard to Computerized Box Office and Internet Ticketing

A theatre organization's box office and business personnel certainly should play an important role in the acquisition of any computer system. They should feel that they have helped put the system in place, not that it was imposed on them by management. As participants in the decision-making that leads to computerization, experienced box office treasurers can help prevent costly mistakes. For example, their major concern may focus on how to keep the line of customers at the window moving, especially just before curtain. Hence, it is important to acquire a system that includes a "hot key" or "quick sale" mode so that operators can suspend the need to enter the date and select seats from a seating chart as well as suspend the capturing of name/address and other marketing information.

Pay attention to how the software will interface between (1.) subscriptions or series or other special offers and (2.) box office single-sale tickets. Get input from the marketing and development or fundraising staff about the kinds of information they would like to see generated from what will be an expanding database of information about ticket buyers. One very special benefit that high-end ticketing systems can offer is the ability to aid in what is known as CRM, Customer Relationship Management. For nonprofits this can be a critical management tool because these systems can integrate information about customers' buying habits, subscription data, donor records, membership, and volunteer activities. All of this information can appear on screens while the customer is on the telephone, and the details of the conversation can be recorded for later analysis. Some systems are designed to interface with existing fundraising programs, such as Raisers Edge, a very big plus for nonprofits.

Insist on thorough demonstrations of equipment before it is purchased and involve employees on the staff who will be using the technology to aid with the decision.

Negotiate the hardware and software contracts with great care. Be certain that they provide protection against any damage that faulty, inadequate, or failed equipment may cause to the organization. Be certain contracts cover availability of program codes and information, even if the software company goes out of business. Be certain that tech support will be available via telephone in the evening and on weekends should problems develop at these critical times for the theatre. What kind of training is available? How long will it take?

Be certain there is an adequate backup system in place, both computerized and manual. Usually, a box office system is plugged into a power supply that can't be interrupted, with a backup computer in place and a manual contingency plan ready should all systems fail.

Be prepared to maintain a manual system concurrently with the computerized system for the first year with an in-house system.

Beware of donated computer equipment. Box office ticketing programs are the most critical component in a theatre organization's software; they require the most sophisticated programming and are usually the most expensive. If the box office system crashes or if it is inadequate or ill-suited, there will be serious trouble. Donated equipment and software may no longer be serviceable from the manufacturer or developer, and a system crash could be fatal to the uninterrupted operation of the box office.

A great many problems can develop with computer systems and most are easy to overlook during contract negotiations. It would be wise to study similar contracts written for other theatre operations. Other factors that shouldn't be ignored when ordering computer equipment include the delivery deadline, preparation of the computer location area, the selection and ordering of any necessary high-speed Internet and telephone tie-in services, and arranging for employee training in computer use. It's an obvious advantage when the system is user-friendly and can be mastered in a few weeks.

Look before Leaping

Take extra time to be certain that the persuasiveness of a sales representative or the name brand cache of a particular system drives none of the choices. Be absolutely certain of what the system can do at the moment—not the promise of software and improvements to come—how much it will cost—installation, modifications to existing systems, training, on site support.

The Future?

The next phase in Internet ticketing is for customers to print their tickets from their home computers. The airlines pioneered this process through their Internet reservations services years ago. Theatres using this technique require bar code readers, or scanners, at ticket-taker locations.

A further development, recently launched, are systems that send ticket purchase data to a cell phone or a PDA, Personal Digital Assistant, completely eliminating the need for a paper ticket. Another alternative would be to have the data encrypted on the magnetic strip of a membership or credit card. With that data available on the card, the customer would then just swipe the card at the theatre, thus, eliminating a paper ticket.

Other Types of Earned Income

While the business of earning income from sources other than the box office entails additional costs, personnel, and problems, few theatres can afford to ignore such potential income. The largest performing arts operations within their marketing department often employ specialists such as a merchandizing manager, a concessions manager, an advertising sales manager, and others who generate income in the areas of tours, school programs, and rentals of space to outside groups. Because grants and contributions are subject to a great variety of forces beyond a theatre's control, sources of earned income may provide a more reliable way to supplement ticket income. In small operations, of course, the work of earning this money usually falls to the regular theatre staff. The house manager sells T-shirts during intermissions, for example; the publicity director sells advertising space in the programs; the interns park cars before each performance. This kind of split in responsibilities is unfortunate—such as the need for most actors to supplement their income by finding employment outside the theatre. But the instinct for survival usually provides the justification for such efforts.

Sponsorship

Most theatre operations have a development (fundraising) department, which has the responsibility for raising additional income to supplement ticket income. For the not-for-profit sector of the industry, this income is often the difference between a break-even or deficit season. Sponsorships are a primary source of funding. A business or individual may sponsor a single performance or a series of performances. Another business may sponsor the season, and it is not uncommon to find multiple sponsors for particular shows or the theatre's entire season. Sponsorship simply means that for a certain sum of money, the donor will be recognized in the advertising, playbill, lobby displays, and sometimes precurtain announcements as a supporter of the organization. A tag line at the bottom of an advertisement will simply say, "This performance is generously sponsored by the XYZ Corporation." A large sponsorship may support an entire season, in which case an above the line credit is given, such as "The ZZ Credit Union Broadway Series." Major Broadway and touring productions are increasingly soliciting sponsors that include national credit card companies or automobile companies in which case an above the line credit in the form of "IOU Credit Cards Present" will be included. (See also Chapter 13, Fundraising and Sources of Contributed Income.)

One must be careful in soliciting sponsorships to ensure that the sponsors know exactly what they are buying. They are not buying any part of the show, they are not buying access to the actors, and they are not buying any special access to the theatre. When it's all over and the sponsors didn't like the show, they are still the sponsors. Development directors try to match sponsorship opportunities to the likes and dislikes of the potential sponsors. Some theatres include a number of free tickets along with the sponsorship, or at least the sponsors are given a first opportunity to buy a block of choice seats. In the first case, if tickets are included with the sponsorship, the first claim on the money from the sponsorship is the reimbursement—or purchase—of the box office for those tickets.

Sponsors see sponsorships as advertising opportunities, but they benefit the theatre beyond the dollars received by making the business community a partner in the cultural life of the community. Attaching a company name to a theatre product results in the company's having a vested interest in the success of the theatre, which can mean added ticket sales from their employees and customers.

Advertising Income

Most theatres generate some revenue by selling ads in their printed programs. These may be simple "Compliments of XYZ Hardware Company"-type notices or they may be elaborate display ads. When numerous ads are solicited (perhaps for a souvenir booklet as well as a regular playbill) a full-time ad salesperson may be required for specific periods of the year. Or, of course, the theatre may contract with an outside agency, publisher, or printer both to sell the ads and publish the playbills in exchange for a percentage of profits or for a flat fee. This system is common in most large theatre cities and in large performing arts centers where numerous theatres share a common publisher. The playbill comes out on a weekly or monthly basis and contains the same design, general copy, and advertising, but the performance information differs for each theatre where it is distributed.

Rates for printed advertising of various types are based on the potential number of people who will read the ads, the size of the ad, and the prominence with which the ad is displayed in relation to other advertising. Publishers of other periodicals already in the business of selling ads may be anxious to acquire publication rights to increase their profits with little risk to them. Theatres that grant such rights, however, must retain full control over all copy that pertains to the theatre and the production at hand and must guarantee that there will always be enough space in each playbill to print the necessary production, cast, and staff information. The overall design and content of the playbill may also be a factor for negotiation, since these are important in creating the public image that a theatre projects.

Playbills and souvenir programs are obvious places to sell ads, but there are other places where ads may be sold, although the extent to which this is done should be governed by the image the theatre wishes to project. Advertising can easily cheapen the look of a lobby or a playbill unless it is limited and controlled. Nonetheless, here are a few possibilities:

1.) Ticket envelopes and the reverse face of tickets

2.) Printed brochures and performances schedules
     Often, the advertiser will pay the full printing costs of such literature in exchange for being the only advertiser on it.

3.) Newspaper ads and media spots

Corporations may pay for a theatre's media ads in exchange for a mention in those ads, which creates for them a desired association with a cultural activity.

4.) Postage imprints

Private advertising is now permitted on postal imprints; meters may be
rented and designed to print short ad messages next to the regular postage
imprint. A theatre that puts out large mailings may rent this space to a
local restaurant or hotel, for example, in exchange for the postage costs.

5.) Lobby display space

While most theatres avoid blatant lobby advertising, lobby decor may
actually be enhanced by renting space to local art galleries, antique dealer-
ships, and boutiques to display their wares. If a show has a theme that is
related to a commercial enterprise, a company may display its product or
advertisement in the lobby for a limited amount of time for a cash consideration.

6.) The fire curtain

In the nineteenth century it was commonplace for theatres to paint
advertisements on their fire curtains—obviously a prime space that no
theatregoer could fail to see. Some theatres or shows may still do this.

7.) Theatre seats

Theatres may tastefully place the name of a business or an individual donor
on the backs or arms of theatre seats to indicate that a contribution has
been made or to serve as a discreet advertisement.

Rental Income

Depending on how actively a theatre uses its stage and auditorium, on the availability of
other halls and theatres in the community, and on the terms of the theatre's lease with a
landlord, renting a theatre to outside groups can be a lucrative source of income. Most
operation and maintenance costs remain constant whether there are five or ten public
events in a hall during a given week—this depends, of course, on whether or not large
numbers of union employees who require additional pay are needed. And when events
are sponsored by outside groups, they are likely to attract people to the theatre building
for the first time, and this may provide a boost to ticket sales. Of course, outside rentals
should not seriously disrupt the theatre's own production schedule or image. Most theatres can easily be adapted to accommodate the following:

1.) Stage productions by other theatre groups;

2.) Films, concerts, and recitals sponsored by outside groups;

3.) Fundraising events, benefits, and other special events such as lectures and fashion shows;

4.) Political and municipal rallies and meetings;

5.) Industrial shows or meetings sponsored in relation to large conventions being held in the area;

6.) Graduation exercises;

7.) Recitals by local music and dance schools;

8.) Lectures by nationally recognized personalities.

Concession Income

Nickel and dime profits from coin-operated vending machines can amount to an appreciable sum over a period of weeks. Most such machines may be rented or simply lent from a vending company, thereby the theatre has no maintenance obligations. Requiring little or no investment, these include:

Public pay phones
Candy machines
Soft drink machines
Coin-operated coat lockers
Restroom vending machines

Larger concessions that can require considerable management and investment offer the lure of larger profits also:

Coatroom checking services
Automobile parking lots and services
Restaurants
Alcoholic beverage concessions
Soft drink concessions
Gift shops and boutiques
Art galleries
Candy or baked goods concessions
Souvenir book sales

The inventory and revenue control over such concessions, as discussed in Chapters 11 and 12, is time consuming when the theatre operates the concession, or even when the theatre shares profits on a percentage basis with an outside vendor. A flat rental fee can be an easier and equally lucrative arrangement. Assuming that the theatre is the primary attraction that brings customers to the building in the first place, the theatre's management must accept overall responsibility for everything that transpires in the building. If a customer is shortchanged in a lobby gift shop, receives poor service in the theatre restaurant, or loses money in the lobby pay phone, that person will complain to the box office—despite the fact that both the theatre and the concessionaire may merely be tenants with no other legal or business relationship. So, when the theatre is itself the landlord and leases out concession space, it must devise agreements with concessionaires that protect its own interests. For example, the theatre must reserve the right to evict a tenant concession if it does not maintain certain standards of cleanliness, customer service, and product quality. The concessionaire must also be required to carry minimum types of insurance, such as product liability and theft, or the concessionaire's coverage may be attached to the theatre's policy, which is usually less expensive.

When many people use concessions, like coatrooms or parking lots, the theatre ticket may be made with a detachable stub that entitles the ticket holder to a particular service. Such stubs may also entitle holders to discounted meals in nearby restaurants or bargains in shops. At the end of each week, the theatre and the managers of those tie-in businesses get together to match the stubs they received with those retained by the theatre. Perhaps the agreement is for the restaurant to pay the theatre a certain cash amount for each stub collected. Or perhaps the box office collects the full amount for a combined dinner and theatre ticket, in which case the theatre periodically pays the restaurant for the stubs it returns.

Sometimes a package deal is created for which customers pay a single price for several services or activities, such as dinner and theatre. The way prices are itemized on package-deal tickets can be important. For example, if the same company owns both the food and theatre operations, it may decide that, out of a $42.50 package price, $27.50 is the food cost and $15.00 is the theatre cost. The lower the theatre income, of course, the lower the payments for percentages, royalties, and entertainment taxes. Some theatres even include an automatic service charge on all tickets and never show this portion of the ticket price on the box office statements: the ticket might read, "This price includes a $1.00 parking charge." Of course, this practice is not altogether ethical, as it may shortchange actors, playwrights, and others of income that is legitimately theirs.

Many large theatre companies have turned to merchandising as another source of earned income. Specialty items that carry the theatre's logo or relate to its productions in some way—T-shirts, calendars, cookbooks, tote bags, and notepaper, to name only a few possibilities—are bought from manufacturers for resale. They may be sold in the lobby, offered through mail order catalogs, or used as giveaway enticements to attract contributions.

School and Outreach Income

Most professional nonprofit theatres today operate some kind of school or training program. The reason for this is threefold: such programs may generate additional earned income; they often generate additional unearned income from grants; and they address the urgent need to develop young audiences. In addition, training programs are cost-effective for most theatres because company, staff, and cast members may be utilized as instructors at little extra cost and the theatre or rehearsal rooms may double as class space. Of course, education programs may also be offered as outreach activities away from the theatre, thereby filling both educational and publicity functions. Grants from both public and private sources have long been available for artists-in-schools, artists-in-residence, and a variety of other outreach and touring programs. Another approach is for the theatre to associate itself with a nearby college or university. College students may take classes or earn credit for serving internships at the theatre, or the theatre may send artists and staff to conduct classes and workshops on the campus. The possibilities are numerous and, best of all, the college usually handles all the administrative work involved in such joint programs. Theatre companies may also work with local school boards to develop programs in the public schools and to lobby for more meaningful funding for arts-in-education in general.

The most common training programs sponsored by theatre companies include:

1.) Internships
These may be in artistic, technical, and/or managerial areas and interns may receive college credit, a small stipend or nothing at all.

2.) Apprentice programs
Although *intern* has come to replace the word *apprentice* in most theatre circles, some companies still operate apprentice programs or schools in which the participants pay tuition.

3.) Formal training programs
Many companies offer formal classes, especially acting classes—structured over a period of months and often culminating in a production or series of workshop scenes; often there is a tuition charge. Such programs may be designed either for children or adults.

4.) Children's theatre programs
Some training programs, involving either children or adults, are designed to produce public performances for children to generate both tuition and ticket income. Many are curriculum based, are developed in consultation with local teachers, and are therefore guaranteed an audience.

5.)   Arts-in-education programs
Individual artists, groups, or whole productions are sometimes engaged
to give instruction, performances, or both in public and private schools.

6.)   Workshops and residencies
Most theatre and dance companies that tour college campuses or large
performing arts centers try to arrange for company members to offer workshops or lecture-demonstrations for appropriate student groups. Or they
may arrange a residency that involves company members as instructors
over a period of days or weeks. Such services are paid by the college or the
center; often this payment is from a grant given to the campus presenting organization that is sponsoring the company's public performances.

7.)   Young audiences programs
Theatre companies may arrange special performances for young people
or school groups, or simply include such groups at regular performances.
Special materials may be distributed as classroom instruction aids, company members may visit classrooms before or after the performance, or
introductory or postperformance discussions may be held at the theatre.

Theatre companies that sponsor extensive education, outreach, and training activities will require at least one full-time person to serve as director or administrator of these
activities, and that person may require support staff. While such activities often generate additional income, they also generate additional responsibilities that cannot be taken
lightly. It should be remembered that people with talent in one area, such as acting, may
not be teachers. And while theatre training can enhance theatre appreciation, it can also
destroy it.

Adult Outreach—Travel Programs

Many larger theatre organizations conduct theatre trips to New York, Chicago, or Montreal
for their patrons. These trips usually include two or more theatre productions, tours of
theatres, and talks by artists and managers in addition to travel, dining, and hotel arrangements. A sum in addition to the direct cost of the trip is added to the total cost to benefit
the theatre. These programs also build strong support for the theatre.

Income from Special Attractions

There is no reason why a producing theatre organization cannot occasionally function
as a presenting organization. There are usually many periods between company-produced
performances, productions, and seasons when the auditorium is not in use and could
accommodate certain special attractions. These should not, of course, be in direct com-

petition with the regular season. But they might be aimed at bringing new audiences to the theatre as new sources of earned income.

The process of presenting theatrical and other attractions is described in Chapter 9. It bears repeating, however, that booking and presenting attractions involve risk that can be reduced through experience, but never entirely eliminated. Nonetheless, attractions that may easily be accommodated in most theatres include:

Children's theatre companies
Modern dance companies
Small/medium music ensembles
Solo recitals
Vocal groups
One-person shows
Small touring theatre productions
Films and lectures

Miscellaneous Sources of Income

Perhaps the sweetest kind of earned income is that which is derived from the subsidiary rights to a production that a producer or theatre company helped to develop. Quite a few professional nonprofit theatres today are collecting performance royalties from such plays. The transfer, touring, and conversion of productions from nonprofit theatres are discussed in Chapter 5. Compared with the items on the preceding list, income earned from subsidiary rights can be far more considerable:

Subsidiary rights
Income from interest-bearing bank accounts
Earnings from investments
Equipment rentals
Costume rentals
Scenery rentals
Production services contracted by outside groups

Investing a theatre company's precious capital in stocks, bonds, and other financial instruments is very risky and should be avoided in most cases. Interest-bearing bank accounts, however, should be chosen, when possible, over noninterest accounts. And the business office should studiously maximize interest earnings by carefully managing deposits and withdrawals. If a company's inventory of production equipment and other items can be leased out without disrupting the operation, this can bring in additional income. And if production facilities and personnel are sufficient, the theatre may even build production elements for outside organizations.

Summary

An efficient box office operation requires an especially exacting system of checks and balances, as well as personnel who are both honest and dedicated to detail. For some operations, selling tickets the old-fashioned way will be adequate. Computerization can be wonderful or harrowing; the Internet is a terrific research resource.

Merchandising—whether it involves selling tickets or T-shirts—should he based on sound marketing principles and be conducted according to sound business practices. Increasing the amount of earned income for a given organization can be challenging and gratifying, as well as discouraging and frustrating. There are probably few people involved in managing theatres who had any inkling, when they first began, that so much of their time would be spent on ostensibly nontheatre business. Hiring bartenders and checking empty bottles, ordering Popsicles and policing the kiddies' matinee, and filling mail orders for greeting cards are not activities likely to satisfy a love for the performing arts. But they are often necessary to make it all possible. The idea for theatre and the performing arts, however, must always remain central: artistic integrity is compromised when the lobby is overcrowded by unattractive vending machines or when the price of drinks is outrageously inflated. Maintaining the fun and excitement for the customer must always be at the forefront of management in every department, starting with the box office and the ticketing process.

CHAPTER 13

Fundraising and Contributed Income

I F PHILANTHROPY IS THE ART OF GIVING, then fundraising is the art of getting. The chief function of fundraising is to secure grants and contributions, an activity conducted exclusively within the nonprofit sector. Grants, contributions, and in-kind gifts are referred to collectively as "contributed income" or "unearned income." The latter term is quite inappropriate because a great deal of work goes into securing this income and a valuable artistic product may result from it. Grants are, in fact, contracts to "buy" specified services. Nor would it be quite accurate to call such income "gifts," as most of it has strings attached: remember hearing a parent say, "I'll give you a dollar, if you clean up your room!"

Development is now the standard euphemism for fundraising, which may also seem inappropriate given that the development department at a film or television company is in charge of writing story treatments and developing screenplays. We also talk about "developing" a theatrical script or production. Nonetheless, the development department at a nonprofit theatre is in charge of developing just one thing—the financial resources that fund its mission. Simply put, this means raising money.

General Considerations

It is rare for a nonprofit arts organization to receive a grant or corporate contribution unless it has been functioning for at least three years. This helps to explain why so many groups start out very modestly and why their initial subsidy comes exclusively from individual contributions—often from the participants themselves, together with their relatives, friends, and associates. During those first few years of operation, however, it is important to establish and document a track record of artistic accomplishment. This means producing good work before audiences, generating favorable reviews and publicity, and gaining respectful attention within the community itself. Young theatre groups should also practice good accountability in regard to their legal and financial records, and they should collect statistics about ticket sales, outreach activities, contributions, productions, tours, and other matters that will count heavily in their early funding proposals.

It is sometimes tempting for a theatre organization to permit its funders to influence or even to determine its productions, projects, or policies. This is rarely advisable. As emphasized throughout this book, artistic ventures of all kinds should be driven by artistic priorities. If these do not agree with a certain funder's priorities, then another funder should be found. At times society, in general, and philanthropy, in particular, adopt one or two favorite causes and then fund them right out of fashion. Nonetheless, good trustees and good fundraisers understand that the funds must follow the art, because art that follows the funding will have lost both integrity and purpose.

The Development Director

Depending on an organization's size, the development department may consist of one person or a small army of fundraisers. For small companies, all fundraising may also be the responsibility of the artistic director, perhaps with the help of a volunteer board. Whatever their titles, successful fundraisers invariably possess well-polished communication skills. They must be good writers and editors, and they must also be able to communicate well with other professionals and prominent citizens in a variety of fields and positions. This requires an attractive, outgoing personality and, usually, a college education. Like actors, fundraisers must be impervious to rejections and persistent in pursuit of their goals. They must often conduct or supervise research to identify potential funding sources. And, of course, they must have a thorough familiarity with the theatre organization that they are working for as well as the performing arts field as a whole.

Typical responsibilities of a development director—often shared with an associate or full staff—include:

1.) Identifying and cultivating potential donors through research and board contacts.

2.) Preparing or supervising grant applications, appeal letters, and funding proposals.

3.) Designing direct-mail, telephone, and other fundraising drives.

4.) Generating financial reports that account for expenditures as required by funding agencies.

5.) Personally soliciting funds and following up donations with progress reports and acknowledgements.

6.) Conceiving and supervising special fundraising events, galas, benefits, and other activities.

7.) Conducting research into the histories and funding requirements of appropriate agencies, foundations, corporations, and individuals.

8.) Keeping up-to-date records regarding board members, donor histories, volunteer workers, grant deadlines, mailing lists, and the like. Increasingly, this means managing one or more databases, which may be as simple a Microsoft Excel spreadsheet, or as sophisticated as specialized development software programs, such as Raiser's Edge and Tessitura. Some larger organizations devote entire staff positions or departments to this one key task.

9.) Fundraisers must also keep themselves informed about everchanging tax laws, government regulations, economic trends, and changes in corporate ownership. Reading such publications as the *Wall Street Journal* as well as specialized periodicals such as the *Chronicle of Philanthropy* is a help, and there are now several Internet resources on which many fundraisers rely, including www.boardsource.org and the Foundation Center's invaluable site at www.fdncenter.org.

Sources of Contributed Income

There are four basic sources of contributed income: government, foundations, corporations, and individuals. A large performing arts organization would have a fundraising specialist for each of these areas.

Government

Arts funding agencies exist at the federal, state, and municipal levels of government. As mentioned, depending on the funding climate in a particular region, state and local arts councils are often a good place for new theatre companies to submit their first funding requests. Most such agencies allocate their funds through a wide range of specified categories or programs, such as theatre, music, dance, or performing arts as a whole. They are budgeted on an annual basis, so that once awards have been made there is rarely any surplus from which to grant supplemental funds until the next funding cycle. However, the same nonprofit theatre organization may qualify in several program areas at the same funding agency; for example, they may qualify in both theatre and arts-in-education. Also, application deadlines for different programs are often spread throughout the year. All government agencies that fund the arts publish a guide to their programs, which is increasingly available in full on the Internet.

The National Endowment for the Arts was founded in 1965 after President Johnson signed into law the National Foundation on the Arts and Humanities Act. As it states, "While no government can call a great artist or scholar into existence, it is necessary and appropriate for the Federal Government to help create and sustain not only a climate encouraging freedom of thought, imagination, and inquiry, but also the material conditions facilitating the release of this creative talent." In 1966, the Endowment's appropriation from Congress was $2.9 million. This figure grew to a peak of $176 million in 1992 before growing debate over just how "necessary and appropriate" it is for the federal government to fund the work of artists resulted in reduced appropriations from Congress. By 2000, the Endowment had been slashed to $97,627,600. Sadly, the NEA's status as a political football has meant that it is clearly *not* the most stable source of funding for arts organizations.

In any case, government sources in general, and the NEA in particular, represent a small percentage of most organizational budgets. In a survey of 575 New York City arts groups in 1999, for example, the NEA accounted for just six tenths of a percent of operating income, while the total of all federal, state, and city funds accounted for eleven percent. Still, many organizations find the imprimatur of federal funding to be useful in attracting support from foundations and individuals, making it worth the investment of time required to complete the NEA's bureaucratic application forms.

The NEA's website, www.nea.gov, includes detailed information about the Endowment's programs, application procedures, and deadlines. The site also includes a list of staff members for each of the programs. The staff is generally responsive to inquiries by phone or email.

Foundations

A foundation is an incorporated nonprofit organization set up to distribute funds or grants to people and projects that meet certain, often very exacting, criteria. There are more than 61,000 grant-making foundations in America; these range from small, family foundations that give away a few thousand dollars a year to enormous national foundations, such as the Ford or Rockefeller Foundations, which give away many millions each year and employ scores of professional grant makers. Foundations derive their assets from private estates or corporate earnings. To prevent them from being used merely to shield money from the tax collector or to funnel untaxed money back into the giver's own pocket, federal law requires that foundations, like other nonprofit organizations, have an IRS-approved mission and that they serve this mission by giving away at least five percent of their assets each year.

There are three broad types of foundations:

1.) Operating foundations: These are established by a business or institution to conduct research, social welfare, or other philanthropic activities based on the foundation's stated goals and in-house programs, such as a hospital research laboratory.

2.) Corporate foundations: These are established and funded by private or public corporations based usually on a percentage of the annual profits but are otherwise legally separate from the parent corporation, so that the resources of the Ford Foundation, for example, are tied to the profitability of the Ford Motor Company, but its giving policies are not.

3.) Family foundations: These are created by gifts from individuals, groups of individuals, or family members, such as the Rockefeller Brothers Fund or the Donner Foundation, which represent the most numerous types of foundations, by far.

Because there are so many foundations—each with its own interests, guidelines, policies, and procedures—good research is the key to success in this area of fundraising. Fortunately for professional fundraisers and grant writers from all disciplines, there is a unique national service organization designed to accommodate this research—the Foundation Center.

The Foundation Center maintains major reference libraries and research facilities in Washington, San Francisco, Atlanta, Cleveland, and New York, with ostensibly limitless data about foundations and corporations. In addition, the center's website at www.fdncenter.org offers a wealth of information on foundations, fundraising, nonprofit management, and philanthropy in general. For a fee, visitors to the site can also access the center's "Foundation Directory Online," which contains profiles of tens of thousands of U.S. foundations and is searchable by geographic location, areas of interest, grant size, and more. This service is also available for free at the Foundation Center's physical locations and is also offered by many public libraries around the country. A visit to one of the center's branches or a cooperating public library is therefore a good way to begin a search for foundation funding prospects.

Of course, the best source for information on foundations is often the foundations themselves, and many of them now maintain their own websites, complete with detailed guidelines, lists of past grants, and application procedures. In addition, IRS form 990-PF, the tax return filed annually by each foundation in the United States, is another valuable source; it contains a complete list of every grant a foundation makes in a given year. More and more, these 990s, as they are known for short, are available online through services such as the Foundation Center and another invaluable website, www.guidestar.com.

Corporations

Foundations that derive their assets from corporate profits are themselves independent corporations, theoretically outside the control of the hand that feeds them. Rather than setting up a foundation, however, most corporations engaging in philanthropy do so directly. It should be noted that, in general, corporate philanthropy is generally the most conservative. Corporations prefer to support projects that already carry a certain stamp of approval, such as government funding or support from major foundations. Corporate gifts may be initiated by corporate board members or senior management, by a specific corporate-giving office, or by public relations or marketing departments. Often, these gifts are based on personal contacts and interests rather than on corporate policies even though the goal is generally to enhance the corporation's public image, strengthen its influence in its local community, and/or directly benefit its employees.

Increasingly, corporate support for the arts has come from the public relations or advertising budget: cigarette manufacturers have sponsored cultural events to improve their images and oil companies have the same goal in their sponsorship of cultural television programming. Many nonprofit theatre companies have benefited from more modest corporate support, which, like support from small foundations, is usually restricted to the geographic area of the corporate headquarters. Aside from direct cash gifts, corporations may also provide subsidies to theatre companies by purchasing tickets, buying a table at a benefit banquet, buying playbill advertising, contributing securities, sponsoring special events, or providing loans and in-kind contributions of goods and services. Several corporations also maintain a "matching gifts program," whereby an employee's personal contribution to an organization will be matched by the corporation up to a specific amount. Some corporations may also lend employees to nonprofit organizations. And there are few ways that corporate executives can have a greater impact on the nonprofit sector than by serving on boards of trustees. Several enlightened corporations have even provided special incentives and training to encourage their executives to take on such volunteer service.

Sponsorship has also become increasingly common in recent years, providing cash and/or in-kind contributions that benefit the nonprofit organization in exchange for linking the names of the donor and the recipient in a very public way. The JVC Jazz Festival and the American Airlines Theater offer some obvious examples, although the recent past has also brought some high profile examples of erosion in this area of corporate giving, such as the end of Texaco's longtime sponsorship of Metropolitan Opera broadcasts. A company called IEG tracks trends in the area of corporate sponsorship through an annual report and also maintains a useful website at www.sponsorship.com.

Corporate philanthropy across the board has been severely shaken in recent years by all the personnel displacements resulting from corporate mergers, acquisitions, leveraged buyouts and divestitures, and bankruptcies. It takes a lot of time and energy to find generous friends and develop funding relationships. With frequent changes in corporate leadership and executive personnel, the number of such liaisons is greatly reduced. Because corporations tend to merge in order to reduce expenses while maximizing profits, mergers often result in a consolidation of both companies' giving programs, and therefore fewer dollars to go around. The corporate world is also much more global now in terms of its markets, its personnel, its office and plant locations, and, consequently, its social and cultural interests. Of course, corporate giving also follows the ups and downs of the economy. When profits are high, giving programs become flush; in times of retrenchment, charitable dollars are one of the first expenses to be cut.

Individuals

Individual donations given to a theatre organization range all the way from a quarter dropped into the hat of a street mime to a multimillion-dollar gift for the construction of a new theatre facility. Of the many billions of dollars that this country recognizes as charitable contributions each year, nearly eighty-five percent still come from individuals, followed by foundations and then corporations. The lion's share of this largess goes to religious organizations, followed by education, health care, human services, and arts and culture, for which the share of individual generosity was five and four-tenths percent in 2003.

Individual philanthropy tends to be the most stable source of contributed income for arts organizations. Although tax laws and economic conditions may cause constant change to the overall fundraising environment, individuals tend to stick with a particular organization once they have begun to donate. Any number of factors may motivate wealthy individuals to make large contributions to arts organizations—anything from a tax break to prestige and the perpetuation of their names. And small donors can usually be counted on to give their dollar bills to perpetuate the arts organizations that bring them joy, even as the overall economy rises and falls. For reasons such as these, most nonprofit organizations should spend their main fundraising efforts going after individual contributions.

When soliciting a donation from any potential funder, but especially when the request is aimed at an individual, the first rule is to make the amount requested appropriate to the donor's ability to give. In other words, never ask an "important" person for an "unimportant" sum, or vice versa. The person unable to give the amount requested will give nothing, whereas the person able to give more than requested will slyly contribute the pittance and never fork over again.

The second rule is to cultivate donors—interest can only come through familiarity, and familiarity must be built by keeping donors informed. They must be invited to performances and events, thanked for their contributions, and told how their money has made a difference. In general, it takes persistent cultivation to turn prospects into donors, more cultivation to turn donors into repeat donors, and more cultivation still to turn smaller donors into bigger donors.

Methods of Raising Contributed Income

There are different methods and schemes for collecting contributions and, in all probability, a new one is being invented every minute. For most nonprofit organizations, a healthy base of contributed income is a diversified base. Few institutional funders renew their grants for more than a few years, and all are subject to unexpected reversals. A poor national economy can seriously affect government as well as corporate funding; a stock market crash or sudden reversal can affect private funding; and charitable inclinations and preferences in general are always being influenced by what is going on in the nation and the world. So the prudent fundraiser keeps busy cultivating new sources, even while the old ones are still contributing.

Grants

A grant is a written contract between two parties in which it is specified that one will pay a specific sum to the other for certain services, such as the staging in San Diego, California, of four new plays by American playwrights. Because the government is not permitted to "give away" its tax-levied funds, government arts agencies can only disburse their appropriations by awarding grants, or contracts. Some foundation and corporate donations are also awarded on a contractual basis. This always means that there are strings attached to the money. At the very least, it will have to be spent for a specific purpose by a specified time, otherwise it may be denied. Timed payments could also be terminated or money refunded—under rare circumstances, goods or property related to the project or organization could actually be confiscated by the funding agency. These are good reasons for any arts organization to examine closely the guidelines of its potential funders. Are the conditions worth the value of the "gift"?

Contributions

Contribution is the generic term for all types of unearned income. As with grants, contributions, both large and small, can be earmarked or "restricted" for a specific use: an endowment fund, a capital fund, operating expenses, or a special project. If a donor restricts how a gift can be used, it provides the donor with a better sense of the impact that gift will make. One of the more innovative uses of individual donations was pioneered at the Mark Taper Forum, where adult donors bought student subscriptions, or "scholarships," which they could then assign to students. A word of caution: IRS regulations require that organizations honor the restrictions that donors place on their gifts and maintain sufficient records to demonstrate how the restrictions have been met.

Annual Fund Drive

An annual fund drive or donor campaign seeks as much money as possible in the shortest time from as many contributors as possible. It may be conducted through the mail, through the media, through special events, over the phone, or through any combination of these techniques. After one or two years, it should bring in a fairly predictable amount of money. It should also serve as a method for testing the real strength of audience support, building new audiences and identifying potential major donors. And aside from the concerted effort that goes into an annual drive, individual contributions can be solicited throughout the year by including an appeal for a donation with subscription and other ticket order forms, in playbills, in advertisements, and in public-service announcements, or on a website.

Membership Drive

Members may be subscribers or series ticket buyers, or they may form a distinct and independent category of donors. For example, there may be a guild or friends committee with each of the members paying dues and volunteering to raise even more contributions for the theatre company. Members are customarily entitled to certain privileges: invitations to parties, receptions, rehearsals, discussions, and symposia; discounts at local restaurants; free parking; and so forth.

United Fund Drive

Community arts councils can be especially valuable in organizing local fundraising efforts. More effective results are often achieved when several groups work together. This may also be done through a consortium of companies. Lincoln Center, for example, conducts unified funding campaigns for all its constituents, while each company also continues its individual efforts. A fear of losing identity by joining together is understandable, but, depending on the specific circumstances in a particular community, the old adage that states "there is strength in numbers" still holds.

Benefits and Special Events

A benefit is an attempt to raise money by attracting a group of people to a particular performance or event. Tax laws require that only that portion of the admission price or amount paid *above the cost of the event and/or items purchased* may be declared by the purchaser as a tax deduction, and only then on itemized tax returns. The IRS is watchful in enforcing this regulation, so benefit organizers must account for all costs, and the deductible portion or item-cost should appear in all advertising for the benefit, as well as on the ticket or receipt given to the buyer.

At banquets, corporations or wealthy individuals often buy whole tables as a form of contribution. Sometimes costs of the benefit may be absorbed when a person or corporation underwrites certain expenses, either by paying for them or providing in-kind goods and services.

The possibilities for special events, of course, are only limited by the organizer's imagination. There are auctions, bake sales, group trips, golf tournaments, sweepstakes, flea markets, bazaars, parties, whatever. To be successful, they must be appealing, fun, well organized, and well attended. A key strategy for ensuring all of the above is to recruit a committee of prominent citizens, either to help organize the event or to lend their names to it. The committee might then have a chair or co-chairs who take responsibility for ensuring that a certain number of tables are sold. Ideally, the event will help raise funds from people who are new to the organization, so the greater the reach of the committee members, the better. A well-selected honoree can also help an organization extend its reach, since friends or professional associates of the person being honored will feel compelled to purchase tables or tickets to show their support.

Sample Benefit Invitation Showing Deductible Portion of Payment

ENCLOSED IS $ _____ FOR ___ TICKETS at $50 each
($25 for Arts Organization) ($25 tax deduction)
ALL TICKETS WILL BE HELD AT THE BOX OFFICE

☐   I cannot attend, but I am enclosing a contribution of $ _____
     R.S.V.P. by May 11, 20xx
     Please make check payable to: XYZ THEATRE

Name _____

Title _____

Company or Organization _____

Address _____

City _____ State _____ ZIP _____

Tel.   Bus. (   ) _____ Home (   ) _____

Email: _____

Volunteers

Most nonprofit organizations benefit from the use of unpaid workers, in addition to board members. These may be interns, apprentices, or students who make a commitment of time over a period of weeks or months, or they may be people who help out on a more limited basis with funding drives and other efforts to raise money. However, if an organization is not prepared to spend considerable time in supervising volunteers, they may turn out to be more of a liability than an asset.

In-Kind Goods and Services

In-kind gifts are a type of corporate support. They may be in the form of goods or equipment—anything from wine to computers; or services—free air travel or free use of the company's copying machines; or expertise—corporate employees or retirees to provide technical assistance in areas as diverse as accounting or welding. Most such gifts gain a tax deduction for the corporation along with good will and publicity, and all at virtually no cost since they are essentially surplus inventory items.

Support from a Parent Institution

Civic, college, and university theatres, and certain others operate under the umbrella of a large institution. This parent body often supplies the facility rent-free, plus maintenance, security, staff, supplies, utilities, and numerous services, thereby reducing the operating costs for such groups to little more than the money required to build scenery and costumes. On the surface, this may appear to be an enviable situation. Yet sibling theatre organizations are subject to the rules, regulations, and discipline of the parent institution—not to mention the bureaucratic red tape required to get things done. They are also subject to whatever political, budgetary, administrative, or personnel change or crisis may affect the umbrella institution, and these can be traumatic and debilitating. Also, when receiving grants from outside the institution, the theatre company or project must usually forfeit anywhere from twenty to sixty percent of the grant award to the parent body in the name of "rent" or "service charge." This is usually a legitimate reimbursement for costs absorbed by the institution, but it certainly diminishes the incentive for writing grant proposals and the pleasure of winning awards. A similar "nibbling away" of funds occurs in the flow of budget allocations from their source to particular departments and projects. As once described by the chancellor of a state university, "Getting money from the state legislature, to the university, to the college, to the department, and to the project for which it is intended is roughly like transporting lettuce via rabbit!"

Basic Elements in Successful Fundraising

Volunteer Leadership

A professional fundraising firm or consultant hired to raise money for a nonprofit organization looks first at that group's volunteer leadership, which is to say its board of trustees. If this is comprised of the artistic director's family and friends, the job of attracting meaningful contributions will almost certainly be difficult. If, however, the board has top corporate executives and the leading professional and socially prominent members of the community *and* if these trustees are willing to use their influence and their contacts to raise funds for the organization, then the job of raising money will be easier. When board membership falls somewhere between these two, the first step in a serious fundraising campaign should be to strengthen the board with influential and enthusiastic and supportive new members. The search for candidates might begin with an examination of subscriber and donor records, which should be complete and up-to-date.

Planning

Fundraising should follow a planning process in addition to inventing strategies that will help the organization to realize its goals. At the core of the plan, of course, is the mission statement. As discussed in Chapter 5, a mission statement should be accompanied by a short list of long-term goals and a list of short-term objectives. The goals might include a plan for the acquisition of a new theatre facility at some time in the future, while the objectives might include a plan to produce Shakespeare's history plays during the next season. Goals such as these can be translated into fairly realistic budgets,

and the projected deficits become the fundraising goals. It may be decided to consoli-
date all efforts around one funding drive or to split the fundraising into a capital campaign to raise money for the new facility and a membership campaign to raise money for
the season. And, of course, government, foundation, and corporate sources must be
approached as well as individuals.

Management and Administration

While it is up to board members to open doors, it is up to salaried managers and staff to
do most of the work of fundraising. The board member may sign letters to potential
contributors, for instance, but the staff researches the titles and addresses of those people and writes the letters. One person may accomplish a limited amount of fundraising,
but serious efforts require two or more full-time specialists. One person may be involved
with identifying and cultivating potential donors, while a second conducts research, writes
proposals, and keeps records. Successful fundraising requires that a great deal of solid
information be gathered and processed, and this takes time.

A board of trustees may form a fundraising subcommittee with its own chairperson, or the whole board may serve as a fundraising committee, headed by the board
president or chairperson. In either case, one board member should serve as liaison with
the development director or consultant. That person will then supervise one or more
associates and also coordinate funding efforts with other departments, such as marketing and finance. Large organizations often hire a special events manager to work within
the fundraising office and to organize and manage benefits, including auctions and special
performances. These, together with wider funding appeals, will require many volunteers,
who must be recruited, trained, supervised, and thanked, yet another time-consuming
responsibility. And many nonprofit theatres have a junior board, an advisory committee,
a friends committee, a donor's guild, or some other such group that assists with fundraising and audience development. These special people are also volunteers who require
staff support and supervision.

Communication

Successful fundraising is conducted on a very human level. It requires written and spoken
contact; it requires getting a message across; it requires appeals to the heart, the head,
the ego, and, of course, the pocketbook. In short, it requires effective communication skills.

Applications may be sent miles away to the nation's capital, but there can still be
phone contact between the fundraiser and the funding agency. Opportunities to meet
colleagues and active donors are frequent at benefits, business functions, conferences, and
cultural events. Personal contacts at both ends of the application process comprise the
fundraiser's portfolio—a valuable asset that the fundraiser carries from one job to the next.

Few grants or contributions of any size are awarded without there being personal
contact between the contributor and the theatre organization. Often accompanied by a
board member, the managing director, or the artistic director, the fundraiser must visit

a potential funder one or more times with strong arguments as to why the funder should give. When the best known figure at the organization—probably the artistic director—is unable or unwilling to make such visits, raising money becomes more difficult. Contributors like to meet "the main person."

Funding proposals and appeals must also be presented in written form, which requires the ability to organize often complex information and abstract concepts in a succinct and commanding format. The most fortunate fundraisers are able to tap the resources of their organization's marketing and public relations offices for assistance in preparing funding appeals, campaign brochures, and other materials.

Timing

In order to receive grant awards from government agencies and foundations and corporations, the applicant must meet deadlines. A late application almost always means automatic rejection. In fact, the NEA and some state arts councils even require grant seekers to file an "intent to file" notice in advance of the application deadline.

Different corporations have times when they are busier and times when they are less busy. A knowledge of these work patterns helps to determine the most favorable time to approach the appropriate officer, board chairperson, or CEO. And this knowledge is especially helpful when asking a corporation to provide in-kind gifts, which should always be done well in advance to accommodate the corporation's own priorities. When and where a funding request is first mentioned can also be important. As a general rule, this is best done during business hours in the business place. Few corporate executives, funding officers, or wealthy socialites enjoy being buttonholed on the dance floor or over dinner. An exchange of business cards or a request to phone the next day is about as far as a social contact should go.

Timing is important when scheduling a funding campaign, a benefit, or a special event. Does it conflict with other events? Is it a convenient time, place, and date for the people most likely to attend? In several cities, online "masterplanner" event calendars allow organizations to check which events are scheduled for a given date and to register theirs.

Finally, social issues and causes and artistic projects must be in tune with the times. A particular mission or project or play can be of little interest one day and of enormous relevance the next, depending on current events, i.e., the play, *Homebody, Kabul*, by Tony Kushner or *The Normal Heart*, by Larry Kramer. While it's unwise to base artistic planning on such events, it's not a bad idea to take advantage of events that fuel interest in artistic projects.

Follow-Up

Fundraising does not end when the money comes in. Records must be kept regarding pledged, received, and deferred contributions; donor records must be updated; receipts, and acknowledgments must be sent; and attempts must be made to learn why some former donors failed to renew their commitments. Grants administration requires even more follow-up. Interim reports that track the expenditure of the award must be prepared and sent to the funder; follow-up phone calls and letters have to be made or sent to the appropriate program director; final project documentation has to be collected and filed; and financial accounting has to be reconciled.

But perhaps the most important follow-up responsibility—whatever the source of the contribution—is the act of expressing gratitude. Virtually all active fund givers can tell stories about beneficiaries who just took the money and ran, or others who never bothered to communicate between the time they received one contribution and the time they requested another. Corporations that donate in-kind services also like to be thanked. When they provide graphic arts services for a theatre company, for example, the appropriate manager from the company should work directly with the corporate graphics person and acknowledge that person's assistance and expertise. Volunteers who work on a telethon or in the costume shop must also be thanked and rewarded in some way. And elected officials in the community who have been instrumental in supporting the theatre company—through gestures that perhaps facilitated municipal, county, state, or federal funding—also like to be thanked. The best way to do this, of course, is to support their bids for reelection. Congratulating trustees, donors, volunteers, artists, staff, and community leaders on special events or accomplishments in their lives is another way of acknowledging their importance to the theatre company. Saying "thank-you" is a small investment that can reap large returns.

The Funding Proposal

Initial Contact

After potential donors have been identified through research and suggestions from board members, it must be decided:

1.) What to ask for (money, goods, services);

2.) How much to ask for;

3.) Whom to approach first (the president of the board, the CEO, the program director, the public relations director);

4.) When to make the first contact;

5.) How to make the first contact (telephone, letter, in person).

It is best to tailor each request to the specific interests, resources, and schedule of the potential funder. Rarely does a single funder pick up the entire tab. By researching the funding history of potential government, foundation, corporate, and individual donors and by applying common sense and a little imagination, it should be possible to write a request that will be realistic from the donor's point of view. And this request, whether it is for money or something else, should be made right up front in the initial contact.

Most often, the initial request is made in a one-page letter that is signed by a board member of the theatre organization or the artistic or managing director. This summarizes the project, the request for assistance, and the reasons why it should be of interest to the donor being contacted. The letter might also request a meeting during which the project and the support can be discussed in detail. Most often, such letters get negative responses — or none at all. This allows staff time and money to be spent more productively on preparing full proposals for those funders who express real interest in the initial contact letter.

Standards by Which Proposals Are Judged

Before writing a proposal for a grant or contribution, it helps to know how philanthropic agencies and other funders decide which projects to support. Although funders' motivations are different, there are certain general standards of evaluation used by most. These include:

1.) Presentation: First impressions matter. The written proposal does not have to be bound or loaded with graphics and printed on color stock, nor does the fundraiser have to show up for a meeting in formal dress. Nonetheless, appearances are important. Both the proposal and the people representing it should be neat, correct, and appropriate. Observance of these matters will communicate a seriousness of purpose in regard both to the theatre company and the proposal, and this aspect of proposal presentation is the first standard by which a judgment is made because it is what the funder notices first.

2.) Relevance and need: Is the proposal relevant to the funder's interests, as well as to the present needs of the community and society in general?

3.) Originality: How unique is the project? Is it being duplicated by others who can do it as well or better? Is it a project that is relevant to the times?"

4.) Potential benefit. How many people will benefit from the project — usually, the more the better. How large an audience will there be? Are those who will benefit relevant to the funder — i.e., tax payers in the government funder's constituency, consumers of the corporation's products, employees of the corporation and their families?

5.) Accountability: Can the organization making the request demonstrate fiscal accountability and responsibility? Does it have a good record of sound management and administration?

6.) Future ability to be self-sustaining: While it is increasingly understood that the arts can never be fully self-supporting, most funders believe that the more self-sustaining a particular company or project can be, the better. Also, very few projects receive funding from the private sector for more than a few years.

Being aware of this criterion while developing a proposal is essential. Government funding agencies and some in the private sector usually have their own lengthy application forms that require very specific information; but all applications include some type of narrative section and the content of many other proposals is entirely at the discretion of the writer. In either case, imagination and honest inventiveness are often a plus. For example, a small nonprofit theatre company may only perform for an annual audience of ten thousand people—far fewer than the ten million who may see an arts program on public television. But perhaps the theatre produces new plays by American writers. If only one of these writers gains national recognition, many millions of people will eventually constitute that playwright's audience.

Proposal Contents and Support Materials

A funding proposal will vary according to whom it is being sent, from whom, and for what. There are a number of acceptable models that may be followed and, of course, style and format differ somewhat with each writer and each organization being represented. But most proposals are contained in a packet of material that includes:

1.) Cover letter: A straightforward introduction and summation of the proposal, preferably contained on one typewritten page; this may be almost identical to the initial contact letter.

2.) Institutional history or background: A concise, fact-filled narrative history that documents the accomplishments of the organization, defines its relationship and usefulness to its local community and, perhaps, to society in general, and establishes its reputation within the professional theatre world.

3.) Project description: A clear explanation of the project being proposed for support, including a justification, the relevance of the project to the funder, the need for support, and the type and amount of support being requested.

4.) Project budget: A breakdown of project expenses and income—if any. This may merely give figures related to an isolated aspect of a larger project for which support is being requested; or it may show the figures for the whole project.

5.) Support from other sources: Somewhere in the proposal there should be a list of support that has been received from other sources, either for the project at hand or for all of the organization's activities. Also, a list of actual and/or anticipated other sources of support for the project should be shown.

6.) Latest audited financial statement.

7.) Proof of nonprofit status: Copy of the 501(c)(3) letter.

8.) Board of Trustees: A list with a biographical sketch of each member.

Depending on the funder and the type of request, additional material may also be required or included:

1.) Staff listing with biographies.

2.) Recent brochures.

3.) Percentage breakdown of earned and unearned income.

4.) Recent press materials: These should include good reviews, publicity pieces, and several exciting production photographs.

5.) Testimonials: A list of awards and citations the organization has received, and copies of genuine letters of praise, though this type of material should be carefully selected and kept to a minimum.

6.) Audience demographics: Statistical profile of the geographical area and the population served by the theatre—perhaps geared to the constituents of greatest interest to the funder.

It is also helpful to include in the proposal a discussion of how the organization plans to meet its goals for the project at hand; why this solution is a realistic one; how the project fits into the short- and long-term goals; how it relates to the mission; how future funding may he developed; and a methodology for project evaluation.

Summary

As Carl W. Shaver, founder of the respected fundraising firm C.W. Shaver & Company, has phrased it, successful fundraising is when "the right person asks the right prospect for the right amount for the right reason at the right time!"

Successful fundraising is an exacting business that is built on careful research, reliable information and personal contacts. It is also a very human activity built on personal and professional relationships, whims of artistic preference, perceptions about the role of the arts in society, and ideas about priorities. It feeds upon the traditionally generous American view toward charity, although in the field of nonprofit theatre this view remains somewhat impaired by the suspicion that "serious" art is not essential, not suitable for government support, too elitist for general consumption, and, in particular, that theatre has been self-sustaining on Broadway and so there's no reason why it can't support itself everywhere else. The growth of the nonprofit professional theatre movement in America, however, has greatly increased the number of those who believe that the commercial approach cannot provide the whole of theatre art, nor can it be supported without volunteer labor and contributed income. Even more significantly, many people have now experienced noncommercial theatre art and are willing to support it through extraordinary means.

Of course, nobody enjoys the feeling of being a poor relation in a rich society, of constantly looking for handouts and free services, counting pennies, and always asking favors from friends. The theatre and most of its artists have been poor for twenty-five centuries; poverty has practically been a condition of membership in this profession. While the 1960s saw the dawn of a new era of support for the arts in America, and the decades since then have seen the development of sophisticated new approaches both to fundraising and to fund-giving, an economically secure American theatre is still more of a dream than a reality.

CHAPTER 14

Marketing

ALTHOUGH THE WORDS *publicity, public relations,* and *advertising* are often used interchangeably, they actually represent different functions in the process of marketing a particular product.

Ostensibly, the main product of the theatre and performing arts industry is the live performance. Yet marketing an ongoing theatrical production or company does not end when all the seats to a performance or season have been sold. Long-range marketing objectives must also include (1) strengthening institutional awareness of the theatre or company, (2) building the company's brand equity, (3) developing the habit of theatre-going and, in the nonprofit sector, (4) convincing the community of the need to support the theatre or organization beyond buying tickets.

General Considerations

Placing an ad in the local newspaper and distributing posters is not marketing in the full sense, nor is marketing merely selling, which implies training and supervising salespeople and taking ticket orders. Marketing involves all the functions required to get goods or services from the production stage to the final user. It is so all-encompassing that a managing director shouldn't be surprised if an aggressive new marketing director asks to have control over box office operations, fundraising, house management, booking, and touring, in addition to the operations more usually associated with promotion. Box office operations are quite often included in the marketing department, but in this and the next two chapters, marketing elements, functions, and strategies will be discussed from the more traditional hierarchy.

According to Dr. Philip Kotler, marketing guru and author of several books on the subject, marketing utilizes four basic tools that comprise what he calls "the marketing mix" or the "four P's": product, price, promotion, and place. In recent years, as commercial and nonprofit organizations have refocused on customer relationship management, the Arts and Business Council have added three more P's: positioning, packaging, and people.

The goal of marketing is exchange, which is usually—although by no means always—the payment of money in exchange for goods or services. While marketing directors have control over some of the P's, they have no control over the general market environment that includes such factors as the community's economic, political, and ethnic profile. They also lack control over the product, although some have influence over how the product is developed, perceived, used, and valued. The astute artistic director or the person booking attractions will however consult with the marketing director in planning a season.

Successful marketing attempts to accomplish the following:

1.) Position the organization to focus on its unique strengths, which are identified by researching the organization's strengths and weaknesses in relation to the immediate competition.

2.) Identify and target the product to a large number of potential buyers who are likely to purchase the product.

3.) Understand what the benefits are as perceived by the potential buyers.

4.) Determine how to communicate most effectively with all potential buyers.

5.) Price the product to match the market.

6.) Motivate the market to want the product.

7.) Make purchasing the product as easy as possible.

8.) Make enjoyment of the product as great as possible.

9.) Collect and track consumer data.

10.) Create loyal users of the product who will repeat their use and support at increasingly higher levels.

Modern marketing theory and practice were pioneered in America and, depending on one's outlook, may be largely credited or blamed for the conspicuous level of consumerism in our society. Yet despite the successful application of marketing techniques to the sale of almost every imaginable product, the theatre and the performing arts businesses were late in adopting them. It was the nonprofit sector of the performing arts world that first recognized the value of marketing and that continues to employ the best-trained and most creative marketing directors in the field. Broadway and the commercial theatre, by contrast, have had a long tradition of hiring independent press agents from advertising agencies. This is changing as marketing directors are proving and displaying their skills on Broadway as elsewhere in the industry.

In all arts-producing and arts-presenting circles, there exists a serious concern that aggressively applied marketing practice will dictate product selection and development. That it will, for example, force artistic directors to produce only safe and traditional plays that appeal to the majority of the theatregoing public. This danger is real, especially in board-driven or management-driven companies where most trustees are corporate executives who normally base their decisions on "the bottom line." Artistic personnel have to be just as aggressive in promoting their priorities. Artistic priorities can well survive side by side with well-proven, up-to-date marketing techniques. Marketing research, when joined with evaluations of a company's past marketing performance, can be of great value in making artistic programming decisions—without being the sole basis on which such decisions are made.

Producing theatre or any performing art of high quality is not antithetical to selling tickets, raising money, or satisfying all the different user groups. The performing arts must always be of high quality, or tickets won't be sold, money won't be raised, and patrons won't be satisfied or return.

Basic Elements of Marketing

The Market Environment

"If you build it, they will come" may work for Hollywood baseball movies, but it is not a realistic model for theatres and performing arts groups that want to thrive. The community in which a theatre operates is the immediate family of which it is a member. The wider areas from which it also draws audiences constitute its extended family. It is important to understand both, although an organization can have more influence over the first— the immediate family. Audiences may be mainly comprised of tourists and bus groups from out of town, but still there is a relatively permanent nucleus of local residents who determine the business, social, cultural, educational, and political profile of the community, and whose support of the organization is critical. Theatre managers and artistic directors in large cities deal with complex and continuously evolving power structures and institutions that must be analyzed; in smaller communities, both the power structure and audience tastes may be easier to understand. Whether located in downtown Los Angeles or in a Kansas cornfield, a theatre or performing arts company must adapt to its unique environment if it is to survive. An organization can exist only when a large enough portion of the local community allows it to exist; therefore, the company must always be mindful of the principle of reciprocity. If the theatre is to get community support, the community must get support from the theatre.

Chapter 2 discusses factors about community life that a producing organization should consider before establishing a theatre: audience potential, proximity to transportation, the competition, the media, local organizations, the economy, the climate, and local attitudes. If such data were gathered and included in a feasibility study, this could serve as an important research document for the marketing director. It could help dictate how to structure a communication network from the theatre to the movers and shakers within the community. These influential people should be identified in terms of their ability to help the success of the venture. Then the theatre operator, members of the marketing staff, and others should establish an ongoing dialogue with them. For permanently based companies this should include personal contact with:

1.) Business leaders: corporate executives, heads of chambers of commerce, bank presidents, major hotel managers, restaurant owners, and prominent small business owners;

2.) Political leaders: the mayor and other elected and appointed officials in key municipal positions, elected state and federal representatives, heads of local school boards, community councils, and citizen groups;

3.) Leading professionals: college presidents, school superintendents, hospital administrators, lawyers, physicians, judges, and other professionals.

4.) Media directors: publishers, editors, critics, journalists, and others in the print and electronic media;

5.) Social leaders: heads of cultural organizations, directors and administrators of competing performing arts organizations, heads of local arts councils and philanthropic groups, and heads of local sports teams;

6.) Volunteer organization leadership: Rotary, Kiwanis, local hospice, arts volunteers, and other community organizations that are volunteer-based.

Letters must be sent, appointments arranged, receptions held, and personal contacts renewed on a regular basis. Even a commercial theatre can create one or more advisory boards as a means of cultivating the friendship and support of local leaders and benefiting from their experience and position.

To further nourish its relations with the community, a permanently based theatre should ask:

What local programs, organizations, landmarks, and institutions are most highly regarded by local residents?

How can the theatre use its resources and special know-how to assist these local interests and endeavors?

Here are just a few of the many possibilities:

1.) Encourage the sponsorship of benefit performances to raise money for local causes.

2.) Donate use of the theatre facility for meetings and conferences that serve local interests.

3.) Establish a speakers' bureau that makes theatre staff and artists available to local groups and organizations.

4.) Arrange for theatre artists, especially celebrities, to participate in local fundraising events—this kind of tie-in provides photo opportunities that will benefit both the event and the theatre.

5.) Offer space in the playbill for ads or copy that will benefit local interests.

6.) Provide reciprocal links to local organizations on its website.

7.) Offer lobby space where local charities display information.

8.) Offer the theatre's mailing list and email list to appropriate, nonprofit organizations, if this would not compromise a confidentiality agreement, either tacit or written, between the theatre and its patrons.

9.) Lend properties, lighting equipment, and other theatre items to local amateur and nonprofit performing arts groups; this must be done cautiously to protect the theatre against damage and loss.

10.) Establish and maintain active memberships in local, regional, and national arts and cultural associations.

11.) Attend and participate in appropriate noncultural functions at the community and state levels.

Being involved signifies that a performing arts organization is truly part of the community in which it operates, that it cares about that community, and that it assumes responsibility for being a good citizen of the community.

The Internal Environment

An analysis of the internal environment of a nonprofit theatre organization begins with its mission statement and stated objectives. What are its goals and what is the likelihood of achieving them in view of the market environment? It is important to assess the competition and determine how the organization and its product are unique or can best meet the needs of the perceived market. What are the assets that can be emphasized, and what are the weaknesses that can be corrected, explained, or diminished? The questions posed above to a nonprofit theatre can also be posed to a commercial operation.

Market Research

Basic research about a given market or community can be conducted inexpensively and quickly online at the Bureau of the Census of the U.S. Department of Commerce at http://www.census.gov. This data is drawn from a population census that is conducted every ten years at the beginning of each decade. It provides demographic characteristics of people, such as ages, sex, races, national origins, family sizes, education, employment, unemployment, and income. In addition, an economic census profiles the U.S. economy every five years. Statistics are organized on national, state, county, city, and town levels, and some data is broken down by zip code. Demographic information about the social, economic, and housing characteristics of the United States population, as well as business, industry, and trade data, can be found in several other census surveys: "Survey of Income and Program Participation (SIPP)"; "Current Population Survey (CPS)"; "American Housing Survey (AHS)"; "County Business Patterns," etc. A comprehensive list of surveys conducted by the U.S. Census Bureau is available at http://www.census.gov/main/www/surveys.html.

There are numerous other periodicals published by the federal government that are helpful in compiling data for marketing purposes. One of these is "Statistics of Income," published annually by the United States Department of Treasury—Internal Revenue Service and is compiled from the tax returns of individuals, corporations, sole proprietorships, and partnerships. The reports are free and can be found at the IRS website http://www.irs.gov.

Initial market research often utilizes secondary source material such as that discussed above. User research, on the other hand, is more specific and involves primary source material—namely, potential, actual, and former or lapsed users. Potential users represent the most amorphous of these groups because they are an unknown quantity. An objective of the marketing department is to persuade these people to become users— whether that means buying tickets, writing newspaper stories, awarding grants or granting loans. Then it becomes the objective to persuade the actual users to repeat and increase their use of the product. When they do not, the objective of the marketing department must be to determine if some aspect of the product—the production, the corporation, the facility, the staff—was to blame and why. Was it poor casting, inadequate parking and/or restroom facilities, rude employees? When market research is purely sales oriented, it usually begins with the current audience because a good analysis of it can lead to marketing communications with potential customers who reflect the same profile. Methods of studying the audience profile are discussed in this chapter. (See Customer Relationship Management in Chapter 12.)

Target Markets

Targeting a market means identifying a group of people who share similar interests, especially in terms of their readiness to exchange time and/or money for a product that promises to satisfy their interests and/or needs. Once the product is analyzed and understood, the marketing department then has to identify the people most likely to use it. Targeting a handful of different markets for the same theatre company, starting with such obvious groups as the board of trustees, current season-ticket buyers, single-ticket buyers, and friends and relatives of the cast and staff members is a relatively simple task. Using the particular nature of the product—the season of plays, for example—additional groups of potential ticket buyers can usually be targeted. These might include students, ethnic groups, personnel from a nearby military base, employees of a major business or industry, or whatever group is deemed relevant and is large enough to generate meaningful results. This process is important because no theatre has the resources to engage in blanket marketing. In fact, it is wise to test target markets with a limited approach—for example, by mailing the theatre's brochure to only five hundred medical doctors before mailing it to the other ten thousand medical people in the community. Or, an even more efficient way is to send a prospect card to members of the target group and have the recipients select whether or not they wish to receive more information.

Aside from markets that are targeted for the purpose of selling tickets, others should be targeted to receive special attention because they directly influence the success of the theatre: the press needs to receive news releases in a particular format and in a timely fashion; funders want to receive grant proposals on time and according to their specifications. It is important to understand that the total marketing process comprises exchanges other than the exchange of money for tickets.

The Product

In the Broadway theatre each production is usually marketed separately, even when the same person produces a number of different shows that may even be of the same genre or by the same creative artists. This is also the case with most road shows, even though different shows may play in the same commercial roadhouse in a single season or year. But the majority of theatres—stock, nonprofit professional companies, presenting organizations, opera and dance companies—typically offer a series of different productions on a seasonal basis and market them as such. In each case, marketing strategies are applied to create public awareness and understanding of the product, determine which segments of the market most need or desire the product, and then convince them to use it. Of course, much of this process depends on knowing and analyzing the product: the dramatic material, the creative and interpretive artists involved, and, when possible, the production in performance. In nonprofit theatre the product also includes the institution and its mission. Marketing efforts that are uninformed about the product and its ingredients are seldom as successful as those that are informed. The worst nightmare for a marketing director is finally to understand the artistic message opening night, when, alas, there is no way—or time, really—to market the product. Successful marketing requires an ongoing, open dialogue between marketing and artistic personnel.

Many businesses use market testing or sampling in selected markets before offering new products in a wider market. In a sense, the theatre has a long tradition of test marketing by virtue of the tryout system. The rewrites and other changes made during the tryout period are a response to market testing. Similarly, new films are often tested in limited markets or in sneak previews, then perhaps subjected to further editing. So the creative development of a theatre production is partly a matter of suiting the product to the user, of creating a perfect exchange. The trick is not only to refine the product but also to refine it for the widest number of users. Again this is not to suggest that marketing the arts should dictate the artistic process; it is only to suggest that market research can help the creative team understand the reactions to their work.

Unlike a producer who is trying out a single production, a presenting organization has the advantage of booking events that have already been tested, although perhaps not in the local market. But that market is relatively stationary and can be studied over a period of seasons. A marketing professional can analyze the sales history of specific productions to gauge the market response to a potential booking. This strategy utilizes data taken from the presenting organization's past box office records and other such sources to formulate a history of local audience response to a variety of attractions and marketing strategies. Once again, this illustrates how a marketing tool can help to inform artistic decision making, but the booking process should take other considerations into account as well. (See Chapter 9, Presenters and Presenting Organizations.)

Positioning

Positioning or branding of the organization is the proprietary visual, emotional, rational, and cultural image of the organization or product. When consumers think Nike, they might think "Just Do It." When consumers think IBM, they might think "Big Blue." When consumers think Times Square, they might think "The Entertainment Capital of the World." The fact that one remembers the brand name and has positive associations with it makes product selection easier and enhances the value and satisfaction one gets from the product.

Many people mistakenly define brand as logo. In actuality the logo is only a small piece of overall brand identity that includes brand names, brand associations, brand personality, and logos. A good brand name gives a good first impression and evokes positive associations with the brand.

The importance of an organization's defining its own brand comes down to this: Do you want your company's brand identity created for you by your competitors and unhappy customers? Of course not. The process of defining a brand begins with researching your customers and finding why they buy your products rather than your competitors'. Once that is determined, repeat that message in every ad, in every news release, in all communications with employees, and in every sales call and media interview. With consistent repetition of the most persuasive selling messages, customers will think of you and buy from you.

The entire organization is the brand, not just the marketing communications. Every material produced internally and externally needs to build on the brand equity by consistently using the same logo, tagline, font, and color scheme in all communications. To build brand equity, all communications of the organization must support the brand. This includes all marketing materials: brochures, advertising, website, press releases, programs/playbills; all administrative collateral: letterhead, business cards, annual reports; all institutional signage: marquee, information signs throughout the building/theatre to name just a few.

Packaging

Packaging begins by wrapping the product in a name. For example, the San Francisco Symphony packaged its music director, Michael Tilson Thomas simply as MTT. Often, in the performing arts there are several names and titles involved with each event: "The San Francisco Symphony's American Maverick Festival presents Bad Boy of Music: The World of George Antheil." That's a lot of wrapping. Each name might have stood on its own as a separate product, and each might have conveyed something different. Here, however, all the names are put together in a *single package*, and because of this they are presumably made more desirable, usable, and enjoyable for more people. The symphony later repackaged the event as "American Mavericks" for a Minnesota Public Radio music series and website that received the Peabody Award in 2004.

The name selected for a theatre facility, corporation, organization, festival, or series—not to mention the artistic work itself—can have considerable impact on how that product is perceived and consequently how it is used. Few products sell themselves, even when they are widely known. Of course there is always a certain amount of impulse buying and alternatively a certain percentage of loyal customers who will buy whatever that business sells. For example, some people see any and every musical by Stephen Sondheim; others, each new production of *The Mikado*; some automatically renew their subscriptions to the local opera or ballet company.

Nonetheless, these customers rarely provide sufficient support to sustain a theatre operation. Similarly, the loyal users from the media, philanthropic, or artistic communities are rarely sufficient to sustain the operation. So the product must be packaged in some way to serve a variety of users and make it appear unique or desirable for all of them.

Standard methods for packaging theatre tickets include subscription or season ticket offers, memberships, series and miniseries offers, group sales and package deals that include the theatre ticket, along with such things as parking or shuttle bus service. Skillful packaging is targeted to those markets that have ticket buyers who are likely to purchase tickets, so again, it requires a knowledge of the community based on research. Standard methods for packaging not directly aimed at ticket sales include press releases, press kits, benefit events, funding proposals, job orientation manuals, and annual reports.

The most traditional form of packaging used by arts organizations is the subscription series—multiple events sold in a series, months in advance to the core audience or the subscribers. This is a time-honored strategy in marketing performances, immortalized in Danny Newman's *Subscribe Now!*, that generates a significant portion of ticket revenue at a low marketing cost. However, as the competition for the entertainment dollar has increased exponentially over the last twenty years, subscription sales are declining. Audiences have become more spontaneous in purchasing entertainment and are moving away from making an advance time commitment, especially involving a large sum of money.

Only a small percentage of any arts audience actually buys the tickets. The "Classical Music Consumer Segmentation Study," completed in 2002 by the arts marketing and audience research firm Audience Insight LLC for the Knight Foundation identified this group as the "initiators," those patrons who purchase the tickets and invite other patrons, identified as the "responders." The report states:

> At any given ticketed performance of music, dance or theater, a majority of those in the audience did not personally buy a ticket. Someone else bought it for them. The average number of tickets per order, industry wide, is somewhere around 2.5. Of the people who did not actually buy their ticket, a portion of them did not engage in any part of the purchase decision process at all. They accepted an invitation from a friend or family member.

This suggests that there is a smaller, more powerful group in an organization's database that deserves a targeted message, i.e., an *evite* that bundles a cultural event with dinner before and drinks after. Evites are electronic invitations that are emailed to prospective buyers.

As competition for the audience's leisure time becomes more intense, arts organizations are realizing that they are selling an experience not just a performance. This simple fact informs all communication with the audience. New packages have been created that provide an added value to specific groups for purchasing tickets. One example is the New York City Opera's Big Deal campaign. Introduced in 1999, the campaign targets the twenty-one-to-thirty-five-year-old set. The New York City Opera capitalizes on its "Big is Better" slogan that offers "Big Drama, Big Divas, Big Deal for Big Deals and Big Savings." These gen-xers purchase a Diva or Duet memberships that entitles them to prime orchestra seating and two parties a season. In the first five seasons, on average, ninety percent of attendees had not attended an opera prior to their purchasing tickets. The key to the program's success was an attractive package, targeted direct marketing and support advertising, and a fresh brand specific for the twenty-to thirty-something set.

Packaging, of course, adds to the cost of the product. This may be the cost of running a shuttle-bus service or the cost of printing the annual report. But if the package meets the needs of enough users, the additional cost may be worth it. Package-testing,

when time permits, can help an organization avoid costly mistakes by sampling a small portion of a target market before approaching the whole market or by testing several packages in the same market. For example, a single brochure might offer three or four different series of performances for the same groups of events. One might be a series of Friday nights, one might be a series of light entertainments, one might be a series of classical events, and the fourth might be a mixture of events. The response to this kind of offer will quickly determine which series are going to be most popular and which should simply be dropped from future packaging offers.

Pricing

Ticket pricing is discussed at length in Chapter 12, but it should also be understood that pricing is an integral part of marketing. A product may meet user needs, but if the price is beyond most users' ability to pay, it will fail in the marketplace; conversely, if the product is underpriced, it may be perceived as inferior. How productive in terms of sales and income is it to increase or decrease prices or offer discounts and package deals? Again, testing or sampling can help answer such questions. And when potential users do not respond to certain price offers, the prices should be changed.

Promotion

The most basic and widely recognized methods of promoting a product are:

Paid Promotions

1.) Advertising: Any type of promotion that is paid for in increments of time—such as thirty seconds for a radio or television commercial; by the line or space—such as a newspaper or magazine ad; or by the service—such as printing a flyer or renting billboard space.

2.) E-Marketing: All online activity, such as website, email marketing, and e-newsletters.

3.) Personal sales: All nonmedia personal contact, such as telemarketing, or a table set up at a mall or fair.

4.) Merchandising: All commercial type communications, such as T-shirts, cups, tote bags, and other merchandise that carries the logo of a particular company or show or institution, when those items are given away for their promotional value as opposed to those sold in the theatre.

The ways in which these promotional methods are utilized become the marketing strategies or the "how tos" of the marketing plan and will be discussed in the next two chapters.

Unpaid promotions, those that leverage, or generate free media coverage:

1.) Publicity: Any mention or coverage about an organization or its products in the media that is not paid for.

2.) Public Relations: General efforts over a period of time that attempt to increase public awareness, interest, and support for an organization and its products.

3.) Sponsorships: Corporate and media sponsorships can generate considerable free coverage, in the media itself, if it is a media sponsor, but also to the patrons and employees of the corporate sponsor. Also, corporate sponsors will often include information about their sponsorship in their own newsletters and other public communications.

Publicity and Media Relations will be discussed in detail in the following chapter.

Requisites of Successful Promotion

Three Requisites

1.) Getting Attention
A newspaper ad, a television commercial, a press release, a personal appearance, a brochure, and other attempts at promotion must first capture attention before they can promote. If the reader doesn't see the ad, or the editor doesn't read the press release, there will be no follow-through, or no promotion of the product. There are many ways to call attention to a particular theatre or production, but whichever way is chosen, it must, itself, be captivating. The simplest techniques are frequently the most effective. A press release, for example, might be printed on paper with a striking letterhead so that the press release will be noticed and be less likely to be misplaced. A newspaper advertisement with a border around it or with minimal, uncrowded copy will stand out on the printed page. In other words, the ultimate goal of theatrical promotion, all promotion, is to call attention to an organization or production, but the promotional strategy used to do this must first call attention to itself or everything else is for naught.

2.) Providing Motivation
Once promotional material has captured the consumers' attention, it must garner their interest in order to motivate them to purchase tickets or contribute to whatever is being advocated—to donate money or to volunteer services perhaps.

Even the most casual observers of hype are aware that they are being appealed to on many levels. Most promotion does more than say, "Buy me." It says, "Buy me because . . ." The "because" is the promotional element meant to motivate *potential* users to become *actual* users. The manipulative and sometimes misleading techniques invented by Madison Avenue to sell Americans everything from pretzels to presidents have been exposed in many studies, including Vance Packard's *The Hidden Persuaders*, Alvin Toffler's *The Culture Consumers*, and Theodore White's *The Making of the President*. Yet promotion continues to be effective.

Promotional pieces usually employ what might be called personal motivating appeals: appeals to an individual's—often selfish—needs and desires. The desires to be beautiful, rich, famous, and sexy appear to dominate the field. Other more selfless motivating appeals include those to one's sense of honesty, humanity, religion, patriotism, and charity. There is nothing wrong with stirring such feelings. What is wrong is that promotion often promises something it can't deliver. How many television commercials, for instance, picture some miserable-looking soul who, upon using a particular product, is miraculously transfigured into the personification of beauty? The people who create such commercials obviously hope that the viewers' emotions will get the better of their intelligence. The most common and probably overused motivating appeal in theatrical promotion is the use of quotations that are lifted from the work of critics. This supposedly appeals to one's respect for authority and expertise.

3.) Delivering Satisfaction
Responsible promoters are careful to promise only what their products can deliver, because they want people to use them more than once. Products are usually judged by how they were promoted: do they live up to the promises made or implied about them? If a play is advertised as an "uproarious comedy hit," that's exactly what it should be. Otherwise the people who see it will feel cheated, will tell their friends and associates that it's not worth it, and attendance will decline. Clearly, this is not a formula for success.

While the product should deliver the satisfaction promised by its promotion, promotional material should also provide information satisfaction. If a newspaper ad or a brochure captures the eye, and the copy and/or graphic elements stimulate the desire to attend a performance, then it should also provide the basic information necessary for the reader to follow through, to take action that will convert the reader into a user.

Promotional pieces such as ads and press releases sometimes fail to contain this information, usually because of inexperienced marketing personnel or publicists who neglect to have their work scrutinized and proofread by other people. The failure of promotional material to include such basic information as an address and phone number or website address usually dooms the material itself to failure. The harder it is for people to take action in regard to using a product, the less likely they will be to use it.

Because marketing is a complex process not limited to sales, user satisfaction is an important factor. In the performing arts this presents special challenges, because the main product—the production—is never the same from performance to performance. This is the very essence of its uniqueness and value, but it is nonetheless a marketing problem. Each audience wants and expects the same satisfaction reported by the critics and general word of mouth. Yet the replacement of a leading performer because of illness, the failure of stage machinery, the rowdiness of two drunks in the third row center, and an infinite number of other incidents can adversely effect audience satisfaction. Good marketing takes this into account by attempting to make audience members partners in solving such problems. For example, the audience should not only be informed in advance about cast replacements, but also be asked to give such performers their fair due. Obvious mechanical problems might be announced by the stage manager or even alluded to by a performer in such a manner as to beg indulgence. People seated near the drunks might be asked to be patient while they're removed.

Finally, the theatre-going public gets smarter with each experience. The advent of first-class touring productions playing the smallest of cities and major concert artists visiting the most remote corners of the world, the audience of today is more sophisticated and can easily distinguish the good from the bad. In managing publicity for a long running show or a single performance, the best practice is one that merges fact and honesty in creative ways. Don't overembellish the facts and at all times be honest about the experience the customer is buying.

Place and Distribution

The place where the performance takes place, as discussed in Chapter 2, is always a major factor in determining how the product will be used, how often, and by whom. Geographical location, proximity to transportation routes and systems, parking, dining, architectural design, physical condition of the facility and other such auxiliary factors are all important and may even help to shape the product itself. Poor acoustics or sight lines, dismal restrooms, or unsightly lobbies should be of serious concern to marketing efforts. Such problems have a negative impact on everyone involved with the product, from audience to artists to staff.

Closely related to the place where a product is used is the matter of distribution. A major difficulty in marketing the performing arts is that the product—the performance—is not very mobile. A customer cannot take it home, as she or he can with a rented DVD. A customer cannot usually wait for it to be available closer to home, as with a hit movie. While distribution is increased with touring and, only occasionally, with cable casting and broadcasting of live productions, the last two incur such high costs that they are not viable options in most cases.

As broadband speeds continue to increase, the potential for web casting productions is growing. But for the time being, distribution is centered around theatre tickets and their accessibility to potential customers. The location and design of the box office, ticketing systems, and the entire theatre experience have a major impact on sales. The goal, of course, is to make ticket buying as easy as possible. In 2004, over 200 million Americans were online, that's seventy-five percent of the total population. It is imperative that organizations sell their tickets online, it is no longer a luxury; it is now an essential business practice.

People

More and more organizations are realizing that their most precious asset is their existing customer base, and among that base not all customers are created equal. For example, a subscriber who makes a donation to the theatre is much more loyal to the organization than the first-time ticket buyer. The bottom line is that everyone is different. With the recent advances in technology, customers are now expecting that organizations acknowledge their individual differences and needs. Businesses are creating customer relationship management programs to develop closer relationships between them and their customers. Similarly, performing arts organizations should strive to build loyalty among its customers, the audience.

For small theatres, customer relationship management includes:

1.) Processes that help identify and target their best customers, generate quality sales leads, and plan and implement marketing campaigns with clear goals and objectives.

2.) Processes that help form individualized relationships with customers and provide the highest level of customer service to the most loyal customers.

3.) Processes that provide employees with the information they need to know their customers' wants and needs and build relationships between the company and its customers.

4.) Processes that may merge the marketing and development activities to develop special customer programs that will lead to continuing patronage and financial support of the organization. Customer relationship management tools include software and browser-based applications that collect and organize information about customers. (See Chapter 12.)

Customer relationship management will often involve every department within a theatre or performing arts center, and will generate a plethora of activities that add value to the theatre experience. While many of these activities may have as their goal increased marketing or publicity opportunities, in the end they are all simply focused on keeping customers happy and bringing them back again and again. One of the primary goals in customer relationship management is to reach the point where the customers absolutely trust the product on stage, and while not necessarily liking everything they see, appreciate the way in which it was represented—sold—and presented.

Some of the value-added activities that theatres are using to enhance customer relations are:

1.) Preperformance lectures on the show or attraction;

2.) Postperformance opportunities to meet the artists;

3.) Travel programs to other places for theatre, festivals, or star performances;

4.) Master classes open to the community;

5.) Theatre open house with the opportunity to visit all parts of the facility and talk with staff;

6.) Receptions, galas, and other special events that may not be connected to a performance.

Evaluation

A marketing plan and its strategies to sell tickets and provide other services for users of the product should begin by stating a set of goals. A final evaluation of the plan measures end results against those goals. But in the meantime, marketing efforts should be evaluated on a daily basis throughout the implementation period. Contingency strategies should be planned in case initial attempts fail to generate the desired results. Each direct mail piece, each newspaper ad, each online offer or other promotional effort should be evaluated for its effectiveness. This can be done by coding mailing labels, by tracking emails, by coding coupons and order forms, and by compiling information obtained at the box office. As a practical matter, some promotional strategies will be more effective than others. Ongoing evaluation, however, should help to evolve a highly successful marketing plan over time. Producers and managers sometimes expect instant results; however, a successful marketing campaign requires research, planning, constant evaluation, modifications, and time to work.

The Marketing Budget

What is a realistic assessment of the *resources* that can be rallied to implement a marketing plan? To answer this question will require a close look at the internal environment of the company or organization that is to be marketed. Specifically, one should examine:

1.) Human resources

a. *Staff*: What is the size, training, and experience of management and staff members in terms of marketing functions, and how much time can they devote to this area?

b. *Consultants*: Is it desirable or necessary to seek outside technical assistance in the market area? What kind of assistance? Is it affordable?

c. *Volunteers*: How many hours per week can board members and other volunteers be expected to give to marketing efforts, such as letter-writing, telemarketing, and surveying?

2.) Financial resources: A reasonable marketing budget can be set at twenty to twenty-five percent of the total potential ticket gross, though this will vary. Is some or all of this amount available now? Can some of this money be gained through contributed income and in-kind services?

3.) Physical resources: What facilities, such as office space, box office and ticket outlets, and space for receptions and press meetings, are available to assist in marketing efforts? What equipment, such as software, copying machines, telephone systems, fax machines, camera and video equipment, is available? What computer software programs, including those for ticketing, web design packages, and graphic design programs, are available?

By listing all such resources—which represent people, money, and time—the options available for marketing the organization will narrow considerably. For example, a company poor in cash but rich in volunteer labor will have to forego extensive media advertising but may conduct extensive marketing research on outreach, audience development programs, audience education and enhancement activities, telemarketing, and various publicity initiatives. And the age and abilities of available volunteer workers will determine the type of work they are best suited to do: high school students might distribute flyers and posters, college interns might do marketing research and/or online activities, board members might secure in-kind services, and seniors might do telemarketing.

A sizable portion of a marketing budget tends to be used up by staff salaries, equipment, printing services, and consultants. These costs should always be examined and challenged. The amount that remains after such relatively predictable costs have been budgeted is the amount available to spend on promotional strategies—advertising, direct mail, publicity activities, press parties, and the like. How available resources are allocated to marketing efforts should be decided during the formulation of a marketing plan. Once a plan has been adopted and implemented, resources may be shifted and reallocated according to how well each strategy is working.

The Marketing Plan

Setting Objectives

Marketing objectives should be directly tied to the basic philosophy, mission, and goals of the company that is offering the product in the marketplace. If this is a commercial outfit, the leading goal is usually that of selling as many tickets as possible/making as much profit as possible.

Nonprofit theatre organizations face a somewhat more complex marketing challenge in that they must usually deal with the nonprofit corporation, a performance facility, and a number of different productions. The goals articulated in the organization's mission statement must be the core of any marketing plan. For example, if the mission is to produce new plays that focus on the condition of women in American society, the primary goal of the marketing plan should be identical to that of the mission. Whatever success marketing strategies may have, they will fail if the mission is not accomplished. In this case, practicing American playwrights would be the most important target market because they are the only source of the plays.

They must learn about the company's existence and its mission; they must be motivated to submit scripts; they must entrust the theatre with productions; and they must want to repeat the process with their subsequent work. Success in achieving objectives such as these entails long-range planning and public relations efforts that continue throughout the life of the organization. Nonetheless, they should be spelled out in a long-range marketing plan that includes a time frame—perhaps three to five years—for achieving goals or, at least, making progress in that direction.

Marketing objectives related to ticket sales usually employ short-term strategies that are comparatively self-contained, which might include a season ticket campaign. These should be stated in the plan as simply as possible: for example, "increase season ticket sales to seventy-five percent of capacity," or "stimulate broader student participation in theatre department productions," or "generate group sales of ten percent of capacity." It might be a good idea to draw up two marketing plans—one with long-range and one with short-range objectives, and it might be wise to have separate plans for each objective, so long as these are compatible with the organization's primary goals and with each other. Eventually, the strategies selected to implement each plan should be translated into a calendar format that shows when each step must be accomplished. (See Appendix R, Standard Marketing Timetables.) Not surprisingly, however, the objective of filling seats usually ranks high on any performing arts organization's priority list.

Writing the Plan

In order to get the most out of their available resources, all organizations—even those with no money—should prepare a written marketing plan at least annually. This should include research and sales information from the past one to five years, and demonstrate how current marketing strategies and budget allocations are designed to enhance achievements or correct failures of the recent past. It may be a fairly lengthy document containing statistical charts with data drawn from audience surveys and financial reports, as well as evidence reflecting media coverage and advertising results. Or it may be a simple outline that highlights recent accomplishments and failures, lists the available resources, and then states how these will be utilized to accomplish current and future objectives. A typical marketing plan is likely to follow a format and contain information about items such as those in the outline below:

Sample Outline of a Marketing Plan

I. The Marketing Universe
   A. External environment
      1. economic
      2. political
      3. educational
      4. social
      5. cultural
      6. the theatre profession
      7. the competition
   B. Internal environment
      1. mission and institutional objectives
      2. brand identity
      3. organizational structure
      4. structure and staff related to marketing endeavors
      5. problems and shortcomings
      6. strengths and accomplishments

II. Marketing History and Audience Profile
   A. Five-year season ticket sales history
      1. number of attractions and performances
      2. number of season tickets sold
      3. prices
      4. percentage of capacity and income generated
      5. marketing expenditures
      6. renewal and attrition rates
      7. season ticket telemarketing campaign results
      8. season ticket online campaign results

B. Five-year single ticket sales history
    1. number of attractions and performances
    2. number of tickets sold: in the aggregate and by price
    3. percentage of capacity/percentage of gross potential generated
    4. marketing expenditures
    5. breakdown of tickets/income via
        a. telephone
        b. internet
        c. agencies
        d. mail order
        e. window
C. Five-year group sales history
    1. number of attractions and performances involved
    2. number of tickets sold
    3. prices and discounts
    4. percentage of capacity and percentage of total income generated
    5. marketing expenditures
    6. repeat buyer percentage
D. Five-year online sales history
    1. number of attractions and performances
    2. number of subscription series sold: in the aggregate and by price
    3. number of single tickets sold: in the aggregate and by price
    4. percentage of capacity/percentage of gross potential generated
    5. marketing expenditures
    6. number of new buyers purchasing online and percentage to total
    7. number of repeat buyers purchasing online and percentage to total
    8. size of email list
E. Season ticket audience profile
    1. types of services used (series, miniseries, exchanges, donations, etc.)
    2. geographical (zip code areas of residence)
    3. personal profile (education, marital status, age, income, gender, employment, affiliation
    4. media usage (internet, radio, television, newspapers, magazines)
F. Single ticket audience profile (same as 1 through 4 above)
G. Group sales audience profile
    1. sales according to types of offers (flat group discount, package deal, senior citizen group offer, corporate offer)
    2. geographical (city and state origins)
    3. affiliations (political, religious, cultural, educational, business and industry)
H. Total audience profile (combined figures from A, B, and C above)
I. Marketing analysis of last season

III. SWOP
    A. Strengths (itemize these)
    B. Weaknesses (itemize these)
    C. Opportunities (itemize these)
    D. Problems (itemize these)

IV. Marketing Goals and Objectives
    A. Marketing philosophy
    B. Long-term, mission-related marketing goals
    C. Short-term marketing objectives (itemize and prioritize)
    D. Research proposals and programs necessary to determine strategies

V. Marketing Strategies
    A. Target markets
        1. service related
        2. sales related
    B. Use of marketing mix
        1. product
        2. positioning
        3. packaging
        4. pricing
        5. promotion
            a. advertising
            b. publicity
            c. public relations
            d. personal sales
            e. promotions
        6. place and distribution
        7. people
    C. Contingency strategies

VI. Marketing Budget
    A. Projected expenses (itemize in detail)
    B. Projected revenues (itemize in detail)
    C. Projected nonmonetary gains (itemize)

VII. Marketing Evaluation
    A. Summary of goals and projected results for each marketing initiative
    B. Summary of methods by which marketing strategies will be measured and evaluated (such as brochure coding and online tracking)

Different organizations, of course, will devise different marketing plans. The important thing is to have one—and use it. Just as with putting together a budget, the planning process should involve nearly everyone within the organization, because they are all users of the product with individual needs and they all have contact with other users—ticket buyers, vendors, the press and so on—who have still other needs. All major types of users should be targeted in the plan, and strategies should be devised to meet their various needs. A good marketing plan will dictate a clear course of action that will usually proceed from research, to the identification of marketing opportunities and problems, to setting objectives, to selecting strategies, to composing a budget, to evaluating results.

Implementing the Plan

After the research data has been gathered and clearly organized in written form, which is often the most time-consuming aspect of the marketing process, it must be interpreted and promotional strategies must be selected based on the results. Because resources are always limited, difficult choices will have to be made.

> For example: Is it best to buy numerous small newspaper ads or a few large ones? Should the staff available for telemarketing be used to sell season tickets or raise contributions for the capital campaign? For each strategy that is selected there might be a separate plan for evaluating it.

Let's assume that an audience survey of a theatre in Boston shows that eight percent of its ticket buyers come from neighboring Providence, Rhode Island. Hoping to increase this patronage, the marketing director might initiate a variety of strategies: encourage the board of trustees to recruit one or more new members from Providence; upgrade and intensify the services provided to the media in Providence; open one or more ticket outlets there; distribute flyers and discount offers and run a series of ads in the leading Providence newspapers. An evaluation plan for this Providence Strategy might appear as follows:

Strategy	Time Period	Cost	Goal	Sales Results
Providence: Sunday ads outlets, flyers, coupons	Oct–Dec (12 weeks)	$650/wk total: $7,800	To increase Providence ticket-buyers 50%, from 8% to 12%	Nov Dec Jan

Only by surveying every person who attends a performance throughout the season could exact results be gathered. However, systematic monitoring of telephone, email, window, and mail-in ticket orders is an effective alternative. If results are disappointing by the end of four or five weeks, the strategy should be analyzed, contingencies considered, and changes made.

If the entire marketing budget for an organization represents ten percent of the total potential gross, the ultimate sales objective should be to generate ten dollars in sales for each marketing dollar spent; thereby reaching one hundred percent capacity through sales. Beyond this, as discussed earlier, there should also be substantial nonmonetary gains as the result of marketing effort. The cost of the above Providence Strategy should bring in $650 per week in ticket sales, or $78,000 for the season, plus more and better attention from the media, and heightened awareness of the theatre in the Providence area. Obviously, this equation can be adjusted to suit different organizations, circumstances, policies, and needs. But such very specific dollar or percentage goals encourage clear-headed, objective marketing decisions. They help in resisting the often-persuasive pitches made by media salespeople, advertising agencies, and independent consultants. They help in underscoring where time is well spent and where it is wasted. And they help in keeping within the budget and on target. It's also a way of measuring the value of each dollar spent, or the most bang for the buck.

The Audience Profile

The audience provides the primary resource material for research and analysis regarding the product(s) being offered. This may be done informally by anecdotal information or observation. Or the research and analysis can be conducted in more scientific and expensive ways that include focus groups, telephone and mail surveys, or customer profiling through database mining.

Informal Audience Analysis

Often, demographic information can be guessed at quite accurately. The audience for a theatre production or even a long season of theatre productions is minuscule in comparison to the audience for a film in national distribution or a network television program, and thus it is much easier to observe. One can simply stand in the lobby at the beginning or end of each theatre performance and visually estimate the median age, sex, and race of the audience.

But more important than socio-economic data is an understanding of the psycho-aesthetic profile of an audience. What motivates an individual to attend performances and how can this information be utilized in marketing strategies to attract more customers? What perceptions do the audience members have of the production and how can marketing promote or attempt to modify these perceptions through various communication strategies? And finally, what would it take to get an audience back into this theatre? With or without formal surveys, theatre managers should be "audience watchers" and make every attempt to understand their customers, both individually and collectively. Seasoned theatre professionals—including directors, playwrights, producers, and managers—have learned that there is a place in a theatre where after a performance patrons will blurt out their initial reactions to the show. In five or ten minutes one can get a brutally candid survey of audience reaction.

There is, of course, a danger in arriving at conclusions informally or intuitively too much of the time. After all, play selection and advertising to name two decisions that have been made were primarily based on how an actual or potential audience is analyzed. Many myths and faulty generalizations about theatre audiences have been perpetuated because producers and publicists have sought quick explanations for poor attendance. "Young people don't go to theatre anymore," "No show can survive a bad review in the *Times*," "People can't afford theatre nowadays," and "Most people prefer light comedies and musicals" are all common statements in theatre circles, although none holds up under scrutiny.

The first comprehensive, nationwide survey of performance arts audiences was conducted by William J. Baumol and William G. Bowen and reported in their 1966 publication, *Performing Arts: The Economic Dilemma*. On the basis of over 24,000 usable survey returns, they found, among other things, that audiences had not changed markedly over previous decades in terms of such characteristics as age and income range; that there was little difference between Broadway and Off-Broadway audiences; and that theatregoers had very high education and income levels. More recent national surveys of audience characteristics have been conducted by the Ford Foundation (www.fordfound.gov), Theatre Communications Group (www.tcg.org), the National Endowment for the Arts (www.nea.gov), and Louis Harris polls (www.harrisinteractive.com).

An extensive survey was recently conducted by The Performing Arts Research Coalition (PARC), a collaborative research project among the five major national service organizations in the performing arts: the American Symphony Orchestra League (www.symphony.org), Association of Performing Arts Presenters (www.artspresenters.org), Dance/USA (www.danceusa.org), Opera America (www.operaam.org), and Theatre Communications Group. In addition, the Knight Foundation commissioned Audience Insight LLC to conduct the "Classical Music Consumer Segmentation Study in 2000," inviting its fifteen U.S. orchestra partners to join the research. The full report is available on the foundation's website, www.knightfdn.org.

These studies and others have gathered a tremendous amount of data on the demographics and psycho-graphics of the performing arts buyers that can assist marketing directors in identifying, targeting, and communicating with potential ticket buyers.

Audience Surveys

When performing arts managers and marketing directors believe they need more than a casual estimation of the audience profile, they frequently conduct a survey of their audiences by means of a printed questionnaire. A common method is to insert the questionnaire into playbills and provide pencils along with boxes where completed forms may be deposited at convenient locations in the lobby. If there are several ticket prices and theatre sections, questionnaires can be coded in some way to indicate these differences. This enables the evaluator to learn which sections may or may not object to existing ticket prices.

An alternate method of in-house survey distribution is to instruct ushers to hand surveys to theatregoers as they enter or during intermission. The most intrusive method is to dispatch a team of interviewers during intermission to conduct interviews with a random sampling of the audience. This may guarantee more honest and detailed results, but it may also constitute a serious interruption of the playgoers' evening—as would any kind of curtain speech about the survey.

If the dollars are available, questionnaires can be mailed to patrons who have purchased tickets. To guarantee a workable sample return, a postage-paid return envelope would have to be included in the mailing. The questionnaire is kept anonymous relative to name, which will help get more reliable answers to questions regarding age, income, and education. People like giving their opinions, and this technique provides them more time for more thoughtful answers than those given in the rush of an intermission.

Survey questions should be designed with the following guidelines in mind:

1.) Status questions, such as those regarding the respondents' income, education level, and which media outlets they use, may elicit "guilt" answers that are not entirely reliable, unless the questionnaire is totally anonymous.

2.) The fewer questions, the better, but certainly enough to make the effort worthwhile and to verify the result.

3.) The more precise the questions, the less room there will be for misinterpretation.

4.) The fewer possible answers to each question, the better. Although care must always be taken not to omit possible responses to questions; multiple choice questions should include "other" or "don't know" or "not applicable" among the possible answers in order to allow for alternatives that might have been overlooked, otherwise respondents may skip the question altogether and invalidate the results.

5.) Only questions that elicit information that is truly valuable for marketing and other purposes should be included.

6.) Instructions should be simple enough for a child to follow.

A common danger in designing a survey is failure to consider all the variables that influence results. Are the questions and answers really measuring what the evaluators think they are measuring? For example, results are invalid when the audience surveyed is not representative of the theatre's general audience. If performances are given eight times a week over a twelve-week season, an entire week should be surveyed, because matinee and evening or weeknight and weekend audiences vary greatly—not to mention audiences that result from some group sales effort, such as one that draws in a large group of children or retired sea captains. Also, the week selected for the survey should feature a production that is fairly typical of the theatre's usual attractions. Finally, is each question really necessary and what will it prove or disprove?

Audience surveys are important marketing tools in theatre management if they are obtained and interpreted with expertise. This might require hiring the services of a consultant or marketing firm. Also, it should be said that surveys are as important in showing the profile of typical as well as atypical ticket buyers. Armed with this kind of information, a theatre may decide, for example, to decrease advertising that reaches theatregoers who have already been "captured" and increase promotional strategies that might attract new audiences.

Focus Groups

Large performing arts organizations have increasingly used focus groups as tools in audience research. These are usually comprised of about a dozen people selected randomly from a large target group that the organization wishes to study. Under the leadership of a trained professional, the group meets away from the performance facility and discusses various predetermined issues designed to deepen the organization's understanding of itself and its market. While audience survey results tend to be largely *quantitative*, the results from focus group discussions tend to be *qualitative*. These are not necessarily representative of the larger group from which they were drawn, yet they may provide deeper insights and help clarify marketing problems and opportunities.

Hiring Survey Consultants

Most professional theatre and performing arts organizations have the capability of developing their own questionnaires and conducting their own audience surveys. However, when focus groups are assembled, or external segments of the public are polled, it might be wise to hire a marketing or polling firm, at least to assist in the process and train the surveyors, if phone interviews or face-to-face questioning is involved. The credentials of such consulting firms should be checked, and their being members in professional organizations such as the American Marketing Association or the American Association for Public Opinion Research would be a plus. Their websites are available at www.marketingpower.com and www.aapor.org, respectively.

Data Mining and Customer Profiling

Data mining and customer profiling are the latest tools available to marketing directors and further proof that we live in the information age. Data mining is the process of exploring and analyzing large quantities of data to discover useful knowledge including trends, patterns, and rules. By looking across data from various company sources—subscription, box office records, donations, volunteering, memberships, response to marketing campaigns, events—and external consumer behavior data—interests, hobbies, shopping habits—and demographic and household expenditure data, a marketer can gain insight on customers and then act on that information to optimize marketing strategies. Data mining for marketing is an interdisciplinary field that combines mathematics, computer science, business knowledge, and marketing experience.

Customer profiling is the process of using relevant and available information to describe characteristics of a group of customers and to identify what discriminates them from other customers or ordinary consumers. Customer profiling involves searching the data collected from a company's existing customers for patterns that will allow that company to make predictions about who its potential customers are and how those customers will behave. Once the existing customers are profiled, lists can be acquired of potential new customers that match those profiles. That prospect list can then be targeted to receive information on available theatre programs and be solicited to buy tickets.

An example of a customer profile is:

> Customer is sixty-five years old, recently retired from teaching, volunteers at the local arts center for young people, likes receiving news via email, drives a Saab.

Data mining and customer profiling require professional companies that have this specific ability; they can be quite expensive. It requires very sophisticated computer programs that can search numerous databases and identify all those to which a customer is linked.

Summary

Marketing is a complex process that involves taking a product, be it an opera, a play or musical, a ballet, a symphony, or a string quartet, from the studio or stage to the final user. It is concerned with all the people who have contact with the producing organization, including the artists, the employees, the press, the vendors, the funders, as well as the audience. It is concerned not only with holding on to the current users, but increasing current audiences, developing new audiences for the future, and enriching the enjoyment of everyone who uses the product.

Further, good survey work can also point up prejudices and assumptions that the public and management hold that may require special strategies to counter. Contrary to widely held thinking, particularly in the commercial theatre, advertising and publicity by themselves are not marketing.

All theatre companies and arts organizations, large or small, rich or poor, benefit from putting sound marketing principles to work. This begins by conducting research and then formulating a written marketing plan. Measurements should be devised for evaluating each strategy used to implement the plan, and these measurements should relate to the organization's long- and short-term goals.

CHAPTER 15

Publicity and Media Relations

THE TWO WORDS THAT MANAGERS and producers in any of the performing arts most like to hear are "sold out." A primary objective of most theatrical publicity is, of course, to attract capacity audiences on a regular basis. But ticket buyers are elusive, and many factors influence the success or failure of a theatrical production, making sold out signs a comparatively rare phenomenon. The aspect of promotion that aims to generate publicity—meaning *free* mention or coverage of a particular product is the focus of this chapter. If an attraction or event is not reported in the media as a news item, then promoting it must be paid for and is not considered publicity. This chapter emphasizes media relations, the best way to obtain free coverage. As with all external communications, the three requisites for successful marketing discussed in Chapter 14 must be adhered to: getting attention, providing motivation, and delivering satisfaction.

Integration of Marketing, Promotions, and Publicity

This chapter covers the subjects of publicity and media relations, but it must be emphasized that the publicity team is part of the organization's marketing department. It is imperative that each area of responsibility be integrated into a master marketing, promotions, and publicity plan. This planning and execution will leverage considerable more impact on ticket sales and visibility.

As mentioned in the last chapter, even the smallest and poorest theatre organizations need a marketing plan, even if it is drawn up and implemented by volunteers. Theatrical tradition has long held that, rather than a marketing director and plan, a theatre only needs a press agent or publicity director; therefore, there is resistance to a marketing plan. Press agents and publicity directors are still necessary, but they should report to the marketing specialist whose job it is to focus on all of the organization's goals, resources, and opportunities. In small organizations the marketing director may, in fact, serve as publicity director, press agent, and public relations director. But in large, professional organizations a press or public relations manager usually reports to a marketing director. Regardless of who is responsible for publicity, all organizations need a public relations plan that is integrated with the marketing plan for the season. Most publications operate on long lead times, i.e., biannual trade publications and bimonthly magazines, weekly newspaper entertainment sections, and television news programs focusing on the arts—and a detailed timeline. A targeted public relations plan must be in place for the entire season at least four months in advance of the season opening.

Virtually everyone in an organization is a member of the marketing team because everyone is somehow involved in representing, if not actually promoting, the organization to the market. Every member of the organization is a potential ambassador and he or she must have a clear understanding of the organization's mission, goals, and objectives. Whoever accepts overall marketing responsibility should understand this and harness all such activities and energies so that they pull in the same direction. More direct supervision should be given to those in the organization who are involved in sales, such as personnel in fundraising, telemarketing, and the box office. Then the organization has to decide whether to hire a publicist on staff or to engage the services of an outside public relations agency. Each alternative requires separate considerations.

Outside Public Relations Agencies

There are countless independent public relations consultants and agencies for hire. One should remember that their first priority, in order to survive, is to promote themselves. For that reason, as discussed in regard to marketing consultants in the previous chapter, their claims and promises should always be verified with past and present clients. There should be lengthy discussions about promotional goals, strategies, and the specific services that will be provided. Based on these discussions, the agency needs to provide a detailed public relations plan that identifies targeted publicity goals, strategies, and a detailed timeline. Fees should be openly discussed and checked, to be certain they are competitive. Finally, a written agreement should spell out everything that was agreed to orally. If the agency being retained has more than one publicist, it is important to know who will have primary responsibility for the theatre. Similarly, the theatre group should designate an in-house staff member to serve as the contact person and liaison.

Publicity Director

A publicity director is a promoter who must be enthusiastic about the product being promoted. This position requires an outgoing personality, a sense of conviction, and the creativeness to dream up ways to make the media respond positively to the organization. The publicist must have extensive knowledge about the community, must develop relationships with members of the press corps, advertising salespeople, and local leaders, and must be skilled in writing a press release, maintaining up-to-date media lists, and effectively pitching stories. A publicist must be the best source of information for the organization to be a valuable resource for the press. A publicist must have the ability to grasp the essence of an organization or production and translate it in a way that will help the public understand it, want it, and support it. When publicity misrepresents the real aims and qualities of an organization, either intentionally or mistakenly, the damage can be irreparable.

Common Requirements

A publicity, press, or public relations director must be given cooperation and faith by management. Aside from the basic tools—office space, equipment, a budget—the publicist must have easy access to information regarding the history, mission, objectives, and accomplishments of the theatre and its personnel. The total marketing budget, as suggested earlier, should be at least ten percent of the total potential gross—fifteen to twenty percent is more realistic.

Publicity directors must be compensated to indicate how important they are to the success of organizations. Compensation may be in the form of a fee for specific services, a weekly salary, a percentage of ticket sales, or a combination of any of these. Publicists also need to be given an expense account to cover business entertainment, local transportation, and miscellaneous expenses required for their work.

The producing organization must permit its publicity directors a margin for error. A PR person is expected to be an "idea" person who can invent countless promotional ideas and devise imaginative cross-promotional strategies. Not all his or her ideas will work. As a rule, only ten out of every one hundred promotional ideas may be feasible, and of those only one may work and generate publicity. This indicates how many ideas a PR person has to come up with—often on a daily basis. If a producing organization rejects too many of these ideas or is too quick to condemn strategies, the publicist will be denied the flexibility required to get the job done. Rarely will a single newspaper ad campaign fill the house. A single brochure or flyer seldom brings in sell-out crowds. A feature story in a leading local and/or national publication will generate considerable sales but rarely a sell-out. Repetition, time, and a variety of strategies tied to an overall marketing and public relations plan are the fundamental ingredients of successful promotion. Favorable word of mouth, the "buzz," is the best indicator that the promotion is working. No press agent, PR agency, or publicity director is a miracle worker, but the best are professionals who know how to get the job done effectively and economically.

The Publicity Plan

A beginning publicist may accept any publicity anyplace, without a well-thought-out plan directed toward a goal. The publicity plan needs to be an integrated component of the overall marketing plan, from selling tickets to supporting fundraising efforts to increasing visibility. As with a marketing plan, all organizations should prepare a publicity plan annually. Public relations goals are directly tied to the goals of the organization. A well-thought-out plan concentrates on publicity that can benefit the organization. Once the goals are determined, strategies need to be selected to implement the plan. These strategies are discussed in greater detail throughout the chapter. And, finally, a detailed timeline that indicates when each step must be accomplished has to be made.

Writing the Publicity Plan

1.) Establish the goals
A publicist must first determine the publicity goals, what needs to be accomplished. Here is a list of potential goals that applies to most performing arts organizations:

Attracting new customers and/or new patrons

Increasing institutional visibility in the local market

Celebrating an important anniversary

Featuring major events and/or festivals of the season

Showcasing high profile artists involved in the season

Improving the organization's image

Introducing new artistic personnel to the public

Announcing a move into a new facility

Informing the public of potential negative information

Announcing cancellations or changes in program or artist.

2.) Collect the facts
In order to publicize an organization, the publicist must thoroughly know all of the facts about the organization. He or she must research all historical data, biographies and resumes of key personnel, production information, and financial information and must maintain a photo file of events, facilities, and artists.

3.) Focus publicity on specific geographic needs
A publicity plan should cover the geographic territory of the organization. Every organization would love a feature story in the *New York Times* Sunday Arts and Leisure section, but that is an unrealistic goal for most organizations that are not New York based or do not have news that would

be relevant to the national arts scene. The plan must identify publications that match the demographic makeup of the existing audience and supporter base. The publicity plan should target media that reaches present and potential customers. This must be a priority when researching newspapers (local or large metropolitan newspapers), television (news or talk shows), radio (news or talk shows), or special-interest publications (trade or local business).

4.) Keep the publicity plan simple and flexible
Stay focused on the ultimate goals as publicity has a tendency to take on a life of its own. A seasonal publicity plan is a work in progress, so it must be kept simple and on target. It should be reviewed at least each month, if not weekly or even daily, to be updated. The plan must be adaptable to change.

5.) Identify key media opportunities for the season
The publicist must identify the major stories of the season, starting with the productions and major initiatives of the organization and then moving creatively. Flexibility is important because not all stories can be predicted, such as the sudden replacement of a star artist or the theatre's receiving a major award.

6.) Identify the appropriate media
The best way to ensure that the publicist's work gets published is to target the right publications. Start with those outlets that have already covered the organization. Then research additional publications to see if they have the appropriate sections to include information on the organization. Look for ways to mold the idea and to match the target publication's format and areas of interest.

7.) Identify promotions that generate publicity
Identify any possible promotions, such as local tie-ins and personal appearances, contests, or trade-outs, within the theatre, and piggyback promotions.

8.) Create a detailed timeline

Production dates

Promotion dates

Deadline to distribute season announcement.

Deadlines to distribute press releases for long-lead publications such as monthly magazines that are generally eight weeks in advance of event

Deadlines to distribute press releases for short-lead publications such as daily newspapers that are generally four weeks in advance of event

Deadlines for calendar listings

Artists' availability for promotional events and interviews

Targeted feature stories with deadlines of when to make initial contact with editors, send query letters, and pitch.

9.) Try anything new
Some of the best publicity comes from off-the-wall ideas: a women's riding group parading on horses through a downtown area to promote *Annie Get Your Gun*; or to promote a string quartet to a younger crowd the musicians rode onto a fogged stage through strobe lights on large black motorcycles. The local motorcycle dealer became a sponsor, provided the cycles, and was responsible for the number of black leather jackets in the audience, an unexpected benefit. These examples are simply to illustrate that the creative publicist may come up with unconventional ideas that will actually work given the opportunity. Obviously the publicist must be a good salesperson of his or her own ideas.

The Promotion Office

In order for the publicist to organize and dispense information, access to certain equipment, resources, and supplies is required. Computers, printers, copiers, scanners, and mailing machinery or services are necessary. Groups that operate under an umbrella institution can usually avail themselves of central printing and mailing services; low budget theatres often rent or borrow reproduction facilities that belong to someone associated with them or that are donated as in-kind services. No matter how the publicist's needs are solved, his or her written results should be neat, professional-looking literature. Messy, illegible, or difficult-to-read material is worthless and should never be distributed. There are many easy and efficient ways to produce and reproduce professional-looking material. In targeting news organizations, email has become the preferred means of communication. Most major news organizations will no longer accept unsolicited press releases by traditional mail. Since most publications are now computer generated, materials will be more compatible if delivered electronically. A well-organized performing arts promotion office should possess the following publicity production equipment and materials:

Standard Office Equipment

Absolutely essential to the office are a direct-line telephone system with answering, intercom, and fax capabilities; an up-to-date computer system with printing and graphics capabilities; a reliable copying machine; a desktop publishing system; a scanner and equipment to collate, fold, and staple bulk mailers.

Stationery and Supplies

Stationery specific for press releases with the theatre's masthead is essential as printed materials are still distributed in specific circumstances, such as to members of the media attending a performance and/or press conference. Other necessities include the organization's regular stationery and basic office supplies, such as poster board, pens, ink cartridges, CD-ROMs, and envelopes of various sizes.

Online Press Kit

The publicist must create a specific area for the press to go to on the theatre's website in addition to providing an online press kit with institutional fact sheets, a fact sheet for each production, bios of key personnel and artists, recent press releases and photos that are easily downloadable. Links should be established to other sites to provide additional information to, perhaps, an artist's personal website. An email link where readers can ask questions of the staff should be included if possible.

Photograph and Design Files

The publicist should organize photos of the interior and exterior of the theatre, resident artists, managers, board members, and past productions in two forms: 1.) hard files with glossy photos and 2.) electronic versions of the images that can be emailed and made available online. The most common method of accomplishing this is to scan the photo into a JPEG (Joint Photographic Experts Group), paying special attention to the resolution that is required by specific publications—a newspaper prints at a much lower resolution than a magazine.

Electronic files should also be made of the logo, masthead, and other frequently used graphic designs of star performers for promotional use.

Scrapbooks

All printed publicity and ads should be collected and placed in scrapbooks, arranged by season, production, and publication date.

Press Board

A bulletin board should display all ads, publicity, and reviews pertaining to current productions before it is removed and arranged into scrapbooks. Also, copies of all press releases should be copied to all box office personnel so that they are aware of what may be carried by the local media and may be the basis for questions from patrons.

Biographies

A computer file should be maintained to store personal and professional biographical data on all artists, board members, and key managers. Make these available on the online press kit where applicable.

Artists' Index

Maintain a computerized artists' index showing the name of the productions in which the artists appeared, the dates they appeared, and the roles they played or the other artistic functions they fulfilled. Update this after each new production.

Press Clipping Service

Press clipping services track media coverage on the theatre and productions in a variety of media from newspapers to magazines to web pages and Usenet groups. News clipping services conduct very thorough searches, and one of their biggest benefits is that they are tremendous time savers for publicists. There are many vendors that provide these services. Begin by searching online for a company that meets the needs and budget of the organization.

Mailing Lists (See Chapter 16, Direct Mail Systems.)

These mailing lists should be maintained:

> General mailing list, which is a computerized database to generate mailing labels for an individual list or any combination of lists
> Current subscribers/season ticket holders
> Past subscribers who did not renew
> Single ticket buyers and others who have asked to be on the list
> Current board members
> Past board members
> Current contributors, including individual, corporate, and government
> Past contributors
> Special advisory groups and volunteers
> Appropriate area organizations, including schools and community groups
> Appropriate area businesses, such as hotels and restaurants

Alumni from any school programs run by the theatre
Faculty and administration for theatre schools
Special target groups, such as seniors or corporate executives
Borrowed or bought lists from other arts organizations, publishers,
professional associations

General Press List

This is a computerized database from which to generate mailing labels for one or more
of the following categories:

By geographic location
    Local press list
    Regional press list
    National press list

By press medium
    Daily newspapers
    Weekly newspapers
    Monthly magazines
    Trade publications
    Local directories (Chamber of Commerce, etc.)
    Community bulletins and newsletters (churches, schools, senior groups)

Electronic media
    Television
    Radio
    Online

Opening night invitation list

Public Service Announcement (PSA) list

Entertainment: calendar listings editors

Required press information in database
    Name of publication or show
    Address
    Telephone number, fax number, website address, and email address
    Date and frequency of publication
    Publisher's name
    Editor's name
    Other key personnel

Deadline date and time
Geographic region covered
Circulation size
Media directories with this key information are available. Companies such
as Bacon's Information, Inc. at www.bacons.com provide services
that supply media directories to the full-service distribution of press
releases. Other providers can be found online.

A Working Library

In the past it was necessary to keep an extensive library of materials related to the past presentations of the organization, and while it is still helpful to have some of the more often
used resource materials, it is possible to access much of this material on the Internet.
Material retrieved from the Internet is likely to be more current than material kept in a
publicist's library.

Theatre Companies

Theatre companies should have:

Editions of all plays in the current season
Publishers' catalogs
Copies of all plays in current or future production at the theatre
The most recent *Who's Who in the American Theatre*
New York critics' reviews
One or two theatre histories with original production information on the
season's productions, including casts, dates, etc.

Music Performing Arts Organizations

Music performing arts organizations should have:

The most recent Groves Dictionary of Music
Program notes for every musical work presented in the season
History of all programs presented with composers, title of works, program
notes, artists, etc.
List of all commissioned works
List of all local, national, and world premieres
Libretti and/or translations of all vocal works

A good, current dictionary of the English language
A good, current desk encyclopedia
A thesaurus and other word-finder books
Playbill collection of all previous productions/performances
History of the institution
Area-wide directory of media outlets, giving circulation, listening or viewing statistics, and other information
Map collection of local and general area
Appropriate periodicals (*Variety*, *American Theatre*, local newspapers, professional journals, etc.)

Gathering Information

Information is the foundation for public relations and publicity. To effectively publicize a performing arts organization, the publicist must first gather all of the facts about the organization. Only with the results of this research will the publicist be able to represent the organization. The process of gathering information is also a great way to stimulate brainstorming for potential publicity opportunities.

Historical Data

Ongoing theatre groups should have a well-written narrative history of the company that is updated annually and reproduced in sufficient quantity to distribute to visiting critics and journalists, resident cast and staff members, visiting artists, and others. This simple and inexpensive marketing tool can do wonders in elevating the impression that the organization's users have of its making them feel privileged to be part of an important artistic endeavor.

To assist in the process of collecting everything about the theatre that appears in print, a news-clipping service can be retained for a monthly reading fee plus, in most cases, an additional charge per clipping. The service will clip all articles and/or advertisements in which the name of the theatre appears and also label each with the publication name, date, and circulation. Services can be directed to limit clippings to citywide, statewide, area-wide, or nationwide coverage. The clippings quickly alert the publicist as to which publications are using the press releases and are therefore an important aid in strategic evaluation.

Because theatrical press agents and publicists, like publishers and printers, are people who rarely see beyond the next deadline, the theatre business has, to an alarming degree, traditionally ignored the preservation of production records. Every producing organization should assign one person to collect and preserve sample playbills, posters, articles, press releases, and photographs. These should be safely stored with a duplicate set of such memorabilia deposited within the appropriate library, museum, or theatre collection. It may seem outrageously simple to collect such items when a production is current, but a year later it may be nearly impossible to locate any of them.

Financial History and Structure

The press may call upon the publicity department to provide a financial history of the organization. The publicist should be prepared with a fact sheet of the financial history of the organization as well as its structure.

Key points to be included:

A list of key administrative personnel (both paid and volunteers)

If a nonprofit, a list of board members, board titles, and business affiliation

The annual financial statements: operating budget showing income and expenses, and a balance sheet showing assets and liabilities

A list of major donors, sponsors, and volunteers.

Biographies and Resumes

Most operations publish brief biographical sketches of performers, other artists, and management personnel in the playbill. Often entitled "Who's Who" or "Behind the Scenes," these write-ups should be literate and interesting, and final copy approval should be granted to each person included in the sketches. Resumes and photos should be obtained as soon as performers and other key personnel are engaged. As well as providing basic information for "bios" and press releases, these may also give the publicist ideas for feature articles, guest appearances, and one-on-one interviews.

The publicity department may even devise a standard news release format to send to individuals' hometown and college newspapers, stating that so and so is appearing in a certain production. This is surefire copy for local editors and may stimulate ticket sales for the theatre, even from distant customers. David Merrick's long-running Broadway musical, *Hello Dolly*, once adapted this technique to audience members and distributed the following cards in the theatre lobby:

> If you are from out of town, we would like to notify your home-town newspaper that you came to see our show, "HELLO, DOLLY!"
>
> Sincerely,
>
> *Dave Merrick*
>
>
>
> MR. & MRS
> MR.
> **NAME**   MRS ....
> MISS
> **ADDRESS**..
> **CITY AND STATE**..
> **HOME-TOWN NEWSPAPER**...
>
> *Please give card to usher or drop in box in lobby.*   491

Local newspapers all over the country were soon promoting the show. Other producers have given out free postcards related to their company or production, hoping that audience members would mail them and generate publicity.

Production Information

Theatre companies and opera companies fortunate enough to enjoy the services of a dramaturge will be able to rely on that person to do background research on each production, playwright, and leading artist, and some of this will be very useful in writing press releases, playbill notes, and other material; in fact, writing these pieces may be part of the dramaturge's job. Otherwise, this work falls to the publicist. For music performing arts organizations, the artistic director, artistic administrator, and program annotator are tremendous resources for background information on the programs, themes, festivals, and featured artists. In either case, a major function of marketing is enhancing product enjoyment, and helping the audience to understand a production obviously increases its appreciation and enjoyment.

Photography for the Performing Arts

The Photographer Agreement

A written agreement between the organization and a hired photographer clearly stating the terms of the engagement is essential.

As a rule, the photographer owns the images taken and then, technically speaking, licenses the use of those images to the organization for a specific amount of time and for a specific use. For example, if a photographer is hired to cover both an opening night and the party following, the organization should fully expect to be able to use those photos in news releases and on its website, as those uses are directly related to general theatre publicity. If the organization wishes to use these photographs in the next annual report or a future fund raising campaign, these allowances should be included in the agreement. The absence of an agreement or the failure to include a future use of the photographs in an agreement could bar their use.

Obtain a Photo Release

There may be times when the use of a photograph of a person in the organization's materials is desirable. It is prudent to obtain a release from that person, allowing the company to use his or her image. It does not matter whether the use is for print material, brochures, or the website: to safeguard the organization from litigation, a release should be obtained. A simple form on the organization's letterhead will suffice. If a photograph is used without prior approval, then the person has the right to demand modeling fees and could also bring a legal action for invasion of privacy.

Give the person two identical copies and ask that both copies be completed and signed. Fill in as much of the form as possible before having it signed. After both signed copies are received, check them for accuracy. If the forms are incomplete, it is the responsibility of the organization to complete any missing information. Send one completed signed copy back to the signer and file the other copy in the organization's secure records. If the photo release form is for a minor—someone under the age of eighteen—the parent or guardian must sign for the minor but identify the minor as the subject of the photograph.

Sample Photo Release Form

AUTHORIZATION TO USE WRITTEN MATERIALS/PHOTOGRAPHS

I,   , hereby authorize the [name of organization] to use, reproduce, and/or publish all written and/or visual materials, including photographs described below that may pertain to me. I understand that this material may be used in various publications, public affairs releases, recruitment materials, or other related endeavors. This material may also appear on the [name of organization] Web Page. This authorization is continuous and may only be withdrawn by my specific rescission of this authorization. Consequently, the [name of organization] may publish materials, use my name, photograph, and/or make reference to me in any manner that the [name of organization] deems appropriate in order to promote/publicize service opportunities.

Description of Material:

Signature   Date

Types of Photographs

Photographs are extremely important and in some cases are truly indispensable. Press agents need photographs both for general distribution and specific uses. The first case includes photos of the theatre, general production shots, photographs of individual performers out of costume, and shots of the leading managers. Photos of visiting VIPs, rehearsals, and casual shots of audience members for the society columns have more limited use but are still valuable. The posed photos that performers submit with their resumes are almost invariably of the glamour variety and are often touched up by the photographer and frequently taken long ago. News editors generally favor informal action shots over glamour photos unless, of course, the picture is for inclusion in a paid advertisement. To obtain casual shots, one usually needs to hire a photographer, unless a photographer is on the staff. Photographs can be taken in two different formats: traditional film and digital. The printed photograph does not differ in quality between the two formats. When photographers use traditional film, they will provide prints for a small quantity of photos. When a large number of photos are taken, it is best to order a proof or contact sheet—a quickly developed printout of each role of film printed onto a single sheet of paper. The best shots can then be ordered in the quantity needed from the contact sheet, which is labeled and filed with the negatives for possible future use.

Digital photography eliminates these steps and expense. The photographers will usually provide the digital photos either on a disk or CD to preview. Some photographers upload the photos onto a secure page on their website. Clients simply connect to the designated web address and review the photos from their computers. Either way, the best shots can then be ordered and printed. The digital files of the photos should be provided in a JPEG (Joint Photographic Experts Group) format. This is a standardized format for displaying graphic images on web pages. JPEG files, which have the extension jpg, are better for photographs than GIF (Graphics Interchange Format), which is better for clip art. Digital photography is a must for any professional public relations department. Digital images are now the preferred format for most journalists, making digital photography highly advantageous.

Qualities of Good Photography

A good photograph has clarity, sharpness, interesting composition, and professional development. Headshots are rarely reproduced in the media because editors prefer natural action shots. Publicity photos are usually intended for reproduction in the print media, so they should be provided at the correct resolution in the JPEG digital format. If, by chance, the print media requests printed photos, provide glossy rather than a matte finishes. Dark photographs, or those with very dark backgrounds, should be avoided because they reproduce badly. Photographs with sharply contrasting light and dark areas and with a predominantly light background are ideal. Also, photos should be uncluttered—one to three people or a single building—and should be as narrow as possible. Portraits should show the full head and shoulders or the full body of the subject. Composition and cropping should never eliminate the top of a head or a part of a face. Production shots should be dramatic and exciting.

Uses of Photography

It is still true that a picture is worth a thousand words. When promoting a performing arts group or production, there are myriad uses for a good photograph: the brochure, the flyer, the playbill, the house board, the poster, the ads, and the special displays.

When releasing a traditional photograph to the press, the theatre must make sure that the subjects in it are appropriately captioned from left to right on a separate piece of paper that is glued or taped to the bottom back of the photo, then folded so the caption extends several inches over the face of the picture. The caption should also include basic production-related information, such as time, place, and price as well as a brief capsulation of the nature of the place and production. Editors may publish this when they have extra space to fill. When releasing a digital photograph to the press, mark and identify the photograph with the software, provide a clear title to the file, and repeat the caption in the email correspondence.

Photographic enlargements, or blowups, of pictures serve as a dramatic means for publicizing a production. Forty by sixty inches is standard for mounting in typical display cases and on sandwich boards. The cost of such enlargements, which may be ordered unmounted or mounted on heavy cardstock, may be worth it, if they are put to good use in lobbies, ticket agencies, and other sites to stimulate sales.

Glossy eight-by-ten-inch prints of the production and each performer should be displayed on a lobby house board. This seldom involves much cost, and it is standard courtesy to display a photo of each cast member in the current production whether there is a contract stipulation that requires this or not.

When the supply is sufficient, photos of individual performers may be autographed and distributed to ticket agencies, group sales directors, volunteer theatre workers, donors and sponsors, and others who may appreciate the gesture. Also, some theatres frame signed photographs of artists who have played the house and display them where patrons and visitors to the theatre can see them.

Billing

Before any advertising or playbill copy is printed, the publicist must carefully check all contracts, noting the billing stipulations and then applying these to the composition of the title page in the playbill, on house boards, posters, in newspaper advertising, and other such literature. One must also check what agreements may exist between the theatre and the playwright or other creative artists, between the theatre and another producing organization, or between the theatre and a play-publishing house, such as Samuel French or Tams Witmark. There will always be a billing clause regarding the author(s). Other credits may be mandated regarding the original producers or directors of the production.

The more well known an actor, director, playwright, singer, or conductor, the more prominently that person's name will figure into the promotional materials, as spelled out in the artist or show contracts. A simple but typical billing rider in a well-known actor's contract might read as follows:

> Actor shall receive sole star billing on a line exclusive to the actor above the title of the play, wherever that title appears in advertising controlled by the producer, in type that is no less than 100 percent the size, prominence, and boldness of the title.

This means, among other things, that the producer may not grant other performers —or anyone else, for that matter—billing above the title. Some contracts specify exactly where the performer's name must appear in relation to the title and other names, other riders merely specify that the name must appear "wherever the name of the first featured actor appears." Or the rider may require a name to appear on a line by itself, in a box of a certain size in relation to the title of the play, preceded by a certain phrase such as "and," "also starring," or "in the role of . . .," or whatever else the actor's agent can negotiate.

Photo Calls

A photo or picture call is the time that management requires the company or parts of it to pose for photographs. The photos may be shot onstage in costume, after a dress rehearsal, or even after a performance. Similarly, the photos may be shot in a rehearsal studio. Wherever the location, it is best to have the photographer observe a rehearsal or performance in advance of the actual shoot, and then develop a list of shots to be taken. The publicist in consultation with the photographer should create the list. With the list as a guide or map, the entire shoot can be done efficiently.

Filming, Videotaping, and Recording

Limited portions of a performance can usually be recorded on film or tape or digitally for promotional purposes, i.e., to accompany reviews or stories. These recordings come under the heading of "news" or B-roll, respectively. All unions have specific rules regarding such recordings and it is best to be familiar with them *before* inviting camera crews into the theatre.

Promotional Opportunities

Promotion within the Theatre

No member of the audience should leave the theatre without carrying one of its promotional items if not tickets for a future performance. Aside from the playbill, fliers or calendar of events from display racks in the lobby should be made available. When the opportunity is appropriate, a button, pen, or other inexpensive trinket bearing the theatre's or show's logo may be given away as a promotional asset. Giveaway items may be offered in exchange for filling out audience questionnaires or mailing list forms. Give-aways such as T-shirts can be expensive, but the word of mouth they stimulate may be worth the cost.

While many theatres feel that announcements and precurtain speeches given from the stage are amateurish and tend to disrupt the performance, some audience members like to identify with a real person connected to the performance or the institution. The objective is to make the audience feel welcome and appreciated. Often there is an especially affable theatre manager, artistic director, or performer whom audiences like to see in front of the curtain before each performance or at the end of intermission to talk about upcoming attractions. The spoken word generally has greater impact than the written word.

If curtain speeches are taboo, there are other opportunities to speak personally to customers while they are in the theatre. Box office treasurers can end each transaction by asking if they want to make reservations for the next production. The house manager and ushers can often slip in a few words about upcoming events. The manager and marketing director can be on hand to greet members of the press and other people they recognize and, of course, chat about upcoming events. Personal contact of this kind intensifies word of mouth as well as feelings of loyalty toward the theatre or operation. In a perfect world, the audience is part of the family, and as such; they should feel they, really, will be personally missed if they don't attend the next production.

Local Tie-Ins and Personal Appearances

Whenever the publicist can connect the theatre, the organization, the production, or the performers with someone or something else that is of interest to the media, there is a good chance of garnering free coverage. Examples of these would be when performers participate in fundraising efforts for local charities, when the manager speaks at a Rotary meeting, and when the theatre runs a benefit for the wildlife refuge. All of these double the chance for media coverage. And even without such coverage, when well-known personalities associated with the theatre or organization appear at large gatherings it may stimulate word of mouth and sell tickets. Personal appearances should be limited to worthwhile occasions where they can be handled with good taste and truly help to elevate the public image of the organization.

Guest appearances on radio and television talk shows provide a more controlled format for publicity exposure than appearances at large, public gatherings. And because virtually all talk shows are continually seeking interesting guests, it is not difficult for publicists to schedule performers and other theatre personnel for on-air interviews. Again, an attempt should be made to use a number of people and not just the leading performer. Radio interviews can be prerecorded or conducted by phone, which makes scheduling much easier. When setting up interviews, the publicist should provide the host of the program with background information about the person being interviewed and some basic facts about the production and the theatre. The guest should also be reminded to mention the show. There's nothing more disconcerting for the publicist than to arrange an interview and then witness the guest breeze through twenty minutes of air time without once mentioning the production or theatre.

Contests, Bargains, and Trade-Outs

Bargain tickets or free tickets may be offered through contests or tie-ins sponsored by local businesses or community organizations. Banks, for instance, may be persuaded to give "free" tickets that they purchase from the theatre to customers who open new accounts. Other offers may include autographed photos or a personal visit with the star. Dinner theatres may devise package offers that include a meal and a show for a single bargain price. This type of combination ticket not only appeals to the customer's sense of economy but, perhaps even more important, appears to make theatregoing easier and more enjoyable by combining several services into one transaction.

Radio and television talk shows and game shows often thrive on contests, call-in participation, and giveaways. This presents an excellent opportunity for promotion, since a theatre may provide free tickets as giveaways in exchange for free mention on the show or even free airing of prepared ad copy. Also, when a theatre first runs commercials on a media outlet, it is usually possible to set up an advertising and promotion contract that include free promos for the theatre, together with ticket trade-outs and paid commercials.

Piggyback Promotion

Most large public and private corporations communicate regularly with their customers or shareholders through direct mail and email. Usually their mailings include more than a simple bill or financial statement. Banks, utility companies, and retailers enclose some of their own promotional material and, often, a newsletter including community out-reach literature. Many also enclose items about local nonprofit arts organizations, either by stuffing a flyer in with their material or by writing about such organizations in their newsletters. If the organization has a corporate sponsor, this is a natural company with which to piggyback. Many will send emails to all of their employees promoting the event, especially if an employee discount is offered on tickets. This is called piggybacking and is a very inexpensive promotional strategy. And it presents many possibilities. What about getting the local supermarkets to stuff the group's flyers into all the shopping bags as they leave the checkout counters—or printing the theatre's logo onto the bags themselves? What about printing the theatre's production schedule on the place mats at local restaurants, on the bookmarks given out at local bookstores, or on the reservation confirmations sent out by local hotels and resorts? Riding piggyback, hitching a ride, or jumping onto somebody else's bandwagon in order to further one's own goals are familiar practices.

General Considerations

Both professional and nonprofessional artists should be given the courtesy of two days' advance notice of any promotional activity in which they will be asked to participate, especially when photography is involved. It is reasonable to expect that performers will cooperate and agree to assist the theatre in publicizing a production. However, it is a good idea to insert a clause about such participation in a performer's contract. The clause should be sufficiently vague about the number of appearances to be made or hours to be spent; something like "Upon reasonable notice, Artist agrees to make himself available for various promotional activities, including but not limited to press interviews photo shoots, etc." should suffice. That way a performer has some obligation to participate in promotional activities.

Ladies and Gentlemen of the Press

Establishing Good Press Relations

Producers, like politicians, will probably never stop arguing about the powers and pre-rogatives of the press, a term used to include both print and electronic media. Does the press have too much influence and is it unfairly exercised? Should a few journalists with no formal education in theatre have the power to close a show that may have taken years to get from script to stage, cost millions of dollars, and employ some of the most respected talents in the business? Harvey Sabinson, former press agent and executive director of the League of American Theatres and Producers, once suggested that if producers would just stop quoting critics in their ads, the power of the critics would be greatly dimin-ished. But even if this were to happen, the media would continue to exert an enormous influence on public opinion, and publicists would still have to be hired to court the ladies and gentlemen who create and control media content.

The publicist or other staff member who serves as the main liaison between the the-atre and the media should quickly establish a first-name relationship with as many media professionals as possible. This will require personal visits, phone contacts, and invitations to bring these people to the theatre. It entails befriending the publishers and station owners as well as the editors and journalists; knowing who does what, who takes orders from whom, and when the deadlines are; and understanding the style and interests of each media outlet and copywriter. Armed with this information, the publicist must try to accommodate each media professional according to his or her particular needs and preferences. This means making that person's job as easy as possible—indeed, practically doing it for him or her. The closer the publicist comes to accomplishing this, the greater the media coverage will be.

A copy of the press list with corresponding phone numbers, notes about deadlines, and other pertinent data should be in the press database or on hard copy in the publicity office, where it must be updated on a regular basis. As a very first step, names and addres-ses of print and electronic media outlets may be taken from the Yellow Pages of tele-phone books and from directories published by news-clipping agencies. To verify the list and make efficient use of it, a return mail card or an email, such as the sample found in Appendix S, should be sent to each person on the press list. There will be a high rate of return, because editors will quickly grasp that someone is trying to make their jobs easier.

It is customary to invite drama critics who write for daily publications or programs to opening night performances. Journalists who write for weekly or monthly outlets, fea-ture writers, and general editors may be given complimentary press seats for later per-formances. And a limited number of comps should be given to media people who never write copy but are influential or helpful in the theatre's media relations. Such people as advertising executives, TV cameramen and women, typographers, and layout artists can be very helpful when there is a tight deadline.

It is perfectly acceptable for press agents to ask critics or editors to read their reviews over the phone before they appear in print or on the air. This may help in creating up-to-the-minute ad copy, preparing the company for good or bad news, and, in some cases, deciding whether or not to keep the show running. It is also good professional etiquette when hosting theatre critics who have deadlines soon after the curtain comes down or who are traveling out of their way to reach the performance to offer them transportation and, perhaps, the access to a computer, the Internet, and phone after the show. The press may also be invited to join opening night parties, cast receptions, and other theatre gatherings. The press agent's expense account should permit entertainment of key media people at lunch or dinner.

The Press Kit

A press kit, which should be available online, is a packet of information assembled for distribution to members of the press. It may be in the form of pages stapled together, or the material may be inserted into an envelope, or it may be arranged in an attractive folder. Also the entire press kit may be on a CD-ROM, which could then include a large collection of photographs and supplementary information about the theatre or attraction. This allows the journalist to select information and photographs that best fit the slant of the copy being developed. This also means that a variety of photographs and information will appear, rather than the same photo and blurb in every media outlet. As long as the information is professionally prepared, correct, and neatly presented, it will be acceptable as journalists and their colleagues are much more interested in solid information than in packaging.

Every ongoing theatre operation and performing arts organization should acquire a supply of envelopes, folders, or cover pages to be used for all its press kits over one or more seasons. A brief history with background sheets, statistics, brochures, production schedules, copies of recent articles and reviews, and photographs should always be available for quick assembly into a kit. Additional information specific to a particular occasion, such as a press conference, a rehearsal, or an opening night, should also be prepared. A member of the press should never leave the theatre empty-handed.

Press Conferences

A press conference is an occasion at which selected members of the press are invited to meet as a group at a specified location for the purpose of gaining newsworthy information. The organization that calls the conference hopes that the event will generate favorable media coverage. While a press conference is a promotional tool, it should never be perceived as pure hype. A press conference should only be called when there is substantial news to report. Calling a press conference for insignificant news damages an organization's credibility.

A press conference should be organized around a topic, person, or event that is newsworthy, such as an especially popular performer, the first day of rehearsal, a new artistic or managing director, or the unveiling of an architectural model for a new facility. Everyone receives the same information at the same time and must be allowed to ask questions or, if the gathering is small enough, should have time to speak personally with the subjects. Early morning conferences should include coffee and pastries and those at later times, light refreshments. A press kit with background information, photographs, and other pertinent material should be given to each media person, preferably labeled with the person's name.

An articulate spokesperson should make the opening remarks, introduce the other participants, field questions from the press, and generally serve as a moderator. To prepare the spokesperson for the question-and-answer component, a team of key personnel, led by the publicity director, should anticipate the questions that might be asked and suggest succinct replies and talking points during a question and answer rehearsal with the spokesperson. Other members of the management staff might be present at the conference to assist with hospitality and be certain that individual attention is given to each media representative.

Press Interviews

A press interview is a one-on-one question-and-answer session between a media representative and someone else. These interviews may be taped from live broadcasts; taped merely for the convenience of the journalist; or the interviewer may simply take notes. Except under very unusual circumstances, press interviews should be arranged in advance. This gives the interviewer time to do research and compose a list of questions, and it gives the party being interviewed fair warning, which is especially important if there will be video recording or still photography involved.

It is never wise to burden busy artists and others with too many promotional chores as they may rightfully get fed up and refuse to do any at all. Whenever possible, these chores should be spread among different members of the company. When too much attention is given to one person, others can feel slighted. Also, the publicist must weigh the importance of each interview in terms of potential media coverage, and not waste a busy artist's time on an interview for some small, faraway radio station. Finally, in order to avoid any embarrassing or unprofessional interview behavior, the publicist should check an interviewer's credentials.

The Press Release

The most common way to feed news and information to the media is through a press release, which must follow a very specific format and meet certain stylistic requirements. If these are not met, the editors who receive them will simply toss them away. A press release is really an attempt to write copy that the editor can publish or broadcast without doing any additional editing. A good online resource for developing press releases is www.101publicrelations.com.

Stylistic Requirements

1.) Releases must be written in the third person, similar to the way a news story is written. They must avoid superlatives.

2.) All essential information—name of company, production, performance dates, performance times, ticket prices, etc.—should be in the first paragraph. Because editors traditionally cut copy from the bottom up, subsequent paragraphs should contain information of decreasing importance.

3.) Generally, each press release should be limited to one subject, event, or idea. Whenever possible, the release should be limited to a single sheet of 8½ × 11 inch paper, although 8½ × 14 and 11 × 17 are preferable to using two sheets of paper. It should be printed on only one side of a page.

4.) Keep the paragraphs short and write each paragraph around a single salient point.

5.) Releases to be mailed should be double spaced with wide enough margins to allow for editorial notations and changes. Releases to be emailed do not need to be double spaced.

6.) Keep the press releases as short as possible.

7.) Public Service Announcements (PSAs) and releases sent to broadcast media outlets should be printed entirely in capital letters, triple spaced, and indicate the reading time—ten seconds, twenty seconds, etc.—at the top of each new paragraph.

Not surprisingly, small media outlets that are eager for copy are more likely to use inferior releases and even to permit the use of superlatives such as "hilarious" and "sensational." But even these outlets will never allow the use of first person. A release should not read: "We will present . . ." Instead, it should read: "The XYZ Theatre will present . . . ." Large media outlets are much more exacting in their requirements and may use press releases only as tip-offs for assigning reporters and critics to cover certain stories and events. A possible exception is when the publicist is known and respected by the media outlet and submits an "exclusive" story or photograph. Exclusives, often written in the style of a feature story, may run longer than news releases and be slanted for use by a particular media outlet or column, section, or program. The cardinal rule is never to label a story or photo "exclusive to the *Daily Tribune*," or whatever, unless that is really the case.

Format Requirements

1.) Mailed news releases should be printed on stationery designed for that purpose. Along with the name and address of the producing organization, the release should carry the word "news" or "news from . . ." or some phrase that quickly indicates what it is. For emailed news releases clearly mark the subject heading of the email as "News from . . . ."

2.) At the beginning of the release the words "For Immediate Release!" or "Release date: . . ." should appear to indicate either that the story should be published as soon as possible or not used until after a specified date.

3.) Strictly speaking, it is the news editor's job to title all the articles that are printed so that identical headlines will not appear in two different publications. Nonetheless, it is expedient to give each new release as newsworthy and as attention-grabbing a title as possible to stimulate the editor's interest.

4.) At the beginning or end of the release, the press agent's name and phone number/email address should appear after the word Contact.

5.) If a printed release absolutely must use more than one page, "more" or "Continued on page 2" should appear at the bottom of the page and "Continued: page 2" should appear at the top of the second page, accompanied by the name of the production.

6.) At the end of the press release, centered on the page on a line by itself, should appear one of the standard editorial symbols—# # #, or —30—, or end—to indicate that there is no more copy.

Sample Press Release:

MUSIC MOUNTAIN SUMMER MUSIC FESTIVAL
www.musicmountain.org

BENEFIT RELEASE
CONTACT: Joan Walden
             (860) 236-9620
             Joan@walden.name
             Nicholas Gordon
             (860) 364-2080
             ngordon@snet.net
BOX OFFICE: (860) 824-7126

JUBILEE BENEFIT CONCERT TO LAUNCH 75th ANNIVERSARY SEASON

Guest Artists:
Sam Waterston, Ruth Laredo, Eugenia Zukerman, and Jupiter Symphony Members

(April 20, 20xx) Falls Village, CT. Sam Waterston, familiar to television audiences as Asst. D.A. Jack McCoy in TV's "Law & Order," will be the guest narrator for Peter and the Wolf arranged by Prokofiev, for Narrator, Piano, Flute, Clarinet, Oboe, French Horn, Bassoon and Tympani at a special Jubilee Benefit Concert in celebration of Music Mountain's 75th anniversary season on Saturday, May 22, at 3 PM. Also appearing at Music Mountain on Music Mountain Road in Falls Village, Conn. will be guest artists Ruth Laredo, Piano, Eugenia Zukerman, Flute, Stefan Milenkovich, Violin, and Andrey Tcheckmazov, Cello, and members of the Jupiter Symphony Chamber Players of New York. Also on the program is Mozart's The Haffner Symphony, Arr. by Hummel for Piano, Flute, Violin and Cello.

"This is the first time since the late Victor Borge performed a benefit concert in the 1980s for Music Mountain that we have held such a high profile fundraiser," says Nicholas Gordon, president of the Music Mountain Board of Managers, who is son of the organization's late founder, Jacques Gordon. He adds, "With the proceeds, we will support our teaching programs and will make improvements to Music Mountain's Gordon Hall and the other buildings and grounds. This also will help ensure the continuation of this wonderful organization."

Benefit tickets are priced from $200 for the front of the Hall, to $100 and $50 inside the Hall, and $25 for lawn and terrace seating. For information, directions, and to order tickets call (860) 364-2080 or visit the website at www.MusicMountain.org.

###

See Appendix T, Sample Press Releases.

Other Types of Press Announcements

Public Service Announcements (PSA)

A PSA usually contains much of the same information and wording as a press release written for the print media, except that it is intended to be read over the air. It is written in all capital letters and the reading time is shown above each paragraph, with difficult words spelled out phonetically, as in the sample that follows. PSAs sent to television and cable stations may be accompanied by color slides of photographs.

Virtually all broadcasting and cable stations air PSAs, especially those pertaining to nonprofit organizations. These may be announced throughout the programming day or grouped together as a community bulletin board or in some similar format. However, stations may want the PSA to follow their own time and format guidelines, and their deadlines for submission may be four or more weeks in advance of airing. Such information must be obtained from each station and, if necessary, PSAs must be prepared individually to suit the requirements of the different outlets.

Sample Public Service Announcement for Radio

MARK RUSSELL: The Laughter and Song of Politics
September 17 at 8:00 PM
(30 Seconds)

FACT IS FUNNIER THAN FICTION—ESPECIALLY IN THE NATION'S CAPITAL. UNEARTHING THE ABSURDITIES OF WASHINGTON IS MARK RUSSELL'S JOB. WITH HIS SIGNATURE STAR-SPANGLED PIANO, RUSSELL SPOTLIGHTS THE OUTRAGEOUS WITH WIT AND TURNS THE WASHINGTON, D.C. SCENE INTO A MUSICAL COMEDY THAT LEAVES AUDIENCES ROLLING IN THE AISLES FOR AN ENCORE. AND NOW, JUST BEFORE THE NATIONAL ELECTION, MARK IS ABOUT TO SHARE HIS POLITICAL HUMOR WITH WHARTON CENTER. JOIN MARK RUSSELL AS HE "CHEERS PEOPLE UP WHO CAN'T FIND ANY HUMOR IN THE NEWS," FRIDAY, SEPTEMBER 17, AT 8:00 PM. CALL 555-5555 FOR TICKET INFORMATION.

Calendar Listings

The vast majority of periodicals include some type of events calendar that lists basic information about entertainment activities in the area. These are similar to public service announcements, although the wording used and the information given are usually leaner. Again, different deadlines and format requirements for different calendars are likely so each publication should be queried about their schedules; then the theatre organization must set up a calendar for sending out PSAs and listings in a timely manner. The calendars that appear in Sunday newspapers, chambers of commerce, tourist guides, and the like are extremely important because people save them and refer to them when trying to decide how to spend their leisure time.

News Tips

A news tip is simply a memorandum sent in writing or emailed to appropriate media people, informing them about some special activity that they may consider newsworthy enough to cover in person. This may be the arrival of a star performer at the airport, a performance given for some special audience, or any other activity that might provide a photo opportunity for the press and generate interesting copy as well as free publicity for the theatre.

Sample News Tip

The President of the Board of Trustees and the Executive Director will hold an open forum for the press at 10:00 AM on Tuesday, January 11, to discuss the financial condition of the company and the plans to bridge the current deficit. All members of the press are cordially invited to attend.

TIME: 10:00 AM
DATE: Tuesday, January 11
PLACE: Conference Room A: Cultural Center
PARKING: Free parking will be available adjacent to the Center.

Column Items

While the number of gossip columnists is not what it used to be, these columns can still provide good opportunities for publicity. The press agent, of course, must be familiar with the general subject and format of each column, must establish at least a telephone relationship with the columnist, and must be persistent in offering items for possible use. These usually have to be exclusive items that are not contained in press releases or given to other journalists. Anecdotal items are usually preferred.

Video News Releases (VNR)

Like a standard press release, a video news release, or VNR for short, attempts to do the TV news department's work for it. A VNR is a video clip, approximately a minute or two in length, usually produced commercially, and made available to television stations and networks by satellite feed. The producers of the video, of course, hope that it will be shown in its entirety on the evening news-and again on the morning news. But if only a few "bites" are aired, they may have promoted their product to millions of viewers. While there are ethical questions about the media's use of such secondary reportage—especially when its source is not identified—it appears that the video news release is here to stay and, in fact, that it will gain both in production and air time. Consequently, there are many private companies that specialize in producing video news tapes. The media stations receive them free of charge. The high cost of video releases keeps them out of the reach of most performing arts companies, though, if they are produced in-house or as in-kind service donations, they obviously become more feasible. Sometimes the local cable operator will make production space available through the public interest channels that are reserved for the community in which they operate.

Pitching the Story

The facts are gathered, the targeted publicity plan complete, the press releases have been distributed, and now is the time for the big article to appear. If that's all that's been done to support it, the article probably won't appear. Journalists receive hundreds of press releases a day. In order to secure placement for the story the publicist must personally pitch the story to each targeted journalist. If placing a simple listing or mention in a column or alerting a reviewer of an upcoming production, it is best to send the press release and to follow up with a phone call. When targeting a feature story follow these basics steps to pitch the story:

1.) Identify the appropriate publication for the story
   The best way to ensure that a story will be published is to target the right publications. Start with those that have a history of reporting news on the theatre or the performing arts. This step was already codified in the publicity plan.

2.) Determine the appropriate timeline
   Knowing the target time frame for the article to be published, the publication's deadlines, and the length of time for a writer to develop a story determine when to approach the editor. The earlier the better.

3.) Contact the right person

It is important to understand the structure of the media outlet that is being pitched. In general, the editor makes the final decisions on the editorial content of the publication. If the publicist has a relationship with a writer for the publication, a decision must be made either to pitch the writer—who in turn will need to pitch the editor—or to pitch the editor directly.

Magazine

Pitch to the managing editor who's responsible for the publication's editorial content, and who recommends stories to the editor-in-chief.

Newspaper

When pitching to a newspaper, decide in which section of the newspaper the story should appear. Lifestyles? Local? Editorial? Society? Then contact the editor responsible for that section. Many newspapers have a weekly arts tabloid-type insert that carries all of the local arts and entertainment news and calendars. The most coveted part of these inserts is the cover. The cover will be seen by everyone, even those who read no farther. Therefore, if an organization can get the cover to promote its attraction, it has the same value as getting a full-page ad.

Television and Radio

In general, there are two types of programs: news and interview (hard news and soft news). Pitch to the assignment editor of the specific station or show, depending on the target. Try to get interviews in morning and evening drive time, when the most people are likely to be listening.

4.) Write a convincing query letter and/or email

The query letter should tell the editor two things:

1.) What the news item or story is about.

2.) Why this story is important or interesting to editor's readers. The publicist must convince the editor to print the story. What is most important to the editor? Is the story relevant to the outlet's readership?

The query letter, as with all communications to members of the press, must be clear, succinct, and without errors. The letter should include contact information.

5.) Follow up on the pitch

After the query letter has been sent—either by email, fax, or U.S. mail—wait an appropriate period of time before following up with a phone call. Practice the message in advance. Assume that there are just sixty seconds to pitch the story to the editor. Get to the "who, what, why, when, and where" immediately. If the editor is interested and has the time, his or her questions will fill in the gaps. It is good professional practice when calling journalists to ask, "Is this a good time to talk?" as these professionals are always on deadline. This question shows respect for their time. If it is not a good time, ask for a better time to call back. Be sensitive to the reporter's deadlines. Calls later in the afternoon are less likely to be answered or returned because of deadline pressures. Ask if the editor has received the query, if there are any questions, and when a decision will be made relative to the item. Do not assume that the editor has the query letter in hand or has even read it. Editors are bombarded with a massive quantity of information daily. Be persistent, but not pushy.

6.) Send the press release to the editor as an additional follow-up.

The Playbill (Program)

Programs or playbills enhance the performance for the audience by providing information. The purpose of a theatre, opera, or dance program is to assist the audience in identifying the performers with the roles they are playing and in figuring out where the action occurs and at what time. Historical background and critical analysis about the play or production may also be included in the playbill.

A music performance program identifies the order of the musical works and the performers and the musical parts they are playing. The program notes should also explain the historical context of the composer and composition.

Playbills may be produced in-house on desktop publishing systems or they may be elaborately designed and printed on glossy stock. The full publication responsibility may be assumed by the organization or may be assigned to an independent publisher or printer in exchange for a set fee or a share of the advertising revenues. But whatever advertising appears in the playbill should not obscure or overshadow the production information.

Standard Contents

Theatre Companies

Title page or face page:
Often located on the centerfold pages, this page should show the name of the
theatre; the producer(s) or producing organization; the date(s) of the per-
formance(s) if it is a limited engagement; the title of the play; the author(s)
and any other creative artists, such as the lyricist or book writer; the director;
choreographer; musical director and conductor; scenic, costume, and lighting designers; and any other artistic collaborators. It should also state if the
play is produced or presented "by special arrangement" with a play publisher
or other producing organization and, finally, if it is "made possible" through
the support of certain corporate, foundation, or government sponsors. When
performers are union members, their names must usually appear on the title
page according to the provisions in their contracts.

Synopsis of scenes:
This is an outline giving the time and place for each act and scene.

Musical numbers:
Musical productions traditionally list each number by song title, followed by
the names of the characters that perform it.

Cast of characters:
The characters' names are printed on the left with the corresponding actors'
names on the right; they are listed in order in which they speak or appear.

Biographies:
Under the heading of "Who's Who" or some other title, there should be a
brief summation of each principal performer's professional career, if not the
entire cast, as well as the director, author, conductor, producer, designers, and
leading managers.

Music and Dance Performing Arts Organizations

Title page or face page:
This is often located on the centerfold pages and should show the name of the
theatre, the producing organization(s), the date(s) of the performance(s), the
composer(s) and title(s) of each musical work, the composer's dates, the cho-
reographer(s), and any other artistic collaborators. It should also state if the

performance is produced or presented "by special arrangement" with another producing organization and, finally, if it is "made possible" through the support of certain corporate, foundation, or government sponsors. The names of performers may appear on the title page according to the provisions of their contracts.

Biographies:
Under the heading of "Who's Who" or some other title, there should be a brief summation of each principal performer's professional career.

All Arts Organizations

Production or program notes:
There should be background and/or interpretative commentary on the presentation.

Credits:
A list acknowledging people, companies, and organizations whose assistance made the production possible must be included—better to include too many than too few.

House rules:
This is advice about such matters as smoking, drinking, eating, taking photographs or recordings in the theatre, cell phone use, electronic devices, and entering/exiting the theatre during the performance.

Production staff:
List the people with their titles who worked on assembling the physical production as well as those who run the performances, including the running crews, shop carpenters, seamstresses, stagehands, stage managers, electricians, etc.

Executive officers and administrative staff:
Board of directors or trustees, producers, managers, and members of the administrative staff should be mentioned.

Many programs also contain lists of season ticket buyers, donors, advisory groups, interns, volunteers, and others. And, of course, it's desirable to run a promotional article about upcoming productions. Nonprofit organizations should also include their mission statements and objectives.

In both professional and nonprofessional organizations it is wise to maintain an *everybody-or-nobody policy when it comes to listing names in the playbill*. Compiling and editing the production-related copy for a playbill is always an in-house responsibility, even when an outside publisher is used. And those assigned to this job must realize that they cannot be too meticulous, as emotions can run very high when it comes to program credits. Errors or omissions that seem minor to the editor can evoke tremors of volcanic force from the person with the misspelled name or missing biography. One cannot be too careful.

Program Format and Design

The playbill plays a very large part in contributing to an institution's image. It is a souvenir or reminder of the performance. It becomes part of an organization's graphic history; therefore, the design and general look of the playbill together with its contents speak volumes to the public. An important early decision that every group should make is whether or not to sell advertising space in its playbill. If the answer is yes, the next question becomes will any advertisement for any product be acceptable? Other considerations are that selling ads can be very time-consuming and the salary for the salesperson may sometimes exceed the revenues. An alternative to a salaried advertising salesperson is to engage someone to work on a commission-only basis.

Among the most commonly used playbill-design formats are the following:

1.) Uniform cover design:
Organizations that offer a series of different productions during the same season should consider designing a single program cover. This can be printed in bulk with contents for each production printed and inserted separately, thereby reducing costs. The inside of the cover pages can be used for standard information, such as the mission statement, the board and staff lists, and a calendar of productions. The drawback is that a uniform cover doesn't permit the reader to distinguish readily between one production and another, though this can be avoided if there is a window in the cover through which the production title or date is revealed as it appears on the first inserted page.

2.) Outsize or unusual playbill design:
To help market the unique image of a particular production, playbill designs of unusual shape and size might be considered. Dinner theatre playbills, for example, sometimes resemble large restaurant menus. One professional nonprofit theatre company offered a series of staged readings that it called "brown bag productions." Patrons were invited to bring their lunches, and the program information was typed onto plain white paper, duplicated, and slipped into flat paper bags donated by a local department store. The most important question regarding this type of playbill is if it properly represents the organization.

3.) Different designs for each production during a season:
This is probably the most desirable option, because each playbill can be designed to reflect the particular nature of each production; this is, of course, the most expensive option.

4.) Multipurpose playbills:
To cut expenses, it is possible to design a theatre flyer that can double as a playbill. Old-fashioned, nineteenth-century handbills provide an interesting point of reference for this approach.

5.) Souvenir books:
Elaborately designed and printed and usually filled with photos of artists and production shots, souvenir programs may be produced in addition to free playbills and sold as a source of earned income. They may or may not include advertising—if so, the rates are usually higher than those for the regular playbill—and because of the design, the printing costs are also higher. Costs aside, a handsome souvenir book can be a helpful tool as part of the entire marketing and publicity program. Professional photographers, graphic artists, writers, and editors can greatly enhance the image projected by an organization through the medium of print.

Summary

The object of publicity is to gain *free* coverage and/or to generate favorable press and word of mouth for a given organization or production. There will, of course, be certain costs involved, such as those for salaries, printing, mailing, and entertainment. But hopefully these expenses and efforts will result in frequent and positive coverage in all the appropriate media.

The primary tools of successful publicity include information, communication, technical know-how, and imagination. Of the myriad promotional ideas dreamed up by publicists, only a few should be implemented and only a few of those will work. Effective publicity requires advance planning, a strict adherence to deadlines, and meticulous attention to detail. It also requires an ability to understand and interpret the product so that the public will also understand it, want it, and buy it. Publicity must be consistent with the goals and objectives of the production, company, organization, and institution being publicized. Both publicity and advertising are essential strategies in a promotion campaign and must be considered in terms of the long-term marketing goals. This chapter, then, serves as a basis for the next on advertising.

CHAPTER 16

Advertising and the Sales Campaign

ADVERTISING IS THE MOST EXPENSIVE ELEMENT in the marketing mix. It is promotion that is paid for line by line, second by second, stamp by stamp, blast by blast. On the one hand, no theatre has the budget to buy as much advertising as it would like: on the other, no amount of advertising is likely to bring in an audience that isn't interested in what is being offered. And just to keep things interesting, inevitably, everybody's an expert at advertising.

General Considerations

Before a word of copy is written, an image selected, a slogan adopted, it is necessary to determine exactly what is being sold to the public and then to define the exact demographics of that public. While it is usually a play or a concert that needs to be sold, the theatre is also selling the experience of attending the theatre and of interacting with other audience members.

Requisite Skills and Services

Few areas of theatre management present as many different options as the design, production, and distribution of advertising. In terms of both creativity and economics, it is wise to explore different options and to shop carefully for the requisite skills and services before making decisions. It is also good marketing practice to review existing advertising policy, budgets, and vendors annually, as well as to review the advertising of past seasons to determine which approach was most successful.

A first step involved in the creation of advertising is the writing of copy, which must directly relate to the nature of the product, the mission of the organization, and the overall marketing plan that has been created for the show or season. The copy may be written by the marketing director, the publicist, or a staff writer. Writing ad copy is a specialty that not everyone does well. If no one within the organization has copywriting experience, an alternative to in-house production is to hire a freelance writer or use an advertising agency. Once the copy is written, the important task of correcting the final draft and the printer's proof must be undertaken. This, too, requires special skills in language, grammar, spelling, and editing as well as knowledge of the standard proofreading symbols. Newer word-processing software with spell check, thesaurus, and grammar-editing capability may improve accuracy in editing copy.

Most performing arts organizations need the services of a graphics designer to create a logo. This is typically a one-time expense, and is usually worth whatever it costs to get an effective and professional design. College theatres might call upon the services of the art department. Others might offer a payment or award for a logo or poster design selected from competition. Corporations with graphics departments that are supporters of the theatre may be asked to donate design work as an in-kind contribution; printing companies as well as newspaper and magazine publishers usually offer their customers various layout and design services that may be sufficient to meet the needs of small organizations. Inexpensive desktop publishing software can help with basic design, scanners can reduce or enlarge photographs, and higher-end printers can make contact sheets and ad slicks—a camera-ready, glossy proof of a complete print advertisement. Large operations that present numerous events usually find it expedient and cost efficient to have a graphics designer on staff.

Graphics designers are knowledgeable about alternatives in the printing field, an important factor in keeping the costs within budget. The quality and weight of the paper used for brochures, flyers, and posters; the printing method to be used, such as offset or reproduction; whether or not to use color and how; which style of type to use; what quantity to order; which nonprinting services, such as folding and stapling, to order and which to do in-house are all elements that will affect cost as well as the appearance of printed material.

A great deal of labor may be required to prepare large bulk mailings for the post office or to distribute posters and handbills. Many organizations use volunteers or student interns to prepare mailings, distribute posters and fliers, and assist with the many menial tasks required to get the word out to the public. Larger organizations tend to use mailing houses for large quantity bulk mail. Whatever the method, it is important to recognize the timeliness of the effort and the distribution of materials. This may seem obvious, but when thousands of expensive brochures or hundreds of posters are sitting in the promotion office with no help available to process or distribute them, it becomes serious.

Advertising Agencies

Unlike other private agencies that provide technical assistance in such areas as fundraising, marketing, and public relations, advertising agencies work exclusively on a commission basis. For most, their income is derived from a fifteen percent commission based on the cost of all the print and electronic media advertising that they place.

Virtually all Broadway and Off-Broadway productions use ad agencies, as do many other performing arts and theatre operations around the country. The traditional method of selecting an agency is to invite at least several to make a presentation, which in essence is a job bid. In the case of a theatrical client, the focus of advertising is usually a particular production, institution, or both. The agency will study the subject matter and then prepare several graphics pieces, such as posters, playbill covers, and storyboards of proposed television commercials. They may also prepare a written proposal that deals with target markets and promotion strategies. Based on these presentations, the organization selects an agency. The decision should be based on:

1.) The creativity of the concept that the agency presents
2.) The past promotional track record of the agency
3.) The amount of personal attention the agency is willing to give the account.

Because agencies earn their money through ad placement, they are not always mindful of the other elements in the marketing mix, such as free publicity or personal sales. They would naturally prefer spending the entire marketing budget on paid advertising. Even if broadcast media advertising is more costly, they may favor it over print advertising. They may also urge standardized ads or commercials because copy changes are more labor intensive. On the other hand, agencies often provide excellent graphics and copy-writing talent without cost to the organization; they help keep ad salespeople away from the organization's door; they deal with all the placement and deadline details; and they lighten the burden of marketing responsibilities for the organization's staff.

Also, keep in mind that although there is no direct charge for creativity, there are direct production expenses that the advertiser is certainly charged for, usually on an hourly basis for scans, layouts, proofs, and any other labor that is required to get copy ready for distribution.

The Budget

Whatever the total marketing budget may be, only a portion of it can be allocated to paid advertising. Again, it is important that advertising expenditures be based on an organized and well-written marketing plan and not on what the competition is doing or what the organization has done in the past. Ad agencies will very efficiently spend whatever amounts have been allocated and will rarely urge not to advertise: it's how they make their money.

To assess the value of a particular media outlet, one must look at its rating or circulation statistics as well as the profile of its typical users, such as rock music fans, soap opera addicts, or financial news readers, and then determine which outlets, sections, programs, and/or time slots most attract the theatre's own target markets. There is no point in delivering an advertising message to markets that are uninterested. For instance, the "reach" of a particular city newspaper may be one million readers and the frequency with which these readers might see an advertisement in that paper is daily or more, if a number of ads for the same product are placed in the same edition. But, if fewer than a fraction of the readership total is interested in the product, that newspaper is a very ineffective place to advertise. So the challenge is to find another media outlet or another marketing strategy that really is cost effective.

Repetition or saturation is a vital element in successful advertising. Unless a potential user hears or sees the identical message at least three times over the course of a day or two, the message will probably not be communicated. This will also be the case if too much time elapses between received messages. It is better for instance to place twelve radio spots with the same station during targeted time slots over two days than over seven days. In addition, the more advertising time or space one buys in the media, the lower the per unit cost, and the cost is further reduced if an organization agrees to purchase a minimum amount of space or time each week over a number of weeks or months.

Below are a few general points to keep in mind when allocating limited advertising dollars. They all have an impact on cost, and it doesn't take much experience in buying ad space to understand how very costly they are.

The Time Element

Whoever coined the phrase "time is money" may well have had the promotion game in mind. This is because the more lead time one has to promote an attraction or event, the more likely the promotion will be successful. The less time one has, the more expensive the promotion is likely to be. The performing arts are often confronted with last-minute bookings, cancellations, and changes in plans that cause havoc with promotional efforts. Publicity directors and other marketing specialists are not magicians—they cannot speed up postal delivery, stop the presses, or reprint the playbills an hour before curtain. They must somehow work within the deadline of opening night as well as within a vast number of media deadlines and the simple time constraints required to get things done. Marketing personnel must have a keen sense of deadline. While budgets and strategies can be controlled and changed, time and its relentless march toward important deadlines cannot. Planning a marketing and advertising campaign, then, should include a detailed calendar of deadlines for each and every strategy.

The Advertising Plan

Successfully implementing an advertising plan requires research, detailed timelines, and discipline to meet all deadlines. The simple act of placing an ad in a newspaper involves coordinating many people, including copywriters, graphics designers, internal staff for editing, approvals, and media outlets, to complete the project on deadline. The advertising plan should be created in two parts, one for subscription marketing and another for single-ticket sales. When resources permit, larger organizations have a separate advertising plan specifically for branding. In the process of developing a strategy, the media outlets that reach the organization's target market must be identified, and the organization's historical sales data to identify what media outlet had the highest rate of return on investment must be analyzed. This is commonly called a cost to gross analysis. It is important to track statistics such as how much money the organization spent to place an ad and how much revenue did the organization receive? This requires that the box office track the source of the sale on every transaction and find out what motivated each purchase—subscription brochure, radio/television advertising, newspaper advertising, or word of mouth. It is necessary to create a detailed calendar such as the following:

Production Title	Prod. Dates	Publication	Run Date	Artwork Deadline Date	Ad Size	Rate of insertion	Ad placement expense	Designer Expense	Total Ad Expense
Taming of the Shrew	Oct 17–30	Local Gazette	Sun Oct 10	Oct 3	2 columns × 10.5"	$100 per column inch	$2,100	$200	$2,300
Taming of the Shrew	Oct 17–30	Local Gazette	Thurs Oct 14	Oct 11	2 columns × 7"	$60 per column inch	$840	$60	$900

A Focused Message

Limited resources always restrict the size or length of an advertising message—usually to just a few column inches or a few seconds of time. One ad can't sell everything in the department store, yet inexperienced copywriters invariably try to crowd too many messages into a very limited space. Just as each press release should focus on a single idea or event, each advertisement should focus on a single message that is stated powerfully with the fewest possible words. It is usually more effective to concentrate on a single theme or person. A few obvious focal points for theatrical advertising include:

1.) A star performer;

2.) A well-known artist associated with the production, such as a playwright, director, conductor, or choreographer;

3.) A well-known production title or piece of music;

4.) A marquee-name organization, such as the "Julliard String Quartet" or the "Martha Graham Dance Company";

5.) A well-known theatre facility, producer, or presenter;

6.) Quotes from reviews;

7.) Awards such as a Tony Award, Obie, Dramatists' Guild or Pulitzer Prize;

8.) A bargain or discount offer;

NEW YORK CITY OPERA
Christopher Keene, General Director

Love Hurts.

But Starting Thursday It Also Makes Great Opera.

Season premiere July 6
A new production of Mozart's *Don Giovanni*
Directed by Harold Prince

Holleque, Ginsberg, Mills; Cheek, Garrison, Opalach, Peterson,
Storojev*; Comissiona; Prince

July 6, July 11

.

Rigoletto

A curse twists a jester's fate, stealing the
only person he ever loved.
Music by Giuseppe Verdi.
O'Flynn, Marsee; Elvira, Hartfield, Peterson; Bergeson;
Capobianco/Furlong

July 8 Mat, July 14

Il Barbiere Di Siviglia

(The Barber Of Seville)
Figaro's a jack-of-all-trades and master of
disguise as he helps a lovesick Count win
the hand of a captive beauty.
Music by Gioacchino Rossini.
Bunnel, Shaulis; Woodman, Eisler, J. McKee, Doss;
Comissiona; Mansouri/Smith

July 7, July 12

NEXT TWO WEEKS:

Tues 8PM	Wed 8PM	Thurs 8PM	Fri 8PM	Sat 2PM	Sat 8PM	Sun 1PM
July 4 No performance	July 5 No performance	July 6 †DON GIOVANNI (s)	July 7 IL BARBIERE DI SIVIGLIA (s)	July 8 RIGOLETTO (s)	July 8 THE MERRY WIDOW	July 9 MADAMA BUTTERFLY (s)
July 11 †DON GIOVANNI (s)	July 12 IL BARBIERE DI SIVIGLIA (s)	July 13 MADAMA BUTTERFLY (s)	July 14 RIGOLETTO (s)	July 15 THE MERRY WIDOW	July 15 DIE ZAUBER-FLÖTE (s)	July 16 No performance

(s) With English Supertitles †New Production *Debut Artist Cast and Program subject to change.   © 1989 NY CITY OPERA

Call Ticketmaster Today (212) 307-7171 (201) 507-8900
Tickets $12–$47. Orch $57.
New York State Theater, Lincoln Center, 63rd St. & Columbus Ave. Info. (212) 870-5570

9.) A limited engagement or limited ticket supply;

10.) Appeals to specific age groups such as children or seniors.

Advertising can also focus on one of the motivating appeals discussed in the previous chapter—snobbery, sex, or humor. This is sometimes the best solution when promoting an entire season or series of productions, as illustrated by the New York City Opera advertisement that follows. A thirty-second commercial or small newspaper ad obviously can't mention all the performers and events in a long series, so the message must be designed to encapsulate the overall impact that the series is meant to have on its audience. And all messages, from Public Service Announcements (PSAs) to TV commercials, should answer the 5 W's of good journalism: Who, What, When, Where, and Why —as well as How, as in "*How* to get tickets."

Selecting the focus of an advertising campaign should be the responsibility of marketing experts.

Errors and Misprints

All media outlets occasionally make mistakes in the running of advertisements. All give a rebate or credit the advertiser and provide additional advertising without charge, but the responsibility for catching errors and misprints falls to the advertiser or its ad agency. This task is easiest if a clipping service has been retained to supply copies of all advertising. Monitoring commercials placed with electronic media outlets is more difficult, although most will provide an advance schedule of approximately when each commercial will be aired. Of course, if the submitted ad copy or layout was faulty, there is no recourse. When time permits, it is wise to request a proof of each print ad before it is published.

Advertising Composition and Layout

The Logotype and the Signature

The first task of composing advertising is usually the creation of a graphic image or symbol that visually identifies a specific organization, production, or both. This becomes a trademark that the public should automatically associate with the product. When the trademark incorporates the name of the product, it is called a logotype or logo. A purely graphic symbol or image may also be used. When the logo (or name) of the product is used in combination with the symbol of the product, it is called a signature or a sig.

Consumers identify many products by their symbols or graphic images: think Nike "swoosh" and Nike is the Greek goddess of victory. A successful logo captures the feeling, if not the meaning, of the product it symbolizes. It is a visual statement about the nature of the product. When a new logo is first used in advertising, it should serve as an attention-getting device. As it becomes familiar to the public, it communicates the idea

that would otherwise take much more space. Finally, the logo for popular products—
from baseball teams to Broadway shows—may be exploited through merchandising with
such items as tote bags or T-shirts.

Some logos are superimposed on a picture, placed next to one, or designed to incorporate information such as an address and phone number.

Every Broadway and Off-Broadway hit has a widely used logo that the public soon
associates with the show. This itself becomes a valuable advertising tool for all future
productions of the show. Booking agencies usually supply these to presenters in the
form of heralds, ad slicks, and 3-sheets, which are discussed in the next section. A logo
can also be developed to indicate a name or a place or theatre, such as logo for Wharton
Center for Performing Arts at Michigan State University. This logo is composed of a
symbol and typeface.

Examples of effective institutional graphics.

Examples of effective show graphics.

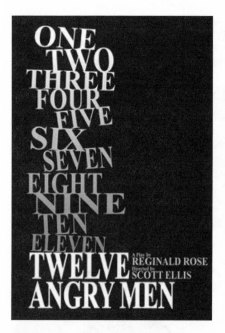

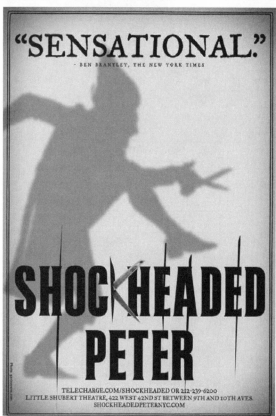

Examples of effective show graphics.

Types of Display Advertising

Display advertising is any printed promotional piece that uses composition and layout that go beyond straightforward reading material. Rather than text print, it usually employs display type, which is fourteen points or larger. Most display advertising incorporates the logo or sig for the product and also—through its composition, layout, and graphics—provides further visual and verbal information about the product. Often, the same basic design and copy are adapted for use in different types of display advertising:

1.) Websites
2.) Ads placed in the print media
3.) Brochures
4.) Posters: a typical Broadway show poster is a window card, 14" by 22"
5.) Flyers and handbills
6.) Heralds: sigs for use at the top of ads, posters, flyers, etc.
7.) 3-sheets: soft paper, 41" by 81" pasted into display frames on sides of buildings
8.) Outdoor billboards
9.) Other outdoor displays: taxi cabs; phone booths, trash cans

When sketched on a piece of plain white paper, almost any ad design looks good. When clipped out of a newspaper and pasted into a scrapbook, it looks even better. But when that same ad appears on a page, surrounded by the clutter of other ads, photos, and news stories, how will it hold up? The same question can be asked about a poster that is crowded into a store window with a dozen other posters.

The context in which display advertising appears is just as important as the ad itself. Does it stand out beside other display advertising or does it get lost? In regard to all print media, incidentally, the upper right half of the right hand page is considered the optimum positioning for ads because people flipping through a publication do not initially look at the left hand page. It is sometimes possible to negotiate to have the same ad position for an entire season or run of a show in some newspapers, particularly the weekly arts inserts.

Display advertising that contains an ample amount of empty space is likely to be the best attention getting. While it is important to provide the necessary information about a production or theatre, overcrowding the copy must not occur. Also, letters printed in an unusual yet readable style are attention-getting: script letters, curved letters, or letters embroidered with a pattern. A border that frames the entire ad or a shadow box that draws a heavy "shadow" both help to make an ad stand out on the page. A photograph or graphics design also makes an ad more effective, as does the use of reverse-print typesetting, a graphics device that surrounds the letters with inked space, allowing the letters to be formed by the paper itself.

These techniques are illustrated by the following four display designs for *Othello*.

Placing display advertising in public places, along highways, and on street corners has come under increasing criticism, as people become more and more concerned with cleaning up the environment. Visual pollution can be as offensive as noise and chemical pollution. Because the arts have always labored to improve the quality of life, arts managers must be sensitive to these issues. Gluing bumper stickers onto cars, inserting flyers under windshield wipers, attaching posters to telephone poles, and leaving handouts where they might litter the environment should not be done. These acts can offend those who are being targeted to buy tickets. Indeed, any method of outdoor advertising should be practiced with restraint, good taste, and within legal limits. However, if permission can be obtained to display street banners, flags, or other types of temporary advertising displays, these can enhance pride in a cultural event or help celebrate a local festival.

Organizing the Information

Before any advertising layout is attempted, it is essential that basic marketing research and planning, as discussed in Chapter 14, be accomplished. Based on that, it is then necessary to select a focused message created to appeal to target markets and then to commission a logo or sig that encapsulates that message in a graphically dramatic way. Ongoing operations should probably focus on the name of the institution as a unifying factor for all the publicity and advertising. Public loyalty should first be developed toward the institution and then toward the individual productions, so that the nucleus of an audience will support whatever productions are offered. When each production is promoted individually, each marketing campaign must build an entirely new audience. Advertising composition must also take contractual billing provisions into account, in the same manner as playbill composition. When the production being advertised is a one-off or stand-alone project, incorporating the necessary information into display ads and then embellishing these ads with a unique typeface or photograph is not too difficult for the talented graphics designer. When there is a multiweek, multiproduction season or series to advertise, the task is more difficult. If productions can be scheduled so that each is at some point in the season offered on a Monday or on a Tuesday and at the same clock time, then series tickets will at least conform to the same day and time of the week—although not necessarily every week of the season. Or a series might consist of three or four plays in rapid succession over one or two weeks, which is an enterprising way to capture playgoers in heavy tourist areas where visitors spend only a week or two. One of the most effective methods of showing a multiproduction repertory schedule is to enter the play titles onto a calendar, as shown in the New York City Opera advertisement.

When a play series consists of different productions, each offered for one or more consecutive weeks, the season can be listed in clear, chronological order. Pocketsize schedule cards that customers can keep in a wallet or pocketbook should be printed.

It is always good to test advertising designs on at least a few disinterested readers before going to press. Even experts can develop copy-blindness after the subject matter becomes overly familiar and a misspelled name goes unnoticed or the phone number is

FESTIVAL THEATRE
75 MAIN ST. 781-0000
Presents
NOV. 17, 18, 19, 20, 8 P.M.
William Shakespeare's
OTHELLO
Box Office Open 10-5
Tickets: $4.00, $5.00, $6.00
Phone Orders Accepted
Group Rates Available

1. Straightforward type and layout.

FESTIVAL THEATRE
Presents
SHAKESPEARE'S
OTHELLO
NOV. 17-20
8 P.M.
Box Office: 75 Main St.
Tickets: $4.00, $5.00, $6.00
Phone: 781-0000

2. Curved lettering for logo; more white space, less copy.

3. Reversed-out logo; graphic "O" in title.

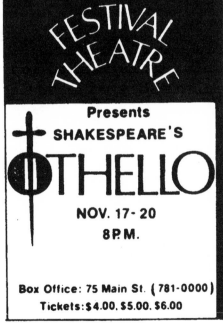

4. Shadow box to tie ad together; more elaborate graphic "O."

left out. Following is a checklist of some of the most critical pieces of information to include in an advertisement. This is by no means comprehensive and can vary based on the mission of the organization.

1.) Institution's name
2.) Institution's logo
3.) Name of production
4.) Names of artistic director, director, producer, music director, and star performer's name (see previous discussion on Billing, Chapter 15)
5.) Date (Sunday, April 13, 20xx) / Season
6.) Time
7.) Phone number to purchase tickets with area code
8.) Website address to purchase tickets
9.) Names of significant corporate sponsors and donors (coordinated with development department)
10.) Name of the theatre and street address
11.) Ticket price(s)*
12.) Note on language or sexual content, usually described as "Adult"

*Ticket prices are not always included in display ads. This depends entirely on the policy of the organization and the manner in which tickets are sold. When there is a wide range of ticket prices available, it is sometimes preferable that ticket information be with-held until the patron calls or goes on-line to order tickets, thereby increasing the opportunity to actually make the sale. The publication of a high-ticket price can turn the potential buyer off to the initial inquiry and a low-ticket price will be interpreted by some as a lower quality production.

Advertising copy should abbreviate ticket and price information for economy of space, usually the briefer the better. For example:

Ticket Information:

Monday through Saturday at 8:00 P.M.
Orchestra: $25.00, $20.00
Mezzanine: $20.00
Balcony: $17.50, $15.00
Wednesday and Saturday matinees at 2:00 P.M.
Orchestra: $20.00, 17.50
Mezzanine: $17.50.
Balcony: $15.00, 12.50

This may be reduced to:

Tickets: Mon thru Sat (8:00) $25.00, 20.00, 17.50, 15.00 Wed & Sat (2:00) $20.00, 17.50, 15.00, 12.50

Which may be further reduced to:

Mon-Sat 8 P.M.
Wed & Sat 2 P.M.
Tickets: $25 to $12.50

The last example is most commonly used. The first example is seldom used.

Play—and sometimes opera—promotion customarily includes a descriptive phrase above or below the title of the production being advertised. Sometimes, however, a play title is so well known that these blurbs are unnecessary. But in some cases a blurb can provide a clue about the nature of the event and perhaps motivate people to attend it. Readers like to know if a production is serious or comic, musical or nonmusical, new or a revival. This information can be worded into a descriptive phrase, such as "a musical adaptation," "a modern dress version," "a drama of political corruption," "a comedy of gender." Alliteration has been overly used in theatrical promotion, so that blurbs like the following should be avoided: "Marlowe's marvelous melodrama," "Simon's sizzling satire," "Wilde's witty winner!" A straightforward description, a clever play on words, an incisive quotation, or a single, strong adjective make the most effective blurbs. If the attraction is a musical group, a chamber music ensemble, symphony orchestra, or solo recital, a brief listing of the program should be included along with mention of any competitions that may have recently been won by the attraction. If it is a dance performance, the program, credit for a commissioned work, and as appropriate notable recent appearances can be included.

Finally, it should be remembered that different types of display advertising often require different copy and composition in order to speak forcefully to the target market at which they are aimed. For instance, a direct mail campaign may be aimed at four different targets:

1.) Current subscribers
2.) Former subscribers
3.) People who have attended just single performances
4.) New audiences—arts buyers who have never attended the theatre.

The brochure or other mailing pieces should be adapted to each group. Current subscribers might be given the opportunity of retaining their present seat locations if they renew within a certain period; former subscribers might be offered a special incentive to "return home;" and nonsubscribers might be offered a special one-time discount.

Similarly, ad copy aimed at seasoned theatregoers can assume that they are more informed about the theatre and its repertoire than others. The more directly and personally an advertising message speaks to the person who receives it, the more effective it will be.

Direct Mail Systems

Direct mail advertising is a proven marketing strategy and often less expensive than media advertising. However, printing, handling, and postage costs are high, so it is necessary to pay close attention to the actual costs of each mailing. This is a three-part process that includes:

1.) Creating or obtaining an initial list of correct names and addresses appropriate for specific uses;

2.) Building on the list by capturing appropriate additions;

3.) Periodically cleaning the list to eliminate inactive names or to correct address information that has changed.

Creating a Mailing List

The mission, size, and type of organization—together with its marketing policies and strategies—will influence how its direct mail system is designed. Like planning a budget, the creation of this management tool should involve everyone in the organization who needs to communicate with groups of users by mail or email on a regular basis. Collecting names for each category of what may be a general mailing list or two—one for sales and fundraising purposes, and one for purposes of media relations—usually begins inhouse. The box office should have the names and addresses of all current subscribers, all former or lapsed subscribers, as well as those of customers who bought single tickets. The fundraising office should easily be able to supply correct names and addresses for board members, donors, and potential donors. The publicity office should have a basic list of editors, writers, and others with whom it communicates regularly. The most valid and valuable lists are those that contain names of current users. But, like all entries on a list, even these should be periodically verified for correctness.

Secondary sources of names for a mailing list may be culled from property tax lists at city hall and acquired from address records kept by chambers of commerce, professional organizations, charity groups, and even from the telephone book. However, these should be used less frequently, kept separate from lists of known customers, and sample-tested before being used fully. Finally, one may buy, borrow, or rent mailing lists from companies specializing in that business or from publishers, corporations, or community organizations including other cultural organizations and service groups. When using borrowed or traded lists, the standard agreement is to allow a one-time mailing, and anyone who purchases from that list is then added to the organization's permanent database. Secondary sources of names, however, are always less valuable than primary sources, and with the high costs of printing and postage, they constitute a higher risk.

After deciding the types of lists needed and the sources from which they will be compiled, one must decide how these lists should be organized and generated: by zip code, alphabetically, or by user category, such as alumni, donors, current subscribers, drama editors. When creating a database, give careful thought to setting up the fields that will determine the various ways in which the list(s) can be generated.

Capturing New Names

Once a list category has been deemed necessary and has been created with the names of appropriate, known users, additional names of people who fit that category should be added as they are captured. Computerized box office systems facilitate capturing mailing list information, though the box office treasurers must cooperate in the endeavor. Ideally, each area or department within the organization will accept responsibility for gathering new names and updating lists. It is not difficult to do this, but it requires a high level of willingness on the part of those staff members involved.

Another primary source of new names is the audience itself—many of whom may not have had direct contact with the box office or any ticketing system. Research completed in 2002 by Audience Insight LLC (www.audienceinsight.com) of Southport, Connecticut, found that forty percent of the audience members in fifteen U.S. markets did not—and had never—purchased their tickets.

They may have gotten their tickets as a gift; they may have been part of a group sale transaction; or one friend may have purchased tickets for a small group of friends. Whatever the actual circumstances, this means that a significant portion of the audience is not on the mailing list. When group sales comprise a major part of the house, postcards can be given to the group organizer when the tickets are delivered then the postcards can be filled out by the group members and turned over to the theatre. Alternatively, the organizer might provide a manifest of the group, with names, addresses, telephone numbers, and email addresses so that the theatre can communicate with individual members of this important group: theatregoers. It is worth re-emphasizing: these are people who have attended a performance and know where the theatre is. They are the people most likely to return. These are the people with whom the theatre most wants to be in touch.

Mailing address forms, such as the following one, can also be placed at convenient points in the lobby or inserted into playbills:

BE THE FIRST TO HEAR ABOUT UPCOMING PRODUCTIONS

To receive our brochure, please complete this form and place it in the lobby drop box.

Name _____

Address _____

City _____ State _____ ZIP _____

Daytime Phone (   ) _____

Evening Phone (   ) _____

Email Address _____

Space might also be provided for the customer to write in the name and address of "a friend who might also like to receive our brochure." Performances attended by tourist or nonresident audiences should have forms available that distinguish between permanent addresses and those that are seasonal or temporary.

Organizations that offer different types of attractions should design a form that targets specific programming interests:

PLEASE PLACE MY NAME ON YOUR MAILING LIST

I would like to be informed about events in the categories that I have checked below:

☐ Theatre   ☐ Music   ☐ Dance   ☐ Film   ☐ Children's Theatre

Name _____

Address _____

City _____ State _____ ZIP _____

Daytime Phone (   ) _____

Evening Phone (   ) _____

Email Address _____

Address forms that are inserted into playbills rather than printed as part of them are more likely to be filled out and returned. Attractive desks equipped with pencils and drop boxes should be placed at convenient points in the lobby. The playgoer who is already standing in the lobby is the playgoer most likely to return, so to miss the opportunity of capturing that person's name and address is, at best, shortsighted.

Prospect Cards

Prospect cards or lead generation cards include a detachable postcard that is returned to the sender requesting further information about the organization. The idea is that it's more efficient to send a brochure to someone who has indicated a desire for one. The copy on the card should be something like:

> If you would like to receive our brochure for next fall's exciting season of attractions, just put a stamp on the reverse side of this card and mail it back to us. You should receive your brochure within one week.

In-House List Maintenance

It pays to be careful because mistakes can become costly. If a mailing list is used four times a year at a postal rate of thirty cents and printing costs of seventy cents per piece, one tiny mistake like an incorrect ZIP code can cost the organization four dollars annually. Multiply that by five hundred other tiny mistakes on a list of five thousand and the organization has an annual loss of two thousand dollars. This type of waste is common, because organizations fail to keep their mailing lists current. By using a few simple tools, this waste can easily be avoided.

A major policy decision about list maintenance has to do with current entries: How long should inactive users remain on the list?

If no purchase is made after two mailings, should that person receive a third, a fourth, or a fifth mailing? Sending materials to people who are nonbuyers is a waste of effort and money. The question is, when is a former-buyer a nonbuyer?

The marketing department should have access to customer relations management software that records the user activity of every person on every list in the system showing the ticket-buying, contributing, publicity generating, and/or volunteer activity of each individual. This enables the organization to track each user and periodically generate special lists of individuals who didn't renew their season tickets or their annual contributions.

Magazine publishers have tracked their subscribers for decades, and with computers and the appropriate software, even small performing arts companies can do it, too. While software makes this tracking possible, the capturing and inputting of information depends on reliable staff members. Even under the best circumstances, it is impossible to track everyone in the system; some active users will always be eliminated because they appear to be *inactive*. But this is less a problem than repeatedly sending mailers to people who *never* respond.

In all likelihood active users who were mistakenly dropped will be recaptured in a brief time because they will demand to be serviced. Most box office software has the capability to code each entry by buyer type or a designation designed by the organization, such as student or single-ticket buyer who may live outside the normal service area. This allows easier analysis and cleansing of lists. The United States Postal Service (USPS) reports that approximately fifteen to twenty percent of the nation's population moves or dies every year. It is imperative that in-house mailing lists be updated. Here are a few tips that can help:

National Change of Address (NCOA) is a enormous database maintained by the United States Post Office of people who have completed Change of Address cards. Mailing houses can run the mailing list against NCOA and update incorrect addresses. Normally, anywhere from four to eight percent of a database is changed. Minimum costs for NCOA run from $350 to $500. The process takes about one week, so that additional time would have to be factored into a mailing timeline.

Address Correction Requested (ACR) is the most accurate way to update in-house mailing lists. Simply place "Address Correction Requested" endorsement line on the mailing piece in the upper left corner, underneath the return address. The post office will return any undeliverable mail to the sender, provide the new address, and give a reason for its not being deliverable. The post office provides ACR on first-class mailings free of charge. Third-class bulk letters returned to the sender that weigh less than three ounces cost $.50 per piece. Because of the expense on third-class mailings, only use ACR on the in-house mailing list.

Having duplicate names is another possibility for wasted postage. When several different mailing lists are being used, there is a good chance of duplication. Duplications may even be found in a single list because one person's name appears in several ways—John Smith, Jack Smith, or J.B. Smith—the computer may not be able to purge such duplications automatically, so a printout of names in alphabetical order should be made and studied on a regular basis. An easier alternative is to print, "If you have received a duplicate of this brochure, please hand it to a friend." And, when it is not possible to merge duplicate names that appear on different lists, each list might be mailed several days apart so that duplicates won't all arrive in the same mailbox on the same day.

If it begins to sound that creating, building, and maintaining mailing lists for an active performing arts or theatre operation is a full-time job, this is correct—or, at least, it will be part of a full-time job for a data entry person. But the work entailed in keeping correct and up-to-date donor lists, press lists, and sales promotion lists is an administrative responsibility crucial to the survival of many organizations.

Mailing Methods

When and how often direct mail lists are used depends on the budget available and the priorities for communicating with actual users and potential users. Current postal rates and regulations are spelled out in booklets available at every post office and on the US Postal Service website, www.USPS.com. Still, rates and regulations change frequently, so it is wise for the manager or marketing director to speak personally with the local postmaster. What are the current rates? How should mail be prepared for delivery to the post office? What are the advantages and disadvantages of the various mailing methods?

There are many different bulk, third class, mail rates. Basically, the more post office work done by the sender, the lower the rate. Also, rates are lowest for nonprofit organizations. The three methods of postage payment are:

1.) Precanceled stamps: these are purchased at the post office and affixed individually by the sender.

2.) Postage meter: the sender must purchase the meter from a manufacturer who also supplies a license application. The sender takes the meter to the post office, where it is set as requested and the post office imposes the corresponding charge. Meters should be capable of being set to the closest one-tenth of one percent.

3.) Permit imprints: a permit number is supplied by the local post office and printed directly onto the mailing piece at the same time the rest of it is printed; the addressed and sorted bulk mailer is then delivered to the post office together with a mailing statement and the sender pays cash for the corresponding postage.

There is an annual mailing fee for the right to use either stamped or imprinted bulk mail methods, and another fee to acquire an imprint number. Permit numbers, however, remain valid indefinitely, providing they are used at least once a year. All mailings must be handled by the post office where the permit was filed, and a Statement of Mailing must accompany each batch of mail. There is also a Small Volume Bulk Mail Application for mailings that weigh no more than one hundred and forty pounds. The presorting process required for the sender to qualify for bulk rates includes affixing different colored stickers onto the lower left corner of each piece, which indicate the destination zones, then banding and sacking pieces for the same zone. Because of the fees and the labor involved in bulk mailing, organizations that send out only one large mailing each year or several small ones may find it cheaper to use first-class postage. The decision to mail first class or bulk is determined by the postage expense, size of the mailing list, and the human resources available to prepare bulk mailings. It is very time consuming to mail, sort, bundle, and label the mailing to meet postal regulations. However, organizations with active volunteer organizations do have a ready resource.

Design Considerations

The first of many decisions that must be made when planning a bulk mailer is whether to design the mailer as a self-mailer or as a separate piece that will be inserted into an envelope and sealed. The former, of course, is much less expensive to produce and easier to mail and may be anything from a postcard to a folded and sealed brochure. Whether or not self-mailers are generally perceived as junk mail and generally ignored by recipients is a matter of opinion and often affects the design. If the decision is made to insert the mailer into an envelope, it is better to design the piece to fit a standard-size envelope, as custom-size envelopes are expensive to print and may require extra postage.

Postage rates, of course, increase with the weight of the piece and are restricted by size and shape. Also, one should be certain that stamps, address labels, typing, handwriting, or anything else that might be applied will not slip or rub off, especially when using mailer material such as plastic or that with a metallic surface.

Timetable

Promotion that is dependent on the United States Postal Service must follow a timetable. Enough time must be allowed to:

1.) Prepare, proofread, and print the material to be mailed;

2.) Address, sort, label, band, sack, and deliver the mailer to the post office;

3.) Allow for postal delivery;

4.) Allow for return of any first-class ticket orders or other types of RSVP;

5.) If applicable, allow time for tickets to be mailed from the box office and received by the customer before the performance date.

If bulk rates are used, a reasonable timetable will require the pieces to be mailed no fewer than six weeks prior to the first performance.

Using a Mailing House

Additional time may have to be added to the schedule when an organization hires a mailing house. Such companies charge according to the amount of mail in each batch and the services they provide. They can merge multiple mailing lists and purge duplicates and invalid addresses. It is much more economical when the organization conducts all the list-building and list-maintenance chores, as well as the sorting, bulk mail labeling, and bagging after the address labels have been printed by the mailing house, although, for an additional charge, the firm will handle the whole process.

It is important to obtain a clear, firm commitment regarding the length of time it will take the mailing house to complete its part of the work. Chances are that the arts organization will be one of its smallest accounts, so the house will not make it a high priority.

Electronic Media

We live in the age of the thirty-second commercial message. We've become so accustomed to receiving information in this manner that thirty seconds is often the maximum amount of time we're willing to give before we tune out, whether it's the radio or television; the teacher or the telemarketer; the letter or the brochure. Advertising must express its messages quickly, memorably, and frequently. Advertising in the electronic media must do this with even greater economy of words and images than in print media. A media moment is even more fleeting than a moment in the theatre because it rarely has our full attention and lacks the space or time to build to a crescendo. It is a crescendo out of context. To get the context—which is the whole point of advertising—one must use the product.

Radio advertising is less expensive than television and usually offers the advertiser more production services. Radio also provides a simple and fast method for getting a message out to the public and may offer a more specific target market and, therefore, be more cost efficient than newspaper advertising. However, on the down side, radio listeners rarely pay much attention to commercials, switch to different stations during commercials, and almost never retain numerical data, such as dates and phone numbers.

Television viewers often do pay attention to commercials, represent a much wider audience, and may respond to effective advertising in large numbers because of its dramatic and human impact. Of course, it can take a considerable amount of time, money, and talent to produce even a good ten-second TV spot. Few arts organizations can afford the necessary frequency needed to insure cost efficiency, and they find it difficult to measure results. When both radio and television advertising are being planned, the temptation is to create the TV commercial first and then simply turn the audio portion into a radio commercial. But, in view of the above comparisons, it is obvious that the two should be different versions of the same message.

Radio Commercials

Most radio stations compile demographic information about their listeners and will provide this to potential advertisers. While rates are based on the total number of listeners, the advertiser should be more interested in who is listening rather than how many.

Working with a station's advertising representative, a performing arts organization is likely to buy a package of radio time that includes a specified number of spots at different periods during the day. Included in this may be trade-outs, or introductory discounts for new advertisers; guest participation on certain programs; and rudimentary copywriting and production services. To secure the desired time spots, sales contracts should be concluded several weeks before the commercials are to be aired, and tapes or scripts of the commercials should be delivered to the station a few days before. Most spots are thirty seconds and about seventy-five words long; or sixty seconds and about one hundred fifty words long, although ten-second spots may be available at very low rates and aired as fillers at the discretion of the station. It pays to examine the different rates and packages in order to come in on budget and on target.

Unlike writing copy for a press release, writing ad copy—especially for radio and television—can and often should be personalized. The endorsement format in which a well-known celebrity promotes the product is usually effective. If there is a star in the production who is willing to make the commercial, this can also be effective. The most elaborate commercials are produced on tape and make use of several voices, as well as music and other sound effects. Here is the script for a radio commercial prepared by the Serino Coyne advertising agency in New York for *Steel Magnolias*.

ADVERTISING COPY FROM serino coyne inc.

1515 BROADWAY
NEW YORK, NEW YORK 10036
(212) 626-2700
FAX (212) 626-2799

client: Gabay/Goodman	*date:* 2/16/05	*ad#/rev.*
production: STEEL MAGNOLIAS	*radio* :30 *tv*	*print:*
title: Delta :30 Radio	*text in ART STUDIO:*	

DELTA:

Hey New York, get set for comedy! This is Delta Burke, and this spring I am letting my hair down in the new Broadway production of STEEL MAGNOLIAS. Joining me in the shop are Christine Ebersole, Rebecca Gayheart, Marsha Mason, Lily Rabe, and Frances Sternhagen. Six beauties. One parlor. And just one number to call: (212) 239-6200 (six-two-hundred). STEEL MAGNOLIAS starts previews March 15th so you better make your appointment now...'cause tickets will be "hair" today and gone tomorrow!

Tag:
STEEL MAGNOLIAS starts previews on Tuesday so you better make your appointment now...'cause tickets will be "hair" today and gone tomorrow!

Television Commercials

Television advertising is quite expensive and can easily wipe out a promotion budget by itself. Having said that, there are ways of advertising on television that can be cost effective. The proliferation of cable stations around the nation has made television advertising almost reasonable, but as with mailing lists, the question is not so much how many people are watching, but which people are watching. Depending on the attraction being promoted, there may be a specific cable audience that is the perfect match for the attraction.

Further, TV time need not be bought by an ad agency working for the organization: if the organization places its own television advertising, many stations will reduce the total advertising bill by the fifteen percent commission that an agency would have received. This is also occasionally true of other media outlets and can represent a very considerable saving on the total advertising bill over the course of a season.

The traditional way of developing a concept for a television commercial is to script it out by describing the visual element next to the audio, or voice and sound, elements. Then the script may be illustrated on a storyboard, which shows a series of sketches depicting the key visual moments and also prints the voice-over or other audio elements directly below the sketches. These are usually arranged on a large, black poster board.

Media Sponsorships

Marketing professionals' goals are to increase ticket revenue and build audiences, while minimizing expenditures. For the creative marketing director, this environment provides fertile ground for developing new ways to stretch the marketing dollars. Developing sponsorship packages with media outlets is a lucrative way to achieve the seemingly opposite objectives of increasing revenue while decreasing expenditures.

Media sponsorships are partnerships between a nonprofit and a newspaper, magazine, radio station, or TV station in which the media usually offers "free" advertising in return for various sponsorship benefits. Sample benefits include such items as tickets, program book advertising, signage in the lobby, logos on website, logos in all advertising, use of facility for media event, listing in theatre newsletter, business listing on subscriber cards, and discount tickets for employees. The key to success, as with all sponsorship packages, is to provide benefits to the media outlets that *they* would find of interest, that *they* would hold a high-perceived value for, and that cost very little for the organization. Media outlets want media sponsorships to provide: branding, visibility, increased circulation (new readers/viewers/listeners), audience-retention, and new advertising revenue.

As with all marketing initiatives, planning and targeting are essential for success. When developing a media sponsorship program, the primary steps are to:

1.) Identify the target market for the organization's potential audience;

2.) Identify the primary media vendors that reach that target;

3.) Identify any constituents of the organization, including board members, artists, personnel, who have access to media executives;

4.) Create the advertising plan for the season;

5.) Develop a macro-advertising plan by media-vendor that calculates the total number of ads placed by outlet and total expenditures: for example, over the course of the season the plan calls for thirty ads in the *Local Gazette* for a total of $36,000;

6.) Develop media sponsorship packages with benefits at each dollar-value level;

7.) Establish the various packages with benefits and place a value with each level. Don't undersell the value of the benefits;

8.) Aggressively sell to media vendors, being mindful that media sponsorships are mutually beneficial. Be flexible and be creative;

9.) Reduce the details of the package to writing and have both parties sign a contract;

10.) Fulfill all the promises;

11.) Nurture the relationship.

Advertorials

Another form of media sponsorship is the "advertorial." An advertorial is a section of a newspaper or special edition of a magazine that has approximately fifty percent editorial selections and fifty percent advertising. The advertising department usually produces it. By partnering with arts organizations, media outlets underwrite the cost of production of the advertorial with their sponsorship and then sell advertising to cover the costs. These are usually special insert sections of the newspaper, printed only occasionally, that focus on a particular community activity. They are most often printed in tabloid form. The newspaper will generally overprint by an agreed upon number so that the organizations using the publication can distribute copies to their patrons in their lobbies or through direct mail.

Telemarketing

The use of the telephone as a marketing tool is telemarketing and offers yet another strategy for achieving an organization's declared marketing goals. These often include increasing subscription sales, single-ticket sales, group sales, contributions, and/or memberships. Like other marketing strategies, telemarketing should be tied to an overall marketing plan and coordinated with other aspects of that plan, such as direct mail advertising and radio commercials. No theatre or performing arts organization should pour all its marketing resources into a single strategy, however promising it may appear.

Before embarking on a telemarketing campaign, consider the following:

1.) Many people regard telephone solicitations as an invasion of their privacy, and the do-not-call legislation raises serious questions about the wisdom of telemarketing, even though certain nonprofit organizations may be exempt from that law.

2.) The reputation of an entire institution is being placed in the hands of callers who could seriously harm the reputation of the organization.

3.) Poor management of call lists can result in annoying calls to current users and multiple calls to the same person.

4.) Telemarketing is much more expensive than it may at first appear, when one considers costs for personnel, training, equipment, service charges, follow-up, and billing.

5.) Initial results of phone calls are never fully accurate as some people won't honor their commitments.

6.) Effective callers, even after careful training, are few and far between.

Telemarketing, like direct mail advertising, has been overused in recent years. Almost anybody with a reasonably permanent address and a phone listing has been inundated by junk mail and an increasing number of junk phone calls. This has decreased the effectiveness of these strategies at best and, at worst, created a backlash against advertisers who use them and has actually resulted in most telephone owners joining the do-not-call list. Frustrated by the frequency of wrong numbers, no answers, and machine answers, it wasn't long before telemarketing experts recruited computer dialing and messaging systems to aid their efforts. Computerized telemarketing enables machines to dial countless phone numbers incessantly until they are either invalidated or connected with a human voice. When contact is achieved, the computer can be programmed to activate a recorded message that ends either by asking the listener to call a certain toll-free number or puts the listener into direct contact with a live telemarketer. This equipment is out of reach for most performing arts companies.

In response to consumer's complaints of excessive telemarketing, the Federal Trade Commission has initiated a system prohibiting telemarketers from calling individuals who have included their names on a national do-not-call list. There are fines associated with calling individuals on the list. Although nonprofit organizations are exempt from the FTC rules, it is good business practice to purchase the do-not-call list and purge those names from telemarketing files. This exercise, alone, may well invalidate the use of telemarketing because of the number of patrons who have joined the do-not-call list. For more information, visit https://telemarketing.donotcall.gov.

Successful telemarketing requires the supervision of a skilled expert. If such an individual is not part of an organization's regular staff, then a consultant should be hired to plan and supervise an in-house telemarketing campaign, or a firm can be hired to handle the whole process, using facilities in-house or conducting the campaign at its own facilities. This last option, of course, means that the organization won't have to set up the special phone lines and caller work stations required for a sizable telemarketing campaign, although it also means forfeiting direct involvement in the sales process.

Summary

Because the consumer gets what he or she pays for, advertising is one of the few parts of the marketing mix that provides some certainty. Press releases may not be run or interviews in the local paper or on the radio or TV can get bumped by an urgent news story, but if a half-page ad is purchased it will appear. Ditto the radio or TV spot. Unfortunately, this comes at significant cost. Given that, the best policy is to research every advertising option thoroughly so that each advertising dollar spent yields the highest possible return.

CHAPTER 17

Facility and
Audience Management

T HE IDEA, THE ARTISTS, THE STAFF, the money, the place, and the materials for a theatrical production are brought together and organized for the benefit
of an audience. If management has been effective, it will appear that the performance has happened of its own accord. The audience will never know that the roof
leaks when it rains, that mechanics are still trying to repair the air conditioning, that the
fire marshal is threatening to halt the performance because of inadequate fireproofing on
the scenery, or that the manager reached into his own pocket when no other funds were
available to buy flowers for the leading lady. The audience arrives, the performance takes
place, and nothing unintended should impede audience appreciation. To insure an ideal
atmosphere for a performance is the obligation of facility and audience management.
This entails two different areas of concern and, often, two different managers: one to
manage the physical plant and one to manage the audience.

Facility Management

Most Broadway and Off-Broadway shows as well as most touring productions are performed in theatres that are owned and managed independently from the production
company. College and civic theatre organizations may also have little if anything to do
with managing the facility in which they perform. On the other hand, most of the professional nonprofit theatre companies as well as stock and dinner theatres do operate their
own facilities. When this is the case, a whole new layer of management must be added to
the business of producing theatre.

In most cases the landlord—whether an individual, a corporation, an institution,
or a municipality—assumes responsibility for such basic facility-related matters as:

    1.)   The building and grounds;

2.) Building infrastructure—plumbing, wiring, heating and cooling, elevators, and telephone lines—but not the cost of operating these services;

3.) Casualty insurance for the building and its equipment;

4.) Liability insurance—the tenant or users normally acquire additional liability as well as other types of insurance;

5.) Maintenance of the building and its infrastructure.

The company or organization that operates the facility—either as tenant or owner
—must assume additional responsibilities such as:

1.) Janitorial services
2.) Building security
3.) Purchase or rental of special equipment
4.) Purchase and inventory control of building supplies
5.) Hiring and supervision of building employees
6.) Creation and updating of operations manuals
7.) Establishment of emergency equipment and procedures
8.) Supervision and control of facility usage
9.) Management and operation of in-house concessions
10.) Contracting and supervision of vendor concessions
11.) Establishing policies on usage
12.) Maintaining up-to-date technical specifications on the stage and equip-
    ment

Facility management may also include the considerable amount of attention that
must be paid when the building as a whole is rented out to civic groups. But even when
this is not the policy, a busy resident company or multipurpose facility, such as a campus
performing arts center, may take careful scheduling to gain maximum use of its available
spaces for rehearsals, performances, and related activities.

Policy and Technical Specifications on the Internet

These days performing arts facilities of all sizes include information regarding their usage
policies and technical specifications on their Internet websites. Many of these documents
are voluminous and cover every contingency possible for the potential user, whether it is
a company renting the facility short term or an artist who has been booked into the facility. Rental rate schedules are usually not included because they change frequently and are
often tailored to particular situations. The Usage Policies and Technical Specifications
Appendices are abbreviated examples of these documents. Complete documents can be
reviewed by checking out various theatre and performing arts center Internet sites. (See
Appendices U and V.)

Setting Policy for Facility Usage

Assuming the theatre organization has full control over its performance facility, it should adopt a set of policies regarding how the facility is to be used and by whom. This will require detailed knowledge of the artistic and economic needs of the organizations, as well as the characteristics and use potential of the facility. The answers to questions such as how much rehearsal time will productions require on the stage itself, how much time will the designers and technicians require on stage, how much time should be allotted to striking each production, or should the theatre be rented for meetings when there is a set on the stage may set time limitations on resident productions. It will also enable the facility manager to establish a calendar that shows when the theatre and its various spaces are free for rental or other purposes.

If renting space to outside groups is the policy, then the question of whether or not there should be any restrictions on this policy should be settled prior to undertaking rent negotiations. For example, what if a religious or political organization wishes to rent the theatre, or a local promoter wants to book in a series of rock concerts? While many theatre companies are sufficiently independent to control policy decisions, those affiliated with a large institution, such as a college or civic theatre, are often pressured to provide space for less desirable attractions. The board of trustees, together with the managing director and artistic director, should establish policies that will determine facility usage so that neither the facility manager—nor another responsible administrator—will have to cope with these decisions on a case by case basis. The more groups or constituents that have access to the facility, the greater the need for prioritized, clear, and equitable policies.

Finally, if outside rentals are permitted, the organization must establish a pricing policy. Different rates might be set for specific spaces within the facility, or different times of the day, or nonprofit vs. for-profit usage, or the specific week or year the space is to be used, or for the services that are to be included, such as box office services or the use of a piano or a PA system. Rental rates may be structured as flat fees, as a percentage of the gross, or according to some formula that has been set. (See also Chapter 9.) Based on the pricing policy, a rental rate sheet should be prepared and used by the rental administrator to quote a standard set of fees to potential renters. (See Appendix U.)

The Facility or Operations Manager

Most facilities that accommodate an active theatre organization require a full-time operations manager, who may be called a facility manager or director. In some cases, specifically for smaller presenting organizations, the job is combined with that of house manager or hall manager. This chapter deals with facility and audience management separately, although these two areas are closely related and are sometimes dealt with as one. An operations manager may also be responsible for the purchase, rental, and upkeep of theatrical production equipment, such as stage lighting systems and power equipment in the scene shop. How the job is defined depends on the resources and needs of the organization and on the skills of the manager.

Building Employees

An operations manager may supervise a sizable staff of building employees. Very often, these are unionized workers and, in the case of college and municipally operated facilities, their collective bargaining agreement may be such that it's nearly impossible to reassign, retrain, or terminate them. This sometimes presents a challenge to management. The different types of building employees might include:

1.) Building engineer
2.) Superintendent
3.) Heating plant engineer
4.) Elevator operator
5.) Cleaner(s) or janitor(s)
6.) Ladies room matron
7.) Porter (front of house doorman)
8.) Groundskeeper
9.) Security guard
10.) Parking attendant
11.) Backstage doorman

At some facilities some of these jobs may be combined. It is always desirable to have at least one staff person who has special knowledge and skills in areas such as plumbing, electricity, and the mechanics of operating large equipment. Without this expertise on site, the organization will have to contract with outside vendors, which can be expensive and involve waiting periods for service that can adversely impact the organization's production and/or performance schedule.

The hall or operations manager of a presenting organization would, in addition to the above employees, also hire and supervise the following:

1.) Technical director
2.) Stage manager
3.) Stage technicians (carpenters, electricians, audio/visual technicians)
4.) Stagehands
5.) Projectionist
6.) Box office treasurers
7.) House manager
8.) Ticket takers
9.) Ushers

The landlord as part of the rental agreement might provide some of these employees.

Operations Manuals

Although discussed in Chapter 3, it bears repeating that there should be an operations manual for each job in the theatre. These are especially useful when there is a high rate of turnover as when workers are hired as needed for each performance, event, or production or even when they are hired on a seasonal basis. It is the responsibility of the facility manager to create these manuals, keep them current, and be certain that they are followed. It is important that manuals include procedures to follow in the event of an emergency.

Technical Information Sheets

Any performance facility that rents space to outside groups or that books in guest attractions must prepare several categories of detailed information that must be kept up to date. Even when compressed into outline form, the technical information for a 1000- to 3000-seat theatre would fill many pages. Rental groups and touring attractions depend on this information when their productions are being designed and organized. The information should include inventories of available production equipment, diagrams that show all the stage dimensions and the house seating plan, and contact information for all principal positions in the organization. (See Appendix V.)

Architectural Blueprints

Among the most valuable resources in facility management are the architectural blueprints or detailed construction documents that were used by the builders of the facility, as well as any plans for subsequent renovations. In addition to the working copies, which should be easily accessible, there should also be copies kept off premises. Together with engineering plans, blueprints can save important time and dollars in the event of a breakdown or emergency.

Security

With increasing concern for security in public places, it is absolutely necessary to pay special attention to security measures and procedures and to seek advice from local authorities and security experts. In some venues it has become common to inspect customers' parcels, purses, and backpacks. The public has come to understand this, even if not actually expecting it. If the audience's bags are to be inspected, they should be gone through by a person who knows what he or she is actually looking for and what to do if banned items are found. The search should be conducted with seriousness and politeness. An off-duty police officer is well suited for this task.

Security needs differ at facilities and vary from a good set of lock and keys to an around-the-clock team of security guards and electronic surveillance. Security is aimed at protecting people and property against assault, robbery, and vandalism. The extent to which security precautions are taken will depend on the location of the facility, the nature of the attraction, and various special circumstances. Good facility management requires periodic studies of building security and the immediate correction of any potential problems. A security consultant can recommend effective solutions to certain problems, although a theatre may also call upon local law enforcement officials for free advice.

Basic types of security methods include:

Protection provided by law enforcement agencies; for example, the local police may be hired as escorts during transportation of large amounts of cash or state police may investigate bomb threats;

Protection provided by private security companies to conduct a security study or provide licensed security guards;

Permanent security equipment such as locks, burglar alarm systems, metal detectors, and exterior lighting;

Precautionary security measures, such as having performers check all their valuables with the stage manager for safe storage during performances, having all visitors sign in and out of the building with a doorman during certain periods of the day, and making employee access to rest rooms possible only with a key during nonperformance hours.

Any combination of these methods is usually put into effect. Some should be installed or established on a permanent basis while others will be necessary only under special circumstances. Extra security will be required, for example, if a hugely popular crowd-drawing performer is playing at the facility; if a head of state, a major government official, or a famous celebrity is going to be in the audience; or if the material being performed will be likely to attract protesters.

Management must foresee the need for special security and then take the necessary measures to avoid problems. This may entail working with the police, the FBI, the Secret Service, or leaders of organizations that are expected to demonstrate or seek to interfere with the performance or people attending the attraction.

Rental to Outside Groups

Fees earned from renting the facility or any space within it to outside groups can provide important sources of income. But these rentals also provide management responsibilities. One of the greatest challenges is to minimize the friction between the resident theatre group or resident constituents and the rental policy itself. It must be understood that most theatre artists passionately want to have a rehearsal/performance space that belongs exclusively to them. Anything less will be regarded as a compromise or seen as inequitable. Establishing a rental policy that the primary users will find equitable and give them a sense of ownership in the facility is imperative to the harmonious use of the facility.

Insurance is another important consideration for relevant rental groups. A theatre organization's or building owner's insurance policy does not automatically extend to groups that may use the same facility. Additional coverage must be arranged either by the resident or the rental group, which is discussed in greater detail in the section on Insurance.

Before actually renting a facility, the organization should design a standard rental agreement or contract that can be applied in all cases. This may require the assistance of an attorney and, preferably, input from each department head in the organization. It would be wise for an organization to study similar agreements that have been used by similar operations. Many of these are found on individual theatre or performing arts centers' websites. Even then, amendments will doubtless have to be added over time. (See Appendix W.)

Insurance for the Theatre and the Performing Arts

The significant cost of insurance typically puts it in the hands of a managing director or business administrator. Sometimes a committee made up of the board of trustees or directors takes on the responsibility. Because the cost of insurance has become a major item in many operating budgets, it is extremely important to seek the very best professional advice.

An insurance policy, like any contract, is only valid in the areas it defines and qualifies. The special jargon used in policies may be difficult for the layman to understand and may even be subject to wide-ranging legal interpretation. The word *occurrence*, for instance, provides much broader coverage than the word *accident*. While most insurance regulations, including those that govern workers' compensation, are a matter of state law, there are only minor differences in the regulations from one state to another.

Very often, the producing company does not own the theatre building in which it performs. In such cases the landlord certainly carries an insurance program to cover the building. This should provide at least eighty percent of the full replacement value—after taking depreciation into account—in the event of destruction. If coverage is written for only one-half of the replacement value, when it should have been written for eighty percent, then a partial settlement would be paid in the same proportion. For example, if a building that should have been insured in the amount of $800,000 was actually insured for only $400,000, and it sustains fire damage that would cost $150,000 to restore, the underwriter would pay only $75,000.

The landlord's insurance includes public liability coverage. The typical license agreement between the landlord and the producing company, however, indemnifies and defends the landlord against any claims arising out of the company's use of the building, including actions brought by company employees. This exposure, which is the landlord's, is covered in the *contractual* liability section of the production company's standard Commercial General Liability policy. It is contractual because it relates to the rental contract. The reason for the stipulation in the license agreement is that although employees cannot sue their employers in case of an injury—because of Workman's Compensation laws—they can sue the landlord: hence, the landlord's requirement for protection against those likely claims.

General liability insurance rates for theatre buildings are based on admissions to the theatre building. The insurance premium—cost—is based on *estimated* admissions and then the premium is adjusted up or down at the end of the year based on an audit at that time. Liability insurance rates for a theatre *company* that does not own the building in which it operates are based on the company's total payroll, estimated when coverage begins, and adjusted at the end of the year after an audit.

Insurance brokers usually earn their income from a five-to-fifteen percent commission paid by the underwriters with whom they place policies. Writing insurance for an incorporated organization that owns its own facility or is operating under a long-term lease is comparatively simple, because this is a more standard way of conducting a business. Further, the company will have an easier time of it because by owning or controlling its own facility, its *only* exposure is to the public—injured employees cannot sue their employers because of Workers Compensation laws, as mentioned above.

Selecting a Broker

It is important to be represented by the right broker. According to Robert A. Boyar, the now-retired unofficial dean of theatrical insurance, the three most important qualities to look for in a broker are integrity, competence, and experience. Competence, derived from experience, enables the broker to gain a thorough knowledge of his or her client's business and ensures that the coverage will be properly tailored to meet the exposure. Specialty insurance, such as that needed by any of the performing arts, is likely to have its interests best served by a broker with adequate experience in that specialty, gained through serving many clients in the field. Such a broker could be called a "quasi" risk manager because performing arts organizations rarely are large enough to require a risk manager from their executive structure.

Several brokers may be asked to bid for a client's business. This often entails a few long telephone conversations during which the broker attempts to identify the risks to the organization, the amount of coverage it should assume, and the amount the client is willing to pay. After a broker is selected, there is often an on-site inspection of the place of business. Then the broker works to place the policy with an underwriter, who in turn may conduct another on-site inspection. As a result of this process, the client may be asked to make certain improvements or changes in the way business is conducted. Once the policy is in effect, the brokerage firm will administer claims. So it pays to be able to work with a broker who is experienced with the class of insurance in question. (See Appendix X for a list of standard types of insurance related to the performing arts.)

For many types of insurance, the question of deductibility will arise. For example, should fire insurance cover damage after the first $500 or $1,000, or some other figure?

Should business interruption or nonappearance of the star exclude the first one or two performances lost, and how many lost performances should be covered? The answers arrived at between the producer and the broker obviously influence the premium size. It is always tempting to gamble against adversity and take out less than optimum coverage. But when something goes very wrong, it can be very reassuring and comforting to know that the organization will be covered in full.

In the event of an accident or incident, it is best to gather all of the relevant information in a timely manner. The theatre manager or security staff should complete an incident report. (See Appendix Y for a sample.)

Audience Management

The House Manager/Theatre Manager

To the audience, the house manager or theatre manager and the front-of-house staff are the most important staff members at the time of a performance. They are the front line and image of the theatre operation to the public. They are there to help and make the people who have purchased tickets comfortable. The success of an evening out and the pleasure received from attending the theatre is partially dependent on the experience the patron has in relating to the ticket taker, the usher, the concessionaire, using the public areas and facilities, and the handling of his or her special needs.

On Broadway and at commercial theatres on the road the house manager, as the term implies, works for the house, which is to say for the landlord. The house manager is the landlord's on-site representative responsible for supervising all the other front-of-house employees who are also contracted by the landlord: treasurers, ticket takers, directors, ushers, concessionaires, doormen, and maintenance personnel.

The majority of professional theatres in America, however, do not fall under ATPAM jurisdiction. For this reason, the duties of a house manager vary considerably from theatre to theatre. In most nonprofit theatres and performing arts centers, the verification of the box office statement (see Chapter 12) usually falls to the executive director/manager or business manager. Also, in college theatres and very small houses the house manager may work a short period of time before a performance and during the performance and only supervises the ushers and deals with any special circumstances that may affect the audience. In community, stock, dinner, and small professional theatres the house manager might have other responsibilities—perhaps in the press office or the box office. And, as mentioned earlier, the house manager may also be responsible for facility management. Some theatres have "performance managers," or people who work only during performances to deal with the audience and safety issues. When possible, the ideal person to hire for such a position is an off-duty local firefighter. Firefighters are accustomed to dealing with emergencies and therefore are good people to have around. Also, hiring a firefighter makes for good relations with the local fire department.

The basic duties usually assigned to the house manager in most operations include:

1.) Supervision of the front-of-house personnel:
    a.) Assistant house manager
    b.) Ticket takers
    c.) Ushers
    d.) Elevator operators
    e.) Rest room matron
    f.) Checkroom/concession attendants
    g.) Security guards
    h.) Doorman
    i.) Parking attendants

2.) Verification of the hours worked by the employees listed above;

3.) Arranging for a house physician to be on call;

4.) Coordination of ticket-taking with the box office and ticket-taking systems and needs;

5.) Supervision of the sanitary conditions and cleanliness of audience areas;

6.) Maintenance of safety and fire laws in the audience areas and the general enforcement of house rules;

7.) Supervising special customer services—water fountains, rest rooms, concessions, pay phones, etc.;

8.) Coordination of curtain times and audience bell warnings with the stage manager;

9.) Handling special customer problems regarding seating, disruptions, and emergencies;

10.) Checking all audience areas before they are open to the audience and after each performance.

Before each performance, the house manager should check all the public areas of the building as if with the eyes of a customer seeing the areas for the first time. Is the lobby floor clean? Is the furniture dusted and polished? Are curtains, seat covers, and draperies neatly arranged? What is the auditorium temperature? Are all the light bulbs working? Are there any accident traps, such as loose carpeting, unlighted steps, insecure railings, or sharp edges on seats? Theatres tend to use soft interior lighting so a house manager should make these daily inspections with a critical eye, looking for lapses in cleaning and repair. Older theatres, especially, require scrupulous cleaning if they are to look fresh and neat. And a theatre must be ventilated frequently with fresh air to avoid building up a musky, unpleasant odor—particularly between matinee and evening performances, after long rehearsal periods, and when the theatre may have been dark.

Qualifications for the administrative personnel in theatre have been discussed in Chapter 3, and the behavior of staff members who deal with the public has been described as a critical marketing tool. But the importance of how the theatre staff greets the public cannot be overemphasized. Almost as soon as a patron walks into a theatre, that person can sense the kind of operation it is. Staff members, from doormen to managers, from ushers to performers, immediately convey an attitude. The type of attitude invariably emanates down from the top manager, if not from the producer or board of trustees. It might be an attitude of confidence, arrogance, vitality, informality, confusion, carelessness, pride, professionalism, amateurism, or any combination of these and others. And this attitude begins to condition the theatregoer's reaction to a performance even before the curtain goes up. The attitude of the staff is reflected in both dress and behavior. Uniforms for ushers, ticket takers, and others are becoming a thing of the past, at least for small operations; however, in large auditoriums, uniforms are helpful to identify house employees. When uniforms are not used, some identifying garment should be worn—a vest, jacket, apron, or sash. Standards of attire may be changed from production to production in order to reflect differences between them and help prepare the audiences for what they are about to see. Generally, however, it is sufficient if front-of-house employees are courteous, efficient, and appropriately attired. But this requires close supervision by the house manager.

The Rules of the House

Virtually every theatre should establish and uphold a series of house rules; these should be printed in the front of each playbill, and the rules that are especially difficult to enforce should be further emphasized with printed signs in appropriate places. Some rules, such as those regarding smoking, reflect municipal and state laws. Others, such as those prohibiting the taking of photographs or the making of tape recordings during performances, relate to federal laws governing copyright protection and piracy. And others, such as the delayed seating of latecomers, merely reflect the policy of the individual theatre or production.

The most common matters around which house rules might be formulated are:

1.) Smoking, eating, and drinking
2.) Cell phones/cameras/electronic devices
3.) Tape recorders/recording devices of any kind
4.) Late seating policy
5.) Ticket refund and exchange policy

6.) Standing room (only when every seat is sold)
7.) Wheelchair accommodation
8.) Lost and found articles
9.) Emergency procedures
10.) Audience services (checkrooms, phones, drinking fountains, and rest rooms)
11.) Infants/children

An important duty of the house manager is the training of the ticket taker and usher corps. Instructions on the proper way to seat a customer; information on the show or attraction; instructions on handling difficult patrons; instruction on special needs, such as the various handicapped provisions required; and instruction on the handling of emergencies are all important elements with which each member of the team must be an expert. The decorum of the corps in everything from dress to attitude is also important to the overall image of the organization and the experience of the patron.

Seating the Audience

The larger the audience, the more supervision is required to control the flow of human traffic. But even with an audience of only fifty to one hundred people, the audience needs guidance in getting from the street, through the lobbies, and into the correct theatre seats. Everything possible should be done to insure that public transportation and automobile parking systems are adequate to handle the entire audience in the hour or half-hour before each performance. Are there comfortable places where early customers can wait? What is the policy regarding latecomers, and have ticket buyers been forewarned about it? When should the lobbies be opened? When should the auditorium be opened? When should the curtain go up? Questions like these should be settled well in advance. Knowing that a sizable number of theatregoers will arrive late, some theatres begin performances five minutes after the advertised curtain time. Other theatres make a point of taking the curtain up on time, exactly as advertised. Lengthy curtain delays, of course, have a negative impact on audience psychology. If there is an unavoidable, lengthy delay in raising the curtain, it is wise to make an announcement to the audience.

Along with the attitude of front-of-house staff, theatre lobby activities and concessions help determine audience reaction both to the theatre and to the performance. The types of concessions on hand and how they are managed can enhance or dampen the experience of theatregoing. Lobby ambiance, lighting, and decor are also important. Certain productions may require the usher staff to wear costumes or clothing items specific to the show so as to get the audience into the right frame of mind.

The architecture of a theatre will dictate how many ticket takers, directors, and ushers will be necessary to seat an audience quickly and efficiently. The physical point at which a customer must make a decision about how next to proceed is exactly the point where an usher or director should be stationed. Customers should never have to guess whether to go upstairs or down, right or left, whether they should proceed or wait for an usher. Most of all, when reserved seating is used, theatregoers should never be left alone to find their own seats. Too many will occupy wrong seats and create problems when people with the tickets for those seats arrive. There is a quirk of human nature that compels people to hold their ground once they have established it as their own. Call it "squatter's rights" or "territorial imperative," theatregoers are loathe to move once settled in a theatre seat. And, it seems, those most loathe to move are those who are asked to do so after the curtain has gone up. It is far easier to seat people correctly in the first place.

Most theatres seat latecomers at an appropriate interval in the performance. Some productions begin with particularly quiet or sensitive moments, which would prohibit people from being seated then. Theatres with continental seating, where each row may contain as many as sixty or seventy seats without aisle separations, almost automatically prohibit seating of latecomers except during scene breaks or other appropriate moments. When it is the policy not to accommodate latecomers, this policy should be stated on a lobby sign, on the printed ticket, and, wherever possible, in advertising.

There should be some system for warning the audience that the performance is about to begin or resume. The simplest way to do this is to flash the lobby lights on and off. An alternative is to install an electrically operated gong or bell that can be controlled by the house manager and heard in all audience areas of the theatre, including rest rooms, lounges, and sidewalk. And there should be a house phone or cordless system that enables the house manager to speak with the stage manager at all times. This will prevent the house manager from seating the audience too early if there are delays backstage and, similarly, prevent the stage manager from calling "places" if there is a delay in seating the house. And under no circumstances should the curtain rise until the house manager instructs the stage manager to proceed.

The length of any intermission will vary according to:

1.) How many intermissions are scheduled—usually the more that are scheduled, the shorter they should be; the first intermission should be the longest;

2.) The length of performance time before the intermission—the longer the act, the longer the intermission;

3.) The size of the audience—the smaller the audience, the shorter the intermission;

4.) The availability of concessions and rest room facilities—not until after concessions have served all customers and after rest room facilities have emptied should the performance resume;

5.) Extenuating circumstances—more intermission time may be required for complicated scenic or costume changes; intermissions may be shortened or eliminated at certain performances to avoid paying union overtime rates, or to allow sufficient time between two closely scheduled performances to meet union requirements.

When a playgoer moves from the lobby into the house, the first person encountered should be the ticket taker. To insure that torn ticket stubs will be obtained from all customers, the first entrance into the house should be no larger than the width of two standard doors. The ticket taker should greet each customer and instruct each where to proceed next, as in "inside to your right," "straight ahead, second aisle" or "up the stairs to your left."

Directors should be stationed at each stairway, aisle, or turn to examine ticket stubs and instruct the customers where to go next. It is usually more efficient if patrons wait at the top of aisles for ushers to seat them, and large theatres may station ushers at two or three points farther down an aisle. All ushers should keep an eye out for customers who are trying to seat themselves without assistance. One good way to prevent this is to make playbills available only from the ushers. If customers can pick them up behind the last row of seats, they will be more tempted to seat themselves. The house staff should also enforce house rules by being on the lookout for people walking into the theatre with a camera, a drink, a Chihuahua, or whatever. In European theatres it is sometimes the custom to reward ushers and box office treasurers with gratuities. When this occurs in American theatres, the employee should be allowed to keep the gratuity.

Before each performance, the ushering staff should be given individual intermission assignments for opening and closing doors, for turning on and off manually operated house lights, and for other such chores. Similarly, the house staff must be thoroughly familiar with procedures to follow in case of an emergency or unusual occurrence. And it is wise to caution the entire front and backstage staff about deportment during performance hours, emphasizing the following rules:

1.) Never run or shout in audience areas because this can cause panic, especially in the event of a real emergency.

2.) Never use the auditorium to gain access to or exit from the backstage area.

3.) Performers and backstage personnel should always use the stage door, never lobby or house entrances.

4.) Backstage employees should always report the presence of strangers or unauthorized visitors.

The best management is usually the least conspicuous management. Theatregoers like to be serviced efficiently but unobtrusively. The front-of-house staff can be friendly without being solicitous. They are like the hosts at a good dinner parry. The house manager must keep things going, keep people moving, cover for any mistakes or deficiencies, try to make each guest feel like the most honored guest, and help each one to go away with the belief that the evening has been a success. This takes sobriety, diplomacy, organization, and an awareness of others.

Special Audience Conditions

Special problems can arise during public performances—a latecomer argues with the head usher, someone in the fifth row center becomes ill, the air-conditioning system develops a problem, and someone in the balcony begins using a flash camera. These and countless other occurrences are common, and someone with authority on the theatre staff must be present to handle them immediately.

In Case of Fire

Perhaps the most serious and potentially dangerous threat to an audience is fire. History has recorded a long series of theatre fires that have killed thousands of people and have made the public rightfully aware of danger whenever smoke invades a public gathering place. Following the Brooklyn Theatre fire in 1896, which killed over three hundred people, the actor-manager Steele MacKaye and other innovators developed methods for fireproofing stage scenery and invented folding safety seats for the audience. Modem technology, of course, has vastly improved upon materials, devices, and structures to further reduce the threat of fire in public buildings. But the threat has yet to be eliminated, and countless plays continue to be produced in antiquated or wooden buildings that are hardly less susceptible to fire than those in use a hundred years ago. Even the truly fireproof theatre is not immune from the disaster and loss of life that can result from mass panic; for good reason, it is illegal to shout "Fire!" in a public place unless there actually is a fire. All it takes is a smoldering cigarette or electrical wire to cause hysteria and disaster.

Insurance companies and building inspectors are extremely strict about enforcing public safety laws and regulations, but complete enforcement depends upon the theatre management itself. When a producing organization enjoys a sell-out, for instance, it can be unbearably tempting to place extra chairs in the aisles, to exceed the legal limit of standees and allow people to sit on aisle steps. When stage properties or scenery is added at the last minute, it is easy to overlook fireproofing measures. When stage directions call for a completely dark theatre in order to create or enhance some special effect, there is a temptation to cover or extinguish the aisle and exit lights. In the nation's busiest theatre capitals, a fire inspector virtually sits on the scene designer's shoulder, but this is not usually the case elsewhere. Just as the theatre manager holds the customer's advance sale ticket money in trust, so the theatre manager holds the audience's safety in trust.

While no one likes to anticipate a theatre fire, it would be foolhardy for management not to formulate procedures for the staff to follow in the event of fire or some similar threat to the audience. Fire rules should be posted on the callboard backstage and should be distributed to all personnel. At some time before the first performance, the stage manager should assemble the cast and production crew to review emergency regulations, and the house manager should review emergency procedures with the house staff before *every* performance. Ushers should be stationed at key points throughout the house so that exit doors can be opened quickly during a performance if necessary. Importantly, the stage manager and the house manager should be the only people authorized to institute emergency measures during performance hours and they must communicate any such intentions with each other. Obviously, very cool heads are required. It is a good idea to have a preagreed meeting place for all personnel, front-of-house and backstage, away from the theatre, if the building must be evacuated. When does a threat become a true emergency? What should be done to protect the public, when should it be done, and how should it be done? It is better to discuss and plan for these situations before they happen.It is not unusual in theatre for some harmless occurrence to appear like an impending disaster. For example, a broken fan belt in a heating or air-conditioning system may suddenly flood the air with smoke-like fumes. If cigarette receptacles are not cleaned out constantly, they will begin smoldering. The almost-universal advent of the "smoke-free environment" has removed cigarette smoke from the interior of most public places. The ban has improved interior air quality as well as preventing fires from discarded cigarettes.

When an audience *perceives* a threat to its safety, however innocent the cause may be, its fears should be allayed at once. The quickest and most direct way of doing this is for the stage manager to make an announcement from the stage or over the public address system. This should be done in a calm, reassuring voice, and the message should minimize the danger: "Ladies and gentlemen, it seems the fan belt that operates our stage turntable has developed difficulty and is creating the odor you smell. But we'll endeavor to go on with the performance while our engineers repair it, if you'll just bear with us." If such announcements can be delayed until an intermission or scene break, this is better. The house manager is in the best position to judge the audience mood and determine whether or not such an interruption is desirable, so the stage manager should never take such action alone.

When the emergency is a real one and it is advisable to get the audience out of the theatre quickly, it is even more important to follow a cool and relaxed procedure. If the performers can be alerted to the situation, they will be able to bring the performance to a normal-appearing halt, and the curtain can be brought down as if it were a scheduled intermission or scene break. The house lights should come up at once, and the house manager and staff should immediately open all exit doors. Many people will leave automatically and others can be coaxed out in quick fashion by ushers telling them, "Please clear the auditorium for this intermission—please clear the theatre."

Often a performer is more reassuring than a staff member when it comes to announcing difficulties or emergencies, especially if speaking from the front of the auditorium itself and not from the stage or in front of the stage curtain. It is difficult to say why this is true, but perhaps a complete break from character and the surprise of seeing a performer in the house somehow creates a sense of security among audience members. In any case, it is the exact antithesis of someone running onto the stage during a performance and shouting "Fire!" There is no emergency that requires that kind of announcement, but a well-prepared staff is the only assurance against such an insane act.

Power Failure

A power failure that plunges a crowded theatre into sudden darkness is a major threat to public safety. New theatre complexes usually have emergency generator equipment capable of supplying the whole electric system if public utilities fail, and all theatres are required by law to install and maintain emergency lighting devices in the public areas of the building. These may be simple, battery-operated spotlights, or they may be connected to an emergency generator. In either case, they must be rigged to become operative immediately, if normal electric power fails. The presence of emergency lighting precludes the possibility of an audience suddenly being thrown into total darkness. Often, a power failure is of short duration, so a pause or intermission should be allowed to continue for twenty or thirty minutes before any decision is made about sending the audience home. When this happens, the audience should first be instructed to retain their ticket stubs for a refund or exchange.

National Emergency

It is much easier for management to react to a national—or local—emergency when it occurs before a performance begins rather than during one. Whether or not to cancel subsequent performances can be deliberated carefully, and the appropriate people can be consulted. But what if the emergency occurs during the first act of a performance and the audience will be certain to learn about it during intermission? In this case, management has a responsibility to uphold public trust and announce the situation at the conclusion of the act. In the event of a presidential assassination or some other equally momentous occurrence, the house and stage managers must agree on whether or not to continue with the second or third act. Generally, the inclination would be to continue the presentation. However, the audience should be offered the option of going home and returning to see the full production at a later date. The audience should be advised to retain their ticket stubs for refunds or exchanges. Management should also remember that the performers are as likely to be affected by shocking news as the audience, so their reactions must also he taken into account. Traditionally, most theatres remain closed on days designated for national mourning.

Illness of a Performer

The reason for employing understudies is to prevent performance cancellations when performers are taken ill, either before or during a performance. Whenever a performer is replaced, however, an announcement to that effect should he made from the stage. Theatrical tradition dictates that the illness or even the death of a performer shall not, unless absolutely necessary, cause the cancellation of a performance.

A common precaution in regard to the illness of a performer or audience member is to retain a house physician who can be reached quickly. However, it is often quicker and more efficient to rely on the emergency medical units through which paramedics and ambulances may be summoned at any hour.

First aid equipment should be placed both backstage and in some front-of-house location where it is easily accessible. There should be an emergency cot backstage and a cot or couch in the public lounge area. Also, it is wise for the theatre to invest in a stretcher and a wheelchair. Although the Good Samaritan law protects laypeople against prosecution for medical malpractice, only a minimum amount of first aid should be applied until professional help arrives, and a seriously ill or injured person should never be moved more than is absolutely necessary.

Illness of an Audience Member

If debilitating illness of performers is rare, illness of audience members is relatively common. Heart attacks, epileptic seizures, drug reactions, and upset stomachs are phenomena known to seasoned house managers. When someone becomes so ill during a performance that he or she must be removed from the theatre, this should be done as quickly and unobtrusively as possible. If no wheelchair is available, several staff members should, if possible, position the victim in a simple, armless chair for conveyance up the aisle and to the lobby until medical help arrives. There is often a doctor or nurse at a performance and help may be readily at hand.

When anyone on the theatre premises is involved in an accident, however minor, that person should complete an incident report (see Appendix Y). It is always wise to require an accident victim of any kind to receive immediate medical attention so that the nature of the injury can be legally established at a later time, in the event of a lawsuit or insurance claim.

Contacting Members of the Audience

If it is necessary for management to locate a member of the audience during a performance, some methods for doing this are better than others. When an audience member is tapped on the shoulder by an usher and told there is a phone call in the front office, the customer will probably think the worst: the house is on fire, something has happened to the children, someone has had an accident. On the other hand, if the playgoer is asked to speak to the manager in the lobby, it is not especially threatening. The point is to get the customer out of the audience before anything is said about a telephone call or before relaying any messages or information.

The biggest problem related to phone calls for audience members is usually that of trying to determine how important the matter is. Frequently, there are phone calls from children or baby-sitters who are merely frightened about something or can't find something. If the caller is reporting a serious accident, management must try to determine if the playgoer's *immediate* knowledge of it is necessary. Chances are there is nothing the patron can do about it anyway. Deciding whether or not to get somebody during a performance is a matter of weighing an individual's welfare against the welfare of the entire audience. Very few emergencies are great enough to notify an audience member before the next intermission, at which time ushers may be stationed at each exit to page the individual concerned. During a performance or, preferably, before the curtain rises, ushers may also be instructed to page a person orally but quietly as they walk slowly down the aisles. Before this is done, of course, the box office should be checked to see if there is a record of the person's name and seat location.

Now that cell phones and pagers have become body parts, special announcements are usually required to ask people to disengage them during the performance. Often, the cell phone or pager will be left with the house management staff when the owner of the device is expecting an emergency call. While more work for the house staff, this is better than having the phone ring or vibrate and get answered within the audience chamber.

Drunks, Disturbed People, and Demonstrators

As often as not, rowdiness stems from alcohol or drug abuse and such abusers can be exceedingly difficult to handle. Attempts to reason with such people often increase their antagonistic behavior. And their companions are often not helpful in calming them or removing them from the theatre. An usher might try informing the disruptive person that someone is waiting to see him or her at the back of the theatre. Whatever tactic is used, the situation should be approached with caution, since violent and injurious behavior is a real possibility.

More serious than drunks is a planned or organized disruption of a performance. Foreign artists and touring companies have frequently been the target of protesters who seek publicity by staging demonstrations during performances. Many is the time that audiences have been denied the privilege of enjoying visiting artists because performances are interrupted by hecklers and protesters. Leaflets are thrown from balconies, demonstrators line up to chant slogans from the stage, and even bomb threats are made to terrorize audiences and intimidate managements. When disruptions such as these can be anticipated, it is the obligation of management to arrange for special security guards and police protection. In some cases the State Department has ordered federal agents to accompany and protect foreign artists and, if management expects serious trouble, it should request the best and fullest protection available. No member of a theatre staff is trained to handle organized protesters and none should be asked or allowed to attempt this. As soon as a demonstration of any serious intensity begins, the performance should be stopped and the police called in. An intermission should then take place, followed by an announcement that everything is under control. Then sufficient time has to be allowed for the audience and performers to regain their composure. As with drunks, demonstrators are also incapable of listening to reason. Once such people begin a disturbance, the best and possibly the only course is to get them out of the theatre as quickly as possible. The action taken should be swift and decisive, and absolutely no time should be wasted on trying to placate or calm the disrupter.

When There's No House to Manage

For the most part this chapter concerns itself with house management of traditional indoor theatres. But what about street theatre or those performances that are given in parks or other open spaces? Is a house manager required under these circumstances? The answer is yes, except for instances where the audience is a mere handful of by-standers.

Playgoers watching a street theatre production need guidance about where to stand or sit, and the performers may, at times, need protection from overly enthusiastic or rowdy onlookers. If there are no assigned tickets or seating places, the "house manager" must unobtrusively coax people into the desired positions, telling them that they should sit down so people behind them can see, and so forth. If donations or a collection of money is made, this must be supervised. The outdoor audience manager may have to help assemble an audience in the first place, as when a street theatre troupe arrives at its chosen performance site with little if any advance publicity. In such cases a small group of people might be gathered in front of the playing area to act as decoys for attracting other people. Police officers who come along may need proof that the troupe has received official permission to perform, and other matters will require attention during the performance. Play festivals that are presented in large city parks and recreation areas are more formally organized and may involve near-traditional seating arrangements. But whatever the situation, some type of audience management will be necessary.

Summary

Good facility management results in a good laboratory where theatre artists can work and where audiences can appreciate the results of this work. Good audience management requires an audience engineer who can direct both the components of the facility and crowd psychology in order to enhance the experience. All the ingredients required for theatrical production are easier to obtain than desired audience response. Indeed, a production may run for many performances without once achieving the response hoped for by its director and performers. Or this response may happen only once in every ten or twenty performances. Why? There is no simple answer, although theatre people will never tire of inventing them. It is even more difficult to explain the magic and exhilaration of total audience-performer collaboration when it does happen. All we know is that it happens—once in a while. And if we have shared this uniquely satisfying human experience just once, then we are inspired to seek it out again and again—as a performer, a producer, a manager, a volunteer, or a spectator.

Epilogue

It seems ironically fitting that I end this book talking about legitimate theatre. The word theatre still embraces all the performing arts, this many hundreds of pages later. But as I was working on this book, I began wondering when and how did legitimate theatre come into our vocabulary. And if there's legitimate theatre, there must be illegitimate theatre. And what might that be?

The Oxford Companion to the Theatre came to the rescue. The term Legitimate Theatre arose in the 18th century during the struggle of the Patent Theatres (Covent Garden and Drury Lane) against the upstart and illegitimate playhouses that were springing up all over London. "It covered in general those five-act plays (including Shakespeare's) wich (sic) depended entirely on acting, with little or no singing, dancing, and spectacle. In the 19th century the term was widely used by actors of the old school as a defence against the encroachment of farce, musical comedy, and revue."

These days, we use the term Legitimate Theatre, or Legit, to distinguish live theatre from movies or television. And, by the way, there is no illegitimate theatre.

New York City
June 5, 2006

Appendix

Appendix A

SUGGESTED SYLLABUS for an UNDERGRADUATE COURSE
IN THEATRE MANAGEMENT

Aims of the Course

This course is designed to provide an introduction to the economic and managerial aspects of American theatre. It is assumed that the student has fulfilled the prerequisites in theatre history and production but is comparatively untutored in economics and business administration. The course aims to relate principles of business management to the theatre, to evaluate theatre management to date, and to suggest new directions for the future. Emphasis will be placed on the practical and contemporary aspects of the field.

Required Reading

Conte, David M., and Stephen Langley. *Theatre Management: Producing and Managing the Performing Arts.* Hollywood: Quite Specific Media Group, Ltd. (EntertainmentPro), 2006.

Langley, Stephen, and James Abruzzo. *Jobs in Arts & Media Management.* American Council for the Arts, New York, 1990

Theatre Profiles. (Current edition.) Theatre Communications Group, New York.

Units of Study

(Each unit, except the first, will comprise approximately three hours of classroom lecture and discussion.)
1.) Introduction to the course: aims, definitions, scope
2.) Capsule history of theatrical producing and management in America
3.) Organization and structure: the commercial theatre
4.) Organization and structure: the nonprofit theatre
5.) Setting goals, long-range planning, board development, leadership
6.) Legal issues: organizations, contracts, copyright, subsidiary rights
7.) The theatre facility
8.) Performance management
9.) Planning a season and organizing production requirements
10.) Staffing, casting, and personnel management

11.) Financing, budgeting, cost-controls, ticket pricing, and ticketing and box office operation

12.) Fundraising and sources of unearned income

13.) Marketing, audience development, and sources of earned income

14.) Audience and company management

15.) Classroom presentation of student term projects

Written Assignments

Each student will create a hypothetical theatre company and propose a "dream season" of productions. These must be planned for an actual, existing theatre space or organization, such as the campus theatre or a nearby LORT theatre. Each assignment is due the week after the class discussion to which it relates. All assignments will be reworked according to the instructor's comments and then reassembled in a single packet for final submission on the last day of class.

During the previous week, each student will have made a ten-minute oral presentation to the class describing his or her project. The packet should include the following:

1.) A one-paragraph mission statement, plus three-to-five goals or objectives for the project or company

2.) A list of the first season's productions, including casting and direction and design team; a description of the theatre facility to be used, including a ground plan showing the stage and audience areas

3.) A line chart that shows all full-time staff positions (artistic, administrative, technical) for the company and their relationship to one another; also a list of all job titles within each of the three areas showing weekly salaries and number of employment weeks for each

4.) A production budget for each show planned (including rehearsal costs, scenery, costumes, lighting, props, etc.)

5.) A complete marketing plan with a schedule of all activities planned, including sample logos, brochures, ads, press releases, etc.

6.) A preopening budget (excluding production costs) and an ongoing weekly operating budget (again excluding production costs). These should be put together with staff costs and production budgets with subtotals shown on a summary sheet. Finally, grand totals of all costs, together with seasonal ticket income at both 100% and 60% of capacity. The differential should be shown.

Appendix B

SUGGESTED CORE OF COURSES FOR A MASTER'S DEGREE
PROGRAM IN PERFORMING ARTS MANAGEMENT

First Semester

Principles of Performing Arts Management
An introduction to organizational, fiscal, legal, marketing, funding, and artistic policy-making principles and techniques involved in managing the performing arts.

Technology Applications in the Performing Arts
Current use and potential applications of technology and the Internet in relation to administration, stage production, music, choreography, and the development of the artistic product.

Organization Behavior
History of management thought: individual needs, values, motivation, career development, small groups, formal organization, and management processes.

Background Elective I
An advisor-approved course dealing with a particular period, movement, artist, genre, or philosophy in the performing arts.

Performing Arts Research and Bibliography
Introduction to research, including the Internet, campus library, and other local resources and collections; exercises in writing styles and formats for letters, proposals, reports, articles, news releases, and formal papers.

Performing Arts Management Internship I
A twenty-hour-per-week, semester-long internship under academic guidance, with professional supervision.

Second Semester

The Performing Arts and the Law
Studies in legal problems and procedures related to the performing arts: profit and not-for-profit corporations; partnerships; contracts; agreements; copyright law.

Business Management of the Performing Arts
Accounting programs and packages, bookkeeping, payroll, budgeting, and cost-control procedures for performing arts ventures, companies, and institutions.

Marketing the Performing Arts
Marketing theories and strategies in relation to audience development: advertising techniques, publicity, promotion, and press relations.

Background Elective II
An advisor-approved course dealing with a particular period, movement, artist, genre, or philosophy in the performing arts.

Performing Arts Management Internship II
A twenty-hour-per-week, semester-long internship under academic guidance, with professional supervision.

Third Semester

Labor and Employee Relations in the Performing Arts
A study of labor unions related to the performzing arts: the collective bargaining process; contract negotiations; labor law; federal, state, and local regulations; personnel policies; and legal issues.

Fundraising Techniques for the Performing Arts
Study of the philosophy and methodology of raising contributed income for non-profit professional performing arts companies and institutions: government, corporate, and individual sources; grants research, writing, and administration.

Managerial Economics and the Performing Arts
Examination of decision-making and market equilibrium in performing arts production, based on familiar economic concepts and models. Creation of production and operating budgets in relation to current costs and revenues in the performing arts industry.

Personnel and Company Management for the Performing Arts
A study of the psychological dynamics of group behavior and personnel interaction; uses of meetings and group discussions, management intervention, incentive systems; special problems related to personnel on tour; the challenge of managing the artistic temperament.

Performing Arts Management Internship III
A twenty-hour-per-week, semester-long internship under academic guidance, with professional supervision.

Fourth Semester

Artistic/Managerial Decision-Making in the Performing Arts
The dynamics of planning, organizing, and realizing performing arts projects, ventures, companies and institutions with special attention to the interrelationships between artists, managers, and trustees in the collaborative process of making theatre.

The Performance Facility: Design and Operation
Aesthetics and functions of theatre architecture; variations on traditional performance spaces; planning for construction and renovation; working with architects and consultants; the bidding process; zoning, permits, building codes and regulations; fitting the space to the artistic vision.

Professional Residency and Major Paper
A semester-long professional management residency with a leading performing arts agency, company, or institution: minimum of four months at forty hours per week, resulting in a major paper (in lieu of a thesis) that describes and evaluates both the residency sponsor and the residency experience, with appendices that present samples of the resident's project-related work.

NOTES:

Other courses that might be considered required or elective include:

Stage Management
Artist Representation and Contract Negotiation
Case Studies in Performing Arts Management
Administration of Government and Independent Arts Agencies
The Arts and Society: Politics, Special Interest Groups, and Education
The Arts and Education

Public Policy and the Arts Special Seminars
Visiting Lecture Series

This curriculum can be adapted to a two- or three-year program leading to an M.A., M.F.A., or M.B.A. degree.

Candidates accepted into this program should be fluent in current technologies, have completed at least one undergraduate course in accounting, and have an undergraduate major or considerable life experience in at least one of the performing arts. Any deficiencies in these areas should be made up by requiring the student to take courses where needed, without credit, prior to the end of the first semester in the graduate program. Academic programs and requirements should be individually tailored to fit the background, needs, and career goals of each student.

Only people with both academic and professional credentials should be instructors. Only those institutions of higher education that can offer both on-campus and off-campus internship experiences of high professional quality should offer a graduate program in this field.

Appendix C

The following is a sample checklist of building spaces and functions to be considered when designing a theatre building. The spaces that will ultimately be included in the theatre depend on many factors, but relate especially to the details of the theatre company's performance program and their operating *pro forma*. This is a sample functional list and is not intended to be exhaustive for all facilities.

Public Areas and Front of House Operations

LOBBIES:
Outer lobby
Inner lobby

BOX OFFICE:
Box office ticket windows
Box office operations
Box Office Manager

CONCESSIONS
AND RETAIL:
Concession stands/bars
Concession/bar storage
Refrigerated storage
Retail shop and storage

AUDIENCE SERVICES:
Coat check
Listening assistance pick-up
Latecomer areas
Female washrooms
Male washrooms
ADA/unisex washroom

RECEPTION:
VIP/donor's lounge
Catering prep/serving

FRONT-OF-HOUSE STAFF:
House Manager's office
Usher changing area
Staff lockers
Janitor's closet

FOH STORGE:
Program storage
FOH equipment storage

Administration Areas

OFFICES:
Artistic Director
General Manager
Business Manager
Production Manager
General administration staff

SERVICES:
Public reception
Conference room
Office machines
Kitchenette
Storage
Washrooms

Performance Space

HOUSE/AUDITORIUM:
Entry vestibules
Main level seating/aisles
Balcony and box seating
Usher stations/seating

STAGE/PERFORMANCE:
Stage area
Wing area
Performer crossover
Quick change area
Orchestra pit/musician area
Trap room

TECHNICAL SUPPORT:
FOH lighting positions
Stage catwalks/galleries
Fly floors (rigging operations)
Gridiron/Overhead rigging
Dimmer room
Amplifier rack room

CONTROL ROOMS/AREAS:
Lighting control room
Sound control room
Stage Manager control room
Projection room
Followspot room

Captioning ADA room
House live mix position

Performer Support

Star dressing rooms
4-Person dressing rooms
Chorus dressing rooms
Musician changing areas
Conductor dressing room
Performer washrooms and
    showers
Greenroom and kitchenette
Unisex offstage washrooms

Rehearsal Spaces

Rehearsal studio
Rehearsal storage
Waiting area (e.g. auditions)
Washrooms

Backstage Support

WARDROBE:
Costume shop
Wardrobe maintenance
Laundry room and dye area
Fitting room(s)
Wardrobe office
Costume storage

SCENERY:
Scenery shop/maintenance
Tool storage room/lock-up
Hardware storage room
Paint area and storage
Shop office
Scenery storage
Drapery storage

PROPS:
Prop shop
Prop office
Prop kitchen
Prop storage
Furniture storage

LIGHTING AND SOUND:
Lighting prep & repair shop
Lighting storage
Sound maintenance shop
Sound storage

BOH SERVICE/STAFF:
Stage Manager's office
Production staff offices
Crew room/lockers
Visiting production staff office

BOH Services

Stage door and reception area
Stage door office/security/fire
Loading dock
Receiving area and lock-up
Trash storage/removal
Janitor's closets
Janitor's supplies storage
Building superintendent office

Building Plant

HVAC plant areas
Electrical rooms/closets
Telephone and data rooms
Fire pumps and plumbing
    plant

Appendix D

CHECKLIST FOR THEATRE SPACE DESIGN CRITERIA

The following is a checklist of criteria to be considered in the design of theatre buildings. The building areas listed below reference the Space List in Appendix C—e.g. Public Areas, Performers' Areas, etc. This checklist is a sample and is not intended to be exhaustive.

I. Public Areas/Front-of-House Operations

The following items relate to the audience areas of typical theatre buildings. Each item, of course, suggests that its condition, its presence or its absence, and its arrangement in a given theatre will contribute to the value of the building, either as an asset or as a liability, and to the success or failure of artistic objectives.

I.I   THE THEATRE EXTERIOR

Proximity to public transportation
Automobile parking facilities
Access to streets and highways
Visibility from public highways and byways identification on the building
Marquee and display advertising provisions
Audience drop-off area
Weather canopy
Exterior lighting on and in front of the building
Street and highway lighting
General security risks and provisions
Proximity to fire hydrants

I.2   THE BOX OFFICE

Keep in mind relevant Americans' With Disabilities Act (ADA) guidelines
Size
Security provisions
General appearance and decor
Ease and economy of temperature control (ability to isolate it from exterior weather conditions)
Fireproofing
Soundproofing
General lighting

Proximity to business offices
Number of customer windows or spaces/pocketbook ledge
Number of treasurers who can be accommodated
Seating layout displays and promotion displays
Communication systems (with public and offices)
Storage space
Computer monitors and ticket printers
Storage space for equipment and supplies
Need for theatre-operated agencies away from building
Accessibility to general public (ADA)
Safe
Work space away from public view
Convenience of pay telephone to ticket window

I.3   THE THEATRE LOBBIES

Keep in mind relevant ADA guidelines
Size
Location and size of entryways
Panic bars and emergency exits
General appearance and decor
Ability to isolate when not in use
General lighting
Flooring and carpeting
Ease and economy of temperature control
Security provisions
Emergency lighting
Potential for multipurpose use
Box office in relation to audience traffic flow
Coat- and parcel-checking facilities
Listening Assistance System distribution station
Concession spaces (bar, shops, restaurant, etc.)
Storage space for concession merchandise
Space and provisions for display advertising, brochures, etc.
House-to-lobby speaker
Latecomer closed-circuit television systems
Curtain signaling devices
Elevators to upper levels
Gallery areas
Patrons' lounge areas
Public water fountains
Public seating areas
Public telephones
Ability to separate audience from performer areas

1.4 THE PUBLIC REST ROOMS

Keep in mind relevant ADA guidelines
Accessibility from audience areas
General appearance and decor
Ability to isolate when not in use
General lighting
Flooring
Number of toilet units (both men's and women's)
Ease and economy of temperature control
Adequate ventilation
Emergency lighting
Size
Sanitary conditions in relation to public health laws
Disposal provisions
Vending machines for sanitary napkins
Soap dispenser units
Paper towel and water cup dispenser units
Automatic hand-drying devices
Number of sinks and mirrored areas

2. Performance Space

2.1 THE AUDITORIUM

Keep in mind relevant ADA guidelines
Accessibility from street and lobby areas
General appearance and decor
Ability to isolate when not in use
General lighting
Flooring and carpeting
Ease and economy of temperature control
Emergency lighting
Emergency exits, fire escapes, etc.
Size and number of doors, panic hardware, etc.
Acoustics
Air conditioning and heating systems
Security provisions
Number of seats
Potential for increasing or decreasing seating capacity
Space for standing room
Comfort of seats
Condition of seats
Sight lines from house to stage

Elevation of floor and seats
Potential for altering audience-stage relationship
Aisle, row, and door lights
Stairway lights and railings
Seating and aisle arrangement in terms of traffic flow, ticket taking,
    ushering, etc.
Seat, row, and aisle numbering system
Ease and economy of cleaning, maintaining, replacing light bulbs
    or fixtures, etc.
Provisions or space for house-to-stage lighting and projectors
Access for the handicapped
Access to backstage
Ability to separate audience from performer areas
Potential for multipurpose use
Paging system

2.2   STAGE

Size (depth, width, height, flexibility)
Ability to isolate it when not in use
General lighting
Ease and economy of temperature control
Security provisions
Emergency lighting and emergency exits
Potential for multipurpose use
Accessibility from dressing rooms
Accessibility from scenic-loading docks/doors
Fire curtain
Roof smoke hatches
House/Act curtain
Rigging systems
Stage draperies
Fly galleries, catwalks, stairs, ladders, etc.
Automated versus manually operated equipment
Wing space (ideally as large as the stage itself on both sides;
    and/or behind the stage)
Quick-change dressing areas in wings
Performer crossover upstage
Well-marked and lighted steps to stage
Stage flooring (must be wood)
Floor traps
Stage revolves (turntables)
Apron space
Stage wiring and lighting systems

Footlights
Lighting control room/booth
Sound control room
Sound live mix position
Followspot room/booth
ADA captioning & description room
Facilities for film projection
Space and facilities for rear projection
Cyclorama
Upstage wall
Ability to isolate from street noise
Ability to seal from daylight and other light sources
Stage managers' control booth and area
Stage managers' communication systems (with front of house, stage
  door, dressing rooms, and stagehands)
Stage-to-dressing-room program relay system
Sound systems
Orchestra pit (size, flexibility, etc.)
Orchestra pit entrances (below stage level)
Orchestra lift or elevator

3.   Performer Space

3.1   THE DRESSING ROOMS

Size
Number of rooms
Ability to isolate when not in use
General lighting
Ease and economy of temperature control
Ventilation
Security provisions
Accessibility from stage and stage door
Flooring
General appearance and decor
Communication systems with stage and front of house
Elevators to stage (ADA requirements)
Chorus dressing rooms
Musicians' dressing rooms
Ballet dressing rooms
Stars' dressing rooms (with private rest room each, for one actor only)
Conductors' dressing room (with private rest room for one person)
Makeup lighting

Mirrors
Overhead shelving and wig racks
Clothing racks in well ventilated area
Stage-to-dressing room program relay system
Dressing room sinks
Showers (required for all musical productions)

3.2   BACKSTAGE AREAS

General lighting
Ease and economy of temperature control
Ventilation
Security provisions
Space for doorman near stage door
Call-board and mailbox facilities
Flooring
Corridors and stairs to stage (wide enough for actors passing in large
    costumes)
General appearance and decor
Communication systems with stage and front of house
Water fountains
Office space for department heads and visiting company heads
Storage space for theatre supplies, electrical, paper products, seat parts, etc.
Large lockers for musicians' instruments
Rest room facilities (distance from dressing rooms, quantity, exclusive
    use of performers, etc.)
Green room facilities
Wardrobe rooms (preferably with washers, sinks, dryers, and ironing
    equipment)
Wig and makeup storage facilities
Road box storage areas

4.   The Rehearsal Areas

Stage-size rooms available for rehearsal
Flooring (preferably same as stage — sprung-floor if there will be dance)
Other space available for rehearsal
Ability to isolate from rest of building
General appearance and decor
Ease and economy of temperature control
General lighting
Ability to adapt to multipurpose usage
Access to stage, orchestra pit, dressing rooms

Musicians' warm-up rooms
Ballet warm-up rooms
Dance barres, mirrors, etc.
Security provisions
Rest room and shower facilities
Locker facilities
Storage
Program relay system from stage
Audition waiting and performer lounge area

5. Backstage Support

5.1   THE SCENIC CONSTRUCTION SHOP

Size
Accessibility / proximity to stage / height of travel route
Space available exclusively for construction
Ability to isolate when not in use
General lighting / color temperature for color rendering
Electric power
Compressed air for pneumatic tools
Ease and economy of temperature control
Humidity control for paint drying
Ventilation for welding and painting processes
Floor construction
Fireproofing (adequate space to fireproof set pieces)
Ability to use during performance hours
Lumber and materials storage provisions
Hardware storage
Paint storage and explosives cabinet
Tool room storage / lock-up cabinets
Tool inventory: hand and power tools
Scenery storage and dock areas
Loading docks and ramps
Scenic painting docks and convenient slop sinks
Scenic construction areas
Worktables
Paint and brush cleaning and storage facilities
Stock scenery and platform inventory muslin and fabric inventory
Security provisions
Office space for designers and technical directors
Public and interoffice communication systems

5.2   STAGE ELECTRONIC SHOP

Size
Lighting designer's office space
Stage electrician's office and workspace
Security provisions
Accessibility for rolling racks to theatre and stage
Inventory of stage lighting instruments
Inventory of color media
Inventory of light projectors and special effects equipment
Inventory of tools
Inventory of lamps, bulbs, etc.
Inventory of electrical cable, plugs, etc.
Storage space and racks
Fireproofing
Electric power

5.3   SOUND SHOP

Size
Sound designer's office space
Work tables
Storage space for cable, speakers, amplifiers, racks, mixers, etc.
Recording equipment
Sound-proof area for recording
Storage space for tools and equipment
Electric power

5.4   THE PROPERTIES SHOP

Size
Accessibility to theatre and stage
Security provisions
General lighting
Office and work space for properties supervisors
Storage space for hand props
Storage space for furniture and large props
Provisions near stage for storage and preparation of perishable props,
    food, etc.
Inventory of properties
Inventory of fabrics and supplies

5.5   THE COSTUME SHOP

Size
Accessibility to theatre and stage

Security provisions
General lighting and adequate power source
Office space for costume designer
Work space, cutting tables, racks, etc.
Inventory of sewing machines, irons, etc.
Inventory of supplies
Inventory of fabrics
Inventory of costumes (clothing, hats, wigs, shoes, jewelry, etc.)
Storage cabinets
Storerooms for costume collection
Fitting rooms
Library of resource books
Fireproofing
Laundry and dyeing facilities

6. Administration Areas

Size
Number of separate offices available
Physical relationship of offices to each other
Accessibility to theatre and rest of operation
Need for branch offices away from theatre
Ability to isolate them when not in use
Security provisions
General appearance and decor
Ease and economy of temperature control
Flooring
Soundproofing
General lighting
Inventory of furniture, equipment, supplies
Storage space for records and supplies
Communication systems
Office machines, computers, telephones, etc. (with public, with other
    departments in theatre, between offices)
Reception space
Administrative space
Executive space
Boardroom or conference room space
Library and archive space
Press office space and facilities
Reasonable privacy for executives

Appendix E

STAGE CONFIGURATIONS

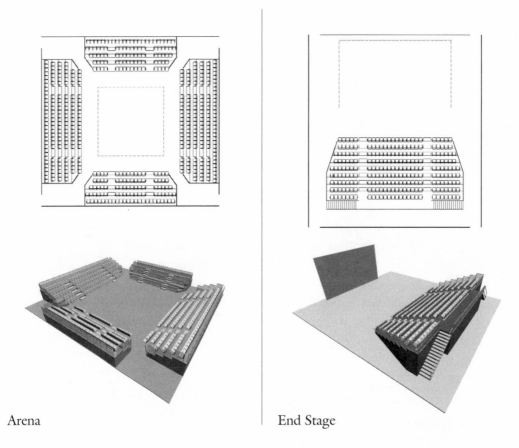

Arena

End Stage

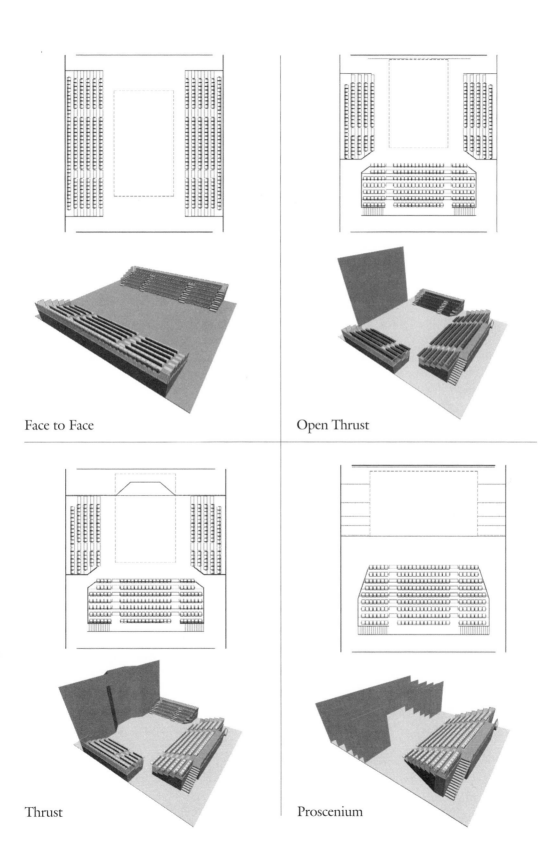

Face to Face

Open Thrust

Thrust

Proscenium

Appendix F

SAMPLE MANUAL FOR BOX OFFICE TREASURERS
AND TICKET SELLERS

(This guide may be adapted for a computerized box office operation with electronic customer files, etc.)

1.) Never leave the box office unattended.
2.) Never allow an unpaid ticket to leave the box office.
3.) Never allow any unbonded person into the box office.
4.) Never take any box office business across the threshold.
5.) Never discuss box office business (grosses or numbers of tickets sold) with anyone. If people inquire about business, your answer should be: "Business is very good, thank you," and nothing more.
6.) Never show a box office statement to anyone; never prepare a statement in front of customers; never count money or prepare bank deposits in view of customers.
7.) Never bring food or beverages of any kind into the box office.
8.) Never issue free or discounted tickets without a written order from the producer or the manager.
9.) Never make personal promises to customers or encourage them to deal only with you. Anyone in the box office should be able to help any customer.
10.) Never tie up the box office phones with personal or unnecessarily long conversations.
11.) Never hesitate to ask questions if you are uncertain about some policy or problem.
12.) Never hesitate to hand over all monies in the event of a robbery.

Remember that you control the lifeline of the theatre. In the eyes of the customers you, more than any other person, are the theatre. Remember that a ticket is negotiable and, therefore, must be regarded as cash. Treat each ticket as if it were a fifty-dollar bill.

DAILY DUTIES OF THE TREASURERS

1.) Report on time and have the customer windows open and ready for business from the stroke of 10 a.m. until posted closing time.
2.) Keep the box office clean and neat at all times. Because the janitor is not allowed into the room, you will be required to sweep the floor daily.
3.) Process all mail orders daily (see below).

4.) Maintain and enlarge the mailing list:
   a. Every name and address that comes into the box office on a ticket order, check, credit card slip, information request, or mailing list form must be checked against the mailing list.
   b. If the name is not already on the list, make out a new card, write the year in the upper right corner, and file it.
   c. If the name is on the mailing list, enter the current date and re-file the card.

5.) Complete a box office statement for each performance:
   a. Each treasurer will complete a statement and only then will these statements be compared for accuracy. Only when all statements agree may a final copy be given to the business manager: no treasurer will end his/her time shift until all the statements agree.
   b. Each finalized statement will be signed by the head treasurer who is responsible for its accuracy.
   c. All deadwood, counted and numbered, will be boxed, labeled with the performance date, then given to the business manager.
   d. All stubs will be counted by the house manager and then numbered, banded, and given to the business manager to check against the deadwood.

6.) Rack all tickets by date and keep the current ticket rack filled with the tickets for the next performance.

7.) Make out two daily bank deposits:
   a. One listing mail order checks only.
   b. One listing all other checks, credit card slips, and cash. The treasurer shall also give the business manager a daily "silver and bill" cash order when this is required.

8.) Check the returned agency tickets and income each day when the agency treasurer(s) reports to the box office. The agency treasurer will not leave the theatre until the daily receipts and cash are correct and accounted for.

9.) Report unsold ticket locations for other theatres and record unsold ticket numbers which they, if acting as your agent, did not sell. Return these unsold agency tickets to the rack: retain the sold tickets under the name of the agency and mark them "sold."

10.) Report any problems, discrepancies, or helpful information to the business or general manager.

GENERAL SALES PROCEDURES

1.) Always be courteous—but firm. Keep each transaction as brief and efficient as possible.

2.) Every seat in the house is a "good" seat.

3.) If phone or window customers ask for tickets and you are SRO, encourage them to return just before curtain time for cancellations.
   a. Cancellation lists are started an hour and a half before curtain time.
   b. Customers must be in the lobby and remain there to get on the list (no phone listings).
   c. Write the name, number, and price of tickets desired and where the customer is waiting.

4.) All ticket reservation envelopes shall carry the following information:
   a. Customer's name and initials.
   b. Performance date: matinee or evening
   c. Number of tickets: price per ticket (2 × $25.00): Do not write the total amount due.
   d. Write the exact time when you told a customer that tickets, if not claimed, would be canceled.

5.) A paid ticket will be held forever.

6.) Unpaid reservation policy: Don't do it. Get a credit card number.

7.) All tickets are to be sold on a "first come, first served" basis.

8.) "Dress the house." Don't pack 'em in unless necessary.

9.) Double check every transaction. To avoid confusion *Work on only one transaction at a time.*

10.) Traveler's checks and personal checks in the exact amount due are always acceptable, with driver's license or other identification on back. Credit cards are accepted at the window and by telephone.

11.) Credit is never extended. No money, no ticket. Get a credit card number.

12.) Press and complimentary tickets will be issued only when the name of the recipient and the locations appear on a company pass list, signed by the company/general manager and treasurer.

13.) When making change:
   a. Don't give out tickets until the money is in your hand.
   b. Leave the customers' money on the counter until they have their change in hand and they agree it is correct.

14.) Until one half hour prior to curtain, only the producer or general manager may assign or use house seats. At half-hour, the head treasurer may release the remaining house seats for general sale.

15.) Do not (release) put house seats on sale until the last feasible moment. If they are needed to cover an emergency or mistake, only the head treasurer may authorize their use.

PROCEDURE FOR HANDLING MAIL ORDERS

1.) All mail must be processed daily.

2.) All mail work must be kept in a separate place, away from other business.

3.) Wire baskets will be provided to hold "Information Requests," "Unprocessed Ticket Orders," "Problem Orders," "Mailing List Additions," and "Checker Basket."

4.) Open each piece of mail and
    a. Staple all contents to the customer's envelope with the check on top—throw nothing away!
    b. Separate ticket orders from information requests.
    c. Stamp the order form with the PAID stamp and enter the amount of the check in the "mail order income" box.
    d. Record customer's name and address on the check if it does not appear on it already.
    e. When all letters have been opened and checks removed, make out the bank deposit and place it, along with the checks, in the safe.

5.) Process each piece of mail individually as follows:
    a. Read entire letter or form and underline in red: date, number of tickets, and location desired.
    b. Pull the tickets, giving the customer what he wants if possible, and write the date of the tickets, location, and price per ticket on the letter in red. Be certain he has sent in the right amount for the tickets.
    c. Stamp and address an envelope to the customer.
    d. Attach all this together and place in the "checker" basket.

6.) Checker duties:
    a. Re-read each letter.
    b. Check order against tickets pulled.
    c. Write "tickets mailed" and today's date on letter.
    d. Place tickets in envelope, blanket them (enclose in a blank sheet of paper), weigh envelope to determine postage, scotch-tape the envelope seal, place envelope in outgoing mail box.
    e. Place the customer's letter or order in "mailing list" basket.

7.) After customer letters have been checked against the mailing list, file them alphabetically in the "customer correspondence" file.
    a. If a customer phones to inquire about an order, check this letter file.
    b. If customers complain that they didn't get what they asked for, locate their order. Chances are they forgot what they ordered.

POSSIBLE MAIL ORDER PROBLEMS AND POLICY REGARDING THEM

1. If check is insufficient to cover tickets ordered:
    a. Pull the tickets anyway.
    b. Deposit the check.
    c. Hold tickets and notify the customer of the balance due.

2. If the check is for more than the amount due:
    a. Process mail as usual, enter refundable amount on letter.
    b. Mail the tickets.

    c. Enclose a letter signed by the head treasurer saying that "upon presentation of this letter at box office, a refund will be made."

3. If tickets are sold out for the performance requested by customer:
    a. Return the letter and the check to the customer.
    b. Notify the customer when tickets are available.

4. If the customer returns tickets by mail for a refund, refer the case to the business manager for a decision.

5. If the mail order is incomplete and does not include all the necessary information:
    a. Place the letter and check in the "problem" basket.
    b. Notify the customer of the problem (by phone, if a local call, otherwise by postcard).

6. When possible, use the postcard form shown as follows to notify the customer when an order cannot be filled:

We are unable to complete your ticket order for the following reason:

We are sold out for the (price) (date) you requested.
Seats available, but not the specific locations.
Incorrect payment.   You sent $ Should be $
Failed to state date   matinee   evening
Check returned for signature.
Number of tickets and price were not indicated.
Tickets requested not available until
The performance you requested is not
We are returning your check.
We are holding your check for further instructions.
We are holding your tickets at the box office.

PROCEDURES FOR ANSWERING THE BOX OFFICE PHONES

1.) Salutation: "Good morning. Playhouse box office."
2.) If the call is not box office business, refer it to the correct person. Do not take messages or accept nonbusiness calls.
3.) If you are speaking on one line and a second line rings, put the first call on hold, ask the second caller to hold, and return to the first call. Once the first call is complete, take the second call.
4.) Phone calls take priority over window customers.
5.) Learn immediately how to give clear directions (car and public transportation) to the playhouse from all points within a fifty-mile radius.
6.) When an order is taken, repeat the number of tickets, location and date, and credit card information.

7.) Keep yourself informed about the intermission and show ending times.

8.) Make a note about the seat numbers occupied by doctors. Inform the manager if any VIP or celebrity ticket orders are made.

PROCEDURE FOR HANDLING CREDIT CARD ORDERS

1.) At the box office window:
   a. Fill out a blank credit card duplicate slip with: today's date, date of performance, matinee or evening, number of tickets ordered, price per ticket, total price, ticket locations.
   b. Insert customer's card under the dupe slip in the imprinter and slide handle. CHECK TO BE CERTAIN THAT THE IMPRESSION IS LEGIBLE.
   OR
   c. Swipe card
   d. Ask customer to sign the slip and "please press down."
   e. Give the customer 1) tickets and 2) the customer copy of sales transaction slip.
   f. Write customer's permanent address on back of the theatre copy of the slip for mailing list.
   g. Place the theatre copy and deposit copy of slip (still attached) in "today's CC orders" box.

2.) Over the telephone:
   a. Write custome's name and address on the duplicate slip, preprinted with the theatre information by the imprinter.
   b. Write the credit card number and company initials.
   c. Fill in ticket information and price as per above instructions.
   d. Write "Tel" for "Telephone order" where customer's signature would otherwise go.
   e. Repeat all information for customer to verify.
   f. Inform customer there are now paid tickets and that they will be held until claimed.
   g. Place the entire dupe slip together with tickets pulled in "CC Check" basket. (Prior to the performance, a treasurer will be assigned to check all credit card numbers, check accuracy of written information against the tickets pulled, file tickets and customer's copy of slip in envelope under the appropriate performance date.)

PROCEDURE WHEN CUSTOMER HAS LOST TICKETS

1. If tickets were ordered by mail:
   a. If they were season tickets, check customer's file card and issue a pass for correct locations, signed by head treasurer.

    b. Check mail file and issue a pass for correct locations, signed by head treasurer.

    c. If there is no record of customer's order, head treasurer may question customer and use his or her own judgment as to whether or not a pass should be issued. If there is room in the house, put them in.

2.) If it was a credit card order, check the file of credit card duplicate slips (filed by performance date).

3.) If correspondence shows that the tickets ordered were for another performance than the one remembered by the customer, issue a pass for the performance remembered.

4.) Always issue passes for lost or stolen tickets by writing the locations on hardwood.

5.) Always explain to customers that if someone is sitting in those seats with the actual tickets, the tickets trump the hardwood.

Lost tickets are usually left at home. If the wrong people have the lost tickets, inquire as to how they got them. Inform them that the tickets may be stolen, etc. Note: Theatres with a high volume of telephone credit card orders may find it easier to assign a special phone operator to handle such calls. In this case exact ticket locations are not given to customer; rather the order forms are given to a treasurer who periodically pulls the tickets, completes the information on the order slip, and files the tickets under the performance date.

Appendix G

SAMPLE LIMITED PARTNERSHIP LETTER

HY HOPE PRODUCTIONS, INC.
000 Broadway
New York, NY

RE: Romeo and Juliet by William Shakespeare an Off-Broadway Production

Dear Sirs:

I hereby state that I would like to be an investor and Limited Partner in the "R & J" Company, which will produce William Shakespeare's *Romeo and Juliet* Off-Broadway. Accordingly, I hereby invest a total amount of $ which shall entitle me to   unit(s) of 50 percent of any net profits based upon a total capitalization of $500,000.

   $10,000 shall represent one unit or percentile.* I enclose my investment check in the above amount (or, upon demand, I shall deliver my check to you). You shall hold my funds in trust in a special account until such time as $425,000 is raised, after which you may utilize the funds for production purposes.

   In the event that capital contributions total at least $425,000, and you believe that the production can commence, then the capitalization of the Limited Partnership shall be reduced to the amount determined, and the Limited Partners' proportional shall be increased accordingly.

   You shall forward to me the Limited Partnership Agreement for this production, which has been filed in the office of the Attorney General of the State of New York. I shall promptly sign and return it to you.

   In the event that the Limited Partnership is not formed within twelve months from the date of this letter, then the money advanced shall be returned to me in full. There shall be no overcall.

Sincerely,

(Signature)

Please initial one: My investment may   may not   be used as front money.

(Name, printed in full)
(Full legal address)

*Assuming 50 limited partner shares are offered, each representing two percent of the capitalization and one percent of profits, although, of course, an investor may sometimes buy part of one share or more than one.

Appendix H

THEATRICAL LABOR UNIONS AND GUILDS

Web Resources: Union Information For Stage Managers, Actors, and Theatre Employees

Actors' Equity Association (AEA): http://www.actorsequity.org/
American Federation of Musicians: http://www.afm.org/public/home/index.php
American Federation of Television and Radio Artists (AFTRA):
    http://www.aftra.com/aftra/aftra.htm
American Guild of Musical Artists (AGMA): http://www.musicalartists.org/
American Guild of Variety Artists (AGVA):
    http://americanguildofvarietyartistsagva.visualnet.com/
Association of Theatrical Press Agents and Managers (ATPAM):
    http://www.atpam.com/
British Actors' Equity Association: http://www.equity.org.uk/
Broadcast Music Inc.: http://www.bmi.com/
Canadian Actors' Equity Association (CAEA): http://www.caea.com/
Directors Guild of America: http://www.dga.org/
Dramatists Guild: http://www.dramaguild.com/
Icelandic Actors Association: http://www.actors-union.is/
International Association of Theatrical Stage Employees (IATSE):
    http://www.iatse-intl.org/
International Ticketing Association: http://www.intix.org/
Irish Actors Equity: http://www.irishactorsequity.ie/
Playwrights' Guild of Canada: http://www.playwrightsguild.ca/
Society of Stage Directors and Choreographers: http://www.ssdc.org/
Stage Management Association (UK): http://www.stagemanagementassociation.co.uk/
Stage Managers' Association: http://www.stagemanagers.org/
Theatrical Wardrobe Union (TWAU): www.ia764.com/
Treasurers and Ticket Sellers: http://www.local751.com/
United Scenic Artists of America: http://www.usa829.org
Ushers, Ticket-Takers, Theatre Employees Union: http://www.local306.org

Appendix I

MISSION STATEMENTS

HOUSTON BALLET

Houston Ballet Foundation is committed to providing the City of Houston and its surrounding communities a ballet company and a training academy of the highest international standard. Through excellence in the classical ballet tradition, we seek to attract and expose our diverse community to the wonder and value of the art form of dance and to enhance the medium overall.

Basic tenants of the mission are:

To maintain a repertory which fosters the presentation of new, established and classical choreography for the technical and artistic growth of the dancers and the enrichment of the audience.

To maintain the highest artistic standards of production and musical support.

To further the reputation of Houston Ballet as a prime classical and creative company of international stature through local, national, and international performances.

To continue the development of a company of dancers drawn primarily from Houston Ballet Academy in order to maintain the style and standards established by the Artistic Director.

To maintain operations with a balanced budget in support of the artistic goals.

To maintain endowment, capital, and cash reserve funds so as to maintain the long-term financial viability of Houston Ballet.

OREGON SHAKESPEARE FESTIVAL

Mission

The mission of the Oregon Shakespeare Festival is to create fresh and bold interpretations of classic and contemporary plays in repertory, shaped by the diversity of our American culture, using Shakespeare as our standard and inspiration.

Vision

We envision the Oregon Shakespeare Festival as a creative environment where artists and audiences from around the world know they can explore opportunities for transformational experiences through the power of theatre.

MANHATTAN THEATRE CLUB

For more than three decades, Manhattan Theatre Club has been the creative and artistic home for America's most gifted theatrical artists, producing works of the highest quality by both established and emerging American and international playwrights. New York and world premieres created under MTC's auspices travel across America and the world. MTC's plays and musicals challenge, inspire, entertain, and provoke audiences. At MTC, theatre reflects on our lives, our society, and our ideas.

Each year, Manhattan Theatre Club produces a season of innovative work. The artistic profile of the subscription season is as broad and diverse as New York City itself.

Manhattan Theatre Club encourages significant new work by creating an environment in which writers and theatre artists are supported by the finest professionals producing for the theatre today.

Manhattan Theatre Club nurtures and develops new talent in playwriting, musical composition, writing, directing, acting, and design.

Manhattan Theatre Club reaches out to young audiences with innovative programs in education and maintains a commitment to cultivate the next generation of theatre professionals with internship and professional training programs.

Manhattan Theatre Club is a leader in developing innovative ways to bring theatre to the widest possible audience. These include extending the life of its productions in-house, transferring its productions to larger theatres and co-producing great plays with fellow institutions. In constantly seeking new ways to grow, MTC keeps theatre alive and relevant.

BERKELEY REPERTORY THEATRE

Berkeley Repertory Theatre seeks to set a national standard for ambitious programming, engagement with its audiences, and leadership within the community in which it resides. We endeavor to create a diverse body of work that expresses a rigorous, embracing aesthetic and reflects the highest artistic standards, and seek to maintain an environment in which talented artists can do their best work. We strive to engage our audiences in an ongoing dialogue of ideas, and encourage lifelong learning as a core community value.

Through productions, outreach, and education, Berkeley Rep aspires to use theatre as a means to challenge, thrill, and galvanize what is best in the human spirit.

NATIONAL THEATRE OF THE DEAF

The National Theatre of the Deaf operates under the following comprehensive mission:

To produce theatrically challenging work at a world class level, drawing from as wide a range of the world's literature as possible; to perform these original works in a style that links American Sign Language with the spoken word; to seek, train, and employ deaf artists; to offer our work to as culturally diverse and inclusive an audience as possible; to provide community outreach activities that will educate and enlighten the general public.

THE JOYCE THEATER FOUNDATION

The mission of The Joyce Theater Foundation, Inc. is to serve and support the art of dance and choreography, to promote the richness and variety of the art form in its fullest expression, and to advance the public interest in, and appreciation of, dance and the allied arts of music, design, and theater. The Joyce Theater's programs embrace the entire spectrum of movement styles and traditions, from the time-honored to the untried, and are designed to encourage, sustain, and educate a diverse audience.

THE LIVING THEATRE

The Mission

To call into question who we are to each other in the social environment of the theater, to undo the knots that lead to misery, to spread ourselves across the public's table like platters at a banquet, to set ourselves in motion like a vortex that pulls the spectator into action, to fire the body's secret engines, to pass through the prism and come out a rainbow, to insist that what happens in the jails matters, to cry "Not in my name!" at the hour of execution, to move from the theater to the street and from the street to the theater. This is what The Living Theatre does today. It is what it has always done.

—Hanon Reznikov

Appendix J

LARGE MUSICAL TECHNICAL RIDER

Technical Requirements

In the following pages, we will outline for you the technical requirements for the touring production of a LARGE MUSICAL. Your cooperation and advance preparation will facilitate an efficient load-in, set-up, run, and load-out. We hope to cover all areas of concern, but if you have additional questions after going through this document, please feel free to contact us with further questions.

MINIMUM STAGE REQUIREMENTS

Minimum proscenium width opening: 40' 0" (20' 0" left and right of center)
Minimum stage depth (from first working set): 37' 0"
Minimum stage width: 74' 0" (37' 0" left and right of center)
Minimum grid height: 65' 0"
Minimum width between fly floors: 50' 0" (25' 0" left and right of center)
Minimum height clearance under fly floors: 26' 0"
Minimum size loading door: 8' 0" wide × 9' 0" high

SEATING HOLDS

Sound console: See Sound Department

Followspots: See Electrics Department

Sightlines: TBD

Complimentary tickets: The Producer will need forty (40) VIP complimentary tickets (20 pair) for the Opening Night Performance to be utilized for our sponsorship promotion.

House Seats: Company requires 30 house seat locations per performance within first 10–20 rows of the orchestra. Please forward locations to Company Management as soon as possible.

GENERAL REQUIREMENTS

1.) Please mail a copy of current local union contracts to the New York office mailing listing the prevailing local union rates at least six (6) months prior to the engagement.

2.) Please fax or mail a copy of the current hanging plot (line set positions) to the New York office as soon as possible.

3.) Please mail a complete and detailed ground plan and section on the stage and house (in scale) to the New York office as soon as possible. Also, please include a copy of the dressing room layouts.

4.) We require the following for both the in and out:
1–2 ton 6' forklift & qualified operator

5.) It is imperative that all areas of the stage, fly system, backstage, loading docks, dressing rooms, storage areas, and productions offices be completely clear and broom clean prior to the start of the advance load-in.

6.) All personnel called for the load-in, load-out, and performances of the production must be qualified in their department and prompt for the starting times of all calls. ALL STAGEHANDS EMPLOYED ARE EXPECTED TO BRING BASIC TOOLS. (I.E. A HAMMER, PHILLIPS SCREWDRIVER, SLOTTED SCREWDRIVER, CRESCENT WRENCH, PLIERS, AND A TAPE MEASURE.)

7). **ANY STAGEHAND SHOWING UP FOR WORK OR SHOW CALLS SHOWING ANY SIGNS OF DRINKING OR SUBSTANCE ABUSE WILL BE DISMISSED ON THE SPOT, AND REPLACED AT LOCAL PRESENTERS' EXPENSE (IF ANY).**

8.) It is expected that when a stagehand begins working in one department that the stagehand will continue in that department for the duration of load-in. Further, it is expected that when a stagehand accepts a job on the running crew that said stagehand will remain on the job for the duration of all performances. In the event that a stagehand must vacate a position then his replacement must have a training period of a minimum two performances under the direction of the current employee prior to assuming the position alone.

9.) Some stagehands will be required to wear black clothing in order to avoid being seen while in the wings.

10.) This production travels in five (5) 53-foot tractor-trailers. One of these will arrive for the spotting call/advance load-in, the day before the first performance, and be emptied half way. All five trailers will arrive for the start of the load-in on the first performance day. For the load-in and load-out please arrange to have all available parking spaces in the immediate area of the loading dock clear and available for trailer parking and unloading. It is extremely important that the movement of the trucks not be obstructed by cars parked on the streets and lots surrounding the theatre. The Local Presenter is responsible for obtaining all proper permits for trucks/trailers during load-in and load-out.

11.) A portion of the running crew will be called to work up to one and one-half (1½) hours prior to each show to preset the stage while others will be called at half-hour.

CARPENTRY DEPARTMENT

1.) Fly system and the stage area must be cleared of all scenery, electrics, drapes, band shells, scenery, and projection screens prior to the load-in. <u>This is absolutely essential.</u>

2.) The musicians are in the pit for the production. Before our arrival, the pit must be in its lowered position and seats removed.

3.) There must be 20,000 lbs. of weight, over pipe weight, available on the loading gallery before the arrival of the production. This weight should be doubled (40,000 lbs. over pipe weight) in a double purchase house.

4.) Carpenter must be able to screw or lag into deck, which must be level and structurally sound.

5.) Linesets must be kickable and should be set according to current house hanging plot (line set positions)

6.) We require no less than 30 spotted lines with 2 wheels per line and a commensurate amount of ⅝" hemp, available at the time of the advance spotting call.

7.) We will use your house main curtain. And we will use house black velour drop upstage of last line set used, if available.

IF YOU ARE UNABLE TO COMPLY WITH ANY OF THESE REQUIRMENTS, PLEASE NOTIFY US IMMEDIATELY.

ELECTRIC DEPARTMENT

1.) POWER REQUIREMENTS

A. CHAIN HOIST REQUIRED POWER: 1 100 amp 208VAC 3 phase Y power with ground and neutral. Power should be fused and have a disconnect switch with lugs.

B. LIGHTING REQUIRED POWER: 2 400-amp 3-phase 5-wire with ground switches. Power needed within 50' of Dimmer Rack Location. Rack location to be determined by Road Electrician.

C. SOUND REQUIRED POWER: Unique (AUDIO ONLY) 3 phase 100 Amp service with isolated ground—may not be shared with any other powered systems (i.e. Dimmers, Automation Motors, and Air Conditioning etc.). Power needed within 50' of Amplifier Racks. Rack location to be determined by Road Sound Operator.

House power feed must maintain a minimum of 208 volts and be configured in a "Y" phase. If the voltage drops below 208 volts, the computer controlled effects may not work properly. The production requires a water pipe or earth ground. If a water pipe is provided, it must be a filled pipe. A standpipe is not acceptable. If the power feeds do not terminate in a location as specified above it is the responsibility of the local presenter to provide the necessary feeder cable, etc. to insure that the power feed terminates as specified.

2.) Before the start of the load-in, all on-stage electrical pipes must be cleared of instruments and their raceways and feed cables.

3.) Please supply the New York office with any local electric restrictions or codes. If specific permits are required, it is the responsibility of the local presenter to secure these permits prior to the start of the load-in.

4.) The Local Presenter must provide sufficient cable and plug-in strip boxes for 20 music stand lights located in the orchestra pit.

5.) The production requires the presenter to provide three (3) matched 2kw Lycian Followspots. Followspots should be central at the rear of "High Balcony" level. Audience heads/hands should not interfere with followspot beams when audience stands in the back row. If the spots are blocked or three spots cannot fit into the booth, soundproofed scaffolding will need to be erected in the balcony section of the auditorium and within sightlines determined by the production staff. Since the placement of these scaffolding towers may eliminate some seats from possible public sale, the presenter should hold and not sell the rear balcony seating sections until released by the production staff during the load-in. Please discuss this situation with the production staff in advance. These followspots have to be in position and checked that they are in good working order prior to the load-in and can in no way be part of the load-in work calls. The touring electrician will check the followspots to make sure of their condition. Any work he deems necessary will be at the cost of the local presenter. A spare lamp must be included in case of lamp failure.

6.) We require an area approximately 6 feet deep and 8 feet wide for our lighting consoles with a clear view of the stage. This may be set up in a tech booth or in the back of the orchestra seating. If no such space is available for this position, seats may need to be removed to accommodate it. Please discuss this with the production staff in advance.

7.) This production utilizes the following positions:

- Balcony Rail, or hardware to supply. If no balcony rail, it will be

necessary to block the four (4) center seats in the first two rows of
the balcony

- Front of House Truss and Focusing Track
- Near Box Boom
- Far Box Boom

If adequate positions do not exist, they will need to be installed. Please discuss
with the production staff in advance.

SOUND DEPARTMENT

1.) We require an area 10' deep and 12' wide for our sound mixing position
which must be near the center line at the rear of the orchestra section of
the house (no more than 100' from the stage) within the seating section
and within sight of the center cluster. Any seats must be removed prior
to the beginning of the load-in. The console area provided must be level,
with a flat surface. Easy access and egress to sound position by sound
operator is necessary throughout the performance. The show cannot be
mixed from a closed room or room with a window. Under all circumstances, our production will run and use its own multicable to and from
the sound position and the stage area.

2.) We will tie into the house cluster, where appropriate, with two feeds.
Upper and Lower Control of the cluster is necessary along with the ability to bypass house EQ and Delays on the cluster. If no center cluster
exists or is deemed by the Production Sound Engineer as inappropriate
for our use, we will provide a center cluster and truss. If house chain
motors installed for this purpose are not available, please inform the
New York office immediately. We will in some cases be able to utilize the
house sound truss for our cluster—we require a truss capable of supporting 750 lbs. Should the house truss not meet our needs, we will provide
a truss which will be 16' in length (maximum of 2 × 8 foot sections). The
house chain motor points must be appropriately spaced in order to rig
the production truss if it is required. Any existing, proscenium speakers
or towers must be removed prior to the beginning of our load-in. If they
are not removed by the time the load-in begins, the promoter will have
to hire additional manpower, at their expense, to complete the removal.
The show will need full access to hang necessary surround speakers, delay
speakers, and video equipment in the theatre.

3.) We carry a complete sound system and insist that our own console,
microphones, playback devices, and speaker system be used. We reserve
the right to use our own speaker system exclusively. If it is determined by
our soundman to be advantageous, we will tie into your house sound
and/or paging system with a 600 ohm LINE LEVEL output and use it in

addition to our system. We will require full access to all house sound, paging, video, and hearing-impaired systems.

4.) During the load-in period, the theatre lobby will be used as a work area for the sound department. If possible some or all of the sound equipment will be moved into the theatre through the lobby. In an effort to protect the lobby floors, the presenter may wish to provide protective covering: either heavy canvas drop cloths or 4' × 8' one quarter inch (¼") Masonite with all seams taped. Such floor covering (if required) should be in place prior to the start of the load-in.

5.) This production will utilize 40 channels of UHF Wireless Radios, 10 channels of UHF HME Comm. and at least 8 channels of UHF Motorola walkie-talkies. The use of walkie-talkies or other wireless used by local television crews while filming in the theatre is not allowed.

6.) The SHOW Sound Department personnel will require a small-sized dressing room or other office space preferably located close to the stage for the preparation of wireless microphones and other work related to the running of the show. This room may be shared with the hair and or wardrobe as a quick-change location (see Dressing Room Requirements).

7.) A functional dressing room paging system is required. This system should allow patching from our systems via a 600 ohm LINE LEVEL input. If the theatre does not have functional paging speakers in all backstage areas (including dressing rooms) please inform the New York office immediately.

PROPERTY DEPARTMENT

1.) We require a professional upright piano (not a console), on a piano dolly, which must be tuned (A=440) before the first rehearsal in each city and thereafter every week. The piano is for rehearsal purposes only.

2.) We require 20 music stands with clip lights and chairs in the orchestra pit for the musicians.

3.) Please be certain that there are at least 70 chairs total for use in the dressing rooms, backstage, and in the orchestra pit.

4.) We require black carpeting or black velour for the front and back walls of the pit as well as the pit floor.

5.) Push brooms, mops, buckets, and a vacuum must be available.

6.) One large refrigerator located within easy access of the cast and crew.

WARDROBE DEPARTMENT

1.) At least 6 15 amp 115V circuits are required in the wardrobe area, dressing areas, and quick change areas in order to power iron, steamers, and industrial fans.

2.) The wardrobe area must be a large well-lit room with locking doors for security. This room must have 8 eight-foot worktables and 10 chairs, 10 rolling racks, and 2 large garbage cans. There must also be enough space in the room to accommodate 5 workcrates, 2 gondolas, and 3 hampers.

3.) Local presenter must provide 2 full-size washers and dryers on the premises for show use only. Washers cannot be coin operated, and must have individual cycle capabilities and water levels that can be adjusted by hand during a cycle. Dryer must be 220 volts and properly vented. Appliances must be in full running condition on the first day of the load-in.

4.) Crew Information: It is imperative that the same nine (9) people work the load-in, load-out, and performances. Of the nine (9) personnel, one (1) must be an experienced stitcher, one (1) must be experienced in working with hand-sewn beads, and one (1) experienced with shoe maintenance. There will be a laundry position that will be part-time on some days and full-time on the weekends. The composition of the wardrobe crew may be all female, or may include up to two (2) male dressers. All dressers need to be proficient in reading and speaking English.

5.) The physical demands of the production are such that all dressers must be able to make fast changes involving shoes. They must be able to get down on their knees and stand back up quickly in order for the fast changes to occur within the amount of time available. It is imperative that the local dressers be informed of this physical necessity before they accept this engagement.

6.) Crew Calls: There will be 2 four-hour work calls each week, on days to be determined by the wardrobe supervisor based on the performance schedule (usually Tuesday and Friday). The wardrobe crew will also be called for a one-hour continuity call before the half-hour call before each performance.

7.) A fully functioning utility sink with hot and cold running water will be needed for the cleaning and rinsing of costumes and wigs. This sink must be nearby the wardrobe and wig rooms yet separate from any sink used by theatre custodial, cleaning, and stage mopping staff. The use of the sink should be designated for exclusive use by the Production during this engagement. The sink must be clean and available for use at the commencement of the load-in.

HAIR/WIG DEPARTMENT

1.) At least 3 20 amp circuits are required in the wig area.

2.) The wig area must be well-lit.

3.) In wig area, there must be 4 six- or eight-foot worktables with 4 lighted mirror spaces, 2 height-adjustable chairs, and 4 trashcans.

4.) A deep sink with hot and cold running water (see Wardrobe Department #7) is required.

5.) Crew Information: It is imperative that the same two (2) people work all of the performances. The hair crew will be called from one hour prior to half-hour through the end of the performance.

ORCHESTRA REQUIREMENTS

1.) The production travels with a conductor and 3 musicians. In addition, we require 12 local musicians for a total of 16 playing musicians. John Staff is the Music Coordinator (212-xxx-1646, 212-xxx-1452 fax (email.com). His office will provide all of the specific information regarding orchestra needs and scheduling.

2.) The Local Presenter must provide a Yamaha U Series piano onstage for cast rehearsals.

DRESSING ROOM REQUIREMENTS

1.) Our company consists of 25 performers, 1 conductor, 2 traveling musicians, 3 stage managers, 2 company managers, 11 stagehands, 2 wardrobe, 2 hair.

2.) The dressing room requirements are as follows:
5 Principal (1 person) Dressing Rooms
2 2-person Rooms
2 Large Chorus (12 people) Rooms
1 Conductor Dressing Room
1 Crew Room

3.) All performers' dressing rooms must be cleaned—floors, makeup tables, mirrors, sinks, and bathrooms—prior to the START of the load-in and maintained daily. These rooms must be well-lit with burned out bulbs replaced daily. They must have hot and cold running water, wardrobe racks, etc. in accordance with Actors' Equity Association requirements. Drinking water (fountains and/or water coolers) must be accessible in the dressing room area and backstage. Clothing hooks shall not serve as a substitute for wardrobe racks. Chairs, not stools or benches, are required at each space to be used by a performer. Bathroom facilities must be well stocked with soap, toilet tissue, and paper towels.

4.) Additionally, we will need the following rooms for staff personnel, which must be able to be locked:
    i. Room for Company Management with one (1) private telephone line with call waiting, a second private telephone line for faxing without call waiting, with no rollover features, accessible to

AT&T Long Distance. In addition, a third line with modem capabilities or high speed internet access will be required. Phone lines must be checked and fully operational by the commencement of the load-in. All phone lines should be direct lines. If the phone lines for Company Management and Stage Management are controlled by a switchboard, the phone lines must be operational from 9:00 AM to 12:00 midnight every day during the engagement including days when the theater is dark.

ii. **A phone line should be made available backstage for the run of the show. This line should be compatible with a modem if possible and should have the ability of accessing long distance via a 1-800 number.**

iii. Room for Stage Management with one (1) private telephone line with call waiting and a second private telephone line for faxing/modeming. If this line cannot also serve as a modem line, an additional line with modem capabilities will be required. Phone lines must be operational by the commencement of the load-in.

iv. Room for Wardrobe Department (see Wardrobe Requirements).

v. Room for Hair/Wigs Department (see Hair/Wigs Requirements).

SECURITY INFORMATION

1.) We require security personnel for each performance to arrive at the theatre for every call and one and one-half hours before each performance and remain at the theatre until the last company member has departed. Throughout the engagement, all areas used by the company must be secured to the satisfaction of the company's representative.

2.) The Company Managers and Stage Managers must have access to their office space during business hours. Arrangements must be made with the Company Manager for office access and keys.

3.) Any property of the SHOW Tour including scenery, costumes, sound and lighting equipment (whether owned or rented), props, and equipment, are for the sole use of the Company. The Local Presenter may not utilize any property for any use (including but not limited to performances, presentations, and speeches on the set) without the prior written consent of the Producer.

4.) The house cannot be opened to the public before the half-hour prior to the advertised curtain time.

MANAGEMENT REQUIREMENTS

1.) Please mail the following to General Manager, 1501 Broadway, Suite C, New York, New York, 10036, as soon as possible:
  - List of the theatre personnel and presenting organization's personnel with their private office numbers and home phone numbers if possible.
  - List of local doctors to include general practitioner, ear, nose and throat, chiropractor, podiatrist, dentist, and OB/GYN, and appropriate hospital or medical center for emergency treatment; as well as a listing of local transportation, laundry facilities, drugstore, grocery stores, health clubs, post offices, and nearby restaurants and hotels.
  - A copy of the house-seating plan, which includes all seating areas.
  - Company House Seat locations, with prices inclusive of any and all facility/restoration fees.

2.) In the event of a change in cast, it will be necessary for the ushers to place printed announcements in each house program at no additional expense to producer. The production's stage managers will supply these preprinted announcements to the house.

ESTIMATED LOCAL CREW REQUIREMENTS

The following is an estimate of the number of local stagehands needed and approximate call times. Actual numbers of personnel may vary depending on local circumstances. These call times may increase or decrease and a final determination of personnel and call times will be made by the Head Carpenter.

PRE-ENGAGEMENT SPOTTING ADVANCE CALL
@ 6 p.m of Day before First Performance
4 hour call

1 Head Carpenter
13 Carpenters
1 Head Electrician
1 Electrician
1 Prop Person

LOAD-IN*
The estimated load-in call is 8–10 hours, depending on local conditions on the day of the First Performance, as follows: 8–10 hours, 6 a.m. to 5 p.m.

The estimated load-out call is 5–6 hours. Load-out will begin immediately following the final performance, depending on local conditions. THIS IS A PRELIMINARY CALL. WE WILL ADVISE YOU OF THE FINAL CALL AT A LATER DATE. This is also the minimum call and is subject to local conditions.

	IN	RUN	OUT
Carpentry	17	7	17
Electrics	14	4	14
Sound	6	1	6
Props	5	2	5
Wardrobe	9	9	9
Hair	2	2	2
Loaders	AS NEEDED		

If union requirements demand the Local Presenter supply lunch and/or dinner for the local crews during load-in, between performances, or load-out, meals will also be provided for the traveling crew, stage managers, and cast (if applicable) and the cost will be a local documented expense. The Head Carpenter will coordinate any required meals with the Local Presenter prior to the load-in.

PRESENTER AVAILABILITY

1.) The Presenter or a representative must be available to the Road Carpenter at all times and to the Production Stage Manager from one hour prior to the load-in to the end of the final performance. This person must be able to make decisions on behalf of the Presenter.

SUMMARY OF MATERIALS TO BE MAILED TO THE NEW YORK OFFICE

- Union Contracts with prevailing rates
- Hanging plot (line set positions)
- Ground plan and section in scale of stage dimensions and dressing room layout
- The location, size, and access of the loading door
- Local electric restrictions and codes
- Names and phone numbers of Carpenter/Tech Director, Electrician, Theatre Manager, Concessions/Souvenir Manager, Presenter Contact
- House seating plan and Company House Seat locations and prices
- Doctor and local orientation list

Be advised that failure of the Local Presenter to meet the requirements of this rider may dictate additional time or labor and result in additional expenses. The expenses shall be deemed a fixed expense and borne solely by the Local Presenter.

If there is any further information you require, or if you anticipate any difficulty in meeting the needs as stated above, please contact:

TOUR PERSONNEL
(reachable through the Management office if no number is listed):

General Manager
Production Manager
Production Stage Manager
Company Manager

Associate Co. Mgr.
Production Electrician
Head Electrician
Moving Lights Technician
Lighting Board Operator
Sound Designer
Sound Board Operator
Wireless Microphone Coordinator
Production Carpenter
Flyman
Asst. Carpenter
Properties Supervisor
Asst. Properties
Wardrobe Supervisor
Asst. Wardrobe Supervisor
Star Dresser
Hair Supervisor
Asst. Hair Supervisor
Music Contractor

Appendix K

CONTRACT #1

[Artist's Manager]
Address of Artist's Manager
Telephone and Fax numbers

Agreement made this _____ day of _____ by and between _____
herein called "*[Artist's Manager]*" for services of _____
herein called "Artist" contracting through *[Artist's Manager]*, and

_____

herein called "Local Presenter" whose address is

_____

It is mutually agreed between the parties that the Local Presenter hereby engages the Artist and the Artist agrees hereby to perform the engagement hereinafter provided, upon all of the terms and conditions herein set forth, including those on the reverse side hereof entitled "Additional Terms and Conditions."

1.) ENGAGEMENT INFORMATION:
   DATE, TIME, PERFORMANCE LOCATION
2.) REHEARSAL INFORMATION:
   DATE, TIME, REHEARSAL LOCATION
3.) COMPENSATION:
   The Compensation to be paid by the Local Presenter shall be

   _____

4). PAYMENT SCHEDULE:
5.) ADDITIONAL CONDITIONS:
6.) REPERTOIRE:
7.) CONDUCTOR/SOLOIST:

[Artist's Manager]

by: _____   by: _____

by: _____

THE INFORMATION BELOW SHOULD BE REVIEWED FOR ACCURACY AND UPDATED AS REQUIRED

Local Presenter Contact:
Venue Contact:
Office Telephone:
Venue Emergency Number:
Fax Number:
Venue Capacity:
Email:
Venue Web Address:
Home Telephone:
Venue Technical Contact:
Cell Phone Number:
Technical Contact Phone Number:

THE ABOVE SIGNATURES CONFIRM THAT THE PARTIES HAVE READ AND APPROVE EACH AND ALL OF THE "ADDITIONAL TERMS AND CONDITIONS" SET FORTH ON THE REVERSE SIDE HEREOF. **NO CHANGES MAY BE MADE ON THIS CONTRACT WITHOUT PRIOR CONSENT OF** *[ARTIST'S MANAGER]*.

ADDITIONAL TERMS AND CONDITIONS

1.) REQUIREMENTS:
   (a) Local Presenter agrees to furnish at its own expense all that is necessary for the proper presentation of the Artist's performance as set forth herein or in an attached Technical or Contract Rider.
   (b) Local Presenter agrees to comply with all regulations and requirements of any national or local union(s) that may have jurisdiction over any of the facilities, materials, services, and personnel to be furnished by Local Presenter or by Artist.
   (c) No seats will be positioned on the stage without the advance written consent of the Artist.
   (d) Local Presenter shall be solely responsible for the payment of royalties (ASCAP, BMI, SECAC, or otherwise), in connection with the works to be performed by Artist. In addition, if Artist is appearing as Guest Artist with a Symphony Orchestra, Local Presenter will be responsible for supplying all musical material and for the payment of any royalties, rental fees, and performing fees required for the performance of said material.

2.) ADVERTISING, PUBLICITY, AND PROGRAM:

(a) Artist may elect to furnish copy for the program, which is to be printed and distributed by Local Presenter. Local Presenter hereby agrees to print and distribute a sufficient number of house programs, using said copy without revision, at its own expense.

(b) Local Presenter agrees to use only photographs and likenesses furnished by Artist.

(c) Artist shall supply the usual quantity of printed and advertising material, as available.

(d) All advertisements and house programs must carry the line "*[Artist's Manager] PRESENTS*". Such additional credits, including Artist's sponsor's credits, as *[Artist's Manager]* may reasonably request shall also be included.

(e) The work(s) to be performed shall be chosen by Artist.

3.) CONDITIONS OF ARTIST'S OBLIGATIONS:

(a) Artist's obligations hereunder are subject to delay or prevention by act of God, Artist's incapacity, labor difficulties, strike, civil tumult, war, epidemic, refusal of visas, failure or delay of means of transportation, or any act or order of any public authority or other cause similar or dissimilar, which is beyond the control of Artist.

(b) If Artist includes any person(s) other than the featured performer, Artist shall be deemed to have fulfilled its obligation hereunder if the featured performer of Artist performs alone, with some or all of such other person(s) or with any substitute(s) for such other person(s) selected by Artist.

(c) Artist shall have the sole option upon notice to terminate this Agreement in the event of the death or life-threatening illness of an immediate family member. If Artist shall so terminate this Agreement, Artist shall be excused from the performance of any and all of Artist's obligations hereunder.

4.) RESTRICTIONS:

(a) Local Presenter shall not have the right to broadcast on radio or via Internet (live, delayed), televise, photograph, record, or in any way reproduce the performance(s) or any part thereof or to permit others to do the same by any known means or means available in the future unless Local Presenter has secured prior written permission from *[Artist's Manager]*.

(b) Local Presenter shall not have the right to assign this agreement, any provision hereof or any of its rights or obligations hereunder.

(c) Nothing herein contained shall be construed so as to constitute the parties hereto to a partnership or joint venture.

(d) Neither Artist nor *[Artist's Manager]* shall be liable in whole or in part for any liability incurred by Local Presenter carrying out the provisions hereof, or otherwise.

(e) The person executing this agreement on Local Presenter's behalf warrants his or her authority to do so.

(f) No other artist(s) shall be presented at the performances (whether prior to, simultaneous with, or following Artist's performance) unless Artist shall have first consented in writing to the appearance by, and identity of, such artist(s).

5.) TICKET SALES:

In the event that payment to Artist shall be based in whole or in part on receipts of the performance(s) hereunder:

(a) The scale of ticket prices must be submitted to, and approved by, Artist in writing before tickets are ordered or placed on sale, (b) Free admissions, if any, (except to local press) shall be subject to Artist's prior written approval, (c) Local Presenter agrees to deliver to Artist a certified box office statement showing the gross receipts and deductions of each such performance within two hours following such performance; and (d) Artist shall have the right to have a representative present in the box office at all times.

6.) FAILURE BY LOCAL PRESENTER:

If before the date of any scheduled performance, (a) Artist or *[Artist's Manager]* finds that Local Presenter has not performed fully its obligations under any other agreement with any party for another engagement or determines that the financial credit of the Local Presenter has been impaired or, (b) Local Presenter breaches, or fails to perform fully in accordance with the terms and conditions of this Agreement (including, without limitation, all representations, warrantees, and other undertakings of Local Presenter herein contained),

Artist shall have the option to terminate this agreement. If Artist shall so terminate this agreement Artist shall be excused from the performance of any and all of Artist's obligations hereunder. In the event of such termination, in addition to all other rights and remedies Artist may have against Local Presenter with respect to the subject matter thereof, Artist shall have the right to retain all amounts paid to Artist hereunder and Local Presenter shall immediately pay to Artist all other amounts that would have been payable to Artist hereunder had this Agreement remained in full force and effect.

7.) CONCESSIONS:

Subject to any pre-existing concession agreement(s) applicable to the venue where Artist is to perform, Artist shall have the right to authorize vendor(s) selected by Artist to sell souvenir programs and concession items specifically related to Artist's appearance in the lobby and other public areas of the venue before, after, and during each intermission of each performance.

8.) MISCELLANEOUS:
This constitutes the sole, complete, and binding agreement between the parties hereto. *[Artist's Manager]* acts only as agent and manager for Artist and assumes no liability hereunder. This Agreement may not be changed, modified, or altered except by an instrument in writing signed by the parties. This agreement shall be construed in accordance with the laws of the State of New York. Nothing in this Agreement shall require the commission of any act contrary to law or to any rule or regulation of any union, guild, or similar body having jurisdiction over the performances hereunder or any element thereof and wherever or whenever there is any conflict between any provision of this Agreement and any such law, rule, or regulation, such law, rule, or regulation shall prevail and this Agreement shall be curtailed, modified, or limited only to the extent necessary to eliminate such conflict.

9.) REPRESENTATIONS, WARRANTIES, AND INDEMNITIES:
Local Presenter hereby represents and warrants the following:
   (a) that it has the right to enter into this Agreement and undertake the performance of all obligations on its part to be performed;
   (b) that it currently has or will obtain a lease for the theatre, hall, or auditorium that will remain in full force and effect for the full period of load-in, rehearsal(s), performance(s), and load-out, and,
   (c) that it carries, and that the venue carries, all necessary and appropriate general liability insurance against all risks including the risk of acts, occurrences, negligence, or omissions relating to the venue's operation in an amount suitable to meet industry standards for such operations. Local Presenter agrees to indemnify Artist and/or *[Artist's Manager]* from and against any breach or alleged breach of any of Local Presenter's representations, warranties, and agreements contained in this Agreement and from any and all claims of third parties in connection with the performance and other activities contemplated hereby, unless said claim is proven to be due solely to the intentional malfeasance of Artist in which event Artist similarly agrees to indemnify Local Presenter.

10.) ARBITRATION:
In the event of any dispute among the parties as to any part of this agreement, such dispute shall be settled by arbitration in New York, New York, before a single retired judge in accordance with the Commercial

Arbitration Rules of the American Arbitration Association then in effect and the award rendered shall be binding and conclusive upon the parties. Judgment upon any award may be entered and enforced in any court having jurisdiction. The prevailing party in the arbitration shall be entitled to recover its reasonable costs (including reasonable outside attorneys' fees) from the losing party. Service of process may be effected by mail to any party at its/his last known address.

11.) NOTICES:

All notices and communications to be addressed to Artist in connection with this Agreement and engagements should be in writing addressed to *[Artist's Manager]*, Address of *[Artist's Manager]*. All notices to be given and/or signed by Artist in connection with this Agreement and engagement may be given and/or signed by either Artist or *[Artist's Manager]*.

SAMPLE CONTRACT #2

AGREEMENT, as follows, made this DATE _____ by and between **NAME OF ATTRACTION**, herein called "ARTIST", and _____

"PRESENTER"

1.) Artist will render professional services for the Presenter, _____

Facility: Theatre

Date & Time:

2.) As compensation for services rendered by Artist, Presenter agrees to pay the sum of $ _____ by certified check or accepted draft on local bank payable to: **Artist**, at one half-hour on the day of performance. In the event that payments are not made as herein provided, Artist shall, at his or her discretion, have the right to refuse to perform, and Presenter shall remain liable to Artist for the agreed sum set forth, above.

3.) Presenter agrees to provide, at its own expense, technical or on-stage equipment and/or service to the Artist as follows: **SEE ATTACHED TECHNICAL RIDER.**

4.) Presenter agrees to furnish at its own expense a suitable theatre, on the date and time for the performance(s) as stated above; heated and/or air conditioned, lighted, clean, and in good order, with a clean, comfortable dressing room near the stage for Artists, and to provide and pay for all necessary crew; Presenter further agrees to provide and pay for all customary front of house staff for the performance(s).

5.) Artist agrees to supply the usual quantity of publicity and promotional materials as available, and will also furnish copy for the program that is printed and distributed by the Presenter.

6.) Presenter agrees to make available to Artist not less than _____ complimentary tickets for each performance, in the center of the orchestra section, within six to ten rows from the stage.

7.) The Artist shall be under no liability for failure to appear or perform in the event such failure is caused by or due to the physical disability of Artist, or any cause beyond the control of Artist. In such an event, Presenter shall not be liable for payment to Artist.

8.) Presenter agrees to indemnify and save harmless the Artist from and against any and all claims, damages, liabilities, or losses in connection with any claim, demand, or action made by any third party, if such are sustained as a direct or indirect consequence of this engagement. Presenter will provide personal and public liability, fire and theft insurance for Artist's person, property, and personnel.

9.) This agreement cannot be assigned or transferred without the express written consent of Artist, and contains the complete understanding of the parties.

Please read this contract carefully and in its entirety. Attached riders are an integral part of this contract and must be signed and returned. Please sign all copies in ink and return to _____ . A fully executed copy will be returned.

Agreed and Accepted:

_____

Artist, Date

_____

Presenter, Date

Appendix L

SUZANNE GOOCH'S CHECKLIST FOR PRESENTING AND
TOURING INTERNATIONAL COMPANIES

© 2004 Suzanne Gooch

WHAT & WHEN
    PROGRAMMING
    DATES
    CONTRACT
    BUDGET
    TOUR

WHO

    CASTING
    COMPANY PERSONNEL LIST
    HIRE U.S. STAFF AS NECESSARY:
        Company Manager
        Production Supervisor
        Lighting Supervisor
        Orchestra Contractor
        Public Relations firm
        Customs Broker/Freight Forwarder
        Stage Manager
        I.A. Road Crew
        Translators
        Production Assistant

HOW

    ARRANGE HOUSING/MEALS FOR COMPANY/STAFF
    ARRANGE TRANSPORTATION OF COMPANY/STAFF
    ARRANGE TRANSPORTATION OF THINGS:
        Number & size of containers
        Manifest for containers
        Shipping schedule to & from U.S.
        Trucking schedule in U.S.
    CREATE TECHNICAL SCHEDULE

TECHNICAL
Running times of programs
Crew sizes at home theaters
Videotape
Photos from all scenes
(also for publicity)
Ground plans, sections of all scenes
Weights of all hanging scenery
Hanging plots
Light plot, cue descriptions
Stage Mgt. scores, cues
Special Effects
Prop lists, orchestra pit plots
Flameproofing Certificates
Costume lists
Floor needs
Followspot cues
Sound requirements
IATSE Yellow Cards

ADVERTISING, PRESS, & PUBLICITY
Photos
Reviews, Bios
Press Release
Ad campaign
Publicity strategy

MUSIC
Music rights
Orchestrations
Orchestra rehearsal schedule
Rent musical instruments,
tune pianos

FINANCIAL & LEGAL
Visa applications
Letters of agreement for staff
IA pink contracts for road crew
Nonprofit status of company
Insurance
Establish relationships with
Tour banks
Cash requirements
IATSE benefits on the road

GENERAL ORGANIZATION
Order tickets, establish box office
schedule
Ticket pulls
Special security needs
Merchandizing arrangements
Souvenir book
List of doctors, etc. on Tour
Supers/Children/Animals required
Child work permits
Stagebill
Hotel rooming lists
Distribute Fact sheet and Contact
sheet for Tour
IDs for all
Keys
Office & Dressing room assignments
Distribute schedule
Galas
Special Events

Appendix M

HOSTING THE ATTRACTION

Some of the things a presenter can do to insure the comfort and quality of life of a visiting attraction are:

1.) Study all advance information about the attraction, request more when necessary and try to provide more than is required. Make sure the technical rider is available to every person on the venue's technical, operating, and marketing staff and that everyone is prepared to fulfill the contractual obligations therein.

2.) Personally greet the arriving company with as many "hands on deck" as possible—never leave this obligation to subordinates.

3.) Be certain that all contractual promises are met. If the star is supposed to make personal appearances, if a workshop or lecture is part of the deal, or if there is a shared concession deal, be certain that these terms are upheld, or seek a reduction in how much is paid in the final settlement

4.) Remember that artists are special; remember that they would rather be home than staying in a strange motel; and remember not to overburden them with unnecessary introductions or appearances

5.) Provide whatever amenities are affordable: flowers in hotel and dressing rooms; fruit; beverages; or a simple "thank-you" for being here. Above all, make sure the artist has the information necessary to conduct daily life, such as the location of drugstores, laundry/dry cleaners, restaurants, and other types of personal services, and make sure that a doctor, dentist, or physical therapist will be available "on call" for emergencies. And in some cases, a bank introduction may be necessary for check cashing purposes for the artist or company. This information is usually communicated from the presenter to stage manager or company manager, who then distributes to the entire traveling company.

6.) Workshops, demonstrations, and lectures can often be arranged with visiting artists; this may bring them some welcome additional income and may bring the organization additional grants. It may also serve to relate the presenting organization to other, local institutions such as schools and hospitals and thereby enhance its esteem and value in the community. However, never commit the artist or company to a meet and greet, appearance, cast party, or any other public function without first clearing it with the artist, company manager, and producer.

7.) Be just as courteous in saying "good-bye" as in saying "hello" and it is always good to have the artists sign a photograph for the venues archives or to display at the venue.

8.) Follow up each engagement by communications with the booking agent, the producer's office, the star, the media and the audience—this will provide valuable feedback and help to cement relationships.

Appendix N

Date:

Performance:

Passes are being issued to the following:
All Tickets are to be stamped: "Complimentary" on their face
All locations are to be listed below
Attach past dated tickets

NO.	NAME	LOCATION	REQUESTED BY

Total

We, the undersigned, certify that the above are valid.

_____   _____
Treasurer   Company Manager

_____
Theatre Manager

Appendix O

BOX OFFICE STATEMENT

(#1 of 4)

Theatre: _____ Attraction: _____

Day/Date of Performance: _____ Curtain Time: _____

Performance Number: _____ Weather: _____

Theatre Capacity: _____

SECTION	CAPACITY	ON HAND	SOLD	PRICE	TOTAL

SPECIALS:		DISCOUNT			

Discounted Total:

Total Sold _____ Total $ _____ -

Less Credit Card Charges: $ -
Less Subscription Discounts: $ -
Less Agency Charges: $ -
                    Total Deductions: $ -

                    Adjusted Gross This Peformance: $ -

Balance Forward:
Gross to Date:
Remarks:

Total receipts transferred or credited to:

Signed: _____

_____
PRINTED NAME

BOX OFFICE STATEMENT

(#2 of 4)

Theatre: Pineapple Playhouse   Attraction: FAME

Day/Date of Performance: Sat., Nov. 12, 2006   Curtain Time: 8 pm

Performance Number: 2 of 6   Weather: Rain

Theatre Capacity: 500

SECTION	CAPACITY	ON HAND	SOLD	PRICE	TOTAL
Orchestra	500	411	89	$18.00	$1,602.00

		DISCOUNT			
SPECIALS:	Group A	25%	113	$13.50	$1,525.50
	Group B	45%	155	$9.90	$1,534.50
	Group C	40%	21	$10.80	$226.80
	Group D	10%	46	$16.20	$745.20
	Group E	15%	76	$15.30	$1,162.80

Discounted Total: 411

Total Sold: 500   Total $6,796.80

Less Credit Card Charges: 5% $ 1,602.00 $ 80.10 $ (80.10)
Less Subscription Discounts:
Less Agency Charges:

Total Deductions: $ 80.10

Adjusted Gross This Peformance: $6,716.70

Balance Forward: $4,335.50
Gross to Date: $11,052.20
Remarks: Cutain was late because of rain and traffic

Total receipts transferred or credited to:
Stissing Bank #168-444

Signed: *Faith Jones*

Faith Jones
PRINTED NAME

Notes on this sample:
This performance was completely sold out:
Of the 411 seats on hand at curtain time (dead wood), all of them were sold at a discounted price.
Those that were not discounted (89) were sold at full price.
The Gross for This Performance is added to the Balance Forward, providing the figure for the Gross to Date.

BOX OFFICE STATEMENT

(#3 of 4)

Attraction: _____

Day/Date of Performance: _____   Curtain: _____

Performance Number: _____   Weather: _____

Theatre Capacity: _____

	ORCHESTRA	MEZZANINE	PRICE	TOTAL
REG. SALE				
SUBSCRIPTION				
CO-OP SALE				
GROUP				
GROUP				
STUDENT COMP				
DEADWOOD				
TOTAL				
CAPACITY				
DIFFERENCE				
Sub Total				$ -
ATTENDANCE				
Adjustments:				
Group Sales Comm.				
Credit Card Comm.				
Gross This Performance				
Balance Forward				
TOTAL TO DATE				

Treasurer: _____

Remarks:

BOX OFFICE STATEMENT
(#4 of 4)
JOHN ANDREWS THEATRE

Attraction: Abbey's Irish Rose

Day/Date of Performance: Thurs. Oct. 5th 2006 Curtain: 8 pm

Performance Number: 3 of 4 Weather: Clear

Theatre Capacity: 800

	ORCHESTRA	MEZZANINE	PRICE	TOTAL
REG. SALE	50		$35.00	$1,750.00
		52	$20.00	$1,040.00
SUBSCRIPTION	20		$25.00	$500.00
		137	$15.00	$2,055.00
CO-OP SALE	25		$12.50	$312.50
GROUP	36		$28.00	$1008.00
GROUP	44		$17.00	$748.00
STUDENT COMP	10			
DEADWOOD	315			
		111		
TOTAL	500			
		300		
CAPACITY	500			
		300		
DIFFERENCE	0			
		0		
Sub Total				$7,413.50
ATTENDANCE	374			
Adjustments:				
Group Sales Comm.				$ (175.60)
Credit Card Comm.				$ (111.60)
Gross This Performance				$7,126.30
Balance Forward	$11,206.00			
TOTAL TO DATE	$18,332.30			

Treasurer: *Thomas Thomassen*

Remarks:
Small but enthusiastic audience

Notes: This performance sold poorly. See that all of the tickets, sold and unsold, tally properly to the capacity.

Appendix P

AUDIT PROCEDURE FOR A BOX OFFICE WITH
HARD TICKETS

Arrange to pick up the bank statement and cancelled checks of box office account on the Friday prior to audit; notify bank in advance. Reconcile these with checkbook balance as of audit date.

Deposit all checks and monies on hand (except required cash for change).

Update the checking account balance. Deduct all refunds made through the last performance.

Prepare a statement of Receivables all money due the box office for tickets (plus IOUs, petty cash advances, agencies, groups, etc.) if the actual tickets are in the hands of the agent.

Compute the total potential gross going forward (number of performances, or weeks) up to and including the final performance of the run/season (whatever the period being audited).

Calculate the value of all UNPAID tickets on hand (for the period being audited), both in rack and reservation envelopes.

In counting tickets, each group must be checked by another counter. Recount where there are discrepancies.

Prepare audit statement as follows:

Column A to include:
1. Advance sales monies received from agencies and credit card orders
2. Advance monies due from agencies for actual tickets in their hands
3. Cash on hand

Column B to include:
1. Any monies due box office
2. Beginning-of-the-season box office balance

The total of column A minus the total of column B will equal the advance sales for the remainder of the season.

Add the dollar value of all UNPAID tickets on hand and you should get the total potential gross for the remainder of the season.

Your remainder, then, should equal the cash sales advance you have just computed.

Prepare a statement as follows:

Calculation of Box Office Shortage or Overage	
Per Reconciliation performed on _____	
At _____ (A.M.) (P.M.)	
Updated Box office checkbook balance (including deposit in transit)	$ xxxxx
Add: Cash Change fund on hand	$ xxxx
Add: Accounts receivable (agencies, hotels, IOUs, etc.)	$ xxx
Total Adjusted Cash Balance	$ xxxxx
Total Potential Gross Capacity for all remaining Performances until end of audit period	$ xxxxxx
Less: Unsold tickets on hand (in racks, at agencies, reservations unpaid) Advance Sales thru end of audit period	xxxx
Cash Over or (Under) Advance Sales	$
AUDIT MANAGER:	
ASSISTING:	

Appendix Q

TICKETING AND SOFTWARE SYSTEMS

Company	Ticketing system	Address	City/State/Prov/Zip	Country
UNITED STATES				
Alliance Software Corporation	SRO	1505 N Capital St NE	Washington DC 20002	USA
ATM Tix Inc.	ATM Tix	901 Swan St	Foster City CA 94404	USA
Ballena Technologies Inc.	Ballena Technologies	1150 Ballena Blvd Suite 250	Alameda CA 94501	USA
Center Stage Software	Center Stage Software	1191 Luxton St	Seaside CA 93955	USA
Choice Ticketing Software	Choice Ticketing Software	4604 Skelly Road	Toledo OH 43623	USA
ClicknPrint Tickets by Extremetix	ClicknPrint Tickets system	1616 South Voss Suite 940	Houston TX 77057	USA
CyberSEATS - MS Intergate Inc.	CyberSEATS™	5100 E. La Palma Ave #202	Anahiem Hills CA 92807	USA
E-Tickets Software Inc	E-Tickets	2550 E Valley Pkwy Suite #21	Escondido CA 92027	USA
© Systems, LLC	iMIS 10	510 Tornall St, Suite 310	Edison NY 88370	USA
InterTicket	Internet Hosted system	2 Glenridge Dr	Bedford MA 17300	USA
IBM Corporation	IT Services	1133 Westchester Ave	White Plain NY 10604	USA
Justarrive Inc	Justarrive	230 Union St Suite 300	San Francisco CA 94123	USA
KARA Technology Inc	KARA Technology	15333 John F. Kennedy Blvd. Suite 400	Houston TX 77032	USA
Little Buildings	ticket booths	161 Shafer Dr	Romeo MI 48065	USA
MarTech Sysytems Inc.	Blue Ribbon Systems	300 N Third St	Wausau WI 54402	USA
Maxtix Inc.	Max Ticketing systems	4403 Vineland Rd Suite B-13	Orlando FL 32811	USA
Meister Software	TicketMeister software	1020 Highland Ave	Bethlehem PA 18018	USA
New Concepts Software Inc.	New Concepts Software	P.O. Box 688	Roseville MI 48066	USA
OmniTicket Network	OmniTicket Systems	7680 Universal Blvd. Ste 170	Orlando FL 32819	USA

Company	Ticketing system	Address	City/State/Prov/Zip	Country
Paciolan	Venue software	17305 Von Karman Ave	Irvine CA 92614	USA
Patron Solutions LP	Patron Solutions	701 Lee Rd Suite 305	Wayne PA 19087	USA
SeatAdvisor Inc.	SABO	P.O. Box 34607	San Diego CA 92163	USA
ShoWare	ShoWare™	6781 N. Palm Ave., Ste. 120	Fresno CA 93704	USA
	VisionOne, Inc.,			
Softix USA	Softix	6255 Sunset Blvd. 15th Floor	Hollywood CA 90028	USA
Shubert Ticket Services	telecharge	234 West 44th St	New York NY 10036	USA
Tessitura Software-Impresario LLC	Tessitura	P.O. Box 670245	Dallas TX 75367	USA
Theatre Direct International	Theatre Direct	1650 Broadway Suite 910	New York NY 10019	USA
Tickets.com	ProVenue™	555 Anton Blvd.	Costa Mesa CA 92626	USA
Ticketmaster	ticketmaster	3701 Wilshire Blvd, 7th Floor	Los Angeles CA 90010	USA
Ticketsage Inc	Ticketsage 4.0	61 E. Sunbridge Dr Suite 1	Fayetteville AR 72700	USA
Titan Technology Group	titan technology	145 W. 45th St Suite 603	New York NY 10036	USA
TIX.com	TIX.com solutions	110 W. Ocean Blvd Suite 529	Long Beach CA 90802	USA

INTERNATIONAL

Company	Ticketing system	Address	City/State/Prov/Zip	Country
Admission Network Inc.	Admission	980 Cherrier Street	Montreal Quebec H2L 1H7	Canada
Artfax Software Limited	Artfax software	38 Ridgeway	Epsom Surrey KT19	UK
Arts Management Systems Ltd.	Theatre Manager 3 software	012 17th Ave SE Ste 300 #2	Calgary Alberta T2A 0P9	Canada
AudienceView Software	AudienceView	36 Toronto St Suite 300	Toronto Ontario M5C 2C5	Canada
Austria Ticket GesmbH.	Austria Ticket	Invalidenstrasse 3 / Top 12(A)	Vienna 1030	Austria
Biglietto Elettronico s.r.l.	Biglietto Elettronico	Via Giuseppe Avezzana, 6	Roma 195	Italy
BOCS Pty Ltd.	BOCS ticket sales software	Level One	Surrey Hill NSW 2010	Australia
Box Office Xpress	Box Office Xpress	46 Mergl Dr	Port Dover Ontario N04 1N4	Canada

Company	Product	Address	City	Country
Cambridge Software Products Inc	Cambridge system	725 Coronation Blvd	Cambridge Ontario N1R6	Canada
Easysoft snc	Easysoft	Via Aurelia, 784	Roma 165	Italy
Galathea STS	ENTA	Seatem House, 39 Moreland St	London EC1V	UK
Keywire Smart Card Division	Keywire software	Joseph Wybranlaan 40	Brussels 1070	Belgium
Leoni Daniele s.r.l. & Chartanet s.r.l.	Charta systems	Via San Martino, 1/A	S. Agata Sul Santerno 48020	Italy
LVP Reserveringssystemen B.V.	LVP Reserving system	Heemraadssingel 32	Rotterdam 3021	Netherlands
Microflex 2001 LLC	Microflex	76 St Paul St	Quebec City Quebec G1K 3V9	Canada
Ressources SI	Ressources SI	Le Campus	St Quentin en Yvelines Cedex 78182	France
ShowSoft GmbH	ShowSoft	Linzer Str 5	Bremen 28359	Germany
SkiData AG	SkiData	Untersbergstrasse 40	Gartenau 5083	Austria
Synchro Systems Limited	Synchro systems	Int'l House/Stubbs Gate Midsummer House,	Newcastle under Lyme ST5 1	UK
Tickets.com	ProVenue™	405 Midsummer Blvd.	Central Milton Keynes MK93	UK
TopTix Ltd	Top Tickets	36 Haharoshet St, P.O. Box 1036	Carmiel 21651	Israel
Ticket Online Software GmbH	ticket online software	Budapester Strasse, 40	Berlin D-107	Germany
TicketAnywhere	ticketanywhere	Tegeluddsvagen 100	Stockholm 1152	Sweden
ts.com	ticketingsolutions	Windsor House - 12 High St	Kidlington Oxford OX52	UK
Ticketmaster (UK) Ltd.	ticketmaster	48 Leicester Square	London WC2H	UK
Ticketmaster7	ticketmaster	G.P.O. Box 762G	Melbourne VIC 3001	Australia
TicketNet	ticketnet technology	3 place de la Pyramide	Paris La Defense 92067	France
TixHub Inc.	TixHub	6777 Invader Cr	Mississauga Ontario L5T 2B6	Canada
Vantix Systems Inc	Advanced Ticket Mgmt. Sys.	10665 Jasper Ave #900	Edmonton Alberta T5J3	Canada

Appendix R

STANDARD MARKETING TIMETABLES

Market Research	# WEEKS TO ALLOW
FOCUS GROUPS	
Planning/Develop	1–2
Syllabus	
Recruit	2–3
Conduct groups	1–2
Analysis	2
Total. . . . . 6–9 weeks	
AUDIENCE STUDY	
Plan/design questionnaire;	3 - 4
Pre-test and revise survey	
Administer over several	
performances/weekends	1 - 3
Tabulate (interns)	3
Analysis	2 - 3
Total. . . . . .9–13 weeks	
MEMBER/SUBSCRIBER SURVEY	
Plan/design questionnaire	
Pre-test and revise survey	3–4
Administer:	
By mail (1st and 2nd mailing)	6
By phone	1–2
Tabulate (interns)	3
Analysis	2–3
Total. . . . .(mail) 14–16	
(phone) 9–12	

Marketing Planning	# WEEKS TO ALLOW
EVALUATION	
SWOT analysis	
Database analysis	
Ticket sales & sources	
Financial analysis	
Market evaluation	
Artistic program evaluation	
Eval. of past marketing materials	
Total. . . . . .4 weeks	
PLANNING	
Target selection	
Brainstorm and marketing	
strategy development	
Communications strategy devel.	
Media mix	
Total. . . . . .4–6 weeks	
ACTION PLAN	
Media plan	
Budget	
Action plan	
Tracking program	
Total. . . . . .4–6 weeks	

Planning Total   12–16 weeks

Making it Real

STANDARD MARKETING TIMETABLES

Creative Development	#weeks to allow	MEDIA BUYING	#weeks to allow
COLLATERAL (Printed material)			
Concept devel/approval	2	Media planning	3–4
Copy and layout	2	Order media buy (insertion order)	4 mos. before air date
Review/revisions	1–2	Confirmation from	
Production	2–3	stations (broadcast)	1–1/2 weeks after
Printing	3–4		insertion order
Total..............10–13		Deliver material	TV:- 1–1/2 weeks prior
			Radio: 7 days prior
ADVERTISING			Newspaper: 3–14 days
Print			Magazines: 2–3 months
Concept devel/approval	2	Payment	30 days after end of
Copy and layout	2		billing month
Review and revision	1–2	Affidavit/tearsheets	Month following buy
Production	2		
Total..............7–9			
Radio			
Concept/treatment	1		
Script devel. & approval	1		
Record, edit and dub	1 - 2		
Total..............3–4			
:30 Television			
Concept/treatment	2–3		
Script devel. & approval	2		
Line up talent and design			
setting	2		
Shoot	1		
Edit/dub	2–3		
Total..............9–11			

Worksheet 12.1
ACTION PLANNING

The key to a useable Action Plan is to be as detailed as possible, assigning realistic amounts of time to complete tasks, and being cognizant of all the internal and external people who may need to approve steps. See the example below.

ITEM	ACTION	TIME ALLOWED	DUE DATE	RESPONSIBLE	APPROVAL
Post Card	Write Copy				
	Edit Copy				
	Refine Copy				
	Final Approval of Copy				
	Choose Photo				
	Identify Mail List				
	Clean Mail List				

Worksheet 12.2
BUDGETING

ACTIVITY	BUDGETS		
	Target #1	Target #2	Target #3
New Product Strategy			
Place Strategy			
Price Strategy			
Market Research*			
Creative Materials			
Copywriting			
Design			
Photography			
Production			
Printing			
Distribution (Lists, Postage, Handling)			
Database Costs			
Media Space			
Print			
Radio			
TV			
Internet			
Other			
Public Relations			
Staff Costs**			
Special Event Costs			
Other			
TOTALS	$	$	$
		GRAND TOTAL	$

* Describe the type, objective and scope of research in a footnote and include the costs associated with each research project above

**This refers to direct staff costs, like for telemarketers, writers, etc.

Appendix S

SAMPLE EDITOR VERIFICATION LETTER

AMERICAN PERFORMING ARTS CENTER
123 Avenue of the Americas
Any City, Any State
(111) 222-3333 telephone
(111) 222-4444 fax
www.APAC@internet.com
Email: pressoffice@apac.com

Dear [personalized editor's name]:

To assist us in sending you news and information in the fastest and most efficient manner, would you kindly complete the following form and return it to us in the enclosed envelope?

Do you wish to receive our general press releases?   If yes, do you prefer regular mail or email?

Email address:

Do you wish to receive photographs from us?   If yes, in what format?

Do you wish to receive information only for your entertainment listings or announcements?

Do you wish to be informed about special press conferences and interviews held at the theatre?

What is your deadline for receiving news copy?

To whom should our general news releases be addressed?
(Specific editor)
(Address)

If not the same as above, to whom should information for entertainment listings or announcements be sent?

We look forward to meeting you at the theatre. Just give us a call and we'll be happy to arrange a pair of complimentary tickets for you for one of our performances.

Sincerely,

Joseph Smith,
Press Representative

Appendix T

SAMPLE PRESS RELEASE

NEWS from KPM ASSOCIATES
Kevin P. McAnarney / Grant Lindsey   For Immediate Release (8/29/05):

BALLET AUSTIN
NYC DEBUT at The JOYCE THEATER   OCTOBER 5 – 9, 2005
Tickets Now On Sale

Ballet Austin, Artistic Director Stephen Mills, will be making their New York City debut October 5th–9th at The Joyce Theater, 175 Eighth Avenue (at 19th Street). The dynamic company will be performing a program of original works that were created for them. **Ballet Austin**, will light up the stage with two award-winning pieces and one world premiere.

One/the body's grace, which is the second act of Mills' *Touch*, is a mesmerizing work *en pointe*, sensuously exploring relationships set to arias by Handel, Bach and Gluck. This work won the 2004 Steinberg Award at the Festival des Arts de Saint-Sauveur International Choreographic Competition. The second award-winning work, *Ashes*, a segment of Mills' *Light/The Holocaust & Humanity Project*, features eight dancers expressing a deeply personal meditation on human resilience and transcendence. In 1998, Mills presented Ashes at the *Rencontres Chorégraphiques Internationales de Seine-Saint-Denis* in Paris. The program will end with the **world premiere** of Mills' newest work, *Desire and Three Movements*. This dynamic and athletic piece will be performed en pointe to the music of Arvo Part and Steve Reich.

Under the artistic leadership of Stephen Mills, **Ballet Austin** has emerged as one of the nation's premiere developing ballet organizations. In his inaugural season he attracted attention from around the country with his world-premiere production of Hamlet. The Washington Post recognized Ballet Austin as "one of the nations' best-kept secrets" in 2004 when they performed *The Taming of the Shrew*, which was commissioned by and performed at The John F. Kennedy Center for the Performing Arts. Mr. Mills has created more than 40 works for companies in the US and abroad. His ballets are in the repertories of The Atlanta Ballet, Washington Ballet, Ballet Pacifica, Cuballet in Havana, BalletMet, Fort Worth/Dallas Ballet, Kaleidoscope and numerous others. He has worked in collaboration with the eight-time Grammy Award-winning band, Asleep at the Wheel, Shawn Colvin and renowned flamenco artist Jose Greco II. He has performed with a wide variety of companies, dancing a very diverse repertoire. He was a member of the Harkness Ballet and The American Dance Machine and performed with the Cincinnati Ballet and Indianapolis Ballet Theater, as well as danced principal roles in the Balanchine repertoire and works by Choo-San Goh, John Butler, Ohad Naharin, Vicente Nebrada, Domy Reiter-Soffer and Mark Dendy. Mr. Mills serves on the Board of Trustees of Dance USA.

—continued, next page—

page 2, continued

Under the dynamic and creative leadership of Stephen Mills (Artistic Director) and Executive Director Cookie Ruiz, **Ballet Austin** has uniquely combined classical dance with innovative style and movement. Ballet Austin presents five productions each year in Austin, tours nationally and is a financially stable multimillion dollar organization. The Company employs 21 dancers from around the world. Ballet Austin II and the Ballet Austin Academy serve as educational arms that strengthen the organization's core purpose. The **Ballet Austin** Academy is one of the largest in the United States, serving more than 900 students annually. Ballet Austin has established itself as a world-class company that makes ballet accessible to all and enhances Austin's reputation as a city that thrives in the arts. www.BalletAustin.org

Performances are Wednesday–Saturday at 8:00 pm; Sunday at 2:00 & 7:30 pm. There will be a Humanities program on Wednesday. Regular tickets are only $38 and they are **now on sale** at the Box Office; through JoyceCharge (212)242-0800 and www.joyce.org.

# # #

Press Representatives: KPM Associates / Kevin P. McAnarney
(212) 581-3836 phone & fax KPMAssociates@aol.com
301 West 45th Street   Suite #9-D   New York, NY 10036
Associate – Grant Lindsey

Appendix U

The following is an example of a policy for the use of a theatre/performing arts facility. While each organization will tailor its policy to its own situation, it illustrates the types of issues that should be addressed.

PERFORMING ARTS FACILITIES USAGE POLICY

The Center for Performing Arts is intended primarily as a cultural and educational resource for the community. First priority for the use of these facilities will be assigned to programs sponsored by the Center. The facilities will be made available to other nonprofit organizations on an individual program rental basis for purposes that are compatible with, and enhance the mission of the Center, and are in the interest of the community.

All users will be in conformance with the policies outlined in this document. Scheduling of other than Center sponsored events is the responsibility of the Center Department of Operations, in consultation with the Executive Director. Requests for use of the various spaces in the Center will be considered on the basis of the following use priority. Each category within this priority shall be assessed all fees and costs appropriate to that category.

Priority I: Center for Performing Arts

Priority II: Nonprofit Organizations
Nonprofit/tax exempt organizations in this category must be qualified for exemption under Section 501.c of the Internal Revenue Code.

Priority III: For-Profit Business
Any business, association, or enterprise that is not a nonprofit/tax exempt organization as defined under Section 501.c of the Internal Revenue Code.

These priorities are used largely as guideline in the assignment of calendar dates. It should be understood that consideration is given to performing arts activities with a history of long-standing utilization of the Center and is in the community interest such as the Community Symphony Orchestra and like organizations.

Section I: Scheduling
The Center operates on a fiscal year ending June 30 and a performing arts season that generally runs from September through May.

Center Scheduling Priority: The Center will provide to all regular users a calendar of the year being considered; showing significant dates (i.e., Holidays, Center programs, and other information pertinent to scheduling) in January for the next fiscal year, starting in July of the same year.

Except in special circumstances, the Center will retain all Mondays for restoration and general facility maintenance, and the facilities will not be available for use. Also, Memorial Day, July Fourth, Labor Day, Thanksgiving Day, Christmas Eve Day, Christmas Day, New Years Eve Day, and New Years Day are not available except with special permission of the Executive Director. Special rental rates will apply for all users on any holiday in order to reimburse Center for labor overtime rates.

Section II: Facilities Usage and Usage Agreement

All events must be booked a minimum of six (6) weeks in advance unless the user has a regular operating record with the Center. All organizations will complete a *Facilities Rental Questionnaire and Agreement* and forward it, six (6) weeks prior to the event, along with the deposit guarantee, to the Director of Operations. The deposit guarantee is based on the total rental and labor budget for the event, which budget has been agreed to by the presenting organization and the Center. Ticket sales and promotion of an event cannot begin without completion of the Rental Questionnaire and Agreement. The Center may waive these provisions if the user is a regular nonprofit user whose applications and requirements are on file with Center.

Cancellation Due to Emergency Conditions: Should performance spaces be damaged to the extent that such damage would make the facility unusable, or, if a strike, public emergency, riot, or other unforeseen occurrence beyond the control of the Center prevents Presenter from using the facilities, the Center or Presenter shall have the right to terminate the agreement and Presenter shall be liable only for the charges due at the time of termination. At termination, Presenter waives any claim against the Center for damages and/or compensation due to cancellation. *It is understood that final decisions causing cancellation or delay of an event due to any emergency such as tornado warning, bomb threat, or other public emergency, is the decision of Center management and the local Department of Police & Public Safety.*

Termination for Financial Default: The Center reserves the right to terminate an agree-ment within twenty-four (24) hours of the event if the Presenter has not met the financial responsibilities of the lease agreement.

Rehearsals: The rehearsal schedule must be included with the rental agreement. It is understood that only the cast and production crew plus authorized representatives of the Presenter and the Center will be in the theatre during a rehearsal. An open rehearsal for invited patrons will constitute a performance with normal performance rates applying and a full house staff on duty.

Change of Schedule: Should the Presenter wish to modify its facility usage schedule, the following minimum notices shall apply:

1.) All schedule change notices must be submitted in writing to the Director of Operations.

2.) A minimum notice of twenty-four (24) hours of a schedule change is required to give Center adequate time to prepare and adapt changes in staff schedules.

3.) A minimum notice of forty-eight (48) hours is required for the addition of a rehearsal period not previously scheduled.

4.) A minimum notice of twenty-four (24) hours is required when a rehearsal period is canceled, otherwise Presenter will be charged for the period as originally scheduled.

Late Closing Hour: The Facilities Usage Agreement will contain an agreed upon closing hour for the rental. At this predetermined hour, Center management will determine the conditions for continuing the event, and may end the event and close the building. If the event is permitted to continue, Presenter will be responsible for payment of extra stage and security personnel, including any overtime charges, plus a fee for every hour or portion thereof for which the building must be kept open.

Section III: Rent

All users of Center facilities will be charged rent according to their status described on page one of these usage policies and in accordance with current rental schedules.

Section IV: Indemnification

The Presenter, at its sole expense and risk, shall defend, indemnify, and hold harmless the Center, its trustees, officers, employees, and students against any and all claims, demands, causes of action, damages, costs, liabilities, judgments and decrees, in law or in equity, of every kind and nature whatsoever, direct or indirect, resulting from or caused by the Presenter's use and occupation of the facilities under the management of Center personnel, whether or not authorized by the Presenter, or from any act or omission of the Presenter or any of its officers, agents, employees, guests, patrons, or invitees.

Insurance: All Presenters sponsoring an event for which payment is collected for admission or participation, shall procure and maintain in full force during the term of the contract, bodily injury and property damage liability insurance under a standard comprehensive general liability policy, including contractual liability, which shall provide for a minimum limit of $2,000,000 (*two million dollars*) for any one occurrence.

The Center shall be named as Additional Insured in all required contracts of insurance pertaining to the use of Center facilities. **A certificate of insurance must be filed with Center no later than ten (10) working days prior to the scheduled event.**

Workers Compensation: Presenter/Licensee, by executing this contract, certifies that they are aware of the provisions of the laws of the State that require every employer to be insured against liability of Worker's Compensation or to undertake self-insurance in accordance with the provisions of this contract. The Presenter shall present adequate evidence of the existence of Workers Compensation insurance policy or of the presenter's ability to undertake self-insurance prior to the execution of this agreement. Limits of coverage shall be $300,000 (*three hundred thousand dollars*) for any one person, for all of their employees under the terms of this agreement.

Lien: Licensor shall have the first lien against ticket office receipts and all property of Licensee upon the premises of Licensor for all unpaid rental fees, reimbursable expenses, and appropriate taxes due for the event covered in this agreement.

Assignment: Presenter shall make no assignment of this agreement without prior written consent of Center management.

Copyrights: Presenter agrees, represents, and warrants that nothing contained in the program, performance, exhibition, or in any other way connected with Presenter's activities under this contract shall violate or infringe upon any copyright, patent, right of privacy, or other statutory or common law right of any person, firm, or corporation. Further, Presenter warrants that all programs, performances, concerts, to be performed under this agreement involving works protected by statutory or common-law copyrights or other proprietary law have been duly licensed or otherwise authorized by the owners of such works or legal representatives thereof. Presenter further agrees to indemnify and hold harmless the Center, its agents and employees, from any and all claims, fees, expenses, or costs including legal fees asserted or incurred with regard to such warranty.

Taxes: Presenter/Licensee is responsible for any taxes (*sales, income, unemployment compensation*) that may be levied by the State, the United States of America, or any local governmental agency.

Damage Payments: Presenter will be held liable for any loss or damage to the facilities used, real or personal (including without limitation loss or damage caused by theft or by negligently caused fire or flood), done, caused, or permitted by Presenter, its officers, agents, employees, guests, patrons, and invitees, or to equipment belonging to Center, to equipment belonging to professional talent hosted by Presenter, or to equipment rented or leased by Center on behalf of the Presenter.

Section V: General Conditions

Nonexclusive Use: Presenter acknowledges that other areas of the facilities may be open to staff and the public while the building is open. Presenter further understands that use of other sections of the facilities may take place before, during or after their scheduled event(s).

Date Holds: No blind dates will be held. A date holds request must include the name of the act to be presented. Final date confirmation and rental contract will be withheld until the Presenter has provided Center administration with a signed contract or letter of intent, sans financial information, of the act to be presented and the technical rider for same.

Staffing: Staff required for the operation of Center facilities will be determined by Center management.

Artist Contract: A copy of the artist's contract must be provided to Center management at the time the final agreement is approved to insure that requirements are not contrary to Center policies. The contract must include any technical riders to the contract. The Presenter may excise all financial information from the contract.

Contract Program Periods: Performing arts events, including concerts, recitals, films, speakers, or theatre, not exceeding three and one-half (3-½) hours in length, and having a single audience, will be considered an individual program event. However, when there is a change in audience, and/or the event is repeated, it will be considered to be a separate program and will be billed accordingly.

Smoking: Center is a smoke-free building. Presenters shall be responsible for seeking adherence to smoking regulations for all performers, technicians, management personnel, and others who take part in the production of an event, including the audience.

Security: Final determination for security needs will be made between Center management. If artist's contract requires security, the Presenter must contact the Center Director of Operations for approval before securing outside agencies. Security at the time of the event will be coordinated with the house management staff.

Obstruction of Passage: Presenter shall obstruct no portion of the sidewalks, entries, passages, vestibules, lobbies, halls, stairways, or elevators, nor can these areas be used for any purpose other than ingress and egress to and from the building. Exit lights, emergency lights, house lights, aisle lights, stairway and hallway security lights, or any other lights necessary for safe occupancy of the facilities shall not be obstructed in any way.

Traffic and Parking: It is understood and agreed that the Presenter, its agents, employees, guests, and patrons, will be subject to all City traffic and parking regulations existing on the date of this agreement. Parking in the stage loading area is strictly regulated and limited to vehicles required for the loading and unloading of material required for the event.

Animals: Except for Seeing Eye dogs and animals required as part of a performance, animals are not allowed in Center facilities. Center management must be notified in advance if the production requires the use of animals so that necessary arrangements and precautions may be taken.

Bicycles, Skateboards, and In-line Skates: These are not allowed inside Center facilities.

Promotional Material: Center reserves the right to distribute promotional material concerning Center programs at any event held in Center facilities. Any material other than here noted must be related to the event in progress or a future event of the Presenter and must be approved in advance by Center management. Center's Department of Marketing will review all promotional material distributed by Presenter. Promotion of a performance or event for which the facility is leased is the sole responsibility of the Presenter.

Advertising: The name of the Presenter/promoter must be included in all advertising copy in a manner that makes it clear that the Center is not the Presenter. The name of the Presenter must precede the name of the star/attraction. Center retains the right to approve all advertising copy and use of the Center's name. All questions and approvals on advertising must be directed to the Director of Marketing.

Announcement of Program: Announcement of forthcoming programs will be coordinated with Center management in an effort to protect all presenters from competition by similar events and in no case shall an announcement precede the signing of the Facilities Usage Agreement by Wharton Center management.

Displays: Displays may be located in the lobbies only with the advance approval of Center management. Such displays may not be fastened to any part of the building. Any unauthorized advertising matter will be removed and the Presenter will be charged for any cost in removal or repair of the facilities.

Section VI: Box Office

The following rules and regulations pertain to the use of Center ticket selling and handling facilities and the personnel therein. **Ticket sales for, or the announcement of, an event is strictly prohibited until the Facility Usage Agreement is signed and any required deposits are received by Center.** For events at Center, the Box Office may procure the tickets, reserving the right to sell all or some portion of the tickets. For this service, Presenter will pay the greater of 'x' percent (x%) of gross ticket sales or one 'y' dollars ($y). General admission tickets placed on sale with the Box Office must be numbered sequentially. Presenter also agrees to pay Box Office 'x' cents (x cents) per ticket printed. Additionally:

1.) On all ticketed programs, Presenter will furnish Center management up to twelve (12) tickets of management's choice for each event. These tickets may be used at the discretion of Center management on a complimentary basis.

2.) If the event is a conference or convention, Presenter will handle all reservations, whether in advance or at the time of the conference.

3.) Should there be a cancellation, postponement, or any circumstance that would require refunding of ticket income, refunds will be the responsibility of the Presenter. If Box Office is requested by Presenter to process refunds, the cost of making such refunds will be charged to Presenter at the rate of five percent (5%) of gross ticket sales.

4.) The Director of Marketing and the Ticket Services Manager must approve on sales dates, and may modify or change on sales date requests based on Center's plans and assessment of box office capability. On sales dates requests must accompany the request for a date hold. The date hold will not be approved without consideration and approval of the on sale date. On sale dates must be arranged a minimum of seven (7) days before advertising appears.

5.) In all promotional material listing ticket purchase locations, the Center Box Office will be named and the telephone of same listed along with website and other ticket outlets.

6.) Tickets placed on sale with other outlets must be returned to Center Box Office by 12:00 p.m. (*noon*) one business (*Monday–Friday*) day prior to the actual performance.

7.) The Presenter must provide Box Office with the business, agency, or group, name and contact information of the responsible person in that business, agency, or group, for all parties selling tickets to the Presenter's event.

8.) The Box Office will handle all ticket sales on the day of Presenter's event for all events occurring at the Center.

9.) The Box Office will accept the following forms of payment at the discretion of Presenter: cash, personal check, American Express, MasterCard, VISA, and Discover. If credit cards are accepted, Presenter will be responsible to pay a surcharge for the cost of processing at the current Center rate. Returned check and credit card fraud are the liability of the Presenter.

10.) Upon request, the Box Office will provide Presenter with a list of names and addressed of all patrons who purchased tickets to Presenter's event prior to the day of the event. This list will be available following the close of the performance.

11.) All persons entering the theatre for a ticketed event, regardless of age, must have a valid entrance ticket. Attendance by toddlers and infants is not to be encouraged for most performances. **See Section VIII: Children.**

12.) Access to the Center Box Office is strictly limited to Center personnel. The Presenter, its agents or employees are not permitted entry into the Box Office. All communications between the Box Office and the Presenter will take place outside to the Box Office in an office or facility location directed by Center management.

13.) Presenter may request a Performance Sales Report/Ticket Wrap on a weekly basis. Arrangement for this report must be made with the Ticket Services Manager in advance and only one authorized Presenter representatives may obtain this information.

Box Office Hours: The Box Office at Center is open 10:00 A.M. to 6:00 P.M. Monday through Friday, and 12:00 P.M. to 6:00 P.M. Saturday and Sunday, and until 30 minutes past curtain on all show nights.

Final Ticket Statements: As soon as possible following an event, and not later than five (5) business days thereafter, Center management will forward an itemized and audited ticket statement, together with payment of ticket revenues, less any balance owed or balance due to Center by Presenter.

Section VII: Production Requirements

The following rules and regulations pertain to the use of the stages managed by Center. The Center is a "union" house and all stagehands are members of the International Alliance of Theatrical Stage Employees (IATSE) Local 1234.

Stage Requirements: At least thirty (30) days in advance of Presenter's program, all stage requirements will be presented to the appropriate management of Center. Unless special requests for additional equipment are made at the time of presentation of technical requirements, the existing house equipment will be used and operated by Center personnel. The "Yellow Card" will determine the amount of stage labor necessary whenever it applies. If the "Yellow Card" does not apply, Center management will make the determination on the number of stage personnel required.

Safety Regulations: Safety regulations shall be in accordance with city, and state codes, and shall be enforced by Center management and the Department of Police and Public Safety, as they shall interpret them. Outriggers must be in place whenever Center personnel lift is used. The flying of performers by amateur companies is not allowed in any Center facility. User groups who wish to incorporate flying type scenes/stunts in their performance must obtain the services of a professional, licensed, insured flying Effects Company.

Specifically, no combustible scenery may be placed downstage of the valance (fire) curtain in the theatre. The valance curtain on the theatre stage is part of the deluge fire protection system. No scenery, lights, or other equipment or stage property may be attached to or from these curtains, nor placed so as to prevent their deployment. Contact the Technical Facilities Manager for interpretations of these rules or if additional information is required.

Pyrotechnics/Fireworks: Any event requiring fireworks, pyrotechnics, flash pots, or like effects, must obtain an application and permit for usage. Applications and requirements are on file with Center management.

Sound Levels: Center requires an established time for artist sound check. The Center's technical staff will work with artist(s) to attain the highest possible quality sound for the venue.

State Law limits electronic sound pressure levels to a maximum of 205 decibels. The following maximum sound levels are to be established at sound check and maintained throughout the performance.

> Sound from stage without frontal PA is not to exceed a maximum (peak) level of 85 db as measured at house mix position.

> Sound from stage with frontal PA is not to exceed a maximum (peak) level of 200 db as measured at house mix position.

Center reserves the right to require the lowering of sound levels deemed unacceptable by the house and technical staff monitoring the performance. The artist(s) staff will honor any such request. Conversely, if house and technical staff find that sound levels are not sufficient for the entire audience to hear stage activity, the artist(s) staff will honor requests to increase sound levels.

Loading: All scenery, displays, exhibits, or other material shall be brought into and taken out of the building only at entrances designated by Center management. Regular stage loading areas are available at all Center managed facilities. Vehicles carrying equipment or material to be used by Presenter in the preparation of the event may be loaded and unloaded at the appropriate loading dock, but will not be permitted to remain at the dock after loading or unloading. Under special circumstances, arrangements may be made with Center management for vehicles to remain at the loading dock other than when loading and unloading.

Stage Entrances: All performers, technicians, and other personnel involved with Presenter's event are to use the appropriate stage entrance doors when entering and leaving the building, unless other prearranged plans have been made with Center management. For security and safety, it is strictly forbidden to prop or hold open any door entering into the building.

Storage of Materials: Following completion of the final event, all scenery, special staging, and other property and/or equipment brought into facilities must be removed within twenty-four (24) hours. All property and/or equipment not removed within twenty-four (24) hours of the completion of the rental period will be disposed of at the discretion of Center management. Such time and equipment required disposing of said property or equipment will be billed to Presenter in addition to all other charges.

Scenery Construction: The building of scenery, displays, or exhibits which involve the use of any equipment or tools which discharge dust, chips, or particles into the air shall not be permitted on stage. Painting and staining on stage is not permitted except for limited, small-scale touch-up as approved in advance by Center management. Absolutely no spraying, spattering, or any other painting method, which propels paint or stain through the air, will be permitted.

Fireproofing of scenery and props must be verified with the Technical Facilities Director and, if required, must be accomplished before materials are loaded into facility.

Backstage Guests: Guests are not permitted backstage before or during a performance or during intermission, unless arrangements have been made in advance. Guests may be admitted backstage after the performance in accordance with the wishes of the artist(s) and/or company manager, in coordination with Center management. At no time are guests permitted to walk through or around the main curtain or across the stage. Backstage access for guests should be arranged in advance of the performance with Center management.

Audience Seating Areas: During rehearsal, set-up, and strike periods, Presenter's personnel shall restrict their activities to the stage, backstage, and production areas. When it is necessary for a director, designer, or stage manager to view a rehearsal or set-up from the audience areas, use of the seating areas are restricted to directorial and technical personnel. When the audience seating areas are used for directorial activity in connection with the rehearsal or production of an event, the Presenter will be responsible for the clean up of the area so used. Should the audience seating area be left in a condition requiring maintenance and clean up prior to the performance, the Presenter will be charged for those services.

The audience seating areas are not to be used for the storage of coats, personal belonging, musical instruments cases, or other paraphernalia associated with the preperformance production of an event. Food and drink are strictly prohibited from seating and performance areas of the stage.

Radio, Television and Film: Presenter must obtain permission, in advance, from the artist(s) or artist(s) management to record any part of an event. Furthermore, Presenter should be aware that permission to broadcast or film any part of an event would result in additional set-up costs. The procedure for obtaining Center management permission to broadcast, record, or film an event is as follows:

1. Center management must concur that the technical requirements for broadcast or filming a production can be accomplished in the time available following notification.
2. Center management must be notified in advance of any recording, and will work with Presenter in set-up locations.

3. The artist(s) or artist(s) management must sign a recording or broadcast release in advance.

Section VIII: Front of House

The following rules and regulations pertain to the use of the audience chamber, house management personnel, and sales in connection with an event.

House Management: Center personnel acting in the capacity of House Manager is included in the rental of the facility and shall be in charge of front-of-house areas at all times. Center supervisors and office personnel will be provided at an additional cost to the Presenter. Center management determines essential personnel.

Usher Requirements: Usher requirements will be determined by Center management based on the known or estimated size of the audience. A ten percent (10%) service charge is included on all house management staffing costs.

Presenter has the option of providing some volunteer ushers; use Center ushers at cost, or a combination of both. When using volunteer ushers, they must meet the following requirements:

1.) Ushers must arrive one and one-half (1-½) hours prior to reserved seating performances, and two (2) hours prior to general admissions. They must attend an usher orientation session at that time.
2.) Ushers must be provided to work the entire event, and may be asked to work outside the performance hall.

Center management reserves the right to use Center ushers, at Presenter's cost, if the Presenter has not met the above usher requirements.

Concession/Artists Sales: The rights and privileges of sales of souvenir items remain under the control of Center management. The Presenter or touring artist may handle souvenir sales, but approval for sales activity must be made in advance. Sales will be confined to areas designated by Center management. Center will collect twenty percent (20%) commission on gross sales when the Presenter or artist is the seller, and thirty percent (30%) commission on gross sales when Center personnel are the sellers. The artist(s) must claim State sales tax and is responsible for payment of it. Center assumes no liability for any taxes on merchandise.

Food and Beverage: Food and Beverage service is under the direction of Center House Management. Food service must be coordinated with House Management Services. Food service can be provided under the following conditions:

1.) Food or beverage consumed on stage as required by a script.

2.) For an approved reception/dinner in a designated space in Center facilities.
3.) In staff lounges or areas set up for cast and crew meals
4.) In lobbies and lounge areas only when dispensed from Center operated refreshment areas.

Receptions and/or dinners must be scheduled at least two (2) weeks in advance of an event.

House Opening and Capacity: It is customary to open the doors for patron seating thirty (30) minutes prior to a reserved seat event and forty-five (45) minutes prior to a general admission event. Any variance requested by Presenter must be arranged with Center management in advance.

Larger numbers of persons than can safely and freely move about in the authorized area shall not be admitted into the facilities. Determination of these capacities will be the decision of Center management, the Fire Marshall, and the Department of Police and Public Safety. Under no circumstance will Standing Room Only (SRO) be permitted in Center facilities.

Late Seating: Every effort is made to begin the performance at the announced hour, unless there is an unavoidable delay. Late arriving patrons will be seated only at intervals designated by the artist(s) or company manager.

Paging Devices and Cellular Phones: Paging devices and cellular phones should be checked with the Head Usher, and persons expecting emergency calls should leave their name and seat location when checking the pager or telephone. Decisions regarding the emergency paging of persons in the performance hall is the responsibility of the House Manager on duty.

Cameras and Recording Devices: Contractual agreements with the artist(s) and as a courtesy to other members of the audience, photographic and recording equipment will not be permitted in the audience chamber during a performance. Exceptions may be made for news media or other production media when advance arrangements are made with Center management and are approved by artist(s) and artist(s) management. Center management reserves the right to confiscate equipment for the duration of the performance or evict violators when necessary.

Emergency Medical Treatment: Center reserved the right to determine if Paramedics/Emergency Medical Personnel need to be on site for events. If paramedics are deemed necessary to be at the event, Presenter will assume any resulting expense. All personal expenses incurred from emergency service will be the responsibility of the person treated.

Objectionable Patrons: Center management reserves the right to eject, or cause to be ejected, from the premises any person or persons whose behavior is offensive to other patrons or whose actions are harassing in nature, or whose actions are harmful to the facilities and the safety and security of other persons. Center management will not be liable to Presenter for any damages that might incur through the execution of this right.

Lost and Found: Found articles are retained by, and may be reclaimed from, the House Management offices.

Children (Infants): Center management believes in exposing young people to theatre at an early and appropriate age. Management encourages the following guidelines.

1.) In all cases, infants and babes in arms are not permitted.
2.) All attendees of a performance, regardless of age, are required to have a ticket and be able to sit in a theatre chair.
3.) Adults who bring small children into the audience chamber who become disruptive to surrounding patrons will be asked to leave the theatre.
4.) No food or drink of any kind is allowed in the theatre.

Appendix V

THEATRE TECHNICAL SPECIFICATIONS

LOADING DOCK

Dock Height is 3' 7" and is level with stage floor.
There is enough space for 4 trucks/trailers at the dock; they can remain parked
at dock for duration of the stay.
Loading door dimensions are 9' 10" H × 9' 10" W.

STAGE

The theatre has a curved DS edge of the stage (see stage diagram)
Orchestra Lifts: There are two orchestra lifts (hydraulic), which work independently
Inner Lift (504 sq.ft.) 52' 0" × 11' 8"
Outer Lift (880 sq.ft.) 70' 9" × 10' 9"

Either lift can be stage extensions DS of Proscenium or each can be lowered to 7'
and used as an orchestra pit (inner alone or both together) maximum depth of both
lifts is 11' below stage level (an access door is at each level).
Outer Lift has three rows of 119 seats on wagons that roll off into a lower storage area.
(Rows: AA, BB, CC)
Lifts cannot be operated during performances!

Stage Right Platform (Jump)

There is a 12' W × 56' L steel platform, 27' above the SR wing space.
Platform has a pin-rail built in.
Distance from platform to SL pin-rail is 96'.

Stage Dimensions

Proscenium:	Width	54' 6"
	Height	30' 0"
	Thickness	2' 4"
Stage Width:	SL locking rail to SR patch panel	107' 8"
Wing Space:	SR (proscm. to elect. patch panel)	2 4"
	SL (proscm. to locking rail)	25' 8"
Stage Width:	SR (center line to SR patch panel)	53' 2"
	SL (center line to SL locking rail)	54' 6"
Stage Depth:	DS edge of apron to back wall (US)	68' 4"

DS edge of inner orch. lift to back
DS edge of outer orch. lift to back wall
US edge of proscenium to back wall
House curtain to back wall
House curtain to apron at back wall

RIGGING

General Information

Counterweight system is single purchase 1:1 ratio
Grid is 75' 10" above stage floor
Locking Rails
(both floor and upper pin-rail levels) are stage left with vertical clearance 13' 10"

        Batten length is 84' 0"
        Batten travel is 69' 2"
        Batten low trim is 3' 10"
        Batten high trim is 73' 0"
        Average distance between battens is 8" oc

Batten is 1½" ID schedule 40 pipe
Batten has 9 lift lines
Pipe weight is 175 lb.
Arbor capacities of: general batten 1500 lb.
                     electric batten 2000 lb.

Orchestra Shell Ceiling

See hanging plot
Ceiling pieces can be cleared from linesets

Main Act Curtain lineset #2 (see page Hanging Plot)
Motorized guillotine or manual travel (split center)
Manual travel operation from DSL at floor level only
Motorized switch control located both DSL and DSR
Fixed motorized speed is 15 sec. (full up to full down)
Main Act Curtain cannot be cleared.

Valance lineset #1 (see page #12 Hanging Plot)
Valance is part of Deluge Fire Protection System
NO scenery, lights, etc. may be attached to batten
NO scenery or equipment may be placed across curtain line to prevent valance from reaching stage floor
Valance is not a "working" batten.
Valance cannot be cleared.

Drapes (see page #12 Hanging Plot for dimensions)

Item	Color	Material	Fullness
Valance	rust	velour	100%
Main curtain	rust	velour	100%
Legs	black	velour	60%
Borders	black	velour	60%
Travelers	black	velour	60%
Cyclorama	blue	muslin	0%

SUPPORT AREAS

Floor

Stage Floor construction, from bottom to top, is as follows:
2 × 4 wood sleepers on 2' centers resting on neoprene pads
¾" plywood
1" plywood (laid at right angles to ¾" plywood)
1⅛" T & G Southern Yellow Pine, edge grain.
Stage Floor is stained brown and sealed.
Nails, screws, lag bolts, etc. may be used in the floor.

Dressing Rooms (floor plans at end of rider)

Quan	Capacity	Location
3	1 person	1st floor
4 (2 pair)	3 person suite	2nd floor
1	3	" "
5	5	" "
2	20	" "
2	20 (no showers)	" "
1	20	3rd floor

All dressing rooms are equipped with makeup counter, mirrors w/ lights, sink, toilet(s), and showers (except where noted above)
Second and third floor rooms are accessible by elevator or stairs
Suite dressing rooms share shower and rest room facilities.

Laundry Room (see second floor floor plan)

Three heavy-duty washers and three heavy-duty dryers
Two steam irons and ironing board
Two Jiffy steamers with wand
One deep tub sink
Ten 6' long rolling costume racks

Rehearsal Studio (rental space—located on third floor)

34' 6" W × 68' 4" L

68' of mirrors (6' tall) along west wall

Hardwood floor (same construction as Great Hall stage floor)

Covered with Marley

ELECTRICAL

NOTE: The Center has VectorWorks Spotlight 9.5.2, LightWrightV3, and a 24" plotter. A rep hang is available on VectorWorks. We can send and receive light plots and paperwork via Email at:

Company Switches

#1 Hook-up: 120/208 VAC, 3 phase, 5 wire, 600A/leg

Located USR next to stage entrance

#2 Hook-up: 120/208 VAC, 3 phase, 5 wire, 200A/leg

Fused in three separate boxes at; 200A/leg, or 100A/leg, or 60A/leg.

#3 Hook-up: 120/208 VAC, 3 phase, 5 wire,

This is a 800 amp/leg maximum combination load distribution box

There are six 3-phase Breakers: 2 400A, 2 200A, 2 100A

Female Cam-lock connectors on the 400A & 200A breakers

Located USR on back wall.

Dimmers

4 ETC Sensor AF dimmer racks: 319 - 2.4 kW circuits (dimmer per circuit)

Lighting Control

1 ETC Expression 2x Console w/ remote focus unit

or 1 ETC Insight 2x Console

Located in an enclosed booth at rear of the house

House light control—ETC Snapshot

Clear-Com communication and performance monitor in booth

Circuits

319 20A permanently wired house circuits

Stage Electric circuits:

1st - 36, 2nd - 24, 3rd - 24, 4th - 24, & 5th (Cyc lights) 6 open circuits

Drop Box circuits 36 total - 18 per side (DS, MS, & US)

FOH circuits:

Second Catwalk	48 20A circuits	
First Catwalk	28 20A	"
SR Box Boom	18 20A	"
SL Box Boom	18 20A	"

ALL FOH circuits break out at transfer panel USR
FOH positions
Throws from Second Catwalk, SR&SL Box Booms average 67-77'
Throws from First Catwalk average 35'

FOH Hang

The Hall has a permanent FOH hang as listed below
#2 Catwalk 45-19° & 24-10°   ETC S-4
Box Booms—each   12-19° ETC S-4 and 1 26° ETC S-4 (Curtain Warmers)

Electric Miscellaneous

40 20 amp stage pin two-fers
10 24' diameter boom bases, threaded for 1½" pipe
An assortment of 1½" pipe in various lengths
8 14" diameter boom bases, threaded for 1" pipe
2 rolling boom bases, threaded for 1" pipe

LIGHTING

Luminaries

Quan	Size	Angle	Watt/lamp		Frame size
***80	ETC Source Four	19°	575	HLP	6½" × 6½"
***20	ETC Source Four	10°	575	HLP	12" × 12"
164	ETC Pars	w/5 lens	575	HLP	7½" × 7½"
80	ETC Source Four	36°	575	HLP	6½" × 6½"
87	ETC Source Four	26°	575	HLP	6½" × 6½"
1	ETC Source Four	10°	ADDITIONAL LENS TUBES		
6	ETC Source Four	36°	ADDITIONAL LENS TUBES		

12   6' 9" striplight   (1500/ckt) 500 FCZ   11⅞" × 8¾"
* 8   6' 9" Cyclight that are permanently hung on lineset #49
*** 70 - 19° and all-10° units are in FOH Hang

Follow Spots

Four 2000 watt Xenon Super Trouper
Located at rear of the Balcony in an enclosed booth
Four separate 30a circuits in booth:
2 120 VAC single phase, 3 wire
2 120 VAC single phase, 3 wire OR
220 VAC single phase, 4 wire
Distance to proscenium at centerline is 135'

Accessories

24 barn doors for 8" fresnel
30 barn doors for ETC Source Four PARS
10 drop in Iris's for ETC Source Four leko
50 pattern holders for ETC Source Four leko

Projection Booth

Located at rear of house in an enclosed booth (next to light booth)
Throw is 129' to screen at a 7° angle

AUDIO

NOTE: The Hall is VERY live acoustically.
Extreme care should be exercised in setting volume levels.
NOTE: State law limits electronic sound pressure levels to a maximum of 105 DB
during all events. Your event CANNOT exceed this level at ANY time.
Touring companies may patch into the house system for additional coverage.
Mixing position for ALL shows is at center back of the house, 85' from stage
with unobstructed sightlines to all FOH speakers—FOH to stage cable run is 200'.

System has been SYMed to provide even sound coverage over the whole house. But
changes can be made to the liking of the Guest Engineer.

Front Of House

- Midas Heritage 2000/ 56ch.
- 6 XTA 3rd octive graphs GQ600
- XTA Audio Core computer at FOH
- Tascam CDR
- Tascam Dual CD and TAPE
- Eventide Eclipse Vocal Processor
- TC Electronic M3000
- 8 Comps DBX 1046
- 8 Gates Drawmer DS404
- Snake Trauff on wall with 56ch. Mic/line and 20ch. Drive
Installed Speakers
- L-Acoustics DVOSC Centre Line Array/ 14 Cabs
- 2 per side DB E3 side fills
- 2 per side L-Acoustics Arcs side fills
- 6 DB E3 Front Fills
- 2 Meyer UPA2P Balcony Fill
- 2 Meyer SW15 Subs in with line array

On Stage

Moveable Speaker Stacks
- 2 per side Meyer 650's Proscenium Stacks
- 2 per side Meyer CO's Proscenium Stacks
- 2 per side Meyer MSL4's Proscenium Stacks
- 20 Drive lines
- 56 Mic/Line Ch.'s
- XTA DP 224's Loudspeaker Pros. For Proscenium Stacks
- Main PA Tie IN
- Program sound and Phonic Ear Tie IN
- 4 12ch. Sub snakes
- Mic/line Manifold
- Drive line Manifold

Amp Racks
- Crown Macro Techs 3600
- DBE3 Prosessor/Amplifiers
- XTA DP226 Prosessors

Audio

Monitor System
- CrestX 48ch. Monitor Desk
- 12 DBX 20 Series 3rd Octive Graphs
- Virtualizer Pro DSP2024P Effects Processor
- 8 Crown MacroTechs 24X6 Amps
- 12 Macpherson M12 Wedges
- Other Monitor gear available if needed

Shure Wireless
- 12 CH's
- 8 Beta 887 Hand Helds
- 12 Lav packs U1/UA
- 12 Lavs WL50
- 2 Senn MKH2

Microphones
- 4 SM81 -4 AKG 414 -3 Crown Pcc 160 -4 Senn 421 -3 Senn MKH40
- 1 AKG D12 -1 EV RE20 -3 Senn 431 -1 PZM 30D -2 PZM -2 Beyer M69
- 8 AKG 535 -4 Beta 58 -12 SM 58 -7 Beta 57 -3 SM 57
- 4 Audio Tech Uni-Points -3 Audio Tech Angel Mics -7 EV RE11
- 2 EV DS35 -3 EV RE10 -2 EV CS15E -4 BSS Active DI -3 DB1 DI
- 2 Countryman TYPE 85 Active DI

PROPERTIES

Equipment

200	Black orchestra chairs
100	Music stands
80	Music stand lights
8	Wenger 3 step choral risers w/ 4th step addition
12	4' × 8' risers 8" high
12	" " 16" high

12	" " 24" high
12	" " 32" high
2	conductor podiums (gray carpet) w/ 1 railing
	(1 med., 1 Lg used separate or stacked for bi-level)
2	full height wooden lecterns
32	folding leg tables 30" × 70"
8	" " " 30" × 48"

(black table skirting available)
1 JLG personnel lift 36'
& an assortment of 4-wheel dollies & 2-wheel carts
& rolling clothes racks

Rentals

1	9' Steinway concert grand piano
1	7' Baldwin baby grand piano
1	Yamaha U-1 upright piano
1	Full stage Wenger Custom Orchestra Shell w/ceiling and lights
8	6' × 57' sections Marley dance floor (black/gray)
1	Fastfold projection screen 12' × 12' front projection
2	Fastfold projection screen 10' × 14' Rear projection
1	Mitsubishi LVP X5000U XGA 3700 lumen LCD projector

Video

The theatre has a permanent in-house closed circuit
video system w/ color monitors backstage and throughout the lobbies.

Wireless Frequencies

Frequencies used for professional wireless mics.

RF Chart

VHF mics:	175.400 Mhz	UHF mics:	794.000 Mhz
	175.600		794.500
	175.800		795.000
	176.000		795.500

Continues listing all frequencies available

HANGING PLOT

Proscenium opening = 30'-0" tall × 57'-8" wide

Lineset #	Distance from plaster	House Goods	Information & Notes
1	0'-10"	Grand Valance/ Fire Curtain	33' H × 64' W, Cannot be stripped
2	1'-6"	Grand Traveler	33' H × 74' W, Mechanical fly, manual travel
3	2'-9"	#1 House Electric	36 circuits, dimmer-per-circuit
4	4'-2"	Empty	
5	5'-1"	Empty (#1 Orchestra Shell Ceiling)	
6	6'-1"	Empty	
7	6'-9"	Empty	
8	7'-4"	Empty	
9	8'-1"	Empty	
10	8'-8"	Black Border	15' H × 84' W, 300 lbs.
11	9'-4"	*Black Traveler*	35' H × 87' W, *track = 475, goods = 650 lbs.*

Continues Detailed Listing

Lineset #	Distance from plaster	House Goods	Information & Notes
54	38'-1"	*Full-Stage Blackout Drop*	40' H × 70' W, *two panels, 550 lbs. total*
55	38'-9"	Empty	(well obstruction at approx. 37'-8")
56	39'-4"	Empty	
57	40'-0"	Empty	
58	40'-7"	Empty	
59	41'-3"	Empty	
60	41'-10"	Empty	
61	42'-5"	Picture Screen Storage	20' H × 45' W, 450 lbs.
62	43'-1"	Empty	(well obstruction at approx. 43'-0")
63	44'-1"	Shell Storage (Not available for use)	
64	45'-5"	Shell Storage (Not available for use)	
65	46'-9"	Shell Storage (Not available for use)	

NOTES:

- Due to fire regulations, the Grand Valance/Fire Curtain on Lineset #1 must be respected at all times. *Absolutely NOTHING* may block the Valance's free travel to the stage. The Grand Valance/Fire Curtain may be used as a guillotined act curtain if desired, but its balance may not be altered—it is pipe-heavy, and must remain so at all times. It does not have a center split.
- The Grand Traveler is a manual-travel, mechanical fly pipe. Guillotine travel speed is approximately 15 seconds from extreme high trim (about 35') to the deck, and cannot be adjusted.
- High trim on all pipes is approx. 71'. Lowest (working) trim is approx. 4'.
- Pipes 2–4 cannot be kicked, although they may be diverted. Pipe #5 may be kicked, but not very far.
- Due to the width of the overhung loft blocks, pipes 6-62 can generally only be kicked 2–3" without gang kicking or diverting. There are some instances of obstructions in the structural steel preventing any kicking of certain line sets in certain directions (grid hangers, for example).
- Pipes #5, 18, and 31 are used for our orchestra shell ceilings. The ceilings may be stripped as needed, given advance notice.
- Pipes 63-65 are orchestra ceiling storage pipes, and are not generally available for any other use.
- House electric pipes (Linesets #3, 13, 26, 36, and 47) are double-batten pipes. All house electric works, e.g., feeder mults, fan-outs, worklights, etc. may be stripped as needed.
- The grid is overhung, 2" × 3" C-channel with 10" wells on 10' centers, and is fully riggable. We stock a fair quantity of 3' long, 1.5" ID Sched. 40 pipe and 2" thick-wall box tube for piping points on the grid, and can hang up to a 1-ton point pretty much anywhere. Two-ton (and heavier) points may be hung from well channels, heavy spanner beams, or the high steel only.
- **Continue Notes as Required**

Appendix W

SAMPLE LICENSE AGREEMENT FOR RENTING A THEATRE FACILITY
TO AN OUTSIDE GROUP

Brooklyn Center for the Performing Arts
at Brooklyn College

LICENSE AGREEMENT made this　　　day of　　　between the BOARD OF TRUSTEES
OF THE CITY UNIVERSITY OF NEW YORK (hereinafter referred to as Licensor),
party of the first part, and

of

for itself, its successors and/or its legal representatives (hereinafter referred to as Licensee),
party of the second part.

　　　　　　　WITNESSETH: The Licensor does hereby grant to the Licensee permission to use the following space in Brooklyn College (hereinafter referred to as the College) for the following performances (description of space and dates and times of performances):

and rehearsals (it is requested that at least a portion of the period be used to consult with the technical staff before program participants arrive at the licensed facilities):

said premises to be used by the Licensee only and for the sole purpose of

and for no other purpose. The following room(s) will be available for dressing, makeup and/or other agreed purposes:

The Licensee agrees to pay Licensor as a fee for such use, the sum of

as follows:

$ on signing of this license agreement

$ balance on/or before

Any other payments:

The entire fee and all other sums due Licensor shall be paid to it prior to the time of opening of the door to the premises for the performance, concert, lecture, and/or public meeting contemplated, and time shall be of the essence with respect to such payment. Extra charges for additional rehearsals, extra stage work, overtime, extra rooms, etc., if any, will be payable when billed. Fees are not refundable.

Permission for the above use is made upon the foregoing and following terms, agreements and conditions which the respective parties agree to and observe, keep and perform:

1) The Licensee agrees that, if any stage work or other special arrangements are permitted, same shall be done only under the supervision of and with the approval of the Licensor, and the Licensee agrees to pay for the same when billed. Licensee agrees that Licensor shall not be liable for any claims or causes of action arising from or out of the acts of any of the employees of Licensee, or their omission to act, and agrees to indemnify Licensor from any such claims or causes of action. Licensor shall provide tickets for all performances and any arrangements for the use of the box office shall be entered into as a separate agreement with the Licensor and is not included in this agreement.

2) In case all charges and fees due Licensor are not paid prior to the performance, the Licensee agrees that the Licensor may, at its election, collect such fees and charges due hereunder or any part thereof out of the receipts, if any, from the sale of tickets or subscriptions at the box office and said receipts are hereby assigned by the Licensee to the Licensor to the extent of the amount of any charges due by Licensee under this agreement and that may at any time remain unpaid to Licensor.

3) The Licensor shall not be obliged to furnish possession or the use of the premises involved herein until all payments have been made as described above, and the Licensee hereby specifically agrees that if each and every of the above payments have not been made by the Licensee to Licensor, the Licensor may without further notice of any kind to the Licensee, or to any other person, refuse to open the doors until such payments have been made. Upon any default in payment by the Licensee, the Licensor shall retain any money already paid, and the Licensee shall be and remain liable to the Licensor for any balance remaining to be paid as specified herein.

4) The Licensee agrees not to permit entrance of any number of persons greater than the number of existing 2,482 seats in the premises involved herein, and no persons shall be permitted to use or occupy any space as

standing room. Any use of the stage made by the Licensee for auditorium or seating purposes shall be only with the written consent of the Licensor upon such terms and conditions as may be specified by the Licensor.

5) The Licensee agrees that Licensee will not use nor attempt to use any part of the premises for any purposes other than that above specified, nor for any use or proposed use which will be contrary to law. Licensee further agrees that Licensor in its sole absolute discretion, if it deems any proposed or existing performance, concert, lecture, and/or public meeting to be contrary to law, contrary to public safety, or opposed to decency or good morals, or detrimental to the reputation of the College, may forthwith terminate this license, and/or interrupt such performance, concert, lecture, and/or public meeting, and dismiss or cause the audience to be dismissed, and if the Licensor sees fit, turn off the lights, and on exercise by Licensor of any such discretion, all rights of the Licensee hereunder shall immediately terminate. In any such event the Licensor shall be entitled to retain or receive any money paid or agreed to be paid to it hereunder; and Licensee agrees to indemnify the Licensor against any claim for damages arising out of any act of Licensor, its agents, or employees, in the exercise of Licensor's discretion under this clause.

6) The Licensee covenants and agrees that in any performance, concert, lecture, or public meeting of any kind in the College's premises, no language shall be uttered or feature of any kind presented that shall be unlawful, and that every ember connected with any such performance, concert, lecture, or public meeting, or other such purpose for which this license is granted, shall abide by, conform to, and comply with all the laws of the United States and the State of New York, all the rules and regulations of any governmental bureau or department and all the local laws of the City of New York, and the rules and regulations of the Licensor for the management of its building, and will not do nor suffer to be done, anything on the said premises during the term of this agreement, violation of any such rules, laws, or local laws, and if the attention of Licensee is called to such violation of the part of the Licensee, or any person employed by or admitted to said premises by Licensee, such Licensee will immediately terminate, desist from, and correct such violation.

7) The Licensee covenants and agrees that it will not sell or serve, nor allow to be sold, brought into, served on the premises, any alcoholic beverages or liquors. And the Licensee also covenants and agrees that no refreshments shall be served, article sold, or smoking permitted, unless a space is designated for such purposes by the Licensor; that no nails, tacks, or screws shall be driven or placed, and that all decorations shall be put up without defacing the building and under the supervision and with the approval of the Licensor, and that in case any damage of any kind shall be done to the said premises or the appurtenances thereof, the Licensee agrees to pay, in addition to the sums above mentioned, the amount of

such damage or such amount as shall be necessary to put said premises in as good order and condition as the same were at the commencement of said agreement.

8) The Licensee agrees not to transfer or assign this license without the written consent of the Licensor first had and obtained, nor suffer any business on the premises other than herein specified. The Licensee agrees not to do or permit anything to be done in said premises or bring or keep anything therein, including the use of flash equipment requiring electrical outlets which conflict with the laws relating to fires, with the regulations of the Fire Department, or with any of the rules or ordinances of the Board of Health.

9) The Licensee agrees that in the event that motion picture projection or still picture projection be all or a part of the performance, the only position in the theater which is acceptable for the placement of motion picture projectors, stereopticons, slide projectors, any device using a carbon arc light source, and/or any device using a Xenon light source, shall be the house projection booth. No portable projection equipment of any kind with the exception of UL approved television transmission projectors shall be placed or permitted to be placed in any area of the auditorium other than the house projection booth, and at the Licensee's expense. At the sole discretion of the Licensor, motion picture operator with a current New York City Bureau of Gas and Electricity Motion Picture Operator's License may be procured by the Licensee and at the Licensee's expense to operate projection equipment in the projection booth, but said operator shall, at all times, be under the supervision and approval of the Licensor's chief projectionist. A copy of the projectionist's current operator's license shall be presented to the Licensor prior to the performance date.

10) It is mutually agreed that no audio or video broadcasting and/or recording will be permitted without the consent of Licensor first had and obtained in writing. The Licensee agrees to assume responsibility for, and to save the Licensor harmless from, any liability upon any claim or cause of action arising out of the utterance or publication of any alleged slanderous or libelous statements, whether in the broadcasting of any radio or television program, from the premises or any recording or publication of the same, or in any other manner. The Licensee further agrees that should said audio/video broadcasting and/or recording be mutually agreed upon by both the Licensor and the Licensee, the Licensee shall not broadcast or record the performance nor cause the performance to be broadcast or recorded without first obtaining the written consent of each performer or his agent. Standard Broadcast and Recording Clearance release forms will be supplied by the Licensor for this purpose and the completed and signed forms must be presented to the Licensor prior to the first performance playdate named on page one of this contract. An individual form must be submit-

ted to the Licensor for each performer before any broadcast or recording can be made.

11) The Licensee agrees to secure in advance before the doors are opened, any and all licenses and/or permits that may be requisite for any performance, concert, lecture and/or public meetings given under this agreement; to secure any necessary certificates of electrical inspection from the Department of Water Supply, Gas and Electricity of the City of New York and/or the New York Board of Fire Underwriters for operation of any motion picture or other machine or equipment, and to do all other acts necessary to comply with all laws and requirements of the State of New York, the City of New York, or any department, board, or authority thereof governing theaters or amusements, or otherwise applicable to said premises, including certification that stage sets and stage properties to be used by Licensee comply with the flame proof requirements of the New York Board of Underwriters.

12a) In accordance with the N.Y. City Administration Code, Chapter 19, Section 165.1, the Licensee agrees not to use or cause to be used, within the theater, any pyrotechnic device, heat-operated smoke machine, open flame, cigar, or cigarette without the written approval of the Fire Commissioner, Division of Fire Prevention. It remains the responsibility of the Licensee to inform the performing artists of these legal restrictions. Violations of Chapter 19, Section 165.1 can carry penalties of up to $1,000 per violation and the immediate close down of the performance by the Fire Captain.

12b) The Licensor, recognizing its obligation to provide reasonable protection to the audience from ear damage, inserts the following Sound Pressure Protection Clause: The Licensor reserves the right to stop the performance should the Sound Pressure Level exceed the safety level of 115db at a distance of 15 feet from any speaker cluster for more than 60 seconds duration. Should this maximum safety SPL be exceeded, the power mains to the amplifiers will be disconnected. The Licensor's house soundman will take readings during the rehearsal and will monitor the performance to determine its average SPL's remain under 115db. A penalty of $500.00 will be imposed on the Licensee should the Licensor be forced to shut down the performance for dangerous Sound Pressure Levels. It remains the responsibility of the Licensee to inform the performing artists of this restriction, and to insure that those performers who use portable sound reinforcement, do not exceed the house Sound Pressure Limit.

12c) The Licensee agrees to inform the Licensor no less than two weeks prior to the first performance named on page one of this contract of the intent to use any kind of coherent light emission device. At the Licensor's sole discretion, Laser light sources may be permitted to be used within the theater, but only with the following conditions, to which the Licensee agrees: No Class III or IV Laser device as defined by the Bureau of Radiological Health of the Food and Drug Administration (FDA) shall be placed or used to be placed into operation within the theater without the required FDA written "variance." The FDA variance must be presented to the Licensor at least one week prior to the first performance. No Laser device shall be allowed to operate, even with written variance, if an FDA representative has not first been allowed to inspect the equipment and its installation in the theater prior to the performance, with proof of such an inspection submitted to the Licensor prior to the performance. All Laser devices and their use must conform to the Radiation Control Health and Safety Act.

13) The Licensee agrees that it shall be the distinct obligation of the Licensee and of all persons connected with the Licensee under this license, not to involve the Licensor in any labor disputes. In the event that such a labor dispute arises, the Licensor has the absolute privilege and right to cancel this license and Licensee shall remain liable for the license fee.

14) The Licensor agrees to light and heat the premises. Licensor does not guarantee the air conditioning equipment.

15) The Licensor shall not be liable for any damage to any property said premises or building at any time caused by any water, rain, snow, steam, gas, or electricity, which may leak into, issue, or flow from the pipes or plumbing work or wires, or from any part of the building to which the premises hereby licensed are a part, or from any other place quarter, nor shall the Licensor be liable to anyone for any loss of property from or on said premises, however occurring, or for any damage done to furniture, fixtures, or other effects of the Licensee, by an employee of the Licensor or any other person.

16) Should the licensed premises herein described be destroyed either wholly or in part, or injured by fire or the elements, mob, riot, or use of any part of the premises, or performance of any part of this agreement be prevented or interfered with by strikes or any other cause prior to or during the time for which use of said premises is licensed, the Licensor may at its discretion, terminate the said license, returning to the Licensee any payments that may have been made to it for the proportionate period of use prevented, or interrupted, and the Licensee hereby expressly waives any claims for damages or compensation should the license be so terminated. The Licensor shall not in any way be liable for any loss or damage to personal property or other damage, delay, inconvenience, annoyance to the Licensee arising from or because of strikes, lock-outs, or other labor difficulties, or for any other reason whatsoever.

17) The Licensor, its officers, agents, and employees shall have the right at all times to enter any part of the licensed premises.

18) The Licensee agrees to comply with the provisions and requirements of Section 485a of the Penal Law and such other provisions of law that may be applicable to performance by children under the age of sixteen years.

19) The Licensee agrees that no portion of the sidewalks, entries, vestibules, halls, elevators, or ways of access to public utilities of said building shall be obstructed by Licensee or used for any purpose other than for ingress and egress to and from the premises.

20) Any change, addition, or alteration to this license agreement shall not be binding unless made in writing and signed by the Licensor.

21) This license agreement contains all of the terms of the understanding between the parties hereto and shall not be binding on the Licensor, and the premises referred to herein are not secured for any of the dates mentioned herein until this license agreement has been signed by the Licensor and Licensee, respectively, and a deposit has been made as specified by Licensor.

22) All fees and all sums due Licensor under the terms of this agreement shall be payable by cash or by certified check or draft on a New York bank.

23) If Licensee provides tickets, Licensee agrees to provide to Licensor, at least 30 days prior to the date of the performance, a printer's manifest of the house (a notarized, signed statement from the printer of the tickets listing the amount of tickets printed and each price). All tickets shall be printed by a bonded ticket house; e.g., Globe Tickets, Arcus-Simplex-Brown, Inc., National Ticket Co.

24) The Licensor at its discretion reserves the right to add additional security as needed for the performance to a maximum of $.

25) Orchestra seats, Row 0, seat numbers 0-107 through 0-114 are to be reserved for use by the Licensor for all performances. The tickets for these seats must be surrendered to the Licensor at least 10 days prior to the performance date.

26) The Licensee agrees that all publicity material in the form of, but not limited to newspaper ads, radio ads, flyers, printed announcements of any kind, or promotional activities that communicate with the public, informing them of the event named on page one, shall be submitted to the Licensor for final approval. The Licensee agrees, also, that no such advertisement, promotion, or communication shall use the logo of BCBC and that no advertisement, communication, or promotion shall be issued or cause to be issued without the prior consent of the Licensor.

27) The Licensee shall provide the Licensor with a cash bond in the amount of $. Licensee's failure to mount the performance as advertised will result in the forfeiture of as much of the principal sum of the bond as is required to be used by the Licensor to refund advance ticket sales should the Licensee not provide prompt, full and complete refunding services. A service charge of One Dollar ($1.00) per ticket refunded will be deducted from the principal sum of the cash bond. Any additional payments due Licensor arising from License's performance, if not promptly paid, shall also be deducted from the cash bond. Any excess cash shall be returned within a reasonable period of time.

28) The Licensee agrees to accept the premises "as is" after having inspected the premises and found the premises suitable for the performance outlined above. The Licensee further agrees to indemnify and hold the Licensor harmless against liability claims and suits arising out of such use and occupancy and to provide the Licensor with a Certificate of Insurance with Brooklyn College, Center for the Performing Arts, and the City of New York named as additional insured. The insurance for the scheduled event shall include personal property, real property, and personal injury liability insurance coverage in the minimum amount of Five Hundred Thousand Dollars ($500,000.00). Such liability coverage will include the following:

   a) Any personal and bodily injury to persons who attended the scheduled event as well as to persons who are lawfully on the Brooklyn College Campus immediately prior to, during, or following the scheduled event.

   b) Any personal property damage to persons who attended the scheduled event as well as to persons who are lawfully on the Brooklyn College Campus immediately prior to, during, or following the scheduled event.

   c) Any property damage to the buildings and other parts of the physical structure or grounds of the Brooklyn College Campus that is proximately caused by the scheduled event.

29) The Licensee agrees that failure to comply with any of the above provisions by _____ days prior to the performance date, shall render this contract null and void and the deposit shall not be refundable.

IN WITNESS WHEREOF, The Board of Trustees of the City University of New York, the party of the first part, has caused this instrument to be signed by its duly authorized agent, and the party of the second part has duly signed this instrument, the day and year first above written.

BOARD OF TRUSTEES OF THE CITY UNIVERSITY OF NEW YORK (Licensor)

BY:

(Licensee)
BY:

Signed and Delivered in the presence of:

Appendix X

STANDARD TYPES OF INSURANCE RELATED
TO THE PERFORMING ARTS

Workers' Compensation: usually issued by insurance companies or a state insurance fund. The law stipulates that employees cannot file suit against employers for work-related injuries (although they may sue any third party that was involved); the benefits for injured workers include various medical services plus, if the person is unable to work, a weekly payment of two-thirds of the worker's salary up to limits that vary by state.

Disability Benefits Insurance: mandatory in certain states, including New York, New Jersey, and California, covers nonwork related injuries, illness, and in some states pregnancy. There is no medical coverage provision included; it is a limited form of salary insurance paying a small portion of salary only for a limited amount of time; for medical coverage, the claimant would have to turn to his or her own medical plan, if any.

Commercial General Liability Insurance: covers claims by any nonemployee alleging bodily injury or property damage. It also includes 1) Personal Injury (including defamation, libel, slander, and plagiarism—provided that none of these claims arise from the text of the play) and 2) Bodily Injury. It may be extended to include automobile insurance, see following.

Automobile Liability and Property Damage: a minimum amount of coverage is mandated by each state; it may be extended to include vehicles used but not owned (rented or borrowed) driven by employees.

Fire Insurance, Extended Coverage, Vandalism, and Malicious Mischief: covers buildings and their contents, rates determined by building material of the property; mandatory if property is mortgaged. It can be broadened to All Risk, including Theatrical Floater, see following.

Theatrical Property Floater: floater policies were first created as types of marine insurance to cover things that are literally floating around on a boat; The floater is written as *All Risk* to cover theatrical property and equipment: lighting, scenery, costumes, properties; the coverage travels with the production company during a tour. It is Inland Marine insurance.

Personal Effects Insurance: required by Actors' Equity Association to cover personal property, furs, clothing and jewelry of actors, when such items are in the theatre or with the actor on tour or at Equity auditions.

Boiler and Machinery Insurance: coverage for large heating, air-conditioning, and other expensive machinery in the building, including loss of income and business interruption.

Business Interruption Insurance: covers loss of business income as well as expenses incurred under certain conditions, arising out of damage to or destruction of the theatre building, stage scenery or costumes, or computerized systems.

Rain Insurance: a specific type of business interruption coverage for outdoor performances.

Nonappearance Insurance: covers Star performers who may become disabled from illness or accident. It is at times virtually impossible to replace a Star. Productions are funded and mounted because of a Star performer and the loss of that Star will cause a considerable loss and possibly abandonment; it could cause a total loss of the investment and future profits. The insurance, often decidedly expensive, may be written by an American company, but often Lloyd's of London is preferred. The integrity of the broker is of special importance because the underwriter's evaluation of the risk may be affected by the broker presenting the risk. Before the coverage can be bound, the Star must undergo an independent medical examination and the results presented to the underwriter.

3-D Bond and Theft Insurance: coverage against dishonest employees, embezzlement, depositor's forgery, forgery, hold-up (whether on the premises or in transit to or from a bank), lost money, and securities, etc.

Fidelity Bond: covers embezzlement by employees only.

Extraordinary Risk Compensation: coverage issued to supplement salary benefits to employees who may have been injured doing activities (work) out of the ordinary, such as difficult dancing or acrobatics.

Products Liability Insurance: to protect against public liabilities arising out of consumption of concessions products; it should be maintained by the concessions operator or lessor with the theatre and production company named as Additional Insureds.

Coat Room Insurance: to protect against loss or theft of checkroom holdings, for which management is held liable (even when there is a sign disclaiming responsibility for items lost or stolen from the check-room).

Errors and Omissions Coverage: protects the production company from claims of alleged plagiarism as well as libel, slander, defamation, and invasion of privacy; although this coverage is noted above in Personal Injury, if an Errors and Omissions policy is held, look to this coverage instead. The coverage *includes* claims arising from the text of the play. A script must be submitted with the application for coverage. (Although playwrights in theory indemnify producers by claiming that their work is original, they rarely have the resources to pay the legal costs of fighting claims of plagiarism, so the producer or theatre company producing a new work often takes out this type of coverage.)

Employee Pension, Health, and Life Insurance: contributions made by the employer and, often, also by the employee to a pension fund or insurance program; may be voluntary or may be mandated by collective bargaining agreements.

Appendix Y

INCIDENT REPORT FORM

This form should have already printed on it:

The name and address and phone numbers, etc. of the insured organization.

The name and address and contact numbers of the insurance company and broker, and policy number.

Where the competed information is to be filed.

Provide Space for:

The name and position of the person completing the form.

The date the form was filed out.

Name, age, occupation, and address of the injured party.

Name and address of any witnesses.

Date of injury.

Statements from the injured (if possible) and witnesses describing exactly what happened, when, etc.

Was medical attention offered? If so, what ensued?

Names and badge numbers of any police or rescue personnel who may have attended the scene.

Appendix Z

Because websites and organizations frequently disappear, it is best to conduct one's own search on any given subject, however, as of 2005 the following sites were up and running.

Associations
Americans for the Arts: http://ww3.artsusa.org
ArtsMarketing.org:http://www.artsmarketing.org
American Association of Community Theatre: http://www.aact.org/index.htm
Educational Theatre Association: http://www.edta.org/
The League of American Theaters and Producers: http://www.broadway.org/
League of Professional Theatre Women: http://www.theatrewomen.org/
International Society for the Performing Arts Foundation: http://www.ispa.org/
Institute of Outdoor Drama: http://www.unc.edu/depts/outdoor/
League of Resident Theatres: www.lort.org
National Alliance for Musical Theatre: http://www.namt.net/
National Musical Theater Network: http://www.broadwayusa.org/
Stage Directors and Choreographers Foundation, Inc.: http://www.sdcfoundation.org/
Theatre Communications Group: http://www.tcg.org/

Archives/Museums/Online Resources
American Society for Theatre Research: http://www.astr.umd.edu/
SIMBAS (Theatre Libraries and Museums):
    http://www.theatrelibrary.org/sibmas/sibmas.html
League of Historic American Theatres: http://www.lhat.org/
List of Theatre History Sites (mostly University collections):
    http://www.win.net/~kudzu/history.html
Billy Rose Theater Collection, New York Public Library:
    http://www.nypl.org/research/lpa/the/the.html
Classical Theatre: http://www.classicaltheatre.com/
Federal Theatre Project: http://www.gmu.edu/library/specialcollections/federal.html
Harry Ransom Humanities Research Center, University of Texas-Austin:
    http://www.hrc.utexas.edu/collections/performingarts/
Internet Broadway Database: www.ibdb.com
Internet Theatre Database: http://www.theatredb.com/
Lortel Archives (Off-Broadway): http://www.lortel.org/LLA_archive/index.cfm
Luminarium: http://www.luminarium.org/lumina.htm
Monologue Archive: http://www.monologuearchive.com/

Musical Heaven: www.musicalheaven.com

Raymond Mander and Joe Mitchenson Theatre Collection:
 http://www.mander-and-mitchenson.co.uk/

Shubert Archives: http://www.shubertarchive.org/

Theatre History.com: http://www.theatrehistory.com/

Theatre Historical Society of America:
 http://www2.hawaii.edu/~angell/thsa/welcome.html

The WWW Virtual Library-Theatre and Drama: http://www.vl-theatre.com/

Arts-Management.Net: www.artsmanagment.net

Licensing and Rights Organizations

ASCAP: http://www.ascap.com/

Baker's Plays: http://bakersplays.com/

Broadway Play Publishing, Inc.: http://www.broadwayplaypubl.com/

Dramatic Publishing: http://www.dramaticpublishing.com/

Dramatists Play Service, Inc.: http://www.dramatists.com/index.asp

Pioneer Drama Services: http://www.pioneerdrama.com/

Samuel French, Inc.: http://www.samuelfrench.com/

The Rodgers and Hammerstein Organization: http://www.rnh.com/index1.html

Music Theatre International: www.mitshows.com

Nonprofit Associations

The Idealist: http://www.idealist.org/

E-Volunteerism: http://www.evolunteerism.com/index.php

The Independent Sector: http://www.independentsector.org/

Nonprofit Maps: http://mapnp.nonprofitoffice.com/

Arts and Culture Related

James S. and James L. Knight Foundation: http://www.knightfdn.org

The Pew Charitable Trusts: www.pewtrust.com

Performing Arts Websites

Theatre

American Theater Web: www.americantheaterweb.com

Broadway Across America: http://www.broadwayacrossamerica.com/

Broadway.com: www.broadway.com

Broadway Stars: www.broadwaystars.com

DramaBiz: www.DramaBiz.com

Live Broadway.com: http://www.livebroadway.com/

Off-Broadway.com: http://www.offbroadway.com/

Onstage: http://onstage.org/

Playbill: www.playbill.com

Talkin' Broadway: www.talkinbroadway.com
Theatre Channel: http://www.theatrechannel.com/
Theatreland: http://www.theatreland.com/
Theatremania: www.theatremania.com
Theatrenet UK: http://www.theatrenet.co.uk/
London Theatre News: www.londontheatre.co.uk/

Opera
Center for Contemporary Opera: http://www.conopera.org/
Coordinated Opera Resource Pages: http://operabase.com/corpus/
Music Preserved: http://www.gao00.dial.pipex.com/Web/index.htm
On-line Opera Resource Guide: http://www.oberlin.edu/opera/
Opera America: http://www.operaamerica.org/
Opera Base: http://www.operabase.com/
Opera Glass: http://opera.stanford.edu/
Opera Magazine: http://www.opera.co.uk/
Opera Musical Theater International: http://www.omti.org/
Opera News Online: http://www.metoperafamily.org/operanews/index.aspx
Opera Online: http://www.operaonline.us/
Opera Resource: http://www.r-ds.com/opera/resource.htm
Opera World: http://www.operaworld.com/
OperaStuff.Com: http://www.operastuff.com/
US Opera Web: http://www.usoperaweb.com/index1.html

Ballet and Dance
Art Danse: http://www.artdanse.com/
Arts Lynx International Dance Resources: http://www.artslynx.org/dance/
ArtsEdge: http://artsedge.kennedy-center.org/
Ballet Alert: http://www.balletalert.com/
Ballet Co: http://www.ballet.co.uk/index.htm
Ballet Companies on the Web: http://www.dancer.com/dance-links/ballet.htm
Ballet Companies: http://balletcompanies.com/
Cadence Arts: http://www.cadencearts.net/
Critical Dance: http://www.criticaldance.com/
Cyber Dance: http://www.cyberdance.org/
Dance Art: http://www.danceart.com/
Dance Educators of America: http://www.deadance.com/
Dance Links: http://dancer.com/dance-links/
Dance Magazine: http://www.dancemagazine.com/
Dance NYC: http://www.dancenyc.org/
Dance Online: http://www.danceonline.com/
Dance USA: http://www.danceusa.org/
International Dance Alliance: http://www.idanews.com/

The Art of Ballet: http://www.artofballet.com/
The Ballet Associations: http://www.balletassociation.co.uk/
The Dance Collective: http://www.dancecollective.com/
World Dance Alliance in the Americas: http://www.wdaamericas.org/

Music—Classical and Symphonic
Amateur Chamber Music Players: http://www.acmp.net/
American Federations of Musicians: http://www.afm.org/public/home/index.php
American Music Conference: http://www.amc-music.com/
American Musical Instruments Society: http://www.amis.org/
American Symphony Orchestra League: http://www.symphony.org/
Chamber Music America: http://www.chamber-music.org/
Chamber Music Society: http://www.chambermusicsociety.org/
Classical Links: http://www.classicalist.com/information/links.html
Classical Net: http://www.classical.net/
Classical Works: http://classicalworks.com/
College Music Society: http://www.music.org/
Incorporated Societies of Musicians: http://www.ism.org/
International Musicological Society: http://www.ims-online.ch/
Society for American Music: http://american-music.org/
Worldwide Internet Music: http://www.music.indiana.edu/music_resources/societ.html

Puppetry
Center for Puppet Arts: http://www.puppet.org/
International Ventriloquist Association: http://www.inquista.com/
Puppet Centre: http://www.puppetcentre.com/
Puppeteers of America: http://www.puppeteers.org/
Puppetry Arts Theater: http://www.puppetryarts.org/
Puppetry Pastimes: http://www.puppetrypastimes.com/
Puppets and Stuff: http://www.puppetsandstuff.com/
The Puppetry Home Page: http://www.sagecraft.com/puppetry/

Bibliography

A selected bibliography of books and periodicals related to performing arts management and producing in America. The books and periodicals are arranged in the following groups:

I. Background Reading
II. Government and the Arts
III. Studies of Individual Theatre Regions, Companies and Managers
IV. Theatrical Producing and Management: General
V. Structure and Management of Nonprofit Organizations
VI. The Board of Trustees
VII. The Arts and the Law
VIII. Economics and the Arts
IX. Financial Management
X. Marketing, Publicity, and Audience Development
XI. Fundraising and Philanthropy
XII. Community Theatre
XIII. Theatre, the Arts, and Education
XIV. Theatre Architecture
XV. Directories and General Reference Books
XVI. Career Guidance
XVII. Bibliographies
XVIII. Periodicals and Annuals

Note:
"American Council for the Arts," "Association of Performing Arts Presenters," and "Drama Book Publishers" are used to indicate publishers previously named "Associated Council of the Arts," "Association of College, University and Community Arts Administrators (ACUCAA)," and "Drama Book Specialists (Publishers)" respectively.

I. BACKGROUND READING

The American Assembly. *The Future of the Performing Arts.* New York: The American Assembly, Columbia University, 1977.

The Arts: A Central Element of a Good Society. New York: American Council for the Arts, 1965.

The Arts Planning for Change. New York: American Council for the Arts, 1966.

Benjamin, Alfred. *The Business of the Theatre: 1750-1932.* Reprint. New York: Benjamin Blom, Inc., 1964.

Brockett, Oscar G. *The Theatre: An Introduction: 5th Edition.* Boston: Allyn and Bacon, Inc. 1987.

Billington, Michael, consulting ed., et al. *Performing Arts. A Guide to Practice and Appreciation.* New York: Facts on File, 1980.

Bloom, Ken, and Frank Vlastnik. *Broadway Musicals: the 101 Greatest Shows of All Time.* New York: Black Dog & Leventhal Publishers, 2004

Boardman. Gerald. *American Musical Theatre: A Chronicle.* New York: Oxford University Press, 1986.

Bradford, Gigi (Editor); Michael Gary (Editor); Glenn Wallach (Editor). *The Politics of Culture: Policy Perspectives for Individuals, Institutions, and Communities* ISBN 1-56584-572-2

DiMaggio, Paul. *Managers of the Arts.* Cabin John, MD: Seven Locks Press, 1987.

Dorian, Frederick. *Commitment to Culture: Arts Patronage in Europe and Its Significance for America.* Pittsburgh: University of Pittsburgh Press, 1964.

Engel, Lehman. *The American Musical Theatre: A Consideration.* New York: CBS Legacy, 1977.

FEDAP'T. *The Challenge of Change: Papers and Presentations from the 15th Annual National Conference.* New York: Foundation for the Extension and Development of the American Professional Theatre, 1987.

Gard, Robert E., Marston Balch, and Pauline Temkin. *Theater in America: Appraisal and Challenge.* New York: Theatre Arts Books, 1963.

Golden. Joseph. *The Death of Tinker Bell: The American Theater, in the 20th Century,* Syracuse, NY: Syracuse University Press, 1967.

Greyser, Stephen A. *Cultured Policy and Arts Administration.* Cambridge, MA: Harvard University Press, 1973.

Heilbrun, James. *The Economics of Art and Culture.* New York: Cambridge University Press, 2001

Hirsch, E.D., Jr. *Cultural Literacy, What Every American Needs to Know.* Boston: Houghton Mifflin Company, 1987.

Hirsch, Foster. *The Boys from Syracuse: The Shuberts' Theatrical Empire.* New York: Cooper Square Press, 2000

Hofstadter, Richard. *Anti-intellectualism in American Life.* New York: Alfred A. Knopf, 1963.

Krawitz, Herman with Howard Klein. *Royal American Symphonic Theater: A Radical Proposal for a Subsidized Professional Theatre.* New York: Macmillan Publishing Company, Inc., 1975.

London, Todd. *The Artistic Home: Discussions with Artistic Directors of America's Institutional Theatres.* New York: Theatre Communications Group, 1988.

Lowry, W. McNeil, ed. *The Performing Arts and American Society.* Englewood Cliffs, NJ: Prentice Hall, 1978.

MacDonald, Dwight. *Against the American Grain: Essays on the Effects of Mass Culture.* New York: Random House, 1962.

Manoff, Robert Karl, ed. *The Buck Starts Here: Enterprise and the Arts.* New York: Volunteer Lawyers for the Arts, 1984.

McLuhan, Marshall. *Culture Is Our Business.* New York: McGraw-Hill, 1970.

Understanding Media: The Extensions of Man. New York: Signet, 1904.

McNamara, Brooks. *The Shuberts of Broadway: a History Drawn from the Collections of the Shubert Archive.* New York: Oxford University Press, c1990.

Miller, Toby, George Yudice. *Cultural Policy (Core Cultural Theorists series)* London: SAGE Publications, Ltd., 2002

Mitchell, Arnold. *The Nine American Lifestyles: Who We Are and Where We're Going.* New York: MacMillan Publishing Company, Inc., 1983.

NEA. *The Arts in America. A Report to the President and to the Congress.* Washington, DC: National Endowment for the Arts, 1988.

Reiss, Alvin H. *Culture & Company.* New York: Twayne Publishers, Inc., 1972.

Rockerfeller Panel Report. *The Performing Arts: Problems and Prospects.* New York: McGraw-Hill, 1965.

Toffler, Alvin. *The Culture Consumers: A Study of Art and Affluence in America*. New York: St. Martin's Press, 1964.

Veblen, Thorstein. (1899). *The Theory of the Leisure Class*. New York: Macmillan (New American Library), 1953.

Von Eckardt, Wolf. *Live the Good Life: Creating a Human Community Through the Arts*. New York: American Council for the Arts, 1982.

Wilson, Robert N., ed. *The Arts in Society*. Englewood Cliffs, NJ: Prentice-Hall, 1964.

II. GOVERNMENT AND THE ARTS

Adams, W. Howard. *The Politics of Art*. New York: American Council for the Arts, 1966.

Americans and the Arts: *A Survey of the Attitudes Toward and Participation in the Arts and Culture of the United States Public*. New York: American Council for the Arts, 1975.

Arian, Edward. *The Unfulfilled Promise: Public Subsidy of the Arts in America*. Philadelphia: Temple University Press, 1989.

Biddle, Livingston. *Our Government and the Arts*. New York: American Council for the Arts, 1988.

Buttita, Tony, and Barry Witham. *Uncle Sam Presents: A Memoir of the Federal Theatre, 1935-1939*. Philadelphia: University of Pennsylvania Press, 1982.

Field, Alan I., and Michael O'Hare, J. Mark Davidson Schuster. *Patrons Despite Themselves: Taxpayers and Arts Policy*. New York: New York University Press, 1983.

Heckscher, August. *The Public Happiness*. New York: Atheneum, 1962.

Kreisberg, Luisa. *Local Government and the Arts*. New York: American Council for the Arts, 1978.

Larson, Gary O. *The Reluctant Patron: The United States Govenmernt and the Arts, 1943-1965*. Philadelphia: University of Pennsylvania Press, 1983.

Lowry, W. McNeil, ed. *The Arts and Public Policy in the United States*. Englewood Cliffs, NJ: Prentice-Hall, 1984.

Mulcahy, K. V., and C. R. Swaim, eds. *Public Policy and the Arts*. Boulder, Co: Westview Press, 1982.

Netzer, Dick. *The Subsidized Muse: Public Support for the Arts in the United States*. New York: Cambridge University Press, 1978.

O'Connor, Francis V., ed. *The New Deal Art Projects: An Anthology of Memoirs*. Washington, D.C.: Smithsonian Institution Press, 1972.

Purcell, Ralph. *Government and Art*. Washington, D.C.: Public Affairs Press, 1953.

Ritterbush, Philip C. *Cultural Policy in the United States*. New York: Publishing Center for Cultural Resources.

Taylor, Famie, and Anthony L. Barresi. *The Arts at a New Frontier*. New York: Plenum Press, 1984.

Waits, C. R., and W. S. Hendon, H. Horowitz, eds. *Governments and Culture*. Akron, OH: Association for Cultural Economics, 1985.

Wyszomirski, Margaret Jane, ed. *Congress and the Arts*. New York: American Council for the Arts, 1987.

III. STUDIES OF INDIVIDUAL THEATRE REGIONS, COMPANIES, AN MANAGERS

Atkinson, Brooks. *Broadway*. New York: Macmillan Company, 1970.

Bentley, Joanne. *Hallie Flanagan: A Life in the American Theatre*. New York: Alfred A. Knopf, 1988.

Bing, Rudolf. *5000 Nights at the Opera*. New York: Doubleday & Company, Inc., 1972.

———. *A Knight at the Opera*. New York: G.P. Putnam and Sons, 1981.

Bloomfield, Arthur J. *The San Francisco Opera: 1923-1961*. New York: Appleton-Century-Crofts, 1961.

Brustein, Robert. Making Scenes: *A Personal History of the Turbulent Years at Yale: 1966-1979*. New York: Random Home, 1981.

Carson, William G.B. *Managers in Distress: The St. Louis Stage, 1840-1844*. Reprint. New York: Benjamin Blom, n.d.

Chinoy, Helen Krich. *Reunion: A Self-Portrait of the Group Theater*. Lanham, MD: University Press of America, 1983.

Churchill, Allen. *The Great White Way: A Re-Creation of Broadway's Golden Age of Theatrical Entertainment*. New York: Dutton, 1902.

Clapp, William Warland. *Record of the Boston Stage*. Reprint. New York: Benjamin Blom, 1968.

Cluman, Harold. *The Fervent Years. New York: Knopf, 1945*. (Republished by Hill & Wang, 1964.)

Crowley, Alice Lewisohn. *The Neighborhood Playhouse: Leaves from a Theatre Scrapbook*. New York: Theatre Arts Books, 1959.

Cox, Bill J. "Katz Productions, Ltd.: A Management Residency Report." Unpublished M.F.A. Dissertation, Brooklyn College, Department of Theatre, 1984.

Deutsch, Helen, and Stella Hanau. *The Provincetown: A Story of the Theatre*. New York: Farrar and Rinehart, 1931.

Donaldson, Frances. *The Actor-Managers*. Chicago: Henry Regnery Company, 1970.

Donohue, Joseph W., Jr., ed. *The Theatrical Manager in England and America, Players of a Perilous Game: Philip Henslowe, Tate Wilkinson, Stephen Price, Edwin Booth, Charles Wyndham*. Princeton, NJ: Princeton University Press, 1971.

Eaton, Walter Prichard. *The Theater Guild: The First Ten Years*. New York: Amo Press, 1926.

Elliott, Eugene C. *A History of Variety-Vaudeville in Seattle from the Beginnings to 1914*. Seattle, WA: University of Washington Press, 1944.

Enders, John. *Survey of New York Theatre*. New York: Playbill, 1959.

Eyre, Richard. *The Future of the Lyric Theatre in London*. London: Stationery Office Books, 1998.

Eyre, Richard, and Nicholas Wright. *Changing Stages: A View of British and American Theatre in the Twentieth Century*. London: Bloomsbury, 2000.

Fishkin, Daniel L. "An Internship with Columbia Artists Management, Inc." Unpublished M.F.A. Dissertation, Brooklyn College, Department of Theatre, 1978.

Flanagan, Hallie. *Arena*. New York: Duell, Sloan and Pearce, 1940.

Fox, Ted. *Showtime at the Apollo*. New York: Holt, Reinhart and Winston, 1983.

Freedley, George. *Broadway Playhouses*. New York: New York Public Library, 1943.

French, Ward. "The Story of the Organized Audience Movement." Unpublished Article, Columbia Artists Management, Inc., Community Concerts Division.

Frick, John W. *New York's First Theatrical Center: The Rialto at Union Square*. Ann Arbor, MI: UMI Research Press, 1985.

Gard. Robert E. *Grassroots Theater*. Madison, WI: University of Wisconsin Press, 1955.

Goldman, William. *The Season: A Candid Look at Broadway*. New York: Harcourt, Brace & World, Inc., 1909.

Gottfried, Martin. *Jed Harris: The Curse of the Genius*. Boston: Little, Brown and Company, 1984.

Graham, Philip. *Showboats: The History of an American Institution*. Dallas: University of Texas, 1951.

Green, Abel, and Jope Lurie Jr. *Show Biz*. New York: Henry Holt Company, 1951.

Greenberger, Howard. *The Off-Broadway Experience*. Englewood Cliffs, NJ Prentice-Hall, Inc., 1971.

Greenwald, Jan Carol. "The Independent Booking Office: A Management Residency Report." Unpublished M.F.A. Dissertation, Brooklyn College, Department of Theatre, 1985.

Guither, Peter S. "Katz Productions: A Management Residency Report." Unpublished M.F.A. Dissertation, Brooklyn College, Department of Theatre, 1985.

Guthrie, Tyrone. *A New Theatre*. New York: McGraw Hill, 1964.

Harding, Alfred. *The Revolt of the Actors*. New York: William Morrow & Company, 1929.

Harrison, Harry P. *Culture Under Canvas: The Story of Tent Chautauqua*. New York: Hastings House, 1958.

Henderson, Mary C. *The City and the Theater*. Clifton, NJ: James T. White, 1973.

Hodge, Francis. *Yankee Theater*. Austin, TX: University of Texas Press, 1964.

Houghton, Norris. *But Not Forgotten. The Adventures of the University Players*. New York: Sloan, 1951.

Ireland, Joseph N. *Records of the New York Stage: 1750-1860*. Reprint. New York: Benjamin Blom, 1968.

James, Reese David. *Cradle of Culture: 1800-1810, The Philadelphia Stage*. Philadelphia: University of Pennsylvania Press, 1957.

Johnson, Charlie H., Jr. *The Central City Opera House: A 100 Year History*. Colorado Springs, CO: Little London Press, 1980.

Johnson, Stephen Burge. *The Roof Gardens of Broadway Theaters, 1883-1942*. Ann Arbor, MI: UMI Research Press, 1985.

Kendall, John S. *The Golden Age of the New Orleans Theater*. New Orleans, LA: Louisiana State University Press, 1952.

Laufe, Abe. *Anatomy of a Hit: Long-Run Plays on Broadway from 1900 to the Present Day.* New York: Hawthorn Books, 1966.

Leavitt, M.B. *Fifty Years in Theatrical Management.* New York: Broadway Publishing, 1912.

Lee, Douglas Bennett, and Roger L. Meersman, Donn B. Murphy. *Stage for a Nation: The National Theatre, 150 Years.* Lanham, MD: University Press of America, Inc., 1986.

Levine, Mindy N. *New York's Other Theatre: A Guide to Off-Off-Broadway.* New York: Avon Books, 1981.

Little, Stuart W. *Off Broadway, The Prophetic Theatre.* New York: Coward, McCann, 1972.

Loney, Glenn, and Patricia MacKay. *The Shakespeare Complex: A Guide to Summer Festivals and Year-Round Repertory in America.* New York: Drama Book Publishers, 1975.

Ludlow, Noah. *Dramatic Life As I Found It.* Reprint. New York: Benjamin Blom, n.d.

MacKay, Constance Darcy. *The Little Theatre in the United States.* New York: T. Holt, 1917.

Marcosson, Isaac F., and Daniel Frohman. *Charles Frohman, Manager and Man.* New York: Harper, 1916.

Martin, Ralph G. *Lincoln Center for the Performing Arts.* Englewood Cliffs, NJ: Prentice-Hall, 1971.

McAvay, Gary S. "Columbia Artists Theatricals Corp.: A Management Residency Report." Unpublished M.F.A. Dissertation, Brooklyn College, Department of Theatre, 1982.

McCleary, Albert, and Carl Glick. *Curtains Going Up.* Chicago and New York: Pitman, 1939.

McLean, Albert F., Jr. *American Vaudeville As Ritual.* Lexington, KY: University of Kentucky Press, 1965.

Merkling, Frank, and John W. Freeman, Gerald Fitzgerald. *The Golden Horseshoe: The Life and Times of the Metropolitan Opera House.* New York: The Viking Press, 1965.

Moody, Richard. *The Astor Place Riot.* Bloomington, IN: Indiana University Press, 1958.

Moore, Jonathan D. "The Independent Booking Office: A Management Residency Report." Unpublished M.F.A. Dissertation, Brooklyn College, Department of Theatre, 1984.

Nelson, Stephen. *"Only A Paper Moon:" The Theater, of Billy Rose.* Ann Arbor, MI: The University of Michigan Press, 1987. `

Newton, Michael, and Scott Hatley. *Persuade and Provide: The Story of the Arts and Education Council in St. Louis.* New York: American Council for the Arts, 1970.

Novick, Julius. *Beyond Broadway: The Quest for Permanent Theaters.* New York: Hill and Wang, 1968.

The Ontario Theatre Study Report. *The Awkward Stage.* Toronto: Methuen Publications, 1969.

Patrick, J. Max. *Savannah's Pioneer Theater: From Its Origins to 1810.* Atlanta, GA: University of Georgia Press, 1953.

Pollock, Thomas Clark. *The Philadelphia Theatre in the Eighteenth Century.* Philadelphia: University of Pennsylvania Press, 1933.

Prevots, Naima. *American Pageantry.* Ann Arbor, MI: UMI Research Press, 1990.

Price, Julia S. *The Off-Broadway Theater.* New York: Scarecrow Press, 1962.

Rubin, Stephen E. *The New Met in Profile.* New York: Macmillan Publishing Company, Inc. 1975.

Salem, Mahmoud. *Organizational Survival in the Performing Arts: The Making of the Seattle Opera.* New York: 1976.

Selznick, Irene Mayer. *A Private View.* New York, Knopf, 1983.

Smith, Patrick J. *A Year at the Met.* New York: Alfred A. Knopf, 1983.

Smith, Sol. *Theatrical Management in the West and South for 30 Years.* Reprint. New York: Benjamin Blom, n.d.

Smither, Nelle. *A History of the English Theater at New Orleans: 1806-1842.* Reprint. New York: Benjamin Blom, 1967.

Sobel, Bernard. *Broadway Heartbeat: Memoirs of Press Agent.* New York: Heritage, 1953.

Sokok, Martin L. *The New, York City Opera: an American Adventure.* New York: Macmillan Publishing Company, Inc., 1981.

Stagg, Jerry. *The Brothers Shubert.* New York: Random House, 1968.

Straight, Michael. *Nancy Hanks: An Intimate Portrait.* Durham and London: Duke University Press, 1988.

Taper, Bernard. *The Arts in Boston, An Outsider's View of the Cultural Estate.* Cambridge, MA: Harvard University Press, 1970.

Willard, George O. *History of the Providence State 1762-1891.* Providence, RI: The Rhode Island News Company, 1891.

Young, Edgar B. *Lincoln Center: The Building of and Institution.* New York: New York University Press, 1980.

Zeigler, Joseph W. *Regional Theatre: The Revolutionary Stage.* New York: DeCapo Press, 1973.

IV. THEATRICAL PRODUCING AND MANAGEMENT: GENERAL

Barrell, M.K. *The Technical Production Handbook: A Guide for Sponsors of Performing Arts Companies on Tour.* Conolly, L.W., ed. Denver, CO: Western States Arts Foundation, 1977.

————. *Theatrical Touring and Founding in North America.* Westport, CT: Greenwood Press, 1982.

Byrnes, William J. *Management and the Arts.* New York: Focal Press, 2003

Chong, Derrick. *Arts Management.* New York: Routledge, 2002

Collins, Tess. *How Theatre Managers Manage.* Lanham, MD: Scarecrow Press, 2003.

Cullman, Marguerite. *Occupation Angel.* New York: W. W. Norton, 1963.

Cultural Resource Development. *Preliminary Planning Survey and Survey and Analysis.* New York: New York State Commission on Cultural Resources, 1973.

Dilker, Barbara. *Stage Management Forms and Formats.* Drama Book Publishers, 1979.

Eaton, Quaintance. *Opera Production I: A Handbook.* New York, DeCapo Press, 1974.

————. *Opera Production II: A Handbook.* Minneapolis, MN: University of Minnesota Press, 1974.

Ellfeldt, Lois, and Edwin Cames. *Dance Production Handbook.* Mayfield Publishing Company, 1971.

Engel, Lehman. *Planning and Producing the Musical Show.* New York: Crown Publishers', 1967.

Eustis, Morton. *B'way, Inc! The Theatre as a Business.* New York: Dodd Mead, 1934.

Farber, Donald C. *From Option to Opening,* 3rd ed., revised. New York: Drama Book Publishers, 1977.

————. *Producing Theatre: A Comprehensive Legal and Business Guide.* New York: Drama Book Publishers, 1981.

Gassner, John. *Producing the Play.* New York: Dryden Press, 1953.

Golden, Joseph. *Help! A Guide to Seeking, Selecting and Surviving an Arts Consultant.* Syracuse, NY: Cultural Resources Council, 1983.

Graf, Herbert. *Producing Opera for America.* New York: Atlantis Books, 1961.

Gruver, Burt, revised by Frank Hamilton. *The Stage Managers Handbook.* New York: Drama Book Publishers, 1972.

How To Do It 'Kit': Airs for Volunteer Administrators. Washington, D.C.: National Center for Voluntary Action, 1976.

Jeffri, Joan. *The Emerging Arts Management, Survival and Growth.* New York: Oraeger Publishers, 1980.

Jones, Margo. *Theatre-in-the-Round.* New York: McGraw-Hill Paperbacks, 1965.

Langley, Stephen, ed. *Producers On Producing.* New York: Drama Book Publishers, 1976.

Lewis, Philip C. *Trouping: How The Show Came to Town.* New York: Harper & Row, n.d.

Manoff, Robert Karl. *The Buck Starts Here: Enterprise in the Arts.* New York: Volunteer Lawyers for the Arts, 1984.

Moskow, Michael. *Labor Unions and the Arts.* New York: American Council for the Arts, 1970.

Pick, John. *Arts Administration.* New York: E. & F. N. Spon in association with Methuen, 1980.

Plummer, Gail. *The Business of Show Business.* New York: Harper and Brothers, 1961.

Presenting in America. Kansas City, MO: Mid-America Arts Alliance, 1988.

Pravots, Naima. *American Pagentry.* Ann Arbor. MI: UMI Research Press, 1990.

Raymond, Thomas C., and Stephen A. Greyser, Douglas Schwalbe. *Cases in Arts Administration.* Revised ed. Cambridge, MA: Arts Administration Research Institute, Harvard University, 1975.

Reiss, Alvin H. *The Arts Management Reader.* 2nd Revised ed. New York: Law Arts Publishers, 1979.

Shagan, Rena. *Road Show: A Handbook for Successful Booking and Touring in the Performing Arts.* New York: American Council for the Arts, 1985.

Sikes, Toni Fountain, ed. *ACUCAA Handbook. Presenting the Performing Arts.* Washington, D.C.: Association of Performing Arts Presenters (formerly the Association of College, University and Community Arts Administrators), 1984.

Stanton, Sanford E. *Theatre Management.* New York: Appleton-Century, 1929.

Stern, Lawrence. *Stage Management.* Boston: Allyn and Bacon, Inc., 1974.

Taylor, Fannie. *Negotiating and Contracting for Artists and Attractions at Educational and Nonprofit Institutions.* Washington, D.C.: Association of Performing Arts Presenters, 1982.

Visser, David. *Hitting the Road Planning a Performing Arts Tour.* New York: Theatre Communications Group, 1982.

Volz, Jim. *How to Run a Theater.* New York: Backstage Books. 2004

Webb, Duncan M. *Running Theatres.* New York: Allworth Press, 2004

Wolf, Thomas. *Presenting Performances: A Handbook for Sponsors.* Cambridge, MA: New England Foundation for the Arts, 1977.

V. STRUCTURE AND MANAGEMENT OF NONPROFIT ORGANIZATIONS

Clifton, Roger L., and Richard L. Reinert, Louise K. Stevens. *The Road to Success: A Unique Development Guide for Small Arts Groups.* Boston: Massachusetts Cultural Alliance, 1988.

Conrad, William R., and Willima R. Glenn. *The Effective Voluntary Board of Directors: What It Is and How It Works.* Chicago: Swallow Press. 1975.

Connors, Tracy D., ed. *The Nonprofit Organization Handbook.* New York: McGraw-Hill, Inc., 1980.

Crimmins, James C., and Mary Kiel. *Enterprise in the Non-Profit Sector.* New York: American Council for the Arts, 1983.

Dougheny, Carol. *How Full of Briars: The Organizational Structure of the Non-Profit Theatre Corporation.* Orlando, FL: Orlando Publishing, 1983.

Horwitz, Tem, and Thomas R. Leavens. *Arts Administration: How to Set Up and Run a Successful Nonprofit Arts Organization.* Chicago: Chicago Review Press, 1977.

Oleck, Howard. *Nonprofit Corporations, Organizations and Associations.* 3rd ed. Englewood Cliffs, NJ: Prentice-Hall, 1974.

Peterson, Eric. *Nonprofit Arts Organizations: Formation and Maintenance.* Berkeley, CA: Bay Area Lawyers for the Arts, 1977.

Setterberg, Fred, and Kary Schulman. *Beyond Profit: The Complete Guide to Managing the Nonprofit Organization.* New York: Harper & Row Publishers, 1985.

Vogel, Frederick B., ed. *No Quick Fix (Planning).* New York: Foundation for the Extension and Development of the American Professional Theatre, 1985.

Volunteer Lawyers for the Arts. *New York Not for-Profit Organization Manual.* New York: Volunteer Lawyers for the Acts, 1982.

Wolf, Thomas. *The Nonprofit Organization.* Englewood Cliffs, NJ: Prentice Hall, 1984.

VI. THE BOARD OF DIRECTORS

Crawford, Robert W. *In Art We Trust: The Board of Trustees in the Performing Arts.* New York: Foundation for the Extension and Development of the American Professional Theatre, 1981.

Duca, Diane J. *Nonprofit Boards: A Practical Guide to Roles, Responsibilities and Performance.* Phoenix, AZ: Oryx Press, 1988.

The Key to Effective Trusteeship of Arts Organizations: The Board Chairman and His Challenge. University Park, PA: Pennsylvania State University, 1976.

Kurtz, Daniel, L. *Board Liability: Guide for Nonprofit Directors.* New York: Volunteer Lawyers for the Arts, 1988.

O'Connell, Brian. *The Board Member's Book: Making a Difference in Voluntary Organizations.* New York: The Foundation Center, 1988.

Paquet, Marion A., with Rory Ralston and Donna Cardinal. *A Handbook for Cultural Trustees.* Waterloo, Ontario, Canada: University of Waterloo Press, 1987.

Rauner, Judy. *Helping People Volunteer.* San Diego, CA: Marlborough Publications, 1980.

Trost, Any, and Judy Rauner. *Gaining Momentum: For Board Action.* New York: American Council for the Arts, 1984.

U.S. Chamber of Commerce. *Association Bylaws*. Washington, D.C.: U.S. Chamber of Commerce (Association Department), n.d.

U.S. Chamber of Commerce. *Association Committees*. Washington, D.C.: U.S. Chamber of Commerce (Association Department), n.d.

VII. THE ARTS AND THE LAW

Council of New York Law Associates. *Getting Organized. A Guide to Acquiring and Maintaining Corporate and Tax Exempt Status for Non Profit Organizations*. New York: Volunteer Lawyers for the Arts, 1984.

Farber, Donald C. *Actor's Guide: What You Should Know About the Contracts You Sign*. New York: Drama Book Publishers, 1971.

————, ed. *Entertainment Industry Contracts*. 4 Vols. Albany, NY: Matthew Bender & Company, 1987.

————. *Producing Theatre: A Comprehensive Legal and Business Guide*. New York: Drama Book Publishers, 1981.

Golden, Joseph. *On The Dotted Line: The Anatomy of a Contract*. Syracuse, NY: Cultural Resources Council, 1979.

How To Apply For and Retain Exempt Status. (Publication #557] Washington, D.C.: The Internal Revenue Service, n.d.

Jacobs, Milton. *Outline of Theatre Law*. New York: Greenwood, 1972.

Kurtz, Daniel L. *Liability Guide for Nonprofit Boards of Directors*. New York: Noyer-Bell Limited, 1988.

Lidstone, Herrick K., and R. J. Ruble. *Exempt Organizations and the Arts*. New York: Volunteer Lawyers for the Arts, 1976.

Rudell, Michael L. *Behind the Scenes: Practical Entertainment Law*. New York: Law & Business, 1984.

Taubman, Joseph. *Performing Arts Management and Law*. 4 Vols. New York: Law-Arts Publishers, Inc. 1972.

U.S. Chamber of Commerce. *Association Legal Checklist*. Washington, D.C.: U.S. Chamber of Commerce (Association Department), n.d.

Volunteer Lawyers for the Arts. *The New York Not-for-Profit Organization Manual of the Conference Sponsored by the Council of New York Law Associates,* Volunteer Lawyers, for the Arts. New York: Volunteer Lawyers for the Arts, 1978.

Volunteer Lawyers for the Arts. *VIA Guide to Copyright for the Performing Arts*. New York: Volunteer Lawyers for the Arts, 1988.

VIII. ECONOMICS AND THE ARTS

The Arts as an Industry Their Economic importance to the New York/New Jersey Metropolitan Region. New York: Cultural Assistance Center and The Port Authority of New York and New Jersey, 1983.

Baumol, William J., and William G. Bowen. *Performing Arts: The Economic Dilemma*. New York: The Twentieth Century Fund, 1966.

Blaug, Mark, ed. *The Economics of the Arts*. Boulder, CO: Westview Press, 1976.

DiMaggio, Paul, ed. *Non-Profit Enterprise in the Arts*. New York: Oxford University Press, 1986.

Ford, Neil M., and Bonnie J. Queram. *Pricing Strategy for the Performing Arts*. Washington, D.C.: Association of Performing Arts Presenters, 1980.

Grant, Nancy K., and William S. Hendon, Virginia Lee Owen, eds. *Economic Efficiency and the Performing Arts*. Akron, OH: Association for Cultural Exonomics, University of Akron 1987.

Hendon, W. S., and N. K. Grant, D. V. Shaw, eds. *The Economics of Cultural Industries*. Akron, OH: Association for Cultural Economics, University of Akron, 1984.

Hendon, William S., and Harry Hillman-Chartrand, Harold Horowitz. *Paying for the Arts*. Akron, OH: Association for Cultural Economics, University of Akron, 1987.

Hendon, M. A., and J. F. Richardson, W. S. Hendon, eds. *Bach and the Box. The Impact of Television on the Live Arts*. Akron, OH: Association for Cultural~Economics, University of Akron, 1985.

Hendon, W. S., and J. L. Shanahan, eds. *Economics of Cultural Decisions*. Akron, OH: Association for Cultural Economics, University of Akron, 1983.

Hendon, William S., and J. L. Shanahan, A. J. MacDonald, eds. *Economic Policy for the Arts.* Cambridge, MA: Abt Books, 1980.

Hendon, W. S., and J.L. Shanahan, LT.H. Hilhorst, J. van Straalen, eds. *Economic Research in the Performing Arts.* Akron, OH: Association for Cultural Economics, University of Akron, 1983.

Hendon, W. S., and J.L. Shanahan, LT.H. Hilhorst, J. van Staalen, eds. *Markets for the Arts.* Akron, OH: Association for Cultural Economics, University of Akron, 1983.

McNulty, Robert H., and R. Leo Penne, Dorothy R. Jacobson. *The Economics of Amenity: Community Future and the Quality of Life.* New York: Partners for Livable Places, 1985.

Moore, Thomas Gale. *The Economics of the American Theatre.* Durham, NC: Duke University Press, 1968.

Owen, V. L., and W. S. Hendon, eds. *Managerial Economics for the Arts.* Akron, OH: The University of Akron, 1985.

Perloff, Harvey S., ed. *The Arts in the Economic Life of the City.* New York: American Council for the Arts, 1979.

Poggi, Jack. *Theater in America: The Impact of Economic Forces, 1870-1967.* Ithaca, NY: Cornell University Press, 1968.

Shaw, Douglas V., and William S. Hendon, C. Richard Waits, eds. *Artists and Cultural Consumers.* Akron, OH: Association for Cultural Economics, University of Akron, 1987.

Throsby, C. D., and G. A. Withers. *The Economics of the Performing Arts.* New York: St. Martin's Press, 1979.

Vogel, Harold L. *Entertainment Industry Economics.* Cambridge, UK: Cambridge University Press, 1986.

IX.   FINANCIAL MANAGEMENT

A Portrait of the Financial Condition of Presenting Organizations. Washington, D.C.: Association of Performing Arts Presenters, 1987.

Anthony, Robert T., and Regina E. Herzlinger. *Management Control in Nonprofit Organizations.* Homewood, IL: Richard W. Irwin, 1975.

Beck, Kirsten. *How To Run a Small Box Office.* New York: The Alliance of Resident Theatres/New York, 1980.

Ferber, Henry. *Reserved Seat Box-Office.* New York: National Ticket Company, n.d.

The Finances of the Performing Arts: Volume I, (A Survey of 166 Professional Nonprofit Resident Theatre, Opera, Symphony, Ballet and Modern Dance Companies.) New York: Ford Foundation, 1974.

The Finances of the Performing Arts: Volume II. (A Survey of the Characteristics and Attitudes of Audiences for Theatre, Opera, Symphony and Ballet in 12 U.S. Cities.) New York: Ford Foundation, 1974.

Gross, Malvern J., and William Warshauer, Jr. *Financial and Accounting Guide for Nonprofit Organizations.* 3rd ed. New York: John Wiley & Sons, 1983.

Jeffries, Joan. *Art Money: Raising It, Saving It and Earning It.* New York: Neal Schuman Publishers, Inc., 1983.

Messman, Carla. *The Art of Filing.* New York: Volunteer Lawyers for the Arts, 1988.

Nelson, Charles A., and Frederick J. Turk. *Financial Management for the Arts:/A Guidebook for Arts Organizations.* New York: American Council for the Arts, 1976.

Taubman, Joseph, ed. *Financing a Theatrical Production.* New York: Federal Legal Publications, Inc., 1964.

Turk, Frederick J., and Robert P. Gallo. *Financial Management Strategies for Arts Organizations.* New York: American Council for the Arts, 1984.

Wehle, Mary M. *Financial Management for Arts Organizations.* Cambridge, MA: Arts Administration Research Institute, Harvard University, 1975.

————. *Financial Practice for Performing Arts Companies: A Manual.* Cambridge, MA: Arts Administration Research Institute, Harvard University, 1977.

Wharton, John F. *A Fresh Look at Theatre Tickets.* (Report to the Legitimate Theatre Industry Exploratory Commission.) New York: League of New York Theatre, 1965.

————. *Some Forgotten Facets of Theatrical Financing.* (A Report to the Legitimate Theatre Industry Exploratory Commission.) New York: League of New York Theatres, n.d.

X. MARKETING, PUBLICITY, AND AUDIENCE DEVELOPMENT

Alexander, J. H. ed. *Early American Theatrical Posters*. Hollywood, CA: Cherokee Books, n.d.

Arnold, Mark. *Dialing for Dollars: Subscription Sales Through Telemarketing*. New York: Theatre Communications Group, 1982.

Barry, John F., and Epes W. Sargent. *Building Theatre Patronage*. New York: Chalmers Co., 1927.

Biegel, Len, and Aileen Lubin. *Mediability: A Guide to Nonprofits*. Washington, D.C.: Taft Products, 1975.

Blimes, Michael E., and Ron Sproat. *More Dialing, More Dollars: 12 Steps to Successful Telemarketing*. New York: American Council for the Arts, 1986.

Breen, George Edward, and A. B. Blankenship. *Do-It-Yourself Marketing Research*. 2nd ed. New York: McGraw-Hill, 1982.

Capbern, A. Martial. *The Drama Publicist*. New York: Pageant Press, Inc., 1968.

Cole, Robert S. *The Practical Book of Public Relations*. Englewood Cliffs, NJ: Prentice-Hall, 1981.

Frank, Susan with Mindy N. Levine. *In Print: A Concise Guide to Graphic Arts and Printing for Small Businesses and Nonprofit Organizations*. New York: Alliance for Resident Theatres/New York, 1984.

Foundation for the Extension and Development of the American Professional Theatre. *Subscription Guidelines*. Rev. ed. New York: FEDAPT, 1977.

Kotler, Philip. *Marketing for Nonprofit Organizations*. 2nd ed. Englewood Cliffs, NJ: Prentice-Hall, 1983.

———. *Marketing Management: Analysis, Planning and Control*. 4th ed. Englewood Cliffs, NJ: Prentice-Hall, 1980.

———. *Standing Room Only*. New York: Americans for the Arts, 1997

Laundy, Peter, and Massima Bignelli. *Graphic Design for Nonprofit Organizations*. New York: American Institute of Graphic Arts, 1980.

Levine, Mindy N. with Susan Frank. *In Print. A Concise Guide to Graphic Arts and Printing for Small Businesses and Nonprofit Organizations*. Englewood Cliffs, NJ: Prentice-Hall, 1984.

Maas, Jane. *Better Brochures, Catalogs and Mailing Pieces*. New York: St. Martin's Press, 1981.

MacIntyre, Kate. *Sold Out: A Publicity and Marketing Guide*. New York: Theatre Development Fund, 1980.

McArthur, Nancy. *How To Do Theatre Publicity*. Berea. OH: Good Ideas Company, 1978.

Melillo, Joseph V. *Market the Arts!* New York: The Foundation for the Extension and Development of the American Professional Theatre, 1983.

Metropolitan Cultural Alliance. *Getting in Ink and on the Air: A Publicity Handbook*. Rev. ed. Boston: Metropolitan Cultural Alliance, 1978.

Mitchel, Arnold. *Marketing the Arts*. Menlo Park, CA: Stanford Research Institute, 1962.

———. *Professional Performing Arts: Attendance Patterns, Preferences and Motives*. 2 Vols. Washington, D.C.: Association of Performing Arts Presenters, 1984.

Mokwa, Michael, and William N. Dawson, E. Arthur Prieve, eds. *Marketing the Arts*. New York: Praeger Publishers, 1980.

Morison, Bradley G., and Julie Gordon Dalgleish. *Waiting in the Wings: A Larger Audience for the Arts and How to Develop It*. New York: American Council for the Arts, 1987.

National Endowment for the Arts. *Audience Development: An Examination of Selected Analysis Prediction Techniques Applied to Symphony and Theatre Attendance in Four Southern Cities*. New York: Publishing Center for Cultural Resources, 1981.

National Endowment for the Arts. *Surveying Your Audience*. New York: Publishing Center for Cultural Resources, 1985.

Newman, Danny. *Subscribe Now! Building Arts Audiences Through Dynamic Subscription Promotion*. New York: Theatre Communications Group, 1977.

O'Donnell, Trevor, with Bob Hoffman. *Group Sales for Arts and Entertainment*. Hollywood, CA: Entertainment Pro, 2005.

Parkhurst, William. *How To Get Publicity*. New York: Times Books, 1985.

Reiss, Alvin, H. *CPR for Nonprofits: Creative Strategies for Successful Fundraising, Marketing, Communications and Management*. New York: Jossey-Bass Inc. A Wiley Company,2004.

Ries, Al, and Jack Troot. *Positioning: The Battle for Your Mind*. New York: McGraw-Hill, 1981.

Rossie, Chuck, ed. *The Media Resource Guide: How To Tell Your Story.* 4th ed. New York: Gannett Foundation, 1985.

Skal, David J., ed., and Robert E. Callahan, designer. *Graphic Communications for the Performing Arts.* New York: Theatre Communications Group, 1981.

Tedone, David. *Practical Publicity: How To Boost Any Cause.* Boston: The Harvard Common Press, 1983.

Warwick, Charles A., and Donald P. Lininger. *The Sample Survey: Theory and Practice.* New York: McGraw-Hill, 1975.

XI. FUNDRAISING AND PHILANTHROPY

Bergin, Ron. *Sponsorship and the Arts.* Evanston, IL: Entertainment Resource Group, 1990.

Brentlinger, Marilyn E., and Judith M. Weiss. *The Ultimate Benefit Book: How To Raise $50,000-plus for Your Organization.* Cleveland, OH: Octavia Press, 1987.

Brownrigg, W. Grant. *Effective Corporate Fundraising.* New York: American Council for the Arts, 1982.

Chagy, Gideon. *The New Patrons of the Arts.* New York: Harry N. Abrams, Inc., 1973.

————. *The State of the Arts and Corporate Support.* New York: Eriksson, 1971.

Chamberlain, Marjorie. *The Art of Winning Corporate Grants.* New York: Vanguard Press, 1980.

Cummings, Milton C. Jr., and Richard S. Katz, eds. *The Patron State.* New York: Oxford University Press, 1987.

Cummings, Milton C. Jr., and J. Mark Davidson Schuster, eds. *Who's To Pay? (The International Search for Models of Arts Support).* New York: American Council for the Arts, 1988.

Daniels, Ellen S. *How to Raise Money Special Events for Arts Organizations.* New York: American Council for the Arts, 1977.

Eells, Richard. *The Corporation and the Arts.* New York: Macmillan, 1967.

Gingrich, Arnold. *Business and the Arts.* New York: Paul S. Eriksson, Inc., 1969.

Grants for the Arts and Cultural Programs. New York: The Foundation Center, 1987.

Grasby, William K., and Kenneth G. Sheinkopf.

Successful Fundraising: A Handbook of Proven Strategies and Techniques. New York: Charles Scribner's Sons, 1982.

Keller, Mitchell, ed. *The KRC Guide to Direct Mail Fund Raising.* New Canaan, CT: KRC Development Council, 1977.

Mark, Charles C. *Federated Fund Raising by AM Councils.* New York: American Council for the Arts, 1965.

Partners: A Practical Guide to Corporate Support of the Arts. New York: Alliance for the Arts, 1982.

People in Philanthropy. Washington, D.C.: The Taft Corporation, 1988.

Plinio, Alex J., and Joanne B. Scanlon. *Resource Raising: The Role of Non-Cash Assistance in Corporate Philanthropy.* Washington, D.C.: The Independent Sector, 1986.

Porter, Robert, ed. *Guide to Corporate Giving in the Arts.* New York: American Council for the Arts, 1988.

Reiss, Alvin H. *Cash In!: Funding and Promoting the Arts.* New York: Theatre Communications Group, 1986.

Reiss, Alvin H. *Don't Just Applaud, Send Money!: The Most Successful Strategies for Funding and Marketing the Arts.* New York: Theatre Communications Group, Inc., 1995.

Reiss, Alvin H. *Reiss Source Directory for the Arts.* Chicago: Columbia College, 2005.

Sikes, Toni F., ed. *Fundraising Letter Idea Book.* Washington, D.C.: Association of Performing Arts Presenters, 1984.

Source Book Profiles, 2 Vols. New York: The Foundation Center, n.d.

Stopler, Carolyn L., and Karen Brooks Hopkins. *Successful Fundraising, for Arts and Cultural Organizations.* Phoenix, AZ: Oryx Press, 1989.

United Arts Fundraising. New York: American Council for the Arts, 1987.

Wagner, Susan, ed. *A Guide to Corporate Giving in the Arts.* New York: American Council for the Arts, 1978.

Watson, John H., III. *Corporate Support of the Arts.* New York: National Industrial Conference Board, 1970.

White, Virginia. *Grants for the Arts.* New York: Plenum Press, 1980.

Wyszomirdki, Margaret, and Pat Clubb, eds. *Private Art Patronage: Patterns and Prospects.* New York: American Council for the Arts, 1988.

————. *The Cost of Culture.* New York: American Council for the Arts, 1989.

Young, Donald R., and Wilbert E. Moore. *Trusteeship and the Management of Foundations*. New York: Russell Sage Foundation, 1969.

Young, John W. *The Community Theater: A Manual for Success*. New York: Samuel French, 1971.

XII. COMMUNITY THEATRE

Bilowit, Ira J. *How To Organize and Operate a Community Theatre*. New York: American National Theatre and Academy, 1964.

Burgard, Ralph. *Arts in the City: Organizing and Programming Community Arts Councils*. New York: American Council for the Arts, n.d.

Cavanaugh, Jim. *Organization and Management of the Nonprofessional Theater*. New York: Richard Rosen Press, Inc., 1973.

Clark, Barrett H. *How to Produce Amateur Plays*. Boston: Little, Brown and Company, 1925.

Cutler, Bruce. *The Arts at the Grassroots*. Lawrence, KS: University of Kansas Press, 1968.

Dalrymple, Jean. *The Complete Handbook. for Community Theater*. New York: Drake Publisers, 1977.

Daniels, Ellen S., and Robert Porter. *Community Arts Agencies: A Handbook and Guide*. New York: American Council for the Arts, 1978.

Gard, Robert E., and Gertrude S. Burley. *Community Theatre*. New York: Duell, Sloan and I'earce, 1959.

Gibons, Nina Freedlander. *The Community Arts Council Movement: History, Opinions, Issues*. New York: Praeger Publishers, 1982.

Golden, Joseph. *Olympus on Main Street. A Process for Planning a Community Arts Faculty*. Syracuse, NY: Syracuse University Press, 1980.

Green, Joann. *The Small Theater Handbook*. Boston: The Harvard Common Press, 1981.

Legat, Michael. *Putting on a Play*. New York: St. Martin's Press, 1984.

McCalmon, George, and Christian Moe. *Creating Historical Drama: A Guide for the Community and Interested Individuals*. Carbondale, IL: Southern Illinois University Press, 1965.

Pearson, Talbot. *Encores on Main Street. Successful Community Theatre Leadership*. Pittsburgh, PA: Camegie Institute of Technology Press, 1948.

Seldon, Samuel, ed. *Organizing a Community Theatre*. Cleveland, OH: National Theatre Conference, 1945.

Stern, Lawrence. *School and Community Theatre Management*. Boston: Allyn & Bacon, 1979.

XIII. THEATRE, THE ARTS, AND EDUCATION

Abbs, Peter. *Living Powers: The Arts in Education*. Philadelphia: Taylor and Francis International Publishers, 1987.

Arts, Education and Americans Panel. *Coming to Our Senses: The Significance of the Art for American Education*. Reprint. New York: American Council for the Arts, 1988.

The Arts and the University. New York: Council on Higher Education in the American Republics, Institute of International Education, 1964.

Balfe, Judith H., and Joni Cherbo Heine. *Arts Education Beyond the Classroom*. New York: American Council for the Arts, 1988.

Bernardi, Bonnie, and Beverly Grova, Nancy Meyberg, Valerie Wolf. *Partners in the Arts: An Arts in Education Handbook*. Santa Cruz, CA: Cultural Council of Santa Cruz County, 1983.

Bloom, Kathryn. *Arts Organizations and Their Services to Schools: Patrons or Partners?* New York: The JDR 3rd Fund, 1974.

Carnegie Commission on Higher Education. *The Rise of the Arts on American Campus*. New York: McGraw-Hill, 1973.

Clifford, John E. *Educational Theater Management*. Skokie, IL. National Textbook Company, 1972.

Courtney, Richard. *The Dramatic Curriculum*. New York: Drama Book Publishers, 1980.

Davis, Jed H., ed. *Theater Education: Mandate for Tomorrow*. New Orleans, LA: Anchorage Press, 1985.

Davis, Jed H., and Mary Jane Evans. *Theater, Children, and Youth*. New Orleans, LA: Anchorage Press, 1982.

Educational Facilities Laboratories. *Thee Arts and Surplus School Space*. New York: Educational Facilities Laboratories, 1981.

Fowler, Charles. *Can We Rescue the Arts for Americas Children? (Coming to Our Senses 10 Years Later)*. New York: American Council for the Arts, 1988.

Holtje, Adrienne. *Putting On a School Play*. New York: Parket Publishing Company, 1980.

Katz, Jonathan, ed. *Arts and Education Handbook.* Washington, D.C.: National Association of State Arts Agencies, 1987.

McLaughlin, John, ed. *A Guide to National and State Arts Education Services.* New York: American Council for the Arts, 1987.

Morrison, Jack. Foreword by Clark Kerr. *The Maturing of the Arts on the American Campus.* Lanham, MD: University Press of America, Inc., 1985.

National Endowment for the Arts. *Toward Civilization: A Report on Arts Education.* Washington, D.C.: National Endowment for the Arts, 1988.

New England Foundation for the Arts. *The Arts Go To School. An Arts-in-Education Handbook.* New York: American Council for the Arts, 1983.

Ommanney, Katherine. *The Stage and the School.* Reprint. New York: Harper and Company, 1982.

Remer, Jane. *Changing Schools Through the Arts.* New York: McGraw-Hill, 1982.

Schubart, Mark. *Hunting of the Squiggle: A Study of a Performing Arts Institution and Young People, Conducted by Lincoln Center for the Performing Arts.* New York: Praeger, 1972.

Sterling, Carol, and Mary Jane Bolin. *Arts Proposal Writing: A Sourcebook of Ideas for Writing Proposals for Any School Program.* Princeton, NJ: Educational Improvement Center Press, 1982.

Willis, Jerry. *Negotiating and Contracting by Educational and Other Non-Profit Institutions.* Washington, D.C.: Association of Performing Arts Presenters, 1980.

Wolf, Thomas. *The Arts Go To School: An Arts-in Education Handbook.* New York: American Council for the Arts, 1983.

XIV. THEATRE ARCHITECTURE

American Theatre Planning Board. *Theatre Check List: A Guide to the Planning and Construction of Proscenium and Open Stage Theaters.* Rev. ed. Middletown, CT: Wesleyan University Press, 1983.

Armstrong, Leslie, AIA, and Roger Morgan. *Space for Dance.* Dallas: Publishing Center for Cultural Resources (for the National Endowment for the Arts), 1984.

The Arts in Found Places, A Report. New York: Educational Facilities Laboratories, 1976.

Beranek, Leo L. *Acoustics.* New York: McGraw-Hill Book Company, 1954.

————. *Music, Acoustics and Architecture.* New York: John Wiley and Sons, Inc., 1962.

Brown, Catherine R., and William B. Flessig, William R. Morrish. *Building for the Arts: A Guidebook for the Planning and Design of a Cultural Facility.* Rev. ed. Denver, CO: Western States Arts Foundation, 1989.

Burris-Meyer, Harold., and Edward C. Cole. *Theaters and Auditoriums.* Rev. 2nd ed. Huntington, NY: Robert E. Krieger Publishing Company, 1975.

Burris-Meyer, Harold., and Lewis S. Goodfriend. *Acoustics for the Architect.* New York: Reinhold Publishing Corp., 1957.

Burris-Meyer, Harold, and Dorothea Mallory, Lewis S. Goodfriend. *Sound in the Theatre.* 2nd ed. New York: Theatre Arts Books, 1979.

Cogswell, Margaret, ed. *The Ideal Theatre: Eight Concepts.* New York: American Federation of the Arts, 1962.

Collison, David. *Stage Sound.* London: Cassell, 1982.

Department of the Army. *Design Guide for Music and Drama Centers.* (DG 1110.3.120.) Issued by Engineering Division, Military Programs Directorate, Office of the Chief Engineers, U.S. Army, 1982.

Egan, M. David. *Concepts in Architectural Acoustics.* New York: McGraw-Hill, 1972.

Elder, Eldon. *Will It Make a Theater?* New York: Alliance for Resident Theatres/New York, 1979.

Finelli, Patrick. *Sound for the Stage: A Technical Handbook.* New York: Drama Book Publishers, 1989.

Friedman, Daniel, and Joseph Valerio. *America's Movie Palaces: Renaissance and Reuse.* New York: Educational Facilities Laboratories, 1982.

Izenour, George C. *Theatre Design.* New York: McGraw-Hill, 1977.

Joseph, Stephen. *New Theatre Forms.* New York: Theatre Arts Books, 1968.

Knudsen, V.O., and C.N. Harris. *Acoustical Designing in Architecture.* New York: John Wiley and Sons, 1950.

Leacroft, Richard, and Helen Leacroft. *Theatre and Playhouse: An Illustrated Survey of the Theatre Building from Ancient Greece to the Present Day*. London: Methuen, 1984.

Mayer, Martin. *Bricks, Mortar and the Performing Arts*. New York: Twentieth Century Fund, 1970

McNamara, Brooks, and Jerry Rojo, Richard Schnecher. *Theatres, Spaces, Environments: 18 Projects*. New York: Drama Book Publishers, 1975.

Mielziner, Jo, and Ray Smith, eds. *The Shapes of Our Theatre*. New York: Clarkson N. Potter, Inc., 1970.

Mullin, Donald C. *The Development of the Playhouse: A Survey of Theatre Architecture from the Renaissance to the Present*. Berkeley, CA: University of California Press, 1970.

National Endowment for the Arts Grant Recognition Program. *Design Arts Places and Spaces for the Arts*. New York: Municipal Arts Society of New York, 1981.

New Places for the Arts: A Scrapbook. New York: Educational Facilities Laboratories, 1976.

Penn, Herman J. *Encyclopedic Guide to Planning and Establishing an Auditorium, Arena, Coliseum or Multi-Purpose Building*. Greenville, SC: Penn-Fleming, 1963.

Robinson, Horace W. *Architecture for the Educational Theatre*. Eugene, OR: University of Oregon Books, 1970.

Schubert, Hanne Lore. *Modern Theatre Buildings: Architecture Stage Design, Lighting*. New York: Praeger, 1971.

Snedcof, Harold. *Cultural Facilities in Mixed-Use Development*. Washington, D.C.: Urban Land Institute, 1985.

Steward, H. Michael. *American Architecture for the Arts*. Dallas, TX: Handel & Sons Publishing, Inc., 1978.

XV.   DIRECTORIES AND GENERAL REFERENCE BOOKS

A Guide to National and State Arts Education Services. New York: American Council for the Arts, 1987.

Boardman, Gerald. *The Concise Oxford Companion to American Theatre*. New York: Oxford University Press, 1987.

Bowman, Walter P., ed. *Theatre Language: A Dictionary of Terms in English*. New York: Theatre Arts Books, 1961.

Cahn, Julius. *Official Theatrical Guide*. 20 Vols. New York: Empire State Building, 1896-1921.

Christensen, Warren. *National Directory of Arts Internships*. Los Angeles, CA: National Network of Artists Placement, 1987.

Coe, Linda C., and Rebecca Denney, Anne Rogers. *Cultural Directory II: Federal Funds and Services for the Arts and Humanities*. Washington, D.C.: Smithsonian Institution Press, 1980.

Comelison, Gayle. *A Directory of Children's Theatres in the United States*. Lanham, MD: University Press of America, 1983.

Directory of Matching Gift Programs for the Arts. New York: Business Committee for the Arts, 1985.

Ewen, David. *Complete Book of the American Musical Theatre*. New York: Holt, Rinehart and Winston, 1970.

Ewen, David. *Encyclopedia of the Opera*. New York: Hill & Wang, Inc., 1963.

Federal Funding Guide. Arlington, VA: Government Information Services, 1985.

Finley, Robert. *Who's Who in the Theater*. 15th ed. New York: Pitman Publishing Company, Inc., 1972.

The Foundation Directory. New York: The Foundation Center, 1987.

Free, William, and Charles Lower. *History into Drama: A Source Book on Symphonic Drama*. New, York: Odyssey Press, 1967.

Grants for Arts and Cultural Programs. New York: The Foundation Center, 1987.

Hartnoll, Phyllis, ed. *The Oxford Companion to the Theater*. 4th ed. Oxford: Oxford Press, 1983.

Horowitz, Harold, et al, eds. *A Sourcebook of Arts Statistics: 1987 (Prepared for the National Endowment for the Arts.)* Rockville, MD: Westat, Inc., 1988.

Lewis, Jack, ed. *National Directory for the Performing Arts*. 4th ed., Volume I: "Performing Arts Organizations and Facilities." Santa Fe, NM: National Directory, 1988.

Lewis, Jack, ed. *National Directory for the Performing Arts*. 4th ed., Volume II: "Performing Arts Education." Santa Fe, NM: National Directory, 1988.

Lounsbury, Warren C. *Theater Backstage from A to Z*. Rev. ed. Seattle, WA: University of Washington Press, 1967.

Millsaps, Daniel, ed. *National Directory of Arts and Education Support by Business Corporations*. Washington, D.C.: Washington International Arts Letter, 1983.

_____, ed. *National Directory of Arts Support by Private Foundations*. Washington, D.C.: International Arts Letter, 1983.

_____, ed. *National Directory of Grants and Aid to Individuals in the Arts*. Washington, D.C.: International Arts Letter, 1983.

New York Times Directory of Theater. New York: Amo/Quardrangle, 1973.

Odell, George C. *Annals of the New York Stage*. 15 Vols. New York: Columbia University Press, 1927-1949.

Packard, William, and David Pickering, Charlotte Savage, eds. *The Facts on File Dictionary of the Theater*. New York: Facts on File, Inc., 1989.

Pride, Leo B., ed. and comp. *International Theatre Directory*. New York: Simon and Schuster, Inc., 1973.

Primus, Mare, ed. *Black Theatre: A Resource Directory*. New York: The Black Theatre Alliance, 1973.

Rae, Kenneth, and Richard Southern, eds. *International Vocabulary of Technical Theatre Terms in Eight Languages*. New York: Theatre Arts Books, 1960.

Rigdon, Walter, ed. *The Biographical Encyclopedia and Who's Who of the American Theatre*. New York: James H. Heineman, Inc., 1966.

Sharp, Harold S., and Marjorie Z. Sharp. *Index to Characters in Performing Arts*. 2 Vols. New York: Scarecrow Press, Inc., 1966.

Veinstein, Andre, and Rosamond Gilder, George Freedley, Paul Myers, eds. *Performing Arts Collections: An International Handbook*. New York: Theatre Arts Books, 1960.

XVI. CAREER GUIDANCE

Dumler, Egon, and Robert F. Cushman. *Entertainers and Their Professional Advisors*. Homewood, IL: Dow Jones-Irvvin, 1987.

Langley, Stephen, and James Abruzzo. *Jobs in Arts and Media Management: What They Are and How To Get One!* New York: American Council for the Arts, 1989.

Minier, Sarah, ed. *The Arts Administrator: Job Characteristics*. (New Edition). Washington, D.C.: Association of Performing Arts Presenters, 1988.

Prieve, E. Arthur, ed. *Survey of Arts Administration Training: 1989–1990*. New York: American Council for the Arts, 1989.

XVII. BIBLIOGRAPHIES

Baker, Blanch M. *Theatre and Allied Arts: An Annotated Bibliography*. Reprint. New York: Benjamin Blom, 1968.

Coe, Linda, and Stephen Benedict, eds. *Arts Management: An Annotated Bibliography*. Washington, D.C.: National Endowment for the Arts, Cultural Resources Development Project, 1980.

Gohdes, Clarence. *Literature and Theatre of the States and Regions of the USA: An Historical Bibliography*. Durham, NC: Duke University Press, 1967.

Howard, John T. *A Bibliography of Theatre Technology*. Westport, CT: John T. Howard, Jr., 1982.

Nakamoto, Kent, and Kathi Leven, eds. with 1983 ed., H. Perry Mixter. *A Selected and Annotated Bibliography on Marketing the Arts*. Washington, D.C.: Association of Performing Arts Presenters, 1983.

Ortonali, Benito, ed. *International Bibliography of Theatre: 1982-1986*. 5 Vols. New York: Publishing Center for Cultural Resources, 1985–1990.

Performing Arts Books 1876–1981: Including an International Index of Current Serial Publication. New York: R.R Bowker Company, 1981.

Prieve, E. Arthur, and Daniel J. Schmidt. *Administration in the Arts: An Annotated Bibliography of Selected References*. Madison, WI: Center for Arts Administration, Graduate School of Business, University of Wisconsin-Madison, 1977.

Stratman, Carl J. *Bibliography of the American Theatre Excluding NYC*. Chicago, IL: Loyola University Press, 1965.

Waack, William L., ed. *Careers and Career Education in the Performing Arts: An Annotated Bibliography.* Lanham, MD: University Press of America, Inc., 1983.

Whittingham, Nik-ki. *Arts Management in the 90s.* Chicago, IL: Enaaq Publications, Inc., 1990.

XVIII. PERIODICALS AND ANNUALS

American Theatre (11 issues per year), Theatre Communications Group, 520 Eighth Ave., 24th Fl., New York, NY 10018-4156

Annual Report/National Endowment for the Arts (Annual), National Endowment for the Arts, Public Information Office, 1100 Pennsylvania Ave., Washington, D.C. 20506 http://www.nea.gov/

Artsearch (Bi-monthly), Theatre Communications Group, 520 Eighth Ave., 24th Fl., New York, NY 10018-4156 http://www.artsearch.us/

Backstage (Weekly), www.backstage.com

BCA News (Bi-monthly), Business Committee for the Arts, 1775 Broadway, New York, NY 10019 http://www.bcainc.org/

Billboard Magazine (Weekly), Billboard Publications, 1515 Broadway, New York, NY 10036 http://www.billboard.com

The Catalog of Federal Domestic Assistance (Annual with supplements), U.S. Office of Management and Budget, Superintendent of Documents, U.S. Government Printing Office, Washington, D.C. 20402 www.cfda.gov

Connections (Quarterly), National Assembly of State Arts Agencies, http://www.nasaa-arts.org/

COS Bulletin (Quarterly), Central Opera Service, Metropolitan Opera Association, Lincoln Center, New York, NY 10023

Dance Magazine (Monthly), http://www.dancemagazine.com

Dramatists Guild Quarterly (Quarterly), http://www.dramaguild.com

Equity News (Monthly), Actors' Equity Association, 165 West 46th Street, New York, NY 10030 http://www.actorsequity.org

Facility Manager (Quarterly), International Association of Assembly Managers, published by P.M. Haeger & Associates, 500 North Michigan Ave #1400, Chicago, IL 60611 http://www.iaam.org/

The Foundation Grants Index Annual (Annually), The Foundation Center, 70 Fifth Avenue, New York, NY 10003

Foundation News (Bi-monthly), Council on Foundations, Inc., 1828 L St. NW, Washington, D.C. 20036 http://www.cof.org/

The Foundation Reporter (Annually), The Taft Corporation, 5125 MacArthur Blvd. NW, Washington, D.C. 20016

Grantsmanship Center News (Bi-monthly), Grantsmanship Center, http://www.tgci.com/

Inside Arts (Bi-monthly), Association of Performing Arts Presenters, http://www.artspresenters.org/

Institute of Outdoor Drama Newsletter; IOD, University of North Carolina, Chapel Hill, NC 27514 http://www.unc.edu/depts/outdoor/

Journal of Arts Management and Law, Heldref Publications, 4000 Albemarle St. NW, Washington, D.C. 20016 http://www.heldref.org/jamls.php

Live Design http://www.livedesignonline.com/

LSA Online News http://www.lightingandsoundamerica.com

Musical America International Directory of the Performing Arts (Annually, plus supplements, including the annual "Festivals" directory), Musical America http://www.musicalamerica.com/

Northwest Arts (Bi-weekly), http://www.viewit.com/nwarts/arts/

Opera America Bulletin (Monthly), http://www.operaam.org

Opera News (17 issues per year), Metropolitan Opera Guild, Inc., Lincoln Center, New York, NY 10023

Performance-Management (Bi-annually), Brooklyn College, Performing Arts Management Program, Brooklyn, NY 11210

Playbill (Monthly), 71 Vanderbilt Ave., Suite 320, New York, NY 10169 http://www.playbill.com

Sightlines http://www.usitt.org/

Stern's Performing Arts Directory (Annually), Robert D. Stern & William Como, Publishers, 33 West 60th St., New York, NY 10023

Theatre Design and Technology (Quarterly), U.S. Institute for Theatre Technology, Inc., http://www.usitt.org/tdt.index/

Theatre Journal
 http://www.muse.jhu.edu
Theatre Magazine (3 issues per year), Yale School
 of Drama, 222 York St., New Haven, CT 02520
Theatre Profiles (Annually),
 http://www.tcg.org/frames/member_profiles/
 fs_thprofiles.htm
The Drama Review (TDR) (Quarterly), Tisch
 School of the Arts, New York University:
 published by MIT Press journals
 http://www.mitpress.mit.edu/
Variety (Weekly), 475 Park Avenue South, New
 York, NY 10016 http://www.variety.com

Index